CO-OWNERSHIP OF LAND

PARTITION ACTIONS AND REMEDIES

To Mum and Dad, with love and thanks

CO-OWNERSHIP OF LAND

PARTITION ACTIONS AND REMEDIES

HEATHER CONWAY
LLB, PhD

Print on Demand Edition

Tottel publishing

Published by
Tottel Publishing Ltd
Maxwelton House
41-43 Boltro Road
Haywards Heath
West Sussex
RH16 1BJ

Tottel Publishing Ltd
Fitzwarren Business Centre
26 Upper Pembroke Street
Dublin 2
Ireland

Reprinted by Tottel Publishing Ltd 2007, 2009

British Library Cataloguing-in-Publication Data
A catalogue record for this book is available from the British Library

ISBN : 978-1-84592-531-4

Typeset by Marlex Editorial Services Ltd, Dublin
Printed and bound in Great Britain by
CPI Antony Rowe, Chippenham, Wiltshire

Foreword

This is a most welcome addition to the growing wealth of texts on Irish property law. At first sight the reader might think that its subject is a somewhat narrow one and of limited interest. However, even the most cursory glance at the text will quickly bring home to the reader that the subject of co-ownership of land is one of considerable extent. It ranges from the very common joint holding of family property, like the matrimonial home, to complex joint ventures involving all kinds of commercial property. Most legal practitioners will find themselves grappling with co-ownership problems on a regular basis.

The major concern which practitioners will have had in recent years is that the law relating to co-ownership of land has had a somewhat troubled history. The interaction between the development of equitable jurisdiction and legislative intervention during the nineteenth century (in particular, the Partition Acts of 1868 and 1876) has not always been clear and has caused the courts in both parts of Ireland some difficulties. The legislation itself was not as well drafted as it might have been and the scope for differing interpretations has come to be realised increasingly in recent times. Underlying some judicial fumbling has been a sense of frustration, stemming from the feeling that the legislation no longer meets the needs of modern family life of commercial practice.

It is the great merit of this book that it deals with all these matters in considerable depth. It deals with the law and practice in both parts of Ireland in a truly scholarly way – combining research and tracing development of the law with a clear statement of the current position. Especially useful is the reference to comparative material drawn from other jurisdictions. Critical comment is made where appropriate and sensible suggestions for reform put forward as appropriate.

Lawyers in Ireland have waited a long time for a book on this subject. I am confident that this book will make them feel that it was well worth waiting for. It is wonderful to see a very young lawyer produce a work of such maturity.

Professor J.C.W. Wylie

November 2000

Preface

Two or more persons often purchase property without making any arrangements as regards what will happen to the property if circumstances change in the future. In the event that shared use and occupation is no longer possible, such persons may agree to divide the property between them, or to sell it and divide the resulting proceeds of sale. Failing this, the law provides a means for one co-owner to compel a sale or division of the property against the wishes of another co-owner, thus releasing the parties from co-ownership and its associated rights and obligations. This book is intended to provide a practical guide to the methods of ending co-ownership and the consequences which flow from this.

A number of people have assisted with various aspects of this book since it began as a PhD thesis in the autumn of 1995. I would like to thank the Hon Lord Justice Campbell, who dealt with a number of general queries in relation to my work. Likewise, Ms Kathleen Finlay, Barrister-at-Law and Dr John Mee, University College Cork provided invaluable assistance on aspects of matrimonial property law in Northern Ireland and the Republic of Ireland respectively. Thanks are also due to Keith Gamble, Holmes & Moffitt Solicitors, Belfast who read and commented on a number of draft chapters.

I would also like to express my gratitude to the various members of staff at Butterworths who were involved in publishing this book. In particular, I wish to thank Ms Ciara Fitzpatrick and Ms Louise Leavy for their patience, efficiency and professionalism. In this respect, I would also like to thank Professor John Wylie, Cardiff Law School for encouraging the publication of this book and for writing its foreword.

Advice and support from colleagues within the School of Law has proved to be invaluable. In particular, I am indebted to Dr Alan Dowling for his unfailing enthusiasm and words of wisdom throughout the last five years. Finally, but not least, thanks to my good friend Dr Cecelia O'Kane for providing sound advice and a sympathetic ear at all times, and to my parents for providing love and support in generous measure.

The law is stated as at 31 July 2000.

Dr Heather Conway

Queen's University, Belfast

November 2000

Contents

Chapter 12 Practice in Partition Actions in Northern Ireland and the Republic of Ireland

Table of Cases

A

B

C

E

F

G

H

K

L

M

P

S

T

Table of Statutes

Ireland: Acts of the Oireachtas (post 1922)

Ireland: Statutory Instruments

Northern Ireland

Northern Ireland: Statutory Rules

United Kingdom: Statutory Instruments

Commonwealth Statutes

Australia

Chapter 1

Introduction

> 'Co-ownership of land has many benefits, especially at its inception. Two or more parties who cannot afford to purchase or maintain desired realty alone may join forces to accomplish a shared purchase. One who desires to give or devise real property to the objects of his or her bounty can do so in a manner treating all equally if that is the desire. For its benefits, however, co-ownership also carries considerable burdens. These burdens are most troublesome when cotenants cannot agree on the use, occupation, improvement or, ultimately, disposition of the shared realty.'[1]

[1.01] Such problems are caused by the unity of possession which is fundamental to co-ownership. Each co-owner is entitled to use and occupy the entire property, subject to a similar right on the part of all the other co-owners.[2] So long as they share in the use and occupation of the land and apportion all associated expenses and income accordingly, few difficulties arise. However, this is not always possible in practice.

[1.02] Co-owners may be unable to agree on a suitable means of exploiting all or part of their land. One joint tenant or tenant in common may simply wish to divide the land and adopt a different use for his share. Alternatively, a co-owner who no longer wishes to be burdened with the responsibilities of land ownership may want to sell the property and realise his investment. Problems may also arise in the event of a personal disagreement between co-owners or the breakdown of a relationship which originally caused them to purchase property as co-owners, such as the end of a joint business venture or failure of a marriage. In these circumstances, relations between the parties may have deteriorated to the extent that shared enjoyment of the property is no longer possible. One co-owner may be deriving more benefit from the property than the others or the land may have fallen into disuse.

[1.03] In the event of such disputes, the only practicable solution may be for co-owners to end this relationship. Partition or sale in lieu thereof destroys the unity of possession which is fundamental to co-ownership and brings co-ownership to

1 *Thompson on Real Property* (1994), pp 445-446.

2 2 *Bl Comm* 181. This rule applies even though one of the co-owners has an additional interest in the property such as a right of residence - *Re Hecker's Estate* (28 April 1994, unreported), High Court (RI).

an end. Upon partition, land is divided into shares commensurate with the respective interests of the co-owners in the entire property. Thereafter, each former co-owner holds a divided share of land in severalty. Sale in lieu of partition involves a sale of the entire property and division of the proceeds of sale between the former co-owners according to their ascertained beneficial interests in the land. In the majority of cases, this provides a more practicable remedy than partition, especially where division of the property in question is inconvenient or impossible.

[1.04] Co-owners may partition or sell their land by agreement. In order to do so, they must all agree on an appropriate scheme of division or sale and implement it accordingly. Failing this, the law provides a means for one or more co-owners to compel partition or sale of the land against the wishes of the others. Proceedings for compulsory partition or sale provide a means of breaking the deadlock where co-owners cannot agree on an expedient means of using or disposing of the land. Since they are not dependant on the agreement of all the co-owners, such proceedings will usually provide a more practicable and widely used means of ending co-ownership than voluntary partition or sale. Joint tenants and tenants in common were first granted a right to compel partition by legislation passed in the sixteenth century.[3] One or more co-owners could force a division of the land by applying to court for such an order. However, such persons could not compel a sale of the land until the enactment of the Partition Acts 1868 and 1876 which empowered the court to substitute the more convenient remedy of sale for physical partition.

[1.05] The Partition Acts remain in force in both Northern Ireland and the Republic of Ireland and thus provide the legislative framework for co-owners who wish to end their relationship. These Acts allow one or more co-owners to compel sale of land against the wishes of the other co-owners by applying to court for an order to this effect and upon satisfying the relevant criteria. In the event of refusing sale, the court may make an order for partition of the property in the alternative. Thus, the Partition Acts allow co-owners to be released from their relationship in the event that common enjoyment of the land is no longer possible. However, proceedings under the Partition Acts are not confined to co-owners themselves. A third party who derives an interest in the land from one of the co-owners, such as a mortgagee or trustee in bankruptcy, may have to bring a partition action in order to secure a sale of the land for the purposes of discharging a debt. This course of action will usually be necessary, since the other co-owners are unlikely to agree to sale in these circumstances.

---

3 Namely, An Act Concerning Joint Tenants and Tenants in Common 1539 and An Act Concerning Joint Tenants for Term of Life or Years 1540, in England and An Act for Jointenants 1542 in Ireland.

[1.06] While there are brief references to the Partition Acts in the major Irish land law texts[4], little has been written on this subject in over a century. Accounts of the immediate post-1868 practice may be found in Foster, *The Law of Joint Ownership and Partition of Real Estate* (1878) and in Walker, *The Partition Acts 1868 and 1876* (2nd edn, 1882). Likewise, discussions of the law on compulsory partition and sale in later editions of *Daniell's Chancery Practice*[5] and *Seton's Forms of Judgments and Orders*[6] do not go beyond the practice in the early twentieth century. The passage of time since the publication of these texts has diminished their practical utility in light of changing social and economic conditions. For example, co-ownership of land has increased dramatically throughout the twentieth century, particularly in the context of home ownership. Land is invariably acquired with the provision of financial assistance from a lending institution which then has associated rights over the property in question. Legislation such as that regulating property rights of spouses in relation to the matrimonial or family home is another recent development which merits consideration.

[1.07] The absence of a modern text dealing with partition actions is matched by a lack of Irish caselaw on the subject. Since the Partition Acts were repealed in England as part of the 1925 property reforms, courts in both Northern Ireland and the Republic of Ireland have not had the traditional benefit of analogous English caselaw.[7] Accordingly, the law relating to compulsory partition and sale of co-owned land in both parts of Ireland has remained largely dormant, with little development until recently. However, recent cases have highlighted a number of deficiencies in this area of law[8], particularly in relation to partition

---

4 See Wylie, *Irish Land Law* (3rd edn, 1997), pp 442-445; Coughlan, *Property Law* (2nd edn, 1998), pp 142-144; and Lyall, *Land Law in Ireland* (2nd edn, 2000), pp 446-450.

5 (8th edn, 1914), pp 1170-1189.

6 (6th edn, 1901), ch 46.

7 The 1925 reforms imposed a system of statutory trusts on co-owned land under the Law of Property Act 1925 (now the Trusts of Land and Appointment of Trustees Act 1996)- see generally Megarry and Wade, *The Law of Real Property*, (6th edn, 2000), ch 9. Despite proposals to impose a similar system of statutory trusts in Northern Ireland and to repeal the Partition Acts accordingly, this is unlikely to happen in the immediate future- see *Final Report of the Land Law Working Group* (1990). The various recommendations put forward by the Working Group are incorporated in a Draft Property (Northern Ireland) Order contained in Vol 2 of the *Final Report*.

8 As regards Northern Ireland, see *Northern Bank Ltd v Haggerty* [1995] NI 211; *Northern Bank Ltd v Adams* (1 February 1996 unreported), High Court (NI); *Glass v McManus* [1996] NI 401; *Fraser Homes Ltd v Fraser Houses (NI) Ltd* [1998] NI 214; and *Ulster Bank Ltd v Carter* [1999] NI 93. As regards the Republic of Ireland, see *O'D v O'D* (18 November 1983, unreported), High Court (RI); *FF v CF* [1987] 1 ILRM 1; and *First National Building Society v Ring* [1992] IR 375.

actions involving lenders and those involving a matrimonial or family home. The extent of the court's discretion when determining partition actions has also been questioned. In addition to this, the apparent lack of Irish caselaw on the Partition Acts may be contrasted with the wealth of Commonwealth caselaw relating to partition and sale of co-owned land. The main provisions of the Partition Acts have been incorporated into legislation governing termination of co-ownership in the majority of Australian states and in New Zealand. A number of Canadian provinces also have legislation which is derived from the Partition Acts. Cases decided in these jurisdictions have identified problems which have not yet troubled Irish courts, and provide a means of resolving such issues which could be adopted accordingly. Such caselaw is often overlooked.

[1.08] This book provides a comparative analysis of the law relating to partition and sale of co-owned land under the Partition Acts in Northern Ireland and the Republic of Ireland, with reference to comparative Commonwealth caselaw where appropriate. It provides advice for co-owners who wish to end their relationship, irrespective of whether such persons are a married couple, co-habitees, family members who inherit or purchase property as joint owners, or persons involved in a joint business venture. The position of third parties with interests in the land such as lending institutions and trustees in bankruptcy is also explored. In particular the book considers:

(a) The factors which courts should take into account in deciding whether to order partition or sale, and the weight to be accorded to the various factors.

(b) The amount of discretion available to courts when determining partition actions, and the consequent likelihood of an order for partition or sale being granted.

(c) The practice where co-owned land is used as security. The first issue which typically arises in this context is the effect of the security on the rights of co-owners vis-à-vis each other as regards seeking an order for partition or sale. For example, can the lender take steps to prevent such an order being made in these circumstances? Assuming that the court makes an order for partition or sale, what effect does it have on the lender? The second issue is whether co-ownership affects the remedies available to a lender for enforcing his security in the event of default, in particular where the security relates to an undivided share of land.

(d) The practice where co-owned property comprises a matrimonial or family home, and whether various statutory provisions regulating property rights of spouses encroach upon the court's jurisdiction to order partition or more likely sale of such property under the Partition

Acts. A matrimonial home may be the subject of a partition action in three situations, namely (i) where a spouse seeks to compel sale of the property following a breakdown in the marital relationship; (ii) where a co-owning spouse has used his share of the matrimonial home as security and subsequently defaults on repayments; and (iii) where a co-owning spouse is declared bankrupt. In situations (ii) and (iii), an issue which typically arises is whether the "innocent" spouse can defeat a request for sale by the lender or trustee in bankruptcy on the basis that the property is a matrimonial home.

(e) The principles to be applied where one co-owner seeks an accounting adjustment as incidental to an order for partition or sale. This often occurs where a co-owner alleges that profits or expenses associated with the property have not been apportioned rateably or that he has been wrongfully excluded from the property. A number of situations are considered, including: (i) whether a co-owner who enjoys exclusive possession of the property must pay an occupation rent; (ii) whether a co-owner who spends money on improvements to the land or who pays all of the outgoings (such as mortgage payments and insurance premiums) is entitled to recover a proportionate share of this expenditure from the other co-owners; (iii) whether a co-owner who receives in excess of his share of rents and profits from the land must account for this; and (iv) whether a co-owner who undertakes to act as the bailiff or agent of the other co-owners is accountable for any profits which he receives in this capacity or for any improper management of the land.

Thus, the following chapters advise co-owners on a suitable means of ending their relationship and the consequences which flow from this.

Chapter 2

Partition or Sale by Mutual Agreement

I Introduction

[2.01] Co-owners of land may agree to end their relationship by dividing the land or by selling the land and dividing the proceeds of sale. Sometimes referred to as voluntary partition or sale, this method of terminating co-ownership is dependent on the agreement of all the co-owners. Once concluded, each former joint tenant or tenant in common is entitled to a divided share of land in severalty or to an aliquot share of the proceeds of sale from the land.

II Partition by Mutual Agreement

[2.02] Voluntary partition involves two stages. Having decided to divide the land, the co-owners should prepare a partition agreement detailing all matters concerning the proposed partition. The parties should then give effect to the agreement by executing the appropriate conveyances or transfers.

A The partition agreement

[2.03] An agreement to partition should be in writing and signed by all the parties[1]. However, an oral agreement to partition which is supported by part performance and which has been acquiesced in for a long time may be enforced in equity[2]. Where the land is held in joint tenancy, the agreement to partition effects a severance[3].

---

1 Foster, *The Law on Joint Ownership and Partition of Real Estate* (1878), p 91. For a form of agreement to partition see Davidson, Wright and Darley, *Davidson's Precedents and Forms in Conveyancing* (4th edn, 1877) Vol I, p 186. Prior to 1677 in England and 1695 in Ireland, an agreement to partition between coparceners could be made by parol: *Litt* s 250 and *Co Litt* 169a. Tenants in common could also partition by oral agreement in certain circumstances if they subsequently perfected the partition by livery of seisin: *Co Litt* 169a. However, an agreement to partition between joint tenants had to be in writing: *Litt* s 290. Following the enactment of the Statute of Frauds 1677 and the Statute of Frauds (Ir) 1695, all agreements to partition had to be in writing or evidenced in writing.

2 See *Ireland v Rittle* (1739) 1 Atk 541 and *Paine v Ryder* (1857) 24 Beav 151 (oral agreement to partition which had been acted on for over twenty years).

3 2 *Bl Comm* 185 and see McClean, 'Severance of Joint Tenancies' (1979) 57 Can Bar Rev 1 at 19. The contrary view expressed in Allnatt, *A Practical Treatise on the Law of Partition* (1820), pp 16-17 appears to be incorrect.

1 Necessary parties

[2.04] The necessary parties to the agreement are those persons who would be required to make a lifetime assurance of each share of the property[4] and must be *sui juris*[5]. However, if one of the co-owners is an infant, trustees of the settlement may consent to and execute the partition on his behalf[6]. If one of the co-owners is a person of unsound mind, these functions are performed by a controller or committee as appropriate[7].

[2.05] Joint tenants and tenants in common of estates in fee simple and estates in fee tail may partition by agreement[8]. Likewise, joint tenants and tenants in common of life estates and leasehold estates may agree to partition land[9]. In these circumstances, partition will be confined to the duration of the limited estate, unless the persons interested in remainder or reversion agree that partition should be permanent and are parties to the agreement[10]. Co-owners of estates in reversion or remainder cannot compel partition or sale since they lack the requisite standing to maintain a partition action[11]. However, such persons may partition their respective estates by agreement[12].

[2.06] An agreement to partition is enforceable both by and against persons deriving their titles from the original co-owners[13].

2 Property that may be partitioned by agreement

[2.07] The types of property that may be partitioned by agreement are the same as those that may be partitioned by order of the court in proceedings for

4 *Anon in Chancery* (1742) 3 Swan 139n.

5 Foster, *The Law on Joint Ownership and Partition of Real Estate* (1878), p 90 and 21 *Halsbury's Laws of England* (1st edn, 1912), p 813.

6 Since land owned by an infant is deemed to be settled land under the Settled Land Acts 1882-1890 - see ch 12 below, para **[12.20]**. As to the procedure in respect of voluntary partition and sale of settled land in general, see paras **[2.23]**-**[2.25]** below.

7 See ch 12 below, para **[12.21]**.

8 In order to bind the issue in tail, the entail must be effectively barred: *Oakeley v Smith* (1759) 1 Eden 261, and see *Neale v Neale* (1837) 1 Keen 672.

9 Allnatt, *A Practical Treatise on the Law of Partition* (1820), p 36 and 21 *Halsbury's Laws of England* (1st edn, 1912), p 813. An agreement to partition between joint tenants for life may be more advantageous to the reversioner or remainderman who may enter the property on the death of one of the joint tenants: Allnatt, *A Practical Treatise on the Law of Partition* (1820), p 36.

10 21 *Halsbury's Laws of England* (1st edn, 1912), p 813 and see *Baring v Nash* (1813) 1 Ves & B 551.

11 See ch 4 below, paras **[4.10]**.

12 See para **[2.07]** below.

13 See *Knollys v Alcock* (1800) 5 Ves 648; *Pearson v Lane* (1809) 17 Ves 101 and *Paine v Ryder* (1857) 24 Beav 151. In Northern Ireland, the provisions of the Contracts (Rights of Third Parties) Act 1999 may also be relevant in this context.

compulsory partition or sale[14]. Thus, co-owners of freehold or leasehold estates may partition by agreement[15]. Likewise, all types of corporeal hereditaments and any estate therein may be partitioned by agreement of the parties[16]. However, partition by agreement is wider than compulsory partition in several respects. For example, estates or interests in reversion or remainder may be partitioned by mutual agreement even though they cannot be partitioned by order of the court[17].

[2.08] Partition by agreement is also possible in situations where the court might refuse to make an order for compulsory partition, for example where partition of leasehold property would be contrary to a covenant in the lease[18]. Likewise, co-owners of land acquired under the Land Purchase Acts and which is subject to an existing annuity might partition the land without the consent of the Department of Finance and Personnel in Northern Ireland[19]. A similar approach may be adopted by co-owners of agricultural land in general in the Republic of Ireland, subdivision of which requires the consent of the Minister[20]. In these circumstances, there is nothing to prevent co-owners from dividing the land if they so choose, albeit that they would expose themselves to an action by the relevant third party (for example, an action for breach of covenant by the landlord). The danger of such action would, however, result in the court refusing an order for compulsory partition in these circumstances[21].

---

14 See ch 4 below, paras **[4.33]-[4.35]**.

15 See ch 4 below, para **[4.33]**.

16 21 *Halsbury's Laws of England* (1st edn, 1912), p 822 citing *Oakeley v Smith* (1759) 1 Eden 261 (agreement to partition estates in remainder and reversion).

17 *Oakley v Smith* (1759) 1 Eden 261. Allnatt, *A Practical Treatise on the Law of Partition* (1820), p 7 states that a reversion may be divided so that one co-owner has a reversion of so many acres and the other co-owner the reversion of the remaining land. Agreements to partition mere expectancies have also been enforced: see *Beckley v Newland* (1723) 2 P Wms 182 and *Wethered v Wethered* (1828) 2 Sim 183. In addition to this, the Court of Chancery could decree specific performance of an agreement to partition copyholds, even though it could not make an order for partition of copyholds until the Copyhold Act 1841 was passed: *Bolton v Ward* (1845) 4 Hare 530 and see ch 4 below, para **[4.33]**.

18 21 *Halsbury's Laws of England* (1st edn, 1912), p 822 and see ch 7 below, paras **[7.23]**.

19 The Department's consent is required for any proposed subdivision of such land: Irish Land Act 1903, s 54(1) and see ch 7 below, para **[7.21]**.

20 Section 12 of the Land Act 1965 and see ch 7 below, para **[7.22]**. The functions of the Land Commission have been transferred to the Minister for Agriculture, Food and Forestry under the Irish Land Commission (Dissolution) Act 1992 (brought into force by the Irish Land Commission (Dissolution) Act 1992 (Commencement) Order 1999). In addition to this, co-owners of land purchased under the Land Purchase Acts and who agree to partition this land may apply to the Minister for leave to do so: the Land Act 1939, s 24. The Minister may implement this scheme of partition: see *In the Matter of the Land Act 1939 and Lands at Glennamaddoo* [1992] 1 IR 297.

21 See ch 7 below.

[2.09] Incorporeal hereditaments may be partitioned by agreement. For example, co-owners may agree to partition rent charges[22]. As regards easements, partition of the servient tenement will not prevent the exercise of the relevant right by the owner of the dominant tenement, while partition of the latter will not prevent the former co-owners from exercising an easement over the servient tenement[23]. However, certain types of incorporeal hereditaments cannot be divided between co-owners. Examples include *profits à prendre* of uncertain character[24] and common rights over land such as fishing and riparian rights[25]. Similar problems may arise where the very nature of the co-owned property precludes partition, such as dwelling houses or single structures[26]. There are a number of methods of circumventing this problem which may be regarded as equivalent to partition of the property in question even though physical division does not take place. For example, co-owners may agree to exercise a particular right in turns or to occupy the property in question for specific months each year (for example, in respect of vacation property)[27]. Where a particular item of property is valued in terms of the profits it generates, co-owners may simply agree to divide the profits[28] or to divide the property in some other manner that ensures equality between them such as taking equal amounts of any produce yielded[29]. However, the parties are

22 See ch 4 below, para **[4.34]**.

23 See ch 4 below, para **[4.34]**.

24 *Co Litt* 164b.

25 See *Menzies v McDonald* (1856) 2 Jur (ns) 575. Problems also typically arose in respect of advowsons (see below) and incidents of a manor (see ch 4 below, para **[4.33]**).

26 In addition to this, partition of a single dwelling (whether by agreement of the parties or by order of the court) requires planning permission and may be contrary to covenants in a lease if the dwelling house is let to several co-tenants: see ch 7 below. Problems may also arise where the property in question is a matrimonial or family home: see chs 9 and 10 below.

27 *Co Litt* 165a and 167b. The former method was common in respect of advowsons which could be 'partitioned' by agreement of the parties or by order of the court: see *Bishop of Salisbury v Phillips* (1699) Carth 505; *Bodicoate v Steers* (1737) 1 Dick 69 and *Johnstone v Baber* (1856) 6 D M & G 439. Because it was impossible to partition an advowson the proper procedure was for the parties to present the rights in turn. However, the Advowsons Act 1708 provided that, following partition, each party was deemed to be seised in severalty of his share of the advowson. As regards coparceners, the right of presentation went to the eldest first: see *Harris and Haies v Nichols* (1583) Cro Eliz 19 and *Buller v Bishop of Exeter* (1749) 1 Ves Sen 340, as well as the case reported at (1341) YB 15 Ed III pl 58 and *Rex v Middleton* reported in *Selden Society: Select Cases Before the King's Council (1243-1482)* pl 1353. In the absence of agreement, the order of presentation between joint tenants and tenants in common was determined by drawing lots: *Seymour v Bennet* (1742) 2 Atk 482 and *Matthews v Bishop of Bath and Wells* (1785) 2 Dick 652.

28 Allnatt, *A Practical Treatise on the Law of Partition* (1820), p 6.

29 *Co Litt* 164b and see *Re Trimmer* (1904) 91 LT 26 (tenants in common received separate dividends on shares in a company).

still regarded as co-owners of the particular item of property in these circumstances[30]. Co-ownership persists unless, for example, one joint tenant or tenant in common sells his interest in the property to another co-owner[31].

3 Matters specified in the agreement

[2.10] The agreement should specify a number of general matters[32]. These include the extent of the parties' respective interests in the land, the date on which the partition is to take effect, and provisions for the subsequent vesting of the allotted shares of the property in severalty. In addition to this, the agreement should specify the manner in which the costs of executing the partition are to be borne by the parties[33] and which party will have custody of the title deeds following partition[34].

[2.11] The agreement should also record matters peculiar to the scheme of partition agreed by the parties. For example, co-owners may wish to exclude certain items of property from the partition, such as mines and minerals located in the land[35]. Alternatively, they may wish to reserve easements that already exist over the land or to grant easements over certain parts of the land to facilitate enjoyment of their respective shares in severalty[36]. Payments of money[37], which are required to correct any imbalance in the value of the divided parcels of land where it cannot be divided into parcels commensurate to the interests of the co-owners, should be included in the partition agreement[38]. Reference should also be made to accounting adjustments which, for example, may be rendered

---

30 For example, where such property is held in a joint tenancy, severance does not occur simply because the parties agree to divide any profits derived from the property: McClean, 'Severence of Joint Tenancies' (1979) 57 Can Bar Rev 1 at 18 citing *Flannigan v Wotherspoon* [1953] 1 DLR 768.

31 *Co Litt* 164a and 165b and 21 *Halbury's Laws* (1st edn, 1912), p 823.

32 Foster, *The Law on Joint Ownership and Partition of Real Estate* (1878), p 91.

33 For example, the entire costs of partition may be borne rateably by the parties in accordance with their shares in the property. Similar rules are applied in respect of costs incurred in a partition action: see ch 12 below, paras **[12.54]-[12.58]**.

34 As to the rules relating to custody of title deeds in general see ch 12 below, para **[12.43]**.

35 See *Darvill v Roper* (1855) 3 Drew 294.

36 Foster, *The Law on Joint Ownership and Partition of Real Estate* (1878), pp 97-99. See further *James v Plant* (1836) 4 A & E 749 and *Re Henderson's Estate* (1874) ILTR 105.

37 Known as 'equality of partition'.

38 For example, in *Ireland v Rittle* (1739) 1 Atk 541 where the land could not be divided into equal halves, one of the parties agreed to pay the taxes on the share of the other co-owner. See further *Hulbert v Hart* (1682) 1 Vern 133. An agreement to partition will not be set aside simply because one of the co-owners has insufficient funds available to him to meet a payment for equality of partition: *Dimsdale v Robertson* (1844) 7 Ir Eq R 536. In the event of non-payment, the sum owed as equality of partition may be recovered with interest from the date on which the first payment was due: *Stewart v Ferguson* (1842) 5 Ir Eq R 157.

necessary as a result of one co-owner's sole occupation of the property or receipt of income from the land[39].

4 Methods of voluntary partition

[2.12] The agreement should specify who is to carry out the valuation and division of the land. Historically, voluntary partition could be carried out in four ways[40] all of which are equally relevant today.

(a) Partition by all of the co-owners

[2.13] This is the most straightforward method of voluntary partition. All of the co-owners acting together decide how the land should be divided and subsequently allocated between them[41].

(b) Partition by one of the co-owners

[2.14] By this method, the land is divided by one of the co-owners and each co-owner selects a portion[42]. However, the co-owner who carries out the division should be given last choice of the divided parcels to avoid any bias in the partition[43].

(c) Partition by a third party

[2.15] Co-owners may appoint a third party to divide the land in a fair and impartial manner[44]. The third party is likely to be a surveyor or person with similar expertise in land valuation[45]. Following partition, the divided parcels of land will be allocated by the third party unless the co-owners can agree on the allocation[46].

(d) Partition by lots

[2.16] This is the most impartial method of voluntary partition. Having employed a third party to partition the land, the subsequent allocation of the

---

39 As to accounting adjustments in general see ch 11 below.

40 See *Litt* ss 243-246 and *Co Litt* 165b-167a.

41 *Litt* s 243 and *Co Litt* 165b. See for example, *Hulbert v Hart* (1682) 1 Vern 133 and *Clarke v Bodkin* (1851) 13 Ir Eq R 492.

42 *Litt* s 245 and *Co Litt* 166b.

43 According to the rule *cujus et divisio, alterius est electio* (when one divides, the other has the right of first choice). As regards coparceners, partition was usually carried out by the eldest sister so that first choice of the divided parcels of land was granted to the second oldest sister, second choice to the third oldest, and so continued with the eldest choosing last.

44 *Litt* s 244 and *Co Litt* 166a. Perhaps one of the earliest recorded instances of partition by this method is reported at (1345) YB 19 Ed III (RS) pl 5. A dispute having arisen over repairs to a mill owned by two brothers as joint tenants, they agreed to partition the mill and employed a third brother to divide the property and to allot the shares.

45 21 *Halsbury's Laws of England* (1st edn, 1912), pp 814-815.

46 With coparceners, this distribution was made according to the privilege of seniority with the eldest coparcener choosing her share (the *enitia pars*) first.

divided parcels is made by drawing lots[47]. The order of selection may be decided by the third party or by mutual agreement of the co-owners[48].

[2.17] These four methods of voluntary partition differ according to the way in which the boundaries of the divided shares of land are determined and subsequently allotted to the respective co-owners. Division of the land may be carried out by one or more of the co-owners themselves, or by a third party nominated by all the co-owners. Likewise, allotment of the divided parcels of land may be determined by mutual agreement of the co-owners, by a third party or by drawing lots. A number of factors may influence the allocation of the divided parcels of land under the first three methods of partition. For example, the fact that one co-owner owns other land adjacent to a divided parcel of land, or has made improvements to a particular area of the co-owned land, or occupies a home or business there may be relevant in this context. Any resulting imbalance in the value of the divided parcels can be remedied by an appropriate payment for equality of partition.

B Execution of conveyances or transfers

[2.18] The agreement for partition itself is not sufficient to terminate co-ownership and vest the individual parcels of land in severalty. The parties must give effect to the agreement by executing appropriate conveyances or transfers. Section 3 of the Real Property Act 1845 provides that a partition will be void unless made by deed. There are two possible methods of achieving this.

[2.19] The parties may execute a deed of partition, stating that they are joint tenants or tenants in common, and that they have agreed to partition the land and the purpose of the deed is to give effect to this agreement. The deed should contain an accurate statement of the parties' titles, a clear and accurate description of the parcel of land to be enjoyed by each party in severalty, and a conveyance or transfer adapted to the parties' respective interests[49]. Alternatively, the parties may simply execute separate mutual conveyances or

[47] *Litt* s 246 and *Co Litt* 167a.

[48] Again, with respect to coparceners, choice of the lots devolved according to the privilege of seniority.

[49] Foster, *The Law on Joint Ownership and Partition of Real Estate* (1878), p 96 and Bythewood and Jarman, *A Selection of Precedents in Conveyancing* (4th edn, 1887) Vol IV, pp 137 and 154 (deed of partition of freeholds between tenants in common). For a more recent form of deed of partition used in respect of registered land see Moir, *Land Registration Manual* (1994), pp 70-72. As regards registered land, a counterpart should be prepared for each party and a new land certificate applied for since only one portion of the land can remain in the existing folio: Moir, pp 70-72.

transfers, delineating the respective parcels of land that they are to enjoy in severalty[50].

III Sale by Mutual Agreement

[2.20] As with voluntary partition, voluntary sale involves two stages. The parties should draw up an agreement for sale, setting out all the factors relevant to sale of the land. For example, the agreement should stipulate the manner in which the sale will take place[51] and the persons who are to have carriage of the sale[52]. It should also state how the proceeds of sale are to be distributed among the parties, as well as providing for any sums to be paid as accounting adjustments and payment of the costs of sale[53].

[2.21] The necessary parties to an agreement to sell are the same as those to an agreement for partition[54]. While the types of property that may be sold by agreement are also the same, the fact that partition of certain property is impracticable or, for example, contrary to a covenant in a lease is irrelevant in the context of sale. Likewise, restrictions on subdivision of agricultural land in the Republic of Ireland or land acquired under the Land Purchase Acts in Northern Ireland are not relevant where co-owners agree to sell this land[55]. As with voluntary partition, an agreement to sell the land and divide the proceeds of sale effects a severance where the parties are joint tenants of the relevant property[56].

---

50 The appropriate form of conveyance or transfer between joint tenants is by release, and in the case of tenants in common by deed of grant. Under the third method of partition noted above, co-owners may join in conveying the property to the third party on trust to convey the respective allotments to them after deciding on a scheme of partition. This approach has two advantages. The co-owners do not have to execute mutual conveyances since no further action is required on their part, and a co-owner who objects to the award cannot subsequently avoid the partition: Bythewood and Jarman, *A Selection of Precedents in Conveyancing* (4th edn, 1887) Vol IV, pp 122-123.

51 For example, whether by auction or private treaty.

52 Whether one or more of the co-owners themselves or a property agent.

53 For example, the entire costs of sale may be deducted from the proceeds of sale before they are distributed between the parties. This is the practice in respect of orders for sale under the Partition Acts: see ch 12 below, paras **[12.54]-[12.58]**.

54 See paras **[2.04]-[2.06]** above. Again, trustees of the settlement will act on behalf of an infant while a person of unsound mind will be represented by a controller or committee.

55 See paras **[2.07]-[2.09]** above.

56 While a mere agreement to sell the land to a third party does not effect a severance (*Re Hughes' Estate* [1920] 1 IR 207 at 211 in which the court held that severance would only occur upon a subsequent division of the proceeds of sale), an agreement to sell the land and to divide the proceeds of sale effects an immediate severance of the joint tenancy: McClean, 'Severence of Joint Tenancies' (1979) 57 Can Bar Rev 1 at 19 citing *Schofield v Graham* (1969) 6 DLR (3d) 88 and *Re McKee and National Trust Company Ltd* (1974) 49 DLR (3d) 689 (joint tenancy severed at the date upon which the agreement was made even though sale was to take place at a later date). See further *Sampaio v Sampaio* (1992) 90 DLR (4th) 122.

[2.22] When a sale of the land has been agreed, the parties must join in executing the requisite conveyance or transfer of the land to the purchaser. The proceeds of sale will then be divided between the parties in the prescribed manner.

IV Partition or Sale by Mutual Agreement Under the Settled Land Acts

[2.23] The provisions of the Settled Land Acts 1882-1890 are relevant where land is subject to a strict settlement[57]. Where two or more persons are in possession of settled land as joint tenants or tenants in common, those persons together constitute the tenant for life[58]. Thus, co-owners of settled land acting together may exercise the powers of the tenant for life, including the power to partition the land and to provide for payment of money as equality of partition[59]. Alternatively, the parties may agree to sell the settled land or any part thereof[60], subject to obtaining the best possible price[61].

[2.24] As tenant for life, the co-owners are obliged to have regard to the interests of all persons entitled under the settlement when exercising these powers[62]. They must give notice in writing to the trustees of the settlement before dividing or selling the land[63], and should supply the trustees with any information reasonably required by them in relation to the proposed partition or sale[64]. Upon

---

57 The Settled Land Acts 1882-1890 confer extensive powers on the tenant for life (as defined by the Settled Land Act 1882, s 2(5)), allowing him to deal with the land free from the constraints of the settlement (see the Settled Land Act 1882, ss 2(1) and 2(3)). In order to protect the interests of the beneficiaries under the settlement and to prevent the tenant for life from abusing his powers, their exercise is supervised by trustees of the settlement (as defined by the Settled Land Act 1882, s 2(8) and the Settled Land Act 1890, s 16). As to the Settled Land Acts in general see Wylie, *Irish Land Law* (3rd edn, 1997) ch 8 and Coughlan, *Property Law* (2nd edn, 1998) ch 11.

58 Settled Land Act 1882, s 2(6).

59 Settled Land Act 1882, s 3. Partition must be made for the best consideration in land or in land and money that can reasonably be obtained: Settled Land Act 1882, s 4(2). Money required for equality of partition may be raised by the tenant for life mortgaging the settled land or any part thereof (Settled Land Act 1882, s 18) or may be paid out of capital money arising under the Act: Settled Land Act 1882, s 21(iv).

60 Settled Land Act 1882, s 3.

61 Settled Land Act 1882, s 4(1). The land may be sold to a third party, or the co-owners may purchase the fee simple in the land themselves by fixing a reserve price and bidding at the auction: Settled Land Act 1882, s 4(4).

62 Settled Land Act 1882, s 53.

63 Settled Land Act 1882, s 45 as amended by the Settled Land Act 1884, s 5. Such notice is also required upon entering into a contract to make partition or sale: see the Settled Land Act 1882, s 31(1).

64 Settled Land Act 1884, s 5(3).

sale of the settled land, the co-owners acting together as tenant for life should join in the conveyance to the purchaser[65]. However, upon partition of the settled land, a conveyance of the divided allotments is made by the trustees of the settlement[66].

[2.25] Following partition, the life-tenants hold divided shares of land in severalty but subject to the terms of the settlement[67]. The partition is binding on the persons entitled in remainder for the duration of the life estate. Upon sale of settled land, the purchaser takes the fee simple estate in the land free from the terms of the settlement. The interests of the remaindermen are overreached and transferred to the proceeds of sale. The purchase money is paid to the trustees of the settlement[68] or into court[69] and invested accordingly[70]. Thereafter, the tenant for life is entitled to the income and the capital is preserved for the remaindermen[71].

V Partition or Sale by Mutual Agreement: Advantages and Disadvantages

[2.26] Partition or sale by mutual agreement involves a relatively simple and straightforward means for co-owners of land to end their relationship if they so desire. Following the division or sale of the land as agreed, each former co-owner is entitled to a share of land in severalty or to a share of the proceeds of sale. This method of terminating co-ownership is likely to be less expensive than compulsory partition or sale. In addition to this, the parties have greater freedom to implement their own ideas, and in particular to implement a scheme of partition which might not be ordered by the court. If one of the co-owners reneges on the agreement to partition or sell the land, the others may be able to obtain a decree of specific performance.

[2.27] However, partition or sale by mutual agreement is dependent on the consent of all the co-owners to every aspect of the associated proceedings. For voluntary partition to be possible, all the co-owners must wish to enjoy their respective shares in severalty. In addition to this, a consensus must be reached as to the manner in which the division and subsequent allocation of the shares is to

65 Settled Land Act 1882, s 20(1). However, if the land is purchased by the co-owners themselves, the conveyances are executed by the trustees of the settlement: Settled Land Act 1890, s 12.

66 Settled Land Act 1882, s 12.

67 Settled Land Act 1882, ss 24(2) and (3).

68 Settled Land Act 1882, s 22.

69 Settled Land Act 1882, s 46(2).

70 The money is invested as directed by the tenant for life or, failing this, at the trustees' discretion: Settled Land Act 1882, s 22(2). For the various methods of investment, see the Settled Land Act 1882, s 21.

71 Settled Land Act 1882, s 22.

be made. Likewise, for voluntary sale to occur, all of the co-owners must wish to convert their interests into money by selling the land and dividing the proceeds. They must also agree on the manner in which sale should be carried out and the proceeds of sale divided between them.

[2.28] If co-owners cannot reach a consensus on any of these matters, partition or sale by mutual agreement may not be possible. In these circumstances, the only option for those persons who wish to end co-ownership is to institute a partition action.

Chapter 3

Historical Development of Partition Actions: Compulsory Partition Prior to 1868

I Introduction

[3.01] Prior to the enactment of the Partition Act 1868, joint tenants and tenants in common of land could end their relationship by agreeing to partition or to sell the land. In the absence of an agreement to sell being reached by all of the co-owners, one party could not compel sale of the land against the wishes of the others during this time. However, if the co-owners could not agree on an expedient division of the property, the parties who wished to enjoy their shares in severalty could compel partition against the wishes of the other co-owners. There were several means by which compulsory partition could be effected. One such method was by private Act of Parliament, although it appears that these were seldom sought in practice[1]. Co-owners could also seek an order for partition under the Inclosure Act 1845 in England[2] or under the Incumbered Estates Court Act 1849 and subsequently the Landed Estates Court Act 1858 in Ireland[3], albeit only in specific circumstances. However, the most common and

1 Historically, private Acts of Parliament were often employed as a means of regulating large family estates where, for example, the presence of numerous trusts or the fact that titles were complicated, or the absence of certain parties precluded the persons interested from obtaining relief at common law or in equity. As regards concurrent interests in land, one co-owner could in effect compel partition by securing a private Act, the sole purpose of which was to effect a division of the land or which directed partition as ancillary to the primary relief granted by the Act: see Lloyd's Estates (Partition) Act 1866 and Brandon's Estate Act 1860. See further 21 *Halsbury's Laws of England* (1st edn, 1912), pp 812-813.

2 Where several persons were interested as joint tenants or tenants in common in a parcel of land allotted by an inclosure, any one of them could make a written request to the Inclosure Commissioners to partition the land: Inclosure Act 1845, s 90 (as extended by the Inclosure Act 1848, s 13). See generally 21 *Halsbury's Laws of England* (1st edn, 1912), pp 824-833 and Foster, *The Law on Joint Ownership and Partition of Real Estate* (1878), pp 164-166 and 184-204.

3 The Incumbered Estates Court and subsequently the Landed Estates Court could make an order for partition in two situations. Firstly, partition could be granted as incidental to sale of an undivided share of land: Incumbered Estates Court Act 1849, s 43 and Landed Estates Court Act 1858, s 79 and see *Re Wilkins* (1855) 4 Ir Ch R 575, as well as *Blake v Jennings* (1861) 12 ICLR 458 and *Re Dane's Estate* (1872) 7 ILTR 46. Secondly, the respective courts could order partition upon such a request by all the co-owners of a particular piece of land, basing the order on the scheme of division and allotment agreed by the parties: Incumbered Estates Court Act 1849, s 45 and Landed Estates Court Act 1858, s 81.

effective means of securing a division of the land was to commence proceedings for compulsory partition.

[3.02] This chapter examines the origins and development of proceedings for compulsory partition, and their transition from common law to equity. The various principles established by Courts of Common Law and, in particular, Courts of Equity form the basis of partition actions today and provide some understanding of the issues which typically arise.

II Compulsory Partition at Common Law

[3.03] Common law distinguished between estates held in coparcenary and those held under a joint tenancy or tenancy in common.

A Compulsory partition by coparceners

[3.04] Prior to 1539 in England and 1542 in Ireland[4], only coparceners had two methods of partition available to them. Like joint tenants and tenants in common, coparceners could partition by mutual agreement. However, coparceners could also compel partition if no such agreement was possible[5]. Since the estate of coparcenary was 'cast on them by law'[6], it was thought that coparceners should not be forced to remain as such where common enjoyment of the land was no longer possible[7]. Thus, the right to seek partition was a common law incident of coparcenary.

[3.05] Proceedings for compulsory partition were commenced by a writ *de partitione facienda*[8], the terms of which were as follows:

---

3 (contd) The latter method may have been resorted to where the parties did not possess all the necessary titles and therefore could not execute a voluntary partition by deed as required by the Real Property Act 1845, s 3.

4 Legislation was introduced in England and Ireland in 1539 and 1542 respectively, enabling joint tenants and tenants in common to compel partition: see paras **[3.11]-[3.13]** below.

5 See Stenton, *The First Century of English Feudalism: 1066-1166* (1932), pp 37-39. Joint tenants and tenants in common had no such remedy available to them: see (1303) YB 30, 31 Ed I (RS) pl 324 and *Litt* ss 290 and 318. Although joint tenants and tenants in common in England could compel partition prior to 1539 by the custom of certain counties (see *Co Litt* 187a and *Fitz Nat Brev*, p 138) it appears that these were exceptional circumstances and did not occur often.

6 Unlike joint tenancies and tenancies in common which usually arise through the acts of the parties themselves.

7 Williams, *Principles of the Law of Real Property* (16th edn, 1887), p 123. See further *Co Litt* 163b and *Ballard v Ballard* (1556) 2 Dyer 128a. Another possible explanation is that because estates in joint tenancy and tenancy in common developed later than estates in coparcenary, when the former eventually became popular the time for inventing new writs had passed and thus joint tenants and tenants in common had to wait for the legislature to apply a remedy: Loyd, 'Partition' (1919) 67 U Pa L Rev 162 at 168.

8 Sometimes referred to as a 'writ of partition'. It appears that this writ was the origin of the term 'parceners' which was used as a convenient shorthand for coparceners: *Litt* s 241 and *Co Litt* 163a.

'Rex, & c. Si A. fecerit, & c., sum B. & c. ostens. quare quum eadem A. & B. insimul & pro indiviso teneant tres acras terrae cum pertin. de haereditate quae fuit M. matris praedict. A. & B. cujus haered. ipsae sunt, in I. eidem B. Partitioni nostrae inde inter eas secundum Legem & consuetudinem regni Angl. faciend. contradic', & eam facere non permittit, minus juste, ut dicit'. & habeas ibi Sum'. & hoc Breve.'[9]

[3.06] The court gave two judgments on the writ[10]. The first[11] directed the sheriff of the county in which the lands were situated to 'go to the lands and tenements etc and ... by the oath of twelve lawful men ... to make partition between the parties'[12]. This involved a number of stages[13].

[3.07] The first stage was to choose twelve knights to assist the sheriff in carrying out a valuation of the land[14]. A writ was issued to the knights from the king, appointing them for this task and ordering them to meet at a particular place with specific instructions for dividing the land[15]. Having ascertained that the coparceners had paid their homage to the relevant chief lords, the writ then directed the knights to make an 'extent and valuation' of the land before dividing it into portions of equal value[16]. If one coparcener received a greater share of a particular property than the others, the latter were compensated for any deficit. This was termed 'owelty of partition' and took the form of additional items of property to equalise the value of the divided shares[17]. Courts of Common Law could not order payments of money as owelty of partition[18].

---

9 *Fitz Nat Brev*, pp 137-138. See further *Litt* s 246 and *Co Litt* 167a. The relevant part of the writ provided that 'the said A. and B. hold together and undivided _ acres of land with the appurtenances, in _, of the inheritance which was _'s, the mother of the aforesaid A. and B., whose heirs they are': *Co Litt* 167 a.

10 *Litt* s 248 and *Co Litt* 168a.

11 Termed *quod partitio fiat inter partes praedictas, de tenementis, cum pertinentiis*: 2 *Cru Dig* 385.

12 *Litt* s 248. Where the lands were in different counties, a separate writ had to be issued to the sheriff of each county. Since the writ of partition commanded the sheriff to go 'in his own person' it could not be executed by a deputy: *Clay's Case* (1583) Cro Eliz 10.

13 See generally *Bracton on the Laws and Customs of England* (1968), pp 208-226.

14 The knights (sometimes referred to as 'justices') were usually unconnected with the parties and therefore impartial.

15 *Bracton on the Laws and Customs of England* (1968), p 209.

16 *Bracton on the Laws and Customs of England* (1968), p 209.

17 *Litt* s 251 and see *Bracton on the Laws and Customs of England* (1968), pp 211-212.

18 Since under the terms of the writ *de partitione facienda*, the land was to be divided according to its true value without any authority for the sheriff or knights to make pecuniary compensation for any inequality: Story, *Commentaries on Equity Jurisprudence* (10th edn, 1870), pp 648-649.

[3.08] The scheme of partition proposed by the knights was then sealed with the sheriff's seal and attached to the writ *de partitione facienda* before both documents were returned to court by the sheriff. Each coparcener was asked if she could show any reason why she or any of the other coparceners should not receive her divided share of the property. If this question was answered in the negative or the court found no substantial ground of action in a particular complaint, the land was divided accordingly. This represented the second judgment on the writ *de partitione facienda*[19]. Since it was the more important of the two, the overall judgment was not complete until the second judgment had been given[20].

[3.09] The next stage was allocation of the divided shares to the coparceners, in most instances by means of an anonymous allotment[21]. The respective parcels of land were written on separate scrolls of paper and handed to an impartial layman who delivered one scroll to each parcener. First choice of parcels usually went to the eldest according to the privilege of seniority, with the youngest choosing last[22]. Finally, delivery of possession was required to complete the partition. The writ *de partitione facienda* merely ordered the parties to assemble before the court to hear the terms of the proposed partition. Another writ had to be issued by the king to the sheriff ordering him to deliver seisin of the divided parcels of land to the parties after partition[23]. This constituted the titles of the coparceners to their respective allotments and no further action was required to complete the partition[24].

B Compulsory partition by joint tenants and tenants in common

[3.10] Joint tenants and tenants in common could not initially compel partition and were at an obvious disadvantage. It was an inevitable consequence of concurrent ownership that disputes arose as to the use and occupation of the

---

19 Termed *ideo consideratum est, per curam quod partitio firma et stabilis in perpetuum teneatur*: *Co Litt* 168a.

20 An alleged error in the proceedings (for example, the absence of the sheriff) had to be examined before the return of the writ *de partitione facienda*: *Clay's Case* (1583) Cro Eliz 10. Once the return had been received and filed, no party could raise such an objection. Where a coparcener was not satisfied with the partition (for example, if she felt that an unfair division had been made) she could bring a writ of error before the court: *Barkeley v Warwick* (1598) Cro Eliz 635. However, such a writ could only be issued after the second judgment had been given on the writ *de partitione facienda*: *Barkeley v Warwick*.

21 *Bracton on the Laws and Customs of England* (1968), p 220.

22 *Bracton on the Laws and Customs of England* (1968), p 220. Alternatively, the allotment of shares could be carried out by the sheriff who would assign a parcel of land to each parcener irrespective of the privilege of seniority: *Litt* s 249 and *Co Litt* 168b.

23 As to the terms of this writ see *Bracton on the Laws and Customs of England* (1968), p 225.

24 *Bracton on the Laws and Customs of England* (1968), p 225.

land, and where they did the only viable solution may have been to end co-ownership. However, joint tenants and tenants in common could only partition or sell the land where they all agreed to do so; if one co-owner refused to consent the others could not force a partition or sale against his wishes[25]. Parliament eventually intervened to provide a remedy[26].

[3.11] The first such legislation was introduced in England in the form of An Act Concerning Joint Tenants and Tenants in Common 1539. In the preamble the legislature acknowledged the problems which had plagued joint tenants and tenants in common:

> '[E]very one of them so being Joint Tenants, or Tenants in common, have like Right Title Interest and Possession in the same Manors Lands Tenements and Hereditaments ... undividedly together with other, and none of them by the Law doth or may know their several Parts or Portions in the same ... and cannot by the Laws of this Realm otherwise occupy or take the Profits of the same, or make any Severance Division or Partition thereof, without either of their mutual Assents and Consents; by reason whereof ... oftentimes of their perverse covetous and malicious Minds and Wills, against all Right Justice Equity and good Conscience, by Strength and Power hath not only cut and fallen down all the Woods and Trees growing upon the same, but also have extirped subverted pulled down and destroyed all the ... Buildings Meadows, Pastures Commons and the whole Commodities of the same, and have taken and converted them to their own Uses ... to the open Wrong and Disherison and against the Minds and Wills of other holding the same Manors Lands Tenements and Hereditaments jointly or in common with them, and they have always been without assured Remedy for the same ...'[27]

[3.12] However, these evils had existed for many years before the legislature attempted to remedy the situation. One author has suggested a different motive for the enactment of this legislation:

> '[T]his fragment of private law, was the silent force of economic pressure, resulting from a new attitude towards land. Feudalism was in decay, commercialism in the ascendant and real property rapidly becoming a form of

[25] See *Fisher v Wigg* (1699) 1 Salk 391. Where a coparcener held land with a tenant in common (if another coparcener had severed her share by alienation) or with a tenant by the curtesy (where a coparcener died leaving her husband to take her share: see *Litt* s 264) the latter were at an obvious disadvantage. While the coparcener could compel partition, the tenant in common or tenant by the curtesy could only partition the land with the agreement of the coparcener: *Co Litt* 175a and 175b.

[26] Thus, the right to compel partition was not a common law incident of a joint tenancy or tenancy in common but was conferred by statute.

[27] This was also stated in the preamble to the equivalent Irish Statute, An Act for Jointenants 1542.

investment. Fractional shares in estates would for all practical purposes remain unmarketable if no means was provided by which a purchaser could dissolve an uncongenial partnership and protect his interests.'[28]

[3.13] The 1539 Act provided that joint tenants and tenants in common of estates of inheritance[29] could compel partition at common law by writ *de participatione facienda*[30] in the 'like Manner and Form as Coparceners by the common Laws of this realm have been and are compellable to do'. The following year, this remedy was extended in England to joint tenants and tenants in common of estates for a term of life or years by An Act Concerning Joint Tenants for Term of Life or Years 1540. Provisions identical to those contained in the 1539 and 1540 Acts were introduced in Ireland by An Act for Jointenants 1542.

[3.14] With the introduction of these 'Statutes of Partition' joint tenants and tenants in common of both estates of inheritance and limited estates were no longer confined to dividing their land by mutual agreement: any one of them could compel partition at common law in the same manner as coparceners[31]. Moreover, joint tenants and tenants in common were entitled to partition as of right[32]. The court was obliged to order partition upon such a request being made and had no discretion to refuse the relief sought no matter how inconvenient partition might be[33]. However, the court's jurisdiction only extended to those estates which were specifically mentioned in the Statutes of Partition. For

---

28 Loyd, 'Partition' (1919) 67 U Pa L Rev 162 at 169.

29 In either their own right or in the right of their wives.

30 It appears that the term '*participatione*' was a misprint of the intended '*partitione*': see *Patel v Premabhai* [1954] AC 35 at 42 per Lord Porter.

31 *Co Litt* 169a and 187a and 2 *Bl Comm* 184-185. See further *Swift v Roberts* (1764) Amb 617. However, there was one difference between the two groups. The right to compel partition was a common law incident of coparcenary, while joint tenants and tenants in common were granted such a right by statute. Accordingly, where land was held by several coparceners and a tenant in common or tenant by the curtesy and one member of each group (a coparcener and tenant by the curtesy or a coparcener and tenant in common) desired partition, they could not join in the same writ *de partitione facienda*: *Ballard v Ballard* (1556) 2 Dyer 128a.

32 The relevant part of the legislation provided that joint tenants and tenants in common 'shall and may be coacted and compelled … to make partition between them'. The words 'shall and may' were regarded as imperative in this context: see University of Alberta Institute of Law Research and Reform Report No 23, *Partition and Sale* (March 1977), p 9 and *Re Hutcheson and Hutcheson* [1950] OR 265. A number of other cases have decided that the words 'shall and may' are to be construed imperatively when used in legislation: see the comments of Lord Hardwicke LC in *A-G v Lock* (1744) 3 Atk 164 at 166 and those of Lord Lyndhurst CB in *Crump v Adney and Page* (1833) 1 Cr & M 355 at 361. See further *Stumper v Millar* (1744) 3 Atk 212.

33 See the comments of Murray J in *Northern Bank Ltd v Beattie* [1982] 18 NIJB 1 at 22.

example, co-owners could not compel partition of copyholds because they were not included in the legislation[34].

[3.15] As with coparceners, a joint tenant or tenant in common seeking partition had to issue a writ *de partitione facienda* against the other co-owners[35]. The court then gave its two-part judgment on the writ[36]. The first directed the sheriff of the county in which the lands were situated to go there and, with the aid of twelve lawful men, to make a valuation of the property before dividing it into parcels commensurate to the interest of each co-owner. Upon return of this inquisition, the second judgment confirmed the proposed partition[37] and was followed by a writ directing the sheriff to deliver seisin to the parties[38]. The titles of the parties to their respective shares were derived from the return of the writ *de partitione facienda* to the court under the sheriff's seal and delivery of seisin by the sheriff; nothing further was required to complete the partition[39].

C Development of the common law action

[3.16] The Statutes of Partition granted joint tenants and tenants in common a right to compel partition at common law. However, there were a number of difficulties associated with this remedy. The process itself was regarded as

---

34 *Scott v Fawcett* (1757) 1 Dick 299. The Statutes of Partition referred to joint tenants and tenants in common dividing 'manors lands tenements and hereditaments'. In *Hanburry v Hussey* (1851) 14 Beav 152, Romilly MR held that these were to be read disjunctively and not conjunctively: for example where partition was sought of a manor, that could be a manor on its own and did not have to be a manor surrounded by other lands, tenements and hereditaments.

35 The Statutes of Partition did not prescribe a particular form of writ *de partitione facienda*, but left this to the discretion of the clerks of the Court of Chancery. During this time, the Court of Chancery had exclusive jurisdiction to issue writs to bring actions in the royal courts: see Wylie, *Irish Land Law* (3rd edn, 1997), pp 84-85 and Kiely, *The Principles of Equity as Applied in Ireland* (1936), pp 3-4. Where the parties were co-owners of an estate of inheritance, the writ could be framed in general terms. As regards limited estates the writ had to be framed in specific terms, stating the respective estates of the parties and the nature of those estates: see *Taylor v Sayer* (1600) Cro Eliz 742 and *Moor and Brown v Onslow* (1600) Cro Eliz 759.

36 See 2 *Cru Dig* 385-386.

37 See *Barkley v Countess of Warwick* (1598) Cro Eliz 635.

38 See *Halton v Earl of Thanet* (1777) 2 Black W 1158. While the court would ignore minor errors in the writ *de partitione facienda* or associated documents (such as spelling errors: see *Yates v Windham* (1587) Cro Eliz 65) more serious errors were corrected by the court. Thus in *Baker v Daniel* (1815) 6 Taunt 193 where the sheriff's return erroneously described the type of estate involved in the partition action, the court amended the return in its second judgment.

39 See Jenks, *Modern Land Law* (1899), p 353 and *Whaley v Dawson* (1805) 2 Sch & Lef 367. Contrast this with the practice in equity: see para **[3.31]** below. If one of the co-owners was under a disability, a partition under the writ *de partitione facienda* was binding on him or her even if it was unequal. This was because the partition was made 'by force of the king's writ, and judgment thereof given ... [and was] made by the sheriff by the oath of twelve men by authority of law; and the judgment [was] that partition shall remain firm and stable for ever': *Co Litt* 171a and 171b. See further Allnatt, *A Practical Treatise on the Law of Partition* (1820), p 64.

'technical and dilatory'[40] and the judgment of the court was dependent on the titles of all the parties to the action, the onus of proving which was on the plaintiff[41]. Problems also arose where the disputed lands were situated in different counties: possession of the divided parcels had to be delivered by the sheriff of that particular county, since the sheriff of one county had no jurisdiction in another[42]. In *Manaton v Squire*[43] the court remarked that, due to the difficulties at common law, the delays were such that a plaintiff often would not see the partition action settled.

[3.17] The legislature attempted to simplify partition actions at common law with the introduction of legislation in 1697[44]. The legislation provided that, following the return of the first judgment on the writ *de partitione facienda*, the court could give a judgment for partition based solely on the declarations of title submitted by the plaintiff where the other co-owners had been given written notice of this return but failed to appear before the court[45]. Partition of the land would be carried out after six days notice to the absent parties and would thereafter be binding on all the co-owners[46]. The Acts also provided that, where the high sheriff could not be present at the proceedings, the writ *de partitione facienda* could be executed by an under sheriff with the assistance of two justices of the county and would take effect as if the high sheriff had been present[47].

---

40 Loyd, 'Partition' (1919) 67 U Pa L Rev 162 at 169.

41 See the comments of Lord Eldon LC in *Agar v Fairfax* (1811) 17 Ves 533 noted at para **[2.?]** below.

42 Foster, *The Law on Joint Ownership and Partition of Real Estate* (1878), p 103.

43 (1677) 2 Free 26.

44 An Act for the easier obtaining Partition of Lands in Coparcenary, Joint Tenancy and Tenancy in Common 1697 and An Act for the more easy obtaining Partition of Lands in Co-parcenary, Jointenancy, and Tenancy in common, and bounding and mearing of Lands (Ir) 1697.

45 An Act for the easier obtaining Partition of Lands in Coparcenary, Joint Tenancy and Tenancy in Common 1697, s 1 and An Act for the more easy obtaining Partition of Lands in Co-parcenary, Jointenancy, and Tenancy in common, and bounding and mearing of Lands (Ir) 1697, s 1.

46 However, the parties could within one year of the partition (or within one year of the end of their disability where they were infants, married women or persons of unsound mind) object to the division on the basis that the plaintiff had misrepresented his title. The court could then set aside the partition or award another: An Act for the easier obtaining Partition of Lands in Coparcenary, Joint Tenancy and Tenancy in Common 1697, s 2 and An Act for the more easy obtaining Partition of Lands in Co-parcenary, Jointenancy, and Tenancy in common, and bounding and mearing of Lands (Ir) 1697, s 2.

47 An Act for the easier obtaining Partition of Lands in Coparcenary, Joint Tenancy and Tenancy in Common 1697, s 4 and An Act for the more easy obtaining Partition of Lands in Co-parcenary, Jointenancy, and Tenancy in common, and bounding and mearing of Lands (Ir) 1697, s 4.

[3.18] These amendments had little impact. By this time, a simpler and more flexible method of obtaining partition had developed in equity and most co-owners had recourse to the Court of Chancery when they sought partition or when a common law partition was unequal or in need of correction[48]. The common law action was eventually rendered obsolete by the abolition of the writ *de partitione facienda* by the Real Property Limitation Act 1833. Thus the Court of Chancery obtained exclusive jurisdiction to determine partition actions[49].

III Compulsory Partition in Equity

[3.19] The transition of partition actions from common law to equity was not a sudden transfer prompted by the abolition of the writ *de partitione facienda*. The equitable jurisdiction to partition had existed concurrently with the common law jurisdiction for centuries.

A Origins of the equitable jurisdiction to partition

[3.20] It appears that the Court of Chancery had assumed jurisdiction in partition actions between coparceners as early as the fourteenth century[50]. As regards joint tenants and tenants in common, most sources indicate that partition actions in equity commenced towards the end of the sixteenth century and gradually encroached on the common law action until the Court of Chancery obtained exclusive jurisdiction following the Real Property Limitation Act 1833[51]. This equitable jurisdiction was well-established by the late seventeenth

---

[48] Loyd, 'Partition' (1919) 67 U Pa L Rev 162 at 169.

[49] Real Property Limitation Act 1833, s 36 provided that no writ of partition could be brought after 31 December 1834.

[50] *Fitz Nat Brev*, p 138 states that partition could be made in equity where one of the coparceners was a ward to the king. See further (1328) YB 2 Ed III (RS) pl 5 and (1341) YB 15 Ed III (RS) pl 42. It is unclear whether this equitable jurisdiction extended to joint tenants and tenants in common before the Statutes of Partition granted them a right to compel partition at common law. Tentative support for this proposition may be found in *Citizens of London v Bishop of Bath* reported in Selden Society, *Select Cases Before the King's Council* (1243-1482), p 8 and in a case noted in Selden Society, *Select Cases in Chancery* (1364-1471) Vol X, p 129. However, it is doubtful whether this course of action was available to joint tenants and tenants in common during this time: see ch 6 below, paras **[6.27]**-**[6.33]**.

[51] See White and Tudor, *A Selection of Leading Cases in Equity* (7th edn, 1897), pp 196-197; 2 *Cru Dig* 388-389; Ballow, *A Treatise of Equity* (1820) Vol 1, pp 18-20; Spence, *Equitable Jurisdiction of the Court of Chancery* (1846), p 654; and Story, *Commentaries on Equity Jurisprudence* (10th edn, 1870), pp 641-646. These indicate that the equitable jurisdiction to partition in respect of joint tenants and tenants in common developed steadily from the reign of Elizabeth I. In *Manners v Charlesworth* (1833) 1 My & K 330 Brougham LC remarked:

> 'A considerable obscurity hangs over many parts of this subject of commission of partition, both as to the origin of the jurisdiction after the statute of Hen. 8, and as to the principles which govern its exercise ... There is no trace of the proceeding, I believe, in this Court before the 40th Elizabeth; and it was of rare and uncertain use as late as the beginning of the reign of Charles I.'

century, Lord Nottingham LC in *Manaton v Squire*[52] remarking that he 'did no more question the jurisdiction of the Chancellor in these cases, than he did whether a gift to a man and his heirs were a fee simple'[53].

[3.21] The original jurisdiction to partition existed at common law under the Statutes of Partition[54]. The equitable jurisdiction to partition developed concurrently with the common law action and was derived from the procedure at law by analogy to the practice under the writ *de partitione facienda*[55]. This remedy of partition 'like so many other equitable remedies, was first introduced for exceptional cases, and afterwards generalised'[56]. It appears that the Court of Chancery assumed jurisdiction because of the inadequacy of the common law remedy of partition and the procedural difficulties associated with such actions:

> 'The Court of Chancery, at first acting only in aid of the common law court, then assuming a concurrent jurisdiction, has at length obtained an almost exclusive jurisdiction over the subject. That it has no original jurisdiction, nor has any express authority from statute, has been acknowledged by those who were most conversant with its jurisdiction, and have best administered it: the general reception it has met with is owing to the advantage it has over the common law court, in being loose and free from all technical restraints; and to the powers it possesses of dealing with and providing for the various interests it may meet with.'[57]

---

51 (contd) In *Norse v Ludlow* (1590) Toth 155n and *Long v Miller* (1594) Toth 155 the Court of Chancery intervened to relieve unequal partitions which had been made by the parties. For examples of other cases decided around this time see *Broughton v Broughton* (1586), *Bab v Dudeney* (1638), *Norbury v Yarbury* (1638-39), and *Windham v Weare* (1639-40), all noted with the report of *Long v Miller* (1594) Toth 155.

52 (1677) 2 Free 26.

53 See further *Earl of Kildare v Eustace* (1686) 1 Vern 419.

54 *Mundy v Mundy* (1793) 2 Ves 122 at 124 and see Allnatt, *A Practical Treatise on the Law of Partition* (1820), p 78.

55 *Miller v Warmington* (1820) 1 Jac & W 484 and *O'Hara v Strange* (1847) 11 Ir Eq R 262. See further para **[3.30]** below.

56 Jenks, *Modern Land Law* (1899), p 352 and see *Agar v Fairfax* (1811) 17 Ves 533. Courts of Equity acted in accordance with the principle of Roman Law '*in communione vel societate nemo compellitur invitus detineri*' (no-one can be kept in a partnership or association against his will): White and Tudor, *A Selection of Leading Cases in Equity* (7th edn, 1897), pp 196-197.

57 Bacon, *A New Abridgment of the Law* (7th edn, 1832), p 509. In *Dodd v Cattell* [1914] 2 Ch 1 at 11 Warrington J commented that '[t]he jurisdiction of the Courts of Equity is a concurrent jurisdiction only, and was resorted to ... owing to the existence of machinery in those Courts more convenient for the purpose than the writ of partition, the only engine available to Courts of Common Law.' See further *Croghan v Grosvenor* (1991) 57 SASR 545 at 547 and the cases cited therein. The equitable jurisdiction to partition developed because of the inadequacy of the common law remedy in the same manner as the Court of Chancery's jurisdiction in cases of dower: see the comments of Langdale MR in *Strickland v Strickland* (1842) 6 Beav 77 at 81.

[3.22] Four factors contributed to the development of the equitable jurisdiction to partition[58].

1 Matters of title

[3.23] A disadvantage of the common law action for partition was the need to establish titles and the heavy burden this placed on the plaintiff especially where the titles were complicated[59]. However, these problems were not so apparent in the Court of Chancery:

> '[C]omplication of titles [is] the true foundation of the [equitable] jurisdiction ... However complicated the titles of the parties might be, still, if they could be thoroughly investigated at law, in the usual course of proceedings in the common law courts, there would seem to be no sufficient reason for transferring the jurisdiction of such cases to the courts of equity. The true expression of the doctrine ... [is] that courts of equity interfere in cases of such a complication of titles, because the remedy at law is inadequate and imperfect, without the aid of a court of equity to promote a discovery, or to remove obstructions to the right, or to grant some other equitable redress.'[60]

[3.24] Under the equitable jurisdiction to partition, the plaintiff had to state his own title with accuracy; if there was no proof of title in the plaintiff the court could not make an order for partition[61]. However, the practice in equity differed significantly as regards the defendants' titles. While the declarations of title had to show unity of possession[62], the plaintiff did not have to show a complete title in the defendants and merely had to establish that they were persons interested in the property[63].

---

58 See Story, *Commentaries on Equity Jurisprudence* (10th edn, 1870), pp 645-653, Bispham, *The Principles of Equity* (10th edn, 1925), pp 764-771 and *Snell's Principles of Equity* (2nd edn, 1872), pp 491-492.

59 See *Agar v Fairfax* (1811) 17 Ves 533 at 552 where Lord Eldon LC referred to the 'extreme difficulty attending the process of partition at Law; where the Plaintiff must prove his title, as he declares; and also the titles of the Defendants; and judgment is given for partition according to the respective titles, so proved'.

60 Story, *Commentaries on Equity Jurisprudence* (10th edn, 1870), p 625.

61 See *Cartwright v Pultney* (1742) 2 Atk 380 where the court stated that the plaintiff had to show a title in himself and not allege generally that he was in possession of a specific share of the property. If a defect in the plaintiff's title was relatively minor, the court would give him an opportunity to perfect his title: *Jope v Morshead* (1843) 12 LJ Ch 190. However, if the plaintiff put forward a very imperfect title the court would dismiss his bill for partition without prejudice to filing a new bill when such defects had been remedied: *Jope v Morshead*. See further *Giffard v Williams* (1869) LR 8 Eq 494 and *Bolton v Bolton* (1868) LR 7 Eq 298.

62 *Miller v Warmington* (1820) 1 Jac & W 484.

63 See *Calmady v Calmady* (1795) 2 Ves 568 and *Baring v Nash* (1813) 1 Ves & B 551. However, the declaration had to show that the shares of the respective co-owners were ascertainable: *Cole v Sewell* (1849) 15 Sim 284.

[3.25] A partition suit in equity could not be used as a means of trying a disputed legal title[64]. While the Chancery Regulation Act 1862 ('Rolts Act') conferred jurisdiction on the Court of Chancery to determine questions of law and fact pertaining to the relief sought[65], the court could only determine incidental legal questions. It could not determine legal questions that formed a substantial ground of the action[66]. In *Slade v Barlow*[67], the plaintiff's bill for partition raised the question of whether, upon construction of the settlor's will under which the plaintiff derived his undivided interest, the estate passed to him under a specific or a residuary devise. The court held that it had no jurisdiction to try such a question in a partition suit, and the bill was ordered to be retained for a year[68].

2 Owelty or equality of partition

[3.26] At common law, if the parcel of land allotted to one co-owner exceeded the value of his undivided interest, the other co-owner was allocated an additional item of property to compensate for this[69]. However, the Court of Chancery could order sums of money to be paid as owelty of partition:

> 'Courts of Equity are not restrained, as Courts of Law are, to a mere partition or allotment of the lands and other real estate between the parties according to their respective interests in the same and having regard to the true value thereof. But Courts of Equity may, with a view to the more convenient and perfect partition or allotment of the premises, decree a pecuniary compensation to one of the parties for owelty or equality of partition. This a Court of Common Law is not at liberty to do.'[70]

64 See White and Tudor, *A Selection of Leading Cases in Equity* (7th edn, 1897), p 198 and *Potter v Waller* (1847) 16 LJ Ch 480.

65 Chancery Regulation Act 1862, Preamble and s 1.

66 See Seton, *Forms of Judgments and Orders in the High Court of Justice and the Court of Appeal* (6th edn, 1901), p 1873 and Walker, *The Partition Acts, 1868 and 1876* (1882), p 64.

67 (1869) LR 7 Eq 298.

68 Similar views were expressed in *Moore v Kempston* (1870) IR 4 Eq 306. See further *Bolton v Bolton* (1868) LR 7 Eq 298n and *Giffard v Williams* (1869) LR 8 Eq 494. However, in *Burt v Hellyar* (1872) LR 14 Eq 160 the court, at the request of the persons interested in the property, allowed incidental legal questions to be decided in the partition action and prefaced the decree for partition with a statement to this effect. This practice continued until the passing of the Judicature Act 1873 and the Judicature (Ir) Act 1877.

69 See para **[3.07]** above.

70 Story, *Commentaries on Equity Jurisprudence* (10th edn, 1870), pp 648-649 and see Reid, 'Partitions in Kind: A Preference Without Favor' (1986) 7 Cardozo L Rev 855 at 859. The term 'owelty of partition' was replaced by the term 'money or compensation for equality of partition': 21 *Halsbury's Laws of England* (1st edn, 1912), p 811. In *Stewart v Ferguson* (1842) 5 Ir Eq R 157 Lefroy B held that, if the defendant refused to pay the sum agreed for owelty of partition, the plaintiff could recover this sum with interest from the date on which the first payment was due.

Thus the Court of Chancery could deal effectively with the rights of the joint owners and do justice between the parties[71].

3 Accounting adjustments

[3.27] Courts of Common Law could not make accounting adjustments between joint tenants and tenants in common as incidental to making an order for partition. A co-owner who desired such an adjustment had to institute a separate action of account[72]. However, the Court of Chancery could direct an account between the parties as incidental to making an order for partition, not under the authority of any statute or upon any general legal principle but upon principles of equity[73]. For example, if one co-owner had ousted the others from the property, the Court of Chancery could order him to pay an appropriate occupation rent[74].

4 Binding estates and interests in reversion or remainder

[3.28] Partition between co-owners of limited estates may be permanent if the persons interested in reversion or remainder consent and are parties to the action[75]. At common law, a decree for partition only bound those persons who were entitled to a subsisting estate; a separate writ had to be issued against the reversioner or remainderman when his estate fell into possession[76]. A decree for partition in equity had the advantage of binding interests in reversion or remainder as well as the co-owners for life or a term of years[77]. Few problems arose where the persons interested in reversion or remainder were ascertainable and could be made parties to the suit. However, a decree for partition in equity bound the persons interested in reversion or remainder even if they could not be made parties, either because they were unborn persons or because it was uncertain who would become entitled upon determination of the limited estate[78].

---

71 See the comments of Bouck J in *Shore v Shore* (1975) 63 DLR (3d) 354 at 356.

72 Story, *Commentaries on Equity Jurisprudence* (10th edn, 1870), pp 648-649. As to accounting adjustments in general see ch 11 below.

73 See *Lorimer v Lorimer* (1820) 5 Madd 363; *Story v Johnson* (1837) 2 Y & C Ex Rep 586; *Gage v Mulholland* (1869) 16 Gr 145 and *Re Jones* [1893] 2 Ch 461. Thus the Court of Chancery intervened 'so as to prevent any injustice or inequality': *Croghan v Grosvenor* (1991) 57 SASR 545 at 548 per Debelle J.

74 See *Pascoe v Swan* (1859) 27 Beav 508 and *Turner v Morgan* (1803) 8 Ves 143.

75 See ch 4 below, para **[4.29]**.

76 Allnatt, *A Practical Treatise on the Law of Partition* (1820), pp 63-64.

77 See Bacon, *A New Abridgment of the Law* (7th edn, 1832), p 510 and Allnatt, *A Practical Treatise on the Law of Partition* (1820), p 78. In *Gaskell v Gaskell* (1836) 6 Sim 643 the court held that the decree for partition would be binding on persons interested in remainder but directed references to the Master to inquire whether the decree would be for the benefit of the future issue of the plaintiff.

78 See *Wills v Slade* (1801) 6 Ves 498 and *Gaskell v Gaskell* (1836) 6 Sim 643.

Such persons could not interfere with the decree for partition when they came into existence or became entitled to an interest[79].

[3.29] A decree for partition in equity required the parties to execute mutual conveyances in order to complete the partition[80]. Under s 30 of the Trustee Act 1850 the Court of Chancery could declare such unborn or unidentified persons trustees of their respective shares, and execute the requisite conveyances on their behalf[81]. The purpose of s 30 was to facilitate the transfer of the legal estate in situations such as this[82]. While the decree for partition bound the equitable interests of all persons not in existence[83], they could not execute the requisite conveyances and the court had to do so on their behalf.

B Comparison of the common law and equitable jurisdictions

1 Common requirements

[3.30] Since the equitable jurisdiction to partition was derived from that at common law, a decree for partition in equity would only usually be granted in the same circumstances as such a decree would have been granted at law[84]. For example, the Court of Chancery could order partition of the same estates and interests as specified by the Statutes of Partition[85], except where it was granted a specific jurisdiction in respect of estates that could not be divided at law[86]. Likewise, the method of proceeding in equity was by analogy to that at common law. The equitable bill for partition was framed in a similar manner to the writ *de partitione facienda*[87]. In the same way as two judgments were given on the writ, the Court of Chancery made two decrees on the bill of partition[88]. However, the equitable jurisdiction to partition was in some respects wider than the equivalent jurisdiction at common law[89]. The Court of Chancery could order partition in situations where it would not have been granted at common law: for example,

---

79 Foster, *The Law on Joint Ownership and Partition of Real Estate* (1878), pp 131-132.

80 See paras **[3.31]-[3.36]** below.

81 See *Bowra v Wright* (1851) 4 De G & Sm 265 and White and Tudor, *A Selection of Leading Cases in Equity* (7th edn, 1897), p 211.

82 *Basnett v Moxon* (1875) LR 20 Eq 182.

83 White and Tudor, *A Selection of Leading Cases in Equity* (7th edn, 1897), p 211 and *Daniell's Chancery Practice* (8th edn, 1914), p 1180.

84 See *Turner v Morgan* (1803) 8 Ves 143; *Miller v Warmington* (1820) 1 Jac & W 484 and *O'Hara v Strange* (1847) 11 Ir Eq R 262.

85 See paras **[3.13]-[3.14]** above.

86 Such as copyholds under the Copyhold Act 1841. The Court of Chancery also retained certain jurisdiction exceptions which had developed at common law: see ch 4 below, paras **[4.36]-[4.69]**.

87 *Lowe v Franks* (1828) 1 Moll 137.

88 *Herbert v Hedges* (1844) 10 Ir Eq R 479 at 488 per Pennefather B.

89 See *Swan v Swan* (1820) 8 Price 518 and *Snell's Principles of Equity* (2nd edn, 1872), p 492.

where the plaintiff could not prove the defendant's title to the property. There was, however, one fundamental procedural difference between partition actions at common law and in equity.

2 *Execution of mutual conveyances*

[3.31] A decree for partition at common law vested the legal estate in the divided shares without any further action on the part of the former co-owners[90]. In contrast, partition in equity was based on the premise of mutual conveyances[91]. A decree for partition only affected the equitable interests and the judgment of the court directed the parties to execute mutual conveyances in order to complete the partition[92]. Since equity acts *in personam*, the decree in equity did not bind the land itself hence the need for such conveyances[93].

(a) Necessary parties and form of conveyance

[3.32] All persons interested in the property had to be joined as parties to the action to facilitate the execution of mutual conveyances[94]. In particular, the persons in whom the legal estate was vested had to be before the court[95]. The plaintiff had to show a good title to the property, unlike the procedure at common law where it was sufficient to allege seisin[96]. Where the plaintiff could not establish his title, the bill was dismissed but without prejudice to filing a subsequent bill[97].

[3.33] The appropriate form of conveyance depended on the type of co-ownership involved. With respect to coparceners the orthodox rule was that, their estate showing characteristics of both joint tenancies and tenancies in common, any transfer of interest could be by release or by grant[98]. As regards joint tenants, partition was by deed of release as opposed to grant[99]. Where the

90 See paras **[3.09]** and **[3.15]** above.

91 *Whaley v Dawson* (1805) 2 Sch and Lef 367 and *Miller v Warmington* (1820) 1 Jac & W 484. See further *A-G v Hamilton* (1816) 1 Madd 214.

92 White and Tudor, *A Selection of Leading Cases in Equity* (7th edn, 1897), pp 204-205.

93 Bacon, *A New Abridgment of the Law* (7th edn, 1832), p 510 and Allnatt, *A Practical Treatise on the Law of Partition* (1820), pp 123-124.

94 *Anon in Chancery* (1742) 3 Swans 157n and see Walker, *The Partition Acts, 1868 and 1876* (1882), p 11.

95 See *Miller v Warmington* (1820) 1 Jac & W 484 and *Whaley v Dawson* (1805) 2 Sch and Lef 367. It was sufficient that such persons were before the court at the second hearing: *Slator v Wilson* (1818) 2 Mol 522.

96 See *Cartwright v Pultney* (1742) 2 Atk 380 and Ballow, *A Treatise of Equity* (1820) Vol 1, p 21.

97 See *Parker v Gerard* (1754) Amb 236 and *Jope v Morshead* (1843) 6 Beav 213. Where the legal title was outstanding, a good equitable title would suffice: *Miller v Warmington* (1820) 1 Jac & W 484 and *Cornish v Gest* (1788) 2 Cox 27.

98 *Co Litt* 200b. Before the Real Property Act 1845 the conveyance was by feofment instead of grant.

land was held under a tenancy in common, partition took place by ordinary conveyances as between strangers and not by release[100]. Section 3 of the Real Property Act 1845 provided that any partition made after 1 October 1845 had to be by deed[101].

[3.34] Since partition in equity required the execution of mutual conveyances, it was customary for the Commissioners' award[102] or the decree of the court to direct the parties to make such conveyances. If an award did not direct the execution of mutual conveyances, it would be set aside[103]. In addition to this, one co-owner could not insist on the receipt of conveyances from all the others as a precondition to executing his conveyance. Since all the parties were under the court order, there was no danger of one co-owner parting with his share before the others had executed their respective conveyances to him[104].

(b) Trustee Act 1850

[3.35] The Trustee Act 1850 altered the relevant law in two respects[105], the first of which related to the practice in partition actions involving persons under a disability. Despite the fact that the court could make an order for partition against an infant, married woman or person of unsound mind[106], partition could not be completed because such persons were unable to execute a valid conveyance of their respective interests[107]. As regards infants for example, partition could not be completed until the infant reached 21 years of age and was able to effectively convey his interest in the property[108]. In these circumstances, the court would decree partition and direct that the parties would be quieted in

99 *Co Litt* 187a.

100 Despite the fact that tenants in common had joint possession, their interests in the land were nevertheless deemed to be several: *Co Litt* 200b and Challis, *The Modern Law of Real Property* (3rd edn, 1911), pp 368-369.

101 The deed of partition had to specify the terms of the partition and any money or property allocated as owelty of partition, the titles of the parties, and covenants for the production of deeds where they were held by one of the co-owners: Foster, *The Law on Joint Ownership and Partition of Real Estate* (1878), p 96.

102 See generally paras **[3.38]-[3.41]** below.

103 *Johnson v Wilson* (1741) Willes 248. Where an award directed the parties to make such conveyances this was sufficient, even though it did not specify which part of the property was to be held in severalty by each co-owner: *Knight v Burton* (1704) 6 Mod Rep 231.

104 *Orger v Sparke* (1861) 9 WR 180.

105 The Trustee Act 1850 also applied to Ireland: Trustee Act 1850, ss 55 and 57

106 See *Martyn v Perryman* (1662) 1 Rep Ch 125 and *Hollingworth v Sidebottom* (1837) 7 LJ Ch 2.

107 See *Brook v Hertford* (1728) 2 P Wms 518, *Tuckfield v Buller* (1753) Amb 197 and *A-G v Hamilton* (1816) 1 Madd 214.

108 However, where an infant's share was vested in a trustee, a conveyance by the trustee was sufficient to vest the legal estate and there was no need for the infant to execute a conveyance when he came of age: *Cole v Sewell* (1849) 15 Sim 284.

possession of the divided allotments until the infant could execute the requisite conveyances[109]. Under the 1850 Act, the Court of Chancery could declare infants and persons of unsound mind trustees of their respective shares within the meaning of the legislation[110]. The court could then execute conveyances on behalf of such persons in order to complete the partition[111].

[3.36] Secondly, in partition actions where the shares of the parties were small and complicated, the Court of Chancery could declare the parties to be trustees of the shares allotted to the other co-owners. The entire property was then vested in a single new trustee under the Trustee Act 1850 with a direction to convey the several shares of land to the respective parties[112]. This avoided the considerable expense associated with execution of mutual conveyances in these circumstances.

C Methods of partition and procedure

[3.37] Proceedings in equity were instituted by means of a bill of complaint praying partition of the land and filed in the Court of Chancery[113]. If the defendant failed to respond to the bill, the Court of Chancery would issue a writ termed a 'subpoena' directing the defendant to appear before it and answer the case presented against him[114]. Assuming that the plaintiff had made the

---

[109] Allnatt, *A Practical Treatise on the Law of Partition* (1820), p 104. An adult co-owner could nevertheless be forced to convey his share immediately where he had brought the partition action (*Tuckfield v Buller* (1753) Amb 197), but not if the action had been brought by the infant (*Brook v Hertford* (1728) 2 P Wms 518).

[110] Trustee Act 1850, s 30 discussed at para **[3.29]** above. It appears that the Trustee Act 1850 did not alter the position of married women. Where property was limited or given to a wife for her separate use, the husband took the legal estate to the property and was considered to be a trustee for his wife: *Bennet v Davis* (1725) 2 P Wms 316. Under the Fines and Recoveries Act 1833 and the Fines and Recoveries (Ir) Act 1834 the concurrence of the husband was necessary to any partition (and execution of mutual conveyances), while partition of the wife's leasehold property was at the sole discretion of the husband. This remained the position until the Married Women's Property Act 1882.

[111] In respect of infants, see *Bowra v Wright* (1851) 4 De G & Sm 265. As regards persons of unsound mind, see *Singleton v Hopkins* (1855) 4 WR 107; *Re Blooman* (1858) 6 WR 178; *Re Molyneux* (1862) 10 WR 512; *Re Sherard* (1863) 1 De G J & Sm 421 and *Moorehead v Moorehead* (1868) IR 2 Eq 492. The law relating to persons of unsound mind was subsequently amended by the Lunacy Regulation Act 1853 and the corresponding Lunacy Regulation (Ir) Act 1871. These statutes provided that a committee in lunacy could partition property jointly owned by a person of unsound mind, and execute the necessary conveyances and pay any sums required for owelty of partition: Lunacy Regulation Act 1853, s 124 and Lunacy Regulation (Ir) Act 1871, s 74.

[112] See *Shepherd v Churchill* (1857) 25 Beav 21 and *Boyce v Woodroffe* (1859) 5 Ir Jur (ns) 57.

[113] 2 *Cru Dig* 389 and 21 *Halsbury's Laws of England* (1st edn, 1912), p 384. As to the procedure for filing such a bill see Bohun, *Cursus Cancellairae: The Course of Proceedings in the High Court of Chancery* (1715), pp 36-38.

necessary declarations of title and that the necessary parties were present, the court would make an order for partition. Partition in equity was carried out by two methods, namely by Commissioners and by reference in chambers.

1 Partition by commissioners

[3.38] By this method, valuation and division of the disputed property was carried out by Commissioners[115]. These were usually experienced surveyors appointed by the co-owners themselves[116]. Each co-owner put forward four names from which two were selected by all the parties in order to establish a commission of four or more Commissioners[117]. When appointed, they were regarded as Commissioners of all the parties and were bound to be impartial[118].

[3.39] Once the interests of the co-owners had been ascertained by the court[119], it would issue a commission to the Commissioners instructing them to divide the land accordingly[120]. This involved the Commissioners carrying out a valuation of the land[121] before dividing it and allocating the various parcels to the co-owners[122]. The scheme of partition and subsequent allotment of divided shares was at the Commissioners' discretion, subject only to compliance with the terms of the original commission[123]. In addition to this, the Commissioners were obliged to make the best partition possible for the benefit of all of the parties[124].

---

114 See generally Horwitz, *Chancery Records and Proceedings* (1995), pp 11-22.

115 See generally 21 *Halsbury's Laws of England* (1st edn, 1912), pp 858-860 and Foster, *The Law on Joint Ownership and Partition of Real Estate* (1878), pp 140-149.

116 *Manners v Charlesworth* (1833) 1 My & K 330 and *Watson v Duke of Northumberland* (1805) 11 Ves 153.

117 It was not usually possible to have fewer than four Commissioners: *Story v Johnson* (1837) 2 Y & C Ex 586. If co-owners could not agree on who should act as Commissioners, the court would select four or more names: *Story v Johnson* and *Watson v Duke of Northumberland* (1805) 11 Ves 153. The court could appoint an uneven number of Commissioners to secure a majority decision: *Howard v Barnwell* (1863) New Rep 414.

118 *Watson v Duke of Northumberland* (1805) 11 Ves 153 at 160 per Lord Eldon LC.

119 The Commissioners had no power to do this: *Agar v Fairfax* (1811) 17 Ves 533. See further *Cole v Sewell* (1849) 15 Sim 284 and *Knox v Mayo* (1858) 9 Ir Ch R 192.

120 See *Manaton v Squire* (1677) 2 Free 26 and *St Leger v Ferguson* (1860) 10 Ir Ch R 488. See further Braithwaite, *The Record and Writ Practice of the Court of Chancery* (1858), pp 233-234. The court could instruct the Commissioners to partition the land in a particular manner: *Warner v Baynes* (1750) Amb 589 and *Foster v Higgins* (1854) 6 Ir Jur (os) 409. In *McNeil v McDougall* (1896) 26 NSR 296 the court directed the Commissioners to allot a specific portion of land to a co-owner who had made significant improvements on that portion.

121 See *Manners v Charlesworth* (1833) 1 My & K 330.

122 Allocation by means of drawing lots could only be used as a last resort: *Canning v Canning* (1854) 2 Drew 234. In dividing the land, the Commissioners could take into account the circumstances surrounding the partition, for example the fact that one of the co-owners already owned land adjacent to or in the same parish as one of the divided parcels: *Canning v Canning* and *Story v Johnson* (1837) 2 Y & C Ex 586. However, the Commissioners could not award sums of money or additional items of property as equality of partition without a special direction of the court: *Mole v Mansfield* (1845) 15 Sim 1.

When the partition had been completed, it was recorded in a certificate and attached to the commission before being returned to court[125]. The certificate was confirmed by the court and partition implemented accordingly, with the parties executing mutual conveyances to complete the process[126].

[3.40] Since the Commissioners were appointed by the co-owners themselves, the court was reluctant to interfere where a co-owner felt aggrieved by the resulting scheme of partition[127]. The court would only intervene if there was an obvious irregularity in the proceedings such as fraud on the part of the Commissioners or negligence amounting to fraud[128]. Thus in *Manners v Charlesworth*[129] where the defendants sought to impeach the certificate merely on the grounds of unfair division, the court dismissed the action[130]. However, the court would interfere if there was a difference of opinion among the Commissioners[131]. The return upon which the court acted had to be made

---

123 *Lister v Lister* (1839) 3 Y & C Ex 540. In the event of any deviation from the commission, the partition could be set aside: *Peers v Needham* (1854) 19 Beav 316.

124 The Commissioners were obliged to consider the best interests of the co-owners (*Calmady v Calmady* (1795) 2 Ves 568 and *Canning v Canning* (1854) 2 Drew 234), and were sometimes likened to arbitrators (*Jones v Totty* (1827) 1 Sim 136). In performing these tasks, the Commissioners had to act together (*Watson v Duke of Northumberland* (1805) 11 Ves 153) and could review any evidence and examine relevant witnesses (*Meers v Lord Stourton* (1711) 1 Dick 21).

125 These documents were termed the 'Commissioners' return': *Stanley v Wrigley* (1855) 3 Sm & G 18. If one of the Commissioners died before the return had been made, the court could appoint a new Commissioner: *Herbert v Lord Beerhaven* (1842) 5 Ir Eq R 23.

126 Since confirmation of the Commissioners' certificate only affected equitable rights, and mutual conveyances were necessary to convey the legal title: Jenks, *Modern Land Law* (1899), p 132.

127 The aggrieved co-owner could either attempt to quash the certificate or oppose its confirmation: *Jones v Totty* (1827) 1 Sim 136 and *Corbet v Davenant* (1787) 2 Bro CC 251. A mere formal error in the Commissioners' return could be corrected in court, but a more fundamental error (such as a miscalculation of the value of the property or non-compliance with specific court directions) had to be corrected by the Commissioners themselves and the certificate returned to them for this purpose: *Rouse v Barker* (1728) Bunb 251. In *Dacre v Gorges* (1825) 2 Sim & St the court found that there had been a procedural irregularity where the Commissioners had included property in their evaluation that should have been excluded.

128 See *Archibald v Handley* (1904) 40 NSR 427 and *In the Estate of Jacob S Thompson* (1835) 2 Green's, NJC 637. In *Lister v Lister* (1839) 3 Y & Coll Ex 540 the court held that, if there was an obvious and substantial error in the Commissioners' partition, the court might infer a fraudulent motive.

129 (1833) 1 My & K 330.

130 Confronted with a similar argument, Stuart VC in *Ames v Comyns* (1867) 17 LT 163 remarked:

> '[I]f the Court could listen to such objections as those now made, I cannot see how any partition could be made.'

131 *Fitzgerald v Massey* (1858) 8 Ir Jur (ns) 229.

unanimously or by a majority of Commissioners[132]. Where equal numbers of Commissioners made inconsistent returns, both returns were quashed since the court could not attach greater weight to one than to another[133]. In these circumstances, the court would either issue a new commission[134] or simply appoint another Commissioner and order a new return[135].

[3.41] Partition by Commissioners was fraught with numerous problems in terms of the amount of work and time involved, the volume of material produced in the Commissioners' reports and certificates, and the associated expense[136]. Accordingly, this procedure gradually fell into disuse.

2 Partition in chambers

[3.42] This method of partition assumed popularity in the mid-nineteenth century[137]. One or more co-owners having brought an action for partition, the court would issue a judgment directing a partition of the land and allowing them to put forward proposals for partition before the judge in chambers[138]. A summons to proceed in this manner would be taken out and served on the opposite parties, and further directions issued upon its return[139]. The proposals submitted by the parties were accompanied by affidavits from surveyors, containing a valuation of the proposed allotments and describing the best means of dividing the land[140]. Following inquiries to establish that all persons interested in the land were parties to the action and the extent of their respective estates and interests[141], the scheme of partition was approved by the court and the parties

---

[132] Where there was a divergence of opinion among the Commissioners, separate returns had to be made: *Canning v Canning* (1854) 2 Drew 234.

[133] *Watson v Duke of Northumberland* (1805) 11 Ves 153 and *Corbet v Davenant* (1787) 2 Bro CC 252.

[134] *Watson v Duke of Northumberland* (1805) 11 Ves 153 and *Corbett v Davenant* (1787) 2 Bro CC 252.

[135] *Canning v Canning* (1854) 2 Drew 434.

[136] See Jones, *The Elizabethan Court of Chancery* (1967), pp 283-284.

[137] It appears that this method was facilitated by the Court of Chancery Acts 1852: Seton, *Forms of Judgments and Orders in the High Court of Justice and the Court of Appeal* (6th edn, 1901), p 1889. As to the procedure in general see Foster, *The Law on Joint Ownership and Partition of Real Estate* (1878), pp 139-140 and *Daniell's Chancery Practice* (8th edn, 1914), pp 1173-1174.

[138] See *Clarke v Clayton* (1860) 2 Giff 333 and *Spike v Harding* (1878) 7 Ch D 871. This method of partition was available even though one of the co-owners was under a disability: *Greenwood v Percy* (1859) 26 Beav 572. See further *Stanley v Wrigley* (1855) 3 Sm & G 18 and *Bull v Bull* (1868) 18 LT 870.

[139] Foster, *The Law on Joint Ownership and Partition of Real Estate* (1878), p 139.

[140] If one of the co-owners was under a disability, another affidavit was required stating that the proposals put forward were for his benefit: *Stanley v Wrigley* (1855) 3 Sm & G 18 and *Greenwood v Percy* (1859) 26 Beav 572.

[141] See the form of order in Foster, *The Law on Joint Ownership and Partition of Real Estate* (1878), pp 172-173.

instructed to execute mutual conveyances to complete the partition[142]. One advantage of proceeding in this manner was the cost involved: co-owners could avoid the expense of proceeding by Commission[143].

D Development of the equitable jurisdiction to partition

[3.43] The equitable remedy of partition was initially viewed as a simpler and more flexible remedy than its common law counterpart[144]. However, weaknesses gradually became apparent. Two factors influenced the practical utility of the equitable jurisdiction to partition. Firstly, the only remedy available to the Court of Chancery during this time was physical partition; the court could not order sale unless all the co-owners agreed to sell the land[145]. Secondly, and perhaps more importantly, the Court of Chancery could not refuse to make an order for partition upon such a request being made[146]: a decree for partition was a matter of right upon proof of title[147]. Since the equitable jurisdiction to partition was derived from that at common law, the Court of Chancery also accorded joint tenants and tenants in common a right to compel partition[148]. Thus one co-owner could force a division of the property no matter how small his interest, and irrespective of any opposition from the other co-owners whether on grounds of inconvenience or a mere reluctance to end their relationship[149].

[3.44] However, physical partition was not without difficulty. Few problems arose where the disputed property could be divided easily, or consisted of several areas of land or several buildings whereby the court could allocate a particular area of land or building to each co-owner with appropriate monetary

142 See *Clarke v Clarke* [1867] 1 ILTSJ 44 and *O'Lone v O'Lone* (1851) 2 Gr 642.

143 Foster, *The Law on Joint Ownership and Partition of Real Estate* (1878), p 140 and *Daniell's Chancery Practice* (8th edn, 1914), p 1174.

144 See paras **[3.18]**-**[3.21]** above.

145 *Ontario Power Company v Whattler* (1904) 7 OLR 198. If one of the co-owners opposed a sale of the property, the court could not make such an order: *Griffies v Griffies* (1863) 11 WR 943.

146 As to the decision in *North v Guinan* (1829) Beat 342, see ch 7 below.

147 See *Parker v Gerard* (1754) Amb 236 and *Baring v Nash* (1813) 1 Ves & B 551. The respective courts in these cases rejected suggestions that partition was discretionary in view of the decision in *Cartwright v Pultney* (1742) 2 Atk 380 which merely indicated that partition would be refused where there was no proof of title in the plaintiff. See further *Cantwell v Hassard* (1858) 7 Ir Ch R 370 and *Griffies v Griffies* (1863) 11 WR 943, and see the comments of Lord Nottingham LC in *Manaton v Squire* (1677) 2 Free 26 noted at para **[3.45]** below.

148 See *Henkel v Henkel* (1937) 276 NW 522 at 525-526.

149 See the comments of Plumer VC in *Baring v Nash* (1813) 1 Ves & B 551 at 554. A co-owner who opposed partition had few options available to him. For example, he could try to persuade the co-owner seeking partition to concur in selling the property by alleging that this would be more beneficial for them than partition. Failing this, he could try to persuade his fellow co-owner that they could both share in the use and enjoyment of the property notwithstanding any prior disagreements that may have prompted the partition action.

compensation for equality of partition if necessary[150]. Instead, problems typically arose where the subject-matter of the action comprised a single item of property that could not be divided easily. The Court of Chancery was obliged to order partition in these circumstances, even if the practical consequence was to diminish the value of the property or render it of no further use to any of the co-owners[151].

[3.45] In the well-known case of *Turner v Morgan*[152] partition was sought of a single dwelling house owned by the plaintiff and the defendant as tenants in common. Lord Eldon LC allowed the matter to stand over in an attempt to force the parties to arrange a scheme of partition. When no agreement was reached, partition was ordered giving the plaintiff all the fireplaces and chimneys, all the conveniences and the only staircase in the house. Despite protests by the defendant, the Lord Chancellor said he was unable to suggest a better scheme of partition and, in any event, was bound by authority[153]. Likewise, in *Nevis v Levene*[154] where the defendant owned four acres in a property comprising several hundred acres and wished to surrender his share rather than submit to an expensive division, the court made an order for partition. In *Warner v Baynes*[155] the parties were tenants in common of an estate containing two water conduits, one of which was used as a cold bath. Despite evidence from a surveyor that partition would cause a substantial depreciation in the value of the property, the court made an order for partition indicating that the difficulty involved was not a

[150] If the subject property comprised different parts, the Court of Chancery did not have to divide each part. For example, in *Earl of Clarendon v Hornby* (1718) P Wms 446 where the defendant was entitled to a one-third share of a house and surrounding parks and land, the court held that not every part of the estate had to be divided. What was important was that the defendant received a share equivalent to one-third in value of the entirety as opposed to one-third of each item of property. See further *Peers v Needham* (1854) 19 Beav 316 and *Lister v Lister* (1839) 3 Y & C Ex 540. However, where the disputed lands were held under different tenures or under several leases, each estate had to be partitioned separately so as to give a portion of each one to every co-owner. The court could not apportion the freeholds to one co-owner and the leaseholds to another: *Re Foley's Estate* (1862) 7 Ir Jur (ns) 402.

[151] 'If there is only one entire subject matter of division, it must be severed into shares, although the difficulty of doing it should be almost insuperable, and although it should be attended with the most palpable inconvenience and even destruction': Allnatt, *A Practical Treatise on the Law of Partition* (1820), p 85. See further Bacon, *A New Abridgment of the Law* (7th edn, 1832), p 511.

[152] (1803) 8 Ves 143.

[153] Counsel for the plaintiff had cited the case of *Benson*, in which a house was partitioned by building a wall up the middle! In *Burley v Moore* (1827) 5 LJ Ch 120 the court divided a set of chambers, giving a doorway to one party and a right of passage through the doorway to the other.

[154] (1744) 3 Atk 82.

[155] (1750) Amb 589.

valid objection to making the decree[156]. It has been said that such partitions were 'as little desirable as that of the living child in the Judgment of Solomon'[157].

[3.46] The practical effect of these decisions may have been indirectly to encourage the parties to agree to a sale of the property rather than face the consequences of an absurd and unworkable partition. A joint tenant or tenant in common who wished to be released from co-ownership could sell his undivided interest in the property. However, it is likely that such shares were less marketable than divided shares of land and would have raised less money than the vendor might have received from a share in the proceeds of sale of the entire property. As co-owners were entitled to partition as of right and the court could only order partition during this time, the equitable remedy of partition was criticised as being too rigid and limited to cope with prevailing conditions[158]. The legislature accordingly moved to remedy the situation by the enactment of the Partition Acts 1868 and 1876[159].

[3.47] The Partition Act 1868 was a fundamental and pragmatic piece of legislation[160]. Whereas the Court of Chancery was formerly restricted to making

---

[156] See further *Manaton v Squire* (1677) 2 Free 26 where the plaintiff and the defendant were tenants in common of a field in respective five-sixths and one-sixth shares. The defendant opposed the plaintiff's request for partition on the basis that there was water at only one corner of the field and the partition would cause obvious inconvenience. Lord Nottingham LC acknowledged the plaintiff's right to partition, remarking that 'it was never known that the aid of this Court was denied to any man who sought for a partition here': see the report in Selden Society, *Lord Nottingham's Chancery Cases* (1961) Vol II, p 566.

[157] Charley, *The Real Property Acts 1874, 1875 and 1876* (3rd edn, 1876), p 354.

[158] Loyd, 'Partition' (1919) 67 U Pa L Rev 162 at 174.

[159] For a post-1868 analysis of the Partition Acts 1868 and 1876 see Foster, *The Law on Joint Ownership and Partition of Real Estate* (1878), pp 111-138 and 154-163; Walker, *The Partition Acts, 1868 and 1876* (1882), pp 23-84; White and Tudor, *A Selection of Leading Cases in Equity* (7th edn, 1897), pp 206-222; *Daniell's Chancery Practice* (8th edn, 1914), pp 1170-1189; and 21 *Halsbury's Laws of England* (1st edn, 1912), pp 834-867. See further Osborne, *The Jurisdiction and Practice of the County Courts in Ireland in Equity and Probate Matters* (2nd edn, 1910), pp 194-206; Carleton, *The Jurisdiction and Procedure of the County Courts in Ireland* (2nd edn, 1891), pp 474-485 and Madden, *The Law and Practice of the High Court of Justice in Ireland in Relation to Proceedings Before the Land Judge* (3rd edn, 1889), pp 301-315.

[160] The preceding Partition Bill was introduced in the House of Lords by the Lord Chancellor on 3 April 1868 (see *House of Commons Sessional Papers* (1867-68) Vol 4, p 1 for the proposed bill), and received Royal Assent on 25 June 1868 (*Hansard's Parliamentary Debates*, Third Series, Vols 191-192). It is interesting that the Bill passed through Parliament without any debate on the proposed changes to the law. The Bill was clearly a government measure, hence its origin in the House of Lords. Yet the absence of any debate on its provisions is perhaps an indication of the perceived need for legislation providing for sale of concurrent interests in land. The Partition Act 1868 was retrospective insofar as it applied to suits for partition commenced before 25 June 1868: *Lys v Lys* (1868) LR 7 Eq 126. However, it did not extend to partition suits in which a decree for partition had been made but not implemented by this date: *Pryor v Pryor* (1875) LR 19 Eq 595.

an order for partition, the 1868 Act empowered it to substitute the more convenient remedy of sale upon certain criteria being satisfied[161]. One author has observed that:

> 'Changing economic conditions and the courts' frequent inability to apportion property fairly, exemplified in *Turner*, precipitated a dramatic shift in English partition law ... [T]he Partition Act of 1868 turned the prevailing partition law on its head by favouring sales over partitions in kind.'[162]

[3.48] The 1868 Act was supplemented by the Partition Act 1876, which introduced a number of procedural changes in relation to the mechanism of partition actions[163]. Following the enactment of the 1868 Act, one or more co-owners could compel sale of co-owned land instead of partition, and enjoy a divided share of the proceeds of sale as opposed to a divided share of the property itself.

---

161 See generally ch 5 below.

162 Reid, 'Partitions in Kind: A Preference Without Favor' (1986) 7 Cardozo L Rev 855 at 859-860.

163 The preceding Bill was brought before the House of Commons on 15 February 1876 (see *House of Commons Sessional Papers* (1876) Vol 5, p 453) and received Royal Assent on 27 June 1876 (*Hansard's Parliamentary Debates*, Third Series, Vols 227-230). During its passage through Parliament, minor amendments were introduced in both Houses: see Charley, *The Real Property Acts 1874, 1875 and 1876* (3rd edn, 1876), pp 353-371. Partition Act 1876, s 2 provided that the Act applied to actions for partition pending on and instituted after 27 June 1876.

Chapter 4

The Partition Acts 1868 and 1876 – Preliminary Matters

I Introduction

[4.01] Although the Partition Acts have been repealed in England and Wales[1], they remain in force in Northern Ireland and the Republic of Ireland. In addition to this, legislation derived from the Partition Acts still governs termination of co-ownership in various Commonwealth jurisdictions. In Australia, the Acts have been incorporated into legislation in Victoria[2], Western Australia[3], South Australia[4], the Northern Territory[5], Tasmania[6] and the Australian Capital Territory[7], while the relevant statutory provisions in New Zealand closely resemble those of the Partition Acts[8]. As regards the practice in Canada, the Partition Acts are still in force in Saskatchewan and the Northwest Territories,

---

1 As part of the 1925 property reforms: Law of Property Act 1925, s 207 and Sch 7. Likewise, An Act Concerning Joint Tenants and Tenants in Common 1539 and An Act Concerning Joint Tenants for Term of Life or Years 1540 have also been repealed in England: Law of Property (Amendment) Act 1924, ss 10, 12(3) and Sch 10. An Act for more easier obtaining Partition of Lands held in Coparcenary, Joint Tenancy and Tenancy in Common 1697 was repealed by the Statute Law Revision Act 1867.

2 Property Law Act 1958 (Vict), Pt IV.

3 Property Law Act 1969 (WA), Pt XIX.

4 Law of Property Act 1936 (SA), Pt VIII.

5 Partition Act 1881 (SA) and see *Johnson v Young* (13 May 1988, unreported) Supreme Court of the Northern Territory of Australia.

6 Partition Act 1869 (Tas).

7 Partition Act 1900 (NSW) as incorporated into the New South Wales Acts Act 1986 (ACT), Pt I. See further the Imperial Acts (Substitution Provisions) Act 1886 (ACT), s 3(3) and Sch 2, Pt IVA. As regards New South Wales and Queensland, termination of co-ownership is governed by the Conveyancing Act 1919 (NSW), Pt IV (as amended by the Conveyancing (Amendment) Act 1930 (NSW)) and the Property Law Act 1974 (Qd) respectively. These Acts provide that, upon an application for partition or sale, the court may appoint trustees to hold the property on a statutory trust for sale or a statutory trust for partition. The land is then vested in trustees who are required to divide or sell it accordingly.

8 Property Law Act 1952 (NZ).

while the main provisions of the Acts survive in modified form in British Columbia[9] and in Prince Edward Island[10].

[4.02] The essence of the Partition Acts (and analogous legislation) is that one or more co-owners may compel sale of the land in the event that common use and enjoyment of the property is no longer possible. However, if a co-owner does not obtain an order for sale, the court may order partition in the alternative[11]. Before considering the main provisions of the Partition Acts and their application, it is necessary to consider a number of preliminary matters that are relevant to proceedings for compulsory partition or sale.

II The *Locus Standi* Test

[4.03] Since partition or sale in lieu thereof destroys the unity of possession inherent in co-ownership, it is axiomatic that partition or sale is only available in respect of lands held in co-ownership[12]. A partition action does not, for example, lie at the suit of a sole tenant for life against the reversioners[13].

[4.04] Co-ownership may arise at law or in equity and may be in respect of an estate vested in possession or an estate in reversion or remainder. However, not all joint tenants or tenants in common can compel partition or sale in the event that one or more of them wishes to end this relationship. In order to maintain a

9 Partition of Property Act 1996 (BC). Sections 6-8 of this Act which enable the court to order sale are virtually identical to the Partition Act 1868, ss 3-5.

10 Real Property Act 1974 (PEI), Pt III. While ss 18-53 of this Act contain comprehensive provisions dealing with virtually every aspect of partition actions, ss 39(1)(a)-(c) which confer jurisdiction to order sale in lieu of partition are derived from the Partition Act 1868, ss 3-5. Other Canadian provinces have revised partition legislation which differs from the Partition Acts 1868 and 1876: see for example the Partition Act 1990 (Ont); Partition and Sale Act 1979 (Alb) now incorporated into the Law of Property Act 1980 (Alb); Law of Property Act 1987 (Man); and Partition Act 1989 (NS). In New Brunswick, partition and sale of concurrent interests in land is governed by the relevant Rules of Court: see the Rules of Court, r 67. However, principles derived from cases decided in these jurisdictions may still provide a useful analogy to the practice under the Partition Acts 1868 and 1876 and suggest methods of solving current issues.

11 See generally ch 7 below.

12 See the comments of Meredith CJCP in *Morrison v Morrison* (1917) 39 OLR 163 at 172 and those of Warrington J in *Dodd v Cattell* [1914] 2 Ch 1 at 11. See further *Jillings v Blewett* (1993) 101 DLR (4th) 604.

13 *Fiskin v Ife* (1897) 28 OR 595 and *Morris v Howe* (1982) 38 OR (2d) 480. In *Stroud v Sun Oil Co* (1904) 7 OLR 704 Britton J refused to make an order for sale on the basis that there was no common title or interest in common between the parties (affirmed on appeal at (1904) 8 OLR 748). See further *Re Morris* (1982) 138 DLR (3d) 113 and *Re Melnychuk and Bassingthwaighte* (1990) 73 DLR (4th) 698.

partition action, the plaintiff must have a legal or an equitable estate or interest in possession in the relevant property[14].

A Legal or equitable estate or interest

[4.05] The plaintiff must have an estate or interest in the property[15]. Thus a security holder who merely has rights over an undivided share of land for the purposes of enforcing his security cannot bring a partition action[16]. In addition to this, the plaintiff and defendant should each be beneficially entitled to an interest in the land[17].

[4.06] Compulsory partition was originally only available to co-owners with a legal estate or interest, but became available to co-owners with an equitable estate or interest when the Court of Chancery assumed jurisdiction in such matters. At common law, since the actual decree for partition vested the legal estate in the divided parcels of land, it was necessary to have this estate before the court[18]. Accordingly, the plaintiff had to have a legal estate in the property in order to maintain a partition action. However, the Court of Chancery would interfere in cases where an equitable title had been set up and which would have precluded a decree for partition at common law[19]. As Fry J explained in *Taylor v Grange*[20]:

> '[Co-owners] would have had no right to partition under the old common law jurisdiction, if they represented no legal interest in the land; but no doubt an equitable owner may obtain a decree for partition, if he be entitled to call for a legal estate which would have entitled him to a partition at common law.'[21]

---

14 See Seton, *Forms of Judgments and Orders in the High Court of Justice and the Court of Appeal* (6th edn, 1901), p 1872 and *Daniell's Chancery Practice* (8th edn, 1914), pp 1170-1171. More recently, this test has been affirmed by Campbell J in *Northern Bank Ltd v Haggerty* [1995] NI 211 and in *Fraser Homes Ltd v Fraser Houses (NI) Ltd* [1998] NI 214 and by Master Ellison in *Northern Bank Ltd v Adams* (1 February 1996, unreported) High Court (NI).

15 See *Angus v Heinze* (1909) 42 SCR 416 and *Morrison v Morrison* (1917) 39 OLR 163.

16 *Northern Bank Ltd v Haggerty* [1995] NI 211 and see generally ch 8 below. See further *Ferrier v Civiero* (6 December 1999, unreported) Ontario Superior Court of Justice.

17 In *Lowe v Franks* (1828) 1 Moll 137 the plaintiffs were beneficial tenants in common under a trust and filed a bill for partition against their trustee as defendant. The court refused to make an order for partition because there was no proper defendant to oppose the action.

18 See 21 *Halsbury's Laws of England* (1st edn, 1912), pp 841-842 and see ch 3 above, paras **[3.09]-[3.15]**.

19 White and Tudor, *A Selection of Leading Cases in Equity* (7th edn, 1897), p 199 and see the comments of Campbell J in *Northern Bank Ltd v Haggerty* [1995] NI 211 at 216.

20 (1879) 13 Ch D 223 at 227 (affirmed on appeal at (1880) 15 Ch D 165).

21 See further the comments of Warrington J in *Dodd v Cattell* [1914] 2 Ch 1 at 8 and those of Overend J in *Hill v Maunsell-Eyre* [1944] IR 499 at 502.

[4.07] A decree for partition in equity directed the parties to execute mutual conveyances of their shares to complete the partition, hence the need for the legal estate to be before the court[22].

[4.08] Thus a joint tenant or tenant in common with an equitable interest in the property and who is entitled to call for the legal estate may compel partition. For example, co-owners who have mortgaged their property may bring a partition action: they retain the equity of redemption and are entitled to the legal estate upon payment of the mortgage money[23]. Other such examples include a plaintiff who claims to be entitled to the interest of one of the co-owners under an agreement to assign or to demise that interest[24], and a plaintiff who has acquired an equitable interest in the common property under a resulting or constructive trust[25].

[4.09] It has been suggested that a joint purchaser under an uncompleted contract of sale cannot maintain a partition action. In *Walsh v Walsh and Webster*[26] the plaintiff was a joint purchaser of land, with a substantial part of the purchase price still payable to the vendor. The plaintiff alleged that, since an unpaid vendor is in the position of a trustee, a purchaser has an equitable interest in the land and may maintain a partition action. Rejecting this argument, Virtue J referred to a number of authorities indicating that a purchaser of land is an equitable owner only in a modified sense[27]. The plaintiff could only bring himself within Fry J's dictum in *Taylor v Grange*[28] if he had paid the purchase money in full and was therefore in a position to call for a transfer of the legal estate. In the present case, the vendor could not be compelled to convey the land because the purchase money was unpaid and there was no guarantee that it would be paid[29]. However, the position may be different in the Republic of Ireland in view of the decision in *Tempany v Hynes*[30].

---

22 See ch 3 above, paras **[3.31]**-**[3.34]**.

23 See ch 8 below, para **[8.09]**.

24 See paras **[4.30]**-**[4.31]** below.

25 This situation typically arises where a spouse or co-habitee contributes to the acquisition of a family home.

26 (1953) 55 WALR 79.

27 See for example, *Wall v Bright* (1820) 1 Jac & W 494.

28 (1879) 13 Ch D 223 at 227.

29 See the comment on this case 'A Novel Claim for Partition' (1955) 28 ALJ 610. Similar arguments were made in *Thomas v Thomas* (1961) 29 DLR (2d) 576 although the court did not find it necessary to decide this issue.

30 [1976] IR 101.

B In possession

[4.10] Only joint tenants and tenants in common who are entitled to possession of the relevant property may compel partition or sale under the Partition Acts[31]. Thus, joint tenants or tenants in common in remainder or reversion cannot maintain a partition action[32]. So long as the plaintiff is entitled to possession and the land is held in co-ownership, it is immaterial that there is no defendant interested in possession[33]. In other words, while co-owners in reversion or remainder cannot bring a partition action, an order for partition or sale may be made against such persons[34].

[4.11] Possession in this sense does not mean physical occupation. Rather the plaintiff must have an estate or interest which is vested in possession or which is coupled with a right to possession of the land[35]. As regards the former, the plaintiff is entitled to possession by virtue of his estate or interest in the land. However, if a particular estate or interest does not confer a right to possession, the plaintiff may be entitled to possession by virtue of a licence or contractual arrangement. One example of this occurs in respect of co-owners who have mortgaged their property: the equity of redemption constitutes an equitable interest in the land, and is typically accompanied by a licence from the mortgagee that the mortgagors are entitled to remain in possession of the property, provided they are not in default[36].

---

[31] See *Evans v Bagshaw* (1870) 5 Ch App 340; *Dodd v Cattell* [1914] 2 Ch 1 and Walker, *The Partition Acts, 1868 and 1876* (1882), p 7. See further White and Tudor, *A Selection of Leading Cases in Equity* (7th edn, 1897), p 199; 21 *Halsbury's Laws of England* (1st edn, 1912), p 840; and *Daniell's Chancery Practice* (8th edn, 1914), p 1171. Similar views were expressed in *Morrison v Morrison* (1917) 39 OLR 163; *Bunting v Servos* [1931] OR 409; *Fidler v Seaman* [1948] OWN 454; *Morrow v Eakin* [1953] 2 DLR 593 and *Nobis Investments Ltd v Atlantic Metal Spinning Co* (30 March 1988, unreported) Ontario Court of Appeal.

[32] See the comments of Murray J in *Tubman v Johnston* [1981] NI 53 at 56-57. Likewise, a bare trustee cannot maintain a partition action. While he has a legal estate in the land, he has no right to possession: *Gillett v Gillett* (1979) 9 RFL (2d) 97.

[33] This may occur where the plaintiff is in possession of the entire property but is simultaneously entitled to different estates in the land. For example, in *Riddler v Dew* (1901) 19 NZLR 708 the plaintiff was in possession of land, but as the tenant for life of one half and the owner in fee simple of the other half. The plaintiff brought an action for partition, making the trustee of the settlement and those interested in remainder defendants. The court held that the plaintiff was entitled to have the land divided; the plaintiff would then know which specific part of the land he held in fee simple and could make improvements to or sell this parcel if he desired.

[34] *Riddler v Dew* (1901) 19 NZLR 708 and see *Tuckfield v Buller* (1753) Amb 197.

[35] See 21 *Halsbury's Laws of England* (1st edn, 1912), pp 840-841. See further the comments of Murray J in *Tubman v Johnson* [1981] NI 53 at 56-57 and those of Master Ellison in *Northern Bank Ltd v Haggerty* (23 March 1994, unreported) High Court (NI), at 9.

[36] See ch 8 below, para **[8.09]**.

[4.12] Although apparently well-established, the reason for this requirement that the plaintiff should be entitled to possession of the land is difficult to ascertain. There is no such express limitation in the sixteenth century Statutes of Partition, which conferred a right to compel partition on joint tenants and tenants in common of 'estates of inheritance' or 'estates for a term of life or years'[37]. Likewise, the Partition Acts simply refer to 'parties interested' in the disputed property. The requirement may have originated in *Co Litt* 167a which states:

> 'Now the word (*tenet*) in the writ of partition always implies a tenant of the freehold. And therefore if one coparcener makes a lease for years, yet a writ of partition lies. But if one or both make a lease for life, a writ of partition does not lie between them: because they do not hold the freehold together, and the writ of partition must be against the tenant of the freehold.'[38]

[4.13] Referring to this extract, counsel for the defendants at first instance in *Evans v Bagshaw*[39] asserted that only a tenant in possession of the freehold could sue out a writ of partition at common law and that equity followed the law in this respect. Prior to this, similar arguments were endorsed by Napier LC in *Cantwell v Hassard*[40]. Thus, it appears that the requirement of an estate in possession existed from the time of Lord Coke and was subsequently adopted by the Court of Chancery when it assumed jurisdiction in partition actions[41]. However, it is suggested that the requirement of an estate in possession cannot be attributed to Coke. He refers to the fact that a coparcener who has made a lease of her share cannot compel partition because she no longer has a freehold estate, as opposed to not having an estate in possession. Both the 1540 Act in England and the 1542 Act in Ireland granted joint tenants and tenants in common of leasehold estates a right to compel partition. Yet the cases referred to in this context appear to have interpreted Coke's comments as establishing that the plaintiff must have an estate in possession.

---

37 In *Re Forster v Forster* (6 March 1980, unreported) Alberta Court of Appeal, Clement JA asserted that the requirement of an estate in possession may be attributed to An Act Concerning Joint Tenants and Tenants in Common 1539 which refers to joint tenants and tenants in common of estates of inheritance who 'have like right title interest and possession' in the lands of which they are seised. However, it is suggested that the 1539 Act was merely referring to difficulties that had arisen as a result of such persons having, *inter alia*, unity of possession.

38 See further Allnatt, *A Practical Treatise on the Law of Partition* (1820), p 53.

39 (1870) 5 Ch App 340.

40 (1858) 7 Ir Ch R 370.

41 Foster, *The Law on Joint Ownership and Partition of Real Estate* (1878), p 130. However, pre-1868 examples of the courts actually stipulating that the *locus standi* test was restricted in this manner are difficult to find.

[4.14] Another reason for this requirement appears to be that persons entitled in reversion or remainder should not be allowed to interfere with the enjoyment of the land by the person or persons currently entitled to possession. The leading judgment in this respect is that of Lord Hatherley LC on appeal in *Evans v Bagshaw*[42]. In this case, a reversioner of a one-sixth interest brought a partition action. Refusing the relief sought, Lord Hatherley stated:

> 'The case, therefore, falls within the ordinary rule that the Court will not allow a partition suit to be maintained by a reversioner. This rule is not merely technical, but is founded on good sense in not allowing the reversioner to disturb the existing state of things. There might be a tenant for life of the whole, and several tenants in common in reversion, in which case the inconvenience would be obviously very great. At all events, the rule is unquestionably settled.'[43]

[4.15] Commenting on this rule, Stout CJ in *Riddler v Dew*[44] stated:

> '[It] was held in ... *Evans v Bagshaw* that a person not entitled to possession cannot sue for partition; but there is an obvious reason for that. If the persons living upon the estate are content, a person whose right to possession has not yet accrued ought not to be allowed to disturb the position.'

[4.16] Likewise, in *Morrison v Morrison*[45] Meredith CJCP remarked:

> 'My opinion is ... that the law of this Province, in this respect, is in accord with that of England; ... that none but those entitled to possession, that is, none but those who really need it, are entitled to partition.'[46]

He continued:

> 'Courts do not sit for the purpose of making orders, entailing great expense, which may be useless: [such as] orders for partition of land at the instance of a person or persons who may never become entitled to any share or interest in the land ...'[47]

[4.17] Thus, if property is given to A for life, remainder to B and C as tenants in common, neither B nor C can compel partition or sale of the land during A's life

42 (1870) 5 Ch App 340.

43 (1870) 5 Ch App 340 at 341.

44 (1901) 19 NZLR 708.

45 (1917) 39 OLR 163.

46 (1917) 39 OLR 163 at 171-172 and cited with approval by Wells J in *Fidler v Seaman* [1948] OWN 454 and by Higgins J in *Re Toronto-Dominion Bank and Morison* (1984) 47 OR (2d) 524.

47 (1917) 39 OLR 163 at 175. See further *Murcar v Bolton* (1884) 5 OR 164 and *Rajotte v Wilson* (1904) 3 OWR 737 in which the respective courts held that a tenant in common in remainder cannot compel partition.

estate. This may be justified on the basis that B and C should not be allowed to interfere with A's enjoyment of the property. For example, B cannot compel partition of the land against C and erect a fence demarcating the boundaries of the respective parcels as this would be contrary to A's rights as life tenant.

[4.18] The *locus standi* test accordingly prevents co-owners of estates in reversion or remainder from compelling partition or sale of the land and disturbing the person or persons who are currently entitled to possession. However, it also prevents co-owners of estates in reversion or remainder from compelling partition or sale of their respective estates. Returning to the above example, B may wish to compel partition of the remainder estate against C in order to identify which portion of land will vest in him when the life estate expires and to facilitate his plans for the future development of the land. Yet B cannot compel partition (or sale) of the remainder estate because he lacks the necessary standing to do so. The fact that the owner of the limited estate (in our example, A) would consent to the proposed partition (or sale) is irrelevant[48].

[4.19] The issue of whether co-owners of estates in reversion or remainder should be allowed to compel partition or sale in these circumstances was considered by the Ontario Appellate Division in *Bunting v Servos*[49]. The plaintiff and defendant were tenants in common of land, subject to their mother's life interest. A majority of the court held that the plaintiff was not entitled to partition of the remainder estate under the Partition Act 1927 (Ont)[50]. Latchford CJ and Fisher JA were of the opinion that the court was bound by *Morrison v Morrison*[51], as well as *Murcar v Bolton*[52] and *Rajotte v Wilson*[53]. Masten JA stated:

> '[W]hile it may be that, on a proper reading of the statute, "lands" includes estates in remainder ... yet the difficulty in [the plaintiff's] way is that he is not entitled to "partition" because ... "partition", as used in the statute, means actual present physical division, among those entitled, of the very property itself, and

---

48 *Cass v Wood* (1874) 30 LT 670. See however *Re Chupryk* (1980) 110 DLR (3d) 108 and *Aho v Kelly* (11 June 1998, unreported) British Columbia Supreme Court (noted at para **[4.23]** below) in which the respective courts made an order for sale of both the limited estate and interest in reversion or remainder where the tenant for life consented to the order and was also entitled to an undivided share of the remainder or reversionary interest.

49 [1931] OR 409.

50 So far as is material the Partition Act 1927 (Ont), s 2 provided that '[a]ll ... tenants in common of any land in Ontario may be compelled to ... suffer partition', while s 3 provided that an application for partition could be made by 'any person interested in land'. 'Land' was defined in s 1 as including 'all estates and interests therein'.

51 (1917) 39 OLR 163.

52 (1884) 5 OR 164.

53 (1904) 3 OWR 737.

> does not mean a declaration regarding future rights in specific property of which the parties may at some future date become entitled to possession.'[54]

[4.20] Masten JA asserted that an order for partition before the determination of the life estate might result in 'grave injustice'[55]. If a parcel of land to be allocated to one of the parties should increase in value before the interest in possession expired, the partition would no longer be equal. He cited as examples land that was located in the suburbs of a rapidly growing city, or the possibility of a valuable oil or mineral deposit being discovered on one portion and not on another. Masten JA concluded that a remainderman who opposed partition should not be 'obliged to forgo his right to an even division at the expiry of the life-estate'[56].

[4.21] The dissenting judges were of the opinion that, because the plaintiff and defendant were tenants in common of an estate in land, the plaintiff was a 'person interested' within the 1927 Act and was entitled to an order for partition. Moreover, an order for partition would not affect the tenant for life. Riddell JA observed that:

> 'It is not proposed to interfere with the life-tenant in any way, either physically or on paper – she is to be left to enjoy her rightful estate in precisely the same way as if no proceedings had been taken in partition. What is proposed to be partitioned has no reference to her estate or possession, but only to the paper-title of the estate in remainder after her death.'[57]

[4.22] Both Riddell JA and Orde JA were of the opinion that *Murcar v Bolton*[58] and *Rajotte v Wilson*[59] had no bearing on the present case. In those cases it was sought to partition the estate of the life tenant; the only parties who would be affected by an order for partition in the present case were the plaintiff and defendant.

[4.23] It is suggested that the views of the minority are to be preferred to those of the majority, and that co-owners of estates in reversion or remainder should be able to compel partition or sale of their respective estates[60]. A number of American and Commonwealth cases have determined partition actions between

---

54 [1931] OR 409 at 416-417.

55 [1931] OR 409 at 417.

56 [1931] OR 409 at 417.

57 [1931] OR 409 at 415.

58 (1884) 5 OR 164.

59 (1904) 3 OWR 737.

60 Albeit that situations in which such persons wish to compel partition or sale may be rare in practice.

co-owners of a reversion expectant on a lease of the entirety[61]. A similar approach has been adopted in respect of partition actions involving co-owners in remainder or reversion subject to a prior life estate[62]. The *locus standi* test restricts the remedies of partition and sale under the Partition Acts to persons having an estate in possession. However, the origins of this test are questionable. The statement in *Co Litt* 167a and the decision in *Evans v Bagshaw*[63] are frequently cited as its basis. As regards the former, the problem identified by Coke was remedied by the sixteenth century Statutes of Partition. The decision in *Evans v Bagshaw*[64] is based on the implications of an order for partition or sale on the life tenant's enjoyment of the property. However, partition or sale of the remainder or reversionary estate will not necessarily affect the owner of the limited estate[65]. Any possible disruption to his enjoyment of the property would be prevented by the jurisdiction exception which exists in respect of third parties. The court does not have jurisdiction to make an order for partition or sale where this would prejudice a third party with rights over the entire property[66]. Thus, it would not be able to order partition or sale at the request of a co-owner of an estate in reversion or remainder where this would prejudice the person currently entitled to possession of the land[67].

[4.24] It is suggested that joint tenants and tenants in common of such estates should be able to compel partition or sale. The *locus standi* test currently restricts partition actions to persons interested in possession. Yet there seems to be no real justification for applying such a limited test. Moreover, the fact that

---

61 See *Woodworth v Campbell* (1835) 5 Paige 518; *Willard v Willard* (1892) 145 United States 116; *Fitzpatrick v Wilson* (1866) 12 Gr 440; and *Robinson v Robinson* (1902) 2 SR (NSW) 197, and see *O'Reiley v Vincent* (1818) 2 Mol 330 and *Graham v Clinton* (1899) 81 LT 717 all cited in 21 *Halsbury's Laws of England* (1st edn, 1912), p 841.

62 See *Re Chupryk* (1980) 110 DLR (3d) 108 in which the Manitoba Court of Appeal held that such persons were 'persons interested' for the purposes of the legislation (applying the dissenting judgments in *Murcar v Bolton* (1884) 5 OR 164 and *Bunting v Servos* [1931] OR 409). In *Re Chapryk* the court made an order for sale at the request of a tenant in common of a two-thirds interest in the remainder estate, the other remainderman (who was also tenant for life of the property) having indicated his support for sale of the land. A similar factual situation arose in *Aho v Kelly* (11 June 1998, unreported) British Columbia Supreme Court, in which Bauman J made an order for sale of land subject to a life estate in favour of the plaintiff, the plaintiff and defendants being entitled in reversion to the extent of one-third and two-thirds respectively.

63 (1870) 5 Ch App 340.

64 As well as that of the respective courts in cases such as *Morrison v Morrison* (1917) 39 OLR 163 and *Murcar v Bolton* (1884) 5 OR 164.

65 See Robinson, *The Property Law Act Victoria* (1992), p 471.

66 See paras **[4.61]-[4.67]** below.

67 For example, a tenant for life or years might be prejudiced by an order for partition if this would affect the manner in which rent is paid or if there is a covenant for future renewal in the lease: see paras **[4.64]-[4.66]** below.

they cannot compel partition or sale is difficult to reconcile with the fact that co-owners in reversion or remainder may divide or sell their interests by mutual agreement[68].

C Persons having *locus standi*

[4.25] There are two principal categories of persons who may compel partition or sale under the Partition Acts.

1 Co-owners

[4.26] A partition action may be maintained by a joint tenant or tenant in common who is entitled to a legal or an equitable estate or interest in possession[69]. The plaintiff may be a joint tenant or tenant in common in fee simple[70] or fee tail[71], or a co-owner of a life estate or leasehold estate[72]. A number of principles have emerged in relation to partition actions by co-owners of limited estates.

[4.27] A tenant for life may bring a partition action against the other tenants for life[73]. Likewise an action for partition may be maintained by a lessee against his co-lessees[74]. In these circumstances, the order for partition or sale is confined to the duration of the limited estate[75]. The reversioners or remaindermen are not necessary parties to the action[76], and the fact that they object will not prevent the

---

68 See ch 2 above, para **[2.05]**.

69 See generally *Daniell's Chancery Practice* (8th edn, 1914), p 1170; 21 *Halsbury's Laws of England* (1st edn, 1912), pp 839-840; and White and Tudor, *A Selection of Leading Cases in Equity* (7th edn, 1897), pp 199-200.

70 See for example, *O'Brien & Cronin Ltd v Dillon* (2 February 1977, unreported) High Court (RI) and *Glass v McManus* [1996] NI 401.

71 See for example, *Brook v Hertford* (1728) 2 P Wms 518; *Tuckfield v Buller* (1753) Amb 197 and *Re Pares* (1879) 12 Ch D 333. See further *Thomas v Gyles* (1691) 2 Vern 232 where it was held that a decree for partition bound the issue, citing *Burton v Jeux* and *Rose v Rose* (both undated).

72 See the cases cited below. Joint tenants and tenants in common of estates of inheritance and limited estates were first granted a right to compel partition by the sixteenth century Statutes of Partition. Co-owners of an estate determinable on marriage (see *Hobson v Sherwood* (1841) 4 Beav 184) and of an estate subject to an executory gift over (see *Greenwood v Percy* (1859) 26 Beav 572 and *Groves v Carbert* (1873) 29 LT 129) could also compel partition at common law under the Statutes of Partition and subsequently in equity. Compulsory partition was also available to tenants by the curtesy: *Co Litt* 175b and see *Stanley v Wrigley* (1855) 3 Sim & G 18.

73 See *Gaskell v Gaskell* (1836) 6 Sim 643; *Williams v Williams* (1899) 81 LT 163 and *Lalor v Lalor* (1883) 9 PR (Ont) 455. As regards land which is subject to a strict settlement, the statutory powers of partition and sale under the Settled Land Acts 1882-1890 (see ch 2 above, paras **[2.23]**-**[2.25]**) are only available where all of the life-tenants agree to exercise these powers. In the absence of such agreement, a co-owner seeking partition or sale of the land will have to bring proceedings for compulsory partition or sale.

74 See *Baring v Nash* (1813) 1 Ves & B 551 and *Heaton v Dearden* (1852) 16 Beav 147.

75 *Baring v Nash* (1813) 1 Ves & B 551.

76 *Baring v Nash* (1813) 1 Ves & B 551.

court from ordering partition or sale[77]. Where the co-owners of the limited estate are joint tenants, it appears that partition benefits the reversioner or remainderman who may enter the land upon the death of a joint tenant as opposed to the surviving co-owner[78].

[4.28] However, compulsory partition or sale is not confined to co-tenants for life or for a term of years *inter se*. A partition action may be maintained even though co-owners have different estates in the disputed property[79]. For example, the court may order partition or sale where one of the parties is a tenant for life of his undivided share and the other an owner in fee simple[80]. Alternatively, one co-owner may be a lessee of an undivided share of land while the other co-owner is entitled to the fee simple of his undivided share[81]. Again, an order for partition or sale is confined to the duration of the limited interest[82].

[4.29] Co-owners of limited estates or interests may desire a permanent partition or sale of the land. The court may make such an order where the persons interested in reversion or remainder consent to this and are parties to the action. Thus, where co-owners for life or years seek a permanent partition or sale, the reversioners or remaindermen must consent to this and be joined as parties to the action[83]. Likewise, where a partition action is between co-owners of a limited estate and an estate in fee simple, the persons entitled to the reversion or remainder of the limited interest must consent and be joined as parties to the action in order for partition or sale to be permanent[84]. Problems may arise in this

---

77 See the comments of Stout CJ in *Riddler v Dew* (1901) 19 NZLR 708 at 711.

78 Allnatt, *A Practical Treatise on the Law of Partition* (1820), pp 36-37.

79 As initially contemplated by An Act Concerning Joint Tenants for Term of Life or Years 1540 in England and An Act for Jointenants 1542 in Ireland.

80 See *Wills v Slade* (1801) 6 Ves 498 and *Riddler v Dew* (1901) 19 NZLR 708 discussed at para **[4.10]** above. For example, a father dies leaving all his property to his children X and Y as tenants in common. X subsequently dies, and under the terms of her will leaves her entire estate to her son Z for life, remainder to her grandchildren.

81 See *Baring v Nash* (1813) 1 Ves & B 551. For example, a father dies leaving all his property to his children X and Y as tenants in common. X subsequently leases her share of the property to a third party.

82 21 *Halsbury's Laws of England* (1st edn, 1912), p 811.

83 *Gaskell v Gaskell* (1836) 6 Sim 643. For example, land is held by A and B for life, remainder to C and D. Co-owner A subsequently brings an action for partition of the land against B. C and D might desire a permanent partition on the basis that they will be able to take a divided share of the land when the remainder estate vests in possession and can plan the future use and development of that share accordingly. However, they must consent to the proposed partition and be joined as parties to the action.

84 See *Baring v Nash* (1813) 1 Ves & B 551. Returning to the examples in para **[4.28]** above, Z may wish to make a permanent partition of the land against Y, and must join the grandchildren as parties to the action and procure their consent. Alternatively, if the lessee of X's undivided share desires a permanent partition against Y, X must consent to this and be joined as a party to the action.

context where one or more persons interested in the property cannot be made a party to the action. This may occur because such persons are not yet in existence[85] or because they are in existence but it is not yet clear who will become entitled in reversion or remainder[86]. In these circumstances, special provisions within the Partition Acts allow the court to dispense with service of notice of the judgment on such persons and to determine the partition action accordingly[87].

2 *Persons deriving an interest from co-owners*

[4.30] A partition action may be brought by a third party who derives an interest in the land from one of the co-owners. This interest may arise by assignment or demise[88], or as the result of an agreement to this effect[89].

[4.31] Partition actions by a third party typically occur in two situations. Firstly, a mortgagee of an undivided share of land may bring an action for sale under the Partition Acts in order to realise his security in the event of default by the mortgagor[90]. Secondly, if a co-owner is declared bankrupt, all his property vests in the trustee in bankruptcy or the Official Assignee as appropriate[91]. The trustee in bankruptcy or Official Assignee may bring an action for sale of the property under the Partition Acts as part of his statutory duty to realise the bankrupt's assets for the benefit of creditors[92].

---

85 Where the persons interested in reversion or remainder are unborn children: see *Wills v Slade* (1801) 6 Ves 498 and *Gaskell v Gaskell* (1836) 6 Sim 643.

86 For example, where the remainder or reversionary interest passes to the heirs of a living person: see *Martyn v Perryman* (1662) 1 Rep Ch 125 and *Basnett v Moxon* (1875) LR 20 Eq 182.

87 Partition Act 1868, s 9 and Partition Act 1876, ss 3-5 discussed in ch 12 below, paras **[12.09]-[12.18]**.

88 See *Story v Johnson* (1837) 2 Y & C Ex 586 and *Williams v Williams* (1862) 10 WR 609.

89 See *Hill v Maunsell-Eyre* [1944] IR 499 at 502 per Overend J citing *Heaton v Dearden* (1852) 16 Beav 147 and *Davies v Davies* (1860) 6 Jur (ns) 1320. See further *Fleming v Hargreaves* [1976] 1 NZLR 123 at 127. In these circumstances, the plaintiff has an equitable interest in the property by virtue of which he is entitled to call for the legal estate.

90 See ch 8 below.

91 The trustee in bankruptcy is charged with administration of the bankrupt's estate in Northern Ireland and the principal legislation is the Insolvency (NI) Order 1989. In the Republic of Ireland, this task is performed by the Official Assignee pursuant to the Bankruptcy Act 1988.

92 The general practice in such partition actions and special rules which apply where the subject matter of the partition action comprises a matrimonial home are considered in chs 9 and 10 below.

93 An application for partition or sale being regarded as a unilateral declaration of an intention to sever by the particular joint tenant: *Munroe v Carlson* [1976] 1 WWR 248 applying *Re Wilks* [1891] 3 Ch 59, and see *Re Sorensen and Sorensen* (1977) 90 DLR (3d) 26.

D Partition actions and severance

[4.32] Where co-owners are joint tenants, the fact that one of them brings a partition action does not effect a severance of the joint tenancy[93]. The joint tenancy is not severed until the court makes an order for partition or sale of the property[94]. Thus, if a joint tenant brings a partition action but dies before an order is made, the property will pass to the remaining joint tenants by survivorship[95]. In contrast, if a joint tenant has obtained an order for partition or sale the joint tenancy is regarded as severed even though a formal judgment for partition or sale was not entered prior to his death[96].

III Property which may be Partitioned or Sold

[4.33] All types of lands, tenements and hereditaments held in co-ownership may be partitioned or sold by order of the court[97]. For example, an order for compulsory partition or sale may be made in respect of freeholds[98]. Likewise, an order for partition or sale may be made in respect of leasehold property[99]. Following partition, the rent owed to the landlord may be apportioned between the former co-owners[100]. However, partition of leasehold property may be refused if division of the property would be contrary to a covenant in the lease[101].

---

93 (contd) A mere statement of intention to sever by one joint tenant does not cause a severance of the joint tenancy: *Corin v Patton* (1990) 169 CLR 540 applying *Patriche v Powlet* (1740) 2 Atk 54, and see *Golding v Hands* [1969] WAR 121 and *Patzak v Lytton* (1984) 9 Fam LR 737.

94 *Grant v Grant* [1952] OWN 641.

95 *Rodrigue v Dufton* (1976) 72 DLR (3d) 16.

96 *Gillette v Cotton* (1979) 99 DLR (3d) 693.

97 See generally 21 *Halsbury's Laws of England* (1st edn, 1912), pp 836-839.

98 While joint tenants and tenants in common of freehold estates have always been able to partition by agreement (see the case reported at (1345) YB 19 Ed III (RS) pl 5; *Eden v Harris* (1576) 3 Dyer 350b and *Re Tann* (1869) LR 7 Eq 434), compulsory partition of such estates was not possible until the sixteenth century Statutes of Partition were passed: see *Fleming v Armstrong* (1864) 34 Beav 109 and *Re Foley's Estate* (1862) 7 Ir Jur (NS) 402. The court may order sale of freeholds under the Partition Acts 1868 and 1876: see *Thompson v Richardson* (1872) IR 6 Eq 596 and *Burnell v Burnell* (1879) 11 Ch D 213.

99 As with freeholds, joint tenants and tenants in common of leasehold estates could not compel partition until the Statutes of Partition granted them such a right: see *Baring v Nash* (1813) 1 Ves & B 551 and *Heaton v Dearden* (1852) 16 Beav 147. The court may order sale of leasehold estates under the Partition Acts 1868 and 1876. For example, in *Rowe v Gray* (1877) 5 Ch D 263 the court ordered sale of ten houses held under a lease by the plaintiff and infant defendant. See further *Burnell v Burnell* (1879) 11 Ch D 213; *Mason v Keays* (1898) 78 LT 33 and *Malayan Credit Ltd v Jack Chia-MPH* [1986] 1 All ER 711.

100 *Ames v Comyns* (1867) WR 74.

101 *North v Guinan* (1829) Beat 342 and *Cantwell v Hassard* (1858) 7 Ir Ch R 370: see ch 7 below, para **[7.23]**. In these circumstances the court is likely to substitute the more convenient remedy of sale.

Although largely of historical interest, the Court of Chancery could order partition of copyholds[102] and subsequently sale of such lands under the Partition Acts[103]. Party walls may be divided by order of the court[104]. However, it is unlikely that the court would order sale of a party wall under the Partition Acts, since this is not a practicable alternative.

[4.34] Compulsory partition is also possible in respect of incorporeal hereditaments such as rent services and rent charges[105]. Likewise, the court may order partition of easements. Where the servient tenement is held in co-ownership and is subsequently partitioned, the owner of the dominant tenement

---

[102] Copyhold Act 1841, s 85 (replaced by the Copyhold Act 1894, s 87). Compulsory partition of copyholds was not possible prior to 1841. There was no reference to either copyholds or customary freeholds in the Statutes of Partition. Furthermore, it was alleged that partition of copyholds would interfere with the rights of the lord by altering the associated rents and services and forcing a different tenant upon him: *Scott v Fawcett* (1757) 1 Dick 299 and *Jope v Morshead* (1843) 6 Beav 213, and see 21 *Halsbury's Laws of England* (1st edn, 1912), p 836. Thus in *Dillon v Coppin* (1833) 6 Beav 217n where the disputed land comprised both freeholds and copyholds, the court ordered that the entire copyhold estate be allotted to one of the parties and the freehold estate to the other party. See further *Clarke v Clayton* (1860) 2 Giff 333 and *Bowles v Rump* (1861) 9 WR 370.

[103] *Burnell v Burnell* (1879) 11 Ch D 213. Manors could be partitioned either by the agreement of the parties (*Melwich v Luther* (1588) Cro Eliz 102 and *Morris v Smith and Paget* (1585) Cro Eliz 38) or by order of the court (*Hanburry v Hussey* (1851) 14 Beav 152). Following partition, each party could hold a separate court in respect of his undivided share: *Cattley v Arnold* (1858) 4 K & J 595. As regards the indivisible incidents of a manor, the profits of the whole could be divided among the co-owners or the parties could take it in turns to enjoy them: *Moor and Brown v Onslow* (1600) Cro Eliz 759. Alternatively, the profits could be allocated to one co-owner who would compensate the others accordingly. Castles built for private use could be partitioned unlike those used for the defence of the realm which could not be partitioned: see Foster, *The Law on Joint Ownership and Partition of Real Estate* (1878), pp 83-84 and paras **[4.37]-[4.39]** below.

[104] The most common type of party wall is a wall forming a boundary between two separate properties. Assuming that the parties are co-owners of this structure (as opposed to one half of the wall being owned outright by each party) one of them may seek partition. In *Mayfair Property Company v Johnston* [1894] 1 Ch 508 the court granted a request for partition by a tenant in common of a wall separating the gardens of two adjoining houses, dividing the wall longitudinally between the two properties. Following a partition in *Morland v Cook* (1868) LR 6 Eq 252, an obligation to maintain a sea wall was imposed on the owners of the respective parts and secured by a charge on these.

[105] Foster, *The Law on Joint Ownership and Partition of Real Estate* (1878), pp 84-85. Following partition, each individual owner has a separate remedy for enforcing the rent service or rent charge: see *Ards v Watkin* (1599) Cro Eliz 637 at 651 and *Rivis v Watson* (1839) 5 M & W 255. Because a rent service is a rent incident to the reversion in the land, it will follow the reversion to which it is reserved on partition: *Ards v Watkin* and *Rivis v Watson*. In *Baxter v Knollys* (1750) 1 Ves Sen 494 it was held that tithes could be partitioned, at least in the Court of Chancery.

is not affected; his easement still exists, notwithstanding partition of the servient tenement[106]. Thus in *Newcomen v Coulson*[107] where a right of way allowed several persons to drive horses and cattle over land in order to reach their own lands, Jessel MR held that where the servient land is partitioned the easement itself is partitioned and goes with every part of the divided land[108]. If the dominant tenement is held in co-ownership and the parties subsequently partition that land, each party may still exercise the easement that exists over the servient tenement[109]. Following partition, the parties cannot exercise a greater right against the owner of the servient tenement than they would have exercised if the property had remained undivided[110]. Such considerations do not arise when the dominant or servient tenement is sold under the Partition Acts. Sale will take place, subject to the easement affecting the land.

[4.35] As regards certain types of incorporeal hereditaments and items of property which cannot be partitioned, the court may achieve a similar result by means of other arrangements between the parties[111]. For example, it might order them to exercise the particular right in turns. However, the court is more likely to apply the more convenient remedy of sale under the Partition Acts in these circumstances[112].

IV Jurisdiction Exceptions

[4.36] There are a number of situations in which the court cannot order partition or sale of co-owned land, even though a co-owner has *locus standi* to maintain

---

106 Since an order for partition cannot prejudice third parties with rights over the entire property: see paras **[4.61]-[4.67]** below. For example, if A has an easement over lands held in joint tenancy by B and C and these lands are subsequently partitioned, A may still exercise that easement over the parcels of land now held by B and C in severalty.

107 (1877) 5 Ch D 133.

108 (1877) 5 Ch D 133 at 141 citing *Harris v Drewe* (1831) 2 B & Ad 164 and *Codling v Johnson* (1829) 9 B & C 933.

109 Thus if X and Y are tenants in common of land and enjoy an easement over land owned by Z, both X and Y may continue to exercise this easement following partition of their land.

110 See *Menzies v Macdonald* (1856) 2 Jur (ns) 575.

111 The various types of property and arrangements which the court might impose are the same as those discussed in relation to voluntary partition between co-owners: see ch 2 above, para **[2.09]**.

112 See for example, *Young v Young* (1871) LR 13 Eq 175n (sale of an advowson under the Partition Act 1868) and *Glass v McManus* [1996] NI 401 (order for sale of a dwelling house). In *Blasdell v Baldwin* (1878) 3 OAR 6 the Ontario Court of Appeal ordered sale of land and an appurtenant water mill privilege upon hearing evidence that partition of the water mill privilege would require large structures to be erected at considerable expense and with high maintenance costs. See further *Union Bank of Canada v Foulds* (1924) 26 OWN 179 and *Lehman v Hunter* (1939) 13 MPR 553.

the action. In these circumstances, the court does not have jurisdiction to make an order[113]. Five such exceptions have arisen.

A Castle for defence of the realm

[4.37] Prior to 1868 the court could not partition a castle used for the defence of the realm on the ground of public policy[114]. Accordingly, an order for sale could not be made in respect of this type of castle under the Partition Acts[115].

[4.38] It has been suggested that this exception survives today, albeit in modified form. In *O'D v O'D*[116], Murphy J described it as a 'somewhat esoteric' exception which involved 'recognition of the principle that partition could not be granted where this conflicted with the public good'. He concluded that '[t]ranslated into contemporary and more mundane circumstances' partition should be refused if it were to prejudice the proper planning of the area in which a building was located[117]. In *Glass v McManus*[118], Girvan J also interpreted this exception as an example of the court refusing to order partition in the public interest, although he did not go so far as to give practical examples. However, it is submitted that both judges have extended this exception beyond its proper scope. Historically, the lack of jurisdiction to order partition of this type of castle appears to have been a strict exception invoked where a division of the property would have threatened the defence of the country. While it may be true to say that this exception was motivated by public policy reasons, it is not indicative of a general rule that partition or sale may be refused if contrary to public good.

[4.39] Applying this to modern circumstances suggests that there is no jurisdiction to order partition or sale where co-ownership of certain property is necessary in the interests of national security. Yet it is difficult to envisage such a situation occurring today. The exception in respect of castles evolved during the period when these were privately owned and were an integral part of defence. Moreover, private ownership may have given rise to situations in which castles were held in co-ownership. Modern examples of defence property may include

113 As distinct from the court exercising a discretion to refuse partition or sale. As to whether such discretion exists in partition actions, see ch 7 below.

114 This exception was said to be '*pro bono publico et pro defensione regni*': Foster, *The Law on Joint Ownership and Partition of Real Estate* (1878), p 83.

115 Since the Partition Acts 1868 and 1876 only allow sale in those circumstances in which a decree for partition might have been made prior to 1868: see ch 5 below, paras **[5.08]-[5.16]**.

116 (18 November 1983, unreported) High Court (RI), at 6-7.

117 (18 November 1983, unreported) High Court (RI), at 7. The relevant planning legislation in Northern Ireland and the Republic of Ireland creates specific problems for co-owners seeking partition of a dwelling house: see ch 7 below. However, such problems arise from restrictions on subdivision contained in the legislation itself, and are not part of a wider jurisdiction exception on the grounds of public policy.

118 [1996] NI 401.

army and navy bases. However, these properties are no longer privately owned: all such property in the United Kingdom is owned by the Ministry of Defence and in the Republic by the State. Accordingly, this exception must be regarded as virtually obsolete.

B Specific types of trust property

[4.40] Under the terms of a trust, two or more persons may be beneficially entitled to property as co-owners. A beneficiary may wish to end this relationship by compelling partition or sale of the trust property. However, the court cannot order partition or sale of trust property if this would override trusts prescribed by the settlor[119]. This may occur where the settlor directs that the property be managed in a specific manner and it must remain vested in the trustees to give effect to this. For example, in *Taylor v Grange*[120] trustees of a testator's will were instructed to work a quarry on the estate and to divide the profits between the testator's daughters. Fry J held that the court had no jurisdiction to order partition or sale of the property under the Partition Acts, since this would have the effect of ending the trusts[121]. Likewise, if property is subject to a trust for sale, the court will not anticipate the execution of the trust by ordering partition or sale of the property. The court's jurisdiction is ousted, irrespective of whether the settlor specifies a particular time at which sale should take place[122] or leaves this to the discretion of the trustees[123].

[4.41] In contrast, one or more beneficiaries may compel partition or sale of trust property if trustees have a mere power of sale. The reason for this appears to be that, even though the settlor has prescribed a means of distributing the property, the trustees are not under a duty to act and consequently may never exercise the power of sale[124]. However, the court may refuse to make such an order where the partition action is brought frivolously, or where the trustees are on the verge of exercising the power of sale[125].

---

119 See White and Tudor, *A Selection of Leading Cases in Equity* (7th edn, 1897), p 196 and 21 *Halsbury's Laws of England* (1st edn, 1912), p 841. The word 'trust' in this sense refers to an active or subsisting trust, and not to resulting or constructive trusts which are imposed by law: see the comments of Murray J in *Northern Bank Ltd v Beattie* [1982] 18 NIJB 1 at 24 and see *Re Forster v Forster* (6 March 1980, unreported) Alberta Court of Appeal.

120 (1879) 15 Ch D 165.

121 Similar views were expressed in *Cass v Wood* (1874) 30 LT 670.

122 See *Swaine v Denby* (1880) 14 Ch D 326 and *Ward v Trustee, Executors and Agency Co Ltd* (1893) 14 VLR 397.

123 *Biggs v Peacock* (1883) 22 Ch D 284 and see the comments of Warrington J in *Dodd v Cattell* [1914] 2 Ch 1 at 11.

124 See *Boyd v Allen* (1883) 31 WR 544 and *Oatley v Oatley* (1898) 19 NSWR (Eq) 129.

125 *Boyd v Allen* (1883) 31 WR 544.

C Agreements regulating the disposal of concurrent interests

[4.42] Co-owners may enter into an agreement that provides for division or sale of their property to be carried out in a certain manner if the parties should wish to end this relationship in the future[126]. In these circumstances, the court cannot make an order for partition or sale if this would be contrary to or inconsistent with the terms of such an agreement[127]. The contractual arrangement between the parties displaces the right to partition or sale, either by preventing the court from making such an order or by restricting the circumstances in which it is available[128].

[4.43] At a cursory glance, it might be thought that an agreement of this nature would be contrary to the policy of the Partition Acts, which provide a means for co-owners to end their relationship in the event of disagreement. The rationale for allowing such agreements appears to be that, although the Partition Acts give joint tenants and tenants in common a right to compel partition or sale, co-owners may restrict or modify that right if they choose[129]. This exception is well established in respect of partnership property[130] and pre-emptive agreements. It has also been suggested that it extends to situations in which co-owners agree not to divide or sell the land, or a co-owner asserts that the plaintiff is estopped from seeking partition or sale[131].

---

[126] Contrast this with voluntary partition (discussed in ch 2 above) where the agreement to partition or sell follows a decision to end co-ownership as opposed to the parties relying on a scheme decided earlier.

[127] 21 *Halsbury's Laws of England* (1st edn, 1912), p 811 and *Thompson on Real Property* (1994), p 454. See further Girard, 'Equitable and Contractual Defenses to Partition' (1966) 18 Stan L Rev 1428.

[128] See *Re McNamara and the Conveyancing Act* (1961) 78 WN (NSW) 1068; *Re Permanent Trustee Nominees (Canberra) Ltd* [1989] 1 Qd R 314; *Ngatoa v Ford* (1990) NSWLR 72 and *Norgard v Norgard* (1996) 20 Fam LR, Lexis transcript. In the majority of cases, the parties will execute a written agreement prescribing the means in which partition or sale of the property should be carried out. The practice in respect of oral agreements is more difficult to ascertain. Notwithstanding the requirements of the Statute of Frauds, courts in America have enforced such oral agreements by employing exceptions to this statute or finding that the agreement has been substantially performed so that a refusal to enforce it would be tantamount to fraud: *Thompson on Real Property* (1994), pp 455-456.

[129] See the comments of Connolly J in *Re Permanent Trustee Nominees (Canberra) Ltd* [1988] 1 Qd R 314 at 322 (citing *Wilson v McIntosh* [1894] AC 129 and *Phillips v Martin* (1890) 11 NSWLR 153) and those of Brennan J in *Nullagine Investments Pty Ltd v Western Australian Club* (1993) 177 CLR 635 at 645.

[130] As defined by the Partnership Act 1890, s 20.

[131] A settlement of matrimonial property on divorce or judicial separation might also be regarded as falling within this jurisdiction exception: see ch 9 below, paras **[9.05]-[9.06]**.

1 *Partnership agreements*

[4.44] Where several business partners are co-owners of land, a partnership agreement will usually regulate the manner in which the property should be distributed upon dissolution of the partnership[132]. The court has no jurisdiction to order partition or sale of partnership property in these circumstances[133]. The agreement excludes (whether expressly or impliedly) the right of any partner to terminate co-ownership under the Partition Acts[134].

[4.45] In the rare event that an agreement does not prescribe any means of distributing property upon dissolution of the partnership, this may be determined under the appropriate partnership legislation[135]. One of the partners may still apply for partition or sale under the Partition Acts in these circumstances[136]. However, the court might refuse to entertain the application and instead distribute the property according to s 39 of the Partnership Act 1890, which deals specifically with this type of situation.

2 *Pre-emptive agreements*

[4.46] Co-owners may agree that, if one of them wishes to sell his interest in the land, the others shall have a 'right of first refusal'[137]. In *Peck v Cardwell*[138] the

[132] The partnership agreement may also provide for a right of pre-emption if one of the partners wishes to sell his share of the property: see *25765 British Columbia Ltd v Bartell Bros Construction Ltd* (1983) 50 BCLR 155.

[133] One of the earliest decisions to this effect is *Dale v Hamilton* (1846) 5 Hare 369 at 398. See further *Redwood v Redwood* (1908) 28 NZLR 260. In *Rigden v Pierce* (1822) Madd & G 353 and *Cook v Collingridge* (1823) Jac 607 the respective courts held that, where a partnership agreement provides for division of such property upon termination of the relationship, this should be construed as meaning sale and division of the proceeds between the parties as opposed to actual physical division.

[134] See the comments of Brennan J in *Nullagine Investments Pty Ltd v Western Australian Club* (1993) 177 CLR 635 at 645-646 and cited with approval by McDonald J in *Tenture Pty Ltd v Costala Pty Ltd* (15 July 1997, unreported) Supreme Court of Victoria. See further *Re Bolous* [1985] 2 Qd R 165 and *Fraser Homes Ltd v Fraser Houses (NI) Ltd* [1998] NI 214.

[135] See *Nugent Sales and Services Ltd v Consolidated Ad Astra Mineral Ltd* (31 December 1975, unreported) Supreme Court of Alberta.

[136] See *Redwood v Redwood* (1908) 28 NZLR 260 and *Fraser Homes Ltd v Fraser Houses (NI) Ltd* [1998] NI 214.

[137] As to rights of pre-emption in general, see the comments of Street J in *Mackay v Wilson* (1947) 47 SR (NSW) 315 at 325. A somewhat bizarre interpretation of such rights was suggested in *Richardson v McGuiness* (12 December 1996, unreported) British Columbia Supreme Court. Counsel for the respondent argued that a pre-emptive right agreed by the parties was inconsistent with the existence of co-ownership and had destroyed the unity of possession, thus preventing the petitioner from compelling sale of premises under the Partition of Property Act 1979 (BC). Rejecting this argument, Holmes J held that the pre-emptive right was merely an arrangement between the parties and a means of enhancing their use and occupation of the property as co-owners.

[138] (1839) 2 Beav 137.

court held that an agreement for the development, subdivision and sale of land under which each tenant in common granted a right of pre-emption to the others prevented the court from ordering partition of the property[139]. More recently, the interaction between pre-emptive agreements and the court's jurisdiction under the Partition Acts and analogous legislation has been considered by the High Court of Australia in *Nullagine Investments Pty Ltd v Western Australian Club*[140].

[4.047] The parties had entered into an agreement, clause 4(b) of which expressly provided that neither would dispose of 'its share or interest' in the property unless it had offered that share to the other party at a price to be mutually agreed. A majority of the court were of the opinion that clause 4(b) only applied to a disposition of its 'share or interest' by each party as opposed to a disposition of the freehold estate. Accordingly, this clause did not preclude either party from seeking partition or sale under s 126(1) of the Property Law Act 1969 (WA)[141], irrespective of whether the plaintiff had previously offered its share to the other party in accordance with the right of pre-emption. Deane, Dawson and Gaudron JJ stated:

> 'As a matter of both law and language, there is a clear distinction between the individual "interest or share" owned by one of two or more tenants in common of a freehold estate in land and the freehold estate itself ...'[142]

They continued:

> 'What cl 4(b) is directed to is a separate sale by one of the two tenants in common of its distinct share or interest ... [I]f the reference in cl 4(b) to a sale or other disposition "by" one tenant in common of "its share or interest in the Land" were construed as extending to a sale or partition of the freehold, cl 4(b) would purport to exclude completely ... any sale or partition of the Land itself.'[143]

[4.48] Dissenting judgments were delivered by Brennan and Toohey JJ. The former was of the opinion that a pre-emptive clause such as this precluded a co-owner from disposing of his interest unless it had been offered to the other party[144]. If the party wishing to sell its interest could apply for an order for sale without giving the other party an opportunity to purchase its share, the pre-emptive agreement would be rendered 'worthless'[145]. Toohey J acknowledged

---

[139] See further *Fletcher v Ashburner* (1779) 1 Bro CC 497.

[140] (1993) 177 CLR 635.

[141] Which corresponds to the Partition Act 1868, s 4: see ch 5 below.

[142] (1993) 177 CLR 635 at 656.

[143] (1993) 177 CLR 635 at 658.

[144] However, Brennan J was of the opinion that this particular clause was an impermissible restraint on alienation because clause 4(b) also prohibited either party from disposing of its interest in the land unless the purchaser covenanted to be bound by the terms of the agreement including clause 4(b).

[145] (1993) 177 CLR 635 at 648.

that clause 4(b) was concerned with the disposition of a co-owner's interest in the land, and was not directly concerned with the sale of co-owned land. However, he continued:

> 'A sale of the land necessarily involves a sale of each co-owner's interest and there is considerable unreality in regarding a sale of the land pursuant to an order of the Supreme Court as not touching the rights and obligations of the parties under cl 4(b). Although s 126 of the [1969] Act speaks of a sale of "the land", that is clearly a compendious way of referring to the estates or interests of the "parties interested" in the land. What is sold pursuant to an order of the Supreme Court is the estate or interest of each co-owner, not some independent entity.'[146]

[4.49] Toohey J concluded that clause 4(b) created a right of pre-emption whereby the party wishing to sell its interest had to offer that interest to the other party. However, if that offer did not result in sale, the party desiring sale could invoke the jurisdiction of the court under the 1969 Act[147].

[4.50] It is submitted that the reasoning of the minority is to be preferred here. Where co-owners enter into a pre-emptive agreement, any person wishing to sell his share or interest must offer that share to the other co-owners. If they refuse this offer or the parties cannot agree on a price, the co-owner desiring sale may sell his share to a third party or bring a partition action[148]. The majority suggested that a co-owner may bring a partition action without offering his share to another co-owner because the entire property is sold in a partition action, not individual interests. However, this ignores the purpose of pre-emptive agreements as giving co-owners a right of first refusal in the event that one of them wishes to be released from the relationship. The Partition Acts provide a second means of achieving this in the absence of a sale to the other co-owners.

3 Agreements prohibiting partition or sale

[4.51] Both partnership agreements and rights of pre-emption modify or restrict the right to apply for partition or sale. Likewise, co-owners may agree not to divide or sell their land for a specific period of time or until a certain event occurs[149]. However, more difficult issues arise in respect of agreements which

---

[146] (1993) 177 CLR 635 at 670.

[147] 'Once a co-owner has offered its interest to the other co-owner in accordance with cl 4(b) and no sale results, it is reading too much into the sub-clause to say that the co-owner wishing to sell may not thereafter apply to the Court for an order for sale': (1993) 177 CLR 635 at 671.

[148] This approach is implicit in the judgment of Holmes J in *Richardson v McGuiness* (12 December 1996, unreported) British Columbia Supreme Court.

[149] For example, in *Re Permanent Trustee Nominees (Canberra) Ltd* [1989] 1 Qd R 314 at 321 Connolly J suggested that co-owners may forego the right to partition or sale for a limited period. See further *Thompson on Real Property* (1994), pp 454-455 and *Nullagine Investments Pty Ltd v Western Australian Club* (1993) 177 CLR 635 at 651-652 where Brennan J referred to the practice in the United States and the fact that courts have held that the remedies of partition and sale may be bargained away for a period which does not exceed the perpetuity period.

prohibit joint tenants and tenants in common from dividing or selling their land. Opinions have differed as to whether co-owners can contract out of the provisions of the Partition Acts completely.

[4.52] In *Wickstrand and Mannix v Cavanaugh and Dillon*[150] Ford J asserted that the right to partition under the Partition Act 1868 may be 'limited, modified or waived' by an express or implied agreement to this effect. Likewise, Myers J in *Stephens v Debney*[151] was of the opinion that a covenant not to apply for partition or sale might prevent such an application. However, a preponderance of authorities suggest that co-owners cannot bargain away the right to apply for partition or sale so as to leave them without any means of ending their relationship. In *Nullagine Investments Pty Ltd v Western Australian Club*[152] Brennan J asserted:

> '[O]ne of the purposes of the Partition Acts is to provide for the termination of co-ownership of land where the co-owners are unable to provide for it or have failed to do so. The remedies afforded by the Partition Acts are created to serve that purpose in the public interest as well as in the interests of the co-owners. On that basis, the co-owners are incapable of bargaining away their right to apply for an order for partition or sale except where the bargain is made as part of an agreement which itself provides for the termination of the co-ownership.'

[4.53] In *ex p Eimbert Pty Ltd*[153] McPherson J likewise remarked that, the right to partition or sale being an incident of the property of a co-owner, the existence of a mere agreement to the contrary should not constitute a bar to such an application[154].

[4.54] Thus it appears that co-owners cannot contract out of the provisions of the Partition Acts. This is prudent. If such agreements were upheld, the effect would be to leave land in the hands of persons who are unable or unwilling to agree on its use and occupation. The law provides a remedy to deal with this specific type of situation. Co-owners should be able to commence proceedings for partition or sale in these circumstances, notwithstanding the existence of an agreement to the contrary. This may be distinguished from partnership property or pre-

---

150 [1936] 1 WWR 113 at 115.

151 (1959) 60 SR (NSW) 468 at 470.

152 (1993) 177 CLR 635 at 651-652.

153 [1982] Qd R 398 at 402.

154 Similar views were expressed in *Landstadt Estates Management Inc v Inland Gulf Properties Inc* (19 October 1998, unreported) British Columbia Supreme Court. See further Adams, 'Partition of Land' (1952) NZLJ 137 where it is suggested that land cannot be transferred to co-owners without a right to compel partition. In *Ngatoa v Ford* (1990) NSWLR 72 at 77 Needham J stated that the court would not uphold a contractual obligation which constituted a restraint on alienation.

emptive agreements since there is a means for co-owners to be released from the relationship, albeit not under the Partition Acts.

4 Estoppel

[4.55] A co-owner may be estopped from claiming partition or sale if the appropriate conditions are satisfied[155]. An estoppel may arise as the result of an informal agreement or arrangement between the parties, or as a result of the conduct of the co-owner seeking partition or sale[156]. For example, in *Lucas v McNaughton*[157] the plaintiff and defendant purchased a dwelling house, which they resided in until the breakdown of their relationship. The defendant opposed the plaintiff's application for partition or sale of the property on the basis that the plaintiff had encouraged an assumption that he would provide for the defendant and her two children by joining in the purchase of the dwelling house. Dismissing the application, the court held that since a contract was a valid defence to an application for partition, promissory estoppel might also be a basis for refusing relief.

[4.56] In *Re Yale and MacMaster*[158] a husband and wife entered into an oral separation agreement whereby the husband paid maintenance to his wife and she remained in the matrimonial home to raise the children of the marriage. It was an implied term of the agreement that the husband would not seek to remove his wife from the home if she fulfilled her part of the agreement. The wife did not seek a lump sum provision when the parties divorced, although the husband's maintenance obligation was incorporated in the decree *nisi*. Galligan J held that the wife had relied on the implied term to her detriment by failing to seek other relief in the divorce proceedings, so that the husband would be estopped from bringing a partition action in respect of the matrimonial home.

5 Position of third parties who derive an interest from one or more co-owners

[4.57] A third party who derives an interest from one or more co-owners will not usually be bound by an agreement between the co-owners regulating the disposal of the land, since he was not an original party to the contract. Thus it should be possible for a mortgagee or trustee in bankruptcy of an undivided share of land to compel sale of property under the Partition Acts without complying with an

---

[155] As to estoppel in general see Cooke, *The Modern Law of Estoppel* (2000).

[156] However, an estoppel may not arise simply because the co-owner seeking sale allowed the defendant to expend large sums of money on the relevant property: *Sheridan Platinum Group Ltd v Madeleine Mines Ltd* (29 June 1994, unreported) Ontario Court (General Division), in which the court found that the defendant had not changed its position in reliance on any action or inaction on the part of the plaintiff which had frequently warned the defendant that money should not be spent without the plaintiff's input.

[157] (1990) 14 Fam LR 347.

[158] (1974) 46 DLR (3d) 167.

agreement between the co-owners and, for example, giving any of them a right of first refusal. Likewise, a purchaser of an undivided share of land should be able to bring an action for sale of property under the Partition Acts without being bound by any right of first refusal conferred on the other co-owners, and could not expect to be given such a pre-emptive right in the event that any such person wishes to dispose of his interest.

[4.58] However, the position in Northern Ireland has been altered somewhat by the provisions of the Contracts (Rights of Third Parties) Act 1999. This Act allows a third party to sue on a contract where the contract provides for this or a term of the contract purports to confer a benefit on him[159]. Thus, where there is an agreement between co-owners regulating the disposal of the land, that agreement should be enforceable by a third party who has acquired the interest of one of the co-owners. For example, a purchaser of an undivided share should be able to enforce a pre-emptive agreement, giving him a right of first refusal in the event of a proposed sale by another co-owner.

[4.59] The 1999 Act does not, however, make a third party subject to the burden of a contract. Therefore, it should be possible for mortgagees or trustees in bankruptcy of an undivided share of land to sell that interest without complying with the terms of an agreement regulating disposal of the land. Equally, there is nothing in the Act to prevent the mortgagee or trustee from compelling partition or more likely sale of the land in these circumstances. The opposing co-owners could not use an agreement of this nature to defeat a partition action by a third party by claiming, for example, that he should have offered them a right of first refusal in relation to that undivided share or that the property in question is partnership property and should be distributed accordingly.

[4.60] As regards an estoppel, it appears that this is capable of binding third parties. Thus, in *Re Yale and MacMaster*[160] where the husband was estopped from compelling partition or sale of the marital home, the court held that a trustee in bankruptcy who derived his interest in the property from the husband was likewise estopped from claiming partition or sale.

D Prejudice to third parties

[4.61] The court cannot order partition if this would prejudice third parties with rights over the entire property[161]. This exception originated in the sixteenth

[159] Contracts (Rights of Third Parties) Act 1999, s 1(1), although the latter option does not apply where it appears that the parties did not intend the term to be enforceable by a third party: Contracts (Rights of Third Parties) Act 1999, s 1(2). A third party may be identified in the contract by name, as a member of a class or as answering a particular description, yet need not be in existence when the contract is entered into: Contracts (Rights of Third Parties) Act 1999, s 1(3).

[160] (1974) 46 DLR (3d) 167.

[161] Contrast this with situations in which the consent of a third party is required before an order for partition may be carried out: see ch 7 below.

century Statutes of Partition. After granting joint tenants and tenants in common the right to compel partition at common law, the Acts concluded:

> 'Provided always, and be it enacted, That no such Partition or Severance hereafter to be made by Force of this act, be nor shall be prejudicial or hurtful to any Person or Persons their Heirs or Successors other than such which be Parties unto the said Partition their Executors or Assigns.'[162]

[4.62] Since the equitable jurisdiction to partition was derived from that at common law, the Court of Chancery also adopted this exception[163].

[4.63] A third party will not necessarily be prejudiced by an order for partition. For example, where co-owners join in creating a mortgage of the property, the mortgagee's rights are not altered if one of them subsequently obtains an order for partition[164]. The parties remain liable to discharge the mortgage payments, and the mortgagee retains the same remedies in the event of default. Similar reasoning applies to the owner of a rent-charge. If the court orders partition at the request of co-tenants under a lease, the parties remain liable to pay the rent due and the landlord may still, for example, forfeit the lease in the event of non-payment[165]. An order for partition does not prejudice an annuitant[166] or someone who enjoys a right of residence on part of the property[167], nor does it prejudice the owners of an easement that extends over lands held in co-ownership[168].

[4.64] The court may order partition so long as a third party would not be prejudiced by division of the land. However, if the rights of a third party would be prejudiced, the court has no jurisdiction to make such an order[169]. This is well

---

162 See An Act Concerning Joint Tenants for Term of Life or Years 1540, s 2 and An Act for Jointenants 1542, s 4.

163 See Allnatt, *A Practical Treatise on the Law of Partition* (1820), p 149; White and Tudor, *A Selection of Leading Cases in Equity* (7th edn, 1897), p 204 and *Daniell's Chancery Practice* (8th edn, 1914), p 1172.

164 See ch 8 below.

165 See the comments of Holmes LJ in *Farrell v Donnelly* [1913] 1 IR 50 at 59-60.

166 Thus in *Hixon v Eastwood* [1868] WN 13 where annuitants were joined as defendants to a partition action, the court held that the action against them should be dismissed. Where land subject to an annuity is sold under the Partition Acts 1868 and 1876, the co-owners remain liable to pay the annuity: *Poole v Poole* [1885] WN 15.

167 *Warwick v Warwick* (21 January 1992, unreported) High Court (NI).

168 See *Newcomen v Coulson* (1877) 5 Ch D 133 noted at para **[4.34]** above. In addition to this, rights of common over land held in co-ownership are unlikely to be affected by an order for partition: Allnatt, *A Practical Treatise on the Law of Partition* (1820), p 149 citing *Agar v Fairfax* (1811) 17 Ves 533.

169 See Wallace, 'Mortgagees and Possession' (1986) 37 NILQ 336 at 355-356 (although it is submitted that the case he cites ie *North v Guinan* (1829) Beat 342 is not an example of prejudice to a third party but a 'futility' case: see ch 7 below). See further *Fraser Homes Ltd v Fraser Houses (NI) Ltd* [1998] NI 214 at 218.

illustrated by the decision in *Cantwell v Hassard*[170]. Persons in whom the shares of coparceners had vested granted a lease for lives renewable forever to a single tenant. The former's interest subsequently vested in the petitioner and respondent in respective one-third and two-third shares, subject to the lease and the petitioner filed a bill for partition. Brady LC at first instance was of the opinion that the court could not order partition, and offered to divide the rent between the parties. This was upheld on appeal. Napier LC suggested that the court could not order partition because of the covenant for future renewal in the lease and the effect that an order for partition might have on the tenant's ability to secure a renewal of the lease. Having referred to the right to a decree for partition in equity, he continued:

> '[T]hough that is perfectly true, it is subject to certain qualifications, and one of those is, that the rights of third persons not before the Court should never be prejudiced. Now see the effect of that here. Behind the back of the parties claiming under the lease, and who have the real and substantial interest, we are pressed to make a separation of the interest out of which the covenant for perpetual renewal is to be satisfied. This might create very great embarrassment in obtaining future renewals, and giving proper effect to the covenants.'[171]

[4.65] The tenant's right to obtain future renewals of the lease would not be affected by an order for partition (since the benefit of the covenant would not be affected by the order). However, an order for partition would render the exercise of that right more difficult since the tenant would have to deal with the petitioner and respondent separately and obtain separate leases from both of them. Accordingly, the tenant would be prejudiced by an order for partition of the property.

[4.66] Although *Cantwell v Hassard* was concerned with the effect of an order for partition on a covenant for future renewal, there are other situations in which a tenant could be prejudiced by a partition of the reversion. One of the most basic duties which a tenant must perform is payment of rent. If several persons are co-owners of the reversion, and the court makes an order for partition of this interest, difficulties arise in relation to payment of rent by the tenant – for example, would he have to pay separate portions of rent to each reversioner; if the tenant failed to pay rent to one of them, what remedies would be available to the latter? It appears that the Lord Justice of Appeal was influenced by these considerations in *Cantwell v Hassard*[172]:

> 'I do not think [the reversioner] ought to be placed in a position to embarrass the tenant for life or the other parties; for if a partition took place, I cannot conceive anything more complicated than the ascertainment of the amount of rent to be payable to each, except, perhaps, the embarrassment which would be caused to

[170] (1858) 7 Ir Ch R 370.
[171] (1858) 7 Ir Ch R 370 at 373.
[172] (1858) 7 Ir Ch R 370 at 374.

> the tenant, who, by his original contract, was to pay but one entire rent. If there were such a partition, how could he pay his rent, so as to avoid actions and distresses?'[173]

In other words, since the tenant would be prejudiced by partition of the remainder estate, the court could not make such an order.

[4.67] Thus the court has no jurisdiction to order partition where this would prejudice third parties with rights over the entire property. Moreover, since the court cannot make an order for partition in these circumstances, it cannot make an order for sale of the relevant property under the Partition Acts[174]. It has been suggested that, if co-owners in reversion or remainder were allowed to compel partition or sale of their respective estates or interests, this jurisdiction exception would prevent any possible prejudice to the life tenant as a result of the order, such as that which occurred in *Cantwell v Hassard*[175].

E Ascertainable shares

[4.68] An action for partition or sale of co-owned land cannot be entertained unless the various parties are interested in ascertainable shares[176]. The reason for this is obvious. The court should know how many persons are interested in the property and the extent of their respective interests in order to divide the land or proceeds of sale accordingly. Thus, in *Miles v Jarvis*[177] Kay J refused to make an order for sale where future born children of a living person were entitled to share equally in the land with ten existing children.

[4.69] As long as the number of shares is ascertainable, any difficulty involved in ascertaining them[178] or the fact that unascertained persons may become interested in a specific share is irrelevant[179].

---

173 However, the courts in *Ards v Watkin* (1599) Cro Eliz 637 and *Rivis v Watson* (1839) 5 M & W 255 held that both rent services and rent charges may be partitioned, with each individual owner then having a separate remedy for enforcing the service or charge.

174 Since the remedy of sale is only available where an order for partition might have been made prior to 25 June 1868 (the date on which the Partition Act 1868 came into force) in a similar factual situation: see ch 5 below, paras **[5.08]-[5.16]**.

175 See para **[4.23]** above. The petition in *Cantwell v Hassard* (1858) 7 Ir Ch R 370 could just as easily have been dismissed on the basis that the petitioner, as a reversioner of an undivided share of land, lacked the necessary standing to maintain a partition action.

176 21 *Halsbury's Laws of England* (1st edn, 1912), p 811. Since an order for partition pre-1868 would not have been granted unless the shares of the various parties were ascertainable (see *Agar v Fairfax* (1811) 17 Ves Jun 533 and *Knox v Mayo* (1858) 9 Ir Ch R 192), an order for sale under the Partition Acts 1868 and 1876 could not be granted in these circumstances: *Miles v Jarvis* [1883] WN 203.

177 [1883] WN 203.

178 *Agar v Fairfax* (1811) 17 Ves Jun 533.

179 21 *Halsbury's Laws of England* (1st edn, 1912), p 842 citing *Wills v Slade* (1801) 6 Ves 498 and *Gaskell v Gaskell* (1836) 6 Sim 643. This may occur, for example, where a tenant for life with remainder to his unborn children seeks a permanent partition or sale: see para **[4.29]** above and ch 12 below, para **[12.29]**.

Chapter 5

Criteria for Ordering Sale – Partition Act 1868 Sections 3, 4 and 5

I Introduction

[5.01] In *Northern Bank Ltd v Adams*[1], Master Ellison devised a two-stage test for determining applications under the Partition Acts. The court should inquire:

> '(a) [whether the plaintiff has] *locus standi* to bring a suit for partition or for sale in lieu ("the *locus standi* test"); and
>
> (b) where there is *locus standi*, whether the court has jurisdiction to make an order for sale in lieu of partition ("the jurisdiction test").'

He continued:

> 'The *locus standi* test is governed by the principle that the plaintiff must be entitled to a legal or equitable estate in possession ... The jurisdiction test is governed by the relevant words in section 4 (or, as the case may be, section 3 or 5) of the Partition Act 1868.'[2]

[5.02] The main provisions of the 1868 Act are ss 3-5 which prescribe the circumstances in which the court may order sale of co-owned land in lieu of partition[3]. Accordingly, a co-owner who wishes to compel sale of the land must bring his action within one of these sections depending on the extent of his interest in the property[4]. This chapter sets out the criteria for proceeding under ss 3-5 and considers the factors that courts should take into account in deciding

1 (1 February 1996, unreported) High Court (NI).

2 (1 February 1996, unreported) High Court (NI), at 14-15. This is subject to the jurisdiction exceptions considered in ch 4 above, paras **[4.36]-[4.69]**. A co-owner who wishes to compel partition or sale of land under the Partition Acts 1868 and 1876 must apply to court for such an order, since the court is overruling the wishes of persons with legal interests in the land: see Cocks, 'Co-ownership: Back to the Partition Acts' [1982] Conv 415 at 418 and 422. The dissenting co-owners are being forced to submit to a course of action which they oppose, and which will alter the nature of their interests. If the court orders partition, they will hold a divided share of land instead of an undivided share. If the court orders sale, each co-owner takes a share of the proceeds of sale.

3 The other main provisions of the Partition Act 1868 and those of the Partition Act 1876 are considered in ch 12 below in relation to the practice in partition actions in Northern Ireland and the Republic of Ireland.

4 Partition Act 1868, s 4 applies to co-owners who are entitled to a half interest or more in the property; Partition Act 1868, ss 3 and 5 apply to co-owners who are entitled to less than a half interest.

whether to order sale. The relevant principles are largely derived from post-1868 case law, as adopted and modified by recent cases in both Northern Ireland and the Republic of Ireland, and from the Commonwealth.

[5.03] Before examining each provision in detail, two matters require attention. Firstly, the proper and necessary parties to an action under the Partition Acts are the same persons who were the proper and necessary parties to a suit for partition prior to the passing of the 1868 Act. Section 9 of the 1868 Act provides that '[a]ny person who, if this Act had not been passed, might have maintained a suit for partition, may maintain such suit against any one or more of the parties interested' without joining all of those persons as defendants, but that 'all persons, who, if this Act had not been passed, would have been necessary parties to the suit' should be served with notice of the judgment on the hearing. Accordingly, s 9 retains the pre-1868 rule that the plaintiff should be entitled to a legal or equitable estate or interest in possession[5], and all other persons interested in the property should be made parties to the action or their absence satisfactorily accounted for[6].

[5.04] Secondly, the court may refuse to order sale under ss 3-5 if the criteria for making such an order are not satisfied[7]. It will be recalled that partition in equity prior to 1868 was a matter of right upon proof of title[8]. The prevailing view in the late nineteenth century was that, because the Partition Acts only altered this practice to the extent of allowing the court to substitute sale for partition, the plaintiff was entitled to either partition or sale – the court could not refuse both[9]. However, there is some disagreement as to whether the court must still order partition or sale, or whether it should be able to refuse both remedies today[10].

II Partition Act 1868

A Section 3 of the 1868 Act

[5.05] Section 3 reads:

> 'In a suit for partition, where if this Act had not been passed a decree for partition might have been made, then if it appears to the Court[11] that by reason of the nature of the property to which the suit relates, or of the number of the parties interested or presumptively interested therein, or of the absence or disability of some of those parties, or of any other circumstance, a sale of the property and a

[5] See ch 4 above, paras **[4.05]-[4.11]**.

[6] See ch 3 above, para **[3.32]**. Partition Act 1868, s 9 is considered in ch 12 below.

[7] Partition Act 1868, ss 3 and 5 provide that the court 'may, if it thinks fit' order sale, while s 4 provides that the court 'shall' order sale 'unless it sees good reason to the contrary'.

[8] See ch 3 above, paras **[3.43]-[3.46]**.

[9] See for example, the comments of Lord Watson in *Pitt v Jones* (1880) 5 App Cas 651 at 661.

[10] See ch 7 below.

[11] As to courts having jurisdiction under the Partition Acts 1868 and 1876 see ch 12 below.

> distribution of the proceeds would be more beneficial for the parties interested than a division of the property between or among them, the Court may if it thinks fit, on the request of any of the parties interested and notwithstanding the dissent or disability of any others of them, direct a sale of the property accordingly, and may give all necessary or proper consequential directions.'

[5.06] It is convenient to consider each provision in its constituent parts. The main elements of s 3 are as follows.

1 'In a suit for partition'

[5.07] These words appear at various intervals throughout the Partition Acts. Initially, cases such as *Teall v Watts*[12] held that a co-owner seeking sale also had to request partition[13]. However, in *Aston v Meredith*[14] Bacon VC held that a sale could be decreed under the 1868 Act, despite the fact that the bill did not seek both partition and sale. This was resolved by s 7 of the Partition Act 1876 which provides that, in an action under the Partition Acts, it is sufficient that a co-owner requests sale of the property and distribution of the proceeds – he does not have to request partition[15]. However, it is common practice for a plaintiff to request sale or partition in the alternative regardless of the fact that he only wants sale, or vice versa[16].

2 'Where, if this Act had not been passed, a decree for partition might have been made'

[5.08] Sections 3-5 of the 1868 Act commence with these words. Following the enactment of the 1868 Act there was disagreement surrounding the interpretation of this opening clause and the extent to which it qualified the court's jurisdiction to order sale. In *Pryor v Pryor*[17] Bacon VC was of the opinion that this clause meant nothing more than 'in any suit for partition'. Thus, any joint tenant or tenant in common could bring an action for sale under the Partition Acts, irrespective of the nature of his interest or the type of property in question.

[5.09] However, subsequent authorities took the view that these words restricted the court's jurisdiction to order sale to those situations in which it had

---

[12] (1871) LR 11 Eq 213.

[13] Similar views were expressed in *Holland v Holland* (1872) LR 13 Eq 406. See further *Parker v Trigg* [1874] WN 27; *Underwood v Stewardson* (1872) 20 WR 668 and *Harper v Bird* (1875) 23 WR 646.

[14] (1871) LR 11 Eq 602.

[15] See *Re Hardiman* (1880) 16 Ch D 360 and *Schnytzer v Wielunski* [1978] VR 418.

[16] See ch 12 below, para **[12.26]**.

[17] (1875) LR 19 Eq 595 at 596.

jurisdiction to order partition prior to the enactment of the 1868 Act. For example, Walker asserted that:

> 'The true meaning seems to be that the Court can only exercise the powers of sale given by the Act where before the Act it could have decreed partition. In other words every action asking a sale under the Act is in the first instance to be tried by the test – could the Court before the 25th of June, 1868[18] have decreed partition in this case? If the test-question must on any account be answered in the negative ... then there is no jurisdiction conferred by the Act to order a sale ... The elaboration cannot be assumed to be meaningless, especially when there is no difficulty in construing it to mean what it says.'[19]

[5.10] More recently, similar views have been expressed by Campbell J in *Northern Bank Ltd v Haggerty*[20]. Considering an action for sale by a creditor with an order charging land, the learned judge referred to s 4 of the 1868 Act and continued:

> 'It follows that it is necessary to consider the circumstances in which a decree for partition might have been made before the passing of the Act ... Since the owner of a charge did not have an estate or interest in possession, prior to the passing of the Partition Act 1868, he would not have been granted a decree for partition and he would not be entitled to an order [for sale] under section 4 of the Act.'[21]

[5.11] Thus, the jurisdiction to order sale under the Partition Acts is dependent on a concurrent jurisdiction to order partition which might have been exercised prior to 25 June 1868 if the plaintiff had asked the court to partition the property in respect of which he now seeks an order for sale.

[5.12] Two practical consequences flow from applying this test. In the first place, only persons who had *locus standi* to compel partition prior to the enactment of the 1868 Act may bring an action under the Partition Acts[22]. Secondly, the court can only order sale of property comprising the subject-

---

18 The date on which the Partition Act 1868 came into force.

19 Walker, *The Partition Acts, 1868 and 1876* (1882), p 27. In *Wickstrand and Mannix v Cavanaugh and Dillon* [1936] 1 WWR 113 Ford J likewise observed that 'the plaintiff's claim to have a sale directed in lieu of partition must be given effect to if the action is one in which before The Partition Act of 1868, ch 40 (Imp) partition would have been decreed'. See further *Joyce v Joyce* [1963] Qd R 139 and the comment on this case at (1963) 37 ALJ 186.

20 [1995] NI 211.

21 [1995] NI 211 at 216-217 and see *Fraser Homes Ltd v Fraser Houses (NI) Ltd* [1998] NI 214. See further the comments of Deane J in *Squire v Rogers* (1979) 39 FLR (Aus) 106 (noted at ch 6 below, paras **[6.49]**-**[6.51]**) and see *Jillings v Blewett* (1993) 101 DLR (4th) 604.

22 See the comments of Master Ellison at first instance in *Northern Bank Ltd v Haggerty* (23 March 1994, unreported) High Court (NI), at 7. This interpretation is confirmed by the relevant wording of the Partition Act 1868, s 9: see para **[5.03]** above.

matter of a partition action if it might have ordered partition of such property prior to 25 June 1868. Thus, if the property would have fallen within one of the jurisdiction exceptions[23] so that the court could not have ordered partition, an order for sale cannot be made[24]. However, the court does not have to consider whether it might have ordered partition of this particular item of property or at the request of this particular plaintiff prior to 25 June 1868. Rather the court must consider whether a decree for partition might have been made in similar circumstances prior to the relevant date[25].

[5.13] This approach avoids two problems. In the first place, if the former test was applied the plaintiff might have to prove that the property comprising the subject matter of the action was held in co-ownership prior to 1868[26]. Secondly, the former test fails to take account of legislation passed since the enactment of the Partition Acts and which affects the court's jurisdiction to order partition or sale of concurrent interests in land. Applying this test suggests that any such legislation passed after 25 June 1868 is not part of the legal context for determining whether an action for partition might have been made before this date. For example, art 48 of the Property (NI) Order 1997 gives chargees and creditors with orders charging land under the Judgments Enforcement (NI) Order 1981 *locus standi* to bring an action under the Partition Acts[27]. If the relevant test was whether a decree for partition might have been made at the request of a chargee of an undivided share of land prior to 25 June 1868, art 48 would be irrelevant. Since a chargee did not have *locus standi* to maintain a partition action at that time, he could not bring an action under the Partition Acts today[28]. However, the court merely has to consider whether a decree for partition might have been made if such legislation had been in force on 25 June 1868. For example, in *Squire v Rogers*[29] the plaintiff and defendant were joint tenants of a leasehold interest which was subject to the provisions of the Darwin Town Area

23 See ch 4 above, paras **[4.36]-[4.69]**.

24 Thus in *Biggs v Peacock* (1883) 22 Ch D 284 at 287 where the plaintiff sought an order for sale of property which was subject to an overriding trust for sale, Bowen LJ remarked:

> 'It appears to me perfectly clear that the Plaintiffs would not have been entitled before the Partition Act to a decree of partition. Therefore it is not within the Partition Act.'

See further the observations of Kay J in *Miles v Jarvis* [1883] WN 203.

25 See the comments of Deane J in *Squire v Rogers* (1979) 39 FLR (Aus) 106 at 118 noted below.

26 This in turn pre-supposes that the particular property existed at this time, which would give rise to problems in respect of buildings constructed after 25 June 1868.

27 See ch 8 below.

28 Likewise, planning legislation (see ch 7 below) which prohibits subdivision of a single dwelling house without the consent of the planning authority would be irrelevant, since the court might have ordered partition of a single dwelling house before the Partition Act 1868 was passed.

29 (1979) 39 FLR (Aus) 106.

Leases Ordinance 1947. The plaintiff brought an action for sale of the land under the Partition Act 1881 (SA). However, the Ordinance prohibited the subdivision of such land. The question arose as to whether the court was deprived of jurisdiction to order partition and consequently sale of the property. Rejecting the argument that the Ordinance was irrelevant insofar as it had been passed in 1947 and the relevant question as regards the jurisdiction to order sale under the 1881 Act was whether a decree for partition might have been made in 1881, Deane J concluded:

> 'The appropriate question, in the circumstances, is whether a decree for partition might, under the law of the colony of South Australia at the time the Partition Act, 1881 (SA) was introduced, properly have been made in respect of the estate of joint tenants under a lease granted in pursuance of a legislative enactment of the colony whose provisions corresponded to the provisions of the Ordinance.'[30]

[5.14] In other words, the plaintiff merely has to show that, had these particular factual circumstances existed in 1868, the court might have made an order for partition. He does not have to prove that the factual circumstances allowing a decree for partition to be made actually existed on 25 June 1868.

[5.15] Despite the reference to those circumstances in which a decree for partition 'might' have been made, a number of cases decided in the late nineteenth century asserted that sale could only be ordered where a decree for partition would have been made prior to 1868[31]. This may have been due to the prevailing view that partition was granted as of right in equity prior to 1868 so that the plaintiff would have been entitled to an order for partition upon making such a request. However, it is suggested that the use of the word 'might' is relevant. As will be discussed later[32], the court may refuse to order partition on the grounds that such an order would be futile because it is within the power of a third party to prevent the order from being carried out. In these circumstances, the court has jurisdiction to order partition and 'might' have made such an order, but chooses not to. However, since the court has jurisdiction to order partition it may order sale of the property under the Partition Acts.

[5.16] To summarise, by virtue of the opening clause of ss 3-5 of the 1868 Act, the jurisdiction to order sale under the Partition Acts is dependent on a concurrent jurisdiction to order partition which might have been exercised in respect of property held in this manner prior to the enactment of the 1868 Act.

---

30 (1979) 39 FLR (Aus) 106 at 118.

31 See for example, *Pitt v Jones* (1880) 5 App Cas 651; *Miles v Jarvis* [1883] WN 203; and *Miles v Jarvis (No 2)* (1883) 50 LT 48. Similar views were expressed in *Porter v Porter* (1888) 37 Ch D 420 and *Roper v Roper* (1907) 41 ILTR 231.

32 See ch 7 below.

3 'On the request of any of the parties interested'

[5.17] Section 3 contemplates a request for sale by any person interested in the disputed property, irrespective of the size of his interest. While there is no such restriction in the section itself, it is well-established that s 3 only applies where the person seeking sale is entitled to less than a half share in the property[33]. The extent of each co-owner's interest will usually be apparent from the title deeds to the property, unless affected by a claim under a resulting or constructive trust[34].

4 'The Court may, if it thinks fit ... direct a sale of the property'

[5.18] The power of sale under s 3 is discretionary[35] and should not usually be interfered with on appeal[36]. In deciding whether to order sale, the court is guided by several factors.

5 'If it appears to the Court that by reason of ... a sale of the property and a distribution of the proceeds would be more beneficial for the parties interested than a division of the property'

[5.19] The court must be satisfied that sale of the property and division of the proceeds would be more beneficial than partition for one or more of the following reasons:

(a) the nature of the property;

(b) the number of parties interested or presumptively interested therein;

(c) the absence or disability of any of those parties; or

(d) any other circumstance[37]

---

33 *Grunert v Grunert* (1960) 32 WWR 509 and see the comments of Joyce J in *Hoggard v Hoggard* (22 November 1996, unreported) British Columbia Supreme Court, in relation to the corresponding provision in the Partition of Property Act 1979 (BC). The position of those persons entitled to half or more is governed by the Partition Act 1868, s 4. Meanwhile, the Partition Act 1868, s 5 applies where the plaintiff's interest affects less than half of the property but he cannot show any reason for preferring sale to partition as required by s 3.

34 Thus in *Hancock v Gibson* [1996] NZFLR 289 where property was originally conveyed to the parties as tenants in common in equal shares, the court held that the plaintiff was only entitled to a one-quarter interest in the property in view of the defendant's contributions.

35 See the comments of Lord Hatherley LC in *Pemberton v Barnes* (1871) 6 Ch App 685 at 693. See further *Re Langdale's Estate* (1871) 6 ILTR 12 and *Grunert v Grunert* (1960) 32 WWR 509.

36 *Dyer v Painter* (1885) 33 WR 806 and *Ontario Power Company v Whattler* (1904) 7 OLR 198. However, it appears that the court's discretion under the Partition Act 1868, s 3 only extends to refusing an order for sale. Various cases decided in the nineteenth century held that the court was then obliged to make an order for partition: see for example, *Dicks v Batten* [1870] WN 173 and *Dyer v Painter* (1885) 33 WR 806. As to whether partition and sale are still regarded as alternatives see ch 7 below.

37 See generally the comments of Lynch J in *Re Langdale's Estate* (1871) 6 ILTR 12 at 12-13.

[5.20] Thus in *Drinkwater v Ratcliffe*[38] where the disputed property comprised buildings surrounded by 30 acres of land which were divisible into 36 shares, the court made an order for sale on account of both the nature of the property and the number of parties[39]. The onus of proof is on the party or parties seeking sale[40], who must allege and prove that sale would be beneficial because of one or more such reasons[41]. Section 3 states that sale of the property must be 'more beneficial than a division'[42]. In *Gilbert v Smith*[43] Jessel MR remarked:

> 'The meaning of the Legislature was that when you see that the property is of such a character that it cannot be reasonably partitioned, then you are to take it as more beneficial to sell it and divide the money amongst the parties.'[44]

[5.21] The corollary of this is that the court may refuse to make an order for sale under s 3 if it is of the opinion that partition is practicable or expedient[45]. The fact that there is evidence to suggest that it would be a good time to sell the property in question is irrelevant in these circumstances[46].

---

38 (1875) LR 20 Eq 528.

39 Likewise, in *Pemberton v Barnes* (1871) 6 Ch App 685 at 694 Lord Hatherley gave an example of the court being able to direct a sale under the Partition Act 1868, s 3 at the request of the owner of a one-tenth share 'if from the nature of the property, or from the number of the persons, the Court thinks it right and reasonable to do so'. See further *Pennington v Dalbiac* (1870) 18 WR 684; *Groves v Carbert* (1873) 29 LT 129; *Higgs v Dorkis* (1872) LR 13 Eq 280 and *Thompson v Richardson* (1872) IR 6 Eq 596.

40 See *Allen v Allen* (1873) 21 WR 842; *Drinkwater v Ratcliffe* (1875) LR 20 Eq 528 and *Prendergast v Mongan* [1913] 1 IR 321. Similar views were expressed on the equivalent provision of the Property Law Act 1928 (Vict) in *Perman v Maloney* [1939] VLR 376.

41 See *Evans v Evans* (1883) 31 WR 495.

42 In *Powell v Powell* (1874) 10 Ch App 131 Lord Cairns LC stated that, in an action for sale under the Partition Act 1868, s 3, the judge had to look at two matters: firstly, who are the parties interested in the property and secondly, would sale of that property then be more beneficial than partition? In *Grove v Comyn* (1874) LR 18 Eq 387 the decree was prefaced with a statement that the court considered sale more beneficial under s 3.

43 (1879) 11 Ch D 78 at 81.

44 Cited with approval by Meredith CJ in *Ontario Power Co v Whattler* (1904) 7 OLR 198 and by Baxter CJ in *Lehman v Hunter* (1939) 13 MPR 553. In *Dyer v Painter* (1885) 33 WR 806 Cotton LJ (commenting on *Gilbert v Smith*) stated that, in an action under the Partition Act 1868, s 3 'when you cannot see how a partition can reasonably be made, a sale should be directed'.

45 *Dicks v Batten* [1870] WN 173. See further *Allen v Allen* (1873) 21 WR 842; *Ontario Power Co v Whattler* (1904) 7 OLR 198 and *Prendergast v Mongan* [1913] 1 IR 321.

46 *Dyer v Painter* (1885) 33 WR 806.

[5.22] Sale must be more beneficial than partition for all the persons interested in the property[47]. In determining this issue the court should apply an objective standard[48]. The term 'beneficial' as used in this context means beneficial in a pecuniary sense – the court should look towards the financial result[49]. Thus, if the costs associated with partition are greater than those associated with sale because of the number of persons interested in the property, sale would be more beneficial than partition under s 3[50]. Likewise, the court may order sale where the resulting purchase money would be greater than the property's current rental income[51], or where a sale of the entire property would fetch a higher price than separate sales of the divided shares following partition[52]. The fact that one of the parties is absent from the area and is therefore unable to enjoy the property or his share if it were partitioned may also be relevant in this context[53]. Where the property is commercial property, the court should consider each party's commercial interests[54]. However, the fact that sale will detrimentally affect a business conducted on the property by one of the co-owners may not deter the court from making such an order[55]. Questions of sentiment that arise, for example, on the proposed sale of family property are also irrelevant in this context[56]. The fact that one of the co-owners has a right of residence in the

---

47 See *Corpn of Huddersfield v Jacomb* [1874] WN 80; *Allen v Allen* (1873) 21 WR 842; and *Gilbert v Smith* (1879) 11 Ch D 78. See further *Jabs Construction Ltd v Callahan* [1992] 1 WWR 748. Contrast this with the views expressed by Denman J in *Fleming v Crouch* [1884] WN 111. Where one of the co-owners is a corporation which has acquired an undivided share of land for public purposes, the interests of the public may be taken into account: *Corpn of Huddersfield v Jacomb* [1874] WN 80.

48 *Pannizutti v Trask* (1987) 10 NSWLR 531 at 540 per Kirby P.

49 *Drinkwater v Ratcliffe* (1875) LR 20 Eq 528 at 533 per Jessel MR. See further the comments of Kearney J in *Hayward v Skinner* [1981] NSWLR 590 at 593 and those of Huddart J in *Jabs Construction Ltd v Callahan* [1992] 1 WWR 748 at 753, as well as *Cryer v Ossher* (5 December 1997, unreported) Supreme Court of New South Wales.

50 See *In the Matter of Softwood Plantations Party Ltd* (17 October 1995, unreported) Supreme Court of the Northern Territory of Australia. In this case, the disputed property was owned by persons entitled to varying sixty-third shares and the evidence suggested that partition would cost over $315,000 while sale expenses would only amount to $7,800.

51 *Drinkwater v Ratcliffe* (1875) LR 20 Eq 528 at 533 per Jessel MR.

52 *Pemberton v Barnes* (1871) 6 Ch App 685 at 695 per Lord Hatherley LC. See further *Sheahan v Cooper* (1 December 1998, unreported) Federal Court of Australia. In *Moss v Zorn* [1991] NWTR 141 the court was influenced by the fact that the parties would have difficulty selling their individual interests in the property, with or without partition.

53 *Moss v Zorn* [1991] NWTR 141.

54 *Jabs Construction Ltd v Callahan* [1992] 1 WWR 748 at 754-755 per Huddart J.

55 *Scates v Scates* [1962] VR 398.

56 *Drinkwater v Ratcliffe* (1875) LR 20 Eq 528 at 533 per Jessel MR.

property will not prevent the court from ordering sale, but may be taken into account on distribution of the proceeds of sale[57].

[5.23] Section 3 states that the court 'may' order sale if it would be more beneficial than partition. A situation could arise in which the court refuses to make an order for sale, even though it is satisfied that sale of the land and division of the proceeds would be more beneficial than partition[58]. However, it is suggested that this is unlikely to occur in practice. The traditional view in partition actions is that the court must order partition if it refuses sale[59]. Therefore, if sale is more beneficial than partition under s 3 the court is likely to order sale especially where partition is impossible or impracticable. Instances of the court refusing to order sale in these circumstances are difficult to find[60].

[5.24] To summarise, the court may order sale under s 3 at the request of any party interested in less than half of the co-owned property, and where that person adduces some reason why sale would be more beneficial than partition for all the parties[61].

B Section 4 of the 1868 Act

[5.25] Section 4 reads:

> 'In a suit for partition, where if this Act had not been passed a decree for partition might have been made, then if the party or parties interested, individually or collectively, to the extent of one moiety or upwards in the property to which the suit relates, request the Court to direct a sale of the property and a distribution of the proceeds, instead of a division of the property between or among the parties interested, the Court shall, unless it sees good reason to the contrary, direct a sale of the property accordingly, and give all necessary or proper consequential directions.'

There are two main elements of s 4.

1 'Party or parties interested, individually or collectively, to the extent of one moiety or upwards in the property to which the suit relates'

[5.26] The person or persons seeking sale under s 4 must be entitled to a half interest or more in the property[62]. However, it was suggested in *Northern Bank*

57 *Re Hecker's Estate* (28 April 1994, unreported) High Court (RI).

58 See the comments of Lowe J in *Carpenter v Sheehan* [1947] VLR 127 at 128 and those of Wright J in *Bay v Bay* (1984) 38 Sask 101 at 103. The Partition Act 1868, s 3 does not state that the court shall order sale if this would be more beneficial than partition; the court's power of sale is discretionary: see para **[5.18]** above.

59 See ch 7 below.

60 See however *Northern Bank Ltd v Adams* (1 February 1996, unreported) High Court (NI), considered in ch 7 below.

61 See generally *Sykes v Schofield* (1870) 14 Ch D 629 and *Re Hardiman* (1880) 16 Ch D 360.

62 See *Daniell's Chancery Practice* (8th edn, 1914), p 1176 and *Pemberton v Barnes* (1871) 6 Ch App 685 at 693.

Ltd v Adams[63] that such persons should be entitled to half or more of the realisable monetary value of the property in order to proceed under s 4. In this case, the Bank had a mortgage affecting a husband's undivided half share of a matrimonial home and applied for sale under s 4. Observing that the house was worth £80,000 while the sum owing to the Bank was approximately £10,000, Master Ellison rejected the Bank's argument that it came within s 4 because its mortgage affected a half share of the estate. He stated:

> 'There is no jurisdiction in the instant case to order a sale under section 4 of the Partition Act 1868 because the realisable value of the plaintiff's mortgage is less than a moiety.'[64]

He therefore concluded that the Bank's action fell under s 3 and not s 4.

[5.27] Although the plaintiff in *Northern Bank Ltd v Adams* was a mortgagee of an undivided share of land, Master Ellison's comments could be applied to partition actions between co-owners *inter se*. This would mean that a co-owner who wanted to bring an action under s 4 would have to show that his undivided interest, if sold, would fetch a sum equivalent to or greater than half the amount that would be raised by a sale of the entirety[65]. Instances of the courts applying such a cumbersome test are difficult to find. It is submitted that Master Ellison was erroneous in applying this test to determine whether a plaintiff was entitled to bring an action under s 4. Section 4 itself refers to persons interested to the extent of 'one moiety or upwards in the property' and not to persons interested to that extent in the realisable monetary value of the property. The relevant authorities clearly favour the former interpretation[66].

2 'The Court shall, unless it sees good reason to the contrary, direct a sale'

[5.28] A co-owner who brings an action under s 4 does not have to establish a particular reason for the court to order sale. Unlike s 3, the court does not have

---

62 (contd) Where an individual co-owner seeks sale under the Partition Act 1868, s 4, the court must be satisfied that he is entitled to at least a half interest in the land: see *Roughton v Gibson* (1877) 46 LJ Ch 366. Where a request for sale is made by two or more co-owners, the collective sum of their interests must be equivalent to or exceed a half interest in the property: see *Re Langdale's Estate* (1871) 6 ILTR 12.

63 (1 February 1996, unreported) High Court (NI).

64 (1 February 1996, unreported) High Court (NI), at 41.

65 Likewise, the Partition Act 1868, ss 3 and 5 would apply where a sale of the plaintiff's undivided interest would fetch less than half the sale value of the entire property.

66 See *Daniell's Chancery Practice* (8th edn, 1914), p 1176 and the cases cited at para **[5.26]** above. See further *Fleming v Hargreaves* [1976] 1 NZLR 123; *Tansell v Tansell* (1977) 35 FLR 272; *Glendinning v Thiessen* (1994) 95 BCLR (2d) 21 and *Grunert v Grunert* (1960) 32 WWR 509 all of which refer to the plaintiff having at least a half interest in the property in question. It follows that the Partition Act 1868, ss 3 and 5 apply to persons interested in less than half of the property.

to consider the nature of the property, the number of parties interested therein, the absence or disability of any of those persons, or any other relevant circumstance[67]. The only factor for the court to consider under s 4 is whether the co-owners who oppose sale have established 'good reason to the contrary'[68]. This requires them to put forward 'special circumstances' which would make it wrong for the court to direct sale[69]. Thus while s 3 requires a co-owner seeking sale to prove that it would be more beneficial than partition, such persons are entitled to sale under s 4 unless the dissenting co-owners can put forward a reason why sale should not be ordered[70]. In *Porter v Lopes*[71] Jessel MR interpreted 'good reason to the contrary' in the following manner:

> '[T]here is an absolute right in the owner of a moiety to require a sale subject to this; unless it sees good reason to the contrary, the Court shall direct a sale ... Therefore [the plaintiff] has an absolute right to a sale unless the Court sees good reason to the contrary. Contrary to what? As I read it, it is contrary to a sale. It can mean nothing else.'[72]

[5.29] However, the issue of whether 'good reason to the contrary' should be given a wide or restrictive interpretation was the subject of judicial debate following the enactment of the Partition Acts.

[5.30] Malins VC at first instance in *Pemberton v Barnes*[73] advocated a wide judicial discretion under s 4:

---

67 See the comments of Jessel MR in *Drinkwater v Ratcliffe* (1875) LR 20 Eq 528 at 530-531.

68 See *Porter v Lopes* (1877) 7 Ch D 358; *Pemberton v Barnes* (1871) 6 Ch App 685; *Drinkwater v Ratcliffe* (1875) LR 20 Eq 528; *Allen v Allen* (1873) 21 WR 842; *Lys v Lys* (1868) LR 7 Eq 126; and *Fleming v Crouch* [1884] WN 111. Discussing the corresponding section of the Partition Act 1911 (Qd) Jeffriess J in *Joyce v Joyce* [1963] Qd R 139 at 154 remarked:

> 'The onus of showing good reason to the contrary is upon the defendant, and if he fails to do so, I must in terms of the section direct a sale. It is not for me to inquire into the reasons why the plaintiff desires a sale.'

See further *Martin-Smith v Woodhead* [1990] WAR 62; *Dew v Riddler* (1900) 19 NZLR 28; *Pillar v Odlin* [1951] NZLR 220; *Re Moore* [1952] NZLR 273; and *Zakoski v Zakoski* (11 June 1984, unreported) Saskatchewan Queen's Bench.

69 *Wilkinson v Joberns* (1873) LR 16 Eq 14 at 16 per Lord Selbourne LC. See further *Bray v Bray* (1926) 38 CLR 543 and *Bay v Bay* (1984) 38 Sask 101.

70 *Hoggard v Hoggard* (22 November 1996, unreported) British Columbia Supreme Court.

71 (1877) 7 Ch D 358 at 363.

72 Thus 'good reason to the contrary' refers to the court having discretion to refuse sale. Various cases decided in the nineteenth century held that upon refusing to order sale, the court had to make an order for partition: see for example *Saxton v Bartley* (1879) 48 LJ Ch 519. As to whether this practice still applies in Northern Ireland and in the Republic of Ireland today see ch 7 below.

73 Reported at (1871) 6 Ch App 685 at 690.

'[Counsel for the plaintiff] says [s 4] is imperative, and no doubt it would have been but for the words "the Court shall, *unless it sees good reason to the contrary,* direct a sale". This leaves it entirely to the discretion of the Court; and the Court, in exercising that discretion, must have regard to all the surrounding circumstances; but above all, it must look ... to the nature of the property and the interests of the parties.'

[5.31] These comments were endorsed by Cotton LJ in *Porter v Porter*[74] who asserted that s 4 'does not make it imperative on the Court to direct a sale'. However, a majority of cases decided at this time took the view that the use of the word 'shall' in s 4 creates a strong presumption in favour of sale. For example, in *Pitt v Jones*[75] Lord Watson described s 4 as 'an imperative enactment' which requires the court to order sale in the absence of 'good reason to the contrary'. Likewise, in *Pemberton v Barnes*[76] Lord Hatherley LC stated that the court is otherwise 'bound' to order sale under s 4, while Hall VC in *Rowe v Gray*[77] referred to the 'right to have sale' under s 4 in the absence of such reason[78]. It is obvious from these and more recent cases that 'good reason to the contrary' is a high hurdle for the parties opposing sale to overcome[79]. If they fail to establish this, the court is bound to order sale. Thus the court's discretion to refuse sale under s 4 is limited and is certainly not as wide as the discretion which it possesses under s 3.

[5.32] This interpretation of s 4 is supported by the fact that, while there are numerous decisions on what *does not* constitute 'good reason to the contrary', there are relatively few cases stating what *does*. It is well-established that co-owners who oppose sale must submit some positive and substantive reason for the court to refuse such an order; mere dissent or opposition to sale is not enough[80]. However, in *Re Langdale's Estate*[81] Lynch J suggested that the court

[74] (1888) 37 Ch D 420 at 426.

[75] (1880) 5 App Cas 651 at 661.

[76] (1871) 6 Ch App 685 at 693.

[77] (1877) 5 Ch D 263 at 264.

[78] See further the comments of Lynch J in *Re Langdale's Estate* (1871) 6 ILTR 12 at 13 as well as *Parker v Trigg* [1874] WN 27 and *Porter v Lopes* (1877) 7 Ch D 358.

[79] See for example, *De Campo Holdings v Cianciullo* [1977] WAR 56 decided under the corresponding provision of the Property Law Act 1969 (WA) and see the comments of Kirby B in *Pannizutti v Trask* (1987) 10 NSWLR 531 at 539 in relation to the corresponding provision of the Partition Act 1878 (NSW). In *Glendinning v Thiessen* (1994) 95 BCLR (2d) 21 at 23 the court referred to the 'very narrow discretion' to refuse sale under the corresponding provision of the Partition of Property Act 1979 (BC). Similar views were expressed by Holmes J in *Richardson v McGuiness* (12 December 1996, unreported) British Columbia Supreme Court, and see *Dobell v Oman* (6 March 1998, unreported) British Columbia Supreme Court.

[80] See the comments of Lynch J in *Re Langdale's Estate* (1871) 6 ILTR 12 at 13 and those of Lord Hatherley LC in *Pemberton v Barnes* (1871) 6 Ch App 685 at 694.

[81] (1871) 6 ILTR 12.

might take dissent into account if it was coupled with other specific factors suggesting that the court should refuse sale. As with actions under s 3 of the 1868 Act, the court is not concerned with questions of sentiment under s 4. For example, the court may order sale of property that is or has been part of a family estate[82]. Likewise, a co-owner cannot prevent sale on the basis that she is unlikely to acquire a reasonably priced equivalent home in the same area[83]. The fact that the property in question is the house in which children of the family were brought up does not constitute 'good reason to the contrary'[84]. A request for sale of a family home may also be granted despite any disruption to the education of a child who is in her last year at school[85].

[5.33] The fact that an order for sale would cause the defendants personal or commercial inconvenience is not sufficient reason for refusing sale under s 4[86]. An order for sale is likely where property is used wholly or principally for business purposes[87], irrespective of any hardship caused by forcing one of the parties to leave the property and relocate his business[88]. The fact that a proposed sale includes a business operated by the dissenting co-owners, which would inflate the sale price and thus increase the amount received by the plaintiff, is irrelevant in this context[89]. Considering a request for sale of commercial property under s 4, Lord Selbourne LC in *Wilkinson v Joberns*[90] remarked:

---

[82] *Pemberton v Barnes* (1871) 6 Ch App 685 and *Porter v Lopes* (1877) 7 Ch D 358.

[83] *Richardson v McGuiness* (12 December 1996, unreported) British Columbia Supreme Court.

[84] See *Smith v Smith (No 2)* [1962] Qd R 132 considering the corresponding provision of the Partition Act 1911 (Qd). In *Peck v Peck* [1965] SASR 293 where a wife opposed her husband's request for sale of a jointly owned home on the basis that he had deserted her and sale would deprive the wife of her home, the court held that this was insufficient reason for refusing to order sale. In *Cattoni v Cattoni* (12 March 1980, unreported) Alberta Queen's Bench, Kerans J made an order for sale of matrimonial property under the Partition Act 1868, s 4 on the basis that it was being used as revenue property (for rental in units) and the wife no longer needed it as her home.

[85] *Bourke v Bourke* [1983] 2 NZFLR 55.

[86] *Bourgeault v Walton* 1998 BCTC Lexis 1271.

[87] Assuming that the parties have not entered into a partnership agreement or a pre-emptive agreement which ousts the jurisdiction of the court: see ch 4, paras **[4.44]-[4.50]** above.

[88] See for example, *Re Franchi and Franchi* (21 August 1980, unreported) Ontario District Court, in which the court made an order for sale under the Partition Act 1970 (Ont) despite the fact that the opposing co-owners occupied both a home and business premises on part of the property. In *Gillespie v Brett* (20 November 1979, unreported) Alberta Queen's Bench, Cormack J made an order for sale of commercial property under the Partition Act 1868, s 4 where the parties could no longer agree on the management of the premises and the appropriate rent to charge tenants.

[89] *Re Franchi and Franchi* (21 August 1980, unreported) Ontario District Court. However, the opposing co-owners may be able to claim an accounting adjustment in appropriate circumstances: see generally ch 11 below.

[90] (1873) LR 16 Eq 14 at 17 and see further the judgment of Bacon VC in *Roughton v Gibson* (1877) 46 LJ Ch 366.

'I can imagine no description of real property to which the policy of that Act would be more applicable than this, of which the value is essentially commercial.'[91]

[5.34] While accepting that occupancy for business purposes by one co-owner is insufficient reason for refusing sale under legislation similar to s 4 of the 1868 Act[92], Hutchison J in *Re Moore*[93] suggested that there might be circumstances in which the court should consider a connection between one co-owner's occupation of the property and his position as co-owner. However, this factor alone is unlikely to amount to 'good reason to the contrary'. As discussed below, partition of the property should be a feasible alternative[94].

[5.35] Irrespective of whether property is used for business or residential purposes, 'good reason to the contrary' is not established by the fact that a sale by auction will not realise the true value of the property[95], or by the fact that a dissenting co-owner offers to purchase the share of the party seeking sale[96]. Where the plaintiff has previously sought to sell his share in the property, the other co-owners cannot argue that the plaintiff should have kept his interest on the market for longer[97]. Suggestions to the effect that it is the wrong time to sell

---

91 Similar views were expressed by Kennedy J in *Martin-Smith v Woodhead* [1990] WAR 62 and by Stable J in *Smith v Smith (No 2)* [1962] Qd R 132. See however, *Schnytzer v Wielunski* [1978] VR 418 discussed at para **[5.42]** below.

92 Namely the Property Law Act 1908 (NZ), s 105(1).

93 [1952] NZLR 273.

94 See paras **[5.37]-[5.39]** below. The fact that property can be divided to accommodate the defendant's business needs does not automatically mean that the court will refuse to order sale under the Partition Act 1868, s 4 and make an order for partition: *Re Moore* [1952] NZLR 273 (defendant was 74 years of age and unlikely to spend many more years in the business so that the proposed partition would be of more benefit to his son and to the other business partner). In addition to this, the fact that an order for sale of commercial property under s 4 would result in a serious reduction of income for the defendant is irrelevant if partition, though practicable, would be economically disadvantageous to the plaintiff: *Polden v Rowling* [1958] NZLR 31.

95 *Lys v Lys* (1868) LR 7 Eq 126.

96 See the comments of Menhennitt J in *Schnytzer v Wielunski* [1978] VR 418 at 421 in relation to the corresponding provision of the Property Law Act 1928 (Vict) citing *Perman v Maloney* [1939] VLR 376 and *Anderson v Anderson* [1957] VR 317. However, Menhennitt J suggested that an undertaking to purchase might be taken into account along with other relevant factors in deciding whether a co-owner has shown good reason for refusing sale and making an order for partition. Sale has also been ordered under the Partition Act 1868, s 4 where the petitioner was unable to deduce title to one-third of the lands in question, but with a direction that a third of the proceeds of sale be retained in court until the title could be made out: *Re Balfour's Estate* (1887) 19 LR Ir 487.

97 *Richardson v McGuiness* (12 December 1996, unreported) British Columbia Supreme Court, where the petitioners had placed the property on the market for several months at less than its market value but had failed to find a buyer.

the property and that sale at a later date would generate more money are unlikely to prevent the court from ordering sale[98]. Likewise, the fact that property is currently operating at a loss is insufficient reason for refusing sale[99].

[5.36] Thus financial considerations are largely irrelevant under s 4. The fact that the plaintiff is motivated by material reasons and simply wants to capitalise on his investment does not constitute 'good reason to the contrary'[100]. In addition to this, a co-owner cannot prevent sale on the basis that it would not produce sufficient money to discharge any debts or incumbrances on the property[101] or that sale will produce a possible monetary loss[102]. While the court may take a proven loss of income into account[103], a mere possibility that the income generated by the proceeds of sale would be less than that derived from the land itself is irrelevant[104]. Complaints that sale will expose the opposing co-owners to significant tax liabilities are also irrelevant[105]. Likewise, the fact that the actions of a neighbouring landowner might render the disputed land less marketable does not constitute 'good reason to the contrary'[106]. The personal

---

98 *Canadian Imperial Bank of Commerce v Mulholland Construction* (28 January 1998, unreported) Ontario Court (General Division), in which Wilkins J regarded expert evidence to this effect as 'conjecture and speculation' and cautioned against the court 'entering into any realm of financial prophecy': Lexis transcript, at 4.

99 *Canadian Imperial Bank of Commerce v Mulholland Construction* (28 January 1998, unreported) Ontario Court (General Division), citing *Sheridan Platinum Group Inc v Madeleine Mines Ltd* (29 June 1994, unreported) Ontario Court (General Division).

100 *Richardson v McGuiness* (12 December 1996, unreported) British Columbia Supreme Court, and *Bourgeault v Walton* 1998 BCTC Lexis 1271.

101 *First National Building Society v Ring* [1992] IR 375. The fact that the opposing co-owner has acted as guarantor on mortgages affecting the entire property does not constitute 'good reason to the contrary' for the purposes of the Partition Act 1868, s 4: *Gillespie v Brett* (20 November 1979, unreported) Alberta Queens Bench (although the court directed that the property should not be sold for less than the amount due on both mortgages in order to protect the respondent from subsequent action by the mortgagees).

102 See *Barnes and Park Place Holdings Ltd v Henshaw* (1980) 5 WWR 755.

103 See *Langmead v Cockerton* (1877) 25 WR 315.

104 See for example, *Rowe v Gray* (1877) 5 Ch D 263 and *Re Langdale's Estate* (1871) 6 ILTR 12. See further *Re Whitwell's Estate* (1887) 19 LR Ir 45. In *Worotniak v Korobejko* (11 August 1988, unreported) Saskatchewan Queen's Bench, Grotsky J made an order for sale of rental property under the Partition Act 1868, s 4 despite the opposing co-owner's attempts to restrain sale by means of an interlocutory injunction.

105 *Gartree Investments Ltd v Cartree Enterprises Ltd and Elgtree Holdings Ltd* (5 June 2000, unreported) Ontario Superior Court of Justice.

106 For example, the court cannot refuse to order sale where the land in question enjoys a view over the surrounding countryside and future building on adjoining land might spoil this view. Rejecting a similar argument in *Porter v Lopes* (1877) 7 Ch D 358, Jessel MR stated that a purchaser of property with a view over surrounding countryside should contemplate the possibility of his view being disturbed by lawful actions carried out on a neighbouring property.

circumstances of the opposing co-owners are also unlikely to persuade the court to refuse sale under s 4[107]. The fact that the defendant has expended money on the property which increases its sale value is relevant in any subsequent accounting adjustment between the parties[108]; it does not, however, affect the substantive relief claimed[109].

[5.37] Opinions have differed over whether the possibility of making a viable partition of the property by itself constitutes 'good reason to the contrary'. In *Re Langdale's Estate*[110] Lynch J asserted that the only material matter 'would be to show affirmatively that it was not a matter of difficulty to make actual partition'. Likewise, Malins VC at first instance in *Pemberton v Barnes*[111] indicated that he would not make an order for sale under s 4 if there was no difficulty in ordering partition. However, the better view appears to be that feasibility of partition does not, *per se*, amount to 'good reason to the contrary'. In *Porter v Lopes*[112] Jessel MR remarked:

> 'When there is some objection to a sale, and, in addition to that, the property can be readily partitioned, of course that does come in aid of what might otherwise not be a sufficient objection to a sale standing alone.'[113]

[5.38] Thus while feasibility of partition should be established as part of 'good reason to the contrary'[114], the opposing co-owners must put forward some other exceptional circumstance which would make it wrong for the court to order sale[115]. Instances of the courts finding that 'good reason to the contrary' exists where partition is impractical are difficult to find. Moreover, partition may not

---

[107] *Re Langdale's Estate* (1871) 6 ILTR 12 (defendants were nuns who opposed sale on the basis that they were unfamiliar with the pitfalls of business and investment and would be unable to invest the proceeds of sale).

[108] See generally ch 11 below.

[109] *Martin-Smith v Woodhead* [1990] WAR 62.

[110] (1871) 6 ILTR 12 at 13.

[111] Reported at (1871) 6 Ch App 685.

[112] (1877) 7 Ch D 358 at 364.

[113] Similar views were expressed by Hall VC in *Rowe v Gray* (1877) 5 Ch D 263. In *Re Moore* [1952] NZLR 273 at 275 Hutchison J stated that 'the fact that property can be readily partitioned comes in aid of the opposition to a sale', and see *Polden v Rowling* [1958] NZLR 31.

[114] Following on from the traditional view that if the court refuses to order sale, it must order partition.

[115] 'In relation to what would constitute good reason to the contrary, the old authorities probably do not go beyond the suggestion that it might be sufficient to show (1) that there are serious disadvantages to a sale *and* (2) that there is no difficulty in achieving a physical partition': Mee, 'Partition and Sale of the Family Home' (1993) 15 DULJ 78 at 84.

be regarded as a practicable alternative under s 4 where a division of the land would require a significant payment of money as equality of partition[116].

[5.39] In addition to this, s 4 simply refers to 'good reason to the contrary' being established. In contrast, s 3 specifically provides that the court may order sale if satisfied this would be 'more beneficial ... than a division of the property'. Therefore, while the court may refuse to order sale under s 3 because it does not regard sale as more beneficial than partition, feasibility of partition by itself cannot be regarded as 'good reason to the contrary' within s 4. It is only one factor that the court may consider when deciding whether to refuse sale under s 4[117].

[5.40] The courts have identified relatively few factors that might be regarded as 'good reason to the contrary' for the purposes of s 4. In *Porter v Lopes*[118] the following were suggested by Jessel MR:

> 'Property may be of a peculiar description so as not to be actually saleable, or, at the time the sale is asked for, may be temporarily very much depreciated in value ... There are cases where the nature of the property was such that you could not well sell it. There are various properties of such a nature; thus, where the property is so attached to some other property, or [has] such a mere dependence on another property as to be almost valueless except in connection with that property, though of very great value in connection with it ... Again you may have very peculiar rights, which cannot be properly divided, attached to property – manorial rights, and rights to game and things of that kind, which could not be properly severed from the land or well sold.'

[5.41] Instances of the courts refusing to order sale in these circumstances are difficult to find. As regards a temporary depreciation in value, McWilliam J in *CH v DGO'D*[119] was of the opinion that this would not constitute 'good reason to the contrary'[120]. However, the learned judge indicated that if the disputed

---

116 As suggested by Jessel MR in *Porter v Lopes* (1877) 7 Ch D 358 and by Hall VC in *Rowe v Gray* (1877) 5 Ch D 263. However, the respective judges indicated that they would have reached the same decision if no such payments had been involved. Feasibility of partition by itself is not 'good reason to the contrary' within the Partition Act 1868, s 4; it is merely one factor which the court has to consider. However, this factor carries less weight if partition involves payments for equality of partition.

117 In *Pemberton v Barnes* (1871) 6 Ch App 685 at 695 Lord Hatherley LC remarked:

> 'The difficulty of partition is dealt with in sect 3, and there is not in sect 4 a single word about the size of the estate or the difficulty of partition; it simply speaks of a case where half the parties interested desire a sale and it provides that they shall have the preponderating voice.'

118 (1877) 7 Ch D 358 at 363-364.

119 (1978) 114 ILTR 9.

120 See further *Pemberton v Barnes* (1871) 6 Ch App 685 and *Adler v Ferguson* [1962] VR 129 where similar views were expressed in relation to the corresponding section of the Property Law Act 1958 (Vict). However, in *Re Whitwell's Estate* (1887) 19 LR Ir 45 Monroe J stated that he had refused to order sale in an earlier case for this particular reason.

property was family land and the conduct of a family member was intended to deter outsiders from bidding at the sale thus causing a depreciation in value, this might be considered good reason for refusing sale[121].

[5.42] In the rare event that courts have actually refused to order sale under s 4, the reason for doing so appears to have been based on the specific circumstances of the case which favoured partition over sale. In *Schnytzer v Wielunski*[122] the parties were tenants in common in equal shares of adjoining shop properties. The defendants opposed the plaintiffs' request for sale under the corresponding provision of the Property Law Act 1958 (Vict), on the basis that they operated a delicatessen business from one of these properties and would suffer financial loss in the event of the court making an order for sale. Menhennitt J stated that the commercial interests of the parties should be weighed against each other in determining whether 'good reason to the contrary' exists[123]. More importantly, several factors favoured making an order for partition in this case. Both properties were of similar size and had been occupied separately by the parties for a number of years prior to the partition action. The properties were also subject to a registered plan of subdivision confirming this arrangement, which would be the same as the partition ordered by the court.

[5.43] In *Saxton v Bartley*[124] the plaintiff's motives in seeking sale and the feasibility of partition were regarded as 'good reason to the contrary' for the purposes of s 4. The plaintiff and Bartley were tenants in common of leasehold property. Following Bartley's death, his widow was entitled to the rent from the property for her life. The plaintiff subsequently brought an action for sale of the property under s 4. Refusing the request for sale, Bacon VC held that the plaintiff was motivated by ill feeling towards the deceased and his family[125]. The plaintiff would not benefit substantially from sale, yet such an order would severely diminish the income received by the deceased's widow. Moreover, partition of the disputed property could be carried out with little difficulty.

---

121 (1978) 114 ILTR 9 at 14.

122 [1978] VR 418.

123 Cases such as *Wilkinson v Joberns* (1873) 16 LR Eq 14 (see paras **[5.33]**-**[5.34]** above) have suggested that there is a strong presumption in favour of sale under the Partition Act 1868, s 4 where the property in question is commercial property. However, Menhennitt J asserted that these cases are not indicative of a general principle that the commercial interests of the parties cannot be taken into account in determining whether 'good reason to the contrary' exists: [1978] VR 418 at 424-426.

124 (1879) 48 LJ Ch 519.

125 Bacon VC referred to *Pemberton v Barnes* (1871) 6 Ch App 685 at 693 in which Lord Hatherley LC suggested that the court might refuse to order sale under the Partition Act 1868, s 4 where it is 'manifestly asked for through vindictive feeling, or is on any ground unreasonable'.

[5.44] Thus the court may refuse to order sale under s 4 if the plaintiff is acting vexatiously or spitefully[126]. However, the fact that one co-owner desires a higher price for the property than the other is willing to pay and brings proceedings for compulsory sale should not be regarded as vexatious. In these circumstances, the plaintiff is merely 'relying upon his legal rights'[127]. Likewise, there is nothing malicious or vexatious in the fact that one co-owner simply wants to realise his share of the property[128]. The court should consider whether the plaintiff is acting vindictively in seeking a sale of the property instead of partition, as opposed to whether he is acting vindictively in issuing the writ[129].

[5.45] Co-owners who oppose sale under s 4 must usually satisfy the court that:

(a) there are exceptional circumstances for refusing sale (such as vexatious conduct on the part of the plaintiff) and

(b) there is no difficulty in making a partition of the disputed property (in practical terms, the opposing co-owners should put forward a scheme of partition to support this)[130].

[5.46] The traditional view has been that the court's discretion to refuse sale under s 4 is limited. However, several recent cases have suggested that 'good reason to the contrary' is not as restrictive as it has been in the past, especially where the partition action relates to a matrimonial or family home[131]. In these cases the respective courts have demonstrated a willingness to consider a wider range of factors as amounting to 'good reason to the contrary' within s 4, notwithstanding that partition of the disputed property is impracticable[132].

[5.47] To summarise, s 4 contemplates sale at the request of co-owners interested to the extent of at least one-half of the disputed property. Section 4 makes it imperative on the court to direct sale, unless 'good reason to the contrary' is established by those co-owners who oppose sale. There is a strong

---

126 See further *Polden v Rowling* [1958] NZLR 31; *Smith v Smith (No 2)* [1962] Qd R 132; and *Schnytzer v Wielunski* [1978] VR 418. Similar views were expressed by Verchere J in *McGreer v Green and the Westminster Mortgage Corpn* (1960) 22 DLR (2d) 775.

127 *Joyce v Joyce* [1963] Qd R 139 at 154 per Jeffriess J.

128 *Re Franchi and Franchi* (21 August 1980, unreported) Ontario District Court.

129 *Schnytzer v Wielunski* [1978] VR 418 at 428 per Menhennitt J.

130 For example, in *Reimer v Robbins* (1982) 24 Man R (2d) 311 the court refused to order partition on the basis that there was no evidence before it as to the value of the land, access or planning restrictions which would provide a basis for the court to make a just and fair division.

131 See for example, *First National Building Society v Ring* [1992] IR 375; *Northern Bank Ltd v Haggerty* [1995] NI 211 and *Northern Bank Ltd v Adams* (1 February 1996, unreported) High Court (NI).

132 See chs 9 and 10 below.

presumption in favour of sale under s 4, and the burden of proof is on the co-owners who oppose sale and seek partition.

C Section 5 of the 1868 Act

[5.48] Section 5 reads:

> 'In a suit for partition, where if this Act had not been passed a decree for partition might have been made, then if any party interested in the property to which the suit relates, requests the Court to direct a sale of the property and a distribution of the proceeds, instead of a division of the property between or among the parties interested, the Court may, if it thinks fit, unless the other parties interested in the property, or some of them, undertake to purchase the share of the party requesting a sale, direct a sale of the property, and give all necessary or proper consequential directions, and in case of such undertaking being given, the Court may order a valuation of the share of the party requesting a sale, in such manner as the Court thinks fit, and may give all necessary or proper consequential directions.'

[5.49] Few partition actions are brought under s 5. However, the interpretation of this section caused most problems following the enactment of the 1868 Act.

1 Independent provision or restriction on sections 3 and 4?

[5.50] Initially, judicial opinions differed as to whether s 5 qualified or restricted ss 3 and 4. Answering this question in the affirmative, Lord Hatherley LC in *Pemberton v Barnes*[133] interpreted s 5 in the following manner:

> 'If we ... look to the 5th section, we shall see how any injustice is guarded against by an enactment which, I think, applies to the 3rd and 4th sections ... Here a wide discretion is given to the Court. The Court may think that a sale under the 3rd or 4th section is rather hard upon the parties who are very anxious not to have a sale; and if they come forward and undertake to buy the share of the party who requests a sale, the Court can give them liberty to do so.'

[5.51] In other words, a request for sale under s 3 or s 4 would be refused where the defendants offered to buy the plaintiff's share in accordance with s 5, and the plaintiff would be compelled to sell his share to them[134].

---

[133] (1871) 6 Ch App 685 at 693.

[134] Similar views were expressed by Webb J in *Trustees, Executors and Agency Company Ltd v Finn* (1891) 17 VLR 609. Considering the effect of identical provisions in the Partition Act 1890 (Vict), ss 3-5, Webb J held that s 5 restricted ss 3 and 4, and that in enacting s 5 the legislature 'made a very wise provision to prevent one of the parties where a sale is ordered, going to the sale and running up the property where the other party desires to acquire it': (1891) 17 VLR 609 at 611.

[5.52] However, in the subsequent case of *Drinkwater v Ratcliffe*[135] Jessel MR held that s 5 did not qualify ss 3 and 4. In his opinion, s 5 conferred an independent jurisdiction to order sale where the plaintiff was entitled to less than half of the property but was unable to proceed under s 3. As regards the owners of a moiety or more, their interests were adequately protected by s 4:

> '[T]he 5th must apply to a case where the Court sees no reason for preferring a sale to a partition. That case is not provided for by the 3rd, nor is it provided for by the 4th section. Where the Court sees no reason at all, still any party interested may apply; and then there is a limit imposed, and the limit is this, that the Court shall not exercise the new power given by the 5th section ... if other people will buy. That is a check upon the new power – not, as it has been supposed to be, a limitation of the 3rd and 4th sections ...'[136]

[5.53] In the earlier case of *Williams v Games*[137], the Court of Appeal held that a co-owner seeking sale could not be forced to accept an undertaking to purchase given by the dissenting co-owners under s 5. Endorsing this decision, Jessel MR described Lord Hatherley's interpretation of s 5 in *Pemberton v Barnes*[138] as a proviso to the effect that 'no sale shall be directed under the 3rd or 4th sections ..., if any other party interested shall undertake to buy the share of the parties asking for sale'. In his opinion, this was contrary to the plain meaning of s 5[139].

[5.54] The matter was effectively resolved by the House of Lords in *Pitt v Jones*[140]. The owners of a three-sixteenths share of land brought an action for sale under the Partition Acts. Affirming the decision of the Court of Appeal, Lords Blackburn and Watson held that this particular case came within s 3 of the 1868 Act, and that s 5 did not qualify either s 3 or s 4[141]. Lord Blackburn reviewed the various authorities and continued:

> '[Section 5] does not say, nor do I think it was intended to say, that a party who requests a sale of the whole must take that valuation; I think it means that if a party presses for a sale, and the Court thinks that the opposing parties in fairness ought either to buy him out or consent to a sale, it may order a sale unless they will agree to take his share at a valuation, in which case the party requesting the sale may either accept that valuation or not. If he does not choose to accept that

135 (1875) LR 20 Eq 528.

136 (1875) LR 20 Eq 528 at 531.

137 (1875) 10 Ch App 204.

138 (1871) 6 Ch App 685.

139 (1875) LR 20 Eq 528 at 531-532. Similar views were expressed by the respective courts in *Roughton v Gibson* (1877) 48 LJ Ch 366 and *Gilbert v Smith* (1879) 11 Ch D 78.

140 (1880) 5 App Cas 651.

141 Again, Lord Hatherley was of the opinion that the Partition Act 1868, s 5 restricted ss 3 and 4: (1880) 5 App Cas 651 at 655.

valuation, he cannot be forced to do so; but will then have his common law right to a partition ... [Lord Hatherley in *Pemberton v Barnes*] did express an opinion that the 5th section was applicable to proceedings under the 3rd and 4th sections, and was intended to give the Court a discretionary power to prevent a sale under these sections if the opposing party was willing to bind himself to take the Applicant's share at a valuation ... I think if this had been intended it would have been properly expressed in the form of a proviso on the 3rd and 4th sections, and not by a fresh substantive enactment ...'[142]

[5.55] Similar views were expressed by Lord Watson, who described s 5 as a 'new and substantive enactment' that enabled a co-owner to obtain a decree of sale unless the others gave an undertaking to purchase his interest[143]. Subsequent cases have confirmed this interpretation of s 5 as a separate provision that does not restrict ss 3 and 4[144].

2 'If any party interested in the property ... requests the court to direct a sale'

[5.56] A request for sale under s 5 may be made by a co-owner who is entitled to less than a half interest in the property, yet who cannot proceed under s 3 because he cannot show any reason why sale would be more beneficial than partition as required by that section[145].

[5.57] It has been suggested that a co-owner seeking sale under s 5 should nevertheless put forward some reason for the court to make such an order. In *Richardson v Feary*[146] North J refused to order sale under s 5 at the request of a

---

142 (1880) 5 App Cas 651 at 659-660.

143 (1880) 5 App Cas 651 at 662-663 (affirming the decisions in *Williams v Games* (1875) 10 Ch App 204 and *Drinkwater v Ratcliffe* (1875) LR 20 Eq 528).

144 Similar views were expressed by Kay J in *Evans v Evans* (1883) 31 WR 495 and by North J in *Richardson v Feary* (1888) 39 Ch D 45, and more recently in *Glendinning v Thiessen* (1994) 95 BCLR (2d) 21 and *Barnes v Kostiuk* (9 March 1999, unreported) British Columbia Supreme Court, in relation to the corresponding provisions of the Partition of Property Act 1979 (BC) and its successor the Partition of Property Act 1996 (BC). See further *Perman v Maloney* [1939] VLR 376 in which O'Bryan AJ held that the Property Law Act 1928 (Vict), ss 222-224 (corresponding to the Partition Act 1868, ss 3-5) were independent of each other. O'Bryan AJ observed that in *Trustees, Executors and Agency Co Ltd v Finn* (1891) 17 VLR 609 (see para **[5.51]** above) the court had only been referred to *Pemberton v Barnes* (1871) 6 Ch App 685 despite the fact that this case had been overruled by *Pitt v Jones* (1880) 5 App Cas 651. Similar views were expressed on the Property Law Act 1928 (Vict), ss 222-224 in *Anderson v Anderson* [1957] VR 317 and on its successor, the Property Law Act 1958 (Vict), ss 222-224 in *Scates v Scates* [1962] VR 398. In *Gray v Dawson* (1912) 31 NZLR 1001 counsel for the plaintiffs sought to distinguish *Pitt v Jones* on the basis that, unlike the Partition Act 1868, ss 3-5, the corresponding provisions in the Property Law Act 1908 (NZ), s 105 were merely contained in separate subsections and thus qualified each other. Rejecting this argument, Cooper J observed that *Pitt v Jones* was not based upon the premise that ss 3-5 were separate provisions but on the ground that the three sections were to be construed together.

145 See *Drinkwater v Ratcliffe* (1875) LR 20 Eq 528.

146 (1888) 39 Ch D 45.

tenant in common of a one-eighth undivided share of land on this basis[147]. This suggestion creates difficulties. A co-owner is only likely to have recourse to s 5 because he is precluded from bringing an action under s 3. It is difficult to envisage a factor which might persuade the court to order sale under s 5, but which does not come within the factors which the court must have regard to under s 3 including 'any other circumstance' the court considers relevant. However, the distinction between the two sections appears to be that under s 5 some reason must be shown for preferring sale to partition, yet it is not necessary to show that sale would be more beneficial than partition as required under the terms of s 3[148]. Thus a co-owner who desires sale may have to rely on s 5 if he cannot prove that sale would be more beneficial in pecuniary terms for all the parties interested in the property.

3 'The Court may, if it thinks fit ... direct a sale'

[5.58] The power of sale under s 5 is discretionary[149]. The court is not obliged to order sale in the absence of an undertaking to purchase from the opposing co-owners[150].

4 'Unless the other parties interested in the property, or some of them, undertake to purchase the share of the party requesting a sale'

[5.59] An order for sale may be granted under s 5 unless one or more co-owners who oppose sale give an undertaking to purchase the plaintiff's share. The plaintiff is not obliged to accept this offer[151]. However, if he refuses to accept it the court cannot make an order for sale of the property and the plaintiff will be

---

147 Since 'the party who applies under Partition Act 1868, s 5 for a sale must shew some reason for it': (1888) 39 Ch D 45 at 49. See however *Drinkwater v Ratcliffe* (1875) LR 20 Eq 528 at 531 in which Jessel MR stated that any party may apply for sale under s 5 'with or without any reason whatever'.

148 21 *Halsbury's Laws of England* (1st edn, 1912), p 845 citing *Richardson v Feary* (1888) 39 Ch D 45 and *Allen v Allen* (1873) 42 LJ Ch 839.

149 See the comments of Lord Blackburn in *Pitt v Jones* (1880) 5 App Cas 651 at 659 and those of North J in *Richardson v Feary* (1888) 39 Ch D 45 at 47-48. Despite suggestions by Lord Watson in *Pitt v Jones* (1880) 5 App Cas 651 at 663 that a co-owner could 'insist for and obtain' a decree for sale under Partition Act 1868, s 5, it is settled that the court has a discretion to order sale under s 5: see 21 *Halsbury's Laws of England* (1st edn, 1912), p 844.

150 See *Richardson v Feary* (1888) 39 Ch D 45. However, if the court refuses to order sale the plaintiff will be granted an order for partition in the alternative: *Richardson v Feary*.

151 See *Perman v Maloney* [1939] VLR 376 and *Norgard v Norgard* (1996) 20 Fam LR, Lexis transcript. Similar views were expressed in *Lougheed Enterprises Ltd v Armbuster* (1992) 26 RPR (2d) 83 and *Jabs Construction Ltd v Callahan* [1992] 1 WWR 748. In *Dibattista v Menecola* (1990) 14 RPR (2d) 157 at 163 Brooke JA observed that the relevant sections of the Partition Act 1980 (Ont) were 'not intended to be a means by which one tenant in common can acquire the interests of the other'. He continued: 'If that was the intention of the Legislature, the section would say so, and the right of first refusal could or would be fairly accorded to one or to the other'. See however *Cattoni v Cattoni* (12 March 1980, unreported) Alberta Queen's Bench.

left with his right to partition[152]. If the plaintiff accepts an undertaking to purchase, the court may order a valuation of his share and make any necessary consequential directions[153].

[5.60] To summarise, s 5 does not qualify ss 3 and 4 of the 1868 Act. Section 5 may be regarded as a type of 'default' provision in that a co-owner is only likely to rely on s 5 if he does not have an interest in a moiety or more of the property and therefore cannot proceed under s 4, but cannot show any reason for preferring sale to partition within the terms of s 3. The court may order sale of the property unless the opposing parties give an undertaking to purchase the plaintiff's share. If he declines this offer, the plaintiff's only remedy will be an order for partition[154].

D Section 6 of the 1868 Act

[5.61] The Partition Acts contemplate one or more co-owners compelling sale of such property against the wishes of the other co-owners. Section 6 of the 1868 Act allows any of the parties interested in the property to bid at the sale, subject to the permission of the court and any conditions it imposes[155]. This provision gives some security to the opposing co-owners – if the court orders sale, they may have an opportunity to retain control of the land by purchasing it at the sale[156].

III Effect of the Partition Acts – a Movement Towards Sale

[5.62] The Partition Acts do not prevent co-owners from dividing or selling their land by agreement if they so desire. However, where no such agreement is forthcoming, the legislation provides a means for co-owners to be released from their relationship and associated responsibilities.

[5.63] While the purpose of the Partition Acts may have been merely to substitute sale for partition in certain circumstances[157], the remedy of sale quickly replaced partition in the majority of cases and this remains the position

---

[152] See the comments of Lord Blackburn in *Pitt v Jones* (1880) 5 App Cas 651 at 659 and see *Williams v Games* (1875) 10 Ch App 204. As to whether courts in Northern Ireland and the Republic are still obliged to order either partition or sale in these circumstances, see ch 7 below.

[153] If the defendant gives an undertaking to purchase and pays the purchase money to the plaintiff, the latter cannot keep this money and at the same time attempt to have a public sale of the property: *Harding v Thomas* (1982) 137 DLR (3d) 715.

[154] See generally *Northern Bank Ltd v Adams* (1 February 1996, unreported) High Court (NI), at 21-22. See further *Schnytzer v Wielunski* [1978] VR 418 and *Martin-Smith v Woodhead* [1990] WAR 62.

[155] See further ch 12 below, para **[12.47]**.

[156] See the comments of Simpson CJ in *Oatley v Oatley* (1898) 19 LR (NSW) Eq 122 at 128 and those of Lord Hatherley LC in *Pemberton v Barnes* (1871) 6 Ch App 685 at 695.

[157] See the comments of Lord Watson in *Pitt v Jones* (1880) 5 App Cas 651 at 661 and those of Simpson CJ in *Oatley v Oatley* (1898) 19 NSWR (Eq) 129 at 127.

today[158]. The reasons for this are obvious. Co-owners may prefer to enjoy a sum of money than to be burdened with the responsibilities of land ownership. In practical terms, it is often easier to order sale of land and division of the proceeds than to order partition[159]. Partition may be rendered difficult by the nature of the property in question[160] or by the number of persons interested therein. Payments of monetary compensation may be required to correct any inequality in the value of the divided parcels of land, while disputes may arise as to which co-owner is allocated buildings or fixtures on the land. Any proposed scheme of partition should serve the interests of all the parties. Yet, the resulting division may enhance the amenity of one co-owner to the detriment of another co-owner[161]. Partition also tends to be more expensive than sale, in view of the associated surveys and valuations, mutual conveyances and the need to create certain rights over the divided portions of land to facilitate their enjoyment in severalty such as easements and access routes[162].

[5.64] Under the Partition Acts, the emphasis is firmly on sale unless sufficient reasons against making such an order are put forward. An order for partition is only likely to be made where a co-owner specifically requests partition and the others do not ask for a sale[163] or where the court refuses to order sale under any

---

[158] Commenting on the effect of analogous legislation contained in the Partition Act 1878 (NSW), Kirby P in *Pannizutti v Trask* (1987) 10 NSWLR 531 at 539 remarked:

> '[W]hereas previously in disputes between co-owners, partition of the property might have been the normal remedy, thereafter, in the circumstances provided, a direction for sale of the property and distribution of the proceeds was to be the normal remedy. Doubtless this new approach reflected the experience of many unsatisfactory partitions where parties in dispute were nonetheless forced, by the remedy of partition, to continue in close association with each other. Doubtless, it also reflected the new economic values and individualism of the nineteenth century, with the view that co-owners should normally be entitled to escape their co-ownership, recoup their funds and spend them as they will.'

See further the comments of Deane J in *Squire v Rogers* (1979) 39 FLR (Aus) 106 at 117.

[159] Likewise, any accounting adjustments which are rendered necessary by the parties' failure to share in expenses or outgoings associated with the property are often easier to make as incidental to an order for sale.

[160] For example, where property is incapable of physical division (single structure or land of an irregular shape) or where part of the land is more valuable in commercial terms than another part. If co-owners wish to divide property (for example, vacation property) by arranging that each should have sole use of it at specific times, difficulties may arise in determining when each party should be allowed to use the property and for how long.

[161] See for example, *Davies v McLaren* (1992) 29 RPR (2d) 127.

[162] In *Rouse v Rouse* (8 March 1999, unreported) Ontario Court (General Division), the court refused to order partition on the basis that a resulting right of way over a portion of the divided land would have interfered with the privacy of that particular co-owner.

[163] See *O'Brien and Cronin Ltd v Dillon* (2 February 1977, unreported) High Court (RI). See further, *De Campo Holdings v Cianciullo* [1977] WAR 56 and *Reimer v Robbins* (1982) 24 Man R (2d) 311.

of ss 3-5 and orders partition in the alternative[164]. Despite the fact that sale was originally introduced as an alternative to partition, it appears that sale is now the preferred remedy.

[164] Another possibility arises where the party seeking sale under the Partition Act 1868, s 5 refuses an undertaking to purchase his share and is left only with his remedy of partition.

Chapter 6

The Repeal of An Act for Jointenants 1542 and the Jurisdiction to Order Partition or Sale Under the Partition Acts

I Introduction[1]

[6.01] A co-owner may seek an order for partition or sale of the land in the event that he wishes to end this relationship. However, this is dependant on the court having jurisdiction to make such an order. At first glance, it would appear that courts in Northern Ireland and the Republic of Ireland possess the requisite jurisdiction: since the Partition Acts are in force in both areas, the respective courts should be able to order partition or sale of land against an unwilling co-owner. However, problems arise upon closer inspection of the wording of ss 3-5 of the Partition Act 1868 and the current state of the law in Northern Ireland and the Republic of Ireland.

II Sections 3-5 of the Partition Act 1868

[6.02] Sections 3-5 of the 1868 Act commence with these words:

> 'In a suit for partition, where, if this Act had not been passed a decree for partition might have been made ...'

[6.03] Following the enactment of the 1868 Act, the judicial consensus was that sale could only be ordered if the court might have ordered partition of the disputed property in similar factual circumstances prior to 25 June 1868[2]. This has been interpreted as requiring the existence of a concurrent jurisdiction to order partition before the court has jurisdiction to order sale under the Partition Acts:

> 'The 1868 Act permitted a sale of the property and a distribution of the proceeds to be ordered by the Court "In a suit for partition, where, if this Act had not been passed, a decree for partition might have been made" ... [I]t was clear from the 1868 Act that the jurisdiction of the court to order a sale and distribution of the

1 This chapter contains material previously published in 'The Repeal of An Act for Jointenants 1542 and the Jurisdiction to Order Partition or Sale Under the Partition Acts 1868 and 1876' (1997) 19 DULJ 1 and reproduced with the kind permission of Round Hall, Sweet and Maxwell.

2 See ch 5 above, paras **[5.08]**-**[5.16]**.

proceeds was conditional upon there being a jurisdiction permitting partition in the particular case to which the application related.'[3]

[6.04] While this may not appear to have any practical consequences for co-owners given the fact that the Partition Acts are still in force, problems arise when the opening words of ss 3-5 are considered in the context of recent legislative changes in Northern Ireland and the Republic of Ireland.

III The Current State of the Law

[6.05] It will be recalled that An Act for Jointenants 1542 granted joint tenants and tenants in common in Ireland the right to compel partition at common law by writ *de partitione facienda*[4]. However, the 1542 Act has been repealed in Northern Ireland by the Statute Law Revision Act 1950 and in the Republic of Ireland by the Statute Law Revision (Pre-Union Irish Statutes) Act 1962[5].

[6.06] It appears that joint tenants and tenants in common can no longer compel partition at common law under the 1542 Act. The problems which might have arisen from the repeal of this Act are all too obvious when considered in the context of ss 3-5 of the Partition Act 1868 and what has been described as the 'parasitic'[6] relationship between the jurisdictions to order sale and to order partition. If the effect of this repeal was that joint tenants and tenants in common could no longer compel partition, two practical consequences would ensue. Firstly, because of the meaning accorded to the introductory words of ss 3-5, it would necessarily follow that joint tenants and tenants in common could not bring an action for sale in lieu of partition and would thus be left without any means of ending their relationship in the event of disagreement as to the continued use and occupation of the property. On a strict interpretation, joint tenants and tenants in common could only partition or sell their property where they all agreed to do so. Secondly, the anomalous situation would arise whereby only coparceners could request sale under the Partition Acts because their right

3 Pearce, 'The Right to Partition and Sale Between Co-owners' (1987) 5 ILT (NS) 36. Similar views were expressed in *Glass v McManus* [1996] NI 401 and *FF v CF* [1987] ILRM 1. See further *Smith v Smith (No 2)* [1962] Qd R 132 at 134 in which Stable J referred to sale being granted under the Partition Act 1911 (Qd) '[w]here the court has jurisdiction to order partition'. Likewise, in *Grunert v Grunert* (1960) 32 WWR 509 at 511 Brownridge J, affirming the dictum of Meredith CJCP in *Morrison v Morrison* (1917) 39 OLR 163 at 168, stated that '[t]he right to partition must first exist before there is a right to sale'.

4 See ch 3 above, para **[3.13]**.

5 Statute Law Revision Act 1950, s 1(1) and Sch 2 and Statute Law Revision (Pre-Union Irish Statutes) Act 1962, s 1 and Schedule. An Act for the more easy obtaining Partition of Lands in Co-parcenary, Joint Tenancy and Tenancy in Common, and bounding and mearing of Lands (Ir) 1697 amending the common law action of partition (see ch 3 above, para **[3.17]**) has also been repealed: Statute Law Revision (Ir) Act 1878.

6 Mee 'Partition and Sale of Family Home' (1993) 15 DULJ 78 at 85.

to compel partition was a common law incident of coparcenary and was independent of the 1542 Act[7].

[6.07] The difficulties produced by such an interpretation are obvious. If correct, joint tenants and tenants in common could not compel partition and accordingly could not bring an action for sale under the Partition Acts, despite the fact that virtually all co-owned property is held in either joint tenancy or tenancy in common. In contrast, coparceners would have both remedies available to them, despite the fact that this form of co-ownership has been abolished as regards intestacy in both Northern Ireland and the Republic and is unlikely to occur today[8]. Yet such a conclusion might be difficult to avoid on a literal interpretation of the successive statutes. However, it is obvious that the respective parliaments did not intend the repeal of the 1542 Act to have such wide-ranging consequences. Two factors support this. In the first instance, while the 1542 Act has been repealed in both parts of Ireland, the Partition Acts remain in force. If the deliberate intention of both parliaments in repealing this statute was to deny the remedies of partition and sale to the vast majority of co-owners, why leave the Partition Acts in force when they would only apply to a diminishing number of coparceners? Secondly and more fundamentally, courts in both jurisdictions have continued to order sale between joint tenants and tenants in common under the Partition Acts, notwithstanding the repeal of the 1542 Act. In *Glass v McManus*[9], Girvan J commented:

> 'It would be a strange result if the repeal of An Act for Jointenants 1542 has inadvertently abolished the right to partition or an order for sale in lieu of partition. The Partition Acts 1868 and 1876 were not repealed and it must be presumed that the legislature intended them to have continued effect. The power of the courts to order partition or a sale in lieu of partition has been continuously exercised since 1950 and has not been questioned in this jurisdiction. Rules of court both in respect of the High Court and the County Court continue to presuppose the Courts' jurisdiction in relation to partition.'

[6.08] The fact that courts in Northern Ireland and the Republic of Ireland continue to order partition and sale notwithstanding the repeal of the 1542 Act raises the fundamental question of how they have overcome the problems created by this repeal. Attempts to circumvent the repeal of the 1542 Act have generated a wealth of case law and academic comment questioning the basis of

---

7 See ch 3 above, para **[3.04]**.

8 Administration of Estates Act (NI) 1955 and Succession Act 1965. The only situation in which coparcenary might still arise is where a tenant in tail dies both without a male heir and without having barred the entail.

9 [1996] NI 401 at 408-409.

the court's jurisdiction to order partition and consequently sale under the Partition Acts.

IV The Saving Provisions in the 1950 and 1962 Acts

[6.09] After expounding the functions of statute law revision, Bennion[10] sounded a cautionary note:

> 'A Statute Law Revision Act is passed to tidy up the statute book by repealing (usually with savings) provisions that are considered obsolete, or otherwise effecting purely technical changes. While saving space in editions of revised statutes, the repeal of spent provisions can be unfortunate. They may need to be referred to in order to construe other provisions that remain alive.'[11]

[6.10] These admonitions are only too apparent when considering the repeal of the 1542 Act[12]. The purpose of statute law revision is merely to remove enactments from the statute books which have been rendered obsolete or which are no longer of any practical consequence. However, in performing this task Statute Law Revision Acts must not alter existing law[13]. To guard against unintentional changes in the law when disused statutes are repealed, the repealing legislation invariably contains a saving aimed at preserving any established rules or practices originating from the Acts thereby repealed[14]. The saving allows such rules or practices to continue to be exercised by the courts, notwithstanding the repeal of the parent legislation. After stating that the various enactments listed in the schedule were repealed, the Statute Law Revision Act 1950 continued:

> '[T]his Act [shall not] affect any principle or rule of law or equity, or established jurisdiction, form or course of pleading, practice or procedure ... notwithstanding

10 Bennion, *Statutory Interpretation* (3rd edn, 1997), p 125.

11 As to statute law revision in general see Simon and Webb, 'Consolidation and Statute Law Revision' (1975) Public Law 285.

12 A likely explanation for the repeal of An Act for Jointenants 1542 is that it was an oversight on the part of the respective parliaments. Both the Statute Law Revision Act 1950 and the Statute Law Revision (Pre-Union Irish Statutes) Act 1962 adopted the format typically employed in statute law revision legislation whereby the main text of each statute contained a general repealing provision and An Act for Jointenants 1542 was listed in the schedule with a number of other statutes and no specific reason was given for the various repeals. This method of repeal has been criticised: Murray, 'When is a Repeal Not a Repeal?' (1953) 16 MLR 50.

13 See *Huffman v North Staffordshire Railway Co* [1894] 2 QB 821 and *Leeds Industrial Co-operative Society v Slack* [1924] AC 851 discussed at paras **[6.15]-[6.16]** below.

14 'A saving is a provision the intention of which is to narrow the effect of the enactment to which it refers so as to preserve some existing legal rule or right from its operation': Bennion, *Statutory Interpretation* (3rd edn, 1997), p 558.

that the same respectively may have been in any manner affirmed, recognised, or derived by, in, or from any enactment hereby repealed.'[15]

[6.11] Commenting on the equivalent provision in the 1962 Act, Barr J in *FF v CF*[16] described the saving as 'a safety-net to prevent ... the inadvertent extinction of any principle or rule of law or equity which is derived from any of the repealed statutes and which is not otherwise provided for in law'.

[6.12] The preponderance of judiciary and academics regard the court's jurisdiction to order sale under the Partition Acts as being dependent on a concurrent jurisdiction to order partition. Both agree that the jurisdiction to partition survives the repeal of the 1542 Act because of this saving in the 1950 and 1962 Acts that the repeal shall not affect 'any principle or rule of law or equity'. The saving acts as a preservation mechanism and performs two essential functions – it retains the right for joint tenants and tenants in common to compel partition (and thus request sale under the Partition Acts), and at the same time prevents the resurrection of the pre-1542 rule that these co-owners can only partition by agreement. However, there is disagreement as to the manner in which the jurisdiction to partition survives the repeal of the 1542 Act. Opinions are divided over whether the saving provisions in the 1950 and 1962 Acts preserve the statutory jurisdiction to partition under the 1542 Act itself ('any principle or rule of law') or whether they preserve the equitable jurisdiction to partition which developed in the Court of Chancery ('any principle or rule of equity').

V Preservation of the Statutory Jurisdiction

[6.13] The decision in *Glass v McManus*[17] suggests that the statutory jurisdiction for joint tenants and tenants in common to compel partition survives the repeal of the 1542 Act. The plaintiff and the defendant were co-habitees, and built a dwelling house which they held as joint tenants. Following the breakdown of their relationship in 1992, the plaintiff made several attempts to sell the property. When the defendant refused to co-operate, the plaintiff sought an order for partition or sale under the Partition Acts. The County Court for the Division of Fermanagh and Tyrone ordered sale of the property and division of the proceeds between the parties; the defendant appealed.

---

[15] Statute Law Revision Act 1950, s 1(1). Statute Law Revision (Pre-Union Irish Statutes) Act 1962, s 2(1) likewise stated:

> 'This Act shall not affect any existing principle or rule of law or equity, or any established jurisdiction, form or course of pleading, practice or procedure, notwithstanding that it may have been in any manner derived from, affirmed or recognised by any enactment hereby repealed.'

[16] [1987] ILRM 1 at 2-3.

[17] [1996] NI 401.

[6.14] The case came before Girvan J in the High Court. Having reviewed the historical development of the jurisdictions to order partition and sale, he concluded that the jurisdiction to order sale under the Partition Acts is dependent on the continued ability of the courts to order partition and acknowledged that an order for sale was more appropriate in this case than partition. The learned judge accordingly had to consider the effect of the Statute Law Revision Act 1950 on the court's jurisdiction to order partition and consequently sale. Girvan J did not doubt that the court retained jurisdiction to order partition notwithstanding the repeal of the 1542 Act. Instead, he had to determine the manner in which this jurisdiction survived the ostensible effect of the 1950 Act.

[6.15] After reciting the saving provision in the 1950 Act, Girvan J referred to the decision in *Leeds Co-operative Society Ltd v Slack*[18]. In this case, the House of Lords had to consider whether courts could award damages in lieu of an injunction under s 2 of Lord Cairns's Act[19], notwithstanding the repeal of that Act. Lord Cairns's Act became law in 1858. Section 16 of the Judicature Act 1873 vested in the High Court of Justice thereby established those jurisdictions which were vested in or capable of being exercised by the Court of Chancery, so that all courts of the Chancery Division could award damages in lieu of an injunction under Lord Cairns's Act. The Statute Law Revision and Civil Procedure Act 1883 repealed Lord Cairns's Act with a saving in s 5 of the 1883 Act that this should not affect any jurisdiction, principle, or rule of law or equity established or confirmed by any enactment so repealed. Several years later, s 5 was repealed by the Statute Law Revision Act 1898 subject to a similar saving provision. Viscount Finlay considered the combined effect of the various enactments and concluded:

> 'It is a truism that a Statute Law Revision Repeal was never intended to alter the law, but merely to remove from the Statute Book enactments which were obsolete or unnecessary ... In my opinion the view presented on behalf of both of the parties ... that the substance of Lord Cairns's Act remains in force in spite of the repeal is correct ... The Judicature Act conferred the power to award damages on the Courts of the Chancery Division and in estimating the damages the principles which Lord Cairns's Act laid down are still applicable by virtue of the saving clause in the Statute Law Revision Act ... The Act itself is now repealed, but the combined effect of s 16 of the Judicature Act 1873 and the saving clause is that the law and practice on this point remain unaltered ... Though the Act is gone, the law which it laid down still exists ...'[20]

---

[18] [1924] AC 851.

[19] Chancery Procedure Amendment Act 1858.

[20] [1924] AC 851 at 862-863.

[6.16] Thus the court could still award damages in lieu of an injunction because the law established by Lord Cairns's Act was unaffected by its repeal. Bennion[21] has remarked that 's 2, and the other sections of Lord Cairns's Act which contain provisions ancillary to s 2, maintain an uneasy existence as repealed provisions which are somehow still in force'. Endorsing both the judgment of Viscount Finlay and Bennion's comments, Girvan J in *Glass v McManus*[22] concluded:

> 'In my view a similar result follows in this case in relation to the Partition Acts. Following An Act for Jointenants 1542 the right of tenants in common and joint tenants to institute suits for partition became well established and deeply rooted in the law of real property. The Partition Acts proceeded from that premise and those Acts were left intact notwithstanding the repeal of the 1542 Act. The Partition Acts would be rendered nugatory if the right to partition was itself regarded as at an end by virtue of the repealing provisions and would make no sense if the ancient common law principle abrogated by the 1542 Act were to be considered to have revived after 1950.'

[6.17] Girvan J was therefore of the opinion that the statutory jurisdiction for joint tenants and tenants in common to compel partition under the 1542 Act survives the repeal of that Act. In other words, while the 1542 Act is removed from the corpus of the statute books the saving provision in the 1950 Act preserves the 'principle or rule of law' laid down by the former Act, so that the court has jurisdiction to order sale under the Partition Acts. The learned judge accordingly ordered sale of the dwelling house and division of the proceeds between the plaintiff and defendant. Having determined the action in this manner, Girvan J did not express an opinion on the effect of the 1950 Act on the equitable jurisdiction to partition[23].

[6.18] There are a number of difficulties associated with this judgment. Girvan J's approach pre-supposes that the statutory jurisdiction to partition existed immediately before the repeal of the 1542 Act[24]. It will be recalled that An Act for Jointenants 1542 enabled joint tenants and tenants in common to compel partition by writ *de partitione facienda*[25]. The abolition of this writ by the Real Property Limitation Act 1833 meant that all subsequent suits for partition had to be brought in the Court of Chancery[26]. For the statutory jurisdiction to compel partition to have survived the repeal of the 1542 Act, this jurisdiction must not have been affected by the 1833 Act despite the fact that

21 Bennion, *Statutory Interpretation* (3rd edn, 1997), p 228.

22 [1996] NI 401 at 410.

23 See para **[6.42]** below.

24 The object of statute law revision being merely to codify existing law and practice, and not to re-enact anything not in force immediately prior to the repealing legislation.

25 See ch 3 above, para **[3.13]**.

26 See ch 3 above, para **[3.18]**.

such suits for partition could no longer be commenced by writ *de partitione facienda*. Girvan J referred to *Mayfair Property Co v Johnson*[27]. In that case, North J alluded to the English Acts of 1539 and 1540 and continued:

> '[Although] no doubt the means prescribed by those statutes, the common law writ of partition, was abolished by the [Real Property Limitation Act 1833, s 36], yet the procedure employed by Courts of Equity in decreeing partition shews either that the writ of partition was merely one mode of carrying out that which the statutes directed to be done, or that Courts of Equity have an independent power to decree partition.'[28]

[6.19] North J felt that it was unnecessary for him to express an opinion on which of these two grounds the Court of Chancery ordered partition after 1833. However, for Girvan J's interpretation to succeed, it necessarily implies that the former approach is correct – the equitable bill replaced the writ *de partitione facienda* as the mode of instituting the partition suit and the procedure in equity was merely another means of exercising the statutory jurisdiction conferred by the 1542 Act.

[6.20] The question of whether the statutory jurisdiction survived the abolition of the writ *de partitione facienda* is in turn dependent on the nature of the remedy granted by the 1542 Act. The relevant part of the Act reads:

> '[A]ll joynt tenants and tenants in commen ... shall and may bee coacted and compelled by vertue of this present act to make partition betweene them ... by writte de participatione facienda ..., in like manner and forme as coparcioners by the common lawes of this land have been and are compellable to do, and the same writte to be pursued at the common law.'[29]

[6.21] It could be argued that the principal effect of the 1542 Act was to provide a statutory right for joint tenants and tenants in common to compel partition – it was merely an incidental feature that this was to be by writ *de partitione facienda* and that the writ should be pursued at common law. In other words, the comma in the penultimate line of the above extract separates the primary objective of the legislation – that is enabling those co-owners to compel partition – from the subsidiary direction of how this is to be achieved. The corollary of this is that, while the 1833 Act abolished the original procedure for seeking partition, it nevertheless left the right to compel partition granted by the 1542 Act intact so that the procedure in the Court of Chancery was an alternative means of exercising the statutory jurisdiction to partition[30]. This jurisdiction

---

27 [1894] 1 Ch 508.

28 [1894] 1 Ch 508 at 513.

29 An Act for Jointenants 1542, s 1.

30 'Upon the abolition of the writ of partition, equity assumed exclusive jurisdiction in cases of partition ...

accordingly forms the basis of the court's power to order sale under the Partition Acts and survives the repeal of the 1950 Act for the reasons given by Girvan J.

[6.22] It is submitted, however, that this view is incorrect, not only because it relies on the location of a punctuation mark as the fundamental basis of the jurisdiction to order sale under the Partition Acts today. The 1542 Act did not simply grant joint tenants and tenants in common a right to compel partition – the relevant authorities clearly show that the 1542 Act granted them a right to compel partition at common law[31]. Accordingly, the remedy of partition which developed in equity could not be regarded as another means of exercising the statutory jurisdiction in view of the separate systems of law and equity in existence prior to the enactment of the Judicature (Ir) Act 1877. If the suggestion is made that after 31 December 1834[32] the equitable bill replaced the writ *de partitione facienda* as the means by which joint tenants and tenants in common could exercise the statutory jurisdiction to compel partition, this poses an insurmountable problem – how could the Court of Chancery order partition under the 1542 Act when it could not administer rules of common law prior to 1877? The Court of Chancery could only administer equitable rules during this time, and could not order partition at common law as prescribed by the 1542 Act[33].

[6.23] Since the 1542 Act granted joint tenants and tenants in common a right to compel partition at common law and the writ *de partitione facienda* was simply the means of exercising this right, it is necessary to determine the effect of s 36 of the 1833 Act on the statutory jurisdiction. Although not concerned with partition, the consequences of abolishing the procedure for exercising a statutory right were discussed in *Kearney v Kearney*[34] in relation to an action of account between tenants in common. Section 23 of the Administration of Justice Act (Ir) 1707 introduced a statutory right for one co-owner to bring an action of account

30 (contd) But the statutes of Henry VIII still provide for a partition being made between tenants in common and recognise the right of the parties to it, although the common law writ was abolished ...': White and Tudor, *A Selection of Leading Cases in Equity* (7th edn, 1897) p 197, citing North J's comments in *Mayfair Property Company v Johnson* [1894] 1 Ch 508 at 513.

31 See ch 3 above, paras **[3.13]**-**[3.15]**. Likewise, *Snell's Principles of Equity* (14th edn, 1905), p 613 refers to 'the common law remedy, which was by writ of partition'. See further Foster, *The Law on Joint Ownership and Partition of Real Estate* (1878), pp 88-89 and see the comments in Wallace 'Mortgagees and Possession' (1986) 37 NILQ 336 at 354-355 noted at para **[6.26]** below.

32 Real Property Limitation Act 1833, s 36 provided that no writ *de partitione facienda* could be brought after that date.

33 This implies that the equitable jurisdiction to partition was an independent jurisdiction: see para **[6.26]** below.

34 (1861) 13 ICLR 314.

against the other co-owners[35]. The provision was, however, subsequently repealed by s 3 of the Common Law Procedure Amendment Act (Ir) 1853 but only in relation to 'personal actions or actions of ejectment in the Superior Courts of Law in Ireland'[36]. In *Kearney*, the court had to determine whether the statutory jurisdiction to order an account between co-owners had been abolished by the 1853 Act. Fitzgerald J commented:

> '[I]n reality [the 1707 Act] did two things; it created a *right* of action by one joint tenant or tenant in common against his co-tenant, as bailiff ...; and it gave as a remedy for enforcing that *right* of action, an action of account ... The statute, therefore, created a right, and gave a remedy to enforce it ... [T]he general intention of the Common Law Procedure Act was to regulate procedure, and remedy, but not to interfere with or take away any right of action. It did interfere with the forms of action; and its general intention was, not to take away rights, but to simplify the remedies for enforcing those rights. My reading of the 3rd section is, that it repeals the [1707 Act] so far as related to the form of the action and procedure, but that the *right* of action was left untouched.'[37]

[6.24] Applying the decision in *Kearney* to the abolition of the writ *de partitione facienda* suggests that the statutory jurisdiction to partition was unaffected by the 1833 Act – joint tenants and tenants in common still had a right to compel partition at common law, albeit that this could no longer be by writ. However, the 1833 Act did not prescribe an alternative means for those persons to exercise the statutory right to partition and, as already noted, the equitable bill could not be considered as an alternative means of proceeding at common law. In addition to this, no other statutes passed after the 1833 Act provided a means for instituting partition suits at common law. Therefore, despite the fact that the 1833 Act did not refer to the 1542 Act and merely abolished the common law writ, the statutory jurisdiction ceased to have any further practical consequence after 31 December 1834[38] because suits for partition could no longer be brought at

---

35 As originally enacted, this provision read:

> '[A]ctions of account shall and may be brought and maintained ... by one joint tenant and tenant in common, his executors and administrators, against the other as bailiff, for receiving more than comes to his just share and proportion, and against the executors and administrators of such joint tenant or tenant in common; and the auditors, appointed by the court where such action shall be pending, shall be and are hereby empowered to administer an oath, and to examine the parties touching the matter in question; and for their pains and trouble in auditing and taking such account, have such allowance as the court shall adjudge to be reasonable, to be paid by the party, on whose side the account shall appear to be.'

This action is considered in ch 11 below.

36 The provisions of the Administration of Justice Act (Ir) 1707, s 23 relating to auditors have also been repealed in Northern Ireland by the Statute Law Revision Act 1950 and in the Republic by the Statute Law Revision (Pre-Union Irish Statutes) Act 1962.

37 (1861) 13 ICLR 314 at 322-323.

38 Albeit that it had fallen into disuse long before this time: see ch 3 above, para **[3.18]**.

common law. The practical effect of the 1833 Act was to render the statutory jurisdiction to partition obsolete, and the equitable jurisdiction took over from this time.

[6.25] As the statutory jurisdiction could not be invoked by joint tenants and tenants in common from 1835 onwards, this jurisdiction could not have formed the basis of the court's ancillary jurisdiction to order sale under the Partition Acts. Moreover, the statutory jurisdiction is not preserved by the saving provision in the 1950 and 1962 Acts as it ceased to be operative over a century before the repeal of the 1542 Act. By deciding that the statutory jurisdiction survives the repeal of the 1542 Act, it is submitted that Girvan J in *Glass v McManus*[39] overlooked both the nature of the 1542 Act and the effect of the 1833 Act on this jurisdiction. In addition to this, submissions in both *Glass v McManus* and *Leeds Co-operative Industrial Society v Slack*[40] to the effect that statutes may remain in force notwithstanding their repeal are unconvincing, and are likely to give rise to problems of interpretation as those Acts will be omitted from subsequent revised editions of statutes[41]. Those difficulties aside, Girvan J's interpretation ignores the decline of the statutory jurisdiction to partition and attrition of the common law remedy by the equitable remedy of partition, which developed in the Court of Chancery. It is suggested that the equitable jurisdiction for joint tenants and tenants in common to compel partition survives the repeal of the 1542 Act and accordingly forms the basis of the court's jurisdiction to order sale under the Partition Acts today.

VI Preservation of the Equitable Jurisdiction

[6.26] The equitable jurisdiction to partition developed concurrently with the jurisdiction at common law[42]. Shortly after the enactment of An Act for Jointenants 1542 (and the corresponding English Acts of 1539 and 1540), virtually all suits for partition were brought in the Court of Chancery. While it may be true to say that the equitable jurisdiction was derived from the 1542 Act insofar as the practices employed by the Court of Chancery were analogous to those at common law under the writ *de partitione facienda*[43], the equitable jurisdiction was nevertheless independent of the 1542 Act[44]. The Real Property

---

39 [1996] NI 401.

40 [1924] AC 851.

41 The *Northern Ireland Statutes Revised* do not include An Act for Jointenants 1542, while the *Chronological Tables of the Statutes 1922 to 1995* in the Republic lists An Act for Jointenants 1542 as repealed in its entirety by the Statute Law Revision (Pre-Union Irish Statutes) Act 1962.

42 See ch 3 above, para **[3.21]**.

43 See ch 3 above, para **[3.28]**.

44 See Pearce, 'The Right to Partition and Sale Between Co-owners' (1987) 5 ILT (NS) 36.

Limitation Act 1833 did not transfer the statutory jurisdiction to partition created by the 1542 Act to the Court of Chancery[45] – by this time, the Court of Chancery was already exercising an independent jurisdiction to partition[46]. Despite the fact that the statutory jurisdiction was not formally abolished until 1833, it had effectively fallen into disuse by the late seventeenth century[47]. The abolition of the common law writ by the 1833 Act, with no alternative means for joint tenants and tenants in common to compel partition at common law, signalled the end of the statutory jurisdiction and granted the Court of Chancery exclusive jurisdiction to determine partition suits[48]. This was confirmed by s 2 of the Partition Act 1868, which specifically conferred jurisdiction to order sale on the Court of Chancery in England and in Ireland. Thus, the equitable jurisdiction to partition may be regarded as a 'principle or rule of equity ... derived ... from' the 1542 Act, which is preserved by the saving provisions in the 1950 and 1962 Acts[49].

[6.27] However, it will be recalled that equity was entertaining suits for partition before the enactment of the sixteenth century Acts[50]. While case law on the subject is sparse, it appears that the Court of Chancery had assumed this jurisdiction by the late thirteenth century[51]. Partition could be made in equity

---

45 As required by Girvan J's interpretation in *Glass v McManus* [1996] NI 401 and contemplated by North J in *Mayfair Property Co v Johnson* [1894] 1 Ch 508.

46 See *Northern Bank Ltd v Haggerty* [1995] NI 211 at 216 in which Campbell J referred to the abolition of the writ *de partitione facienda* by the Real Property Limitation Act 1833 and continued:

> 'The courts of equity, which were already exercising a concurrent jurisdiction ... continued to exercise this jurisdiction after 1833 ... and it then became an exclusive jurisdiction.'

Explanatory notes accompanying the Statute Law Revision (Pre-Union Irish Statutes) Bill 1962 suggested a similar explanation for the repeal of An Act for Jointenants 1542, stating that it was virtually repealed by the Real Property Limitation Act 1833, s 36.

47 See ch 3 above, paras **[3.18]-[3.20]**.

48 See Foster, *The Law on Joint Ownership and Partition of Real Estate* (1878), pp 88-89 and Goodeve, *The Modern Law of Real Property* (4th edn, 1906), p 236.

49 This view is succinctly expressed by Wallace, 'Mortgagees and Possession' (1986) 37 NILQ 336 at 354-355:

> '[T]he purpose of the ... [Act for Jointenants 1542] was to create a right to partition enforceable *at common law*. The equitable jurisdiction which developed concurrently could not therefore be dependent upon the statute although it may have been derived from it by analogy. In time the equitable jurisdiction virtually ousted the Writ of Partition procedure and that writ ... was eventually abolished by ... the Real Property Limitation Act 1833. Thereafter the equitable jurisdiction in respect of partition was of an exclusive nature and the Act of 1542 was obsolete. The fact that the equitable jurisdiction survived its ultimate repeal by the Statute Law Revision Act 1950 is surely not in doubt because section 1 of that Act provides that no repeal thereby made affects "any principle or rule of ... equity or established jurisdiction".'

50 See ch 3 above, para **[3.20]**.

51 See for example, *Citizens of London v Bishop of Bath* (1295) noted in Selden Society, *Select Cases Before the King's Council (1243-1483)*, p 8.

where an infant coparcener was a ward to the King[52]. More importantly however, coparceners who were not under disability could compel partition in equity, notwithstanding that they could already compel partition at common law[53]. It is not clear whether this equitable jurisdiction extended to joint tenants and tenants in common before they were granted a right to compel partition at common law. Yet it is necessary to determine whether the Court of Chancery had such jurisdiction prior to 1542 in Ireland (and 1539 in England). If joint tenants and tenants in common could compel partition in equity before parliament granted them such a right, this poses a vital question: what effect would the statutory jurisdiction have had on the pre-existing equitable jurisdiction?

[6.28] A similar question has arisen in a number of landlord and tenant cases dealing with the equitable jurisdiction to relieve against forfeiture in relation to covenants other than for payment of rent[54]. The issue arising in these cases was whether, once Parliament had intervened to provide a statutory jurisdiction to relieve against forfeiture in such situations[55], there continued to exist an inherent jurisdiction that had been exercised by Courts of Equity[56]. In *Abbey National Building Society v Maybeech*[57], Nicholls J held that the equitable jurisdiction had not been abrogated by the statutory provisions culminating in s 146 of the Law of Property Act 1925. However, on the same day as Nicholls J delivered his judgment, the contrary view was taken by the Court of Appeal in *Official Custodian for Charities v Parway Estates Developments Ltd*[58]. Dillon LJ remarked:

> 'Where the legislature steps in with particular legislation in a particular area, effect must be given to that legislation, and in that particular area, any wider

---

52 See *Fitz Nat Brev*, p 168 and Challis, *The Modern Law of Real Property* (3rd edn, 1911), p 376.

53 The resulting partition was 'equivalent to the judgment given between parceners on a writ *de partitione facienda*': (1341) YB 15 Ed III pl 42.

54 It appears that the equitable jurisdiction to relieve from forfeiture for non-payment of rent was not impliedly removed by subsequent legislation dealing with the subject. The purpose of that legislation was merely to modify and limit the existing equitable jurisdiction: see *Bilson v Residential Apartments* [1992] AC 494 at 511-512 per Browne-Wilkinson VC. Furthermore, in *Shiloh Spinners Ltd v Harding* [1973] AC 691 the House of Lords held that Courts of Equity have jurisdiction to relieve against forfeiture for breaches of covenant other than those for the payment of money.

55 Law of Property Act 1925, s 146 which replaced the Conveyancing Act 1881, s 14 and the Conveyancing and Law of Property Act 1892, ss 2 and 4.

56 The statutory provisions did not expressly oust this equitable jurisdiction. Rather the question to be determined was whether the legislation had cut down the equitable jurisdiction by implication.

57 [1985] Ch 190.

58 [1985] Ch 151 and cited with approval by Walton J in *Smith v Metropolitan City Properties Ltd* [1986] 1 EGLR 52.

> equitable jurisdiction is ousted ... The provisions of ... [section 146] make no sense unless they are regarded as comprehensive within that particular area.'[59]

[6.29] This conflict was resolved by the Court of Appeal in *Bilson v Residential Apartments*[60]. Browne-Wilkinson VC and Parker LJ were of the opinion that a tenant could no longer invoke the equitable jurisdiction to relieve against forfeiture, the former stating:

> 'I have reluctantly come to the conclusion that the inherent equitable jurisdiction to relieve from forfeiture for willful breach of covenant (other than a covenant for the payment of rent) has been extinguished by reason of Parliament having legislated comprehensively in this field.'[61]

[6.30] The decision in *Bilson* suggests that where a pre-existing equitable jurisdiction is comprehensively legislated on by parliament, the statutory jurisdiction can by implication supersede the former jurisdiction[62]. Applying this to An Act for Jointenants 1542, if joint tenants and tenants in common could compel partition in equity before 1542, this equitable jurisdiction should be regarded as having been ousted by the statutory jurisdiction under the 1542 Act. When the writ *de partitione facienda* was abolished by the Real Property Limitation Act 1833, the statutory jurisdiction was at an end and it must be assumed that the pre-1542 equitable jurisdiction was revived at this time[63].

[6.31] While it is not disputed that equity had a concurrent jurisdiction to order partition between coparceners prior to 1542, it is difficult to ascertain whether that jurisdiction extended to joint tenants and tenants in common. There is an instance of such a petition being made in Chancery between 1432 and 1443 in respect of land devised by will to two brothers as joint tenants[64]. Alleging that his brother was in sole occupation of the land and had taken all of the profits, the plaintiff petitioned the Chancellor of England to partition the land, acknowledging that no such remedy was available to him at common law[65]. This suggests that the Court of Chancery may have assumed jurisdiction in suits for

---

59 [1985] Ch 151 at 165.

60 [1992] AC 494 (reversed on different grounds by the House of Lords at [1992] 1 All ER 141).

61 [1992] AC 494 at 516. See however the dissenting judgment of Nicholls LJ at 525:
'Statutes are not to be construed as to take away the jurisdiction of superior courts, unless they do so by express words or by necessary implication.'

62 To similar effect is the decision in *Harrison v Tew* [1990] 1 All ER 321.

63 See *Delaney v Jones* [1939] IR 623 in which Meredith J had to consider the effect of the Landlord and Tenant Law Amendment (Ir) Act 1860, s 70 dealing with an application by a tenant for an order restoring him to possession under the equitable jurisdiction formerly exercised by the court. He concluded that 'so long as s 70 was in force that equitable jurisdiction was in abeyance, but that once it ceases to apply the equitable jurisdiction is revived': [1939] IR 623 at 629.

64 Selden Society, *Select Cases in Chancery (AD 1364-1471)* Vol X, p 129.

partition between joint tenants and tenants in common over a century before they were granted a right to compel partition at common law[66]. Yet, there is no record of whether a partition of the land was made by the Chancellor. In *Citizens of London v Bishop of Bath*[67] decided in 1295, the relevant part of the report states that 'most pleas such as ... partition of land are lately, by bill and not by writ of the king, drawn into the exchequer'[68]. However, it is not clear whether this extends to joint tenants and tenants in common or whether it is simply referring to the established practice in respect of coparceners.

[6.32] Various arguments can be made supporting and refuting the proposition that the Court of Chancery could order partition between joint tenants and tenants in common prior to such a right being granted at common law. It is possible that equity intervened because those co-owners had no remedy of partition at common law and were at a considerable disadvantage. Story[69] has asserted that, because the common law writ was only available to coparceners during this time, the Court of Chancery intervened in two situations. The first occurred where a tenant in common or tenant by the curtesy held lands with the remaining coparceners[70]. Secondly, Story suggests that the Court of Chancery could grant relief to joint tenants and tenants in common since they could not compel partition at common law during this time[71]. However, he does not venture to cite actual cases in which the Court of Chancery made such an order. That aside, if joint tenants and tenants in common could compel partition in equity prior to the respective 1539 and 1542 Acts, the decision in *Bilson* suggests that this jurisdiction should have been in abeyance until 1833. Yet the

---

65 '[T]he seid Thomas hath continually occupyed soule and taken alle the hole profitz contrarie to lawe, conscience, and the wille of the seid William the fadyr, and will not suffre yor seid bisecher to occupy ... and thus your seid bisecher may nought aprowe his part of the seid londes because ther is no particion made ther offe, for the which particion to be made ther is no accyon atte common lawe, and thus particion ther offe may [not be had, save through your] gracious eyed ... Wherefore please hit your gracious lordeship to consider these premisses and [to grant a writ] directe to the seid Thomas upon a certain peyn to apper afore you in the chauncerie at a day by you limitted, and thanne [and] there to make particion of the seid londes and tenements ...': *Select Cases in Chancery (AD 1364-1471)* Vol X, p 129 at 130-131.

66 See the comments of Potter J in *Henkel v Henkel* (1937) 276 NWR 522 at 525.

67 Noted in Selden Society, *Select Cases Before the King's Council (1243-1483)*, p 8.

68 Selden Society, *Select Cases Before the King's Council (1243-1483)*, p 8 at 10.

69 Story, *Commentaries on Equity Jurisprudence* (10th edn, 1870), pp 643-644.

70 The former could not compel partition because they could not bring a writ *de partitione facienda* against the coparceners: see ch 3 above, para **[3.10]**.

71 'Until the Statute[s] of ... Henry VIII ..., no writ of partition lay at law for a joint tenant or tenant in common. And yet the grossest injustice might have arisen, if a Court of Chancery could not, in such a case, have interposed, and granted relief, upon the analogy to the legal remedy': Story, *Commentaries on Equity Jurisprudence* (10th edn, 1870), p 643.

relevant case law clearly shows that the equitable jurisdiction to partition persisted between the passing of these Acts and the abolition of the writ of partition in 1833[72].

[6.33] Even if the decision in *Bilson* were applied to partition suits between joint tenants and tenants in common, this would not alter the fact that the equitable jurisdiction to partition formed the basis of the power of sale under the Partition Acts and survives the repeal of the 1542 Act. However, it is suggested that the better view is that the Court of Chancery could not order partition between joint tenants and tenants in common before they were granted such a right at common law and that the equitable jurisdiction to partition during this time was confined to coparceners. Instances of the Court of Chancery actually making such an order are difficult to find. Furthermore, the relevant case law dates Chancery's jurisdiction in respect of joint tenants and tenants in common as emerging after the enactment of the 1539 and 1542 Acts[73]. As Lord Loughborough LC observed in *Mundy v Mundy*[74], the Court of Chancery had no original jurisdiction to partition, this being a proceeding at common law. Thus the Court of Chancery could only order partition between joint tenants and tenants in common after the 1539 and 1542 Acts granted them a right to compel partition at common law.

[6.34] The theory that the equitable jurisdiction to partition survives the repeal of the 1542 Act has been put forward by a number of academics[75]. However, judicial support for this proposition has been more reserved, at least in the Republic of Ireland. In *O'D v O'D*[76] the disputed property was a matrimonial home which the plaintiff and defendant owned as beneficial joint tenants. Following the breakdown of the marriage, the husband sought an order for sale of the property under the Partition Acts. The Circuit Court refused to order sale but made an order for partition. On appeal, counsel for the husband initially argued that the court's jurisdiction to order partition between joint tenants and tenants in common was conferred by the 1542 Act. When his attention was drawn to the repeal of this statute, counsel argued that the court could nevertheless order partition under the equitable jurisdiction. Murphy J referred to the somewhat surprising repeal of the 1542 Act and continued:

> 'Counsel for the Plaintiff/Appellant was driven to argue that the jurisdiction to decree partition ... is now exercisable in accordance with the principles which the

[72] See for example, *Long v Miller* (1594) Toth 155; *Manaton v Squire* (1677) 2 Free 26; *Mundy v Mundy* (1793) 2 Ves 122; and *Agar v Fairfax* (1811) 17 Ves 533.

[73] See ch 3 above, para **[3.20]**.

[74] (1793) 2 Ves 122 at 124.

[75] See Wallace 'Mortgagees and Possession' (1986) 37 NILQ 336 at 354-355 (noted at para **[6.26]** above) and Pearce, 'The Right to Partition and Sale Between Co-owners' (1987) 5 ILT (NS) 36 at 36-37. See further Mee 'Partition and Sale of Family Home' (1993) 15 DULJ 78 at 80-81 and Lyall, *Land Law in Ireland* (2nd edn, 2000), p 446.

[76] (18 November 1983, unreported) High Court (RI).

authorities show as having been established by the decided cases in respect of the practice of the Courts of Chancery. Whilst it is clear that a separate equitable jurisdiction arose ... I confess to having some hesitation in accepting that principles which evolved as to the manner in which a statutory jurisdiction might be exercised could survive the repeal of that statute.'[77]

[6.35] However, 'assuming rather than accepting'[78] that the equitable jurisdiction survived the repeal of the 1542 Act, the learned judge set aside the order for partition but refused to order sale of the property on the basis that such an order would be inconsistent with the provisions of the Family Home Protection Act 1976[79].

[6.36] It is submitted that Murphy J's comments in *O'D v O'D* overlook two fundamental points. In the first place, the equitable jurisdiction did not simply consist of principles prescribing the manner in which the statutory jurisdiction to partition should be exercised. While the equitable jurisdiction to partition may have been derived from the latter by analogy to the practice under the writ *de partitione facienda*, it was nevertheless an independent jurisdiction. Secondly, it is difficult to understand Murphy J's unwillingness to accept that those principles could survive the repeal of the 1542 Act as this appears to ignore the purpose of saving provisions included in statute law revision legislation. These provisions are specifically intended to preserve such principles or rules of law or equity, even though they may have been derived from (or recognised or affirmed by) the repealed legislation.

[6.37] Two years later, the same issue arose in *FF v CF*[80]. Again the plaintiff and defendant were joint tenants of a matrimonial home. On an action by the husband for sale of the property under the Partition Acts, the Circuit Court held that it could order sale despite the repeal of the 1542 Act. The wife appealed to the High Court, arguing that the plaintiff's right to sale was dependent on the ancillary right to partition which had been removed, albeit inadvertently, by the repeal of the 1542 Act. Barr J held that the right of a joint tenant or tenant in common to compel partition was retained by the saving provision in the 1962 Act[81]. The learned judge remarked:

---

77 (18 November 1983, unreported) High Court (RI), at 8-9.

78 (18 November 1983, unreported) High Court (RI), at 9.

79 As to the effect of the Family Home Protection Act 1976 on the court's jurisdiction under the Partition Acts 1868 and 1876 see ch 10 below.

80 [1987] ILRM 1.

81 Barr J derived support for this view from Official Reports of the debate on the preceding Statute Law Revision Bill in *Dáil Éireann*. However, the use of parliamentary debates to ascertain the intention of the legislature has been questioned: see Power, 'Parliamentary History as an Aid to Statutory Interpretation' (1984) Statute Law Review 38.

> 'It is clear ... that in passing the 1962 Act the Oireachtas had no intention of interfering with any active legal right or principle of law which might have been created by or derived from any of the statutes which it was decided to repeal.'[82]

[6.38] This might suggest that Barr J was of the opinion that the statutory jurisdiction to partition survives the repeal of the 1542 Act[83]. Yet, the fact that he was referred to and considered the decision in *O'D v O'D* could equally suggest that Barr J regarded the equitable jurisdiction to partition as unaffected by the 1962 Act[84]. The judgment is not clear in this respect.

[6.39] The decision in *FF v CF* removed some of the reservations expressed by Murphy J in *O'D v O'D* as to whether the court retained *any* jurisdiction to order partition following the repeal of the 1542 Act. However, these decisions prompted the Irish Law Reform Commission to consider the problems caused by this repeal. It concluded:

> 'It is unsatisfactory that in such a significant matter there should be a doubt as to what the law is and it is suggested that to avoid doubt the statutory power of partition should be restored.'[85]

[6.40] This recommendation has not been implemented. It is regrettable that the Commission did not consider the merits of simply adopting the view that the equitable jurisdiction to partition survives the repeal of the 1542 Act, yet perhaps understandable in view of the decisions in *O'D v O'D* and *FF v CF*. In the meantime, this explanation provides a solution to the potential difficulties raised by the repeal of the 1542 Act prior to any such change in the law being introduced. Moreover, there appears to have been some confusion as to the current state of the law in the Republic. The Commission referred to s 16(f) of the Judicial Separation and Family Law Reform Act 1989. This section empowered the court, when granting a decree of judicial separation, to make an order for partition of property under the Partition Acts. Acknowledging that the 1989 Act was restricted to married couples the Commission concluded:

---

82 [1987] ILRM 1 at 3.

83 See Pearce, 'The Right to Partition and Sale Between Co-owners' (1987) 5 ILT (NS) 36 at 37 where the author treats Barr J's judgment as advocating the preservation of the statutory jurisdiction to partition created by An Act for Jointenants 1542. Similar views were expressed in Duncan and Scully, *Marriage Breakdown in Ireland* (1990), pp 314-315.

84 While Barr J did not expressly endorse the decision in *O'D v O'D* (18 November 1983, unreported) High Court (RI), he did not reject Murphy J's assumption that the equitable jurisdiction still exists. See Mee 'Partition and Sale of Family Home' (1993) 15 DULJ 78 at 81 and Wallace 'Mortgagees and Possession' (1986) 37 NILQ 336 at 355 both of which regard the decision in *FF v CF* [1987] ILRM 1 as advocating the preservation of the equitable jurisdiction to partition.

85 *Report of the Irish Law Reform Commission on Land Law and Conveyancing Law: (1) General Proposals* (1989), p 9.

> 'It has been suggested ... that the restoration of the power of partition will not of itself solve all the difficulties that present themselves, particularly in the cases of matrimonial property, and that the court should also be given power to order a sale of the property as an alternative to partition.
>
> We therefore recommend that ... a statutory provision should be introduced restoring the statutory power of partition and empowering the court to order a sale of the property in lieu of partition.'[86]

[6.41] The Commission's recommendation that the statutory power of partition be restored is understandable in view of the problems it perceived as being caused by the repeal of the 1542 Act. Yet it is difficult to understand why the Commission went on to recommend that this statutory provision should also empower the court to order sale in lieu of partition. Section 16(f) of the 1989 Act was a declaratory provision which merely confirmed the rights of co-owning spouses under the Partition Acts. While the repeal of the 1542 Act has cast doubt on the ability of courts in both parts of Ireland to order partition, there is no doubt that the Partition Acts remain in force in both jurisdictions. Notwithstanding the repeal of the 1542 Act, the courts have continued to order sale in lieu of partition. The decision in *O'D v O'D* aside, the courts have never doubted that they have such jurisdiction. More importantly, statute law revision does not alter the existing law. If the 1950 and 1962 Acts had removed the courts' jurisdiction to order sale under the Partition Acts by the repeal of the 1542 Act, then this would have been contrary to the fundamental principle behind the repealing Acts. It is submitted that the Commission's recommendation that courts be empowered to order sale in lieu of partition is unnecessary. There is no need to legislate for a power to order sale when such power exists under the Partition Acts. The respective Statute Law Revision Acts did not affect this jurisdiction to order sale against the wishes of an unwilling co-owner.

[6.42] In contrast to the position in the Republic of Ireland, support for the preservation of the equitable jurisdiction to partition may be found in several Northern Irish cases. While Girvan J in *Glass v McManus*[87] eschewed any consideration of this 'interesting and difficult point' by his endorsement of the *Leeds Co-operative* case, the learned judge did not disregard the possibility of the continued existence of the equitable jurisdiction[88]. Discussing the plaintiff's

---

86 *Report of the Irish Law Reform Commission on Land Law and Conveyancing Law: (1) Further General Proposals* (1989), p 9.

87 [1996] NI 401.

88 '[I]t should not be overlooked that equity not infrequently sought to temper the perceived inadequacies and shortcomings of the common law by the development of equitable principles and independently of An Act for Jointenants 1542 equity may well have evolved an equitable right to partition in respect of jointly held property': [1996] NI 401 at 410-411.

request for sale under s 3 of the 1868 Act, Master Ellison in *Northern Bank Ltd v Adams*[89] commented:

> 'It was ... submitted for the plaintiff that the relief sought [*viz* sale] was a statutory legal remedy. I cannot accept that submission in full. Although the bank is seeking relief under statutory provision, the remedy of partition was, immediately before the Partition Act 1868, an equitable one and would continue to be treated on such a basis after that Act.'

[6.43] Although in *Northern Bank Ltd v Adams* Master Ellison did not have to deal specifically with the repeal of the 1542 Act and its consequences, this was one of the issues that arose in the subsequent case of *Fraser Homes Ltd v Fraser Houses (NI) Ltd*[90]. After reviewing the historical background to partition actions, Campbell J continued:

> 'The equitable jurisdiction may have been derived from the Act of 1542, but it was independent of the Act. When the writ *de partitione facienda* was abolished in 1833 equitable partition had supplanted the statutory jurisdiction. In 1950 when the Act of 1542 was repealed by ... the Statute Law Revision Act 1950, the equitable jurisdiction was preserved ...'[91]

In other words, the independent equitable jurisdiction to partition survives the repeal of the 1542 Act.

[6.44] It is submitted that preservation of the equitable jurisdiction to partition provides a more satisfactory solution to the problems created by the repeal of the 1542 Act than retention of the statutory jurisdiction. This statutory jurisdiction was rendered obsolete by the abolition of the writ *de partitione facienda* in 1833, at which time the Court of Chancery assumed exclusive jurisdiction. The equitable jurisdiction thus formed the basis of the ancillary power of sale under the Partition Acts. As it was derived from the statutory jurisdiction by analogy to the practice at common law under the writ *de partitione facienda*, the equitable jurisdiction to partition survives the repeal of the 1542 Act as a 'principle or rule of ... equity ... derived from' that Act[92].

VII An Alternative Solution?

[6.45] The preceding solutions to the problems caused by the repeal of the 1542 Act are based on the premise that the jurisdiction to order sale under the

89 (1 February 1996, unreported) High Court (NI), at 11-12.

90 [1998] NI 214. The principal issue in this case was whether the court has discretion to refuse an application for partition: this is discussed in ch 7 below.

91 [1998] NI 214 at 216-217.

92 Statute Law Revision Act 1950, s 1(1) and the Statute Law Revision (Pre-Union Irish Statutes) Act 1962, s 2(1).

Partition Acts is dependent on the court possessing a concurrent jurisdiction to order partition of the disputed property, which might have been exercised prior to 25 June 1868. This interpretation of the opening words of ss 3-5 of the 1868 Act is borne out by the weight of both judicial authority and academic comment[93]. However, the possibility has been raised that the operation of the Partition Acts is not dependent on an existing jurisdiction to partition.

[6.46] In *Patel v Premabhai*[94] the plaintiff and defendant were tenants in common of adjoining plots of land in Fiji. The plaintiff sought an order for partition or sale of the property under s 4 of the 1868 Act[95]. However, s 5 of the Fiji Subdivision of Land Ordinance (1937) prohibited the 'subdivision' of land into uneconomical portions without the prior approval of the Subdivision of Land Board[96]. This raised the question of whether the Ordinance had removed the plaintiff's right to partition the land and with it his right to sale under the 1868 Act. Vaughan CJ at first instance decided that the Ordinance did not either expressly or by implication remove the court's jurisdiction to order partition, and ordered sale of the land[97]. This was reversed by the Fijian Court of Appeal, which held that subdivision was the same as partition, and because the disputed land could not be partitioned no order for sale was possible[98]. The plaintiff appealed to the Privy Council. Rejecting the defendant's submission that a decree for partition inevitably included an order for division, the Privy Council held that the Ordinance did not prohibit the making of an order for partition. It only prohibited the carrying out of the order by division of the land. Accordingly, this particular situation was one in which 'a decree for partition might have been made' and the plaintiff was entitled to sale[99].

[6.47] One of the plaintiff's submissions in this case is relevant to the question of the court's jurisdiction to order partition. It was argued on behalf of the defendant that, division being the essence of partition, the court could no longer order partition without the consent of the Board and therefore could not order sale in those circumstances. Counsel for the plaintiff submitted that the reference in s 4 of the 1868 Act to making an order for sale where 'if this Act had not been passed, a decree for partition might have been made' did not require that the court might order partition of the property when the case was being decided. Rather, counsel asserted that 'on the true construction of s 4 …

93 See the cases and comments noted at para **[6.03]** above and at ch 5 above, paras **[5.08]**-**[5.16]**.
94 [1954] AC 35.
95 The Partition Act 1868 was applied to Fiji by the Supreme Court Ordinance of Fiji 1875.
96 Subdivision of Land Ordance (1937), s 3 provided that 'subdivide' includes 'partition'.
97 [1954] AC 35 at 37.
98 [1954] AC 35 at 37-38.
99 This aspect of the judgment is considered further in ch 7 below.

where under the law in force at the commencement of the Act a decree for partition might have been made, a decree for sale could be made'[100]. Delivering the judgment of the Privy Council, Lord Porter described the plaintiff's argument in the following terms:

> 'On ... behalf [of the appellant/plaintiff] it is maintained that section 4 of the Act of 1868, when it uses the words "where if this Act had not been passed, a decree for partition might have been made", is dealing only with the situation as it existed before that date. If, it is said, such a decree might have been made before 1868, then a sale may, or in certain circumstances must, be granted. *It matters not that division or, indeed, partition may be prohibited at a later time. The only question is, could partition have been decreed before the Act of 1868 was passed.* The wording is not "*might be* made", but "*might have been* made", and such an expression, it is contended, *points to the position as it existed in 1868 and not to the state of the law at a later period.* If it had been desired to prohibit the remedy of sale in lieu of partition it would, it is maintained, have been easy to do so in plain terms, but *a mere prohibition of partition in the future would not have this result.*'[101]

Lord Porter did not find it necessary to consider this question, preferring to base his judgment on the view that a decree for partition did not include an order for division.

[6.48] The implications of the plaintiff's submission in *Patel v Premabhai* as regards the repeal of An Act for Jointenants 1542 are obvious. The words 'might *have been* made' in ss 3-5 of the 1868 Act are retrospective, and indicate that the relevant time for determining whether the court has jurisdiction to order partition is the law in existence when the 1868 Act was passed. Thus the repeal of the 1542 Act arguably has no effect on the court's jurisdiction to order sale under the Partition Acts as sale can be decreed where partition might have been ordered in those circumstances before 25 June 1868. If the wording in ss 3-5 had read 'might *be* made', this would imply that the court's jurisdiction to order sale under the Partition Acts is dependent on a contemporary jurisdiction to order partition, as the word 'be' points to a state of affairs in the future. Therefore, it could be argued that the jurisdiction to order sale under the Partition Acts is independent of a concurrent jurisdiction to order partition, and that the repeal of the 1542 Act is of no practical consequence.

[6.49] The co-existence of the jurisdictions to order partition and sale was considered by the Federal Court of Australia in *Squire v Rogers*[102], the facts of which are similar to *Patel*. The court had to consider whether it had jurisdiction

---

[100] [1954] AC 35 at 38.
[101] [1954] AC 35 at 45 (emphasis added).
[102] (1979) 39 FLR (Aus) 106.

to order partition and consequently sale of a leasehold interest that was subject to an Ordinance prohibiting the division of such interests[103]. The defendant drew attention to the words '[i]n a suit for partition, where, if this Act had not been passed a decree for partition might have been made' in s 4 of the Partition Act 1881 (SA) and argued that, because the Ordinance precluded the making of such a decree, the court had no jurisdiction to order sale. Delivering the judgment of the court, Deane J stated:

> '[T]he threshold problem concerns the identification of the temporal reference point for determining the legal context in which the question whether a decree for partition might otherwise have been made falls to be answered. Is the relevant context that into which the Partition Act, 1881 (SA) was introduced, namely, the law of the colony of South Australia at the time that Act commenced operation? Or is it the law operating at the time and in the place of the institution of the relevant proceedings ...? Or is it the law operating at the time when the order for sale was made ...? Or is it some other, and if so what, legal context?'[104]

[6.50] Deane J referred to the enactment of the Partition Act 1868 in England and to the fact that thereafter virtually all decrees were for sale of the property. He continued:

> 'In these circumstances, it would seem unlikely that it was the legislative intent that the general jurisdiction to make an order for sale should be confined to those circumstances in which, under the law as it might from time to time in the future exist, the increasingly rare order for actual partition of the relevant property might be made. It would seem more likely that it was the legislative intent that the circumstances in which the general jurisdiction to make an order for sale should exist *would be those in which an order for partition might have been made at the time when the Act first spoke. The use of the words "might have been made" (and not "might be made") lends some support for the latter construction which is, in my view, the correct one*. The words "if this Act had not been passed" were, on that construction, necessary for the reason that the temporal reference point is the time when the Act first operated ...'[105]

[6.51] Applying the decision in *Patel v Premabhai*[106], Deane J concluded that, since a decree for partition and an order for subdivision were separate matters, the Ordinance did not deprive the court of jurisdiction to make a decree for partition or 'deprive the present proceedings of their character as an action for

---

[103] See ch 5 above, paras **[5.13]-[5.14]**. As in *Patel v Premabhai* [1954] AC 35, s 29 of the relevant Ordinance provided that each parcel of land was to be occupied under the lease as one undivided parcel, subject to s 29A which provided for an application to be made to subdivide such land.

[104] (1979) 39 FLR (Aus) 106 at 116-117.

[105] (1979) 39 FLR (Aus) 106 at 118 (emphasis added).

[106] [1954] AC 35.

partition where, if the relevant Partition Act had not been passed, a decree for partition "might have been made"'[107].

[6.52] At a cursory glance, it might appear that the decision in *Squire v Rogers* provides some support for the plaintiff's submission in *Patel v Premabhai*. However, *Squire v Rogers* is simply referring to the temporal reference point for determining when the court's jurisdiction to partition might have been exercised. The relevant authorities clearly state that the jurisdiction to order sale under the Partition Acts is dependent on the court having a concurrent jurisdiction to order partition of property held in this manner, which might have been exercised prior to 25 June 1868[108]. While it is not disputed that the opening clause of ss 3-5 of the 1868 Act is retrospective, this only refers to the temporal point for determining when this concurrent jurisdiction to partition might have been exercised. It should not be interpreted as suggesting that, so long as the jurisdiction to order partition between joint tenants and tenants in common existed prior to 25 June 1868, it is irrelevant whether this jurisdiction still exists today[109].

[6.53] While this interpretation was central to the plaintiff's submission in *Patel*, the Privy Council did not express an opinion on the matter. Moreover, *Patel* was not specifically concerned with the repeal of the statute which originally created the right for joint tenants and tenants in common to compel partition and its effect on the court's associated jurisdiction to order sale under the Partition Acts. If adopted, the plaintiff's submission in *Patel* would present a more fundamental problem. It fails to take account of the fact that, if the jurisdiction to partition no longer existed, joint tenants and tenants in common would be unable to compel partition today if they did not want the property to be sold or if the circumstances of the case resulted in the court refusing to make an order for sale under the Partition Acts.

VIII A Theoretical Problem?

[6.54] The repeal of the 1542 Act is essentially a theoretical as opposed to a practical problem. Courts in both Northern Ireland and the Republic of Ireland have continued to exercise the jurisdiction conferred by the Partition Acts since the respective Statute Law Revision Acts were passed, and have determined the

---

107 (1979) 39 FLR (Aus) 106 at 119.

108 See ch 5 above, paras **[5.08]-[5.16]**. The fact that the jurisdiction to order sale under the Partition Acts 1868 and 1876 is related to the prevailing law when the Partition Act 1868 was passed supports the proposition that the equitable jurisdiction to partition survives the repeal of An Act for Jointenants 1542.

109 In other words, the question is not simply whether partition might have been ordered prior to 25 June 1868, but rather whether partition might have been ordered if these particular factual circumstances had existed prior to this date.

majority of partition actions without questioning the effect of the repeal of the 1542 Act[110]. The manner in which the jurisdiction to order partition survives the repeal of the 1542 Act is of no practical consequence to the outcome of the case – whether this jurisdiction is statutory or equitable does not alter the factors which the courts must consider in deciding whether to order partition or sale, nor does it affect the execution of the relevant order. However, the matter should be clarified in view of the lack of consensus that exists as to the manner in which the jurisdiction under the Partition Acts survives the repeal of the 1542 Act. As illustrated above, the most satisfactory explanation is that the equitable jurisdiction to partition is unaffected by the repeal of the 1542 Act. Thus because the courts may still order partition, they can make an order for sale of concurrent interests in land under the Partition Acts.

110 See for example, *Tubman v Johnston* [1981] NI 53; *Ulster Bank Ltd v Shanks* [1982] NI 143; *Northern Bank Ltd v Beattie* [1982] 18 NIJB 1; and *Robin Rainey t/a R Mc A Rainey & Sons v Derek James Weatherup and Another* (13 December 1996, unreported) High Court (NI). As to the Republic see *CH v DGO'D* (1978) 114 ILTR 9; *First National Building Society v Ring* [1992] IR 375; *Rubotham v Young* (23 May 1995, unreported) High Court (RI); and *Rubotham v Duddy* (1 May 1996, unreported) High Court (RI).

Chapter 7

Partition or Sale – A Matter of Right?

I Introduction

[7.01] A co-owner who wishes to end this relationship by compelling partition or sale of the relevant property may wish to be advised on the likelihood of securing such an order. The equitable jurisdiction to partition survives the repeal of An Act for Jointenants 1542 and forms the basis of the corresponding jurisdiction to order sale under the Partition Acts[1]. Instances in which courts have refused to exercise any discretion when granting equitable relief are difficult to find. This might suggest that the remedies of partition and sale under the Partition Acts should likewise be discretionary. However, courts have traditionally declined to follow this practice in partition actions. This chapter examines the options available to courts in Northern Ireland and the Republic of Ireland when determining partition actions and considers whether the respective courts are confined to making an order for either partition or sale in these circumstances.

II Historical Background

[7.02] The sixteenth century Statutes of Partition granted joint tenants and tenants in common a right to compel partition at common law[2]. Since the equitable jurisdiction to partition was derived from that at common law, the Court of Chancery also regarded partition as a matter of right upon proof of title[3]. One co-owner could compel partition no matter how small his interest in the property, and notwithstanding any objections from the other co-owners[4].

[7.03] The Partition Act 1868 conferred jurisdiction on the Court of Chancery to substitute the more convenient remedy of sale for physical partition of concurrent interests in land. However, the court could not refuse both partition and sale[5]. Since partition was granted as of right in equity prior to 1868 and the

---

1 See generally ch 6 above.

2 See ch 3 above, paras **[3.13]**-**[3.14]**. See further the comments of Lord Wilberforce in *Ceylon Theatres Ltd v Cinemas Ltd* [1968] AC 792 at 802-803.

3 See for example, *Cantwell v Hassard* (1858) Ir Ch R 370 at 373 in which Napier LC remarked: '[T]here can be no doubt that the grant of a partition is in a sense not a matter of discretion in Equity. A commission of partition is in this Court as much a matter of right as the old writ of partition was in a Court of Law.'

4 See generally ch 3 above, paras **[3.43]**-**[3.46]**.

5 Assuming of course that the plaintiff had *locus standi* to maintain the action and that none of the jurisdiction exceptions applied to the particular case: see generally ch 4 above.

legislation provided for sale instead of partition, the court was obliged to order either partition or sale. Thus, in *Pitt v Jones*[6] Lord Watson remarked:

> 'Before the passing of the Partition Act the Respondents would have had an absolute right to a decree of partition; and it appears to me that the leading purpose of the Act ... was to enable the Court to substitute, in certain cases, sale and distribution for division, which was the only remedy previously competent ...'

[7.04] Walker[7] likewise observed that:

> 'The right to institute the action is the same as ever; but since the Act of 1868, there is no longer the old right to partition, sale being generally substituted in lieu of it. The right to relief is the same; the relief itself is in most cases changed.'

[7.05] The relevant nineteenth century authorities did not dispute the fact that the court had discretion within ss 3-5 of the 1868 Act to refuse an order for sale[8]. However, the prevailing view was that partition and sale were alternatives, so that the automatic consequence of refusing to order sale was an order for partition[9]. In other words, because the 1868 Act only modified the equitable jurisdiction to partition to the extent that the court could substitute sale for partition in circumstances prescribed by ss 3-5, the plaintiff had an absolute right to either partition or sale. Sale was introduced strictly as an alternative to partition, not as an alternative to maintaining the status quo and allowing the parties to remain co-owners despite the wish of one or more such persons to end that relationship[10].

III Current Practice in Northern Ireland and the Republic of Ireland

[7.06] A question which typically arises in partition actions today is whether courts are still restricted to making an order for partition or sale under the Partition Acts in accordance with the post-1868 practice, or whether they may

6 (1880) 5 App Cas 651 at 661.

7 Walker, *The Partition Acts, 1868 and 1876* (1882), pp 14-15.

8 Partition Act 1868, ss 3 and 5 provide that the court 'may, if it thinks fit' order sale, while s 4 provides that the court 'shall' order sale 'unless it sees good reason to the contrary'.

9 See for example, *Dicks v Batten* [1870] WN 173 and *Dyer v Painter* (1885) 33 WR 806 (decree for partition where sale refused under the Partition Act 1868, s 3), and *Richardson v Feary* (1888) 39 Ch D 45 (partition ordered instead of sale under the Partition Act 1868, s 5). As regards the Partition Act 1868, s 4 see *Saxton v Bartley* (1879) 48 LJ Ch 519, and see *Re Whitwell's Estate* (1887) 19 LR Ir 45 at 48 in which Monroe J referred to an earlier case in which he had declined to order sale under s 4 but had left the plaintiffs 'to their right of partition'.

10 See the comments of Highness J in *Bray v Bray* (1926) 38 CLR 542 at 546. For a more recent example of this approach see *Moss v Zorn* [1991] NWTR 141.

adopt a more flexible approach. A divergence of opinion has emerged in recent years between courts in Northern Ireland and those in the Republic as to whether they have discretion to refuse both partition and sale under the Partition Acts.

[7.07] The following discussion does not consider the practice in partition actions involving spouses and the matrimonial home. While the general principles that have emerged from such cases may be relevant in this context, the burgeoning wealth of legislation regulating property rights of spouses in relation to the matrimonial home and its impact on partition actions merits separate consideration[11].

A Northern Ireland

[7.08] In Northern Ireland the prevailing view is that the court must order either partition or sale – it cannot refuse both. The leading judgment is that of Murray J in *Northern Bank Ltd v Beattie*[12]. The plaintiff brought an action for sale of a matrimonial home under the Partition Acts. Having observed that the 1868 Act introduced the more convenient remedy of sale as a substitute for partition, Murray J continued:

> 'My reading of the law is that if the owner or mortgagee demands a sale this is strictly an alternative remedy to a physical partition and if physical partition is not practicable then sale is the only possible order. I draw attention to the words "a sale ... instead of a division of the property" in s 4 – indeed they also appear in s 3 [sic][13] – and I record that I asked Counsel for authority for the proposition that sale can be refused for "good reason" in a case where physical partition is not practicable. No such authority was produced and I certainly have not been able to find any myself: indeed the cases point against any such proposition being good law.'[14]

[7.09] In other words, the wording of the 1868 Act indicates that partition and sale are alternatives, so that the court's discretion is restricted to choosing between them. Wallace has endorsed Murray J's comments as in keeping with the peculiar nature of the equitable jurisdiction to partition and the fact that the Court of Chancery regarded a decree for partition as a matter of right[15]. More

---

[11] See chs 9 and 10 below.

[12] [1982] 18 NIJB 1.

[13] Although the words 'sale ... instead of a division' are used in the Partition Act 1868, ss 4 and 5, these words do not actually appear in s 3 which refers to the court ordering sale if this would be 'more beneficial ... than a partition'.

[14] [1982] 18 NIJB 1 at 23-24. This approach was also implicit in Murray J's judgments in *Tubman v Johnston* [1981] NI 53 and *Ulster Bank Ltd v Shanks* [1982] NI 143.

[15] '[B]efore one can fully endorse the reasoning of Murray J ... one must decide whether or not the equitable jurisdiction is of a discretionary nature. If, as is normally the case in equity, the jurisdiction is discretionary, then the logic of the decision in *Northern Bank Ltd v Beattie* is undermined to the extent that it was based on the assumption that the Bank *must* be granted *either* partition or sale.

recently, this dictum has been affirmed by Girvan J in *Glass v McManus*[16] and in *Ulster Bank Ltd v Carter*[17], the learned judge taking the view that partition and sale are alternatives so that the court cannot refuse both[18]. Likewise, in *Fraser Homes Ltd v Fraser Houses (NI) Ltd*[19] Campbell J observed that the court is bound to order partition or sale; it does not have a discretion as is usually the case in equity[20].

[7.10] Thus, it appears that courts in Northern Ireland have adopted the post-1868 practice in partition actions and must order either partition or sale upon such an application being made. If the court refuses relief this goes to standing[21] or to jurisdiction[22] rather than the court exercising a discretion to refuse both partition and sale. This apparent lack of discretion is the consequence of the pre-1868 practice of the Court of Chancery and the effect of the Partition Acts in substituting sale for division. While it may not achieve the most desirable result and has prompted suggestions that the law should be reformed[23], a co-owner's right to either partition or sale seems to be the only possible outcome as the law currently stands.

[7.11] However, this view has not met with universal support. In *Northern Bank Ltd v Adams*[24] the plaintiff had a second mortgage affecting a husband's undivided share of a matrimonial home which he and his wife owned as joint tenants. The Bank sought partition or sale of the property under s 4 of the 1868 Act. Master Ellison conceded that partition of the house was impractical, and went on to consider whether the Bank was entitled to an order for sale. He

---

15 (contd) However, it would seem that in this particular area equity regarded a decree as a matter of right and not one to be considered in the light of considerations, such as hardship, which would normally come into play in the exercise of an equitable jurisdiction': Wallace, 'Mortgagees and Possession' (1986) 37 NILQ 336 at 355-356. The author restated this view in 'Mortgages and Charges', *Second Annual Review of Property Law* (1995) 35 at 37.

16 [1996] NI 401.

17 [1999] NI 93.

18 However, in *Ulster Bank Ltd v Carter* [1999] NI 93, Girvan J doubted whether this should be the position as regards spouses and the matrimonial home: [1999] NI 93 at 105 and see ch 9 below, para **[9.44]**.

19 [1998] NI 214.

20 See further Valentine, *Civil Proceedings – The Supreme Court* (1997), p 435 and Valentine, *Civil Proceedings – The County Court* (1999), p 37.

21 As, for example, where the owner of a charge brought an action for partition or sale prior to art 48 of the Property (NI) Order 1997 coming into force: *Northern Bank Ltd v Haggerty* [1995] NI 211 and see ch 8 below.

22 See the comments of Campbell J in *Fraser Homes Ltd v Fraser Houses (NI) Ltd* [1998] NI 214 at 218.

23 See generally paras **[7.60]-[7.65]** below.

24 (1 February 1996, unreported) High Court (NI).

observed that partition is an equitable remedy but that, until recently, authorities such as *Northern Bank Ltd v Beattie*[25] had suggested that there was 'minimal flexibility available to the court'[26] and that it was difficult to resist an application for sale where partition was impracticable. Master Ellison referred to *Northern Bank Ltd v Haggerty*[27] in which Campbell J suggested that 'good reason to the contrary' within s 4 of the 1868 Act may now be interpreted more widely in the context of legislation regulating the property rights of spouses. According to Master Ellison, a more liberal interpretation not only recognised modern legislative changes in respect of property rights of spouses[28], but was also in keeping with the general principle that equitable relief is discretionary so that the court may refuse both partition and sale.

[7.12] Having decided that the Bank's action came within s 3 of the 1868 Act as opposed to s 4[29], Master Ellison went on to consider the nature of the court's jurisdiction under s 3. Observing that the court has a discretion to order sale under this section, he referred to *Gilbert v Smith*[30] in which Jessel MR interpreted s 3 as meaning that, where partition is impractical, sale should be regarded as more beneficial. According to Master Ellison, Jessel MR did not actually stipulate that, where property cannot reasonably be partitioned, the court must order sale under s 3 and has no further discretion in the matter. Master Ellison continued:

> 'The section's permissive wording – "may if it thinks fit" – can in my view only mean that the legislature contemplated the possibility that the court, having found sale at least better than partition, might in some circumstances refuse both partition and sale – or at least, acting on equitable grounds, consider imposing a stay or condition on an order for sale[31]. Had the legislature wanted sale to be

25 [1982] 18 NIJB 1. Master Ellison also referred to Wallace's comments in the respective articles noted at para **[7.09]** above.

26 (1 February 1996, unreported) High Court (NI), at 12.

27 [1995] NI 211 at 217.

28 Master Ellison referred to the Family Law (Miscellaneous Provisions) (NI) Order 1984 (now the Family Homes and Domestic Violence (NI) Order 1998) and the Insolvency (NI) Order 1989, art 309. The effect of this legislation on partition actions involving spouses is considered in ch 9 below.

29 See ch 5 above, paras **[5.26]**-**[5.27]**.

30 (1879) 11 Ch D 78 discussed at ch 5 above, para **[5.20]**.

31 Master Ellison was of the opinion that he could postpone sale under the Judicature (NI) Act 1978, s 86(3) which provides that 'a court, acting on equitable grounds, may stay any proceedings or the execution of any of its processes subject to such conditions as it thinks fit'. Wallace has argued that the purpose of s 86(3) is to verify the continued exercise of existing equitable powers rather than permitting judges to devise new powers when they are of the opinion that a strict application of established rules would be too severe: 'Mortgages and Charges', *Third Annual Review of Property Law* (1996) 7 at 24-25. However, courts in Northern Ireland may now postpone an order for sale under the Property (NI) Order 1997, art 49: see paras **[7.63]**-**[7.64]** below.

> imperative under the section if more beneficial than a partition, presumably it would have used the imperative "shall", but it did not. I respectfully suggest that a finding that the section confers a genuine discretion where physical partition would – as is common ground in the instant case – clearly be unreasonable would be in keeping not only with the plain language of the section, but also with modern thinking and circumstances including the recent legislative changes protecting spouses ...'[32]

[7.13] Although largely concerned with the effect of provisions regulating the property rights of spouses on partition actions, these particular comments are applicable to partition actions in general. The decision in *Adams* suggests that the court is not confined to making an order for either partition or sale under the Partition Acts. Master Ellison's judgment appears to be based on the premise that partition, being an equitable remedy, is discretionary, and that the words 'may, if it thinks fit' in s 3 and 'unless it sees good reason to the contrary' in s 4 give the court discretion to refuse sale, even though partition of the relevant property is impractical[33].

[7.14] However, this aspect of the judgment is open to criticism. Master Ellison's comments that partition is discretionary because it is an equitable remedy ignore the peculiar nature of the equitable jurisdiction to partition. Unlike other equitable remedies, the Court of Chancery granted partition as of right by analogy to the practice at common law[34]. The Partition Acts only modified this jurisdiction to the extent that the court could substitute sale for partition, hence the traditional view in Northern Ireland that the court's discretion is restricted to making an order for either partition or sale. The words 'may, if it thinks fit' in s 3 and 'unless it sees good reason to the contrary' in s 4 only refer to the court

[32] (1 February 1996, unreported) High Court (NI), at 24-25. A similar meaning can presumably be attributed to the words 'may, if it thinks fit' in the Partition Act 1868, s 5. Where the plaintiff requests sale under s 5 and no undertaking to purchase is proffered by the parties resisting sale, the court may refuse both partition and sale. Alternatively, if an undertaking to purchase is given and the plaintiff refuses to accept this, he may not have a right to an order for partition. Master Ellison also appears to have taken the view that the court has discretion to refuse both partition and sale under the Partition Act 1868, s 4. Earlier in his judgment at 19-20 he stated:

> '[G]iven ... the relevant finding about "good reason" in the *Haggerty* case, I think it arguable that even where physical partition is impracticable, the approach set out later in this judgment vis-à-vis section 3 might broadly be applied also to determine whether "good reason" exists in applications by mortgagees which are otherwise covered by section 4 ... The possible of interpretation of section 4 I have suggested assumes however that, post *Haggerty*, the economic viability of physical partition need no longer be regarded as a pre-condition for a finding of "good reason" against sale.'

[33] While accepting that partition and sale are usually regarded as alternatives, Valentine, *Civil Proceedings – The Supreme Court* (1997), p 435 supports Master Ellison's comments that both partition and sale should be regarded as discretionary remedies since the former is an equitable remedy.

[34] See ch 3 above, paras **[3.43]-[3.46]**.

having discretion to refuse sale, and the automatic consequence of such a refusal is that the court must order partition[35].

[7.15] In order to establish 'good reason to the contrary' for the purposes of s 4, an opposing co-owner must usually demonstrate that partition is a feasible alternative to sale and that there are special circumstances which would make it wrong for the court to order sale[36]. Therefore, if partition is impracticable it will be difficult for the defendant to establish 'good reason to the contrary' since this is usually regarded as good reason for ordering partition instead of sale[37]. As regards s 3, the court 'may, if it thinks fit' order sale if this would be more beneficial than partition. It is not disputed that the permissive wording of s 3 contemplates sale being refused even if it would be more beneficial than partition. Considering the equivalent section of the Property Law Act 1928 (Vict), Lowe J in *Carpenter v Sheehan*[38] interpreted this section as:

> 'vesting a discretion in the Court rather than merely conferring a power which the Court is bound to exercise in favour of the applicant once the latter has shown that sale would be more beneficial than division.'[39]

[7.16] Yet it is difficult to envisage a situation in which the court might refuse to order sale under s 3 when, by definition, it has already decided that sale is more beneficial than partition. The fact that partition is impracticable would seem to reinforce this. Thus, as Jessel MR suggested in *Gilbert v Smith*[40] sale should usually be regarded as more beneficial than partition in these circumstances[41].

---

35 See para **[7.05]** above. See further Wallace, 'Mortgages and Charges', *Third Annual Review of Property Law* (1996) 7 at 22:

> '[T]he purpose of the Partition Act was to give the court jurisdiction to order a sale in lieu of partition; not a discretion to refuse both remedies. The balance of authority suggests that prior to the 1868 Act partition was available to a co-owner *as of right*. If this suggestion is correct, the only effect of the Act is to enable courts to order sale *instead* of partition in appropriate circumstances; not to deny both.'

36 See ch 5 above.

37 See the comments of Bray CJ in *Tansell v Tansell* (1977) 35 FLR (Aus) 272 at 275 in relation to the corresponding section of the Law of Property Act 1936 (SA). In *Revell v Baker* [1984] 3 NZFLR 20 Henry J observed that 'good reason to the contrary' under the Property Law Act 1952 (NZ), s 140(1) enables the court to order partition instead of sale but not to decline both, and see *McMahon v McMahon* [1996] 3 NZLR 334.

38 [1947] VLR 127 at 128.

39 The learned judge restated this view in *Scates v Scates* [1962] VR 398 but left open the question of whether the court must order partition if it refuses to order sale.

40 (1879) 11 Ch D 78.

41 Partition is unlikely to be impracticable where an application is made under the Partition Act 1868, s 5. It will be recalled that s 5 is essentially a default provision and will only be invoked where a co-owner is precluded from relying on s 3 because he cannot show any reason for preferring sale to partition. Therefore, if partition of the relevant property is impracticable, he is more likely to apply under s 3 since sale of the property and division of the proceeds is likely to be more beneficial in pecuniary terms than partition.

[7.17] The court has a discretion to refuse to order sale under ss 3 and 4 where partition is impracticable[42]. However, in light of the prevailing view that partition and sale are alternatives under the Partition Acts and that a co-owner is entitled to one or the other, the likelihood of the court ordering sale in these circumstances must be regarded as considerable. As Murray J indicated in *Northern Bank Ltd v Beattie*[43], instances in which the courts have refused to order sale where partition is impracticable are difficult to find[44]. Furthermore, the discretion to refuse sale under ss 3 and 4 has traditionally only been exercised where partition of the relevant property was a practicable alternative[45].

1 Futility cases – consent of a third party to partition

[7.18] Master Ellison's suggestion in *Northern Bank Ltd v Adams*[46] that the court may refuse to order both partition and sale in certain circumstances may be explicable in terms of an order for partition being futile. Three situations may be identified in which the consent of a third party is required before an order for partition may be implemented[47].

(a) Planning legislation

[7.19] The principal planning legislation in Northern Ireland is the Planning (NI) Order 1991, while the Local Government (Planning and Development) Act 1963 is the principal legislation in the Republic[48]. Although neither statute specifically refers to partition or sale of concurrent interests in land, both prescribe a restriction on the division of dwelling houses that may affect co-owners. Article 11(1) of the 1991 Order defines development as including 'the making of any material change in the use of any buildings or other land'. Article 11(3) continues:

---

42 In *Clarke v Clarke* (1974) 48 DLR (3d) 707 Allen JA referred to the Partition Act 1868, ss 3-5 laying emphasis on the words 'if it thinks fit' in ss 3 and 5 and the words 'unless it sees good reason to the contrary' in s 4. He continued at 711:

> 'In my view the italicized phraseology found in these sections clearly indicates that the Court has some discretion with regard to the granting of the remedy of sale in lieu of partition. The proposition that because partition is a matter of right, sale must be ordered when physical division is impracticable, is one which I am not prepared to accept.'

See further *Kornacki v Kornacki* (1975) 21 RFL 400 and *Elligott v Elligott* (1977) 6 AR 282.

43 [1982] 18 NIJB 1.

44 See further *Norgard v Norgard* (1996) 20 Fam LR, Lexis transcript in which the court held that it could not refuse to order sale if partition was impracticable or not sought by either party.

45 See the cases noted at para **[7.05]** above.

46 (1 February 1996, unreported) High Court (NI).

47 The following discussion considers the law in Northern Ireland and the Republic as similar issues arise in both jurisdictions.

48 For an exposition of the relevant law in the respective jurisdictions see Dowling, *Northern Ireland Planning Law* (1995) and Galligan, *Irish Planning Law and Procedure* (1997).

For the purposes of this Article -

(a) the use as two or more separate dwelling-houses of any building previously used as a single dwelling-house involves a material change in the use of the building and of each part thereof which is so used ...

[7.20] Similar provisions may be found in the 1963 Act[49]. Accordingly, if co-owners of a dwelling house desire partition so that each one of them can thereafter occupy his divided share as such, this constitutes a material change of use and requires planning permission[50]. The alterations to the property that are necessary to implement the order for partition require planning permission[51].

(b) Land acquired under the land purchase scheme/agricultural land

[7.21] Subdivision of land acquired under the land purchase scheme is subject to a number of statutory restrictions[52]. As regards Northern Ireland, s 54(1) of the

---

[49] Local Government (Planning and Development) Act 1963, ss 3(1) and 3(3).

[50] Planning (NI) Order 1991, art 12 and the Local Government (Planning and Development) Act 1963, s 24(1). In Northern Ireland planning applications are determined by the Department of the Environment, while such applications in the Republic are dealt with by planning authorities as defined by the Local Government (Planning and Development) Act 1963, s 2(2). As to what amounts to conversion into two or more separate dwellings, see *Ealing Borough Council v Ryan* [1965] 2 QB 486.

[51] Instances of courts in Northern Ireland and the Republic considering whether partition of a single dwelling house conflicts with planning legislation are difficult to find. However, a similar issue has been addressed in a number of Canadian cases. Various Canadian provinces have enacted legislation which prohibits subdivision of land without consent from the relevant authority, and which would include subdivision by a court order in a partition action: *Re Wensel and Wensel* (1976) 72 DLR (3d) 1. For example, the Planning Act 1970 (Ont), s 33a provided that, in an action for partition under the Partition Act 1970 (Ont), notice had to be given to the Minister of Housing who was then entitled to be heard at the proceedings. Cases such as *Re Hay and Gooderham* (1979) 24 OR (2d) 701 and *Re Barchuk and Valentini* (1980) 107 DLR (3d) 510 held that compulsory partition did not come within s 33a. However, in *Cochrane v Cochrane* (1980) 108 DLR (3d) 395 (cited with approval in *Van Harten v Van Harten* (1980) 15 RPR 161) the court declined to follow these cases and held that where the principal purpose of an application for partition was to avoid and render nugatory the procedures required by the Planning Act, the court should not exercise its discretion in favour of partition. See further *Attorney-General for Ontario v Harry; Attorney-General for Ontario v Yeotes* (1979) 23 DLR (3d) 332. However, in *Re Kuz and Kuz* (1980) 118 DLR (3d) 525, Galligan J held that the effect of the Planning Act 1970 (Ont), s 33a was that planning considerations had to be taken into account as a relevant factor before the court could order partition, but the mere fact that partition might lead to violation of the language and intent of subdivision control provisions should not prevent the court from ordering partition. Section 50(20) of the Planning Act 1990 (Ont) now provides that an order under the Partition Act 1990 (Ont) will not have effect unless each part of the land could be divided without contravening this section or consent is given to the court.

[52] As to the land purchase scheme in general see Cherry, *The Irish Land Law and Land Purchase Acts, 1860 to 1901* (3rd edn, 1903) and Cherry and Maxwell, *The Irish Land Acts, 1903 and 1904* (1904).

Irish Land Act 1903 provides that, where such land is subject to an outstanding annuity, the land shall not be subdivided without the consent of the Department of Finance and Personnel[53]. Any attempted subdivision without prior consent is void[54] and the Department may sell the holding[55]. Thus, if a co-owner of land acquired under the land purchase scheme wishes to partition the land, he must obtain the consent of the Department of Finance and Personnel if the purchase advance has not been paid off[56].

[7.22] As regards the Republic of Ireland, land acquired under the land purchase scheme after 1923 could not be divided without the prior consent of the Land Commission, irrespective of whether the outstanding annuity had been paid off[57]. Section 12 of the Land Act 1965 now provides that 'agricultural holdings' cannot be subdivided without the consent of the Minister[58]. Any attempted subdivision of the land without consent is void, and the Minister may vest the land in him[59]. Thus, if a co-owner of agricultural land in the Republic wishes to partition this land he must obtain the prior consent of the Minister.

(c) Covenants in leases

[7.23] Where several persons are co-owners of leasehold property, the tenancy agreement may contain covenants that would allow the court to refuse an order for partition in the absence of the landlord's consent to what would otherwise be a breach of covenant. Although a lease is unlikely to contain a covenant expressly prohibiting or restricting partition, it may contain a covenant prohibiting subdivision or preventing subdivision without the consent of the

---

53 See *Foley's Case* [1957] NI 130. The Northern Ireland Land Act 1925 retained the existing land purchase scheme in Northern Ireland following the partition of Ireland in 1921. The remaining functions of the Land Commission were transferred to the Department of Finance and Personnel by the Finance Act 1963.

54 Northern Ireland Land Act 1925, s 3(1).

55 Irish Land Act 1903, s 54(1).

56 This is likely to be of little practical relevance in Northern Ireland today. The land purchase scheme was completed by 1937 and most of the outstanding annuities have been paid off: Northern Ireland Land Purchase (Winding Up) Act 1935 and see Wylie, *Irish Land Law* (3rd edn, 1997), p 46.

57 Land Act 1923, s 65 and *Re Morris* (1940) 74 ILTR 235. Prior to 1923, the position in the Republic was the same as the present position in Northern Ireland.

58 See further the Land Act 1965, s 13. Land Act 1965, s 12(8) defines agricultural holdings as 'substantially agricultural or pastoral' holdings, whether or not purchased under the Land Purchase Acts. The functions of the Land Commission have been transferred to the Minister for Agriculture, Food and Forestry under the Irish Land Commission (Dissolution) Act 1992 (brought into force by the Irish Land Commission (Dissolution) Act 1992 (Commencement) Order 1999).

59 Land Act 1965, ss 12 and 13. Alternatively, the Minister may retrospectively consent to the purported subdivision: Land Act 1965, s 12(3).

landlord. Another typical covenant is one that prohibits or restricts the making of alterations to the property, such as those that would be required to implement an order for partition[60]. Alterations to the property on partition may also be contrary to a covenant against waste[61].

(d) Third party consent

[7.24] If the third party consents to partition in these circumstances, the court may make an order for partition[62]. If the third party has not been approached, the court might adjourn the partition action to see whether consent could be obtained[63]. However, the court is unlikely to make an order for partition where the co-owner seeking partition has approached the third party and the latter has indicated that consent will be refused. The problem which arises in this context is whether the court's refusal to order partition should be regarded as falling within the established jurisdiction exception which exists as regards prejudice to third parties, or whether these cases should be regarded as 'futility' cases in which the court exercises a discretion to refuse partition.

2 *Jurisdiction or futility?*

[7.25] It might be thought that the court's refusal to order partition where the consent of a third party is likely to be refused goes to jurisdiction. The court cannot make an order for partition if this would prejudice third parties with rights over the entire property[64]. Thus, if the planning authority, Department of Finance or Minister, or landlord have indicated that they would not consent to partition of the relevant property, it is arguable that the court does not have

60 A covenant prohibiting or restricting assignment is not breached by partition: see *Foley v Gallagher* (1877) 2 LR Ir 35 (affirmed at (1877) 2 LR Ir 389).

61 A tenancy agreement will often contain an express covenant to this effect, but in the absence of this a covenant prohibiting waste will be implied by common law or by the Landlord and Tenant Law Amendment (Ir) Act 1860 (Deasy's Act), ss 26-34.

62 This consent should be given at the hearing of the partition action: Carleton, *The Jurisdiction and Procedure of the County Courts in Ireland* (2nd edn, 1891), p 1292 and Osborne, *The Jurisdiction and Practice of the County Courts in Ireland in Equity and Probate Matters* (2nd edn, 1910), pp 655-656.

63 See *Roper v Roper* (1907) 41 ILTR 231 and *Farrell v Donnelly* [1913] 1 IR 50 at 58. The consent of the third party to partition is not a condition precedent to instituting a suit for partition: *Prendergast v Mongan* [1913] 1 IR 321. Alternatively, the court might make an order for partition which is conditional on the plaintiff securing the necessary third party consent: see the Property (NI) Order 1997, art 49 (discussed at paras **[7.63]**-**[7.64]** below) and *Squire v Rogers* (1979) 39 FLR (Aus) 106. In this case, Deane J suggested at 119 that provisions requiring the consent of a third party to partition might lead the court 'either to frame a decree for partition in such a way as to ensure that the necessary approval for subdivision was obtained before the decree could be carried into effect … or to provide, by ancillary orders, for the actual making of an application for approval of the necessary subdivision'.

64 See ch 4 above, paras **[4.61]**-**[4.67]**.

jurisdiction to make the order sought[65]. The advantage of explaining the court's refusal to order partition in this manner is that it accords with the prevailing view that the court can only order partition or sale under the Partition Acts. Jurisdiction exceptions aside, a plaintiff is entitled to partition as of right with the possibility of an order for sale being made in the alternative.

[7.26] However, this interpretation is not without difficulty. The opening words of ss 3-5 of the 1868 Act indicate that the jurisdiction to order sale under the Partition Acts is only exercisable where the court has a concurrent jurisdiction to order partition of property held in this manner which might have been exercised prior to 25 June 1868[66]. If there is no jurisdiction to order partition of the subject property in the absence of necessary third party consent, then the court does not have jurisdiction to make an order for sale. For example, in *Roper v Roper*[67] a tenant in common of land held under a lease requested sale under s 3 of the 1868 Act. Cooke J held that the court did not have jurisdiction to order sale, since the land could only be partitioned with the landlord's consent and the plaintiff had not secured this consent. This would also apply to actions for sale of the other types of property described above. For example, if the planning authority were unlikely to consent to partition of a dwelling house, the court would be prevented from ordering sale under the Partition Acts. This would have significant practical implications, not only for co-owners themselves but also for lending institutions whose security is restricted to an undivided share of a dwelling house and whose only method of realising that security is by an order for sale under the Partition Acts. The decision in *Roper* aside, instances of the courts refusing to order sale of a dwelling house, leasehold property, agricultural land or land acquired under the Land Purchase Acts because a third party would not consent to partition are difficult to find[68]. Why should a co-owner who

---

65 See for example, Wallace, 'Mortgagees and Possession' (1986) 37 NILQ 336 at 355-356 and the comments of the respective courts in *Roper v Roper* (1907) 41 ILTR 231 and *Cantwell v Hassard* (1858) 7 Ir Ch R 370 discussed below. In *Fraser Homes Ltd v Fraser Houses (NI) Ltd* [1998] NI 214 at 218 Campbell J left open the question of whether such cases should be explained on the basis of prejudice to third parties and therefore outside the jurisdiction of the court, or as examples of the court declining to make an order which might be futile and therefore 'doing nothing in vain'.

66 See ch 5 above, paras **[5.08]**-**[5.16]**.

67 (1907) 41 ILTR 231.

68 The courts have ordered sale of a dwelling house without questioning whether the planning authority would have consented to partition of such property, both in the context of partition actions involving co-owners themselves (see for example *Glass v McManus* [1996] NI 401) and those involving lenders (see for example *Northern Bank Ltd v Beattie* [1982] 18 NIJB 1 and *First National Building Society v Ring* [1992] IR 375). Likewise, the prior consent of the Minister or Department of Finance is not a pre-requisite to an order for sale under the Partition Acts: see 'Jurisdiction to Partition Holdings Under the Land Purchase Acts' (1913) 47 ILTSJ 101, and see *Prendergast v Mongan* [1913] 1 IR 321 and *Farrell v Donnelly* [1913] 1 IR 50.

desires sale of such property under the Partition Acts have to procure an unnecessary third party consent to partition in these circumstances?

[7.27] Furthermore, a third party who has indicated his opposition to partition would not actually be prejudiced by such an order. In the unlikely event of the court making an order for partition notwithstanding his objections, the third party has two options available to him. He may choose to accept the order and allow the co-owners to implement the partition decreed by the court. Alternatively, he may take steps to prevent the order for partition from being enforced. For example, the planning authority might commence enforcement proceedings, while a landlord might forfeit the lease for breach of covenant[69]. Since the third party could take positive steps to defeat the order, his rights would not be prejudiced if the court ordered partition in these circumstances.

[7.28] It is suggested that the court has discretion to refuse partition in these circumstances because an order for partition might be futile. The defining characteristic of these 'futility cases' is the power of a third party to defeat the order of the court. Where the consent of a third party is necessary before an order for partition can be carried out, the court is unlikely to order partition if the third party objects to division of the property and may subsequently take steps to render the order useless[70]. In practical terms, the court will be loathe to make a 'paper judgment' – there is little point in making an order which cannot be enforced[71]. The court does have jurisdiction to order partition in these circumstances, but elects not to do so because of the possibility of the third party subsequently defeating the order[72]. However, the fact that the court has jurisdiction to order partition means that it also has jurisdiction to order sale of these three particular types of property notwithstanding the third party's objections to partition – a decree for partition 'might have been made' in these circumstances although it could not have been enforced without the necessary third party consent[73].

---

69 Likewise, the Department of Finance might cause the particular holding to be sold, while the Minister might vest the land in him.

70 Since partition is an equitable remedy and 'equity like nature does nothing in vain'.

71 It is suggested that this is similar to the position where the court is asked to make an order for specific performance of a contract and the consent of a third party is necessary for the contract to be performed: see Spry, *Equitable Remedies* (4th edn, 1990), pp 125-127.

72 See for example, *Crawford v Durrant* (1998) 156 DLR (4th) 292 in which the Manitoba Court of Appeal held that, while the court has jurisdiction under the Law of Property Act 1987 (Man) to make an order for partition upon the application of any person interested in land, the court may refuse to make the order it if would conflict with other legislation, such as the Planning Act 1987 (Man).

73 Commenting on such cases and the use of the word 'might' in the Partition Act 1868, ss 3-5, Mee has observed that 'the Partition Acts are broad enough to give a remedy in some of the rare cases where physical partition would not be available': Mee 'Partition and Sale of Family Home' (1993) 15 DULJ 78 at 83 citing *Prendergast v Mongan* [1913] 1 IR 321 considered below.

[7.29] One of the earliest decisions on this point is *North v Guinan*[74] in which Hart LC refused to partition a dwelling house and premises held under a lease on the ground that this would be contrary to a covenant in the lease prohibiting waste. He remarked:

> 'A series of decisions has settled, that a commission of partition is due of common right to every tenant in common, however minute his share, even though the division might diminish, or possibly destroy the value to both ...[75] The partition of the house must re-model and re-construct the fabric of the building, and it would throw some discredit on the jurisdiction of the Court, if the landlord, disliking the alterations, should, in defiance of the decree, enter for the waste committed, and turn both parties, with the Court and its decree, out of doors.'[76]

[7.30] Thus, if the court ordered partition the landlord might prevent the parties from carrying out the decree by obtaining an injunction to restrain them from committing waste. While the decision in *North v Guinan* has been interpreted as a prejudice to third parties jurisdiction exception[77], the basis of the decision was the power of the landlord to render useless the order for partition[78].

[7.31] In *Prendergast v Mongan*[79] the plaintiff and defendants were tenants in common of land held under a statutory tenancy under the Land Law (Ir) Act 1881. The plaintiff brought an action for sale of the land under s 3 of the Partition Act 1868, and the question arose as to whether the court could make such an order in the absence of the landlord's consent to an order for partition as required by s 5 of the 1881 Act. Dodd J drew attention to s 3 of the 1868 Act, and to the fact that the court had to consider whether a decree for partition 'might have been made' but for the operation of the 1881 Act, as opposed to whether a decree for partition 'would' have been made. Referring to *North v Guinan*, he stated that the court did have jurisdiction to order partition of the subject property but elected not to do so because a third party could discredit the order by rendering it useless. He continued:

> 'The Court, in other words, having jurisdiction, will refuse a decree where a person outside the Court can treat the decree with discredit.'[80]

---

74 (1829) Beat 342.

75 Citing *Turner v Morgan* (1803) 8 Ves 143.

76 (1829) Beat 342 at 344-345.

77 See *Cantwell v Hassard* (1858) 7 Ir Ch R 370 at 373 (discussed at ch 4 above, paras **[4.64]**-**[4.66]**) and Wallace, 'Mortgagees and Possession' (1986) 37 NILQ 336 at 355-356.

78 See further *Witchard v Witchard* (1975) 6 ACTR 31 in which Blackburn J observed that a decree for partition of a leasehold interest would be refused if execution of the decree would involve waste.

79 [1913] 1 IR 321.

80 [1913] 1 IR 321 at 326. *North v Guinan* was also interpreted as a futility case by Murphy J in *O'D v O'D* (18 November 1983, unreported) High Court (RI): see para **[7.42]** below.

[7.32] Applying this to the present case, Dodd J concluded that the court had jurisdiction to order sale of land held under a statutory tenancy notwithstanding the absence of the landlord's consent to partition. Since the court had jurisdiction to order partition in these circumstances, an order for partition 'might' have been made and the court could make an order for sale[81].

[7.33] Although concerned with the effect of statutory provisions requiring the consent of a third party to sale on the court's jurisdiction to order sale under legislation similar to the Partition Acts, a number of Australian cases have also interpreted this requirement as allowing the court to refuse sale where the order would be futile in the absence of consent. In *Blennerhassett v Blennerhassett*[82] former spouses were co-owners of a matrimonial home subject to a mortgage to the Director of War Service Homes. Section 4 of the War Service Homes Act 1918-1949 provided that, where a dwelling house or land was subject to such a mortgage, a transfer of any interest or share in the property could not take effect without the consent of the Director. The husband brought an action for sale of the property in lieu of partition under the Property Law Act 1928 (Vict). Lowe J held that the War Service Homes Act did not oust the court's jurisdiction to order sale of this type of property under the 1928 Act[83]. Moreover, an order for sale in this case would not be futile, since the Director had indicated that he would consent to a transfer of the property[84].

[7.34] Other cases support the view that the court has jurisdiction to order partition (and consequently sale) despite objections from a third party, by distinguishing between making an order for partition and carrying out the order. In *Patel v Premabhai*[85] the Privy Council held that the Fiji Subdivision of Land

---

[81] Tacit support for this proposition may also be found in the judgment of the Lord Chancellor in *Farrell v Donnelly* [1913] 1 IR 50 at 58. A judgment mortgagee of a tenant in common of land acquired under the Land Purchase Acts and subject to an existing annuity brought an action for sale under the Partition Act 1868, s 3. The question arose as to whether the court had jurisdiction to order sale, notwithstanding the fact that the plaintiff had not obtained the consent of the Land Commission to partition as required by the Land Law (Ir) Act 1881, s 30 and the Irish Land Act 1903, s 54. The Lord Chancellor held that, since the plaintiff was not attempting to have the land subdivided, he was not offending against any obligation to the Land Commission and its consent was not necessary.

[82] [1957] VR 214.

[83] 'The Court must of course in exercising its jurisdiction observe any statutory or other requirements, but so long as it does so, I do not think its jurisdiction is interfered with': [1957] VR 214 at 216. Lowe J declined to follow *Bielefield v Bielefield* [1956] QWN 4 in which Stanley J refused to order sale under the Partition Act 1911 (Qd) in similar circumstances because the provisions of the War Service Homes Act had ousted the court's jurisdiction under the 1911 Act.

[84] Similar views were expressed by Virtue J in *Fairweather v Fairweather* (1957) 59 WALR 25 in relation to the court's jurisdiction under the Partition Act 1878 (WA).

[85] [1954] AC 35 and discussed in ch 6 above, paras **[6.46]-[6.47]**.

Ordinance 1937, which prohibited division of land without the consent of the Subdivision of Land Board, did not prohibit the making of an order for partition since a 'decree for partition' and a 'division' of land were separate matters. The Ordinance merely prevented the carrying out of the order by division of the land. Accordingly, the case was one in which 'a decree for partition might have been made' within the 1868 Act and the plaintiff was entitled to sale. Lord Porter remarked:

> '[Land] is not divided merely because an order for partition is made: there is nothing to prohibit the making of such an order. What is forbidden is the carrying out of the order by actual partition unless and until the approval of the board, set up by the Ordinance, has been obtained ... The making of a decree is not prohibited, and as such a decree might have been made (though it could not be implemented by actual division of the property) a direction for sale of the property is permissible under the terms of the Act of 1868.'[86]

[7.35] Similar views were expressed by Deane J in *Squire v Rogers*[87] in relation to analogous restrictions in s 29 of the Darwin Town Area Leases Ordinance 1947:

> 'The requirement of s 29 ... that the land be held and occupied as one undivided parcel would not preclude the actual making of a decree for partition. The making of such a decree would not, in itself, involve a division of the holding or occupation of the land in respect of which the decree was made ... [Section 29] might, in certain circumstances, lead the court to decline to make an order for partition on the grounds that it would be futile to do so (*North v Guinan* ...). There is nothing, however, in the provision of s 29 ... which deprives the court of its jurisdiction to make a decree for partition or which operates to deprive the present proceedings of their character as an action for partition where, if the Partition Act had not been passed, a decree for partition "might have been made".' [88]

[7.36] Since the court has jurisdiction to make an order for partition in these circumstances, its refusal to do so can only be explained on the basis of the court exercising a discretion because the order might be futile. The court has jurisdiction to order partition of a single dwelling house, leasehold property and property acquired under the Land Purchase Acts or agricultural property

---

86 [1954] AC 35 at 47-48. See however *Witchard v Witchard* (1975) 6 ACTR 31 at 35 in which Blackburn J expressed difficulty in reconciling the decision in *Patel v Premabhai* with 'the multitude of cases in which courts have refused to make orders the execution of which would be unlawful'.

87 (1979) 39 FLR (Aus) 106 at 119 and discussed in ch 5 above, paras **[5.13]-[5.14]**.

88 See further *Joyce v Joyce* [1963] Qd R 139 and the note on this case at (1963) 37 ALJ 186, as well as *Henderson v Henderson* [1963] WAR 112 and *Sovova v Ovjan* (1987) 87 FLR (Aus) 170.

notwithstanding the fact that the relevant third party objects to partition. His consent is not a pre-requisite to the court making an order for partition but to the carrying into effect of the order. However, it is likely that the court will refuse to make an order for partition in these circumstances because of the possibility of the third party preventing it from being implemented and thus rendering the order useless. Yet, because a decree for partition 'might have been made' here, the court has jurisdiction to order sale of these types of property under the Partition Acts.

[7.37] An obvious disadvantage of interpreting these cases as futility cases is that it introduces an element of discretion into partition actions when courts have consistently denied that any such discretion exists. Claims that an order for partition is at the discretion of the court in these circumstances sit uneasily with the traditional view that partition is granted as of right, and arguably opens the door to discretion. However, it is suggested that the fact that partition is discretionary in these three situations does not encroach significantly on the traditional view that the plaintiff has a right to either partition or sale under the Partition Acts. Two factors support this. Firstly, the discretion to refuse to order partition on the ground of futility is confined to these three particular situations. These cases should not be interpreted as advocating a general discretion for the court to refuse partition where it feels this would be justified in the circumstances of a particular case[89].

[7.38] Secondly, even though an order for partition may be futile, the court still has jurisdiction to make such an order and consequently retains jurisdiction to order sale under the Partition Acts. An order for sale is the preferred remedy in the majority of partition actions today[90]. Where an order for partition would be futile, the likelihood of the court making an order for sale of the disputed property must be regarded as considerable. Moreover, sale can be ordered in these circumstances without any need for consent from the third party. Master Ellison's comments in *Northern Bank Ltd v Adams*[91] that the court may refuse to order both partition and sale are explicable in terms of the court exercising its discretion under ss 3 and 4 of the 1868 Act to refuse an order for sale of a dwelling house[92], and then refusing to order partition of the property because such an order would be futile without the consent of the planning authority[93].

---

89 Likewise, factors such as hardship, which would usually be relevant to the exercise of an equitable jurisdiction are still irrelevant in this context.

90 See ch 5 above, paras **[5.62]-[5.64]**.

91 (1 February 1996, unreported) High Court (NI).

92 In this case, a matrimonial home.

93 A similar result would arise in respect of partition actions involving property acquired under the Land Purchase Acts in Northern Ireland and agricultural land in the Republic, or leasehold property where partition would be contrary to a covenant in the lease.

However, the arguments made earlier[94] in relation to the court refusing to order sale where partition is impracticable are equally relevant in this context. It is difficult to envisage a situation in which the court would refuse to order sale under s 3 or s 4 where an order for partition would be futile[95]. There is little doubt that an order for sale under s 3 would be more beneficial than partition here[96]. The fact that an order for partition would be futile might amount to 'any other circumstance' which the court may consider under s 3[97]. As regards s 4, 'good reason to the contrary' is usually only established where partition of the disputed property is feasible and special circumstances exist which would make it wrong for the court to order sale. Accordingly, owners of less than a moiety may find it difficult to resist sale under s 4 where an order for partition would be futile[98]. One of the few situations in which the court might refuse both partition and sale in these futility cases is where a co-owner specifically asks for partition and the others do not request sale[99]. However, the court may be able to devise a scheme of partition whereby that particular item of property is awarded to one co-owner and a different item of property of equivalent value is given to another co-owner, thus avoiding the need for any third party consent[100].

[7.39] The current position in Northern Ireland may be summarised as follows: where a partition action is properly constituted[101] and does not come within one

---

94 See paras **[7.14]-[7.17]** above.

95 However, the practice may be different as regards partition actions involving the matrimonial home: see generally chs 9 and 10 below.

96 In *Hoggard v Hoggard* (22 November 1996, unreported) British Columbia Supreme Court, Joyce J stated that, where land was incapable of division (for example because it's located in the Agricultural Lands Reserve), then sale was not only more beneficial than partition under the equivalent section of the Partition of Property Act 1979 (BC) but that it was necessary.

97 *Prendergast v Mongan* [1913] 1 IR 321 at 326 per Dodd J.

98 For example, in *Martin-Smith v Woodhead* [1990] WAR 62 at 69 Kennedy J remarked that, if partition is not feasible, a co-owner interested to the extent of a moiety is entitled to an order for sale under legislation derived from the Partition Act 1868, s 4. Once again, the Partition Act 1868, s 5 is unlikely to be relied on in these circumstances since it only applies where owners of less than a moiety of the property can show no reason for preferring sale to division, and sale will usually be preferable where partition would be futile.

99 In these circumstances, it has been suggested that the court should not order the property to be sold if the third party consent to partition cannot be obtained and should leave the plaintiff to apply for a further order: *De Campo Holdings v Cianciullo* [1977] WAR 56 at 60 per Jones J. However, a note on this case at (1977) 51 ALJ 325 suggested that Jones J should have moulded his order to take account of future contingencies and other necessary steps citing *Dougan v Ley* (1946) 71 CLR 142. See further *Reimer v Robbins, Reimer and Glover* (1982) 24 Man R (2d) 311 in which Dewar CJQB refused to order partition in the absence of any information as to planning restrictions which would provide the court with a basis upon which to make a fair and just division.

100 *Witchard v Witchard* (1975) 6 ACTR 31.

101 In other words, the plaintiff has *locus standi* and the court has jurisdiction to make the order sought.

of the few situations where an order for partition would be futile, a plaintiff has a right to either partition or sale. Even if the action does fall within one of the futility cases, the likelihood of the court making an order for sale must be regarded as considerable.

B Republic of Ireland

[7.40] The relatively rigid application of the post-1868 practice in Northern Ireland may be contrasted with the current practice in the Republic of Ireland. The leading case is *O'D v O'D*[102] in which a husband sought an order for sale of a matrimonial home under the Partition Acts. The Circuit Court refused to order sale but made an order for partition. The husband appealed, arguing that as a joint tenant he had a right to an order for partition, or that in any event this was a suit where 'a decree for partition might have been made' under s 4 of the 1868 Act. As the owner of a moiety of the property he was entitled to sale unless the court saw 'good reason to the contrary'.

[7.41] Murphy J considered both the origin and the nature of the right to partition. Having reviewed the circumstances which led to the enactment of the 1542 and 1868 Acts, he observed that authorities such as *Turner v Morgan*[103] supported the proposition that a decree for partition in the Court of Chancery prior to 1868 was regarded as a matter of right. However, he continued:

> '[T]he existence of these precedents does not establish conclusively that the order is of right or that the Court is without discretion in the matter.'[104]

[7.42] Murphy J cited *North v Guinan*[105] as an instance of the court exercising discretion to refuse partition, and interpreted this as in keeping with the general principle that the court will not usually make an order that would be futile[106]. The learned judge also referred to the fact that a castle used for defence of the realm could not be partitioned, and interpreted this as an example of the court exercising discretion to refuse partition.

[7.43] Murphy J derived further support for his claims that a plaintiff is not entitled to an order for partition from a number of early practitioners' texts. In particular, he referred to a form of order in Osborne's *Jurisdiction and Practice of the County Courts in Ireland*[107] directing preliminary inquiries to be carried

[102] (18 November 1983, unreported) High Court (RI).

[103] (1803) 8 Ves 143.

[104] (18 November 1983, unreported) High Court (RI), at 6.

[105] (1829) Beat 342.

[106] 'It seem to me that ... [*North v Guinan*] represents both good law and good sense. In general principle the Court would not ordinarily make an order which would be futile. Clearly it is inappropriate to make an order directed to parties to proceedings when its execution depends upon the co-operation of parties not bound by the order': (18 November 1983, unreported) High Court (RI), at 6.

[107] Osborne, *The Jurisdiction and Practice of the County Courts in Ireland in Equity and Probate Matters* (2nd edn, 1910), pp 655-656.

out before a surveyor was appointed to survey the land and prepare a map of the proposed partition. Inquiries were ordered as to the persons interested in the land and for what estates and interests, and whether they were parties to the suit; the existence of any agreement prohibiting subdivision; the availability of the landlord's consent to partition if required; and the consent of the Commissioners of Public Works or the Land Commission where necessary[108]. Murphy J concluded:

> 'This procedure seems to me to confirm that the making of the actual order of partition does and always did require the Court to be satisfied by evidence made available to it or to an officer of the Court that it was a proper case in which to make the particular order sought.'[109]

[7.44] As no such evidence had been adduced in the present case and no inquiries directed, Murphy J was of the opinion that the order for partition made by the Circuit Court could be set aside on this ground alone. However, he went on to consider the effect of the repeal of the 1542 Act on the jurisdiction to partition. Assuming that the equitable jurisdiction to partition survived the repeal, Murphy J stated that the exercise of this jurisdiction was 'necessarily subject ... to the proper discretion of the Court'[110]. After considering the relevant provisions of the Family Home Protection Act 1976, Murphy J also refused to order sale of the property[111].

[7.45] Murphy J's ruling that partition is discretionary conflicts with the traditional view that a co-owner is entitled to either partition or sale under the Partition Acts. The court may have a limited discretion to refuse partition where the order would be futile because it cannot be enforced without the consent of a third party. However, it has been suggested that these cases may have little practical consequence because the court is likely to substitute the more convenient remedy of sale in these circumstances. In contrast, Murphy J appears to have taken the view that the court possesses a general discretion to refuse partition that is not confined to futility cases. The court has discretion whether to order sale under the Partition Acts[112]. Futility cases aside, where sale is refused it does not automatically follow after *O'D v O'D* that the plaintiff has a right to partition because, according to Murphy J, the remedy of partition is

[108] Similar inquiries were directed in Carleton, *The Jurisdiction and Procedure of the County Courts in Ireland* (2nd edn, 1891), p 1292 and in a number of orders in Seton, *Forms of Judgments and Orders in the High Court of Justice and the Court of Appeal* (6th edn, 1901), pp 1851-1860.

[109] (18 November 1983, unreported) High Court (RI), at 7-8.

[110] (18 November 1983, unreported) High Court (RI), at 9.

[111] See generally ch 10 below.

[112] See para **[7.05]** above.

discretionary. In other words, the automatic consequence of refusing sale is no longer partition in the Republic of Ireland.

[7.46] However, there are a number of problems associated with this judgment. It is difficult to see why Murphy J so readily dismissed numerous precedents which established that partition was traditionally granted as of right in equity prior to 1868[113]. If the equitable remedy of partition had been discretionary, it is difficult to imagine a more appropriate case for refusing it than *Turner v Morgan*[114]. Yet Lord Eldon LC in that case stated that he was bound to order partition. Murphy J appears to have been influenced by the court's refusal to order partition in *North v Guinan* and where the disputed property was a castle used for defence. However, *North v Guinan* is an example of the court refusing partition on the ground of futility, while the exception in respect of a castle used for defence goes to jurisdiction rather than discretion[115].

[7.47] Likewise, the inquiries directed in Osborne's *County Court Practice* do little to support Murphy J's assertion that partition is discretionary. The need for consent to partition from a landlord or Commissioners of Public Works or the Land Commission[116] constitutes a limited exception on the ground of futility where such consent is refused. However, the existence of an agreement prohibiting partition is another example of the court lacking jurisdiction to order partition[117]. As regards inquiries into the estates and interests of the persons interested in the property and whether those persons are parties to the action, these are merely procedural requirements which have to be satisfied before the court orders partition or sale under the Partition Acts. The court must be satisfied that the co-owners are interested in ascertainable shares[118], and that they are parties to the action or their absence is satisfactorily accounted for under s 3 of the Partition Act 1876[119]. While this may delay proceedings, it does

---

113 See ch 3 above, paras **[3.43]-[3.46]**.

114 (1803) 8 Ves 143 and discussed in ch 3 above, para **[3.45]**.

115 See ch 4 above, paras **[4.37]-[4.39]**. Mee, 'Partition and Sale of Family Home' (1993) 15 DULJ 78 at 81-82 argue that references to the court being able to refuse partition in these two specific situations are not indicative of a general discretion in partition actions:

> 'It is submitted that the "discretion" to which Murphy J referred does not extend beyond a consideration of these two matters and that otherwise partition must be available automatically upon proof of title. Centuries of precedent in the Courts of Equity have established the right of a co-owner (subject to the sensible statutory alternative of sale in lieu) to determine that co-ownership through the partition jurisdiction. In the absence of further legislation, there is no justification for the Irish Courts to interfere now with this fundamental principle.'

See further *Glass v McManus* [1996] NI 401 at 407 in which Girvan J described these particular situations as 'very limited exceptions to what was regarded as a general right to partition'.

116 Now the Department of Finance in Northern Ireland and the Minister in the Republic.

117 See ch 4 above, paras **[4.51]-[4.54]**.

118 Again this is a jurisdiction exception: see ch 4 above, paras **[4.68]-[4.69]**.

119 See ch 12 below.

not alter the practice that the plaintiff is entitled to an order for partition or sale when the various requirements are satisfied. These inquiries are not indicative of a general discretion to refuse relief.

[7.48] There are persuasive arguments in favour of courts in the Republic being confined to making an order for either partition or sale where the action is properly constituted and an order for partition would not be futile. Yet, notwithstanding criticisms of *O'D v O'D*, the current practice appears to be that courts have discretion to refuse both partition and sale[120].

IV Current Position in the Commonwealth

[7.49] Courts in both Australia and New Zealand have to a large extent adopted the post-1868 practice under the Partition Acts and thus usually confine themselves to making an order for either partition or sale. In contrast, Canadian courts have demonstrated a more flexible approach in determining partition actions between co-owners of land.

A Australia

[7.50] In the majority of Australian states, the legislation that currently governs compulsory partition and sale of concurrent interests in land is derived from the Partition Acts and the provisions which confer jurisdiction to order sale closely resemble ss 3-5 of the 1868 Act[121]. The respective courts have accordingly taken the view that partition and sale are alternatives, and that a co-owner is entitled to one or the other. For example, in *Bray v Bray*[122] Knox CJ expressed the following view on the Partition Act 1900 (NSW)[123]:

> 'So far as I can see, the object of the Act was to provide an alternative remedy to partition ... I think it is clear that ... what the Court has to consider is which is the better course for all parties between two alternatives, namely, is it better that there should be a partition or that there should be a sale ...'

[7.51] Endorsing these comments, Menhennitt J in *Schnytzer v Wielunski*[124] stated that 'the only alternative to sale is partition', while Bright J in *Peck v Peck*[125] asserted that there is 'an absolute right to partition, however

[120] See, however, the earlier case of *CH v DGO'D* (1978) 114 ILTR 9 in which McWilliam J appears to have taken the view that partition and sale are alternatives under the Partition Act 1868, s 4.

[121] See ch 4 above, para **[4.01]**.

[122] (1926) 38 CLR 542 at 545.

[123] The Partition Act 1900 (NSW) was derived from the Partition Act 1868 and governed partition and sale of land in New South Wales prior to 1 January 1931 when the statutory trust structure was introduced by the Conveyancing Act 1919 (NSW): see below.

[124] [1978] VR 418 at 422.

[125] [1965] SASR 293 at 300.

inconvenient, unless as a strict alternative sale is ordered'[126]. Likewise, Brennan J in *Nullagine Investments Ltd v Western Australian Club*[127] referred to a co-owner's right 'to either an order for partition or an order for sale'[128].

[7.52] The question of whether the court is obliged to order partition or sale has also arisen in New South Wales and Queensland, notwithstanding that the relevant legislation differs from the Partition Acts[129]. As regards the former, termination of co-ownership is governed by the Conveyancing Act 1919 (NSW)[130]. Section 66G(1) of the 1919 Act provides that the court 'may' appoint trustees to hold the property on a statutory trust for sale or a statutory trust for partition. A number of cases initially suggested that the court had no discretion under this section, and that it was obliged to appoint trustees for the purpose of either dividing or selling the land[131]. However, the better view appears to be that the court has discretion whether to make an order in these circumstances[132]. Section 66G(4) of the 1919 Act provides that the court 'may' appoint trustees to hold the property on a statutory trust for partition if it is shown that partition would be more beneficial than sale for the owners of more than half in value of

---

[126] Bright J described an order for sale as a 'statutory graft on the right to partition' ([1965] SASR 293 at 296) and see the comments of Simpson CJ in *Oatley v Oatley* (1898) 19 LR (NSW) Eq 122 at 127.

[127] (1993) 177 CLR 635 at 645.

[128] Similar views were expressed by Jones J in *De Campo Holdings v Cianciullo* [1977] WAR 56 at 58 and by Kennedy J in *Martin-Smith v Woodhead* [1990] WAR 62 at 69. In *Norgard v Norgard* (1996) 20 Fam LR, Lexis transcript the court held that it had no discretion to refuse relief entirely when an order for partition or sale was sought under the Property Law Act 1969 (WA) and that it could not refuse to order sale if partition was impracticable or not sought by either party. See further *Tansell v Tansell* (1977) 35 FLR 272.

[129] See ch 4 above, para **[4.01]**.

[130] See generally Butt, *Land Law* (3rd edn, 1996), pp 259-266.

[131] Applying the decision in *Re Fettell* (1952) 52 SR (NSW) 221, Kearney J in *Hayward v Skinner* (1981) 1 NSWLR 590 at 593 observed that:

> 'Mandatory effect is given to the word "may" in sub-s (1) because sale or partition are now the rights inherent in co-ownership ... Section 66G confers the choice of partition or sale, but it is an entitlement of a co-owner to have one or the other.'

See further *Re Cordingley* (1948) 48 SR (NSW) 248 in which it was held that partition and sale are true alternatives under the Conveyancing Act 1919 (NSW), s 66G.

[132] For example, in *Re Jackson and the Conveyancing Act* (1951) 52 SR (NSW) 42 Hardie J held that the court was not obliged to order either partition or sale because the word 'may' in the Conveyancing Act 1919 (NSW), s 66G(1) was permissive. See further *Stephens v Debney* (1959) 60 SR (NSW) 468 (and see the note on this case at (1960) 34 ALJ 23); *Ngatoa v Ford* (1990) 19 NSWLR 72; and *Williams v Legg* (1993) 29 NSWLR 867. In *Re McNamara and the Conveyancing Act* (1961) 78 WN (NSW) 1068 Myers J held that the Conveyancing Act 1919 (NSW), s 66G did not impose an absolute duty on the court to make an order, albeit that the court did not have a general discretion to refuse relief because of hardship or unfairness.

the property[133]. However, the court is not obliged to make such an order simply because partition is shown to be more beneficial than sale[134].

[7.53] As regards Queensland, s 38(1) of the Property Law Act 1974 (Qd) provides that the court 'may' appoint trustees to hold co-owned property on a statutory trust for sale or a statutory trust for partition. In *ex p Eimbert Ltd*[135] the court held that, the right to partition and sale being an incident of co-owned property, it was difficult to conceive of circumstances in which the discretion (if any) conferred by the word 'may' in s 38 would be exercised. However, this approach was criticised in *Re Permanent Trustee Nominees (Canberra) Ltd*[136]. While conceding that there are few defences to partition actions based merely on the circumstances of the parties, Connolly J was nevertheless of the opinion that the jurisdiction under s 38 is not mandatory[137].

B New Zealand

[7.54] Co-owners may compel partition or sale under s 140 of the Property Law Act 1952 (NZ), the provisions of which closely resemble ss 3-5 of the Partition Act 1868. It is well established that the court must make an order for either partition or sale upon such an application being made[138]. Thus, in *Polden v Rowling*[139] McCarthy J conceded that in the event of refusing partition 'sale must be ordered'[140]. The only alternatives available to the court are partition or sale – it cannot refuse both[141].

---

[133] An application under the Conveyancing Act 1919 (NSW), s 66G(4) to show that partition would be more beneficial than sale can be made by any co-owner, no matter how small his share: *Pannizutti v Trask* (1987) 10 NSWLR 531. The onus is on him to prove that partition would be more beneficial: *Larkham v Barber* (18 November 1997, unreported) Supreme Court of New South Wales.

[134] See the comments of Kearney J in *Hayward v Skinner* (1981) 1 NSWLR 590 at 593 and cited with approval by McLaughlin M in *Golby v Golby* (6 September 1996, unreported) Supreme Court of New South Wales. This is similar to the position as regards sale being ordered instead of partition under the Partition Act 1868, s 3: see ch 5 above, paras **[5.17]-[5.24]**.

[135] [1982] Qd R 398.

[136] [1989] Qd R 314.

[137] [1989] Qd R 314 at 321.

[138] See Hinde, McMorland and Sim, *Land Law* (1979) Vol 2, p 934. Similar views were expressed in relation to the Property Law Act 1908 (NZ), s 150 which formerly governed partition and sale of concurrent interests in this jurisdiction. For example, Hutchison J in *Re Moore* [1952] NZLR 273 at 274 observed that 'the Court must decree either a partition or a sale, there being no other course open'. See further Adams, 'Partition of Land' [1952] NZLJ 137 at 138 citing *Gray v Dawson* (1910) 12 GLR 511, and see *Pillar v John Odlin and Co Ltd* [1951] NZLR 220.

[139] [1958] NZLR 31 at 36.

[140] To similar effect is *Bourke v Bourke* [1983] NZFLR 55. The property in question (a family home) being incapable of partition, the court held that it was bound to order sale under the Property Law Act 1952 (NZ), s 140.

[141] See *Hargreaves v Fleming* [1975] NZLR 209; *Revell v Baker* [1984] 3 NZFLR 20; and *McMahon v McMahon* [1996] 3 NZLR 334.

[7.55] However, s 140 has been criticised as lacking in flexibility, and the New Zealand Law Commission has proposed new draft legislation to regulate compulsory partition and sale of concurrent interests in land[142]. This would allow the court to make an order for sale of the property and division of the proceeds, an order for partition or an order requiring one co-owner to purchase the share of another co-owner at a fair and reasonable price[143]. In determining whether to make such an order the court must have regard to a number of specific factors, including the extent of the applicant's interest in the property[144], its nature and location and the hardship caused to the applicant by refusing such an order compared with the hardship caused to any other person by making an order[145]. These proposals are obviously intended to allow courts to adopt a more versatile approach when determining partition actions. However, they have not been carried forward to date.

C Canada

[7.56] As regards the province of Saskatchewan where the 1868 Act remains in force, the prevailing view appears to be that the court must order either partition or sale. For example, in *Bay v Bay*[146] Wright J held that, while the court has discretion whether to order sale under the 1868 Act, a co-owner has an absolute right to partition if the court refuses to order sale[147]. A similar approach has been adopted in the Northwest Territories[148]. In addition to this, a number of cases decided prior to the repeal of the Partition Acts in Alberta[149] held that the

[142] Namely the Draft Property Law Act, ss 254-257 and see New Zealand Law Commission Report No 29, *A New Property Law Act* (1994). For an overview of the proposed draft partition legislation see *McMahon v McMahon* [1997] NZFLR 145.

[143] Draft Property Law Act, s 254(1). The legislation states that the court 'may' make any such order.

[144] As well as the number of other co-owners and the extent of their shares.

[145] Draft Property Law Act, s 256. Other factors which the court must have regard to are legal requirements or restrictions associated with division of the particular property, contributions by a co-owner towards improvements to or maintenance of the property, and any other relevant consideration: Draft Property Law Act, s 256.

[146] (1984) 38 Sask R 101.

[147] Cited with approval by Barclay J in *Bay v Bay* (1986) 5 RFL (3d) 59 and see *Grunert v Grunert* (1960) 32 WWR 509. However, in *Zakoski v Zakoski* (11 June 1984, unreported) Saskatchewan Queen's Bench and *Coburn v Coburn* (25 July 1984, unreported) Saskatchewan Queen's Bench, it was held that co-owners have a *prima facie* right to partition or sale under the Partition Act 1868 applying decisions of the British Columbia courts in *Bergen v Bergen* (1969) 68 WWR 196 and *Harmeling v Harmeling* (1975) 5 WWR 688.

[148] *Moss v Zorn* [1991] NWTR 141.

[149] By the Partition and Sale Act 1979 (Alb), the provisions of which are now contained in the Law of Property Act 1980 (Alb).

remedies of partition or sale under the Partition Acts were a matter of right and not of judicial discretion[150].

[7.57] The more flexible approach demonstrated by courts in other Canadian provinces may be explained by the different legislative provisions regulating compulsory partition and sale which are in force there[151]. For example, both s 2 of the Partition Act 1990 (Ont) and s 2 of the Partition of Property Act 1996 (BC) provide that joint tenants and tenants in common 'may be compelled' to partition or sell the land[152]. Thus, such remedies are at the discretion of the respective courts[153]. However, a co-owner who seeks partition or sale has a *prima facie* right to relief[154], and it has been said that the court's discretion in

---

[150] See *Wickstrand and Mannix v Cavanaugh and Dillon* [1936] 1 WWR 113; *Adelman v Adelman* [1949] 1 WWR 112; and *Robertson v Robertson* [1951] 1 WWR 183. However, this right could be suspended if, for example, there was a dispute as to ownership of the land: see *Kulczycki v Kulczycki* [1949] OWN 177 and *Hicks v Kennedy* (1956) 4 DLR (2d) 320 and see ch 12 below, para **[12.32]**. In *Clarke v Clarke* (1974) 48 DLR (3d) 707 and *Elligott v Elligott* (1977) 6 AR 282 the respective courts also held that a co-owner was entitled to partition or sale under the Partition Acts 1868 and 1876 (the refusal to order relief in these cases may be attributed to the fact that the subject property comprised a matrimonial home: see ch 9 below, para **[9.33]**). It appears that the legislative changes did not alter this position in view of the word 'shall' in the Partition and Sale Act 1979 (Alb): *Ferguson v Coles* (27 February 1981, unreported) Alberta Court of Queen's Bench and *Westlock Foods v Bonel Properties Ltd* (1981) 33 AR 1.

[151] It will be recalled that a number of Canadian provinces have revised partition legislation which differs from the Partition Acts 1868 and 1876: see ch 4 above, paras **[4.01]**.

[152] Similar directions are contained in the Law of Property Act 1987 (Man), s 19; the Partition Act 1989 (NS), s 4; and the Real Property Act 1974 (PEI), s 19. While the provisions of both the Partition of Property Act 1996 (BC) and the Real Property Act 1974 (PEI) which confer jurisdiction on the respective courts to order sale are virtually identical to the Partition Act 1868, ss 3-5 (see ch 4 above, para **[4.01]**), the permissive wording of the legislation allows the court to adopt a more flexible approach.

[153] In *Re Hutcheson and Hutcheson* [1950] OR 265 it was held that the use of the word 'may' in the relevant legislation did not impose an absolute duty on the court to order partition or sale. The Ontario Court of Appeal rejected suggestions that the court was without discretion to refuse an order in light of statements to this effect in *Byall v Byall* (1942) 3 DLR 574 and *Morrison v Morrison* (1917) 39 OLR 163 – such cases did not take account of legislative changes in Ontario and merely adopted the pre-1868 practice of the English Court of Chancery in cases such as *Baring v Nash* (1813) 1 Ves & B 551. Similar problems were associated with the judgment of the Manitoba King's Bench in *Szmando v Szmando* [1940] 1 DLR 222. In *Evans v Evans* [1951] 2 DLR 221 the British Columbia Court of Appeal likewise held that the word 'may' conferred discretion to refuse relief, and see *Rayner v Rayner* (1956) 3 DLR (2d) 522. Prior to the legislative changes, it appears that partition or sale was granted as of right: *Davis v Davis* [1954] 1 DLR 827 and see *Ontario Power Co v Whattler* (1904) 7 OLR 198.

[154] See *Davis v Davis* [1954] 1 DLR 827 in which Laidlaw JA stated that each case should be determined on its particular facts and circumstances, and *Brown v Brown* [1953] 1 DLR 158. See further *McGreer v Green and Westminster Mortgage Corpn* (1960) 22 DLR (2d) 775 and *Davies v McLaren* (1992) RPR (2d) 127.

such cases is 'severely limited'[155]. As regards conditions governing the exercise of this discretion, a co-owner or other person interested in such land in Ontario is entitled to an order for partition or sale unless he acts vexatiously, oppressively or maliciously[156]. The fact that a co-owner simply wants to realise his share of the property does not constitute vexatious or malicious behaviour[157]. Likewise, a mortgagee of an undivided share who seeks sale in the event of default is not acting in this manner but merely exercising his rights[158]. The fact that a family situation has deteriorated to the extent that it is no longer possible for the parties to operate as co-owners and one of them subsequently commences proceedings for partition or sale is not regarded as malicious, vexatious or oppressive conduct[159]. As regards commercial property, the court may make an order for sale of such property notwithstanding that one of the co-owners may have to relocate his business[160] and despite suggestions that sale would expose the opposing co-owners to significant tax liabilities[161]. The fact that the plaintiff has refused an offer to purchase her share from the opposing co-owners is irrelevant in this context[162]. In addition to this, the court may order

155 *Bergen v Bergen* (1969) 68 WWR 196 at 197 per Seaton J. See further *Canadian Imperial Bank of Commerce v Mulholland Construction* (28 January 1998, unreported) Ontario Court (General Division); *Fellows v Lunkenheimer* (25 November 1998, unreported) Ontario Court (General Division); and *Caple v Dolman* (26 November 1999, unreported) Vancouver Registry. In *Michaud v Michaud* (1980) 29 NBR (2d) 591 Abbis J expressed similar views on the corresponding legislation in New Brunswick.

156 See for example, *Davis v Davis* [1954] 1 DLR 827; *Arlow v Arlow* (1990) 27 RFL (3d) 348; *Fellows v Lunkenheimer* (25 November 1998, unreported) Ontario Court (General Division); and *Kalita v Freskiw* (10 December 1998, unreported) Ontario Court (General Division). A co-owner of land in Manitoba likewise has a *prima facie* right to partition or sale in the absence of vexatious or oppressive conduct: *Klemowich v Klemowich* (1954) 14 WWR 418; *Zazalak v Zazalak* (1992) 82 Man R (2d) 153; and *Fergus v Fergus* (12 June 1997, unreported) Manitoba Court of Appeal.

157 *Re Franchi and Franchi* (12 August 1980, unreported) Ontario District Court. In this case, the court made an order for sale notwithstanding that the opposing co-owners resided in a house on the property and occupied a business on part of the land. The applicant's ability to enjoy his inheritance was regarded as more important. The court will not refuse relief simply because the plaintiff is motivated by a change in financial circumstances, and he has not otherwise acted vexatiously, maliciously or oppressively: *Brown v Brown* [1953] 1 DLR 158.

158 *Canadian Imperial Bank of Commerce v Mulholland Construction* (28 January 1998, unreported) Ontario Court (General Division).

159 *Peters v Peters* (8 May 2000, unreported) Ontario Supreme Court of Justice, in which the court made an order for sale of cottage property owned by three brothers as tenants in common.

160 *Re Franchi and Franchi* (12 August 1980, unreported) Ontario District Court, noted above.

161 *Gartree Investments Ltd v Cartree Enterprises Ltd and Elgtree Holdings Ltd* (5 June 2000, unreported) Ontario Superior Court of Justice.

162 Since there is nothing malicious, vexatious or oppressive in the plaintiff wanting to obtain the highest possible price for the property, which might only be determined by placing the property on the market: *Gartree Investments Ltd v Cartree Enterprises Ltd and Elgtree Holdings Ltd* (5 June 2000, unreported) Ontario Superior Court of Justice.

partition or sale even though it would cause such persons difficulty or inconvenience[163].

[7.58] In British Columbia, a co-owner or other interested person has a *prima facie* right to partition or sale unless 'justice' requires that the order be refused[164]. For example, the court may make an order for partition or sale of commercial property[165], unless the latter would be premature in the sense that co-owners who oppose sale have not been given an opportunity to consider offers to purchase from a third party[166]. As regards family property, the fact that a co-owner simply wants to realise her share of the property may not prevent the court from ordering sale[167]. Any inconvenience that might result from an order for partition or sale is irrelevant in this context[168]. However, an order for sale may be refused on considerations of justice, even though partition of the property in question is impracticable[169]. The plaintiff must not be motivated by malice or spite, or by a desire to be vexatious or oppressive[170].

---

[163] *Brown v Brown* [1953] 1 DLR 158 and *Davis v Davis* [1954] 1 DLR 827. In *Re Dibattista and Menecola* (1990) 74 DLR (4th) 569 Brooke JA held that the court should order sale under the terms of the legislation if sale would be more advantageous to the parties than partition and the latter was not feasible. However, in *Rouse v Rouse* (8 March 1999, unreported) Ontario Court (General Division), the court refused to order partition of vacation property owned by the first and second wives of the deceased – division of the property would require a right of way which would interfere with the privacy of the occupants.

[164] See *Harmeling v Harmeling* (1975) 5 WWR 688; *Woodson v Protheroe* (1995) 17 RFL (4th) 104; and *Caple v Dolman* (26 November 1999, unreported) Vancouver Registry. In the latter case Humphries J rejected the 'serious hardship' test put forward in *Dobell v Oman* (6 March 1998, unreported) British Columbia Supreme Court.

[165] *Richardson v McGuiness* (19 December 1996, unreported) British Columbia Supreme Court and *Bourgeault v Walton* (18 August 1998, unreported), British Columbia Supreme Court (valid commercial reasons for wanting sale and partition impracticable).

[166] *Landstadt Estates Management Inc v Inland Gulf Properties Inc* (19 October 1998, unreported) British Columbia Supreme Court, in which Melnick J was of the opinion that an order for sale would be premature in these circumstances. The learned judge also remarked that there was nothing to suggest that the parties' bank would call in a partnership loan if an immediate sale did not take place, as claimed by the applicant.

[167] *Hoggard v Hoggard* (22 November 1996, unreported) British Columbia Supreme Court, in which the court ordered sale of a parcel of land inherited by siblings as tenants in common, but refused to order sale of another portion in the hope that the parties would reach a negotiated solution. It appears that the position is the same in respect of commercial property: *Richardson v McGuiness* (12 December 1996, unreported) British Columbia Supreme Court.

[168] *McGreer v Green and Westminster Mortgage Corpn* (1960) 22 DLR (2d) 775.

[169] See *Cleathero v Cleathero* (1955) 14 WWR 473 in which the court refused to order sale of property which was the wife's only means of supporting herself (wife was involved in the raising of birds, and the property was unique and well-suited for this purpose) yet partition was impracticable.

[170] *McGreer v Green and Westminster Mortgage Corpn* (1960) 22 DLR (2d) 775; *Bergen v Bergen* (1969) 68 WWR 196; and *Reitsma v Reitsma* (1975) 3 WWR 281.

[7.59] The onus of proving that an order for partition or sale should not be made is on the opposing parties[171], and the plaintiff must come to court 'with clean hands'[172]. The legislation confers discretion on the respective courts when determining partition actions, giving the courts a measure of flexibility to determine each case according to its particular merits and to refuse relief in appropriate cases. For example, British Columbia retains the basic structure of the Partition Acts but within a more flexible legislative framework. However, the fact that there is a *prima facie* right to partition or sale suggests that there is still a strong presumption in favour of a co-owner being granted the relief sought and thus releasing him from this relationship when disagreement prevents co-owners from continuing as such. In addition to this, where the rules laid down for the exercise of the court's discretion have been complied with and nothing has been put forward to deprive a co-owner of his right to partition or sale, this discretion is at an end and the order must be made[173].

V A Need for Reform?

[7.60] A literal interpretation of the relevant legislation suggests that courts are restricted to making an order for either partition or sale under the Partition Acts. Since partition was granted as of right in equity prior to 1868 and the Partition Acts only modified this to the extent of introducing a statutory alternative of sale, the court should order either partition or sale upon such an application. It is suggested that the court does have discretion to refuse an order for partition if this would be futile in the sense that a third party could prevent the order from being carried out. However, in keeping with the traditional view that partition and sale are alternatives, the fact that partition is futile is likely to tip the balance heavily in favour of sale and render it difficult for the opposing co-owners to persuade the court to refuse sale.

[7.61] Such a strict approach yields several advantages. A co-owner who wishes to end this relationship may do so notwithstanding the opposition of the other

---

[171] *Re Franchi and Franchi* (21 August 1980, unreported) Ontario General Division and *Caple v Dolman* (26 November 1999, unreported) Vancouver Registry.

[172] *Szuba v Szuba* [1951] 1 DLR 387 and *Harmeling v Harmeling* (1975) 5 WWR 688. In *Rayner v Rayner* (1956) 3 DLR (2d) 522 the court refused a husband's request for sale of a house occupied by his wife on this ground. Sullivan J found that the husband had instituted the action out of spite, and that the husband's treatment of his wife had been 'oppressive, vindictive and unfair': (1956) 3 DLR (2d) 522 at 528. For the doctrine of 'clean hands' to apply, the plaintiff's objectionable conduct must have arisen in the course of the present proceedings and not in the context of other separate proceedings: *Melvin v Melvin* (1975) 58 DLR (3d) 98 (husband's refusal to abide by an order for custody of the children in divorce proceedings was not relevant in a subsequent partition action).

[173] *Re Roblin & Roblin* [1960] OR 157.

co-owners. Both the sixteenth century Statutes of Partition and the Partition Acts were enacted for this specific purpose. Since co-owners often purchase property without making any arrangement as to what will happen in the event that they cannot agree on the use or disposition of the land, the law provides a means for the parties to terminate their relationship and thus avoid stalemate. In these circumstances there is little point in forcing such persons to remain in an acrimonious and ultimately unprofitable relationship against their will, with the result that the land may fall into disuse or one co-owner no longer derives any enjoyment from the property and is prevented from realising his investment. The fact that the court is usually restricted to making an order for partition or sale makes for certainty and accords with the principle of law established since Roman times that no-one can be kept in a partnership or association against his will[174]. The likelihood of an application for partition or sale succeeding in these circumstances may persuade the other co-owners to reach some sort of arrangement for the division or sale of the land, thus avoiding the time and expense of going to court and being forced to submit to an order to this effect.

[7.62] However, the fact that the court's discretion is so circumscribed may operate harshly in some cases. Under the Partition Acts there is a strong emphasis in favour of allowing a co-owner who brings the action to be released from this relationship, in most cases by means of an order for sale of the land in lieu of partition. The court cannot usually consider the personal circumstances of the respective parties to the action. For example, the court may order sale notwithstanding that the property in question comprises a family estate, or that one of the parties operates a business from the property or resides there[175]. The opposing co-owner therefore loses control of the land (and possibly his home and livelihood) and has to be content with a proportionate share of the proceeds of sale. Likewise, the court is not usually obliged to consider the financial circumstances of the parties, and the fact that an order for sale may cause them financial hardship (for example, in terms of not being able to afford a similar property or through a loss of business) is largely irrelevant. Circumstances may arise in which courts would like a greater measure of flexibility in determining partition actions.

[7.63] A preponderance of case law on the subject suggests that the court's discretion under the Partition Acts is limited to making an order for partition or sale, subject to the criteria in ss 3-5 of the 1868 Act being satisfied. Courts in the Republic of Ireland have succeeded in avoiding this, and have demonstrated a tendency to refuse both forms of relief. This practice is largely attributable to

---

174 See ch 3 above, para **[3.21]**.

175 See generally ch 5 above.

Murphy J's ruling in *O'D v O'D*[176] that partition is discretionary, the corollary of which is that a plaintiff no longer has a right to partition if the court refuses to order sale under the Partition Acts. Several recent cases in Northern Ireland have indicated that judges would like more flexibility in determining partition actions[177]. Some measure of flexibility has been achieved by art 49 of the Property (NI) Order 1997. Article 49 reads:

> 'Without prejudice to Article 309 of the Insolvency (Northern Ireland) Order 1989[178], where on the request under the Partition Acts of a party interested (or a person treated as such under Article 48[179]) a court makes an order for partition or sale, the court, on making the order or at any time before its enforcement, may also –
>
> (a) impose such stay or suspension; or
>
> (b) impose such conditions,
>
> as, in the circumstances of the case, it thinks fit; and it may revoke or vary any such stay, suspension or conditions.'[180]

[7.64] However, it has been suggested that art 49 does not go far enough[181]. Having made an order for partition or sale, the court can simply postpone enforcement of the order or attach conditions which must be satisfied before the order can be carried out. The court cannot refuse to make an order under the Partition Acts[182]. Recent reports from the Law Reform Advisory Committee for Northern Ireland and the Office of Law Reform have questioned whether the court should be given a general power to decline to make an order under the Partition Acts in specific circumstances[183].

---

[176] (18 November 1983, unreported) High Court (RI).

[177] For example, in *Ulster Bank Ltd v Carter* [1999] NI 93 at 100 Girvan J suggested that a wider discretion would 'enhance the flexibility of the court to achieve a just result in any given case'. See further *Northern Bank Ltd v Adams* (1 February 1996, unreported) High Court (NI).

[178] See ch 9 below, paras **[9.72]**-**[9.80]**.

[179] Namely chargees and creditors with an order charging land under the Judgments Enforcement (NI) Order 1981: see ch 8 below.

[180] Property (NI) Order 1997, art 49 came into force on 1 September 1997: Property (1997) (Commencement No 1) Order (NI) 1997. Although there is no legislative equivalent in the Republic of Ireland, courts in this jurisdiction have demonstrated a similar approach in partition actions: see ch 12 below, para **[12.42]**.

[181] See the comments of Girvan J in *Ulster Bank Ltd v Carter* [1999] NI 93 at 100.

[182] See *Peck v Peck* [1965] SASR 293 at 299-300 in which Bright J observed that postponing an order for sale under legislation similar to the Partition Acts 1868 and 1876 merely defers enforcement but 'does not go to the right to an order'.

[183] Law Reform Advisory Committee for Northern Ireland Discussion Paper No 5, *Matrimonial Property* (1999) which suggests that courts should have such discretion at least in respect of applications by spouses or by mortgagees or chargees of spouses: p 24 and see ch 9 below, paras **[9.37]** and **[9.71]**.

[7.65] As the law currently stands, courts should confine themselves to making an order for either partition or sale under the Partition Acts or equivalent legislation. However, this aspect of partition actions may be subject to reform in the future.

[183] (contd) Likewise, the Office of Law Reform Consultation Paper, *Orders Charging Land and the Innocent Spouse: Balancing the Interests – A Review of Article 48 of the Property (NI) Order 1997* (July 1999) questioned whether courts should have discretion to refuse sale under the Partition Acts 1868 and 1876 even though partition of the property in question would be impracticable or impossible, and queried whether this should be in all such proceedings or only where it was necessary to protect the occupation rights of non-debtor spouses and co-habitiees: pp 19-21.

Chapter 8

Concurrent Interests in Land as Security

I Introduction[1]

[8.01] Concurrent interests in land may be used as security in a number of situations. The most common scenario occurs where several persons purchase property with financial assistance from a bank or building society. Likewise, improvements to co-owned land or its development may be financed by a loan. Where one or more co-owners incurs a debt, the person to whom it is owed may seek to enforce that debt by converting it into a species of security on the land. The use of concurrent interests in land as security raises two interesting issues. The first relates to the effect of the security on the rights of co-owners vis-à-vis each other. Considerations that may arise are whether co-owners can still compel partition or sale in the event of a dispute over the continued use and occupation of the land, and the implications for both the co-owners and the lender. The second relates to the means in which a lending institution can realise its security if co-owners default on repayments, especially where the security is restricted to an undivided share of land. This chapter sets out the principles that apply in this context, and attempts to clarify the practice which has emerged from the relevant case law.

[8.02] Two introductory matters require attention, the first of which relates to the terminology used throughout this chapter. While the term 'mortgage' is frequently used in a generic sense to denote both mortgages and charges[2], it is used solely in the former context here. Although for practical purposes there is little difference between the two types of security, this distinction is warranted by substantive differences that arise when each is considered in conjunction with the Partition Acts. Likewise, references to a 'mortgage' or a 'charge' do not include the security created by a judgment debt entered against land. The term 'judgment creditor' is employed as a convenient shorthand to denote the owner of an order charging land or judgment mortgage. Secondly, while a significant number of partition actions concerning land used as security relate to spouses

---

1 This chapter contains material previously published in 'Nearly, But Not Quite- Partition Actions in the Wake of Article 48 of the Property (NI) Order 1997' (1999) 50 NILQ 166 and reproduced with the kind permission of SLS Legal Publications (NI).

2 See for example, the Conveyancing Act 1881, s 2(vi) which defines 'mortgage' as including 'any charge on any property for securing money or money's worth'.

and the matrimonial home, the ensuing discussion sets out the general principles which apply in such actions[3]. The practice in relation to matrimonial homes and the statutory provisions regulating property rights of spouses which may be relevant in this context are considered in separate chapters[4].

II Property Subject to a Mortgage

[8.03] The distinguishing feature of a mortgage is that it involves a transfer of interest from borrower to lender[5]. A mortgage may be created by all of the co-owners or by one co-owner over his undivided share of the property. Each transaction has different practical consequences where co-owners wish to end their relationship and as regards the means in which the mortgagee can enforce his security in the event of default.

A Mortgages created by all of the co-owners

[8.04] Where all of the co-owners join in executing a mortgage, the mortgagee's security extends to the entire property[6]. The mortgagee takes a legal or equitable estate in the property, depending on whether he has been given a legal or equitable mortgage, while the co-owners retain the equity of redemption in the property. As co-mortgagors, the co-owners are jointly and severally liable to discharge the sums payable to the mortgagee[7].

[8.05] Where the co-owners are joint tenants, execution of a mortgage by all of them does not sever the joint tenancy[8].

---

3 Northern Irish cases relating to the matrimonial home may nevertheless be useful in establishing general principles applicable to partition actions involving lenders. In contrast, Irish cases involving the matrimonial home provide little assistance since these are typically decided by reference to the Family Home Protection Act 1976, which regulates dealings with the family home.

4 See chs 9 and 10 below.

5 *Santley v Wilde* [1899] 2 Ch 474 per Lindley MR and see the comments of Buckley LJ in *Swiss Bank Corpn v Lloyds Bank* [1982] AC 584 at 585. For an exposition of the law on mortgages in Northern Ireland and the Republic of Ireland see Wylie, *Irish Land Law* (3rd edn, 1997), chs 12 and 13; Lyall, *Land Law in Ireland* (2nd edn, 2000), ch 23; and Coughlan, *Property Law* (2nd edn, 1998), ch 17.

6 It is assumed here that there are no invalidating factors such as undue influence or misrepresentation which might restrict the mortgagee's security to an undivided share of the property: see paras **[8.16]-[8.18]** below.

7 Where two or more persons incur a debt, they are jointly and severally liable to discharge that debt and a co-owner who pays more than his share has a right to a contribution from the others: see ch 11.

8 Since all the joint tenants are acting together: *Re Hayes' Estate* [1901] 1 IR 207 and see *Re Allingham* [1932] VLR 469.

1 Position of the mortgagee

[8.06] If the co-owners default on repayments the mortgagee has a number of remedies available for enforcing his security[9]. For example, the mortgagee might bring an action for debt or appoint a receiver to manage the property. However, the principal remedy is sale of the mortgaged property, preceded by an order for possession to facilitate sale[10]. Because the mortgagee's security relates to the entire property, there is no question of an action for sale being brought under the Partition Acts. Where the mortgage was created by deed[11], s 19 of the Conveyancing Act 1881 confers a statutory power of sale on the mortgagee which arises once the debt has become due and is exercisable in accordance with s 20 of the 1881 Act[12]. Where the mortgage was not created by deed[13], the mortgagee may apply to court for a declaration that the outstanding payments are well-charged on the property and for an order for sale[14].

[8.07] The Partition Acts may, nevertheless, have some application where there are several joint mortgagees of the entire property, albeit that this may be more theoretical than practical. The co-mortgagees take a conveyance of the mortgaged property as tenants in common[15], and appear to have *locus standi* to

---

9 These remedies are discussed in Wylie, *Irish Land Law* (3rd edn, 1997), pp 717-743; Lyall, *Land Law in Ireland* (2nd edn, 2000), pp 788-812; and Coughlan, *Property Law* (2nd edn, 1998), pp 374-382. See further Thompson, *Repossession of Property on Mortgage Default* (1993).

10 An order for possession may be made under the court's inherent jurisdiction: *Re O'Neill* [1967] NI 129. Where the property comprises or includes a dwelling house, courts in Northern Ireland may postpone an order for possession if it appears that the mortgagor will be able to pay any sums due under the mortgage within a reasonable time: Administration of Justice Act 1970, s 36 and Administration of Justice Act 1973, s 8. The relevant factors for exercising this statutory jurisdiction are discussed in *Cheltenham & Gloucester Building Society v Norgan* [1996] 1 All ER 449, but see *National and Provincial Building Society v Lynd* [1996] NI 47. As to the mortgagee's right to possession see para **[8.39]** below.

11 Namely all legal mortgages and all equitable mortgages subject to the exceptions noted below.

12 Conveyancing Act 1881, s 20 provides that the power of sale is exercisable when one of three conditions is satisfied, namely:

(i) non-payment of mortgage money for three months following service of a notice requiring such payment, or
(ii) non-payment of interest for two months, or
(iii) failure to comply with a provision in the mortgage deed or the Conveyancing Act 1881 other than a covenant for payment of money.

As to the application of the proceeds of sale, see the Conveyancing Act 1881, s 21(3).

13 Namely an equitable mortgage by deposit of title deeds unaccompanied by a memorandum under seal and a contract to create a legal mortgage not executed by deed.

14 Wylie, *Irish Land Law* (3rd edn, 1997), pp 731-732.

15 Depending on the type of mortgagee created, the mortgagees take a legal or an equitable interest in the property as tenants in common: *Drake v Templeton* (1913) 16 CLR 153.

bring a partition action[16]. In theory, any one of them could bring an action for partition or sale of the mortgaged property against the wishes of the other mortgagees and, more importantly, against the wishes of the mortgagors. However, this would almost certainly never occur in practice. Apart from the fact that it is difficult to see any reason why a co-mortgagee would want to divide or sell the property itself, it is likely that the peculiar nature of the mortgage transaction would prevent him from bringing such an action. The primary consideration here would not be the position of the other mortgagees, but the position of the mortgagors. Since the mortgagors are regarded as the owners of the property in equity[17], it is unlikely that the court would make an order for partition of the property at the instance of a mortgagee when this might have significant practical implications for the mortgagors.

[8.08] Likewise, it is a fundamental aspect of the mortgage transaction that the mortgagor may redeem the mortgage by repayment of the mortgage debt. Accordingly, even if a co-mortgagee could obtain an order for sale under the Partition Acts, any sale would be subject to the equitable rights of the mortgagors, the practical effect of which would be to render the land unmarketable. There is no means of allowing the rights of the mortgagor to be overridden in an order for sale under the Partition Acts. Even if there were, it is inconceivable that a court would order sale if the effect of the order was to destroy the rights of a borrower who was not in default under the mortgage.

2 Position of the mortgagors

[8.09] It is well-established that a mortgage created by all the co-owners does not prevent one or more of them from compelling partition or sale of the mortgaged property under the Partition Acts[18]. Yet this pre-supposes that the

---

15 (contd) This rule prevails regardless of whether each mortgagee has advanced an equal share of the money or whether the conveyance of the property has been made to them jointly: *Rigden v Vallier* (1751) 3 Atk 731. The practice where there are two or more co-mortgagees must be distinguished from the practice where there are two or more successive mortgagees. Here each mortgagee has individual rights and remedies against the mortgaged property and priority is determined according to the normal rules: see Wylie, *Irish Land Law* (3rd edn, 1997), pp 775-789.

16 The *locus standi* test requires that the plaintiff has a legal or equitable estate or interest which is vested in possession or carries with it an immediate right to possession: see ch 4 above.

17 *Blake v Foster* (1814) 2 Ball & B 389 and see Wylie, *Irish Land Law* (3rd edn, 1997), p 687.

18 See for example, *Martyn v Perryman* (1662) 1 Rep Ch 125 and the cases cited below. See further White and Tudor, *A Selection of Leading Cases in Equity* (7th edn, 1897), pp 200-201 and *Daniell's Chancery Practice* (8th edn, 1914), pp 1170-1171. Inquiries may be directed to ascertain whether there are any incumbrances affecting the property, the amount due under each and the priority of the incumbrances: see the form of order in Seton, *Forms of Judgments and Orders in the High Court of Justice and the Court of Appeal* (6th edn, 1901), pp 1856-1857 and see *Fawthrop v Stocks* [1884] WN 118.

mortgagors have the requisite *locus standi* to maintain such an action. The mortgagors, by virtue of their equity of redemption, retain an equitable interest in the property[19] that satisfies the first aspect of the *locus standi* test. Yet, this equitable interest does not confer any right to possession. The fact that the mortgagors are regarded as the owners of the mortgaged property in equity[20] is irrelevant since equity cannot contradict the common law rule that the right to possession passes to the mortgagee upon execution of the mortgage[21]. However, the mortgagee will almost certainly grant the mortgagors a licence to occupy the property for the duration of the mortgage term so long as they are not in default[22]. In other words, the mortgagors' entitlement to possession is not derived from their equitable interest but from the mortgagee's licence or permission to occupy the property[23]. The mortgagors therefore have an equitable interest coupled with an immediate right to possession.

[8.10] It is a fundamental aspect of the law on partition that an order for partition or sale does not prejudice third parties with rights over the property[24]. Cases such as *Sinclair v James*[25] accordingly held that, where a mortgage had been created by all the co-owners, the mortgagee was not a necessary party to a subsequent partition action and did not have to be served with notice of the judgment[26]. This practice still applies today[27]. Since a mortgagee of the entirety

---

19 See *Casburne v Inglis* (1738) 2 Jac & W 194 and *Lloyd v Lander* (1821) 5 Madd 282.

20 *Blake v Foster* (1814) 2 Ball & B 389 and see Wylie, *Irish Land Law* (3rd edn, 1997), p 687.

21 See generally paras **[8.39]-[8.40]**, below.

22 See Wylie, *Irish Land Law* (3rd edn, 1997), p 751 and Lyall, *Land Law in Ireland* (2nd edn, 2000), p 789.

23 Such possession is incidental to enjoyment of their equitable interest by the mortgagors.

24 See ch 4 above, paras **[4.61]-[4.67]**.

25 [1894] 3 Ch D 554.

26 In *Sinclair v James* [1894] 3 Ch D 554, the disputed property was subject to several joint mortgages, as well as a mortgage affecting the plaintiff's undivided share. The several mortgagees and the plaintiff's mortgagee having been joined as parties, the action was dismissed against the former. North J remarked at 556:

> 'To take the case of the overriding mortgagees, I cannot see any reason why they should be parties to the action, and no partition of the interests of persons entitled to the equity of redemption can affect them. A partition of the equity of redemption cannot diminish or affect their rights.'

Similar views were expressed in *Swan v Swan* (1820) 8 Price 518; *Watkins v Williams* (1851) 3 Mac & G 622; and *Waite v Bingley* (1882) 21 Ch D 674. See further Foster, *The Law on Joint Ownership and Partition of Real Estate* (1878), p 7; Osborne, *The Jurisdiction and Practice of the County Courts in Ireland in Equity and Probate Matters* (2nd edn, 1910), p 196; and *Daniell's Chancery Practice* (8th edn, 1914), p 1173.

27 Valentine, *Civil Proceedings – The Supreme Court* (1997), p 435 and *Northern Bank Ltd v Adams* (1 February 1996, unreported) High Court (NI), at 14. See further *Eagles v Eagles* [1960] VR 400 and *Fulton v 523 Nominees Pty Ltd* [1984] VR 200 and see Robinson, *The Property Law Act Victoria* (1992), p 474.

is not a necessary party and his consent is not required, he cannot prevent the co-owners from dividing or selling the mortgaged property[28]. However, the order for partition or sale is subject to the rights of the mortgagee; these rights can only be altered with the mortgagee's consent.

[8.11] Where the court makes an order for sale under the Partition Acts, the standard form of order is that the property be sold:

> 'free from the incumbrances of such of the incumbrancers as shall consent, and subject to the incumbrances of such of them as shall not consent.'[29]

[8.12] If the mortgagee consents to sale any sums owed to him under the mortgage are paid out of the proceeds of sale, and the balance paid to the former co-owners. If the mortgagee does not consent, then the property is sold subject to the mortgage. However, in practical terms it may prove difficult to sell the property if the mortgagee does not consent. A prospective purchaser is unlikely to purchase property that is subject to a subsisting mortgage. In these circumstances, the co-owner who desires sale of the property may have to redeem the mortgage prior to bringing the partition action. This would allow sale of the property free from any incumbrance. However, this course of action may prove difficult. All the co-owners should usually concur in redeeming a joint mortgage[30]. If only one co-owner wishes to redeem, he must pay the entire

---

27 (contd) In *Martin-Smith v Woodhead* [1990] WAR 62 the court held that, while a mortgagee of the entirety is not a necessary party, he should be considered in relation to the form of order made. In *Witchard v Witchard* (1975) 6 ACTR 31 counsel for the defendant conceded that a mortgagee of the entirety was not a necessary party to a partition action, but argued that the court should not order sale without the mortgagee's concurrence. Rejecting this argument, Blackburn J held that the court did not require a mortgagee of the entirety to consent to a sale of the mortgaged property as its security would not be affected by such an order. Contrast this with *McMahon v A F Wade Pty Ltd* [1983] WAR 152 at 155 in which Pidgeon J remarked:

> 'The mortgagee would have taken a mortgage of the whole of the land and each co-owner would have been a party to it and a co-owner's action in doing this would have affected his right to claim a sale in lieu of partition. The mortgagee may not wish to have his mortgage paid out.'

Similarly, in *Kluss v Kluss* [1947] 2 WWR 379 Williams CJKB stated that partition was not available as of right where there was an incumbrance on the property, and that the incumbrancer should be made a party to the action to determine whether he consented to partition.

28 Contrast this with the futility cases discussed in ch 7 above, which require the consent of a third party before an order for partition can be made.

29 *Waite v Bingley* (1882) 21 Ch D 674 at 683-684. See further Seton, *Forms of Judgments and Orders in the High Court of Justice and the Court of Appeal* (6th edn, 1901), pp 1856-1857; *Sinclair v James* [1894] 3 Ch 554; *McMahon v A F Wade* [1983] WAR 152; and *Fulton v 523 Nominees Pty Ltd* [1984] VR 200.

30 Beddoes, *A Concise Treatise on the Law of Mortgages* (1893), p 153 citing *Bolton v Salmon* (1891) 2 Ch 48.

mortgage debt[31], since an individual co-owner has no right to redeem his share separately[32]. This might not be possible in financial terms. If the mortgagee did not agree to redemption, the mortgagor would have to apply to court to exercise his right assuming that the date for redemption had passed[33].

[8.13] Where the court makes an order for partition, this is in respect of the equity of redemption in the property[34]. The mutual conveyances between the former co-owners which are necessary to complete the partition only affect their equitable interests in the property[35]. Following partition the mortgagors remain jointly and severally liable to discharge the mortgage payments as the mortgage still attaches to the entire property, even though it is held in divided shares[36]. Thus the mortgagee may still have recourse to the entire property in the event of default. If a mortgagor wishes to sell his share of the property after partition, he can only do so on the condition of redeeming the mortgage by discharging the outstanding payments[37].

[8.14] However, while it may be true to say that a mortgagee is not a necessary party to an action for partition, such an order may have wider implications for the respective parties than an order for sale. With the emergence of 'a real-

31 *Adams v Keers* (1920) 46 OLR 523.

32 See *Welman v Warren* (1709) 2 Eq Cas Abr 595; *Marquis of Cholmondeley v Lord Clinton* (1820) 2 Jac & W 1; and *Davis v White* (1869) 16 Gr 312.

33 Wylie, *Irish Land Law* (3rd edn, 1997), pp 760-764. Even if this date had passed, the mortgagor would have to comply with the formalities for doing so as prescribed by the court and the mortgage document itself.

34 *Sinclair v James* [1894] 3 Ch D 554 and *Daniell's Chancery Practice* (8th edn, 1914), p 1170. See however, *Fleet v Fleet* (1925) 28 OWN 193.

35 While it is usually necessary to have the legal title before the court in order to execute the requisite conveyances on partition (or sale) that is not the case here. Partition is subject to the mortgagee's rights and is only in respect of the equity of redemption: Walker, *The Partition Acts, 1868 and 1876* (1882), p 11. A conveyance of the legal estate will only take place when the mortgage debt has been discharged and the lender has to reconvey the property – in these circumstances, he will have to execute separate conveyances to each party in accordance with his/her undivided share as instructed by the joint borrowers.

36 The parties, while no longer co-owners, are still co-mortgagors. In *Fulton v 523 Nominees* [1984] VR 200 at 205 Tadgell J suggested that this practice would only apply where the mortgagee consented to partition. If he did not consent, then the mortgage would have to be redeemed citing *Gibbs v Haydon* (1882) 30 WR 726. However, the latter case was a partition action involving a mortgagee of an undivided share of land where the practice differs significantly: see para **[8.24]** below.

37 See *Adams v Keers* (1920) 46 OLR 523. Again, if only one of the co-owners wishes to redeem, he must pay the entire mortgage debt and comply with the formalities outlined above. It may be possible for a co-owner to secure a mortgage on his share of the land following partition in order to redeem a prior joint mortgage: see *McMeekin v Shuter* (1914) 31 WN (NSW) 107.

property-mortgaged-to-a-building-society-owning democracy'[38], lending institutions have moved to protect their interests in property used as security. Mortgages are invariably granted subject to a comprehensive set of conditions prescribing the borrower's obligations and setting out the rights and remedies of the lender in the event of default. These are likely to contain a covenant prohibiting the borrower from doing anything that might prejudice the value of the lender's security while any part of the mortgage debt is outstanding. If the borrower is in breach of covenant, the mortgagee may seek to enforce his security. As regards partition actions between co-mortgagors, this covenant does not alter the fact that the mortgagee cannot take any steps to prevent partition because he is not a necessary party to the action – the order may still be made without the mortgagee's consent. However, the mortgagee may take action if he becomes aware that the property has been partitioned and is of the opinion that the value of the security has diminished accordingly. While such action is unlikely where the mortgage payments are still being met in full, the mortgagee might seek to enforce his security if, for example, partition has resulted in the end of a viable business enterprise formerly conducted on the property or division of the land has reduced its development potential.

B Mortgages created by one of the co-owners

[8.15] Different considerations arise when the mortgagee's security only extends to an undivided share of one co-owner. This typically occurs where the mortgagee initially believes that his security comprises the interests of all the co-owners, but subsequently discovers that it is restricted to an undivided share[39].

1 Circumstances giving rise to a mortgage of an undivided share of land

[8.16] Where title to the property is in joint names, the mortgagee's security will be so restricted if the mortgagor has forged the signature of another co-owner on the documents executing the mortgage[40] or where the other co-owner was not a party to the mortgage[41]. Even if the other co-owner consents to the mortgage,

---

[38] *Pettitt v Pettitt* [1969] 2 All ER 385 at 414 per Lord Diplock.

[39] It is possible that co-owners may specifically intend the mortgage to be confined to an undivided share, although this is rare in practice. Because of the difficulties associated with enforcing this type of security (see below) lenders will usually be reluctant to grant a mortgage of an undivided share of land.

[40] However, there is some doubt as to whether the security extends to the forger's share of the property in these circumstances or whether the entire transaction is void. For the former view see *First National Securities v Hegerty* [1984] 3 All ER 641; *Canada Life Assurance Co v Kennedy* (1978) 21 OR (2d) 83; *Ahmed v Kendrick* (1987) 56 P & CR 120; and *National Commercial Banking Corpn of Australia v Hedley* (1984) NSW Conv R 55-211 (appealed on different grounds). For the contrary view, see *Penn v Bristol and West Building Society* [1995] 2 FLR 938 (case went to appeal on another point) and *Flourentzou v Commonwealth Bank of Australia* (23 May 1997, unreported) Supreme Court of New South Wales.

[41] See for example, *Fulton v 523 Nominees* [1984] VR 200 and *GNR v KAR* (March 1981, unreported) High Court (RI).

this consent may be ineffective if it has been procured by undue influence[42] or by some other vitiating factor such as fraud or deception[43].

[8.17] Where the mortgagor is the sole legal owner, another person may assert a prior beneficial interest in the property[44]. If the mortgagee had actual or constructive notice of this interest, the rights of the beneficial co-owner take priority to those of the mortgagee and the security is restricted to the mortgagor's undivided beneficial interest in the land. The criteria for determining whether the mortgagee's interests are subordinate to prior interests affecting the land by virtue of the doctrine of notice are contained in s 3(1) of the Conveyancing Act 1882[45]. In practical terms, it may be difficult for the mortgagee to deny that he had actual notice of an equitable co-owner[46]. However, the concept of constructive notice raises more difficult issues, since the mortgagee must have carried out the reasonable inquiries and inspections prescribed by s 3(1) to avoid being fixed with such notice. A number of rules may be discerned from the relevant case law.

[8.18] What constitutes 'reasonable inquiries' is determined by an objective standard[47]. If the mortgagee fails to inquire whether there are other persons having any interest in the property, he will be fixed with constructive notice of a prior equitable interest[48]. However, this is subject to two qualifications. Firstly, a

---

41 (contd) A mortgage will only bind the share of the party who signed the relevant documents: *Katsaitus v Commonwealth Bank of Australia* (1987) 5 BPR 12,049 (mortgage documents executed on the basis that both husband and wife would sign them, but wife subsequently refused to do so).

42 See *Barclay's Bank plc v O'Brien* [1992] 4 All ER 983 and *CIBC Mortgages plc v Pitt* [1994] 1 AC 200. For a review of the relevant authorities since these cases see *Royal Bank of Scotland v Etridge (No 2)* [1998] 4 All ER 705 and Draper, 'Undue Influence: A Review' [1999] Conv 176. The burden of proof is on the party alleging that the lender had notice of any undue influence: *Barclay's Bank v Boulter* [1999] 4 All ER 513.

43 See *Northern Bank Ltd v Adams* (1 February 1996, unreported) High Court (NI).

44 This beneficial interest may be established by means of a resulting or constructive trust, but must be a prior beneficial interest. If the beneficial interest was acquired after the mortgage was created, the mortgagee's interest takes priority - *K v K* (October 1980, unreported) High Court (RI).

45 See Pearce, 'Joint Occupation and the Doctrine of Notice' (1980) 15 Ir Jur (NS) 211; Wallace, *Occupiers' Rights and Constructive Notice* (1982); and Conlon, 'Beneficial Interests, Conveyancers and the Occupational Hazard' (1985) 79 Gaz ILSI 59.

46 For example, if a prior beneficial interest was disclosed to the mortgagee prior to execution of the mortgage.

47 See *Northern Bank Ltd v Henry* [1981] IR 1 and *Allied Irish Banks Ltd v McWilliams* [1982] NI 157. A lender need not be unduly suspicious, but merely has to act as a reasonably prudent lender would act in those circumstances having regard to all matters known to him at that particular time: *Woolwich v Comm* (27 July 1999, unreported) Court of Appeal. However, the fact that a lender has complied with standard conveyancing practices is irrelevant if he has failed to make the appropriate inquiries: *Roche v Peilow* [1985] IR 232.

48 See *Northern Bank Ltd v Beattie* [1982] 18 NIJB 1 and *Northern Bank Ltd v Henry* [1981] IR 1.

mortgagee will not be fixed with constructive notice of matters that he might reasonably have expected the person claiming the beneficial interest to have volunteered[49]. Secondly, the mortgagee's interest will take priority if this person knew that the mortgage was being executed or was necessary to purchase the property[50]. Since the decision in *William's & Glyn's Bank Ltd v Boland*[51], it has become standard practice for lending institutions to inquire whether there are any persons over the age of 17 in occupation of the property being used as security prior to the execution of the mortgage. These persons will be required to sign a consent form, postponing their present and future interests or rights in the property in favour of the mortgagee as a precondition to granting the mortgage. This allows the mortgagee to enforce his security in the event of the mortgagor defaulting on repayments, and goes a substantial way towards eliminating the perils of constructive notice[52].

2 Severance

[8.19] Where the co-owners are joint tenants, creation of a mortgage by one of them effects a severance by partial alienation so that the mortgagor becomes a tenant in common with the remaining co-owners who continue to hold their shares as joint tenants[53]. The joint tenancy is not restored when the mortgage debt is discharged and the lender reconveys the interest to the mortgagor[54].

---

49 For example, where the person asserting a prior beneficial interest was present during discussions with the bank manager about creation of the mortgage, but did not disclose this interest: *Ulster Bank Ltd v Shanks* [1982] NI 143. See further *Northern Bank Ltd v McNeill* (14 February 1986, unreported) High Court (NI) and *Midland Bank Ltd v Farmpride Hatcheries Ltd and Willey* (1981) 260 EG 493.

50 *Bristol and West Building Society v Henning* [1985] 2 All ER 606. The fact that the resulting mortgage is for a sum greater than that which was originally suggested is irrelevant: *Abbey National Building Society v Cann* [1990] 1 All ER 1085. In *Doherty v Doherty* [1991] 2 IR 458 a husband and wife made a joint statutory declaration (as required under the terms of the Family Home Protection Act 1976: see ch 10 below) that the family home was in the sole name of the husband when applying for a mortgage of the property. The court held that, as a result of the wife's conduct and declaration, there was no duty on the lender to inquire whether she had any beneficial interest in the property and the wife was estopped from asserting her interest in priority to that of the mortgagee (applying *Harrison v Harrison* (20 June 1989, unreported) High Court (RI)).

51 [1980] 2 All ER 408.

52 However, a consent form may be invalid if the relevant signature has been obtained by undue influence or by fraud or misrepresentation: see *Midland Bank plc v Cooke* [1995] 4 All ER 562.

53 *York v Stone* (1709) 1 Salk 158 and *Re Pollard's Estate* (1863) 3 De G J & Sm 541. See further *Lyons v Lyons* [1967] VR 169, although the position is different in Australia as regards Torrens land since a mortgage of such property operates in the same way as a charge: see paras **[8.57]**-**[8.58]** below. In this context, it is irrelevant whether the mortgage is legal or equitable, since an equitable mortgage of an undivided share of land also effects a severance: see *Re Sharer* (1912) 57 Sol Jo 60 and Mendes Da Costa, 'Co-Ownership Under Victorian Land Law' (1962) 3 Melb Univ Law Rev 433 at 447, but see the comments of Meagher JA in *Guthrie v Australia and New Zealand Banking Group Ltd* (1991) 23 NSWLR 672 at 680.

54 *Re Pollard's Estate* (1863) 3 De G J & Sm 541 and see McClean, 'Severance of Joint Tenancies' (1979) 57 Can Bar Rev 1 at 12.

3 Position of the mortgagor and the other co-owners

[8.20] Where the mortgage only affects an undivided share of land, the alternatives of partition or sale under the Partition Acts are still available to any co-owner wishing to enjoy his share in severalty. However, a distinction should be made in respect of a partition action by the mortgagor and an action by a co-owner whose share is not incumbered.

(a) Partition actions by the mortgagor

[8.21] The mortgagor retains his equity of redemption and therefore has *locus standi* to maintain a partition action against the other co-owners[55]. However, the mortgagee must be made a party to the action[56]. The reason for this appears to be that the character of the mortgaged property will be altered by an order for partition or sale so that the mortgagee's security may be affected by the order[57]. Furthermore, the person in whom the legal estate is vested should usually be before the court[58].

[8.22] Where the relief sought is partition, the nature of the mortgagee's security would be altered by such an order. As North J explained in *Sinclair v James*[59]:

> 'It cannot be said that [a mortgagee of an undivided share] ... has no interest in a partition of the property. His mortgage is the mortgage of an undivided [share] of an equity of redemption. If a partition were made he would be the mortgagee of a divided share ...'[60]

[8.23] If the mortgagee consents to partition, the mortgagor's divided share remains subject to the mortgage[61]. However, it is doubtful whether a mortgagee

---

55 See para **[8.09]** above. It is submitted that White and Tudor, *A Selection of Leading Cases in Equity* (7th edn, 1897), p 200 is erroneous in suggesting that a mortgagor of an undivided share cannot bring a partition action unless his mortgagee joins because he does not have the necessary possession.

56 Osborne, *The Jurisdiction and Practice of the County Courts in Ireland in Equity and Probate Matters* (2nd edn, 1910), p 196 and Valentine, *Civil Proceedings – The Supreme Court* (1997), p 435. See further *Catton v Banks* [1893] 2 Ch 221; *Sinclair v James* [1894] 3 Ch 554; *Re McCully* (1911) 23 OLR 156; and *Fulton v 523 Nominees* [1984] VR 200. In *McDougall v McDougall* (1868) 143 Gr 267 where an order for partition was made at the request of a mortgagor of an undivided share without joining his mortgagee, it was suggested that the mortgagee might be made a party at the Master's office.

57 White and Tudor, *A Selection of Leading Cases in Equity* (7th edn, 1897), p 200 and the authorities referred to below.

58 In order to be bound by the judgment and to facilitate execution of the requisite conveyances on partition or sale: see ch 12 below, para **[12.07]**.

59 [1894] 3 Ch 554 at 556.

60 See further 21 *Halsbury's Laws of England* (1st edn, 1912), p 840 and *Fulton v 523 Nominees Pty Ltd* [1984] VR 200.

61 The fact that the mortgagee had notice of the proposed partition yet failed to object may be regarded as tantamount to consent: *581352 Ontario Ltd v Greenbanktree Power Corpn* (1994) 71 OAC 338.

would agree to this in practice. Lending institutions are careful to ensure that the mortgagor's actions do not alter the value of their security. Although the mortgagee may still seek possession and sale of the mortgagor's share if he defaults following partition, sale of a divided share of land might not realise as much as a proportionate part of the value of the entire property upon sale. The mortgagee would certainly oppose partition where the realisable monetary value of this divided share would not be sufficient to discharge the mortgage debt, but where a sale of the entirety would raise enough money to discharge this debt from the mortgagor's share of the proceeds of sale[62].

[8.24] If the mortgagee does not consent, the mortgagor cannot compel partition without first redeeming the mortgage[63]. In *Gibbs v Haydon*[64] where the plaintiff had mortgaged his share of the land and subsequently brought a partition action, Fry J remarked:

> 'In my judgment the plaintiff has, by the execution of the mortgage, lost his right to partition. As a general rule a mortgagor cannot enforce any rights against the mortgagee unless he is at the same time prepared to redeem the mortgage. It is therefore wrong that the character of the property in the hands of the mortgagee should, upon the application of the mortgagor, be altered and the mortgagee not paid off.'[65]

[8.25] In *Oatley v Oatley*[66] Simpson CJ interpreted these remarks as meaning that, where the mortgagee objects to partition, the mortgagor's right to partition is not lost but merely suspended until redemption of the mortgage. However, it appears that the mortgagor cannot combine a claim against his mortgagee for redemption and a claim for partition against the other co-owners in the same action, the rationale for this being the fundamentally different nature of the two proceedings[67].

---

62 The amount secured by the mortgage may exceed the value of the mortgagor's share if the mortgagee initially believes that the mortgage extends to the interests of all the co-owners but subsequently discovers that it is restricted to that of the mortgagor.

63 See *Dalton v Hayter* (1844) 7 Beav 313. As to the relevant formalities see para **[8.12]** above.

64 (1882) 30 WR 726.

65 Similar views were expressed in *Watkins v Williams* (1851) 3 Mac & G 622; *Sinclair v James* [1894] 3 Ch 554; *Oatley v Oatley* (1898) 19 NSWR (Eq) 129; *Re McCully* (1911) 23 OLR 156; and *Fulton v 523 Nominees* [1984] VR 200. See further *Daniell's Chancery Practice* (8th edn, 1914), p 1171; Beddoes, *A Concise Treatise on the Law of Mortgages* (1893), p 128; and 21 *Halsbury's Laws of England* (1st edn, 1912), p 840. This rule is not altered by the fact that the mortgagee of the undivided share is one of the other co-owners: *Gibbs v Haydon* (1882) 30 WR 726 and *Oatley v Oatley*.

66 (1898) 19 NSWR (Eq) 129 at 132.

67 *Sinclair v James* [1894] 3 Ch 554 and *Oatley v Oatley* (1898) 19 NSWR (Eq) 129. The other co-owners are not necessary parties to the mortgagor's action to redeem his mortgage: Beddoes, *A Concise Treatise on the Law of Mortgages* (1893), p 153.

[8.26] Similar rules apply where the relief sought by the mortgagor is sale in lieu of partition. If the mortgagee consents to sale, the property is sold free from the mortgage and the outstanding debt deducted from the mortgagor's share of the proceeds of sale. However, if the mortgagee does not consent, the property is sold subject to the mortgage affecting the mortgagor's share[68]. Again, the mortgagor may seek to redeem the mortgage prior to bringing the partition action to ensure a realistic prospect of sale.

[8.27] Despite the fact that the mortgagee is a necessary party to a partition action in these circumstances and may not consent to the proposed division or sale of the property, this is not an example of a futility case[69]. In one sense the mortgagee's refusal to consent here has wider implications for the mortgagor in that he may be prevented from obtaining both partition and sale[70]. However, withholding of consent does not present a permanent obstacle to the mortgagor obtaining relief under the Partition Acts. If the mortgagor waits until the date of redemption, he can redeem the mortgage and bring an action for partition or sale of the property.

(b) Partition actions by the other co-owners

[8.28] A co-owner whose interest is not subject to the mortgage may compel partition or sale of the property under the Partition Acts. While the mortgagee is a necessary party to the action[71], the fact that he objects to the proposed division or sale is irrelevant in this context. In *Hill v Maunsell-Eyre*[72] Overend J provided the following analogy:

> 'A shareholder in a company takes his shares subject to the company's statutory right to alter its articles ..., and I am of the opinion that similarly a mortgagee who takes a mortgage of an undivided share of property takes it subject to the statutory rights of co-owners to seek partition or sale in lieu thereof.'

[8.29] Likewise, in *McMahon v A F Wade*[73] Pidgeon J remarked:

> 'If the plaintiff shows he is entitled to a sale ... then the legal owner of the remaining interest must submit to a sale and I consider this must apply in respect of any person who holds a lesser interest, including an encumbrance in the undivided share of the other party ... [A]nyone acquiring an undivided share or

---

68 *Oatley v Oatley* (1898) 19 NSWR (Eq) 129 and *Fulton v 523 Nominees* [1984] VR 200, and see the form of order in *Waite v Bingley* (1882) 21 Ch D 674 noted at para **[8.11]** above.

69 See ch 7 above.

70 In futility cases, the third party consent is only necessary to make an order for partition, but an order for sale may be made in the absence of such consent.

71 As the nature of his security will be altered by such an order.

72 [1944] IR 499 at 505.

73 [1983] WAR 152 at 155.

interest in such a share knows that it is being acquired subject to the rights of the other co-owners to apply for a partition ...'[74]

[8.30] Where the relief sought is physical partition, the mortgage attaches to the mortgagor's divided share following partition and the other co-owners take their respective shares free from any incumbrance[75].

[8.31] However, a divergence of opinion has arisen in two Australian cases as regards the appropriate form of order where a co-owner of an unincumbered share seeks sale in lieu of partition. In *McMahon v A F Wade*[76], the first and third defendants were tenants in common of a plot of land. The first defendant mortgaged his share to the second defendant. The third defendant subsequently transferred her interest to the plaintiff who brought an action for sale. Pidgeon J had to determine whether he could order the land to be sold free from the second defendant's mortgage. The first defendant submitted that no such power existed and referred to the form of order made in cases such as *Waite v Bingley*[77]. He argued that if the land was sold subject to the mortgage he would receive a share of the proceeds of sale, whereas if it was sold free from the mortgage the proceeds would be applied towards reducing a debt which he did not wish to have reduced. Pidgeon J accepted that, in view of this argument, the court should usually order property to be sold subject to incumbrances. However, he concluded that where a partition action was brought by a co-owner of an unincumbered share the property should be sold free from an incumbrance affecting the share of another co-owner since:

> '... it would be completely unsaleable if offered with this particular encumbrance and the effect of the encumbrance would therefore be that it deprives the ... co-owner of the right he would otherwise have for a sale.'[78]

---

[74] See further the comments of Shadwell VC in *Cooper v Fisher* (1841) 10 LJ Ch 221 at 222 and those of Kekewich J in *Catton v Banks* [1893] 2 Ch 221 at 227.

[75] See for example, *Bisson v Luciani* (1982) 37 OR (2d) 257. See further *Fulton v 523 Nominees* [1984] VR 200 at 206-208 and the cases of *Jackson v Pierce* (1813) 10 Johnson's Reports 413 and *Wright v Vickers* (1876) 81 Pa 122 discussed therein. In *Fulton* Tadgell J remarked that the plaintiff in these circumstances would not have to procure the redemption of his co-tenant's mortgage if the mortgagee opposed the division. However, it is difficult to see how the plaintiff could procure such a redemption even if it were necessary. The mortgage exists only between the co-tenant and his mortgagee, and the plaintiff as a third party cannot compel the mortgagee (or the mortgagor) to redeem the mortgage if he does not want to.

[76] [1983] WAR 152.

[77] Namely, that the land be sold free from the incumbrances of the incumbrancers who consent and subject to the incumbrances of those who do not consent: see para **[8.11]** above.

[78] [1983] WAR 152 at 154.

Pidgeon J accordingly ordered that the land be sold free from the second defendant's mortgage and that the first defendant's share of the proceeds of sale be paid to the former to satisfy the mortgage debt.

[8.32] The opposite view was taken in *Fulton v 523 Nominees*[79]. Again a tenant in common of land brought a partition action against the other tenant in common whose share of the land was subject to a mortgage. Tadgell J raised the issue of whether the plaintiff was entitled to partition or sale of the property free from the mortgage without obtaining the mortgagee's consent or redeeming or procuring the redemption of his co-tenant's mortgage. The learned judge held that after partition the mortgage would affect the defendant's share of the land, since an incumbrancer of an undivided share takes his security subject to the right of the other co-owners to compel partition. To hold otherwise would mean that any co-owner could thwart partition by mortgaging his share[80].

[8.33] However, Tadgell J declined to apply the same reasoning to an order for sale, taking the view that the property could only be sold subject to the mortgage since the lender's rights could not be affected against his wishes by an order of the court. Partition or sale could not affect a mortgagee's interest[81], and this would be infringed if the property were sold free from the mortgage and the mortgagee's interest became a proportion of the proceeds of sale. Tadgell J based his decision on a number of cases decided in the New York Court of Chancery[82], pointing out that legislation had been introduced in several American States to facilitate sale of property free from mortgages affecting an undivided share. He concluded:

> 'Any modification of a mortgagee's rights by virtue of a sale could only be achieved pursuant to statute and no such statute exists in this State. I have, therefore, no jurisdiction to despoil the mortgagee's rights under the third mortgage by directing that [the mortgagor] discharge it upon any sale.'[83]

The plaintiff having accepted that the land could not be sold if offered subject to the defendant's mortgage, Tadgell J declined to order sale but without prejudice to the plaintiff's right to seek partition in subsequent proceedings.

---

79 [1984] VR 200.

80 [1984] VR 200 at 207 citing the American cases of *Wright v Vickers* (1876) 81 Pa 122 and *Loomis v Riley* (1860) 24 Ill 307.

81 Reference was made to several cases decided in the New York Court of Chancery including *Wotten v Copeland* (1823) 7 Johnson 140 and *Sebring v Mercerau* (1827) 9 Cowen 344, and to *Swan v Swan* (1820) 8 Price 518 and *Eagles v Eagles* [1960] VR 400.

82 Citing *Harwood v Kirby* (1829) 1 Paige 469 and *Dunham v Minard* (1834) 4 Paige 440.

83 [1984] VR 200 at 209.

[8.34] It is submitted that the decision in *McMahon v A F Wade*[84] is to be preferred on this point. While it is impossible to say whether the outcome would have been different if Tadgell J had been referred to this case, at least one commentator[85] has expressed a preference for the approach taken by Pidgeon J. There are a number of difficulties associated with Tadgell J's judgment. Firstly, it seems unfair that a mortgagee of an undivided share should be in a better position to resist sale in these circumstances than his mortgagor. The former derives his interest in the property from the mortgagor and takes his interest subject to the right of the other co-owners to compel partition or sale. The following dictum of Strong J in *Girard Life Insurance, Annuity and Trust Co v Farmers' and Mechanics' National Bank*[86] is instructive:

> '[T]he argument from the inconvenience of selling subject to encumbrances upon the interests of some of the parties, is not without weight. In many cases it would render partition practically impossible. It would produce great difficulty and uncertainty in the distribution, and it would exhibit the anomaly of a right conferred by one tenant in common superior to that which he never possessed.'

[8.35] Secondly, the decision in *Fulton v 523 Nominees*[87] appears to frustrate the purpose of the Partition Acts in that it is extremely unlikely that land could be sold subject to existing incumbrances. Yet a co-owner who has not mortgaged his share should not be prejudiced by the fact that another co-owner has. As Cromarty J remarked in *Bisson v Luciani*[88], 'the rights of ... innocent co-owners should not be fettered by the acts of ... other [co-owners]'. It is difficult to see why Tadgell J in *Fulton* was influenced by the possibility of a co-owner defeating partition by mortgaging his share of the property, but did not consider the possibility of a co-owner defeating sale by similar means. Thirdly, the cases cited by Tadgell J provide little support for his decision since the majority of them were dealing with partition actions where land was subject to a mortgage created by all the co-owners or where the action was brought by a mortgagor of an undivided share. While courts in Northern Ireland and the Republic have not yet been confronted with this issue, it is submitted that Pidgeon J's judgment in *McMahon v A F Wade* is to be preferred.

[8.36] Thus, a mortgagee of an undivided share should not be able to prevent another other co-owner from procuring sale of the property, assuming that the relevant criteria in either of ss 3-5 of the 1868 Act are satisfied. The mortgagee should be in no better position to prevent such an order being made than the co-

---

84 [1983] WAR 152.

85 Robinson, *The Property Law Act Victoria* (1992), pp 469-470.

86 (1868) 57 Pa 388 at 396.

87 [1984] VR 200.

88 (1982) 37 OR (2d) 257 at 261.

owner whose interest is incumbered. Applying the decision in *McMahon v A F Wade*, the property should be sold free from the mortgage. The mortgagor's share of the proceeds of sale should be paid to the mortgagee to discharge the mortgage, and the balance (if any) given to the mortgagor[89].

4 Position of the mortgagee

[8.37] If the mortgagor defaults, the mortgagee will want to enforce his security. While the mortgagee may seek an order for possession of the mortgaged property followed by an order for sale[90], the exercise of these remedies is complicated by the fact that the mortgage only relates to an undivided share of land. It has been said that a mortgagee who seeks possession in these circumstances 'will be setting off on a fool's errand'[91]. In *Tubman v Johnston*[92] Murray J held that a mortgagee of an undivided share is not entitled to an order for possession against a co-owner whose interest is not subject to the mortgage, and doubted whether the court had jurisdiction to make such an order[93]. The rationale for this appears to be that any order for possession that could be made in these circumstances would have no effect on the other co-owner since he was not a party to the mortgage. The only option available to the court would be to make an order that the mortgagee is entitled to possession along with the co-owner whose interest is not incumbered. Even if an order for shared possession were theoretically possible, it would be of little practical benefit to the mortgagee. Apart from the difficulties of enforcing the order, especially in matrimonial situations[94], the order would not assist the mortgagee in procuring a sale because his power of sale in these circumstances is restricted to the mortgagor's undivided share of the property. Most prospective purchasers would be unwilling to purchase an undivided share of land, and even if sale did take place it would probably be at a reduced price, which might not be sufficient to discharge the mortgage debt[95].

---

89 If his share of the proceeds of sale was not sufficient to discharge the mortgage debt, the mortgagor would remain personally liable to discharge the shortfall to the mortgagee: *McMahon v A F Wade* [1983] WAR 152.

90 See para **[8.06]** above.

91 Wallace 'Mortgagees and Possession' (1986) 37 NILQ 336 at 352.

92 [1981] NI 53 at 56.

93 Citing *William & Glyn's Bank Ltd v Boland* [1980] 2 All ER 408. Similar views were expressed by the Court of Appeal in *Albany Home Loans Ltd v Massey* [1997] 2 All ER 609.

94 For example, the court 'ordering a husband out of his matrimonial home to make way for a male stranger' (*Tubman v Johnston* [1981] NI 53 at 56 per Murray J) or a husband being in contempt of court if he returned to the property at his wife's invitation (*Albany Home Loans Ltd v Massey* [1997] 2 All ER 609 at 612 per Schiemann LJ citing *Alliance Building Society v Austen* [1951] 2 All ER 1068).

95 See the comments of Murray in *Tubman v Johnston* [1981] NI 53 at 56. However, a sale of the mortgagor's undivided share might be a viable proposition.

[8.38] As Murray J explained in *Tubman v Johnston*[96], the appropriate way for a mortgagee of an undivided share of land to enforce his security is to bring an action for sale of the property under the Partition Acts[97]. However, the efficacy of the Partition Acts in providing a solution to the problems facing a mortgagee of an undivided share in these circumstances depends on two criteria being satisfied, namely:

(a) that the mortgagee has *locus standi* to bring a partition action and

(b) that the court has jurisdiction to make the order sought.

(a) The locus standi *test*

[8.39] The *locus standi* test requires that the plaintiff has a legal or equitable interest vested in possession or conferring an immediate right to possession. Where the security takes the form of a legal mortgage the position is relatively straightforward. The mortgagor's estate in the property is conveyed to the mortgagee and the mortgagee has, by virtue of this estate, a right to possession[98]. Accordingly, a legal mortgagee may maintain a partition action in these circumstances since he has a legal estate in possession[99]. This is not altered by the fact that, in most instances, the mortgagee will elect not to enforce his right to possession and will allow the mortgagor to remain in occupation as his licensee so long as the mortgagor is not in default[100] – the mortgagee's right to

---

95 (contd) By analogy to the solution proffered by Wallace relation to orders charging an undivided share of land, the mortgagee could procure a sale of the mortgagor's undivided interest whereupon the purchaser would obtain *locus standi* to bring an action for sale of the property under the Partition Acts 1868 and 1876: Wallace,, 'Mortgages and Charges' *Second Annual Review of Property Law* (1995) 35 at 36-38 discussed at para **[8.80]** below.

96 [1981] NI 53 at 56-57.

97 See further *Ulster Bank Ltd v Shanks* [1982] NI 143; *Northern Bank Ltd v Beattie* [1982] 18 NIJB 1; *Bank of Ireland v Young* (13 February 1992, unreported) High Court (NI); and *Northern Bank Ltd v Adams* (1 February 1996, unreported) High Court (NI), as well as Hunter, *Notes on Procedure by Originating Summons and in Actions by Mortgagees* (2nd edn, 1985), p 22.

98 See the comments of Harman J in *Four-Maids Ltd v Dudley Marshall Properties Ltd* [1957] Ch 317 at 320 and those of Dillon J in *Westminster City Council v Haymarket Publishing* [1980] 1 WLR 683 at 686. However, a mortgagee must exercise this right in good faith and for the purposes of enforcing his security: *Albany Home Loans Ltd v Massey* [1997] 2 All ER 609.

99 This is implicit in Murray J's judgment in *Ulster Bank Ltd v Shanks* [1982] NI 143 at 150-151, and see *Northern Bank Ltd v Beattie* [1982] 18 NIJB 1. In *Deer v Laroque* (1982) 141 DLR (3d) 190 Geatros J held that a lender who had been assigned the interest of a joint tenant as security for a loan was not entitled to possession and could not maintain an action under the Partition Act 1868 (although the assignment in this particular case was not absolute).

100 For example, by an express or implied term in the mortgage deed restricting the mortgagee's right to possession while the mortgagor makes regular payments: see *Birmingham Citizens Permanent Building Society v Caunt* [1962] 1 All ER 163.

possession is merely suspended during this time[101]. If the mortgagor defaults, the situation changes. The mortgagee has a remedy of sale under the Partition Acts and in order to exercise that remedy he elects to enforce his right to possession[102], revoking the licence which he gave to the mortgagor[103]. Notwithstanding this practice, a legal mortgagee of an undivided share of land has an estate in possession and therefore has *locus standi* to bring a partition action[104]. The mortgagee may bring a partition action without the concurrence of his mortgagor[105], although the latter is a necessary party to the action, as are the co-owners whose interests are not subject to the mortgage[106].

[8.40] Where the mortgage is an equitable one, the position is more complicated. Although he has no estate vested in him[107], an equitable mortgagee does have an equitable interest in the mortgaged property[108] and accordingly satisfies the first aspect of the *locus standi* test under the Partition Acts. However, problems arise

---

101 Although a mortgagee of an undivided share has *locus standi* to bring a partition action even when the mortgagor is not in default, the court would be unlikely to entertain such an action for the reasons discussed at paras **[8.07]-[8.08]**, above.

102 The mortgagee may join a claim for possession with an action for sale of the property in order to facilitate sale with vacant possession: see for example, *Northern Bank Ltd v Beattie* [1982] 18 NIJB 1.

103 Thus in ordering possession the court is not granting a remedy but enforcing an existing right. It has been suggested that, in view of statutory and judicial curtailment of the mortgagee's right to possession (for example, under the Administration of Justice Acts 1970 and 1973) it is no longer correct to refer to this as a 'right': see Clarke, 'Further Implications of Section 30 of the Administration of Justice Act 1970' [1983] Conv 293 at 300 and the comments of Lord Denning MR in *Quennell v Maltby* [1979] 1 All ER 568. However, see Bamforth, 'Lord Macnaghten's Puzzle: The Mortgage of Real Property in English Law' (1996) 46 CLP 207 at 237-238 and the decision of the Court of Appeal in *Ropaigealach v Barclay's Bank plc* [1999] 4 All ER 235.

104 The *locus standi* test being based on the fact that the lender has an estate in possession as opposed to being in actual physical possession of the property: see the comments of Murray J in *Tubman v Johnston* [1981] NI 53 at 56-57. However, a number of Canadian cases have suggested that a mortgagee of an undivided share will not be able to bring a partition action while the mortgagor is still in possession: see *Mulligan v Hendershott* (1896) 17 PR (Ont) 227 and *Re Garnet and McGoran* (1980) 30 OR (2d) 742. In *Re Toronto-Dominion Bank and Morison* (1984) 47 OR (2d) 524 the mortgagee of a co-owner's interest brought an action for sale of the property under the Partition Act 1980 (Ont). Dismissing the application, Higgins J held that the bank did not have the necessary standing to bring the action since, *inter alia*, it had not commenced any action for possession against the mortgagor and had not attempted to go into possession.

105 *Robinson v Aston* (1845) 9 Jur 224 and *Davies v Davies* (1860) 6 Jur (NS) 1320.

106 The mortgagor and the other co-owners will be joined as defendants: Valentine, *Civil Proceedings – The Supreme Court* (1997), p 431.

107 Fisher and Lightwood, *Law of Mortgage* (8th edn, 1969), p 315.

108 Wylie, *Irish Land Law* (3rd edn, 1997), p 732.

in respect of the second aspect of this test. There is a lack of consensus as to whether an equitable mortgagee has a right to possession by virtue of his interest in the mortgaged property. A number of authorities have taken the view that an equitable mortgagee has no right to possession at law because he does not have a legal estate in the property[109]. In contrast, other authorities suggest that an equitable mortgagee is nevertheless entitled to possession in equity:

> 'It is generally said that an equitable mortgagee has no right to take possession. Certainly he has none at law, for he has no legal estate. But in equity he should be entitled to the same rights as if he had a legal mortgage, and there would seem to be no reason why he should not take possession under the doctrine in *Walsh v Lonsdale*[110] for the basis of an equitable mortgage is the creation of the relationship of mortgagor and mortgagee forthwith, rather than a mere contract for a future mortgage.'[111]

[8.41] The question of whether an equitable mortgagee of an undivided share of land has *locus standi* to bring a partition action depends on which line of authorities is followed. If an equitable mortgage gives rise to an interest in possession, equitable mortgagees would have the necessary standing to proceed under the Partition Acts. However, if the alternative view is correct, this would have serious implications for equitable mortgagees of an undivided share of land. The *Tubman v Johnston*[112] principle prevents a mortgagee of an undivided share of land from exercising his normal power of sale. Whereas a legal mortgagee could avail of the Partition Acts, this would not be available to an equitable mortgagee since the latter would not have the necessary standing to maintain a partition action[113]. An equitable mortgagee of an undivided share of

---

[109] See Coote, *Law of Mortgages* (9th edn, 1927), p 823; *Barlcay's Bank Ltd v Bird* [1954] Ch 274 and 32 *Halsbury's Laws of England* (4th edn, 1982), p 309. See further Valentine, *Civil Proceedings – The Supreme Court* (1997), p 432 and *Patel v Bank of India* (26 November 1997, unreported) Court of Appeal.

[110] (1882) 21 Ch D 9.

[111] Megarry and Wade, *The Law of Real Property* (6th edn, 2000), p 1214 citing *ex p Bignold* (1834) 4 Deac & Ch 259; *Trichborne v Weir* (1892) 67 LT 735; *Antrim County Land, Building and Investment Co Ltd v Stewart* [1904] 2 IR 357; and *Spencer v Mason* (1931) 75 SJ 295. Similar views are expressed in Fisher and Lightwood, *Law of Mortgage* (8th edn, 1969), p 315 and in Wylie, *Irish Land Law* (3rd edn, 1997), p 733 citing *National Bank Ltd v Hegarty* (1901) NIJR 13 and *Re O'Neill* [1967] NI 129. See further Wade, 'An Equitable Mortgagee's Right to Possession' (1955) 71 LQR 204.

[112] [1981] NI 53.

[113] An equitable mortgagee's remedy of possession may be of little assistance here, since his possession would not be derived from or incidental to the enjoyment of his estate or interest as required for the *locus standi* test under the Partition Acts.

land would therefore be left without an effective means of realising his security in the event of default[114].

[8.42] This difficulty has not yet been raised in Northern Ireland or the Republic of Ireland. Indeed a number of cases have decided that an equitable mortgagee does have *locus standi* to maintain an action under the Partition Acts[115]. However, given the apparent conflict over whether an equitable mortgage confers a right to possession on the mortgagee, doubts must exist as to whether such a course of action is available to an equitable mortgagee of an undivided share of land. One possible means of allaying these doubts is legislative intervention in the form of a simple statutory provision to the effect that equitable mortgagees do have *locus standi* to bring an action under the Partition Acts.

(b) The jurisdiction test

[8.43] Having satisfied the *locus standi* test, the plaintiff must bring his action under either of ss 3-5 of the 1868 Act[116]. Which section the mortgagee elects to proceed under will be determined by the extent of his interest in the mortgaged property, which in turn depends on the extent of the mortgagor's interest. In *Northern Bank Ltd v Adams*[117] Master Ellison asserted that the size of the mortgagee's interest should be determined by the value of his loan as a fraction of the realisable monetary value of the property. This has been criticised as

---

[114] It appears that the Property (NI) Order 1997, art 48 provides little assistance to equitable mortgagees in these circumstances. Article 48 grants chargees of an undivided share of land *locus standi* under the Partition Acts (see para **[8.62]** below). Although the Property (NI) Order 1997 does not define a 'charge' as including an equitable mortgage, Walker C in *Shea v Moore* [1894] 1 IR 158 at 168 stated that 'every charge is not an equitable mortgage, though every equitable mortgage is a charge'. An equitable mortgagee might therefore be regarded as an 'owner of a charge' for the purposes of art 48. However, it may be straining the language of art 48 somewhat to suggest that a charge by implication includes an equitable mortgage in the absence of a specific statutory direction to this effect in the Property (NI) Order 1997. Although a 'mortgage' under the Property (NI) Order 1997 includes a 'charge' and the terms 'mortgagor' and 'mortgagee' are to be construed accordingly (art 2(1)), this does not mean that an equitable mortgagee is a chargee for the purposes of the legislation.

[115] For example, Bacon VC in *Davenport v King* (1883) WR 911 described both legal and equitable mortgagees as 'persons interested' for the purposes of the Partition Acts 1868 and 1876, while in *Hill v Maunsell-Eyre* [1944] IR 499 at 505 Overend J remarked that a mortgagee of an undivided share has a right to partition or sale under the Partition Acts 1868 and 1876 'although he may not have the legal estate in the mortgaged premises'. More recently, similar views have been expressed in *Northern Bank Ltd v Beattie* [1982] 18 NIJB 1; *Northern Bank Ltd v Haggerty* [1995] NI 211; and in *Northern Bank Ltd v Adams* (1 February 1996, unreported) High Court (NI).

[116] See generally ch 5 above.

[117] (1 February 1996, unreported) High Court (NI), at 15-18.

being at variance with the language of the Partition Acts and the relevant authorities[118]. Moreover, *Wallace*[119] has observed that:

> 'It is no exaggeration to say that the Master's [ruling] ... involved a refusal, on the basis of limited authority, to be bound by centuries of wisdom about the fundamental nature of mortgages which have traditionally been regarded as vesting the entire estate provided as security in the mortgagee subject to a proviso entitling the mortgagor to a re-conveyance (in the case of a mortgage by transfer) or a surrender (in the case of a mortgage by demise) upon payment of all sums due.'[120]

[8.44] Since the mortgagee's security attaches to the interest mortgaged by the co-owner, the amount of money secured by the mortgage is irrelevant in this context. If the mortgagor's fractional share of the property equals or exceeds one-half, the mortgagee may proceed under s 4; if that share is less than one-half, the mortgagee may proceed under either s 3 or s 5. However, s 5 will seldom be relied on – a mortgagee should have little difficulty in establishing that sale of the property would be more beneficial than partition as required by s 3[121].

[8.45] The relief sought by the mortgagee in these circumstances will invariably be an order for sale. Where the property does not fall within one of the futility

---

[118] See ch 5 above, paras **[5.26]-[5.27]**.

[119] 'Mortgages and Charges' *Third Annual Review of Property Law* (1996) 7 at 21-22. See further Wylie, *Irish Land Law* (3rd edn, 1997), p 443.

[120] Master Ellison cited *Davenport v King* (1883) 49 LJ Ch 92 and *Hill v Maunsell-Eyre* [1944] IR 499 in support of his proposition. As regards the former, he observed that the headnote refers to mortgagees 'to the extent of one moiety in value' seeking partition. However, the headnote to the same case reported at (1833) 31 WR 911 refers to them as 'parties interested' in the property. In *Hill v Maunsell-Eyre* equitable mortgagees requested sale under the Partition Act 1868, s 4. Master Ellison stated that Overend J in this case made an order for partition but not sale, even though the plaintiffs' mortgage affected half of the property, and 'good reason to the contrary' had not been shown. According to Master Ellison, this could 'only be explained on the basis that "the extent of one moiety or upwards" in section 4 was interpreted as a reference to the realisable monetary value': (1 February 1996, unreported) High Court (NI), at 18. Overend J did not actually stipulate that the plaintiffs had to be entitled to one-half of the value of the property, and ordered an inquiry as to whether persons interested to the extent of a moiety or more 'in the said lands' requested sale: [1944] IR 499 at 506.

[121] However, in the unlikely event of a mortgagee bringing an action under the Partition Act 1868, s 5, the co-owner whose share was not subject to the mortgage could give an undertaking to purchase the mortgagee's interest and thus retain control of the land: see the comments of Master Ellison in *Northern Bank Ltd v Adams* (1 February 1996, unreported) High Court (NI), at 22.

exceptions so that the court must usually order partition or sale[122], an order for sale is likely in view of the difficulties associated with ordering partition in these circumstances[123]. It follows that a mortgagee should have little difficulty establishing that sale is more beneficial than partition under s 3. Co-owners resisting sale under s 4 may have considerable difficulty in establishing 'good reason to the contrary', the latter being demonstrated by the fact that there are exceptional circumstances for refusing sale and that partition is a viable alternative[124].

[8.46] Where the property falls within one of the futility exceptions so that the court has a discretion to refuse partition if the requisite third party consent is not obtained, this is likely to be of little practical consequence. Two factors support this. Firstly, the fact that partition is futile will probably tip the balance in favour of ordering sale, the court being aware that if it refuses sale the plaintiff will be left without relief[125]. Therefore it may be easier for a mortgagee to establish that sale is more beneficial than partition under s 3, and correspondingly more difficult for opposing co-owners to show 'good reason to the contrary' under s 4. Secondly, courts are often reluctant to make an order that will prevent a mortgagee from enforcing his security since such orders may prejudice further advances from lenders in analogous situations[126]. This approach is implicit in Murray J's judgment in *Ulster Bank Ltd v Shanks*[127]. Having decided that the

---

122 See ch 7 above.

123 If the court made an order for partition, the mortgagee would simply take the mortgagor's divided share of the property subject to the mortgage. In these circumstances, the court might order partition followed by a sale of the share subject to the mortgage: see *Hill v Maunsell-Eyre* [1944] IR 499.

123 The amount owing to the mortgagee would be paid from the proceeds of sale, while the other co-owners would continue to hold their shares as such. However, this is unlikely to occur in practice. In practical terms, it would only be a viable proposition where the mortgaged property comprised an area of land that could be divided without difficulty and which did not fall within one of the futility exceptions. More importantly, if there were prior or subsequent mortgages affecting the entire property, this particular share of the land could only be sold if its mortgagor redeemed all the outstanding mortgages: see para **[8.12]** above.

124 The fact that sale will not raise sufficient money to discharge the mortgage debt is not sufficient reason for refusing such an order under the Partition Act 1868, s 4: *First National Building Society v Ring* [1992] IR 375.

125 Furthermore, even if an order for partition of a dwelling house was possible in these circumstances, it would almost certainly be refused. Such an order would be tantamount to making an order for shared possession thereby raising the spectre of the mortgagee sharing occupation of the property with the co-owner whose share is not subject to the security: see para **[8.73]** above.

126 See the comments of Murray LJ in *Allied Irish Banks plc v McAllister* [1993] 5 NIJB 82 at 105.

127 [1982] NI 143.

wife's beneficial interest in the matrimonial home did not take priority over the bank's mortgage, he continued:

> 'If it is any comfort to the wife, however, it seems to me that since her undivided equitable share in the house is only a one-third one, and since the physical partition between the parties of the single modest dwelling house involved in this case would be out of the question, the wife, even if she had won her contest with the Bank on the mortgagee summons, would, at the end of the day, have had no prospect of avoiding an order for sale under the Partition Acts.'[128]

[8.47] Instances of the court refusing sale at the request of a mortgagee of an undivided share of land are difficult to find[129]. In this respect, a mortgagee who seeks to enforce his security under the Partition Acts is in a better position than a mortgagee of the entire property, the latter's power of sale being restricted by the terms of the Conveyancing Acts 1881-1911 or by the court as appropriate[130].

[8.48] As with the typical remedies available to a mortgagee, an action under the Partition Acts should not be brought until default 'by reason of its being inconsistent with the redemption proviso'[131]. The co-owners who did not join in creating the mortgage are in no better position to resist sale under the Partition Acts at the suit of a mortgagee than if the action had been brought by another co-owner. They will be unable to prevent sale of the property, even though the mortgage does not extend to their interests[132]. The order will direct the mortgagor and the other co-owners to deliver up possession of the property, and to join in any conveyance of the property[133]. The proceeds of sale are divided among the parties in proportion to their beneficial interests in the property, the mortgagor's share being paid to the mortgagee to discharge the mortgage debt[134].

---

128 [1982] NI 143 at 151. Likewise in *Northern Bank Ltd v Beattie* [1982] 18 NIJB 1 at 24 Murray J remarked that counsel for the wife 'faced an insurmountable hurdle in asking me to refuse a sale and yet leave the Bank without any relief by way of physical partition'.

129 See however the comments of Master Ellison in *Northern Bank Ltd v Adams* (1 February 1996, unreported) High Court (NI) (see ch 7 above, paras **[7.11]**-**[7.17]** and the criticisms of this approach).

130 Mee, 'Judgment Mortgages, Co-Ownership and Registered Land' (1999) 4 Conveyancing and Property Lawyer 28 at 29.

131 *McMahon v A F Wade* [1983] WAR 152 at 155 per Pidgeon J. In theory, there is nothing to prevent a mortgagee of an undivided share bringing an action for sale under the Partition Acts 1868 and 1876 where the borrower is not in default, since the former is in the position of a co-owner: Mee, 'Judgment Mortgages, Co-Ownership and Registered Land' (1999) 4 Conveyancing and Property Lawyer 28 at 29-30. However, this is unlikely to occur as sale in the absence of default would be contrary to the mortgagor's right to redeem.

132 However, as regards the practice where the mortgaged property comprises a matrimonial home, see chs 9 and 10 below.

133 See ch 12 below.

134 If this share exceeds the outstanding mortgage debt, any surplus will be paid to the mortgagor.

[8.49] A mortgagee of an undivided share cannot prevent an action for sale[135] by a prior or subsequent mortgagee under a mortgage created by all the co-owners and, conversely, such a mortgagee cannot prevent a partition action by a prior or subsequent mortgagee whose security relates to an undivided share[136]. The other mortgagees should be made parties to the action[137]. The court will direct inquiries as to their priority and the amount owing to each mortgagee, and payment will be made accordingly[138]. Where a mortgagee of an undivided share brings a partition action, the fact that a prior or subsequent lender suggests that it is the wrong time to sell the property and that more money could be obtained by delaying sale is irrelevant[139]. In these circumstances, there is no duty on the mortgagee to wait until the best time to sell the property[140]. Likewise, a mortgagee will not be estopped from bringing a partition action simply because he failed to take steps to realise his security at an earlier date[141].

III Property Subject to a Charge

[8.50] Unlike a mortgage, a charge does not involve a transfer of interest from borrower to lender[142]. A chargee merely has certain rights in relation to the land for the purpose of enforcing his security[143]. This distinction has important practical consequences for a chargee of an undivided share of land who wishes

---

135 In this context, the mortgagee's usual remedy of sale.

136 See *Davenport v King* (1883) WR 911 and *Hill v Maunsell-Eyre* [1944] IR 499.

137 32 *Halsbury's Laws of England* (4th edn, 1982), p 400 and see ch 12 below. If they are not joined as parties to the action, they must be served with notice of the judgment.

138 See the form of order in *Waite v Bingley* (1882) 21 Ch D 674 at 684 noted at para **[8.11]** above. See further *Ulster Bank Ltd v McCullough* (25 September 1989, unreported) High Court (NI).

139 *Canadian Imperial Bank of Commerce v Mulholland Construction* (28 January 1998, unreported) Ontario Court (General Division).

140 Assuming that the mortgaged property is sold under reasonable circumstances and at a fair market price: *Canadian Imperial Bank of Commerce v Mulholland Construction* (28 January 1998, unreported) Ontario Court (General Division).

141 *Canadian Imperial Bank of Commerce v Mulholland Construction* (28 January 1998, unreported) Ontario Court (General Division). In this case the parties were mortgagees of certain lands, and the petitioner sought an order for sale under the Partition Act 1990 (Ont). The petitioner had waited several years before commencing the partition action and, prior to this, the parties had shared various expenses associated with the land. However, Wilkins J rejected arguments that this created a waiver or estoppel on the part of the Bank – there was nothing to suggest that it had ever surrendered its rights under the Partition Act 1990 (Ont).

142 See *Patriche v Powlet* (1740) 2 Atk 54; *Northern Banking Co Ltd v Devlin* (1924) 58 ILTR 118; and *Swiss Bank Corpn v Lloyd's Bank Ltd* [1982] AC 584.

143 Wylie, *Irish Land Law* (3rd edn, 1997), p 622. As to creation of a charge on registered land in Northern Ireland, see the Land Registration Act (NI) 1970, s 41 and Sch 7, Pt I, para 1(2). In the Republic, virtually identical provisions are contained in the Registration of Title Act 1964, s 62.

to enforce his security in the event of default. That aside, the position of the respective parties as regards charges created by all the co-owners and those created by one co-owner over his undivided share is similar to that in relation to mortgages.

A Charges created by all the co-owners

[8.51] Where all of the co-owners join in creating a charge, the chargee's security extends to the entire property, and the parties are jointly and severally liable to discharge any sums owing to the chargee[144]. As with mortgages, creation of a charge by all of the co-owners does not effect a severance where the parties hold the land as joint tenants[145].

1 Position of the chargee

[8.52] In the event of default, the chargee has essentially the same remedies as are available to a mortgagee in these circumstances[146]. Thus the chargee may bring an action for debt or appoint a receiver to manage the property. However, in the majority of cases the chargee will seek an order for possession[147] followed by sale of the property[148]. Since the chargee's security affects the interests of all the co-owners, the Partition Acts are irrelevant here[149].

2 Position of the borrowers

[8.53] As with mortgages, a charge created by all the co-owners does not prevent any of them from compelling partition or sale of the property[150]. The only difference here is that the co-owners do not derive their *locus standi* from an

---

144 Since the charge represents a joint debt: see ch 11 below.

145 Since the charge extends to the interests of all the joint tenants: see para **[8.05]** above.

146 See para **[8.06]** above.

147 Unlike a mortgagee, a chargee has no right to possession because he has no estate in the land. However, a chargee has a statutory remedy of possession which allows him to apply to court for such an order: Land Registration Act (NI) 1970, Sch 7, Pt 1, para 5(2) and the Registration of Title Act 1964, s 62(7).

148 Both the Land Registration Act (NI) 1970, Sch 7, Pt 1, para 5 and the Registration of Title Act 1964, s 62(6) extend to chargees of registered land the power of sale available to a mortgagee under the Conveyancing Act 1881, s 19. Since this power of sale only applies where the mortgage was created by deed, it does not apply to an equitable charge by deposit of land certificate or to an agreement to create a legal charge not executed by deed. In these circumstances, the chargee must apply to court for an order declaring the outstanding sum well-charged on the land and for an order for sale.

149 Where there are two or more joint chargees, there is no prospect of one of them seeking partition or sale of the incumbered property against the wishes of the other chargees and the co-owners for the reasons discussed above: see paras **[8.07]-[8.08]**. Moreover, chargees in the Republic of Ireland do not have *locus standi* to bring an action under the Partition Acts 1868 and 1876: see paras **[8.60]-[8.61]** below.

150 See for example, *Glass v McManus* [1996] NI 401.

equity of redemption. Instead, because creation of a charge does not involve a transfer of interest in the property, the borrowers retain a legal or equitable estate in possession. As in the case of mortgages created by all the co-owners, the chargee will not be prejudiced by partition or sale of the property and need not be made a party to the action[151].

B Charges created by one of the co-owners

[8.54] The circumstances in which a charge may be restricted to an undivided share of land are similar to those discussed in relation to mortgages.

1 Circumstances giving rise to a charge of an undivided share of land

[8.55] Where title to the property is in joint names, the security will only attach to the borrower's interest where he has forged the signature of another co-owner on the document creating the charge, or if the latter's consent to the transaction has been obtained by undue influence, fraud or misrepresentation[152]. However, where the property is in the sole name of the borrower and a co-owner with a partial beneficial interest is asserting priority over the charge, the practice in respect of registered land is subject to one important caveat. The doctrine of notice has no application to registered land. Instead, the priority of these competing interests is determined on the basis of whether the person asserting the beneficial interest was 'in actual occupation of the land ... save where upon inquiry made of such person, the right [was] not disclosed'[153]. This right will be protected as an overriding interest and will bind subsequent lenders and purchasers of the land in the absence of registration. Where an overriding interest is binding on a chargee, the charge only extends to the borrower's undivided share of the land.

[8.56] A number of general points may be discerned from the relevant case law. The question of what amounts to actual occupation is one of fact, determined by the circumstances of each case[154]. However, there must be physical presence on the land[155], with some degree of permanence and continuity[156]. A person who claims an overriding interest of this nature need only occupy part of the

---

[151] See paras **[8.10]-[8.14]** above.

[152] See para **[8.16]** above.

[153] Land Registration Act (NI) 1970, Sch 5, Pt 1, para 15 and Registration of Title Act 1964, s 72(1)(j).

[154] *Williams & Glyn's Bank Ltd v Boland* [1980] 2 All ER 408.

[155] Not merely some legal entitlement to possession: *Williams & Glyn's Bank Ltd v Boland* [1980] 2 All ER 408 at 413 per Lord Wilberforce. However, occupation need not be personal and may be by means of an employee or agent: *Strand Securities Ltd v Caswell* [1965] Ch 958 and see the decision of the Court of Appeal in *Lloyds Bank plc v Rosset* [1989] Ch 350.

[156] *Abbey National Building Society v Cann* [1990] 1 All ER 1085. However, a temporary absence from the property does not mean that the person claiming an overriding interest ceases to be in actual occupation: *Chhokar v Chhokar* [1984] FLR 313 and *Kingsnorth Finance Ltd v Tizard* [1986] 1 WLR 783.

property[157], and may share occupation with the borrower[158]. Thus, a chargee might take his security subject to the rights of the borrower's family members[159]. As regards the time for establishing actual occupation, the relevant date is that on which the charge was created[160]. A chargee will not be bound by a beneficial interest if the chargee made inquiry of that person and the latter did not disclose his interest. Where such an interest is disclosed, the chargee will usually secure his position by insisting that the beneficial co-owner signs a consent form[161]. If the chargee is unaware of this prior equitable interest or fails to make any inquires of the beneficial co-owner, his overriding interest will usually be binding on the chargee. However, this is subject to two qualifications. Firstly, such an interest will not be binding on the chargee if the beneficial co-owner led the chargee to believe that he had no interest in the property or that his interest would not take priority to that of the chargee[162]. Secondly, the chargee will take priority where the charge was created to facilitate a purchase of property and the person asserting an overriding interest was aware of its creation or that the charge was necessary to acquire the property[163].

2 Severance

[8.57] Where co-owners are joint tenants, it might seem correct in principle that creation of a charge by one of them should cause a severance of the joint tenancy in the same manner as a mortgage created by one joint tenant[164]. However, a fundamental difficulty which arises in this context is that a charge does not involve a transfer of interest from lender to borrower. Various Australian and Canadian cases have held that, in these circumstances, there is no alienation and thus no severance of the joint tenancy[165]. Although Irish courts have yet to

---

157 *Hodgson v Marks* [1971] Ch 892.

158 Such occupation does not have to be inconsistent with the borrower's enjoyment of the property: *Williams & Glyn's Bank Ltd v Boland* [1980] 2 All ER 408.

159 Although it appears that a child cannot be regarded as someone in actual occupation in these circumstances: *Hypo-Mortgage Services Ltd v Robinson* The Times, 2 January 1997 .

160 *Abbey National Building Society v Cann* [1990] 1 All ER 1085 in which the House of Lords held that the relevant date is that on which the transaction takes place and not the date of registration. This excludes any possibility of a chargee being bound by a beneficial interest that came into existence in the period between creation of the charge and its registration.

161 See *Bank of Ireland v Young* (13 February 1992, unreported) High Court (NI). See further Morgan, 'Mortgagees and Occupiers: Overriding Interests in an Age of Consent' [1997] Conv 402 discussing the decision in *Woolwich Building Society plc v Dickman* [1996] 3 All ER 204.

162 See para **[8.18]** above.

163 *Paddington Building Society v Mendelsohn* (1985) 50 P & CR 244.

164 See para **[8.19]** above.

165 See *Lyons v Lyons* [1967] VR 169; *Power v Grace* [1931] 1 DLR 801 (affirmed on appeal at [1932] 2 DLR 793); and *Re Sorensen and Sorensen* (1977) 90 DLR (3d) 26. In Australia, similar views have been expressed in relation to mortgages of Torrens land which operate in the same way as a charge and thus do not involve a transfer of interest from borrower to lender: see the comments of McInerney J in *Lyons v Lyons* [1967] VR 169 at 173 and those of Smithers J in *Re Murrell* (1984) 57 ALR 85 at 96.

address the issue, it appears that similar reasoning would apply[166]. As regards Northern Ireland, art 50 of the Property (NI) Order 1997 specifically provides that creation of a charge by one or more joint tenants (but not all of them) causes a severance[167].

[8.58] The position in Northern Ireland aside, the fact that severance does not take place in these circumstances may operate unfairly[168]. Upon the death of the borrower, the property passes to the surviving joint tenants free from the charge since the interest in respect of which the charge was originally granted no longer exists[169]. The chargee's only option is to bring a personal action against the deceased's estate to recover the outstanding debt[170]. Where the other joint tenants predecease the borrower, the chargee's security extends to the entire property[171].

3 *Position of the borrower and the other co-owners*

[8.59] Once again the remedies of partition and sale under the Partition Acts are still available to the borrower and to the co-owners who did not join in creating the charge. However, the chargee is a necessary party to the action because the nature of his security will be altered by an order for partition or sale[172]. When ordering partition or sale, the court should apply the same principles as discussed above in relation to mortgages created by one co-owner[173].

4 *Position of the chargee*

[8.60] If the borrower defaults, the chargee will wish to realise his security. Applying the *Tubman v Johnston*[174] principle, the chargee is not entitled to an order for possession against the co-owner who did not join in creating the charge. This effectively precludes the chargee from exercising his normal power of sale in these circumstances. A mortgagee can overcome this difficulty by

166 Wylie, *Irish Land Law* (3rd edn, 1997), pp 440-441.

167 This provision was prompted by the decision in *Northern Bank Ltd v Haggerty* [1995] NI 211 discussed at paras **[8.76]-[8.78]** below.

168 See the discussion in Butt, *Land Law* (3rd edn, 1996), pp 244-245 and the cases cited therein. Although these refer to the practice as regards mortgages of Torrens land, similar reasoning would apply as regards charges of an undivided share of land in general. See further Mendes Da Costa, 'Co-Ownership Under Victorian Land Law' (1962) 3 Melb Univ Law Rev 433 at 448 and 454.

169 See the comments of McInerney J in *Lyons v Lyons* [1967] VR 169 at 180-181 and those of Tadgell J in *Sinn v National Wetminster Finance Ltd* [1985] VR 363 at 366.

170 Since the borrower's personal covenant to repay the debt remains enforceable against his estate: Butt, *Land Law* (3rd edn, 1996), p 244 and Mendes Da Costa, 'Co-Ownership Under Victorian Land Law' (1962) 3 Melb Univ Law Rev 433 at 448.

171 See *Penny Nominees Pty Ltd v Fountain (No 3)* (1991) 5 BPR 11,284.

172 See paras **[8.21]** and **[8.28]** above.

173 See paras **[8.20]-[8.36]** above.

174 [1981] NI 53 and see paras **[8.37]-[8.38]** above.

bringing an action for sale under the Partition Acts. However, the inherent nature of a charge presents a fundamental obstacle to a chargee of an undivided share of land proceeding in this manner. Since a chargee does not acquire any estate or interest in the land used as security, he does not satisfy the *locus standi* test under the Partition Acts and cannot bring an action for sale[175]. In other words, a charge on an undivided share of land 'creates a security which, in practice, may be incapable of realisation'[176].

[8.61] In the Republic of Ireland, it appears that a chargee of an undivided share of land may be left without an effective means of enforcing his security if the borrower defaults[177]. While s 62(6) of the Registration of Title Act 1964 confers on a registered chargee for this purpose 'all the rights and powers of a mortgagee under a mortgage by deed' it is unlikely that this would include the right to compel partition or sale under the Partition Acts[178]. Nevertheless, a chargee of an undivided share may be able to procure a sale of that share since s 62(6) of the 1964 Act includes 'the power to sell the estate or interest which is subject to the charge'. In these circumstances, the chargee could sell the borrower's interest in the property and the purchaser would thereby acquire *locus standi* to bring an action for sale of the entire property under the Partition Acts[179].

[8.62] In Northern Ireland, this problem has been remedied in the wake of the decision in *Northern Bank Ltd v Haggerty*[180]. Article 48 of the Property (NI) Order 1997 provides that:

---

175 See the comments of Campbell J in *Northern Bank Ltd v Haggerty* [1995] NI 211 at 217. It appears that this issue was not raised in *Bank of Ireland v Young* (13 February 1992, unreported) High Court (NI), where the court ordered sale under the Partition Acts 1868 and 1876 at the request of a chargee.

176 Wallace, 'Mortgagees and Possession' (1986) 37 NILQ 336 at 358 and see Wallace, 'Mortgages and Charges' *Second Annual Review of Property Law* (1995) 35 at 38-39. The chargee's remedy of possession provides no assistance here.

176 (contd) Even if an order for possession could be made against the share of a co-owner which was not subject to the charge, a remedy of possession is not the same as entitlement to a legal or equitable estate in possession: see the comments of Costello J in *Gale v First National Building Society* [1987] ILRM 30.

177 Wylie, *Irish Land Law* (3rd edn, 1997), pp 444-445. See further Mee, 'Partition and Sale of Family Home' (1993) 15 DULJ 78 at 86-87 and Mee, 'Judgment Mortgages, Co-Ownership and Registered Land' (1999) 4 Conveyancing and Property Lawyer 28 at 29-30.

178 Mee, 'Judgment Mortgages, Co-Ownership and Registered Land' (1999) 4 Conveyancing and Property Lawyer 28 at 30. A similar argument was rejected in *Northern Bank Ltd v Haggerty* [1995] NI 211: see paras **[8.76]-[8.78]** below.

179 As suggested by Wallace, 'Mortgages and Charges' *Second Annual Review of Property Law* (1995) 35 at 36-38 in relation to orders charging an undivided share of land: see para **[8.80]** below.

180 [1995] NI 211.

> 'The owner of a charge (including a charge under Article 46 of the Judgments Enforcement (Northern Ireland) Order 1981[181]) on land in co-ownership (that is to say, held jointly or in undivided shares) may make a request under the Partition Act 1868 and the Partition Act 1876 for an order for partition, or for sale and distribution in lieu of partition, and shall be treated as a party interested for the purposes of those Acts.'[182]

[8.63] Thus, a chargee of an undivided share of land in Northern Ireland now has *locus standi* to maintain a partition action[183]. To date, there is little authority on the practical application of art 48 in relation to charges. As regards the jurisdiction test, one difficulty, which may arise is deciding under which section of the 1868 Act the chargee should proceed, since a charge is for a specific sum as opposed to a specific estate in the property[184]. It is submitted that the determining factor here should be the fractional share of the borrower over which the charge extends[185]. Even though a chargee does not have an estate in the land, the chargee's action derives from his security over the estate of the defaulting borrower. Accordingly, if the borrower's interest in the property is equivalent to or exceeds one-half, the chargee's action should be brought under s 4 of the 1868 Act; if this interest is less than one-half, the action should be brought under s 3 or s 5 as appropriate[186].

[8.64] In deciding whether to order partition or sale, the court should apply the same principles as discussed above in relation to mortgages. Once again the relief sought will invariably be an order for sale. The chargee will have to show that sale is 'more beneficial' than partition under s 3, while the parties resisting sale under s 4 must establish 'good reason to the contrary'. In practical terms, the chargee is likely to be granted an order for sale, irrespective of whether the property falls within one of the futility exceptions[187].

---

181 See paras **[8.66]-[8.85]** below.

182 Property (NI) Order 1997, art 48 came into force on 1 September 1997: Property (1997) Order (Commencement No 1) Order (NI) 1997.

183 See the comments of Girvan J in *Ulster Bank Ltd v Carter* [1999] NI 93 at 101.

184 See the comments of Campbell J in *Northern Ireland Bank Ltd v Haggerty* [1995] NI 211 at 217. See further Mee, 'Partition and Sale of Family Home' (1993) 15 DULJ 78 at 86 and Mee, 'Judgment Mortgages, Co-Ownership and Registered Land' (1999) 4 Conveyancing and Property Lawyer 28 at 31.

185 Instead of the charge as a fraction of the realisable monetary value of the property. This issue was not specifically addressed in *Ulster Bank Ltd v Carter* [1999] NI 93 at 101.

186 Although a chargee is unlikely to rely on the Partition Act 1868, s 5, since he should have little difficulty in establishing that sale would be more beneficial than partition as required by the Partition Act 1868, s 3.

187 See the comments of Girvan J in *Ulster Bank Ltd v Carter* [1999] NI 93 at 101 although the learned judge suggested that the position might be different as regards partition actions involving spouses (see generally chs 9 and 10) and see generally paras **[8.45]-[8.49]** above.

IV Property Subject to an Order Charging Land or Judgment Mortgage

[8.65] Where one or more co-owners incurs a debt, the person to whom it is owed (the judgment creditor) may obtain judgment for the amount due. The judgment creditor may enforce this judgment by converting the debt into a species of security on the debtor's land, known as an order charging land in Northern Ireland and a judgment mortgage in the Republic of Ireland.

A Northern Ireland – orders charging land

[8.66] The current system for enforcing judgments was introduced in 1969[188], and the principal legislation is contained in the Judgments Enforcement (NI) Order 1981. Under this system, all High Court and County Court judgments are enforced by the Enforcement of Judgments Office ('the EJO'). For present purposes, the most important jurisdiction exercised by the EJO is the making of orders charging land[189].

[8.67] Articles 46-52 of the 1981 Order prescribe the only methods in which a money judgment is enforceable against land[190]. Under art 46(1), the EJO may impose an order charging the debtor's land for securing payment of the judgment debt[191]. However, the order does not take effect until the charge thereby imposed or a notice of the order is registered by the creditor in the Land Registry, or the order is registered by the creditor in the Registry of Deeds as appropriate[192]. An order charging land has the like effect as a charge on the land created by the debtor in favour of the creditor[193], and ceases to have effect 12 years from the date of the judgment[194].

---

188 By the Judgments (Enforcement) Act (NI) 1969 and see Trimble, 'Judgments (Enforcement) Act (NI) 1969' (1970) 21 NILQ 359. This replaced the system of judgment mortgages, which still operates in the Republic of Ireland.

189 As to the practice of the EJO in making such orders see Wylie, *Irish Land Law* (3rd edn, 1997), pp 803-806 and Valentine, *Civil Proceedings – The Supreme Court* (1997), p 335. See further *Allied Irish Banks plc v McAllister* [1993] 5 NIJB 82.

190 Judgments Enforcement (NI) Order 1981, art 45.

191 An order charging land may be made absolutely or subject to conditions: Judgments Enforcement (NI) Order 1981, art 46(2).

192 Judgments Enforcement (NI) Order 1981, art 46(3). As to the procedural requirements for registration, see art 50. In addition to this, a pending action affecting unregistered land must be registered in the Registry of Deeds (Judgments Enforcement) (NI) Order 1981, art 117(a) and Registration of Deeds Act (NI) 1970, s 3), and one affecting registered land must be registered in the Land Registry (Judgments Enforcement (NI) Order 1981, art 117(b) and Land Registration Act (NI) 1970, s 39 and Sch 6, Pt I, para 8).

193 Judgments Enforcement (NI) Order 1981, art 49. This is irrespective of whether the land in question is registered or unregistered.

194 Judgments Enforcement (NI) Order 1981, art 47.

1 Orders charging land where all the co-owners are debtors

[8.68] Where all the co-owners have incurred the debt that gave rise to the judgment, they are jointly and severally liable to discharge that debt[195]. Imposition of an order charging land in these circumstances does not effect a severance where the co-owners are joint tenants[196].

(a) Position of the judgment creditor

[8.69] In the event of non-payment, art 52(1) of the 1981 Order confers on the judgment creditor the power of sale of a mortgagee under a mortgage by deed within the Conveyancing Acts 1881-1911. The judgment creditor also has power to convey the debtor's estate in the land, and to apply to court for possession for the purposes of sale[197].

(b) Position of debtors

[8.70] Any one of the joint debtors may still maintain an action under the Partition Acts in these circumstances. Since the imposition of such an order does not involve the transfer of any estate or interest to the judgment creditor[198], each co-owner retains his original estate in the property and therefore has *locus standi* to bring such an action. As with mortgages and charges created by all of the co-owners, the judgment creditor is not a necessary party to the action, and an order for partition or sale may be made without affecting his rights[199].

2 Orders charging land where one of the co-owners is a debtor

(a) Circumstances giving rise to an order charging an undivided share of land

[8.71] Article 46(1) of the 1981 Order states that the EJO may impose such an order 'on any ... land or estate in land of the debtor'. Where the debtor and the other co-owners of the land are co-owners at law, the order will only affect the debtor's estate if the other co-owner was not a party to the transaction incurring the debt in respect of which the order has been made[200]. Even if the other co-owner was a party to the transaction, his or her consent will be invalid if it has been procured by fraud or undue influence[201].

---

195 Since it represents payment of a joint debt: see ch 11 below.

196 Since the order charging land extends to the interests of all the co-owners, and see para **[8.05]** above.

197 Judgments Enforcement (NI) Order 1981, arts 52(1)(a) and (b) respectively.

198 An order charging land being equivalent to a charge: Judgments Enforcement (NI) Order 1981, art 49.

199 See paras **[8.10]**-**[8.14]** above.

200 See for example, *Northern Bank Ltd v Haggerty* [1995] NI 211 and *Rainey & Sons v Weatherup and Weatherup* (13 December 1996, unreported) High Court, both of which are discussed below.

201 See *First National Securities v Hegerty* [1984] 3 All ER 641.

[8.72] Where title to the property is in the sole name of the debtor but another co-owner establishes a prior equitable interest, the practice may be summarised as follows: since the making of an order charging land is not a transaction for valuable consideration[202], the judgment creditor's security is subject to all prior equitable estates and interests in the property irrespective of whether he had notice of them[203] or whether they were disclosed to the judgment creditor upon prior inquiry. In these circumstances, the order charging land only extends to the debtor's undivided interest.

(b) Severance

[8.73] Prior to the decision in *Northern Bank Ltd v Haggerty*[204] it was assumed that an order charging land imposed against the share of one joint tenant effected a severance[205]. Since art 49 of the 1981 Order provides that an order charging land has 'the like effect as a charge on that land created by the debtor in favour of the creditor' and such an order does not confer any interest in the land on the judgment creditor, the decision in *Haggerty* also cast doubt on whether an order charging land severed a joint tenancy. Such doubts have now been removed by art 50 of the Property (NI) Order 1997[206].

(c) Position of the borrower and other co-owners

[8.74] An order charging the debtor's undivided share of land does not prevent him or the other co-owners from maintaining a partition action. The judgment creditor is a necessary party to the action since the nature of his security will be affected by the order, and the court should apply the same criteria in ordering partition or sale as discussed above in relation to mortgages and charges[207].

(d) Position of the judgment creditor

[8.75] If a judgment creditor wishes to enforce an order charging an undivided share of land, the *Tubman v Johnston*[208] principle prevents him from exercising the power of sale conferred by art 52 of the 1981 Order. In these circumstances, a judgment creditor would have to bring an action for sale under the Partition Acts. However, the status accorded to an order charging land under the 1981 Order is relevant in this context.

---

202 *In the Matter of Folio 3540 Co Tyrone* [1991] 273.

203 See however *Allied Irish Banks Ltd v McWilliams* [1982] NI 157.

204 [1995] NI 211.

205 See Wallace, *Land Registry Practice in Northern Ireland* (2nd edn, 1987), pp 85-86 and Moir, *Land Registration Manual* (1994), p 69.

206 See para **[8.57]** above.

207 See paras **[8.20]-[8.36]** above.

208 [1981] NI 53 and see paras **[8.37]-[8.38]** above.

[8.76] In *Northern Bank Ltd v Haggerty*[209] the Bank obtained a judgment against the husband (the first defendant) for approximately £14,000. Several months later the EJO made an order charging the husband's undivided share of the matrimonial home, which he and his wife (the second defendant) owned as joint tenants. The Bank brought an action for sale of the property under the Partition Acts, with delivery of possession as a consequential remedy. Master Ellison dismissed the action because the Bank lacked the necessary standing to maintain a partition action.

[8.77] Counsel for the Bank argued that, notwithstanding the restriction on the powers of enforcement available to a judgment creditor imposed by art 45 of the 1981 Order[210], the owner of an order charging land was not precluded from bringing a partition action. He contended that a chargee has *locus standi* to maintain a partition action since 'persons interested' under s 4 of the Partition Act 1868 must include the owner of a charge and thus a judgment creditor[211]. After reviewing the relevant authorities[212] Master Ellison concluded that, since a chargee did not have *locus standi* to bring a partition action, a judgment creditor such as the Bank was in exactly the same position. He also rejected counsel's alternative argument that the power of sale conferred on a judgment creditor by art 52 of the 1981 Order included the power to order sale under the Partition Acts[213]. Describing this line of reasoning as 'too tortuous'[214], Master Ellison alluded to the restrictive wording of art 45 and the absence of any reference to the Partition Acts in arts 46-52 of the 1981 Order[215].

---

209 (23 March 1994, unreported) High Court (NI).

210 See para **[8.67]** above.

211 Since the Judgments Enforcement (NI) Order 1981, art 49 grants an order charging land the status of a charge. Counsel referred to *obiter* remarks of Murray J in *Tubman v Johnston* [1981] NI 53 that the owner of an order charging an undivided share of land should bring a partition action to enforce his security. However, these remarks have been criticised as overlooking the fact that a judgment creditor lacks the necessary standing to maintain a partition action: Wallace (1986) 37 NILQ 336 at 358.

212 (23 March 1994, unreported) High Court (NI), at 6-11.

213 Counsel had asserted that:

(i) the referable 'powers of sale' in the Judgments Enforcement (NI) Order 1981, art 52 were all those enjoyed by a mortgagee under a mortgage by deed, whether or not these were under the Conveyancing Acts 1881-1911, and

(ii) in light of judicial authority that a mortgagee has standing to bring a partition action, these 'powers of sale' would include a power of sale in lieu of partition.

214 (23 March 1994, unreported) High Court (NI), at 16.

215 Two factors appeared to influence this aspect of Master Ellison's decision. Firstly, he stated that, if parliament had contemplated a judgment creditor having standing to bring a partition action, it would have conferred something more on the creditor than the power to sell the 'estate of the debtor', presumably since sale under the Partition Acts 1868 and 1876 involves a sale of the estates of all the co-owners and not just that of the debtor.

[8.78] This decision was affirmed by Campbell J on appeal[216], who held that art 45 of the 1981 Order restricted the Bank's powers to those set out in arts 46-52. Accordingly, the only power of sale available to the Bank was that of a mortgagee under a mortgage by deed as prescribed by art 52. Furthermore, even if a judgment creditor was not confined to exercising this power of sale, he could not avail of the jurisdiction under the Partition Acts since, by analogy to a chargee of an undivided share of land, he lacked the necessary standing to do so[217]. Rejecting the Bank's argument that the owner of a charge is the owner of an estate by virtue of s 45(2) of the Interpretation Act (NI) 1954[218], the learned judge explained this provision as meaning that the word 'estate' as used in legislation includes a charge; it does not mean that a charge (and, *a fortiori*, an order charging land) is an estate in land giving the owner *locus standi* to maintain a partition action[219]. Dismissing the application, Campbell J remarked that the 1981 Order had left a judgment creditor of an undivided share of land 'without a satisfactory means of realising his security'[220].

[8.79] In *Rainey & Sons v Weatherup and Weatherup*[221], the defendants were brothers and owned land as tenants in common. Each had a charging order affecting his undivided share of the land that had been imposed at the instance of the same judgment creditor (the plaintiff), albeit relating to separate debts. The plaintiff applied for possession and sale of the land under art 52 of the 1981 Order. This was refused on the basis that the plaintiff had different charges arising from separate judgments and relating to different parts of the land, as opposed to a charge over the entire fee simple. However, the plaintiff was also prevented from bringing a partition action since it lacked the necessary standing to maintain the action[222].

---

215 (contd) Secondly, he was of the opinion that the apparent discretion to grant possession to a judgment creditor for the purposes of sale did not correlate with the fact that when sale is ordered under the Partition Acts 1868 and 1876 an order for possession must be made (unless given up voluntarily), nor was it consistent with *locus standi* to bring a partition action: (23 March 1994, unreported) High Court (NI), at 17.

216 [1995] NI 211.

217 [1995] NI 211 at 215-217.

218 So far as is material, the Interpretation Act (NI) 1954, s 45(2) provides that:

> 'In any enactment passed after the commencement of this Act "estate", when used with reference to land, includes any ... charge ...'

219 [1995] NI 211 at 218.

220 [1995] NI 211 at 218. For an analysis of Campbell J's judgment see Wallace, 'Mortgages and Charges' *Second Annual Review of Property Law* (1995) 35 at 35-39.

221 (13 December 1996, unreported) High Court (NI).

222 The issue does not appear to have been raised in several other Northern Ireland cases where an order for sale under the Partition Acts 1868 and 1876 was made at the suit of a judgment creditor:

[8.80] These decisions had serious practical implications for the enforcement of judgment debts affecting an undivided share of land. A judgment creditor had no means of enforcing his security if the debtor failed to reduce the debt, and might have been prevented from recovering the debt after 12 years since the charging order would cease to have effect. One commentator[223] suggested that these difficulties could be overcome by the judgment creditor selling the debtor's interest in the property, this being facilitated by art 52(1) of the 1981 Order which confers on the creditor 'the power to convey by deed the estate of the debtor in the land'[224]. While acknowledging that sale of an undivided share of land would almost certainly fetch a lower price than sale of the entire land, it was suggested that such a purchase might appeal to 'bargain hunters' shrewd enough to realise that they would thereby acquire *locus standi* to bring an action for sale of the entirety under the Partition Acts[225]. In these circumstances, the judgment creditor would be concerned solely with obtaining sufficient money to discharge the debt owed to him.

[8.81] Such difficulties prompted legislative intervention. Article 48 of the Property (NI) Order 1997[226] grants owners of an order charging land under the 1981 Order *locus standi* to maintain an action under the Partition Acts. Thus a creditor with an order charging an undivided share of land can force a sale of the entire property as a means of enforcing his security. However, problems still exist. In *Ulster Bank Ltd v Carter*[227] an order charging the debtor's undivided share of a matrimonial home was made in July 1997. Several months later, the Bank brought an action for sale of the premises under the Partition Acts in accordance with art 48 of the 1997 Order. However, Girvan J held that the Bank was not entitled to an order for sale because art 48 does not apply to orders charging land that were created before 1 September 1997[228]. He referred to *L'Office Cherifien Des Phosphates v Yamashita-Shinniho Steamship Co Ltd*[229] in

---

222 (contd) *Northern Bank Ltd v Bell* (9 May 1988, unreported) High Court (NI); *Ulster Bank Ltd v McCullough* (25 September 1989, unreported) High Court (NI); *Northern Bank Ltd v Moore* (4 June 1991, unreported) High Court (NI); and *William Ewing t/a Ewing Brothers v McCann* (26 January 1993, unreported) High Court (NI).

223 Wallace, 'Mortgages and Charges' *Second Annual Review of Property Law* (1995) 35 at 36-38.

224 The land is conveyed 'freed from all estates in the land inferior to the charge, but subject to all estates in the land having priority to the charge': Judgments Enforcement (NI) Order 1981, art 52(1)(a).

225 Wallace, 'Mortgages and Charges' *Second Annual Review of Property Law* (1995) 35 at 37. A similar solution has been suggested in a number of Canadian cases: see *Re Craig* [1929] 1 DLR 142 and *Morrow v Eakin* [1953] 2 DLR 593.

226 See para **[8.62]** above.

227 [1999] NI 93.

228 The date on which this provision came into force: see para **[8.62]** above.

229 [1994] 1 AC 486, and in particular the views expressed by Lord Mustill at 525 approving the judgment of Staughton LJ in *Secretary of State for Social Security v Tunnicliffe* [1991] 2 All ER 712 at 724.

which the House of Lords held that a statute should not be construed retrospectively if the consequences of doing so were so unfair that parliament could not have intended such a construction. Applying this to art 48, Girvan J asserted that a retrospective interpretation would prejudice co-owners whose interests were not subject to the creditor's security since these interests were 'materially affected' by the enactment of art 48[230].

[8.82] Whereas a non-debtor co-owner was secure in his/her possession of co-owned property prior to 1 September 1997, that person could now be required to yield up possession to facilitate sale under the Partition Acts at the request of a judgment creditor whose security affects the interest of the other co-owner. According to Girvan J, the interests of a non-debtor co-owner are thus prejudiced when an order charging land is made against the interest of the debtor: it is creation of the security which results in the creditor acquiring *locus standi* to maintain a partition action, and ultimately leads to sale of the property. After art 48 came into force, the possibility of a creditor enforcing his security under the Partition Acts and the impact on a non-debtor co-owner were relevant factors for the EJO to take into account in deciding whether to make an order charging the debtor's interest. However, this would not have occurred in respect of orders charging land made before the commencement date of art 48 since there was no prospect of the creditor bringing a partition action at this time:

> '[I]t is clear that a pre-commencement date charge (... a "non-partitioning charge") differs from a post-commencement date charge (... a "partitioning charge"). In deciding whether to make a charge the EJO has to exercise a discretion taking into account all relevant considerations. The impact of such an order on immediately affected third parties must be a relevant consideration. What the EJO must or may take into account in deciding whether to make a non-partitioning charge will in some and perhaps in the majority of cases differ from what should or might be taken into account in deciding whether to make a partitioning charge.'[231]

[8.83] Girvan J suggested that in the wake of art 48, a non-debtor co-owner should be notified of a proposal to make an order charging land against the interest of another co-owner[232], and that the former should be given an opportunity to make representations to the EJO[233]. This would not have been the practice prior to 1 September 1997.

---

230 [1999] NI 93 at 101.

231 [1999] NI 93 at 102.

232 Endorsing the judgment of Carswell LCJ in *Hallmark Furniture Ltd v Collins* [1998] NI 4 at 8.

233 For example, that the debtor has other resources available to discharge the debt, or that there was an agreement or understanding between the parties that the premises should not be sold for a specific period: [1999] NI 93 at 104.

[8.84] Since art 48 only applies to orders charging land created after 1 September 1997, it follows that creditors with an order charging land created before this date do not have *locus standi* to bring an action under the Partition Acts. However, it would be incorrect to suggest that such persons are still without any means of enforcing their security in these circumstances. The judgment creditor can simply apply to the EJO to make a new order charging the debtor's share of the land and then bring an action for sale under the Partition Acts in accordance with art 48[234]. Thus, a prospective interpretation of art 48 is essentially inconvenient for the judgment creditor, as opposed to creating a substantive obstacle to enforcement of his security under the Partition Acts.

[8.85] As with chargees, whether a judgment creditor proceeds under s 3 or 4 of the Partition Act 1868 should be determined by the fractional size of the co-owner's interest to which the order charging land attaches[235]. The judgment creditor will almost certainly seek an order for sale. Once again the likelihood of the court ordering sale in these circumstances must be regarded as considerable, irrespective of whether the property falls within one of the futility exceptions[236].

B Republic of Ireland – judgment mortgages

[8.86] The current system for enforcing judgments of the High Court and Supreme Court which require payment of a sum of money to a 'judgment creditor' is that established by the Judgment Mortgage (Ir) Act 1850[237]. Under s 6 of the 1850 Act, a judgment mortgage may be registered against 'any lands, tenements, or hereditaments of any nature or tenure' of which the debtor 'is seised or possessed at law or in equity'. Registration is effected by the judgment creditor[238] filing an affidavit in the court in which judgment was entered against

233 (contd) Girvan J also suggested that, as regards matrimonial property, the rights and interests of a spouse would be matters which the Enforcement of Judgments Office should consider in deciding whether to make an order against the other spouse's interest. The provisions of the Family Homes and Domestic Violence (NI) Order 1998 may be relevant in this context: see ch 9 below.

234 As suggested by Girvan J in *Ulster Bank Ltd v Carter* [1999] NI 93 at 100. While the judgment creditor would have to pay a second enforcement fee, this amount would be added to the judgment debt and enforced as part of the order charging land. Alternatively, Girvan J suggested that the creditor could consider other methods of enforcement including proceedings against the debtor under the Insolvency (NI) Order 1989.

235 See para **[8.63]** above.

236 See paras **[8.45]-[8.49]** above.

237 As amended by the Judgment Mortgage (Ir) Act 1858. For an overview of this system see Wylie, *Irish Land Law* (3rd edn, 1997), pp 792-803; Lyall, *Land Law in Ireland* (2nd edn, 2000), pp 776-778; and Coughlan, *Property Law* (2nd edn, 1998), pp 388-389. The Judgment Mortgage (Ir) Acts 1850 and 1858 only apply to certain judgments of the Circuit Court as prescribed by the Circuit Court (Registration of Judgments) Act 1937.

238 Or where there is more than one judgment creditor in respect of the same judgment, by any one of them: Judgment Mortgage (Ir) Act 1858, s 4 and *Re Kane* [1901] 1 IR 520.

the debtor. The affidavit must contain details of the judgment, and a copy of the affidavit must be entered in the Registry of Deeds[239] or Land Registry[240] as appropriate.

[8.87] The rights enjoyed by the judgment creditor depend on whether his security relates to unregistered or registered land. As regards the former, s 7 of the 1850 Act provides that registration of the affidavit in the Registry of Deeds operates to:

> 'transfer to and vest in the creditor ... all the lands, tenements and hereditaments mentioned therein, for all the estate and interest of which the debtor mentioned in such Affidavit shall at the time of such registration be seised or possessed ...'

[8.88] Section 7 continues that this is subject to redemption upon payment of the judgment debt. In other words, registration of such an affidavit on unregistered land creates a mortgage and the judgment creditor takes the debtor's estate or interest in the land as security. If the debtor fails to discharge the debt, the judgment creditor has largely the same remedies as those available to a mortgagee on default[241]. However, where the land is registered land, s 71(4) of the Registration of Title Act 1964 provides that registration of such an affidavit operates 'to charge the interest of the judgment debtor'. In the event of default, the judgment creditor has such rights and remedies for enforcing the charge as may be conferred on him by order of the court[242]. The judgment creditor does not take the debtor's estate or interest in the land, but merely has certain rights in relation to the property for the purposes of enforcing the security.

[8.89] Thus the position of a judgment creditor of unregistered land is analogous to that of a mortgagee, while the position of a judgment creditor of registered land is analogous to that of a chargee. This distinction is of fundamental importance where a judgment mortgage only affects the interest of one co-owner.

1 Judgment mortgages where all the co-owners are debtors

[8.90] Where all the co-owners incurred the debt that has resulted in imposition of the judgment mortgage, they are jointly and severally liable to discharge that

---

239 *Re Flannery* [1971] IR 10.

240 Registration of Title Act 1964, s 71(1).

241 Wylie, *Irish Land Law* (3rd edn, 1997), p 801 and see para **[8.06]** above. However, it appears that the most common method of enforcement is a declaration that the debt is well- charged on the land followed by an order for sale.

242 Registration of Title Act 1964, s 71(4) and see Fitzgerald, *Land Registry Practice* (2nd edn, 1995) ch 8.

debt[243]. Registration of a judgment mortgage against all the co-owners does not cause a severance where the parties are joint tenants[244].

(a) Position of the judgment creditor

[8.91] In the event of default, the judgment creditor may enforce his security in the manner described above, depending on whether the judgment mortgage relates to unregistered or registered land.

(b) Position of the debtors

[8.92] Where a judgment mortgage affects the interests of all the co-owners, any one of them may bring proceedings for partition or sale of the land as a means of ending their relationship. Co-owners retain the equity of redemption in the property where the judgment mortgage relates to unregistered land and thus have *locus standi* to bring a partition action in these circumstances. Where the security relates to registered land, co-owners retain their original estate in the property since no transfer of interest to the judgment creditor has occurred. By analogy to the practice in respect of mortgages and charges, the judgment creditor is not a necessary party to the action and will not be affected by an order for partition or sale[245].

2 Judgment mortgages where only one of the co-owners is a debtor

(a) Circumstances giving rise to a judgment mortgage of an undivided share of land

[8.93] The circumstances in which a judgment mortgage affects an undivided share of land are the same as those discussed in relation to orders charging land in Northern Ireland[246]. In these circumstances the judgment mortgage only extends to the debtor's undivided share of the land.

(b) Severance

[8.94] Registration of a judgment mortgage against the share of a joint tenant of unregistered land effects a severance[247]. This appears to be based on the fact that registration of the security involves a transfer of the debtor's rights to the

243 Since it represents a joint debt: see ch 11 below.

244 Since the judgment mortgage extends to the interests of all the joint tenants: see para **[8.05]** above.

245 See paras **[8.10]**-**[8.14]** above.

246 See paras **[8.71]**-**[8.72]** above. As with orders charging land in Northern Ireland, registration of a judgment mortgage is not a transaction for valuable consideration: see the comments of Kennedy CJ in *Re Murphy and McCormack* [1930] 322 at 327 and see *Tempany v Hynes* [1976] IR 101. As regards judgment mortgages affecting registered land see further the Registration of Title Act 1964, s 71(4) and see *Re Strong* [1940] IR 382.

247 *McIlroy v Edgar* (1881) LR Ir 521 and *Provincial Bank of Ireland v Tallon* [1938] IR 361. See further *Containercare Ltd v Wycherley* [1982] IR 143.

creditor under the 1850 Act[248]. It seems wrong in principle that a different rule should apply to a judgment mortgage imposed against a joint tenant of registered land. However, the latter transaction does not involve any transfer of interest to the judgment creditor and in this respect is similar to a charge. Thus it appears that registration of a judgment mortgage against a joint tenant of registered land does not cause a severance with similar consequences for the respective parties[249].

(c) Position of the debtor and the other co-owners

[8.95] Where a judgment mortgage only extends to the debtor's interest, the debtor or other co-owners may still compel partition or sale. The judgment creditor is a necessary party to the action, and in deciding whether to order partition or sale, the court should apply the same principles as discussed in relation to mortgages and charges[250].

(d) Position of the judgment creditor

[8.96] If the debtor fails to discharge the debt, the judgment creditor may wish to enforce his security. However, there are important practical differences between a judgment mortgage of an undivided share of unregistered land and an undivided share of registered land.

[8.97] Where a judgment mortgage relates to unregistered land, the *Tubman v Johnston*[251] principle prevents the judgment creditor from exercising his normal remedy of sale. In these circumstances, the judgment creditor will have to seek an order for sale of the entire property under the Partition Acts as a means of realising his security. Since registration of the judgment mortgage transfers the debtor's estate or interest in the property to the judgment creditor, the latter has *locus standi* to maintain a partition action in these circumstances[252]. Whether the judgment creditor proceeds under s 3 or s 4 of the 1868 Act will be determined by the fractional size of the debtor's interest in the property[253]. Again the court

---

[248] In other words, the position is the same as a mortgage affecting the share of one joint tenant: see para **[8.19]** above.

[249] See paras **[8.57]-[8.57]** above. See further McAllister, *Registration of Title in Ireland* (1973), p 210 and Fitzgerald, *Land Registry Practice* (2nd edn, 1995), pp 129-130. A number of Canadian cases have also held that registration of a judgment against a joint tenant does not sever the joint tenancy: see *Re Young Estate* (1968) 66 WWR 193; *Sunglo Lumber Ltd v McKenna (*1974) 48 DLR (3d) 154; and *Canadian Imperial Bank of Commerce v Martin* (11 February 1985, unreported) British Columbia Supreme Court.

[250] See paras **[8.20]-[8.36]** above.

[251] [1981] NI 53 and see paras **[8.37]-[8.38]** above.

[252] See *Farrell v Donnelly* [1913] 1 IR 50 at 56-57.

[253] Thus in *Farrell v Donnelly* [1913] 1 IR 50 the debtor being entitled to a two-ninths undivided share of land, the judgment creditor brought an action for sale under the Partition Act 1868, s 3 and alleged that sale was more beneficial than partition.

should usually make an order for sale, irrespective of whether the property falls within one of the futility cases[254].

[8.98] However, the position is more complicated where a judgment mortgage relates to registered land. In these circumstances, registration of a judgment mortgage does not involve a transfer of the debtor's estate or interest in the property to the judgment creditor. Accordingly, a judgment creditor does not have *locus standi* to bring an action for sale of the entire property under the Partition Acts in the event of non-payment by the debtor. In this respect, the judgment creditor's position is identical to that of a chargee in the Republic of Ireland[255].

[8.99] It appears that this difficulty was not raised in *First National Building Society v Ring*[256]. The plaintiff obtained judgment against the husband (the first defendant) for approximately £160,000 and subsequently converted this into a judgment mortgage over a family home, title to which was registered in the joint names of the husband and his wife (the second defendant). When the husband failed to discharge this debt, the plaintiff sought a declaration that the debt was well-charged on his share of the family home and an order for sale under s 4 of the Partition Act 1868. Denham J did not question whether the plaintiff as a judgment creditor of an undivided share of registered land had the necessary standing to maintain the partition action. On the contrary, she appeared to take the view that the plaintiff was in the same position as a judgment creditor of unregistered land, stating that the husband's interest in the home was 'vested in the plaintiff'[257]. Denham J went on to determine the case on the basis of whether the wife had demonstrated 'good reason to the contrary' within s 4 of the 1868 Act[258].

[8.100] Notwithstanding the decision in *First National Building Society v Ring,* it appears that judgment creditors of an undivided share of registered land cannot rely on the Partition Acts as a means of enforcing their security. Instead, they are confined to exercising such rights and remedies as may be conferred on them by order of the court under s 71(4) of the Registration of Title Act 1964. It is unlikely that the court would order a sale of the entire property under s 71(4) in the absence of any specific statutory jurisdiction to make such an order[259].

254 See paras **[8.45]-[8.49]** above.

255 See paras **[8.60]-[8.61]** above.

256 [1992] IR 375.

257 [1992] IR 375 at 381.

258 This aspect of the judgment is considered in ch 10 below.

259 Mee, 'Partition and Sale of Family Home' (1993) 15 DULJ 78 at 87-88 and Mee, 'Judgment Mortgages, Co-Ownership and Registered Land' (1999) 4 Conveyancing and Property Lawyer 28 at 30.

Moreover, sale of the entire property would involve an unwarranted interference with the rights of the co-owner whose share of the property is not subject to the judgment mortgage[260], while the *Tubman v Johnston*[261] principle would prevent the court from making an order for possession against such a person.

[8.101] The only option for the judgment creditor in these circumstances may be to procure a sale of the debtor's undivided share of the property. Yet there are several difficulties associated with this approach. Sale of an undivided share of land may not generate the same price as a sale of the entire property[262]. That aside, the remedies available to a judgment creditor in the event of default are at the discretion of the court, and are subject to any restrictions or conditions on their exercise as may be imposed by the court[263]. Thus, sale of the debtor's undivided share of the property is likely to be of less benefit to the judgment creditor than a sale of the entire property under the Partition Acts.

[8.102] It is unfair that such an arbitrary divergence in practice should exist between judgment creditors of unregistered land and those of registered land, the former being able to enforce their security under the Partition Acts while the latter cannot do so due to lack of standing. In the majority of cases, a judgment creditor of registered land will be unaware of this anomaly when he lends money or the debtor incurs the debt that leads to subsequent registration of the judgment mortgage. The judgment creditor is only likely to discover that he cannot maintain an action under the Partition Acts when he commences proceedings to enforce his security, by which stage it will be too late – the debtor may have incurred a substantial debt which he is unwilling or unable to discharge, and the judgment creditor may be left without any substantive means of recovering this.

[8.103] There is a need for reforming legislation to be introduced in the Republic of Ireland to remedy the problems facing both chargees and judgment creditors of an undivided share of registered land. Such persons should be entitled to apply for sale (or partition) under the Partition Acts as a means of enforcing their security in these circumstances. The reforms implemented in Northern Ireland by art 48 of the Property (NI) Order 1997 may prove useful in this context[264].

---

260 Mee, 'Judgment Mortgages, Co-Ownership and Registered Land' (1999) 4 Conveyancing and Property Lawyer 28 at 30.

261 [1981] NI 53 and see paras **[8.37]-[8.38]** above.

262 Although an undivided share of land may prove to be marketable in light of the suggestion put forward by Wallace in this context: see para **[8.80]** above.

263 Registration of Title Act 1964, s 71(4). Contrast this with an action under the Partition Acts 1868 and 1876 where the court is usually obliged to order partition or sale: see ch 7 above.

264 See Mee, 'Judgment Mortgages, Co-Ownership and Registered Land' (1999) 4 Conveyancing and Property Lawyer 28 at 31-32.

Chapter 9

Co-Ownership of the Matrimonial Home and Partition Actions Involving Spouses in Northern Ireland

I Introduction[1]

[9.01] While spouses may be co-owners of other types of property, the matrimonial home will usually represent the main asset of the parties[2]. Three situations may arise in which spouses are involved in a partition action relating to the matrimonial home. The first is where the marital relationship breaks down and one spouse wishes to realise his or her share in the property. The second and perhaps more common situation occurs where one spouse has used his or her share of the matrimonial home as security and defaults on repayments. In these circumstances, the security holder may bring an action for sale of the property under the Partition Acts. The third situation which may arise is where one of the spouses is declared bankrupt and the trustee in bankruptcy attempts to realise that spouse's share in the matrimonial home to reimburse creditors.

[9.02] Where a partition action relates to the matrimonial home, the preferred order is likely to be one for sale due to the practical difficulties associated with partition in these circumstances and the fact that an order for partition may be

---

1 This chapter contains material previously published in 'Nearly, But Not Quite- Partition Actions in the Wake of Article 48 of the Property (NI) Order 1997' (1999) 50 NILQ 166 and reproduced with the kind permission of SLS Legal Publications (NI).

2 In most situations a husband and wife will be joint tenants at law through choice. However, spouses may be tenants in common at law or in equity by reason of severance of the joint tenancy having occurred. Where legal title to the matrimonial home is vested in one spouse, the parties may nevertheless be co-owners in equity if the other spouse can establish a beneficial interest in the property under a resulting or constructive trust: see generally Lawson, 'The Things We Do for Love: Detrimental Reliance in the Family Home' (1996) 16 Legal Studies 218; O'Hagan, 'Quantifying Interests Under Resulting Trusts' (1997) 60 MLR 420; and Barlow and Craig, 'A Matter of Trust: The Allocation of Rights in the Family Home' (1999) 4 Legal Studies 468. A recent report from the Law Reform Advisory Committee for Northern Ireland has proposed that beneficial ownership of a joint residence (or primary residence) of spouses should automatically vest in both spouses as joint tenants unless the parties execute a written agreement expressly stating otherwise: Law Reform Advisory Committee for Northern Ireland Discussion Paper No 5, *Matrimonial Property* (1999).

3 Conversion of a single dwelling house into two dwelling houses constitutes a material change in use that requires planning permission: see ch 7.

futile[3]. This chapter considers the position of spouses in partition actions involving the matrimonial home and, in particular, whether various statutory provisions regulating property rights of spouses in relation to the matrimonial home allow the court to adopt a more flexible approach[4].

II Partition Actions Between Spouses

[9.03] The distribution of matrimonial property on the breakdown of a marriage may be achieved by a number of methods, some of which may result in spouses becoming involved in proceedings under the Partition Acts.

A Practice on or after judicial separation or divorce

[9.04] When a marital relationship has broken down, either spouse may petition for a decree of divorce or judicial separation under the Matrimonial Causes (NI) Order 1978[5]. In the absence of agreement between the parties as to the continued use and occupation of the matrimonial home, the petitioner may also ask the court to make an appropriate order for ancillary relief in relation to the property. The 1978 Order contains extensive provisions for the court to make property adjustment orders regulating the property rights of the spouses and adjusting their respective financial positions on or after granting a decree of divorce or judicial separation[6]. In practical terms, the court can make any order it thinks fit in relation to the matrimonial home[7].

[9.05] While there is no bar in theory to a spouse bringing an action for sale of a matrimonial home under the Partition Acts in these circumstances, it is suggested that the Partition Acts have little practical application here. Parliament has provided legislation to deal with this specific problem in the form of provisions for making property adjustment orders. The 1978 Order therefore provides a more appropriate jurisdiction for resolving disputes relating to the matrimonial home that may arise on judicial separation or divorce than the Partition Acts[8]. Once the jurisdiction of the court under the 1978 Order has been

---

3 (contd) Most actions for sale of a matrimonial home will be brought under either s 3 or s 4 of the Partition Act 1868. A person interested in less than half of the matrimonial home is unlikely to rely on the Partition Act 1868, s 5, since he should be able to establish that sale would be more beneficial than partition as required by s 3.

4 For an exposition of matrimonial property law in general in Northern Ireland see O'Halloran, *Family Law in Northern Ireland* (1997), ch 20.

5 Matrimonial Causes (NI) Order 1978, arts 3(1) and 19 respectively.

6 Matrimonial Causes (NI) Order 1978, art 23(2).

7 Matrimonial Causes (NI) Order 1978, art 26(1) empowers the court to make one or more of the following orders: an order for a transfer of property, an order for settlement of property, and an order for variation of settlement. The matters which the court must have regard to in deciding how to exercise its powers under art 26 are contained in art 27 (as amended by the Matrimonial and Family Proceedings (NI) Order 1989, art 6). These are discussed in para **[9.37]** below.

invoked by a petition for judicial separation or divorce, the court is unlikely to entertain an application for sale under the Partition Acts. If a spouse was permitted to bring such an action in these circumstances, this could operate unfairly against the other spouse. Taking the view that the court should order partition or sale under the Partition Acts, the former could, in theory, force a sale of the matrimonial home against the wishes of the other spouse on judicial separation or divorce[9]. This would be difficult to reconcile with the court's discretion to make any order it thinks fit under the property adjustment provisions of the 1978 Order. The range of orders available to the court would depend on which statute the petitioner brought his action under[10].

[9.06] Following judicial separation or divorce, either spouse could bring an action for sale of the matrimonial home under the Partition Acts[11]. However, a pre-existing property adjustment order under the 1978 Order may prevent the court from making an order for sale in these circumstances. If, for example, a property adjustment order allows a spouse and children of the marriage to remain in the matrimonial home, the court is unlikely to entertain a partition action brought by the other spouse since an order for sale would be contrary to the property adjustment order. Thus, in *Clarke v Clarke*[12] the court refused to order sale of a matrimonial home under the Partition Acts where the husband had been ordered to pay his wife a lump sum, which was to be secured as a charge on the property[13]. Again, this may be viewed as a type of jurisdiction exception: the jurisdiction under the Partition Acts is ousted because the property adjustment order regulates the use and occupation of the property or the circumstances in which the parties may dispose of the property[14].

---

8 In other words, this is similar to the jurisdiction exception that has been suggested in respect of partnership property: see ch 4 above, paras **[4.44]-[4.45]**.

9 The likelihood of an order for sale under the Partition Acts 1868 and 1876 being considerable because of the difficulties associated with partition.

10 For example, in *Tansell v Tansell* (1977) 35 FLR (Aus) 272 at 299 Jacobs J remarked that, to order sale or partition of a matrimonial home pursuant to a partition action by one spouse at the same time as proceedings for judicial separation or divorce would be to 'cut across and almost certainly frustrate the powers exercisable by the Family Court' in the latter proceedings. In *Irwin v Irwin* (9 March 1978, unreported) British Columbia Supreme Court, Legg J refused to order sale of a matrimonial home in lieu of partition on the basis that the parties' circumstances were subject to change as a result of pending divorce proceedings in which the wife was claiming maintenance and an order in respect of the property.

11 Assuming that the property was still held in joint ownership.

12 (1974) 48 DLR (3d) 707.

13 However, if a property adjustment order directs the parties to retain the matrimonial home for a specified period of time, the court might entertain a partition action by either spouse after the prescribed period of time has elapsed: *Norgard v Norgard* (1996) 20 Fam LR, Lexis transcript.

B Judicial separation or divorce not available

[9.07] If judicial separation or divorce is not available, either spouse could conceivably use the Partition Acts to compel sale of the matrimonial home[15]. For example, a husband may wish to divorce his wife but she will not consent to the decree and he does not have any other grounds upon which to present the petition. Should the husband nevertheless wish to realise his share in the matrimonial home, he could bring an action for sale of the property under the Partition Acts. As there is no petition for judicial separation or divorce, the jurisdiction under the 1978 Order is not exercisable and the court cannot make an appropriate property adjustment order. The court would probably have no option but to entertain the husband's application under the Partition Acts and to determine the action accordingly. However, if the wife subsequently applied for a decree of judicial separation or divorce before the partition action had been determined, the court might adjourn the partition action and deal with the matrimonial home under the 1978 Order[16].

[9.08] Alternatively, spouses may enter into a separation agreement, the terms of which might regulate occupation of the matrimonial home following the breakdown of the marital relationship[17]. For example, an agreement may provide

---

[14] Again this is by analogy to the jurisdiction exception in respect of partnership property and agreements regulating the disposal of concurrent interests: see ch 4 above, paras **[4.42]-[4.45]**.

[15] See the comments of Jacobs J in *Tansell v Tansell* (1977) 35 FLR (Aus) 272 at 301.

[16] Several Australian cases are illustrative of this approach. In *Tansell v Tansell* (1977) 35 FLR (Aus) 272 the husband applied to the Supreme Court under the Law of Property Act 1936 (SA), s 69 for an order for sale of the matrimonial home in lieu of partition. Five days later, the wife applied to the Family Court under the Family Law Act 1975 (Cth) for, *inter alia*, an order that she and the children be granted exclusive possession of the home. The issue before the Supreme Court was whether the Family Law Act deprived it of jurisdiction to entertain the husband's application after the wife had invoked the jurisdiction of the Family Court, in the absence of such specific statutory direction to this effect. Answering the question in the affirmative, Bray CJ asserted at 280:

> 'I cannot think that the Federal Parliament could have intended either that there should be concurrent proceedings in the State and federal courts leading to diametrically opposed conclusions or that a spouse who is faced with the prospect of the matrimonial home being sold over his or her head, albeit in accordance with legal title, should be without ... redress, at least when an arguable case of fault justifying principal matrimonial relief could have been presented to the court.'

However, he insisted that this did not mean that the husband's partition action was dismissed; instead, it 'remain[ed] in a state of suspended animation and [could] be revived if, for example, the proceedings in the Family Court [were] discontinued': (1977) 35 FLR (Aus) 272 at 286. These comments were cited with approval by Fisher J in *Re D'Onofrio* (1986) 65 ALR 545, and see *Williams v Williams* (1979) 38 FLR (Aus) 199.

[17] A separation agreement may, however, be set aside where the conduct of one spouse in forcing the other spouse to sign the agreement amounts to duress: *Bradley v Bradley* (4 April 2000, unreported) Ontario Supreme Court.

for one of the spouses to remain in occupation of the matrimonial home[18]. In these circumstances, it is likely that a non-occupying co-owner would be prevented from compelling partition, or more likely sale of the property under the Partition Acts where such an order would be contrary to the terms of the agreement between the parties. The agreement would oust the court's jurisdiction under the Partition Acts[19]. However, there must be some form of express agreement between the parties regulating the occupation of the matrimonial home[20] and the relevant wording must be explicit[21]. In addition to this, a separation agreement may effect a severance where spouses are joint tenants of the matrimonial home or other relevant property[22].

C Related issues

[9.09] Irrespective of whether spouses seek an order for sale of a matrimonial home under the Partition Acts following judicial separation or divorce, or in situations where such a decree is not available, two issues arise which require attention and which may impact on such proceedings.

---

18 In these circumstances, the non-occupying spouse is not ousted from the property so as to give rise to a claim for occupation rent: *Coburn v Coburn* (25 July 1984, unreported) Saskatchewan Queen's Bench and see ch 11 below, para **[11.18]**.

19 This is implicit in the decision in *Fergus v Fergus* (12 June 1997, unreported) Manitoba Court of Appeal, discussed below. In *Hicks v Kennedy* (1956) 4 DLR (2d) 320 Egbert J refused to order sale of a matrimonial home because of a post-nuptial settlement whereby the parties had transferred the property into their joint names, regarding this settlement as 'good reason to the contrary' for the purposes of the Partition Act 1868, s 4. (The case was reversed on appeal but on different grounds: (1957) 6 DLR (2d) 567.) In *Re Forster v Forster* (6 March 1980, unreported) Alberta Court of Appeal, Clement JA suggested that a separation agreement allowing the husband to have use and occupation of the matrimonial home prevented the wife from compelling partition or sale of the property due to lack of standing. Such use and occupation necessarily required the husband to have possession of the matrimonial home, so that the wife's position was analogous to that of a reversioner.

20 The mere fact that such property was occupied by spouses during the subsistence of marriage would not suffice (as suggested by Girvan J in *Ulster Bank Ltd v Carter* [1999] NI 93 at 105).

21 Thus in *Fergus v Fergus* (12 June 1997, unreported) Manitoba Court of Appeal, where the separation agreement merely allowed the wife to remain in possession of the family home until the parties agreed to sell it, the court held that the agreement did not prevent the husband from applying for partition or sale under the Law of Property Act 1987 (Man). Twaddle JA observed that the legislation was designed to avoid stalemate and that to oust this jurisdiction by agreement 'would require explicit language which is unmistakable in intent': Lexis transcript, at 3. Moreover, such an agreement would only be relevant between co-owners themselves and would not bind third parties (such as lenders) unless the circumstances of a particular case gave rise to an estoppel: see ch 4 above, paras **[4.57]-[4.60]**.

22 For example, an agreement to sell such property and to divide the proceeds of sale effects a severance: see *Schofield v Graham* (1969) 6 DLR (3d) 88 and *Sampaio v Sampaio* (1992) 90 DLR (4th) 122 (initial separation agreement effected a severance despite the fact that the husband subsequently agreed to purchase his wife's share in the property, and irrespective of the fact that the agreement described the property as being held under a joint tenancy).

1 Family Homes and Domestic Violence (NI) Order 1998

[9.10] The provisions of the Family Homes and Domestic Violence (NI) Order 1998 may affect the court's jurisdiction to order sale of a matrimonial home under the Partition Acts. The relevant provisions of the 1998 Order came into force in February and March 1999[23], replacing earlier legislation to this effect in the Family Law (Miscellaneous Provisions) (NI) Order 1984.

(a) Rights of spouses vis-à-vis each other under the 1998 Order

[9.11] Article 4 of the 1998 Order confers 'matrimonial home rights'[24] on a spouse with no proprietary interest[25] and on a spouse with a mere equitable interest in the property[26]. The 1998 Order contemplates two types of application in respect of the matrimonial home, the second of which is more important for present purposes. A spouse with matrimonial home rights may apply to court for an order allowing him or her into occupation of the property, or enforcing his or

22 (contd) A separation agreement giving one spouse a right to sell the property amounts to a severance (*Fraser v Atkinson* (27 October 1982, unreported) Alberta Queen's Bench) as does an agreement permitting a husband or wife to continue to reside in the property but which stipulates that the other spouse is to join in a subsequent sale of the property (*Paterson v Paterson* (1979) 108 DLR (3d) 234) or that the property should be sold if the occupying spouse does not meet certain conditions (*Re McKee and National Trust Co Ltd* (1975) 56 DLR (3d) 190 in which the court also held that a subsequent transfer of other property to the spouses as joint tenants did not affect this). Likewise, in *Van Gruting Estate v Van Gruting* (10 August 1993, unreported) British Columbia Supreme Court, a separation agreement which required the husband to make several lump sum payments to his wife in respect of her interest after which the property was to be transferred to the husband effected a severance, even though the husband died without having completed all the payments. Similar views have been expressed in a number of Australian cases: see *Abela v Public Trustee* (1983) 8 Fam LR 951 and *Pfeiffle v Pfeiffle* (1989) 13 Fam LR 692 (separation agreement which provides for a future sale of the property and its occupation until sale effects a severance), and see *Calabrese v Miuccio* (1984) 9 Fam LR 526 (agreement to divide property between spouses amounts to a severance even though it has not been approved by the court as required under the Family Law Act 1975 (Cth)). See further *Re Pozzi* (1982) 8 Fam LR 157 (agreement between spouses to sell certain property and divide the proceeds of sale amounts to a severance, even though the parties have not agreed on the extent of their respective shares in the property).

23 Family Homes and Domestic Violence (1998 Order) (Commencement No 1) Order (NI) 1999 and Family Homes and Domestic Violence (1998 Order) (Commencement No 2) Order (NI) 1999.

24 Formerly 'rights of occupation' under the Family Law (Miscellaneous Provisions) (NI) Order 1984.

25 Family Homes and Domestic Violence (NI) Order 1998, arts 4(1) and 4(2).

26 Family Homes and Domestic Violence (NI) Order 1998, art 4(9) noted in para **[9.20]** below. As with rights of occupation under the Family Law (Miscellaneous Provisions) (NI) Order 1984, matrimonial home rights are only available in respect of a dwelling house which has been occupied by spouses or was intended to be occupied by them as a matrimonial home: Family Homes and Domestic Violence (NI) Order 1998, art 4(7).

her right to remain in the matrimonial home[27]. Alternatively, if a spouse with matrimonial home rights is already in occupation of the matrimonial home, he or she has:

> 'a right not to be evicted or excluded from the dwelling house or any part of it by the other spouse except with the leave of the court ...'[28]

[9.12] In these circumstances, the other spouse may apply to court for an order terminating these rights. Under the 1998 Order, a person who is entitled to occupy a dwelling house by virtue of a beneficial interest may apply to court for a range of orders under art 11(3)[29], including an order restricting or terminating the respondent's matrimonial home rights[30]. In deciding whether to make such an order, the court is required to have regard to a number of factors[31]. These include the housing needs and housing resources of each party[32], their financial resources and conduct in relation to each other and otherwise[33]. However, an order under art 11 is essentially at the discretion of the court.

[9.13] Article 11 of the 1998 Order also appears to contemplate an application for an order terminating rights in respect of the matrimonial home being necessary where spouses are co-owners at law. The 1998 Order does not confer matrimonial home rights on such persons since they are entitled to occupy the

---

27 Family Homes and Domestic Violence (NI) Order 1998, art 11(1) contemplates applications by a spouse with matrimonial home rights for an 'occupation order' in respect of a dwelling house which is, has been or was at any time intended to be the home of the applicant and an 'associated person', the definition of which under art 3(3) includes spouses. The relevant orders are contained in the Family Homes and Domestic Violence (NI) Order 1998, arts 11(3)(a) and (b), and the court must have regard to the factors contained in arts 11(6) and (7) in deciding whether to make such an order (see para **[9.12]** below).

28 Family Homes and Domestic Violence (NI) Order 1998, art 4(2).

29 Family Homes and Domestic Violence (NI) Order 1998, art 11(1). Again such applications are only possible in respect of a dwelling house that is, has been or was at any time intended to be the home of the applicant and the other spouse: see para **[9.11]** above.

30 Family Homes and Domestic Violence (NI) Order 1998, art 11(3)(f). Although such orders are also referred to as 'occupation orders' under the legislation, they will hereafter be referred to as 'orders terminating' rights to avoid confusion.

31 Family Homes and Domestic Violence (NI) Order 1998, art 11(6).

32 And of any 'relevant child' as defined by the Family Homes and Domestic Violence (NI) Order 1998, art 3(2).

33 The court must also consider the likely effect of an order or refusal of such on the health, safety or well-being of the parties and of any relevant child: Family Homes and Domestic Violence (NI) Order 1998, art 11(6). In addition to this, art 11(7) states that the court must consider whether the applicant or a relevant child would be likely to suffer significant harm (see art 2(2)) as a result of the respondent's conduct if the order were not made. If the answer is yes, the court must make the order, unless doing so would cause just as much or more significant harm to the respondent or any relevant child.

property by virtue of having a legal estate. However, art 11(1) refers to occupation orders being made at the request of a person who is entitled to occupy a dwelling house by virtue of a beneficial estate, which would include spouses who are legal co-owners of a matrimonial home[34]. In these circumstances, the court may make an order prohibiting, suspending or restricting the respondent's right to occupy the dwelling house where he or she is so entitled by virtue of a beneficial estate[35]. Again, the court must take into account the factors discussed above.

(b) Rights against the other spouse and sale under the Partition Acts

[9.14] If spouses are co-owners of a matrimonial home at law or in equity and the husband brings an action for sale of the property under the Partition Acts in the event of being unable to petition for judicial separation or divorce, the 1998 Order may affect the court's jurisdiction to order sale. The 1998 Order places the right of spouses to occupy the matrimonial home and the regulation of this right on a statutory footing. Accordingly, the husband may have to obtain an order under art 11(3) terminating his wife's rights in respect of the matrimonial home before the court makes an order for sale under the Partition Acts. In other words, an application for sale of the matrimonial home in lieu of partition should be preceded or accompanied by an application under the 1998 Order.

[9.15] An order terminating the wife's rights is essentially at the discretion of the court. If the court were to exercise this discretion in favour of the wife and refuse to end her right to occupy the matrimonial home, the court might subsequently refuse to make an order for sale of the property under the Partition Acts. Likewise, if the husband had failed to make an application under the 1998 Order, this might affect the court's decision on whether to order sale of the matrimonial home under s 3 or s 4 of the 1868 Act[36]. In these circumstances, the court might be reluctant to order sale if the terms of the 1998 Order have not been complied with, and might refuse the relief sought or postpone sale until such an application is made[37]. However, in the event of refusing sale, the court would be unlikely to make an order for partition of the matrimonial home in the alternative since this would be both impracticable and futile.

---

34 In other words, where spouses are co-owners of a matrimonial home at law, the Family Homes and Domestic Violence (NI) Order 1998 merely regulates their respective rights to occupy the property.

35 Family Homes and Domestic Violence (NI) Order 1998, art 11(3)(e).

36 For example, the provisions of the Family Homes and Domestic Violence (NI) Order 1998 might enter into the court's consideration of what amounts to 'good reason to the contrary' under the Partition Act 1868, s 4, this being given a wider interpretation in relation to spouses (see the comments of Campbell J in *Northern Bank Ltd v Haggerty* [1995] NI 211 at 217). Alternatively, the Family Homes and Domestic Violence (NI) Order 1998 might influence the exercise of the court's discretion under the Partition Act 1868, s 3 despite the fact that sale of a matrimonial home would be more beneficial than partition as required by this section.

37 The court may postpone an order for sale under the Property (NI) Order 1997, art 49: see ch 7 above, paras **[7.63]**-**[7.64]**.

[9.16] If the court were to proceed with the partition action and make an order for sale of the matrimonial home in the absence of an application by the husband under the 1998 Order, what would be the position of the purchaser? In these circumstances, it appears that the purchaser would take good title to the property. Under the order for sale, the wife would be required to join in the conveyance of the property to the purchaser, and could not use her rights in respect of the matrimonial home to defeat sale, since they merely regulate her position vis-à-vis her husband and are not binding on the purchaser. However, the position may be different where a wife with a mere equitable interest in the matrimonial home has registered a matrimonial charge under the 1998 Order in respect of the property[38].

[9.17] A similar situation would arise in respect of partition actions between former spouses, since the 1998 Order also regulates the rights of such persons to occupy the matrimonial home[39]. Applications under art 11 are not confined to spouses, and may be made in respect of a dwelling house occupied by former spouses as a matrimonial home[40]. Thus, where former spouses are co-owners of a matrimonial home at law, and either one of them seeks an order for sale of the property under the Partition Acts this should be accompanied or preceded by an application for an order terminating the other spouse's rights under art 11(3) of the 1998 Order[41]. Likewise, where former spouses are co-owners of a matrimonial home in equity and title to the property is vested in the sole name of the husband, he should seek a similar order in respect of his former wife's rights before seeking sale of the matrimonial home in lieu of partition. A similar application would be required by the former wife in the event that she desires a sale of the property. However, in these circumstances, she might apply under either art 11 or art 13 of the 1998 Order. Article 13 contains specific provisions for regulating the property rights of former spouses in relation to the matrimonial home where a former spouse has no interest in the property or has a mere equitable interest[42]. While it does not confer matrimonial home rights on

38 See paras **[9.19]-[9.24]** below.

39 This is a new feature of the legislation. Under the Family Law (Miscellaneous Provisions) (NI) Order 1984, there was no provision for regulating property rights of former spouses in relation to the matrimonial home.

40 Family Homes and Domestic Violence (NI) Order 1998, art 11(1) contemplates an order under art 11(3) being made at the request of a person with a beneficial interest in a dwelling house where the property is, has been or was intended to be the home of that person and an 'associated' person, the definition of which under art 3(3) includes former spouses.

41 For example, an order under Family Homes and Domestic Violence (NI) Order 1998, art 11(3)(e): see para **[9.13]** above.

42 Family Homes and Domestic Violence (NI) Order 1998, arts 13(1) and 13(11). Such an application can only be made in respect of a dwelling house that was or was at any time intended by former spouses to be their matrimonial home: Family Homes and Domestic Violence (NI) Order 1998, art 13(1).

such persons, art 13 gives them standing to apply to court for a range of orders[43], including an order prohibiting, restricting or suspending the respondent's right to occupy the dwelling house[44]. However, the application of art 13 to former spouses with a mere equitable interest in the matrimonial home is without prejudice to their ability to make an application under art 11[45].

[9.18] As with spouses, the provisions of the 1998 Order might affect the court's decision whether to order sale of a matrimonial home at the request of a former spouse. However, in the absence of an appropriate application under the 1998 Order, such rights would not be binding on a subsequent purchaser of the property. Any rights that former spouses have under the 1998 Order only exist vis-à-vis the other former spouse, and there is no question of such rights binding third parties. Moreover, applications for sale of a former matrimonial home under the Partition Acts may be rare in practice. The situations in which former spouses would remain joint owners of the matrimonial home after divorce or judicial separation are not likely to arise frequently: in these circumstances, co-ownership may have come to an end as part of the relevant financial arrangements between the parties. Even if former spouses were to remain co-owners of the matrimonial home, the court's jurisdiction under the Partition Acts may be ousted by the terms of a property adjustment order between the parties[46].

(c) Rights of spouses against third parties under the 1998 Order

[9.19] The protection conferred on non-owning spouses by the 1998 Order is twofold, regulating their respective rights in the matrimonial home as regards each other and also as against third parties[47]. A spouse with no proprietary interest in the matrimonial home enjoys matrimonial home rights under the 1998

43 Family Homes and Domestic Violence (NI) Order 1998, arts 13(2)-(5).

44 Family Homes and Domestic Violence (NI) Order 1998, art 13(5)(c). In deciding whether to make such an order, the court must have regard to a number of factors. Under art 13(6), the court must take into account the same factors as it is required to have regard to under art 11(6): see para **[9.12]** above. In addition to this, it must consider the amount of time that has elapsed since the parties ceased to live together and the length of time since the marriage was dissolved or annulled, as well as the existence of any pending proceedings between the parties such as an application for a property adjustment order under the Matrimonial Causes (NI) Order 1978, art 26: Family Homes and Domestic Violence (NI) Order 1998, art 13(6). Family Homes and Domestic Violence (NI) Order 1998, art 13(8) also requires the court to apply a 'significant harm' test (discussed at para **[9.12]** above in relation to applications under art 11).

45 Family Homes and Domestic Violence (NI) Order 1998, art 13(12).

46 See para **[9.06]** above.

47 Such protection against third parties does not extend to former spouses since the Family Homes and Domestic Violence (NI) Order 1998 merely regulates their respective rights in relation to the matrimonial home. It does not confer matrimonial home rights on such persons that would take effect as a matrimonial charge and which could be registered against a subsequent purchaser of the property: see below.

Order[48]. Article 5 of the 1998 Order provides that his or her matrimonial home rights will be protected by the court as a matrimonial charge which, if registered in accordance with art 6, will be binding on a subsequent purchaser of the property[49]. Article 6(1) provides that a 'matrimonial charge' on a legal estate may be registered in the Land Registry or Registry of Deeds. Article 6(3) continues:

> 'A matrimonial charge shall be void as against a purchaser of an estate affected by the charge, unless the charge is registered before the purchaser:
>
> (a) enters into a contract to purchase that estate; or
>
> (b) takes as security for the payment of a sum of money –
>
> (i) the deposit of documents of title in pursuance of section 50 of the Land Registration Act (Northern Ireland) 1970, or
>
> (ii) in the case of unregistered land, the deposit of title deeds, in relation to that estate.'[50]

[9.20] While it may be true to say that the primary purpose of the 1998 Order is to protect a spouse with no proprietary interest in the matrimonial home[51], certain parts of the Order apply where spouses are co-owners of a matrimonial home either at law or in equity. As regards the former, the court's jurisdiction is confined to regulating their respective rights[52]. However, where spouses are co-owners of a matrimonial home in equity only, the 1998 Order goes further than merely regulating their respective rights to occupy the property. Article 4(9) of the 1998 Order reads:

> 'Without prejudice to any rights which arise by virtue of an equitable estate, a spouse who has only such an estate is to be treated for the purpose of determining whether he has matrimonial home rights as not being entitled to occupy the dwelling house by virtue of that estate; and this Article shall apply accordingly where each of two spouses is so entitled.'[53]

---

48 See para **[9.11]** above.

49 A 'purchaser' is defined in the Family Homes and Domestic Violence (NI) Order 1998, art 2(2) as 'any person who, for valuable consideration, takes an estate in land'.

50 For the appropriate documentation to be lodged in the Land Registry where a spouse wishes to register a matrimonial charge see Moir, *Land Registration Manual* (1994), pp 108-110 (discussing the former practice under the Family Law (Miscellaneous Provisions) (NI) Order 1984). The implications of the Family Homes and Domestic Violence (NI) Order 1998 for lenders whose security is restricted to an undivided share of a matrimonial home are considered in paras **[9.57]-[9.69]** below.

51 See the comments of Wood J in *Barnett v Hassett* [1981] 1 All ER 80 on the Matrimonial Homes Act 1967, the original legislation in England.

52 Since spouses who are joint tenants or tenants in common of a matrimonial home at law already have a common law right to occupy the property by virtue of their status as legal co-owners.

53 In other words, the Family Homes and Domestic Violence (NI) Order 1998 confers matrimonial home rights on such persons, even though they have a common law right to occupy the property by virtue of their status as equitable co-owners.

[9.21] Identical directions were contained in art 4(12) of the Family Law (Miscellaneous Provisions) (NI) Order 1984 and were based on s 1(11) of the Matrimonial Homes Act 1983, the equivalent English legislation at that time[54]. This Act replaced the Matrimonial Homes Act 1967. However, as originally enacted, the 1967 Act did not confer statutory 'rights of occupation' (the forerunner to matrimonial home rights) on a spouse with a beneficial interest in the matrimonial home. Such rights were not introduced until 1970[55], and appear to have been prompted by *Gurasz v Gurasz*[56] in which the Court of Appeal held that the 1967 Act only conferred rights of occupation on a spouse without any proprietary interest in the matrimonial home.

[9.22] The purpose of the 1970 amendment allowing a spouse with an equitable interest to claim statutory rights of occupation was to fortify her position vis-à-vis third parties. A spouse with no proprietary interest could register her matrimonial charge under the 1967 Act in order to protect herself against a subsequent purchaser of the property. However, since the 1967 Act did not confer rights of occupation on a spouse with an equitable interest in the matrimonial home, that spouse had nothing to register under the Act and her equitable interest could be defeated by a *bona fide* purchaser for value without notice. Thus, art 4(11) of the 1984 Order allowed a spouse with an equitable interest in the matrimonial home to protect herself against a purchaser by registering her matrimonial charge (derived from her statutory rights of occupation) in order to avoid having to rely on the doctrine of notice as a means of protection. Article 4(9) of the 1998 Order likewise contemplates registration of matrimonial home rights for this purpose. As regards a spouse with legal title to the matrimonial home, his or her legal rights are good against a purchaser and will take priority irrespective of whether or not the purchaser had notice of those rights.

(d) Rights against third parties and sale under the Partition Acts

[9.23] The fact that matrimonial home rights may take effect as a registered matrimonial charge has implications for partition actions where spouses are co-owners of a matrimonial home in equity. Assuming that a wife has an equitable interest in a matrimonial home, title to which is in the sole name of the husband who later brings an action for sale of the property under the Partition Acts, the wife's registered matrimonial charge will be binding on a subsequent purchaser of the property following the order for sale made in the partition action. However, under art 8(1) of the 1998 Order, it will have been a term of the contract of sale that the husband would procure cancellation of the registration

---

[54] The relevant legislation in England is now contained in the Family Law Act 1996.

[55] By the Matrimonial Proceedings and Property Act 1970, s 38, inserting s 1(9) of the Matrimonial Homes Act 1967.

[56] [1969] 3 All ER 822 and see *Tarr v Tarr* [1973] AC 254.

of the charge at his own expense before completion. In these circumstances, unless the wife has signed a release of her matrimonial charge[57], the husband will have to apply to court under art 11 of the 1998 Order[58] for an order terminating his wife's matrimonial home rights in the property which would allow the charge to be cancelled in the register[59]. Either way, the purchaser seems adequately protected so far as the wife's matrimonial charge is concerned[60].

[9.24] What is the position, however, where the husband is unable to secure an order cancelling the wife's matrimonial home rights and consequently her registered matrimonial charge under the 1998 Order[61]? It is submitted that the court would be unlikely to make an order for sale of the matrimonial home under the Partition Acts in these circumstances. While it could in theory make an order for sale, unless the court were also to order the charge to be cancelled (assuming that the court had power to do so, which is extremely unlikely[62]), sale of the property would be subject to the wife's rights under her registered matrimonial charge, the practical effect of which would almost certainly be to render the property unmarketable. Furthermore, it would be unlikely to make an order for partition of the property in the alternative in view of the fact that such an order would usually be impracticable and futile. Thus, under the terms of the 1998 Order, a spouse with a mere equitable interest may be able to resist an action for sale of the matrimonial home under the Partition Acts[63]. The position is different

---

57 As contemplated by the Family Homes and Domestic Violence (NI) Order 1998, art 10(1).

58 See para **[9.12]** above.

59 Family Homes and Domestic Violence (NI) Order 1998, art 9(1) provides that 'registration of a matrimonial charge may be cancelled where– ... (c) the spouse's matrimonial home rights have been terminated by an order of the court'. In addition to this, art 10(2) provides that, where a contract is made for the disposal of an estate in a dwelling house which is affected by a registered matrimonial charge, the matrimonial home rights giving rise to this charge shall be deemed to have been released upon either '(a) the delivery to the purchaser of such documents as are required to effect cancellation of the registration of the matrimonial charge; or (b) the lodging of such documents in the Land Registry or Registry of Deeds, as the case may require', whichever event occurs first.

60 However, if the purchaser were to complete the sale before cancellation of the charge or without its release by the wife, he would be bound by the registered matrimonial charge and would not take good title to the property.

61 It will be recalled that an order under the Family Homes and Domestic Violence (NI) Order 1998, art 11 is essentially at the discretion of the court: see para **[9.12]** above.

62 Since the appropriate means of cancelling the wife's matrimonial charge is for the husband to apply to court under the Family Homes and Domestic Violence (NI) Order 1998 in proceedings brought for that purpose.

63 Likewise, a spouse with no proprietary interest in a matrimonial home could thwart her husband's attempts to sell the property (albeit that he would not have to apply to court for an order for sale) in the event that the husband was unable to procure the cancellation of her registered matrimonial charge under the Family Homes and Domestic Violence (NI) Order 1998.

insofar as a wife with legal title is concerned. She could not rely on the 1998 Order to defeat an action for sale of the matrimonial home in these circumstances since her rights in relation to the property do not constitute a matrimonial charge. However, a spouse with legal title should be adequately protected by virtue of having a legal estate[64].

2 Criteria for ordering sale in partition actions between spouses

[9.25] Partition of a single dwelling house will usually be both impracticable and futile, so that there is likely to be a strong presumption in favour of sale of a matrimonial home under the Partition Acts upon such an application by a spouse or former spouse. An issue which may arise in this context is whether the court should adopt a more flexible approach in deciding whether to order sale, and whether the position of the parties as spouses or former spouses and associated status of the matrimonial home should impact on the otherwise strong presumption in favour of sale. In other words, should the court's discretion under the Partition Acts be wider in these circumstances than it might otherwise be in partition actions where the subject property is not a matrimonial home?

[9.26] Instances of courts in Northern Ireland determining partition actions between spouses or former spouses are difficult to find[65]. However, this particular factual situation has been considered in a number of Commonwealth cases.

(a) Australia

[9.27] Various Australian cases have suggested that the fact that parties to a partition action are husband and wife should not alter the settled practice in such actions. In *Peck v Peck*[66] Bright J remarked:

> 'Except ... insofar as there is an *ad misericordiam* discretion to defer enforcement of an order, I would deal with partition proceedings between husband and wife in the same way as any other partition proceedings ... There is an absolute right to partition, however inconvenient, unless, as a strict alternative, sale is ordered.

64 In these circumstances, the court might nevertheless refuse a request for sale of a matrimonial home by a spouse with legal title by analogy to the policy of the Family Homes and Domestic Violence (NI) Order 1998 and the protection that it confers on spouses with no proprietary interest and with a mere equitable interest in the matrimonial home. Similar arguments arise in respect of applications for sale of a matrimonial home by a creditor with an order charging land: see paras **[9.61]-[9.69]** below.

65 As illustrated in paras **[9.43]-[9.44]** below, most of the Northern Irish case law on partition actions involving spouses has arisen in the context of applications by third parties such as lenders.

66 [1965] SASR 293 at 300 and cited with approval by Fisher J in *Re D'Onofrio, ex p Blyth* (1986) 65 ALR 545.

The onus in the present case is on the wife who opposes sale. On the facts before me she has not discharged the onus and a sale should be ordered.'

[9.28] Similar views were expressed by Bray CJ in *Tansell v Tansell*[67]:

> 'A proceeding for partition and sale arises solely out of the co-ownership of property. The principles on which such a proceeding falls to be decided ... are exactly the same whether the co-owners are husband and wife or not ... The relief sought, and the principles deciding the grant or refusal of that relief, depend solely on co-ownership and in no way on the matrimonial relationship.'[68]

[9.29] These cases suggest that judges should not derogate from the established practice in partition actions simply because the parties are spouses. In addition to this, courts in this jurisdiction have ordered sale of a matrimonial home despite the fact that this might prejudice a possible reconciliation between spouses and despite objections to sale based on the fact that the property in question was the home in which children of the family were brought up[69].

(b) Canada

[9.30] In contrast, a more flexible approach has been adopted in numerous Canadian cases dealing with partition actions between spouses. It will be recalled that a majority of Canadian provinces have revised partition legislation by virtue of which co-owners of land have a *prima facie* right to partition or sale. Despite suggestions that the court's discretion is still limited in these circumstances[70], a wider range of factors have been taken into account in

---

[67] (1977) 35 FLR (Aus) 272 at 277.

[68] Likewise, in *Macrae v Macrae* (1962) SR (NSW) 142 at 144-145, Evatt CJ and Sugerman J stated:

> 'The incidents of a joint tenancy as between husband and wife do not differ from those of a joint tenancy as between other persons ... The husband is entitled as an incident of the joint tenancy, amongst other things, to bring about a sale of the entirety, with a view to ultimate division of the proceeds of sale ...'

See further the comments of McLelland J in *Re Fettell* (1952) 52 SR (NSW) 221 at 228.

[69] See *Witchard v Witchard* (1975) 6 ACTR 31 and *Smith v Smith (No 2)* [1962] Qd R 132, the respective courts taking the view that these considerations did not amount to 'good reason to the contrary' for the purposes of legislation similar to the Partition Act 1868, s 4. In *Peck v Peck* [1965] SASR 293 where a wife opposed her husband's request for sale of a jointly owned home on the basis that he had deserted her and sale would deprive the wife of her home, the court regarded this as insufficient reason for refusing to order sale.

[70] See *Michaud v Michaud* (1980) 29 NBR (2d) 591 in which Abbis J held that the court has discretion to refuse partition or sale of matrimonial property, but that this discretion is severely limited citing *Bergen v Bergen* (1969) 68 WWR 196. See further *Re MacDonald and MacDonald* (1976) 73 DLR (3d) 341 at 346 in which Steele J asserted that the discretion to refuse partition or sale 'must be exercised on narrow grounds' and see *Boeckler v Boeckler* (1987) 15 BCLR (2d) 134. Contrast this with *Silva v Silva* (1990) 75 DLR (4th) 415 in which the Ontario Court of Appeal referred to the limited discretion to be exercised in partition actions where the parties are not spouses.

determining whether to exercise this discretion, such factors being peculiar to the position of the parties as spouses and the status of the matrimonial home[71]. A number of general principles may be discerned from the relevant case law.

[9.31] Co-owners of land in Ontario have a *prima facie* right to partition or sale, unless such an order would be vexatious, malicious or oppressive[72]. In the event that partition or sale would jeopardise substantial rights in relation to the matrimonial home, the application should be dismissed until the spouses' respective rights have been determined under the relevant matrimonial legislation[73]. However, if no such conflict arises, the court may determine the partition action accordingly. The fact that one of the spouses merely wishes to realise his or her interest in the matrimonial home does not usually amount to vexatious or oppressive behaviour[74]. In addition to this, the court is unlikely to refuse to order sale merely because sale would inconvenience the spouse and children who occupy the home[75]. The fact that the occupying spouse may have to

---

71 See below. Such factors have been applied in respect of partition actions both between spouses and between former spouses. In *Re MacDonald and MacDonald* (1976) 73 DLR (3d) 341 it was suggested that, once a married couple had divorced, they were on the same footing as two strangers as regards partition actions involving the matrimonial home. However, in *Re Yale and MacMaster* (1974) 46 DLR (3d) 167, Galligan J held that, where the parties were formerly husband and wife and the property in question was a matrimonial home which continued to provide security for one of the spouses and young children of the marriage, this factor should be given considerable weight. In addition to this, a number of Canadian cases have applied a 'relative hardship' test (see paras **[9.31]-[9.32]** below) to partition actions between former spouses: see, for example, *Fernandes v Fernandes* (1976) 65 DLR (3d) 684; *Cook v Cook* (9 September 1977, unreported) British Columbia Supreme Court and *Re Kneebone and Matheson* (1981) 124 DLR (3d) 538.

72 See ch 7 above, para **[7.57]**. In *Walters v Walters* (1992) 92 DLR (4th) 398, Wright J suggested that the onus of proof should be reversed in partition actions between spouses, giving the applicant a *prima facie* right to partition or sale if he could show that the resisting spouse was unreasonably withholding her consent to such an order.

73 Currently the Family Law Act 1990 (Ont), and see *Silva v Silva* (1990) 75 DLR (4th) 415 and *Martin v Martin* (1992) 85 DLR (4th) 115, followed by the respective courts in *Walters v Walters* (1992) 92 DLR (4th) 398 and *Varty v Varty* (22 September 1994, unreported) Ontario Court of Justice (General Division). Similar views were expressed in *Binkley v Binkley* (1988) 14 RFL (3d) 336 and *Batler v Batler* (1989) 18 RFL (3d) 211 in relation to corresponding legislative provisions which preceded the Family Law Act 1990 (Ont).

74 *Cudmore v Cudmore* (21 February 1997, unreported) Ontario Court of Justice (General Division). However, an order for sale may be refused in these circumstances if the hardship which would be caused to the opposing co-owner by making such an order would outweigh the hardship suffered by the plaintiff (who merely wishes to realise his interest in the property) upon refusing sale: *Re Knowlton and Bartlett* (1984) 16 DLR (4th) 209 and see below. See further *McFadden v McFadden* (1972) 5 RFL 299 in which Costello J held that the needs of the father and children for a stable home life would be preferred to the financial needs of the wife who sought an order for sale of the matrimonial home.

75 See, for example, *Brown v Brown* [1953] 1 DLR 158; *Davis v Davis* [1954] 1 DLR 827; and *Re Perkins and Perkins* (1972) 31 DLR (3d) 694.

apply for additional maintenance as a result of such an order is irrelevant in this context[76]. An order for sale is also likely where an opposing spouse no longer resides in the matrimonial home[77], or where sale of the property and division of the proceeds would provide sufficient funds to purchase other suitable accommodation[78]. The court may give the opposing spouse an opportunity to purchase the share of the party seeking sale[79], and may postpone sale to facilitate this[80]. Alternatively, he or she may be given a right of first refusal upon the court making an order for sale of the matrimonial home[81]. In addition to this, a number of cases have applied a test of 'relative hardship' in determining whether to order sale of a matrimonial home in lieu of partition[82]. This involves weighing

---

[76] *Re Perkins and Perkins* (1972) 31 DLR (3d) 694 and *Re MacDonald v MacDonald* (1976) 73 DLR (3d) 341. Contrast this with the approach of courts in British Columbia, discussed in para **[9.32]** below.

[77] *Breau v Breau* (1989) 22 RFL (3d) 108.

[78] See *Brown v Brown* [1953] 1 DLR 158 (husband's financial situation had changed for the worse; matrimonial home too large and costly for the wife to maintain and she could find more suitable and less expensive accommodation) and *Cudmore v Cudmore* (21 February 1997, unreported) Ontario Court of Justice (General Division) (sale of matrimonial home and associated farm property would leave both spouses with sufficient funds to purchase other suitable accommodation). Similar views have been expressed in relation to the Law of Property Act 1987 (Man). In Manitoba, either spouse is entitled to an order for partition or sale so long as he or she comes to court 'with clean hands' and the other party cannot show that the order would be oppressive or vexatious: *Shwabuik v Shwabuik* (1965) 51 WWR 549; *Magne v Magne* (1990) 65 Man R (2d) 241; and *Carnahan v Carnahan* (1994) 94 Man R (2d) 67). In *Zazalak v Zazalak* (1992) 82 Man R (2d) 153 the court ordered sale of a matrimonial home on the basis that the husband and children had various other reasonable options for accommodation. Contrast this with *Fergus v Fergus* (12 June 1997, unreported) Manitoba Court of Appeal, in which the court observed that sale of the matrimonial home would probably have been refused if the children of the marriage had still been residing in the property. In *Kluss v Kluss* [1947] 2 WWR 379 the court ordered sale of matrimonial property which was subject to a judgment against the husband for the support and maintenance of his wife, but ordered that the husband's share of the proceeds of sale should be paid into court as security for such payments.

[79] *Dearing v Dearing* (26 November 1991, unreported) Ontario Court of Justice (General Division), in which Stortini J asserted that, in family cases, each party should be accorded such an opportunity.

[80] Although the court is unlikely to postpone sale if there is no prospect of the opposing co-owner acquiring the necessary financial means to purchase this share: *Cudmore v Cudmore* (21 February 1997, unreported) Ontario Court of Justice (General Division).

[81] In which case the price of the other co-owner's share would be fixed by the market: *Arlow v Arlow* (1990) 27 RFL (3d) 348). The court should not permit the opposing co-owner to purchase the other spouse's interest at a price fixed by the court (*Wilson v Wilson* (1988) 14 RFL (3d) 98 and *Batler v Batler* (1989) 18 RFL (3d) 211 in which the respective courts stressed the need to achieve the market value of the property by selling it on the open market).

[82] See, for example, *Cmajdalka v Cmajdalka* (1973) 11 RFL 302; *MacDonald v MacDonald* (1973) 13 RFL 248; and *Re Yale and MacMaster* (1974) 46 DLR (3d) 167 (Galligan J in the latter case declining to follow *Re Perkins and Perkins* (1972) 31 DLR (3d) 694 in which the court held that sale would not be refused simply because it would cause hardship to the spouse who occupied the family home).

the hardship which might be caused to the plaintiff by refusing such an order against that which might be caused to the defendant by ordering sale. For example, in *Klakow v Klakow*[83] and *Baker v Baker*[84] the respective courts refused to order sale of a matrimonial home because the husbands were disabled and unemployable, while the wives would not suffer significant hardship if the order was refused because they were financially independent and had accommodation elsewhere. Likewise, in *MacDonald v MacDonald*[85] sale was refused on the basis that the husband had a modest income and would be unable to provide similar accommodation for himself and the children of the marriage, yet the wife was able to support herself[86].

[9.32] In British Columbia, a co-owner has a *prima facie* right to partition or sale unless justice requires that this right be denied[87]. A number of situations have emerged in which notions of justice might persuade the court to refuse or to postpone sale in partition actions between spouses[88]. For example, an order for sale has been refused where a non-custodial spouse has been unable or has refused to pay an adequate amount of child support (the children and custodial spouse residing in the matrimonial home)[89]. Likewise, sale may be postponed where its effect would be to increase the expenses of the spouse who is residing in the matrimonial home to the extent that she would require an increase in child

---

83 (1972) 7 RFL 349.

84 (1973) 14 RFL 256.

85 (1973) 13 RFL 248.

86 A similar decision was reached by the New Brunswick Supreme Court in *Melvin v Melvin* (1975) 58 DLR (3d) 98 (husband occupying the former matrimonial home, and wife living with another man; only real hardship for the wife would be a delay in the conversion of her share of the property into cash) and by the Prince Edward Island Supreme Court in *Re Kneebone and Mathseon* (1981) 124 DLR (3d) 538 (husband occupying the former matrimonial home along with the children of the marriage and his present wife, and could not afford to purchase another home; petitioner had also remarried and shared a home with her new husband). In *Re Yale and MacMaster* (1974) 46 DLR (3d) 167, Galligan J applied the relative hardship test to an application for sale of a matrimonial home by the husband's trustee in bankruptcy. Refusing sale, the learned judge drew attention to the fact that the wife was working part-time and was able to keep up the modest mortgage payments on the property, yet would be unable to make a down payment on a similar property if the matrimonial home was sold. In contrast, any potential hardship to the husband's creditors was small – they would receive their money, albeit at a later date, with the value of the secured property increasing steadily in the meantime.

87 See ch 7 above, para **[7.58]**. Partition of Property Act 1996 (BC), ss 6-8 which enable the court to order sale closely resemble the Partition Act 1868, ss 3-5.

88 For a useful summary of the relevant principles see *Woodson v Protheroe* (1995) 17 RFL (4th) 104. In *Watts v Watts* (1951) 4 WWR 566 the court held that different considerations should be taken into account when a spouse seeks partition than when partition is sought by a partner.

89 *Hoyer v Hoyer* (1982) 41 BCLR 27; *Pacheco v Pacheco* (1988) 18 RFL (3d) 275; and *Wundele v Wundele* (1994) 99 BCLR (2d) 1.

or spousal support payments[90], or where the property is required for housing a spouse and dependent children[91]. The court may refuse to order sale where the equity in the matrimonial home is so small that sale might result in little or no surplus to divide between the parties[92], or where a share of the proceeds of sale of the matrimonial home would not be sufficient for the occupying spouse to purchase alternative accommodation[93]. Sale has also been refused on the basis that it might prejudice a possible reconciliation between spouses[94]. In addition to this, a co-owner seeking partition or sale in British Columbia must not be motivated by malice or spite, or by a desire to be vexatious or oppressive[95]. However, in this context oppression has been interpreted as 'economic oppression', so that an order for sale may be refused if the spouse who occupies the matrimonial home and who opposes sale would be unable to cope financially if the property was sold[96]. In contrast, the court is likely to order sale where this

---

90 *Greenlees v Greenlees* (1981) 23 RFL (2d) 323, and see *Boeckler v Boeckler* (1987) 15 BCLR (2d) 134 (sale would have resulted in increased maintenance payments, yet the plaintiff spouse had failed to make such payments in the past).

91 *Bashi v Bashi* (17 June 1991, unreported) British Columbia Supreme Court. However, in *Madill v Madill* (1988) 31 BCLR (2d) 368 the court made an order for sale of a matrimonial home on the basis that the parties' dependent children were nearing the age of majority and the husband had consistently paid both child and spousal maintenance.

92 *Philips v Philips* (1980) 19 RFL (2d) 193.

93 *Harmeling v Harmeling* (1975) 5 WWR 688 in which the British Columbia Court of Appeal refused to order sale of a matrimonial home which was purchased primarily with the husband's money to provide for his retirement. The husband here was over 70 years old and his half of the proceeds of sale (along with his other assets) would not be sufficient to provide him with alternative accommodation. An order for sale is likely where the spouse who occupies the matrimonial home has sufficient financial resources to purchase a similar home: see *Woodson v Protheroe* (1995) 17 RFL (4th) 104 (wife had financial means to purchase comparable accommodation in the area; husband discharging his child support obligations and was likely to continue to do so) and *Hancock v Hancock* (13 April 1995, unreported) British Columbia Supreme Court (wife could purchase a suitable home in the area with manageable mortgage obligations; desirable that children should have stability, but this did not require them to continue living in the traditional family home).

94 *Watts v Watts* (1951) 4 WWR 566. In *Steele v Steele* (1960) 67 Man R 270 the court also considered the likelihood of a reconciliation between the parties. Contrast this with the Australian case of *Witchard v Witchard* (1975) 6 ACTR 31 noted at para **[9.29]** above.

95 See ch 7 above, para **[7.58]** and see *Rayner v Rayner* (1956) 3 DLR (2d) 522.

96 See *Korolew v Korolew* (1972) 7 RFL 162 and *Reitsma v Reitsma* [1975] 3 WWR 281. In *Meadows v Meadows* (21 October 1974, unreported) Vancouver Registry No 29771 (discussed in *Reitsma*) Berger J held that an order for sale of a matrimonial home would amount to economic oppression where the husband had a reasonably good income, but the wife who occupied the matrimonial home was working in an unskilled job and earning significantly less money. However, in *Reitsma* the court held that an order for sale would not amount to economic oppression where the wife would receive a substantial equity in the matrimonial home on sale and was receiving regular maintenance payments from the husband.

would be economically beneficial for the parties[97]. Despite suggestions that personal inconvenience or hardship caused by an order for sale is irrelevant[98], the latter may be a relevant factor if it amounts to economic oppression[99]. In addition to this, a number of such cases have applied a 'relative hardship' test in partition actions between spouses[100].

[9.33] The practice in such cases may be distinguished on the basis that they were decided under legislation that confers a *prima facie* right to partition or sale, and thus differs fundamentally from the Partition Acts. Nevertheless, they are indicative of a wider range of factors being taken into account in partition actions between spouses. In addition to this, a number of cases decided in Alberta prior to the repeal of the Partition Acts asserted a discretion to refuse both partition and sale where the disputed property comprised a matrimonial home[101]. For example, in *Kornacki v Kornacki*[102] the court refused to order partition or sale of a matrimonial home under the Partition Acts because the wife and infant children of the marriage were living in the property[103]. Likewise, in *Elligott v Elligott*[104] the court was of the opinion that the interests of the wife and

---

96 (contd) In contrast, Seaton J in *Bergen v Bergen* (1969) 68 WWR 196 refused to order sale of a matrimonial home where the wife was barely able to survive in financial terms and renting alternative accommodation with her share of the proceeds of sale would only provide a short-term solution. Despite the fact that the husband here was also in dire financial circumstances, Seaton J found that he was acting oppressively in seeking sale and did not come to court 'with clean hands'.

97 *Wells v Wells* (16 November 1977, unreported) British Columbia Supreme Court (wife's share of the proceeds of sale would allow her to purchase alternative accommodation with similar mortgage obligations, and husband prepared to continue his current maintenance obligations; extensive and expensive repairs required to maintain matrimonial home).

98 *Bergen v Bergen* (1969) 68 WWR 196.

99 *Reitsma v Reitsma* [1975] 3 WWR 281.

100 See, for example, *Fernandes v Fernandes* (1976) 65 DLR (3d) 684 (sale of the matrimonial home would not result in hardship for the wife since an existing maintenance order could be varied to provide her with increased financial provision) and *Bashi v Bashi* (17 June 1991, unreported) British Columbia Supreme Court. See further *McAra v Haisch* (27 September 1991, unreported) British Columbia Supreme Court (mere fact that an opposing spouse has grown accustomed to a high standard of living and will have to move from a large and expensive property into rental accommodation is not sufficient to displace the plaintiff's *prima facie* right to sale where he is responsible for all payments on the existing property). Where the court's decision on whether to grant or refuse sale would cause some inconvenience and hardship to either spouse in any event, the plaintiff's *prima facie* right to relief should prevail: *Cook v Cook* (9 September 1977, unreported) British Columbia Supreme Court.

101 Notwithstanding that the remedies of partition or sale under the Partition Acts 1868 and 1876 were otherwise regarded as a matter of right in Alberta: see ch 7 above, para **[7.56]**.

102 (1975) 21 RFL 400.

103 However, the court suggested that the wife might be awarded less maintenance if permitted to remain in the matrimonial home.

104 (1977) 6 AR 282.

six-year-old son of the marriage would be best served by allowing them to remain in the matrimonial home, and accordingly refused the husband's request for sale[105].

(c) Northern Ireland

[9.34] Under the Partition Acts, the court's discretion is usually restricted to making an order for either partition or sale[106]. The fact that the subject matter of the action comprises a matrimonial home should give rise to a strong presumption in favour of sale, given the practical difficulties associated with partition in these circumstances. For example, there is little doubt that an order for sale of such property would be more beneficial than partition for the purposes of s 3 of the 1868 Act. Likewise, 'good reason to the contrary' for the purposes of s 4 requires substantives reasons for refusing sale combined with the fact that partition of the property is a practicable alternative, which would not be the case in respect of a matrimonial home.

[9.35] It is unclear whether courts in Northern Ireland will continue to follow the established practice under the Partition Acts, or whether they will adopt a more flexible approach in partition actions between spouses and former spouses. In proceedings under the Partition Acts, the court is not required to have regard to specific factors such as the needs of any children and the financial resources of the spouses. However, it may be somewhat dogmatic to assert that such actions should be determined in the same manner as those between co-owners in general. In these circumstances, the courts may be willing to take account of a wider range of factors peculiar to the matrimonial relationship and associated status of the matrimonial home in deciding whether to order sale. Such factors might include ongoing maintenance and other financial obligations, as well as the needs of a spouse and dependent children who are residing in the matrimonial home[107]. In the absence of direct case law on the subject however, the extent to which courts in Northern Ireland will consider themselves bound by the narrow discretion which exists under the Partition Acts, or whether they will adopt a more flexible approach when determining partition actions between spouses and former spouses remains to be seen.

[9.36] Another possible argument in favour of courts in this jurisdiction applying a more flexible approach in partition actions between spouses and

---

105 In *Cattoni v Cattoni* (12 March 1980, unreported) Alberta Queen's Bench, Kerans J suggested that the court might refuse to order partition or sale under the Partition Acts 1868 and 1876 where children still resided in the matrimonial home. However, the learned judge made an order for sale of the matrimonial home in this particular case, since the property was being used by the wife as a source of revenue and she no longer needed it as a home.

106 See ch 7.

107 In addition to this, the court's jurisdiction under the Partition Acts 1868 and 1876 may be ousted by a property adjustment order or separation agreement (see paras **[9.06]** and **[9.08]** above), or where the circumstances of the case give rise to an estoppel (see ch 4 above, paras **[4.55]**-**[4.56]**).

former spouses is the fact that other legislation has conferred more extensive powers on the courts when determining property disputes between such persons than they would otherwise have in relation to property disputes between strangers[108]. For example, judges may take account of a wide range of factors in deciding whether to make a property adjustment order under the Matrimonial Causes (NI) Order 1978[109], and may make any order they think fit upon an application in respect of title to or possession of matrimonial property under s 17 of the Married Women's Property Act 1882[110]. As the law currently stands, it is submitted that courts should not take these provisions into account when determining partition actions between spouses and former spouses in respect of a matrimonial home or other such property. Each provision applies in a different context. The court cannot simply transpose principles derived from applications under matrimonial legislation onto applications under the Partition Acts because the parties to and subject matter of both actions are the same. However, this may change in the future.

[9.37] A recent report from the Law Reform Advisory Committee for Northern Ireland has proposed that the court should have a general power to decline to make an order under the Partition Acts in respect of applications by spouses, and that, when determining such applications, the court should have regard to the matters which it is obliged to take into account under the Matrimonial Causes (NI) Order 1978[111]. In other words, judges would have to consider all the circumstances of the case, with first consideration being given to the welfare of any minor child of the family[112]. Other relevant factors would include the income, earning capacity, property and other financial resources which each spouse had or was likely to have in the future; their respective financial needs, obligations and responsibilities both now and in the foreseeable future; any physical or mental disability of any of the parties; and the contribution which each spouse made or was likely to make in the foreseeable future to the welfare of the family[113].

---

108 See the decisions in *Northern Bank Ltd v Haggerty* [1995] NI 211 and *Northern Bank Ltd v Adams* (1 February 1996, unreported) High Court (NI), discussed at paras **[9.43]**-**[9.45]** below.

109 See para **[9.37]** below.

110 Married Women's Property Act 1882, s 17 is considered in detail at paras **[9.50]**-**[9.56]** below.

111 Law Reform Advisory Committee for Northern Ireland Discussion Paper No 5, *Matrimonial Property* (1999), p 44. The relevant factors are contained in the Matrimonial Causes (NI) Order 1978, art 27 (as amended by the Matrimonial and Family Proceedings (NI) Order 1989, art 6).

112 Matrimonial Causes (NI) Order 1978, art 27(1).

113 Matrimonial Causes (NI) Order 1978, art 27(2). Other factors listed in art 27(2) include the standard of living previously enjoyed by the family; the age of each party to the marriage and its duration; and the conduct of the spouses, if that conduct is such that it would be inequitable to disregard it.

D Proceedings under section 17 of the Married Women's Property Act 1882

[9.38] The court may order a sale or division of matrimonial property under s 17 of the Married Women's Property Act 1882 where a dispute arises between spouses in relation to the title to or possession of such property. The relevant principles for determining such applications and the effect of s 17 on partition actions involving spouses are discussed below.[114]

E Partition actions between cohabitees

[9.39] The position of persons living together in a cohabiting relationship merits consideration at this point. Cohabitees may purchase a home as co-owners[115]. Unlike spouses, no legislation exists to regulate the distribution of such property between cohabitees when their relationship breaks down. If the parties cannot reach an agreement on the disposal of the property or its continued use and occupation, either one of them may commence proceedings for sale under the Partition Acts. In these circumstances, the difficulties associated with physical partition of a dwelling house would usually give rise to a strong presumption in favour of sale. However, the provisions of the Family Homes and Domestic Violence (NI) Order 1998 may be relevant in this context.

[9.40] The 1998 Order regulates the rights of cohabitees and former cohabitees to occupy a dwelling house that represents the home of the parties[116]. As with spouses and former spouses, an application under art 11 of the 1998 Order may be made in respect of a dwelling house occupied by cohabitees and former

---

[114] See paras **[9.50]-[9.56]** below.

[115] The Law Reform Advisory Committee for Northern Ireland has proposed that beneficial ownership of a joint residence (or primary residence) of 'qualifying cohabitants' should automatically vest in both of them as joint tenants unless the parties execute a written agreement expressly stating otherwise: Law Reform Advisory Committee for Northern Ireland Discussion Paper No 5, *Matrimonial Property* (1999). The report defines 'qualifying cohabitants' as persons who have either:

(i) been living together in the same household as husband and wife for at least two years within the last three years, or

(ii) had a child by their relationship and have been living together in the same household as husband and wife.

[116] Again, this is a new feature of the legislation. Under the Family Law (Miscellaneous Provisions) (NI) Order 1984, there was no provision for regulating property rights of cohabitees or former cohabitees in relation to their homes.

[117] Family Homes and Domestic Violence (NI) Order 1998, art 11(1) contemplates an order under art 11(3) being made at the request of a person with a beneficial interest in a dwelling house where the property is, has been or was intended to be the home of that person and an 'associated' person, the definition of which under art 3(3) includes cohabitees and former cohabitees.

cohabitees as their home[117]. Thus, where such persons are co-owners of a dwelling house at law, and either one of them seeks an order for sale of the property under the Partition Acts this should be accompanied or preceded by an application for an order terminating the other cohabitee's rights under art 11(3) of the 1998 Order[118]. Likewise, where cohabitees or former cohabitees are co-owners of a home in equity and title to the property is vested in the sole name of the male partner, he should seek an order in respect of his partner's rights before seeking sale of the home in lieu of partition. A similar application would be required by the female partner in the event that she desires a sale of the property. However, in these circumstances, the female partner may apply under either art 11 or art 14 of the 1998 Order. Article 14 contains specific provisions for regulating the property rights of cohabitees or former cohabitees in relation to a dwelling house where such persons have no interest in the property or have a mere equitable interest[119]. While it does not confer matrimonial home rights on cohabitees or former cohabitees, art 14 gives them standing to apply to court for a range of orders[120], including an order prohibiting, restricting or suspending the respondent's right to occupy the dwelling house[121]. However, the application of art 14 to cohabitees or former cohabitees with a mere equitable interest in a dwelling house is without prejudice to their ability to make an application under art 11[122].

---

[117] (contd) Family Homes and Domestic Violence (NI) Order 1998, art 3(1)(a) defines cohabitees as 'a man and a woman who, although not married to each other, are living together as husband and wife'. References to former cohabitees should be construed accordingly but do not include cohabitees who subsequently marry each other: art 3(1)(b).

[118] For example, an order under the Family Homes and Domestic Violence (NI) Order 1998, art 11(3)(e): see para **[9.13]** above.

[119] Family Homes and Domestic Violence (NI) Order 1998, arts 14(1) and 14(11). Such an application can only be made in respect of a dwelling house that is, was or was at any time intended to be lived in together by the parties as husband and wife: art 14(1).

[120] Family Homes and Domestic Violence (NI) Order 1998, arts 14(2)-14(5).

[121] Family Homes and Domestic Violence (NI) Order 1998, art 14(5)(c). In deciding whether to make such an order, the court must have regard to a number of factors. Under art 14(6), the court is obliged to consider the same factors as in relation to an application under art 11(3) (see para **[9.12]** above). In addition to this, it must consider the nature of the parties' relationship, the length of time during which they lived together as husband and wife and since they ceased to live together, whether there are any children who are children of both parties or for whom both parties have parental responsibility, as well as the existence of any other pending proceedings such as those relating to legal or beneficial ownership of the property. Family Homes and Domestic Violence (NI) Order 1998, art 14(8) also requires the court to apply a 'significant harm' test (discussed at para **[9.12]** above in relation to applications under art 11).

[122] Family Homes and Domestic Violence (NI) Order 1998, art 14(12). In other words, the position is the same as that in respect of former spouses discussed at paras **[9.17]-[9.18]** above.

[9.41] Thus, a cohabitee or former cohabitee who seeks an order for sale of the family home under the Partition Acts should apply under the 1998 Order in respect of his partner's rights in the property. If he fails to do so, the court may take this into account in deciding whether to make an order for sale of the property under the Partition Acts. However, if the court were to proceed with the partition action and make an order for sale in the absence of any such application under the 1998 Order, the purchaser would nevertheless take good title to the property. A cohabitee or former cohabitee who opposes sale cannot use his or her rights under the 1998 Order to defeat sale and they will not bind a subsequent purchaser of the property. Any rights that such persons have under the 1998 Order only exist vis-à-vis the other partner; there is no question of such rights binding third parties[123].

[9.42] Another issue which may arise in this context is whether courts should adopt a more flexible approach in partition actions between cohabitees and former cohabitees than in partition actions in general. The possible arguments for doing so are less persuasive in this context than in respect of partition actions between spouses. For example, the absence of any specific legislative framework regulating the property rights of cohabitees on the breakdown of their relationship (aside from the limited protection under the 1998 Order) suggests that they should not be treated in a special manner, and that the traditional practice should apply in partition actions involving such persons. Likewise, there are currently no plans to reform the law in this respect[124]. Thus, as the law currently stands, it appears that the likelihood of a cohabitee or former cohabitee obtaining an order for sale of a family home under the Partition Acts must be regarded as considerable.

III Partition Actions by Lenders

[9.43] Situations may arise in which one spouse incumbers his or her interest in the matrimonial home. In these circumstances, a lender will have to bring an action under the Partition Acts to realise his security in the event of default, and there is usually a strong presumption in favour of an order for sale to facilitate

---

123 In addition to this, since the Family Homes and Domestic Violence (NI) Order 1998 does not confer matrimonial home rights on cohabitees or former cohabitees, they do not have a matrimonial charge on the property which could be registered in order to secure protection against third parties as in the case of spouses. Thus, cohabitees and former cohabitees are in the same position as former spouses as regards third parties: see paras **[9.17]-[9.18]** above.

124 For example, the recent report from the Law Reform Advisory Committee for Northern Ireland only proposes that courts should have discretion to refuse relief under the Partition Acts 1868 and 1876 in partition actions involving spouses: Law Reform Advisory Committee for Northern Ireland Discussion Paper No 5, *Matrimonial Property* (1999) discussed at para **[9.19]** above.

repayment of the outstanding debt[125]. Cases such as *Northern Bank Ltd v Beattie*[126] and *Ulster Bank Ltd v Shanks*[127] held that the fact that the property in question comprised a matrimonial home merely reinforced this presumption in favour of sale, in view of the practical difficulties associated with an order for partition. Objections to sale based on the fact that the property was not merely a form of security but also the home of the 'innocent' spouse (and perhaps children of the marriage) were irrelevant in this context[128]. However, several recent cases have suggested that the court may consider the effect of legislation regulating the property rights of spouses in relation to the matrimonial home and consequently exercise a wider discretion to refuse a request for sale of such property under the Partition Acts by a lender.

[9.44] In *Northern Bank Ltd v Haggerty*[129] the plaintiff's request for sale of a matrimonial home under s 4 of the 1868 Act was refused due to lack of standing[130]. Counsel for the wife had suggested that, if the Bank could apply for sale of a matrimonial home under the Partition Acts, this would deprive the court of the wide discretion which it possesses under certain statutory provisions regulating the property rights of spouses[131]. However, Campbell J was of the opinion that 'good reason to the contrary' for the purposes of s 4 'may now be interpreted more widely than it has been in the past'[132]. This suggests that 'good reason to the contrary' is a lower hurdle to overcome today, and that the courts may take matrimonial property legislation into account when exercising their discretion to refuse sale under s 4. Campbell J's comments were endorsed by Master Ellison in *Northern Bank Ltd v Adams*[133] as 'in keeping with recent legislative changes dealing with the rights of spouses'[134]. In *Adams*, the plaintiff brought an action for sale of a matrimonial home under the Partition Acts. Determining the action under s 3 of the 1868 Act, Master Ellison suggested that

125 See generally ch 8.

126 [1982] 18 NIJB 1.

127 [1982] NI 143.

128 Likewise, an order for sale of a matrimonial home under the Partition Acts 1868 and 1876 has been granted at the request of a lender in a number of other cases without the court questioning the status of the property in question: see *Ulster Bank Ltd v McCullough* (25 September 1989, unreported) High Court (NI); *Northern Bank Ltd v Moore* (4 June 1991, unreported) High Court (NI); *Bank of Ireland v Young* (13 February 1992, unreported) High Court (NI); and *William Ewing t/a Ewing Brothers v McCann* (26 January 1993, unreported) High Court (NI).

129 [1995] NI 211 (Campbell J).

130 See ch 8 above, paras **[8.76]-[8.78]**.

131 The specific statutory provisions referred to are considered below.

132 [1995] NI 211 at 217.

133 (1 February 1996, unreported) High Court (NI), and considered at ch 7 above, paras **[7.11]-[7.17]**.

134 (1 February 1996, unreported) High Court (NI), at 12-13 judgment.

these recent legislative changes supported the proposition that the words 'may if it thinks fit' in s 3 allow the court to refuse to order sale of a matrimonial home, even where partition is impracticable[135].

[9.45] Both cases suggest that the court now has a wider discretion to refuse an order for sale of a matrimonial home under the Partition Acts because of the proliferation of legislation regulating the property rights of spouses. In other words, the difficulties associated with partition in these circumstances do not necessarily tip the balance heavily in favour of sale and make it difficult for the opposing co-owner to resist such an order. The respective courts in *Haggerty* and *Adams* cited a number of specific provisions regulating the property rights of spouses as encroaching upon the court's jurisdiction under the Partition Acts upon an application for sale of a matrimonial home by a lender.

A Section 30 of the Law of Property Act 1925 and Article 309 of the Insolvency (NI) Order 1989

[9.46] In *Northern Bank Ltd v Adams*[136], Master Ellison asserted that the court should consider both s 30 of the Law of Property Act 1925 and art 309(3) of the Insolvency (NI) Order 1989 in deciding whether to order sale of a matrimonial home under the Partition Acts at the request of a security holder[137].

[9.47] Section 30 of the 1925 Act contemplated applications by trustees for sale and beneficial co-owners of land in England and Wales in the event of disagreement as to whether the trustees should execute the trust for sale or exercise any of their powers (including the power to partition) under ss 28 and 29 of the 1925 Act[138]. There is no equivalent provision in Northern Ireland. Article 309(3) of the 1989 Order regulates partition actions by a trustee in bankruptcy where the subject property comprises a matrimonial home which the bankrupt and his spouse or former spouse own as joint tenants or tenants in common[139]. Under both s 30 and art 309(3) the court 'may make such order as it thinks fit' and has discretion to refuse both partition and sale. In deciding whether to

---

135 In *Ulster Bank Ltd v Carter* [1999] NI 93 at 101 Girvan J referred to the normal practice under the Partition Acts 1868 and 1876 whereby a lender whose security affects an undivided share of a matrimonial home will usually be entitled to an order for sale of the property and the innocent spouse ejected from the premises to facilitate sale. However, he left open the question of whether certain legislative provisions regulating the property rights of spouses might be relevant in this context: [1999] NI 93 at 105.

136 (1 February 1996, unreported) High Court (NI).

137 Although the plaintiff in *Northern Bank Ltd v Adams* (1 February 1996, unreported) High Court (NI) was an equitable mortgagee, the same principles would apply to partition actions by lenders in general.

138 Law of Property Act 1925, s 30 has now been replaced by the Trusts of Land and Appointment of Trustees Act 1996, s 14.

139 Insolvency (NI) Order 1989, art 309(3) is discussed at paras **[9.76]-[9.78]** below.

exercise that discretion, the court is guided by a number of factors, which Master Ellison applied to the factual situation in *Adams*[140]. He examined the extent to which the Bank's interests would be prejudiced by an order postponing sale, the conduct and financial resources of Mrs Adams, the needs of Mrs Adams and her children, and the Bank's conduct in its dealings with her[141]. Master Ellison concluded that the Bank was entitled to an order for sale of the matrimonial home, but postponed sale for 18 months[142].

[9.48] It is difficult to understand why Master Ellison regarded s 30 of the 1925 Act and art 309 of the 1989 Order as relevant to the question of whether the court should make an order for sale of a matrimonial home under the Partition Acts. Whilst acknowledging that the wording of both provisions differed substantially from the relevant provisions of the Partition Acts, Master Ellison was nevertheless of the opinion that they all conferred 'similar kinds of discretion in similar contexts'[143]. However, both s 30 and art 309(3) contemplate applications by co-owners that differ substantially from those under the Partition Acts. As regards the former, the 1925 Act reformed the law of co-ownership in England and Wales by imposing statutory trusts for sale on such land. Applications for sale of concurrent interests in land were regulated by s 30 and the Partition Acts repealed accordingly[144]. Likewise, art 309(3) of the 1989 Order provides that the court may make any order it thinks fit under the Partition Acts in one specific factual situation: namely where a partition action is brought by a trustee in bankruptcy and relates to a matrimonial home. It is not indicative of a wide discretion in partition actions in general[145].

[9.49] Thus, it is submitted that the court's discretion under s 30 of the 1925 Act and art 309(3) of the 1989 Order (as well as the factors that it takes into account when exercising that discretion) are not relevant considerations in an application for sale of a matrimonial home under the Partition Acts by a security holder[146].

---

[140] As regards the Insolvency (NI) Order 1989, art 309(3), the factors which the court must consider are prescribed by art 309(4) of that Order: see para **[9.77]** below. Law of Property Act 1925, s 30 did not prescribe any factors for the court to consider upon such an application (contrast this with an application under the Trusts of Land and Appointment of Trustees Act 1996, s 14 where the court is obliged to consider factors specified in s 15 of that Act). However, Master Ellison in *Northern Bank Ltd v Adams* (1 February 1996, unreported) High Court (NI) applied the factors which would have been taken into account where a lender applied for sale under the Law of Property Act 1925, s 30 as derived from cases such as *Lloyds Bank plc v Byrne* [1993] 1 FLR 369 and *Barclays Bank plc v Hendricks* [1996] 1 FLR 258.

[141] (1 February 1996, unreported) High Court (NI), at 41-48.

[142] Under the Judicature (NI) Act 1978, s 86(3): see ch 7 above, para **[7.12]**.

[143] (1 February 1996, unreported) High Court (NI), at 27.

[144] Wallace, 'Mortgages and Charges', *Third Annual Review of Property Law* (1996) 7 at 23. See further the comments of Murrary J in *Northern Bank Ltd v Beattie* [1982] 18 NIJB 1 at 24-25.

[145] See Wallace, 'Mortgages and Charges', *Third Annual Review of Property Law* (1996) 7 at 23-24.

B Section 17 of the Married Women's Property Act 1882

[9.50] Counsel for the wife in *Northern Bank Ltd v Haggerty*[147] suggested that the court should dismiss the Bank's request for sale under the Partition Acts because of the jurisdiction conferred by s 17 of the Married Women's Property Act 1882[148]. Counsel submitted that, if the Bank could bring an action under s 4 of the 1868 Act, the court would be deprived of the discretion which exists under s 17 because it is trite law that sale must be ordered under s 4 unless 'good reason to the contrary' is established. It is clear that, in line with previous case law on s 4[149], counsel regarded 'good reason to the contrary' as a high hurdle to get over, and was of the opinion that the discretion available to the court under s 17 of the 1882 Act probably would not satisfy this. However, Campbell J regarded this argument as inconclusive because of his wider interpretation of 'good reason to the contrary'[150]. This suggests that the court's discretion under s 17 may be a relevant factor in determining partition actions by lenders[151].

1 Section 17 proceedings

[9.51] Section 17 of the 1882 Act allows the court to determine disputes between spouses over the title to or possession of property. The court may make 'any order [it] thinks fit', including an order for sale[152]. A number of cases initially suggested that s 17 allowed the court to make such orders as it thought just and reasonable in all the circumstances of the case[153]. However, it is now well established that s 17 is procedural and merely permits the court to determine property disputes between spouses according to established legal principles[154]. Furthermore, it can only declare the existing legal and equitable property rights of the spouses, and cannot order the transfer of any proprietary rights between them[155]. Thus, the court's discretion under s 17 is more restricted than the wording of the provision might suggest. Section 17 proceedings are

---

146 Likewise, such provisions would not be relevant in partition actions between spouses or former spouses *inter se*.

147 [1995] NI 211 (Campbell J).

148 As extended by the Law Reform (Husband and Wife) Act (NI) 1964, s 3.

149 See ch 5 above, paras **[5.28]-[5.45]**.

150 See para **[9.44]** above.

151 Although the plaintiff in *Northern Bank Ltd v Haggerty* [1995] NI 211 was a creditor with an order charging land, the same arguments would apply in respect of partition actions by lenders in general.

152 Matrimonial Causes (NI) Order 1978, art 55 extends the Married Women's Property Act 1882, s 17 to spouses in void, annulled or dissolved marriages, while the Family Law (Miscellaneous Provisions) (NI) Order 1984, art 16(2) provides that, where an agreement to marry is terminated, s 17 applies 'as if the parties had been married'.

153 See, for example, *Fibrance v Fibrance (No 2)* [1957] 1 All ER 357; *Ulrich v Ulrich* [1968] 1 All ER 67 and the decision of the Court of Appeal in *Gissing v Gissing* [1969] 2 Ch 85.

typically brought by a spouse wishing to establish a beneficial interest in the matrimonial home through direct or indirect contributions[156]. If the court decides that she has acquired such an interest, it may order a sale of the matrimonial home and division of the proceeds between the spouses in the same proceedings[157]. Alternatively, that spouse might seek a declaration of her beneficial interest under s 17 and either join this with proceedings for sale of the matrimonial home under the Partition Acts or subsequently institute separate proceedings under the Partition Acts.

2 *Section 17 and partition actions involving spouses*

[9.52] Instances of courts in this jurisdiction considering the interplay between s 17 and the Partition Acts are difficult to find. However, a number of Canadian cases have considered the effect of proceedings under s 17 or equivalent statutory provisions on the court's jurisdiction to order sale of matrimonial property in lieu of partition.

[9.53] This issue initially arose in the context of the so-called 'deserted wife's equity'. A number of English cases decided in the 1950s and early 1960s asserted that a deserted wife had a right to remain in the matrimonial home and

---

[154] See the decision of the House of Lords in *Gissing v Gissing* [1970] AC 777 and see *Pettitt v Pettitt* [1971] AC 886. Similar views were expressed in relation to provisions resembling the Married Women's Property Act 1882, s 17 in *Macrae v Macrae* (1962) SR (NSW) 142, and in *Thompson v Thompson* (1961) 26 DLR (2d) 1; *Kearney v Kearney* [1970] 2 OR 152; *Re Hearty and Hearty* [1970] 2 OR 344; and *Michaud v Michaud* (1980) 29 NBR (2d) 591.

[155] In *McFarlane v McFarlane* [1972] NI 59 the Northern Ireland Court of Appeal emphasised that the Married Women's Property Act 1882, s 17 is procedural only and cannot confer a beneficial interest on a spouse which he or she would not otherwise have. See further *Toner v Toner* [1972] NIJB; *McKeown v McKeown* [1975] NI 139 and *Watters v Watters* [1979] 3 NIJB.

[156] See Valentine, *Civil Proceedings – The County Court* (1999), pp 38-39 and Valentine, *Civil Proceedings – The Supreme Court* (1997), p 430. The court's jurisdiction under the Married Women's Property Act 1882, s 17 is not restricted to the matrimonial home, but extends to all types of matrimonial property.

[157] See Valentine, *Civil Proceedings – The County Court* (1999), p 38 and Valentine, *Civil Proceedings – The Supreme Court* (1997), p 430 both citing *McFarlane v McFarlane* [1972] NI 59. It appears that the court may also order a division of matrimonial property under the Married Women's Property Act 1882, s 17: Valentine, *Civil Proceedings – The County Court* (1999), p 38 and Valentine, *Civil Proceedings – The Supreme Court* (1997), p 430. However, instances of the court ordering sale pursuant to s 17 do not occur often because of the range of property adjustment orders available on judicial separation or divorce under the Matrimonial Causes (NI) Order 1978: Valentine, *Civil Proceedings – The Supreme Court* (1997), p 430. The latter are sought more frequently because they do not depend on the applicant establishing a beneficial interest in the matrimonial home. In addition to this, a spouse may not be able to rely on s 17 if the proceedings raise complex issues – s 17 provides that a spouse may apply 'in a summary way', and see the comments of Craig JA in *Harmeling v Harmeling* (1975) 5 WWR 688 at 701.

that this right was a proprietary right[158]. The practice subsequently emerged in Ontario whereby an application under the Partition Act 1950 (Ont) for sale of a matrimonial home occupied by a deserted spouse would be postponed until an application had been made under s 12 of the Married Women's Property Act 1960 (Ont)[159] to determine his or her rights in relation to the property[160]. However, this notion of a 'deserted wife's equity' was eventually rejected by the House of Lords in *National Provincial Bank Ltd v Ainsworth*[161].

[9.54] Other Canadian cases have focused on the effect of proceedings under the equivalent sections of the relevant Married Women's Property Acts and partition actions between spouses in general. The court's jurisdiction under these provisions is only exercisable where a dispute arises in relation to title to or possession of matrimonial property[162]. Upon such an application, the court may make an order for sale or division of such property as incidental to declaring existing property rights[163], or may postpone an associated partition action where such proceedings are joined with an application under the equivalent of s 17[164].

---

158 See, for example, *Bendall v McWhirter* [1952] QB 466.

159 Equivalent to the Married Women's Property Act 1882, s 17.

160 See *Re Jollow and Jollow* [1954] OR 895; *Rush v Rush* (1960) 24 DLR (2d) 248; and *Re Cates and Cates* [1968] 2 OR 447. Accordingly, the spouse seeking sale of the matrimonial home in these circumstances would have to apply under both the Partition Act 1950 (Ont) and the Married Women's Property Act 1960 (Ont): see *Re Perkins and Perkins* (1972) 31 DLR (3d) 694; *Re Maskewycz and Maskewycz* (1973) 44 DLR (3d) 180; and *Lindenblatt v Lindenblatt* (1974) 48 DLR (3d) 494. See further Silverman, 'Husband and Wife – Desertion by Husband – Matrimonial Home' (1967) 47 Can Bar Rev 366; Glenn, 'Partition – Weighing of Relative Hardship – Interrelationship of the Partition Act and the Married Women's Property Act' (1976) 54 Can Bar Rev 149 and Newcombe, 'Partition Actions Between Spouses in Ontario' (1977) 28 RFL 129. See however the Australian case of *Smith v Smith (No 2)* [1962] Qd R 132 in which Stable J was of the opinion that the fact that a wife intended to apply under the Married Women's Property Acts 1890-1952 (Qd), s 21 for an order that she be permitted to stay in the matrimonial home when deserted by her husband did not amount to 'good reason to the contrary' within the Partition Act 1911 (Qd), s 4 (equivalent to the Partition Act 1868, s 4).

161 [1965] 2 All ER 472. Approving the decision in *Thompson v Earthy* [1951] 2 KB 596, Lord Hodson stated at 478-479 that the rights of a deserted wife were mere personal rights that did not run with the land. Thus, the mere fact that a spouse has been deserted does not deprive the other spouse of his right as a co-owner to compel partition or sale of the matrimonial home: see *Peck v Peck* [1965] SASR 293. However, while a deserted spouse does not have proprietary rights in the matrimonial home simply by virtue of being a deserted spouse, he or she may have matrimonial home rights under the Family Homes and Domestic Violence (NI) Order 1998 which may be relevant in this context.

162 If spouses do not raise any questions as to title or possession, this jurisdiction is not available: *Martin v Martin* (1992) 89 DLR (4th) 115 (decided in relation to the Family Law Act 1986 (Ont), s 10 and distinguishing the decision in *Arlow v Arlow* (1990) 27 RFL (3d) 348). In Ontario, the relevant statutory provision is now contained in the Family Law Act 1990 (Ont), s 10.

However, a number of cases have asserted that disputes relating to title to or possession of matrimonial property cannot be assimilated to an action for compulsory partition or sale of such property, and that each type of application is regulated by its own particular procedure. Considering the interaction between s 12 of the Married Women's Property Act 1950 (Ont) and the Partition Act 1950 (Ont), Chevrier JA in *Re Jollow and Jollow*[165] remarked:

> '[I]n my opinion an action for partition and sale ... is fundamentally different from an action between husband and wife ... where the question between them is as to the title to or possession of property. The conduct of each action is regulated by its own respective procedure.'[166]

[9.55] In addition to this, cases such as *Re MacDonald and MacDonald*[167] and *Silva v Silva*[168] have emphasised that the court's discretion under the equivalent of s 17 is much wider than it's corresponding discretion under legislation governing compulsory partition and sale of co-owned land[169]. Under the former, the court may make such order as it thinks fit[170]. In contrast, in a partition action, the court is usually restricted to making an order for either partition or sale in view of the applicant's *prima facie* right to relief[171]. Moreover, the apparently wide discretion that exists in respect of disputes as to title to or possession of matrimonial property cannot influence partition actions between spouses[172].

---

163 See *Cudmore v Cudmore* (21 February 1997, unreported) Ontario Court of Justice (General Division). Family Act 1990 (Ont), s 10 specifically authorises the court to make an order that the property in question be partitioned or sold for the purpose of realising the spouses' respective interests.

164 As initially held in respect of cases involving deserted spouses: see para **[9.53]** above. Similar views have been expressed in relation to proceedings between spouses in general: see *Silva v Silva* (1990) 75 DLR (4th) 415 and *Cudmore v Cudmore* (21 February 1997, unreported) Ontario Court of Justice (General Division).

165 [1954] OR 895 at 912.

166 Although Chevrier JA delivered the dissenting judgment in this case, the principle issue before the court was whether a deserted spouse had a right to remain in occupation of the matrimonial home in these circumstances. The learned judge held that, due to the separate nature of the two types of proceedings, proceedings under the Married Women's Property Act 1950 (Ont), s 12 could not bar those under the Partition Act 1950 (Ont), even in the context of deserted spouses. Similar views were expressed in *Dickson v Dickson* [1948] OWN 325. See however the comments of Hardie JA in the Australian case of *Re Jackson and the Conveyancing Act* (1951) 52 SR (NSW) 42 at 46 in relation to an application under the Conveyancing Act 1919 (NSW), s 66G (see ch 7 above, para **[7.52]**) and the Married Women's Property Act 1901 (NSW), s 22.

167 (1976) 73 DLR (3d) 341.

168 (1990) 75 DLR (4th) 415.

169 See further the comments of Roach JA in *Re Jollow and Jollow* [1954] OR 895 at 902.

170 Albeit that the court must follow established legal principles in determining the application: see *Re Hearty and Hearty* [1970] 2 OR 344 and para **[9.51]** above.

171 See generally para **[9.31]** above in relation to the current practice in Ontario.

[9.56] Applying these cases to the corresponding practice in Northern Ireland and the relationship between proceedings under s 17 of the Married Women's Property Act 1882 and the Partition Acts, a number of principles emerge. Section 17 only applies where there is a dispute over title to or possession of property between spouses. If there is no such dispute, then the jurisdiction is not exercisable. Where there is such a dispute, the court may determine the matter accordingly and order sale of the property[173]. In these circumstances, an order for sale is at the discretion of the court and the rights of both spouses will be given equal weight. Alternatively, an application under s 17 of the 1882 Act may be joined with an application for sale of the property under Partition Acts[174]. In these circumstances, the s 17 application should be determined before the partition action. However, when dealing with an application for sale of a matrimonial home or other matrimonial property under the Partition Acts, the wider discretion that the court possesses under s 17 of the 1882 Act is irrelevant. The court's jurisdiction under s 17 and in partition actions between spouses arises in different contexts, and the former should not interfere with the otherwise strong presumption in favour of sale of such property under the Partition Acts. Furthermore, if the court's discretion under s 17 of the 1882 Act is irrelevant in the context of disputes between spouses, it would also be irrelevant where a partition action is brought by a security holder.

C Family Homes and Domestic Violence (NI) Order 1998

[9.57] It was suggested in *Northern Bank Ltd v Haggerty*[175] that the Family Law (Miscellaneous Provisions) (NI) Order 1984 might encroach upon the court's jurisdiction to order sale under the Partition Acts at the request of a creditor with an order charging an undivided share of a matrimonial home. While the 1984 Order has been replaced by the Family Homes and Domestic Violence (NI) Order 1998 the same arguments apply in this context.

[9.58] The 1998 Order confers matrimonial home rights on spouses with no proprietary interest and with a mere equitable interest in the matrimonial home.

---

[172] See, for example, *Byall v Byall* (1942) 3 DLR 574 in which Urquhart J rejected suggestions that the Married Women's Property Act 1937 (Ont), s 12(1) was a relevant factor for the court to take into account when determining partition actions between spouses under the Partition Act 1935 (Ont).

[173] Or possibly a division of the property: see para **[9.51]** above.

[174] In *Macrae v Macrae* (1962) SR (NSW) 142 the court held that it had no jurisdiction under the equivalent section of the Married Women's Property Act 1901 (NSW) to grant an order in the nature of an injunction restraining a spouse from applying for compulsory sale of matrimonial property under the Conveyancing Act 1919 (NSW), s 66G.

[175] (23 March 1994, unreported) High Court (NI) (Master Ellison) and [1995] NI 211 (Campbell J).

It will be recalled that, under arts 5 and 6 of the 1998 Order, such rights take effect as a matrimonial charge which will bind a subsequent purchaser of the legal estate if registered before he enters into a contract to purchase that estate or acquires the appropriate documents of title as security for payment of a sum of money[176]. However, the implications of the 1998 Order for lending institutions whose security is restricted to an undivided share of a matrimonial home depend on the nature of the security held.

1 Mortgagees and chargees

[9.59] Should the security take the form of a mortgage or a charge, the 1998 Order has few practical consequences for the security holder notwithstanding that the definition of 'purchaser' in art 2(2) of the 1998 Order includes a mortgagee or a chargee. Take as an example a matrimonial home in the sole name of a husband, where his wife has acquired an equitable interest in the property under a resulting or a constructive trust. If the husband creates a mortgage or a charge on the property and the lender takes his security subject to the wife's prior equitable interest, the lender will have to bring an action for sale under the Partition Acts in the event of default by the husband. The provisions of the 1998 Order aside, it is likely that the lender would succeed in a partition action[177]. However, the 1998 Order envisages the wife's matrimonial charge having priority over a mortgage or a charge by virtue of the wife having registered her matrimonial charge prior to creation of the security[178]. If the lender takes his security subject to the wife's matrimonial charge, it might be argued that the court should not order sale of the matrimonial home under the Partition Acts. To allow a mortgagee or chargee to obtain an order for sale in these circumstances would defeat the purpose of the 1998 Order by denying the wife the protection it confers on her where she has registered her matrimonial charge.

[9.60] However, this particular situation is unlikely to arise in practice for two reasons. In the first place, it requires the wife to have taken the positive step of registering her matrimonial charge, which in turn pre-supposes that she is aware of the protection afforded by the 1998 Order. There is a sense in which this legislation confers mere 'paper rights' which have little practical utility. Secondly, if the lending institution discovers that the wife has registered a matrimonial charge on the property, the wife will almost certainly be required to sign a consent form as a pre-condition to the grant of the mortgage or charge[179].

---

[176] See paras **[9.19]-[9.22]** above.

[177] See, for example *Ulster Bank v Shanks* [1982] NI 143 and *Northern Bank Ltd v Beattie* [1982] 18 NIJB 1, as well as ch 8.

[178] As prescribed by the Family Homes and Domestic Violence (NI) Order 1998, art 6(3).

[179] See ch 8.

Accordingly, the wife must have registered her matrimonial charge *and* the lender must have failed to secure his position by means of a consent form before the wife can resist an order for sale under the Partition Acts. The likelihood of the court refusing to order sale in these circumstances because of the provisions of the 1998 Order must therefore be regarded as a theoretical as opposed to a practical possibility.

2 Creditors with an order charging land

[9.61] However, more substantive issues arise where the security takes the form of an order charging land under the Judgments Enforcement (NI) Order 1981. Article 2(2) of the 1998 Order defines a 'purchaser' as any person 'who, *for valuable consideration*, takes an estate in land'[180]. In the case of *In the Matter of Folio 3540 Co Tyrone*[181] Murray LJ held that the making of an order charging land is not a transaction for valuable consideration. This finding has serious practical consequences for a creditor with an order charging an undivided share of a matrimonial home. Returning to the above example, if a wife has a mere equitable interest in a matrimonial home, registration of her matrimonial charge under the 1998 Order is essential in order for her to take priority over a mortgagee or chargee of her husband's interest and perhaps resist an action for sale under the Partition Acts by the former[182]. However, where a creditor has an order charging the husband's interest in the matrimonial home, it seems that the wife does not even have to register her matrimonial charge in order to take priority over the creditor since he is not a 'purchaser' for the purposes of the 1998 Order. The creditor takes his security subject to the wife's matrimonial charge, irrespective of registration. Consequently, it might be argued that the court should not make an order for sale under the Partition Acts at the request of a creditor with an order charging land in these circumstances since his security is necessarily subject to the wife's matrimonial charge under the 1998 Order.

[9.62] It follows that the 1998 Order may enable a spouse with an equitable interest in a matrimonial home to resist an action for sale under the Partition Acts by a creditor with an order charging the other spouse's interest in the property. Similar observations may be made in respect of a spouse with no proprietary interest in a matrimonial home. Where there is an order charging land against the other spouse in these circumstances, the creditor may exercise his normal power of sale[183] since his security is not restricted to an undivided share of land. However, since a spouse with no proprietary interest has matrimonial home rights giving rise to a matrimonial charge under the 1998

180 Emphasis added.

181 [1991] NI 273.

182 This, of course, assumes that the wife's equitable interest preceded the creditor's charge.

183 Under the Judgments Enforcement (NI) Order 1981, art 52: see ch 8.

Order, the court might refuse to order sale of the property as the creditor's security is subject to this matrimonial charge, registered or not.

[9.63] This raises the question of whether a spouse with a legal estate in a matrimonial home may also resist an action for sale under the Partition Acts by a creditor with an order charging the estate of the other spouse. At a cursory glance, this question might be answered in the negative – since the 1998 Order does not confer matrimonial home rights on spouses who are co-owners at law[184], the spouse whose interest is not subject to the creditor's security does not have a matrimonial charge on the property which might induce the court to refuse an order for sale under the Partition Acts. However, the policy of the 1998 Order may be relevant in this context. If a spouse with no proprietary interest in a matrimonial home and a spouse with an equitable interest in a matrimonial home may be able to resist an action for sale by a creditor as a result of the protection conferred on them by the 1998 Order, it would produce a strange result if a spouse with a legal estate could not do so. Where a spouse with a legal estate in the matrimonial home opposes a request for sale in these circumstances, the court might refuse to order sale by analogy to the policy of the 1998 Order and the protection that it gives to spouses with no legal estate in such property.

[9.64] Support for this proposition may be found in *Northern Bank Ltd v Haggerty*[185] in relation to the corresponding provisions of the Family Law (Miscellaneous Provisions) (NI) Order 1984[186]. In this case, the spouses were joint tenants of the matrimonial home at law. Counsel for the wife referred to the decision in *In the Matter of Folio 3540 Co Tyrone*[187] and argued that a spouse without legal title was protected against a judgment creditor by virtue of her matrimonial charge under the 1984 Order. Counsel submitted that, when enacting the 1984 Order, the legislature could not have intended to place a spouse with a legal estate in a matrimonial home in a worse position than a spouse without such an estate. Delivering the judgment at first instance, Master

---

[184] Family Homes and Domestic Violence (NI) Order 1998 merely regulates their respective rights in relation to the matrimonial home: see para **[9.13]** above.

[185] (23 March 1994, unreported) High Court (NI) (Master Ellison) and [1995] NI 211 (Campbell J).

[186] Family Law (Miscellaneous Provisions) (NI) Order 1984, art 4(1) and 4(12) conferred 'rights of occupation' on spouses with no proprietary interest and with a mere equitable interest in the matrimonial home, while arts 5 and 6 provided that these rights constituted a matrimonial charge on the property which could be registered against third parties. Family Law (Miscellaneous Provisions) (NI) Order 1984, art 3(1) also defined a 'purchaser' as someone 'who, for valuable consideration, takes an estate in land'.

[187] [1991] NI 273.

Ellison doubted whether an order for sale under the Partition Acts would be made in such cases:

> '[I]t seems to me that a wife who has no proprietary interest in the matrimonial home, and who accordingly enjoys the benefit of a matrimonial charge under Article 5 ... may well find herself in a position to resist an action for possession to enforce an order charging land registered against the home after her matrimonial charge came into being. Furthermore, since the existence of a matrimonial charge is not dependent on its registration, and since Article 6 ... only deals with priority vis-à-vis a "purchaser of an estate" ... it seems to me that ... a spouse without a proprietary interest need not even register her matrimonial charge to have standing to resist eviction on the application of a creditor with an order charging land registered against the entire estate in the matrimonial home. If this view of the law is correct, and if the Bank's arguments about standing for partition were also correct, a wife without any proprietary interest in the property would seem to be in a much stronger position than one who owns a [share] ... in the home to resist eviction on foot of an order charging land against her husband's interest. In my view, that would be a very anomalous result indeed.'[188]

[9.65] While he did not mention that the 1984 Order also conferred protection on a spouse with a mere equitable interest in a matrimonial home, Master Ellison nevertheless recognised the divergence in practice which might arise by virtue of the 1984 Order between a spouse with no proprietary interest in a matrimonial home and a spouse with a legal estate when resisting an action for sale by a creditor with an order charging land. The fact that the 1984 Order extended to spouses with a mere equitable interest would surely have reinforced his opposition to an order for sale being made in such cases. On appeal, Campbell J described counsel's submission as a 'persuasive argument' that tended to confirm his conclusion that a judgment creditor could not maintain a partition action[189].

[9.66] Although raised as a theoretical difficulty in *Haggerty*, the question of whether a creditor with an order charging an undivided share of a matrimonial home can obtain an order for sale under the Partition Acts has become a substantive issue since such persons were granted *locus standi* to bring a partition action by art 48 of the Property (NI) Order 1997[190]. However, the decision in *Ulster Bank Ltd v Carter*[191] also suggests that the provisions of the 1984 Order (and consequently the 1998 Order) may be relevant in these circumstances. Girvan J had to consider whether a spouse with legal title could resist an action for sale by a creditor with an order charging the other spouse's

---

188 (23 March 1994, unreported) High Court (NI), at 18-19.

189 [1995] NI 211 at 217.

190 See ch 8 above, para **[8.62]**.

191 [1999] NI 93.

share of the matrimonial home in light of art 48. The learned judge referred to the views expressed by Campbell J in *Haggerty*, and continued:

> '[T]he position of spouses raises special considerations and problems which are not fully or clearly addressed by the provisions of the 1997 Order ... The spouse of a debtor may be faced by a charge affecting the property which effectively undermines his or her right to occupy the premises. Parliament has clearly sought to protect the interests of spouses without a legal interest in premises by the 1984 Order and it is unfortunate that the legislature has either overlooked spouses with a legal joint interest or accidentally or deliberately deprived them of the protection conferred on spouses without a title. It is unlikely that this was a deliberate policy since it produces an absurd and unjust result. In balancing the interests of the creditor against a debtor spouse as against the interests of the non-debtor spouse with a joint interest it is not inevitably the case that justice or fairness demands that the scale should come down in favour of the creditor.'[192]

[9.67] In other words, the court might refuse to order sale of a matrimonial home in these circumstances because a non-debtor spouse without legal title would have been protected by the 1984 Order (now 1998 Order) and to decide otherwise would prejudice a spouse with legal title. However, having determined the case by reference to the prospective application of art 48[193], Girvan J did not find it necessary to express a final opinion on this particular issue.

[9.68] These cases suggest that the court's jurisdiction to order sale of a matrimonial home under the Partition Acts at the request of a creditor with an order charging land may be qualified by the 1998 Order, irrespective of whether the spouse who opposes sale has a legal or an equitable estate in the property. For example, the court might regard the protection conferred by the 1998 Order as 'good reason to the contrary' under s 4 of the Partition Act 1868. Alternatively, it might persuade the court to refuse to order sale under s 3 of the 1868 Act even though sale would be more beneficial than partition. In this particular context, the court's discretion to refuse sale of a matrimonial home under the Partition Acts may indeed be wider today. Furthermore, if the court did refuse to order sale, it would be unlikely to make an order for partition in the alternative. Apart from the fact that a judgment creditor would almost certainly not want an order for partition, division of a matrimonial home will usually be both impracticable and futile. The court might make an order for partition in exceptional cases, but the likelihood of it actually doing so is remote.

[9.69] While a creditor with an order charging an undivided share of a matrimonial home now has *locus standi* to bring a partition action, art 48 of the Property (NI) Order 1997 may not improve his position in view of the protection

---

192 [1999] NI 93 at 99.

193 See ch 8 above, paras **[8.81]-[8.84]**.

which the 1998 Order confers on a spouse with an equitable interest in a matrimonial home who resists an action for sale under the Partition Acts and the implications this may also have for a spouse with a legal estate in a similar situation. The 1998 Order provides a means of protecting the 'innocent spouse' in these circumstances, albeit at the expense of the creditor. However, the creditor is not without redress and may commence proceedings under the Insolvency (NI) Order 1989. In these circumstances, the likelihood of obtaining an order for sale of a matrimonial home is considerable, especially where an application for sale is made one year or more after the vesting of the bankrupt's estate in the trustee[194].

D Overview and proposals for reform

[9.70] In partition actions involving lenders and the matrimonial home the court is performing a pragmatic balancing exercise, weighing the interests of the 'innocent' spouse who wishes to remain in the property against a lender who wishes to realise his security. The provisions of the 1998 Order aside, it is submitted that it will usually be difficult for an innocent spouse to persuade the court to refuse to order sale under the Partition Acts at the request of a security holder. In view of the traditional bias in favour of allowing a lender to realise his security in the event of default by the borrower, the court may be loathe to move away from the strong presumption of sale under the Partition Acts in these circumstances, even though the subject property comprises a matrimonial home.

[9.71] However, the Law Reform Advisory Committee for Northern Ireland has suggested that courts should have a general power to decline to make an order under the Partition Acts in respect of applications by mortgagees or chargees of spouses and that, when determining such applications, the court should have regard to the matters which it is obliged to take into account under the Matrimonial Causes (NI) Order 1978[195]. If this proposal were to be implemented, the court would be able to give more weight to the needs of the innocent spouse (and any children of the marriage) and could refuse a lender's request for sale of the matrimonial home in appropriate circumstances. However, judges might nevertheless be cautious in exercising too liberal a discretion in favour of spouses. In these circumstances, the security aspect of the transaction may be a relevant factor – for example, preventing lenders from enforcing their

194 See paras **[9.76]**-**[9.80]** below.

195 Law Reform Advisory Committee for Northern Ireland Discussion Paper No 5, *Matrimonial Property* (1999), p 44. The relevant factors are contained in the Matrimonial Causes (NI) Order 1978, art 27 (as amended by the Matrimonial and Family Proceedings (NI) Order 1989, art 6) and were discussed at para **[9.37]** above.

96 The following dictum of Lord Browne-Wilkinson in *Barlcay's Bank plc v O'Brien* [1994] 4 All ER 417 at 422 is instructive:

security might prejudice subsequent loans secured against matrimonial homes[196]. Furthermore, even if the court was granted a discretion to refuse relief in these circumstances, the position of an 'innocent spouse' may not improve significantly. In the event of being unable to secure an order for sale of the property under the Partition Acts, the lender might commence proceedings against the debtor under the Insolvency (NI) Order 1989 and would be likely to obtain an order for sale of the matrimonial home[197].

IV The Practice on Bankruptcy

A General principles

[9.72] The Insolvency (NI) Order 1989 is the principal legislation governing personal insolvency in Northern Ireland[198]. When a person is adjudicated bankrupt, all property belonging to or vested in him at the date of the bankruptcy order becomes available for the benefit of his creditors[199]. The property vests in the trustee in bankruptcy ('the trustee') who is an insolvency practitioner appointed by the Official Receiver for Northern Ireland[200]. The trustee's function is to administer the bankrupt's estate[201].

[9.73] If a joint tenant or tenant in common is declared bankrupt, his undivided share of the land vests in the trustee in bankruptcy[202]. The trustee in bankruptcy may bring an action for sale of the land under the Partition Acts[203]. In these

---

196 (contd)

> '[I]t is important to keep a sense of balance in approaching these cases. It is easy to allow sympathy for the wife who is threatened with the loss of her home at the suit of a rich bank to obscure an important public interest, viz the need to ensure that the wealth currently tied up in the matrimonial home does not become economically sterile. If the rights secured to wives by the law renders vulnerable loans granted on the security of matrimonial homes, institutions will be unwilling to accept such security, thereby reducing the flow of loan capital to business enterprises. It is therefore essential that a law designed to protect the vulnerable does not render the matrimonial home unacceptable as security to financial institutions.'

197 See paras **[9.76]-[9.80]** below.

198 For an account of the practice on personal insolvency in Northern Ireland and the various provisions of the Insolvency (NI) Order 1989, see Hunter, *Northern Ireland Personal Insolvency* (1992).

199 Insolvency (NI) Order 1989, art 11. For the definition of property, see art 2(2).

200 See Hunter, *Northern Ireland Personal Insolvency* (1992), chs 3 and 13.

201 See Hunter, *Northern Ireland Personal Insolvency* (1992), ch 14.

202 Where co-owners are joint tenants, the vesting of the bankrupt's interest in the trustee in bankruptcy effects a severance of the joint tenancy by involuntary alienation: *Morgan v Marquis* (1853) 9 Exch 145, and see *Re Ali* (1987) 34 DLR (4th) 259 and *Re Francis, ex p Official Trustee in Bankruptcy* (1988) 82 ALR 333.

203 See the cases cited in para **[9.78]** below.

circumstances, there is likely to be a strong presumption in favour of the court making an order for sale notwithstanding the objections of the non-bankrupt co-owner, since the trustee is under a statutory duty to realise the bankrupt's property for the benefit of his creditors[204].

B Bankrupt's property comprising a matrimonial home

[9.74] The 1989 Order makes special provision for cases in which the bankrupt's estate includes a dwelling house that he and his wife occupy as a matrimonial home[205]. Where spouses are joint tenants or tenants in common of a matrimonial home at law or in equity, the trustee in bankruptcy may bring an action for sale under the Partition Acts if he fails to reach an agreement on sale of the property with the spouses.

1 Bankrupt's spouse and matrimonial home rights

[9.75] Where title to the matrimonial home is in the sole name of the husband and the spouses are co-owners in equity, the partition action should be preceded or accompanied by an application under art 11 of the Family Homes and Domestic Violence (NI) Order 1998 if the wife has registered a matrimonial charge in relation to the property under the 1998 Order[206]. In these circumstances, art 309(2) of the 1989 Order provides that the wife's charge continues to subsist and is binding on the trustee in bankruptcy and persons deriving title under the trustee. However, the trustee may apply to court for an order under art 11 of the 1998 Order terminating the wife's matrimonial home rights, thereby enabling the trustee to sell the matrimonial home[207]. Upon such an application, the court shall make such order as it thinks just and reasonable under art 11 of the 1998 Order having regard to the factors set out in arts 309(4) and 309(5) of the 1989 Order[208].

2 Criteria for ordering sale

[9.76] Irrespective of whether spouses are co-owners of the matrimonial home at law or in equity, the trustee in bankruptcy is likely to apply for sale under either s 3 or s 4 of the Partition Act 1868, depending on the extent of the bankrupt's interest in the property[209]. However, art 309(3) of the 1989 Order authorises the court to depart from the normal practice of ordering either partition or, more likely, sale under the Partition Acts in these circumstances. Article 309(3) reads:

---

204 See the comments of Goff J in *Re Densham (A Bankrupt)* [1975] 1 WLR 1519. See further *Re Solomon* [1967] Ch 573. However, a request for sale may be refused if the circumstances of a particular case have given rise to an estoppel between the original co-owners which subsequently binds the trustee in bankruptcy: *Re Yale and MacMaster* (1974) 46 DLR (3d) 167 and see ch 4 above, para **[4.60]**.

205 'Dwelling house' is defined in the Insolvency (NI) Order 1989, art 9(1).

206 See generally para **[9.19]** above.

207 Insolvency (NI) Order 1989, art 309(2)(b) and the Family Homes and Domestic Violence (NI) Order 1998, art 12.

208 These factors are discussed in paras **[9.77]-[9.80]** below.

> 'Notwithstanding any provision of the Partition Acts 1868 and 1876, where a person and his spouse or former spouse have a legal or equitable estate in a dwelling house vested in them jointly or as tenants in common and that person is adjudicated bankrupt, in a suit for partition maintained by the trustee of the bankrupt's estate, the High Court may make such order as it thinks fit.'

[9.77] Thus, art 309(3) permits the court to adopt a more flexible approach and contemplates the court refusing both partition and sale of the matrimonial home in appropriate circumstances[210]. In exercising this discretion, the court must have regard to the factors set out in art 309(4) of the 1989 Order. These are:

(a) the interests of the bankrupt's creditors,

(b) the conduct of the spouse or former spouse, so far as contributing to the bankruptcy,

(c) the needs and financial resources of the spouse or former spouse,

(d) the needs of any children, and

(e) all the circumstances of the case, other than the needs of the bankrupt.

[9.78] In *Official Receiver for Northern Ireland v Kearney*[211] Girvan J made an order for sale of a matrimonial home on the basis that there was nothing to outweigh the interests of the creditors under art 309 – the wife was estranged from the bankrupt and the children of the marriage were no longer residing in the property[212]. Reference has already been made to the fact that a request for

---

209 Partition Act 1868, s 5 will seldom apply since a trustee in bankruptcy should have little difficulty in establishing that sale would be more beneficial than partition as required by s 3 where the bankrupt is entitled to less than a half share in the matrimonial home.

210 In other words, the wording of the Insolvency (NI) Order 1989, art 309(3) indicates that it is intended to avoid the normal practice of ordering either partition or sale where a partition action is brought by a trustee in bankruptcy in respect of a matrimonial home: see Wallace, 'Mortgages and Charges', *Third Annual Review of Property Law* (1996) 7 at 23-24. See further Hunter, *Northern Ireland Personal Insolvency* (1992), p 185 where the author remarks that the court is not restricted by the otherwise 'narrow discretion' under the Partition Acts 1868 and 1876 and that the Insolvency (NI) Order 1989, art 309(3) renders the decision in *Northern Bank v Beattie* [1982] 18 NIJB 1 (see ch 7 above, parsa **[7.08]-[7.09]**) irrelevant in the context of an application by a trustee in bankruptcy. Property (NI) Order 1997, art 49 (see ch 7 above, paras **[7.63]-[7.64]**) does not attempt to restrict the court's discretion under the Insolvency (NI) Order 1989, art 309(3) – the former provision commences with the words '[w]ithout prejudice to Art 309 of the [1989 Order]'.

211 (13 January 1999, unreported) High Court (NI).

212 Sale of a matrimonial home has also been ordered in respect of applications by a trustee in bankruptcy which have fallen outside the Insolvency (NI) Order 1989: see, for example, *Official Receiver for Northern Ireland v Dawson* (2 December 1992, unreported) High Court (NI) and *Official Assignee for Bankruptcy for Northern Ireland v Beattie* (1992) 12 NIJB 11. The Insolvency (NI) Order 1989 only applies where the bankruptcy petition was presented on or after 1 October 1991: Insolvency (NI) Order 1989, Sch 8, para 8(1).

sale by a trustee in bankruptcy will usually be granted[213]. The fact that the property in question comprises a matrimonial home is unlikely to affect this to any significant degree. Cases decided under the corresponding legislative provisions in England and Wales[214] have suggested a strong presumption in favour of sale of a matrimonial home in these circumstances. For example, in *Re Citro (A Bankrupt)*[215] Nourse LJ suggested that the voice of the creditors should usually prevail over the voice of the non-bankrupt spouse, and described any distress which the latter might suffer as a result of loosing his or her home as a mere consequence of debt[216]. Despite the fact that the English legislation for determining disputes involving co-owners[217] is more flexible than the Partition Acts and confers a wider discretion on the courts, they have nevertheless adopted a relatively narrow approach as regards requests for sale of a matrimonial home by trustees in bankruptcy.

[9.79] In addition to this, art 309(5) of the 1989 Order provides that:

> 'Where such an application is made or such a suit is maintained after the expiration of one year from the vesting ... of the bankrupt's estate in a trustee, the High Court shall assume, unless the circumstances of the case are exceptional, that the interests of the bankrupt's creditors outweigh all other considerations.'[218]

[9.80] In *Re Holliday (A Bankrupt)*[219], exceptional circumstances were found to exist where the husband's creditors were not pressing for payment, and the husband had been declared bankrupt on his own petition, which he had presented in a tactical attempt to avoid a property adjustment order being made against him. In addition to this, several recent cases have granted a short

[213] See para **[9.73]** above.

[214] Namely the Insolvency Act 1986, s 336 which makes similar provision in relation to an application for sale of a matrimonial home by a trustee in bankruptcy under the Trusts of Land and Appointment of Trustees Act 1996, s 14 (formerly the Law of Property Act 1925, s 30).

[215] [1991] 1 FLR 71 and see Lawson, 'Bankruptcy and the Family Home - *Re Citro*' [1991] Conv 302.

[216] See further *Re Bailey (A Bankrupt)* [1977] 1 WLR 278 and *Re Lowrie* [1981] 3 All ER 353, as well as *Barclay's Bank plc v Hendricks* [1996] 1 FLR 258.

[217] Namely the Trusts of Land and Appointment of Trustees Act 1996, s 14.

[218] If the court nevertheless decides to postpone sale of the matrimonial home in these circumstances, the terms of the suspension order are essentially at the discretion of the judge. An appellate court would be reluctant to interfere unless it was clear that that judge had misdirected himself in law or erred in principle - see *Claughton v Charalamabous* [1999] 1 FLR 740 in which the court also suggested that it would be inappropriate to attempt to lay down guidelines as to what might constitute "exceptional circumstances" when parliament had neglected to do so in the relevant legislation.

[219] [1980] 3 All ER 385.

postponement of sale on serious health grounds[220]. However, instances of courts postponing sale for a lengthy period on the grounds of exceptional circumstances occur less frequently.[221] Likewise, so-called 'ordinary family suffering' as a result of being made homeless upon sale of the family home will not be regarded as exceptional by the courts[222]. Accordingly, where the trustee's application for sale under the Partition Acts is made after one year, the likelihood of the court ruling in his favour must be regarded as considerable, notwithstanding the ostensibly wide discretion conferred by art 309 of the 1989 Order. In these circumstances, the difficulty of defending such an application may strengthen the trustee's position when negotiating vacation and sale of the matrimonial home with the bankrupt and his spouse[223].

V The Human Rights Act 1998

[9.81] The Human Rights Act 1998 gives further effect to the provisions of the European Convention on Human Rights in domestic law and came into force on 2 October 2000[224]. It is likely that the 1998 Act will impact on property law in general, and more specifically on dealings with the matrimonial home and other

[220] For example, in *Re Bremnar (A Bankrupt)* [1999] 1 FLR 912 exceptional circumstances were found to exist where the elderly wife was caring for the bankrupt who had suffered a stroke and recently been diagnosed with inoperable cancer. The wife opposed the action on the basis of a need to care for her husband and offered to consent to sale taking place three months after his death. In *Re Raval (A Bankrupt)* [1998] 2 FLR 718 the court postponed sale for one year on the basis that the wife had suffered from paranoid schizophrenia in the past and vacating the matrimonial home was likely to trigger a relapse in her condition. However, it rejected the wife's suggestion that sale should be postponed for five years since this would prejudice the husband's creditors.

[221] In *Claughton v Charalamabous* [1999] 1 FLR 740 the court postponed sale of a matrimonial home until the bankrupt's wife ceased to reside in the property. The wife suffered from renal failure and osteoarthritis which severely restricted her mobility, and had a reduced life expectancy, all of which were regarded as "exceptional circumstances." Moreover, the creditors would receive nothing from a sale of the matrimonial home since all the proceeds would be consumed in costs. In *Judd v Brown* [1998] 2 FLR 360 the bankrupt's wife had been recently diagnosed with ovarian cancer and had undergone extensive surgery. Harman J held that this amounted to "exceptional circumstances" and that the threat of having to leave the family home could affect the wife's chances of recovery. In his opinion, this was clearly distinguishable from problems such as simply having to move house or rearrange children's schooling. In these circumstances, it was not appropriate simply to postpone sale for several months in the hope that the wife's health problems might be resolved by this time.

[222] Richman, 'Using the Human Rights Act to Save the Matrimonial Home' (2000) NLJ 1102 at 1103.

[223] Hunter, *Northern Ireland Personal Insolvency* (1992), p 186.

[224] Human Rights Act 1998 (Commencement No 2) Order 2000.

family property[225]. In this context, the 1998 Act may also impact on partition actions involving the matrimonial home. A number of suggestions have been put forward.

[9.82] A recent report from the Office of Law Reform[226] has suggested that the notification procedure in respect of orders charging land made by the Enforcement of Judgments Office ('the EJO') raises a number of human rights concerns. As the law currently stands, there is no provision for non-debtor co-owners to receive notice of intention to make an order charging the debtor's undivided share of the land. In *Ulster Bank Ltd v Carter*[227] Girvan J drew attention to this problem in the context of spouses and the matrimonial home and the fact that such an order would interfere with the non-debtor spouse's right to quiet enjoyment and possession of the property[228]. In his opinion, lack of notice could be construed as being in breach of Article 1 of the First Protocol to the European Convention on Human Rights, which confers a right to peaceful enjoyment of one's possessions[229]. Thus, provision may have to be made for non-debtor spouses and other co-owners to be notified by the EJO in respect of its intention to make an order charging the land in question[230]. This in turn might affect the EJO's decision on whether to make such an order, and consequently the lender's ability to enforce his security under the Partition Acts.

[9.83] The 1998 Act may also have implications for partition actions brought by a trustee in bankruptcy in respect of a matrimonial home. There is usually a strong presumption in favour of the court making an order for sale of the

---

225 See generally Howell, 'The Protection of Rights of Property in Land Under the Human Rights Act' in Betten (ed), *The Human Rights Act 1998 – What It Means* (1999) ch 7 and Howell, 'Land and Human Rights' [1999] Conv 287.

226 Office of Law Reform Consultation Paper, *Orders Charging Land and the Innocent Spouse: Balancing the Interests - A Review of Article 48 of the Property (NI) Order 1997* (July 1999), pp 13-15.

227 [1999] NI 93 at 103-104.

228 The learned judge referred to *Hallmark Furniture Ltd v Collins (t/a Furniture Direct)* [1998] NI 4 at 8 in which Carswell LCJ suggested that the making of such an order by the Enforcement of Judgments Office without notice to the person most directly affected by the order was a breach of the rules of natural justice.

229 Article 1 of the First Protocol to the European Convention on Human Rights further states that:

> 'no one shall be deprived of his possessions except in the public interest and subject to the conditions provided for by the law and by the general principles of international law.'

230 Although the issue was initially raised in the context of spouses in *Ulster Bank Ltd v Carter* [1999] NI 93, any amendment to the existing notification procedure would have to extend to non-debtor cohabitees and co-owners in general to avoid falling foul of Article 14 of the European Convention of Human Rights: see Office of Law Reform Consultation Paper, *Orders Charging Land and the Innocent Spouse: Balancing the Interests – A Review of Article 48 of the Property (NI) Order 1997* (July 1999), p 15.

property under the Partition Acts in these circumstances, notwithstanding the ostensibly wide discretion that exists under art 309 of the Insolvency (NI) Order 1989[231]. However, it has been suggested that Article 8 of Schedule 1 of the 1998 Act may be relevant in this context, and could be used to allow a bankrupt's family to remain in their home for as long as is necessary[232]. Article 8 concerns the right to respect for private and family life, including respect for one's home. The mere fact that the trustee's application is in respect of a family home might be regarded as 'exceptional circumstances' under art 309(5) of the 1989 Order, thus allowing the court to exercise a broader discretion to refuse the relief sought[233]. Another possibility is that both Article 8 and Article 1 of the First Protocol may impact on actions for compulsory sale of the family home in general, and that the court's discretion in such cases should, as a result, usually be exercised in favour of preserving the home[234].

[9.84] It is impossible to predict the effect that the 1998 Act may have on this area of the law and in respect of transactions involving the matrimonial or family home in general. However, in light of the above suggestions, the court may be able to exercise a wider discretion in partition actions involving spouses[235].

---

231 See paras **[9.76]-[9.80]** above.

232 Richman, 'Using the Human Rights Act to Save the Matrimonial Home' (2000) NLJ 1102. Although the author was referring to the corresponding practice in England under the Insolvency Act 1986 and applications for sale under the Trusts of Land and Appointment of Trustees Act 1996, the same principles would apply in respect of the Insolvency (NI) Order 1989 and applications for sale of a matrimonial home under the Partition Acts 1868 and 1876.

233 Richman, 'Using the Human Rights Act to Save the Matrimonial Home' (2000) NLJ 1102 at 1104. The author also suggests that depriving the bankrupt's family of their home is not in the public interest and therefore falls foul of Article 1 of the First Protocol to the European Convention on Human Rights (see para **[9.82]** above), under which a legal or natural person can only be deprived of his possessions in the public interest: Richman, 'Using the Human Rights Act to Save the Matrimonial Home' (2000) NLJ 1102 at 1104.

234 Richman, 'Using the Human Rights Act to Save the Matrimonial Home' (2000) NLJ 1102 at 1104. Although referring to the practice under the Trusts of Land and Appointment of Trustees Act 1996, similar reasoning might apply in respect of applications for sale of a family home in general under the Partition Acts 1868 and 1876.

235 This discretion may also extend to partition actions involving cohabitees. The wording of both Article 8 and Article 1 is wide enough to include such persons. In addition to this, Article 14 of the European Convention of Human Rights, which provides for non-discrimination on various grounds, may be relevant in this context.

Chapter 10

Co-Ownership of the Matrimonial Home and Partition Actions Involving Spouses in the Republic of Ireland

I Introduction

[10.01] As with the corresponding practice in Northern Ireland, spouses who are co-owners of a matrimonial or family home[1] in the Republic of Ireland may be involved in a partition action in three situations[2]. In the first place, a spouse who wishes to realise his or her share in the property upon failure of a marriage may commence proceedings of this nature. Secondly, a lender whose security is restricted to an undivided share of a family home may bring an action for sale under the Partition Acts in the event of default by the borrower. The third situation that may arise is where one of the spouses is declared bankrupt and the Official Assignee seeks an order for sale of the family home to reimburse the bankrupt's creditors.

[10.02] The difficulties associated with partition of a family home combined with the fact that such an order may be futile suggest that there should be a strong presumption in favour of sale under the Partition Acts[3]. However, the practice in the Republic of Ireland differs from that in Northern Ireland in two material respects. In the first place, the current practice in the Republic is

---

1 The latter term is more commonly used in the Republic of Ireland, and will be employed throughout this chapter.

2 The family home will often represent the main asset of the parties. While spouses will frequently be joint tenants at law through choice (with added incentives under the Family Home Protection Act 1976, s 14: see para **[10.04]** below), they may be tenants in common at law or in equity as a result of severance having occurred. Where legal title to the family home is vested in one spouse, a husband and wife may nevertheless be co-owners of the property in equity under a resulting or constructive trust – as to the relevant principles, see the articles noted at ch 9 above, para **[9.01]**. Despite various proposals to reform the law in the Republic of Ireland so that ownership of a family home would automatically vest in spouses as joint tenants, these proposals have not been implemented: see generally Shatter, *Family Law* (4th edn, 1997), pp 826-827 and pp 833-839.

3 See generally ch 7 above. Most actions for sale of a family home are likely to be brought under the Partition Act 1868, s 3 or s 4. A person interested in less than half of a family home is unlikely to rely on the Partition Act 1868, s 5 since he or she should be able to establish that sale would be more beneficial than partition as required by s 3.

unclear following the decision in *O'D v O'D*[4] in which Murphy J was of the opinion that partition is discretionary so that the court is not obliged to order partition if it refuses to make an order for sale under the Partition Acts[5]. Thus, the extent to which legislation regulating the property rights of spouses in the Republic of Ireland has influenced partition actions involving a family home and, in particular, the extent of the court's discretion under the Partition Acts is more difficult to ascertain. Secondly, the general practice in transactions relating to the family home in the Republic of Ireland has been substantially altered by the Family Home Protection Act 1976.

[10.03] This chapter considers the position of spouses in partition actions relating to the family home in the three situations identified above. However, it is convenient to digress slightly at this point and to discuss the main provisions of the 1976 Act, and in particular those which may influence the court's jurisdiction under the Partition Acts[6].

II Family Home Protection Act 1976

[10.04] The Family Home Protection Act 1976 has been described as 'a remedial social statute enacted to protect the interest of the non-owning spouse in the family home'[7]. The Act confers protection on a spouse without legal title in a family home by preventing the other spouse from unilaterally disposing of or creating interests in the property without the former's consent[8]. Assuming that

---

4 (18 November 1983, unreported) High Court (RI).

5 For an overview of the decision in *O'D v O'D* (18 November 1983, unreported) High Court (RI) and criticisms of Murphy J's approach see ch 7 above, paras **[7.40]-[7.48]**.

6 For an exposition of matrimonial property law in the Republic of Ireland in general see Shatter, *Family Law* (4th edn, 1997) ch 15; Walls and Bergin, *The Law of Divorce in Ireland* (1997) chs 5 and 6; and Lyall, *Land Law in Ireland* (2nd edn, 2000), ch 17. Reference may also be made to Duncan and Scully, *Marriage Breakdown in Ireland* (1990), chs 11 and 12.

7 *Bank of Ireland v Purcell* [1989] IR 327 at 333 per Walsh J. For an overview of the Family Home Protection Act 1976, see Shatter, *Family Law* (4th edn, 1997), pp 723-772; Lyall, *Land Law in Ireland* (2nd edn, 2000), pp 476-507; Wylie, *Irish Conveyancing Law* (2nd edn, 1996), pp 569-593; and Coughlan, *Property Law* (2nd edn, 1998), pp 437-456.

8 See for example, *Nestor v Murphy* [1979] IR 326 and *Hamilton v Hamilton* [1982] IR 466. A 'family home' is defined in the Family Home Protection Act 1976, s 2(1) as 'primarily a dwelling in which a married couple ordinarily reside'. It also comprises a dwelling in which a spouse whose protection is in issue ordinarily resides or, if that spouse has left the other spouse, ordinarily resided in before leaving. Family Home Protection Act 1976, s 2(2) (as amended by the Family Law Act 1995, s 54(1)) defines a 'dwelling' as any building or part of a building occupied as a separate dwelling, including any garden or other land usually occupied with the dwelling which is subsidiary and ancillary to it, required for amenity and convenience, and not used or developed primarily for commercial purposes. It also includes a structure which is not permanently attached to the ground and a vehicle or vessel (whether mobile or not) which is occupied as a separate dwelling.

title to a family home is vested in the husband, his wife will be protected irrespective of whether she has a beneficial interest in the property[9]. Under the 1976 Act, the written consent of the wife is a pre-condition to a valid conveyance of any interest in the property. Section 3(1) states that:

> 'Where a spouse, without the prior consent in writing of the other spouse, purports to convey any interest[10] in the family home to any person except the other spouse, then, subject to subsections (2), (3) and (8) and section 4, the purported conveyance shall be void.'

[10.05] Section 1(1) of the 1976 Act defines a 'conveyance' as including a mortgage or transfer of property, and also an enforceable agreement to make any such conveyance[11]. Consent must be given prior to the relevant conveyance[12], and must be voluntary and fully informed consent[13]. However, a general written consent to a future conveyance of the family home will suffice[14]. Where the wife alleges that a conveyance is void for lack of consent under s 3(1), she must bring proceedings to have the conveyance declared void within six years[15].

---

8 However, the Family Home Protection Act 1976 does not apply to a house which is merely intended to be occupied as a family home: see *National Irish Bank Ltd v Graham* [1995] 2 IR 244 (prior written consent of non-owning spouse not required in respect of a mortgage which is used to purchase the family home, and spouses cannot take possession of the property until the loan transaction is complete).

9 The Family Home Protection Act 1976 encourages spouses to place a family home in joint ownership – s 14 provides that where spouses create a joint tenancy in the family home the transaction is exempt from stamp duty, land registration or Registry of Deeds fees and court fees.

10 Family Home Protection Act 1976, s 1(1) defines 'interest' as 'any estate, right, title or other interest, legal or equitable'.

11 As with sales of land in general, house sales are carried out in two stages, namely the contract of sale followed by the deed of conveyance or transfer. If the wife consents at the contract stage, the husband does not have to procure her consent to the subsequent conveyance or transfer: see *Kyne v Tiernan* (15 July 1980, unreported) High Court (RI).

12 Consent given after the conveyance has taken place cannot retrospectively validate the conveyance: *Bank of Ireland v Hanrahan* (10 February 1987, unreported) High Court (RI).

13 *Bank of Ireland v Smyth* [1995] 2 IR 459 and see Mee, 'The Family Home Protection Act: The Practical Implications of *Bank of Ireland v Smyth*' (1996) 14 ILT 188 and 209. Thus, consent will be invalid if it has been procured by duress, misrepresentation or fraud: see for example, *Bank of Nova Scotia v Hogan* [1997] 1 ILRM 407. However, the purchaser may nevertheless take good title to the property if he is a 'purchaser for full value' within the meaning of the Family Home Protection Act 1976, s 3(3)(a) (see para **[10.06]** below) and as such did not have actual, constructive or imputed notice of the relevant vitiating factor.

14 Family Home Protection Act 1976, s 3(9) (as inserted by the Family Law Act 1995, s 54(1)). For example, the wife need not consent to sale to a specific purchaser – it is sufficient that she gives a general consent to sale of the property at some stage in the future.

15 Family Home Protection Act 1976, s 3(8)(a)(i) (as inserted by the Family Law Act 1995, s 54).

[10.06] Section 3(1) merely provides a statutory right of veto, and does not confer any proprietary right on the wife[16]. However, this statutory right of veto is not absolute. The wife's consent is not required where a conveyance is made by the husband in pursuance of an enforceable agreement made before their marriage[17], or where the family home is conveyed to a *bona fide* purchaser for full value[18]. Likewise, consent is not necessary in respect of a conveyance to a purchaser for value by someone other than the husband[19]. Thus, a third party such as a mortgagee or Official Assignee in Bankruptcy may execute a valid conveyance of the family home without procuring the wife's prior written consent[20]. The 1976 Act also provides a means of avoiding a series of invalid transactions – if the husband without his wife's consent conveys the family home to another party who then conveys the property to a *bona fide* purchaser for value, the latter will nevertheless obtain a valid title[21]. The onus of proving that a conveyance is valid under the 1976 Act is on the person alleging this[22].

[10.07] Assuming that the wife's consent is required under s 3(1), s 4 of the 1976 Act allows the court to dispense with this requirement if the wife refuses or is unable to consent[23]. Three situations are identified in which such an order may be made. The first is where the court considers it unreasonable for the wife to withhold consent[24]. In reaching this decision, the court must take account of all

---

16 *Guckian v Brennan* [1981] IR 478.

17 Family Home Protection Act 1976, s 3(2).

18 Family Home Protection Act 1976, s 3(3)(a). For the purposes of s 3, a purchaser is defined as a 'grantee, lessee, assignee, mortgagee, chargeant or other person who in good faith acquires an estate or interest in property': Family Home Protection Act 1976, s 3(6). In *Somers v Weir* [1979] IR 94 the Supreme Court held that this reference to 'good faith' incorporates the doctrine of notice under the Conveyancing Act 1882, s 3 (considered in ch 8 above, paras **[8.17]-[8.18]**). However, the Family Home Protection Act 1976, s 3(7) extends the doctrine of notice in this context, by fixing a purchaser with notice of information acquired by his agent in any capacity (albeit that the relevant information still must have been acquired in the course of the same transaction: see the comments of McWilliam J in *H & L v S* [1979] ILRM 105 at 108). As to the meaning of 'full value' for the purposes of the Family Home Protection Act 1976, s 3(3)(a), see s 3(5).

19 Family Home Protection Act 1976, s 3(3)(b). See generally Lyall, 'Conveyancing – The Family Home Protection Act 1976 and Conveyances Other Than by Spouses' (1984) 6 DULJ 158

20 However, the provisions of the Bankruptcy Act 1988, s 61 will be relevant in respect of any such conveyance by the Official Assignee: see paras **[10.68]-[10.74]** below.

21 Family Home Protection Act 1976, s 3(3)(c).

22 Family Home Protection Act 1976, s 3(4). See further *Allied Irish Banks plc v Finnegan* [1996] 1 ILRM 401 and *ICC Bank plc v Treacey* (10 March 1997, unreported) High Court (RI).

23 Family Home Protection Act 1976, s 4(1).

24 Family Home Protection Act 1976, s 4(2). The onus of proving that withholding consent is 'unreasonable' rests on the husband (or prospective purchaser see below) as the person seeking an order dispensing with consent: *Somers v Weir* [1979] IR 94. What amounts to a reasonable or unreasonable withholding of consent should be determined by an objective standard: *Hamilton v Hamilton* [1982] IR 466.

the circumstances of the case including the needs and resources of both spouses and of any dependent children of the family[25]. Where the wife has been offered alternative accommodation, the court must consider its suitability having regard to the respective degrees of security of tenure in the family home and in the alternative accommodation[26]. Secondly, the court must make an order dispensing with consent under s 4 where the wife has deserted and continues to desert her husband[27]. In this context, desertion includes conduct on the part of a spouse that results in the other spouse 'with just cause, leaving and living separately and apart from him'[28]. Thirdly, the court may make an order dispensing with consent under s 4 where the wife is incapable of giving consent by reason of unsoundness of mind or other mental disability, or where she cannot be found after reasonable inquiries[29]. An order under s 4 may be made at the request of the husband or a prospective purchaser of the family home[30]. However, an application must be made before the relevant conveyance takes place – the court cannot make an order under s 4 retrospectively dispensing with the wife's consent[31].

[10.08] The 1976 Act provides another means of protection for the wife as a non-owning spouse. Section 12 provides for a system of registration that allows the wife to register a notice in the Registry of Deeds or Land Registry stating that she is married to a person having an interest in such property or land[32]. Registration ensures that a subsequent purchaser of the family home cannot maintain the defence of *bona fide* purchaser in the event of the wife not giving prior consent to the transaction[33]. However, registration is merely subsidiary to

25 Family Home Protection Act 1976, s 4(2)(a).

26 Family Home Protection Act 1976, s 4(2)(b).

27 Family Home Protection Act 1976, s 4(3). Unlike the other provisions of s 4, which state that the court 'may' make an order dispensing with consent in appropriate circumstances, s 4(3) states that the court 'shall' make such an order in the event of desertion.

28 Family Home Protection Act 1976, s 4(3).

29 Family Home Protection Act 1976, s 4(4), which states that the court may make such an order 'if it appears ... to be reasonable to do so'.

30 *Hamilton v Hamilton* [1982] IR 466.

31 Since the Family Home Protection Act 1976, s 3(1) requires the wife's 'prior' written consent to the conveyance, and see *Somers v Weir* [1979] IR 94.

32 Family Home Protection Act 1976, s 12(1). Registration is effected pursuant to the Registration of Deeds Act 1707 or the Registration of Title Act 1964 as appropriate, and is exempt from stamp duty and Registration of Deeds or land registry fees: Family Home Protection Act 1976, s 12(3).

33 If a wife fails to register such a notice, this is not evidence in itself that a purchaser could have no prior notice of her rights under the Family Home Protection Act 1976: Family Home Protection Act 1976, s 12(2).

the wife's statutory right of veto under the 1976 Act, and is apparently seldom carried out in practice[34].

III Partition Actions Between Spouses

[10.09] The distribution of matrimonial property on the breakdown of a marriage may be achieved by a number of methods, some of which may result in spouses becoming involved in proceedings under the Partition Acts.

A Practice on judicial separation or divorce

[10.10] Significant changes to the law relating to judicial separation and divorce have been implemented in the Republic of Ireland during recent years. Divorce *a mensa et thoro* has been available since 1870[35], and the principal legislation is now contained in the Judicial Separation and Family Law Reform Act 1989 and the Family Law Act 1995. Prior to the enactment of the 1989 Act, the court's jurisdiction was limited to granting a decree of judicial separation; it could not make ancillary orders as part of the proceedings. If a spouse wanted the court to determine financial and property issues, the only way to achieve this was to institute an appropriate action along with the separation proceedings or to bring such an action after the decree of judicial separation had been granted[36]. However, the 1989 Act permitted the court to resolve financial and property issues between spouses in separation proceedings by making an appropriate order for ancillary relief.

[10.11] Divorce has only been available in the Republic of Ireland since February 1997, and the relevant legislation is contained in the Family Law (Divorce) Act 1996. As with proceedings for judicial separation since 1989, the court when granting a decree of divorce may make a wide range of ancillary orders in relation to financial or property issues arising between the spouses.

1 Property adjustments orders

[10.12] When a marital relationship has broken down, either spouse may petition for a decree of divorce or judicial separation[37]. In the absence of agreement between the parties as to the continued use and occupation of the family home[38],

---

34 Lyall, *Land Law in Ireland* (2nd edn, 2000), p 492. Registration requires a positive step on the part of the wife, which presupposes that she is aware of the protection conferred on her in this respect.

35 See the Matrimonial Causes and Marriage Law (Ir) Amendment Act 1870.

36 It appears that the absence of ancillary relief was one of the reasons why judicial separation was rarely sought prior to 1989: Shatter, *Family Law in the Republic of Ireland* (2nd edn, 1981), p 140.

37 As to the grounds for obtaining a decree of judicial separation, see the Judicial Separation and Family Law Reform Act 1989, s 2. As to the grounds for obtaining a decree of divorce, see the Family Law (Divorce) Act 1996, s 5 and Article 41.3.2° of the Constitution of Ireland.

38 The term 'family home' in the Family Law 1995 and Family Law (Divorce) Act 1996 has the same meaning as in the Family Home Protection Act 1976: see para **[10.04]** above.

the petitioner may also ask the court to make an appropriate order for ancillary relief in relation to the property. The range of ancillary orders available to the court in relation to matrimonial property on judicial separation and on divorce is contained in Part II of the 1995 Act and Part III of the 1996 Act respectively. Both Acts provide for the making of property adjustment orders which, in practice, allow the court to make any order it thinks fit in relation to the family home[39]. In addition to this, s 15 of the 1995 Act and s 19 of the 1996 Act allow the court to order sale of property specified in the property adjustment order, 'being property in which, or in the proceeds of sale of which, either or both of the spouses concerned has or have a beneficial interest, either in possession or in reversion'. The court may impose any consequential or supplementary provisions on the order for sale as it considers appropriate in the circumstances[40].

[10.13] As with the corresponding practice in Northern Ireland, the court would be unlikely to entertain a separate application for sale of the family home under the Partition Acts in these circumstances. Both the 1995 and 1996 Acts provide a more appropriate jurisdiction for determining disputes relating to the family home on judicial separation or divorce[41]. However, the court may order partition or sale of matrimonial property under the 1995 and 1996 Acts.

2 Miscellaneous ancillary orders

[10.14] The 1995 and 1996 Acts empower the court to make a number of ancillary orders on or after granting a decree of judicial separation or divorce. These include specific ancillary orders relating to the family home, and ancillary orders under various statutory provisions. While the latter could be obtained by spouses in separate proceedings, the purpose of including them in the 1995 and 1996 Acts is to avoid multiple proceedings[42]. Section 10(1) of the 1995 Act[43] reads:

---

39 Family Law Act 1995, s 9(1) (as amended by the Family Law (Divorce) Act 1996, s 52(b)) and the Family Law (Divorce) Act 1996, s 14(1) which state that such orders may be made on or at any time after granting a decree of judicial separation or divorce. The court may make one or more of the following orders: a property transfer order, a property settlement order, an order varying an ante-nuptial or post-nuptial settlement and an order extinguishing or reducing the interest of either spouse under any such settlement. In deciding whether to make these orders, the court must have regard to the factors listed in the Family Law Act 1995, s 16 and in the Family Law (Divorce) Act 1996, s 20: see para **[10.15]** below.

40 Family Law Act 1995, s 15(3) and the Family Law (Divorce) Act 1996, s 19(3). These include provisions specifying the manner of sale, and directing that the order for sale shall not take effect until a specified event occurs or a specified period expires.

41 Again, this may be regarded as a type of jurisdiction exception as in the case of partnership property: see ch 4 above, paras **[4.44]**-**[4.45]**.

42 Shatter, *Family Law* (4th edn, 1997), p 907.

43 As amended by the Family Law (Divorce) Act 1996, s 52(2).

> 'On granting a decree of judicial separation or at any time thereafter, the court, on application to it in that behalf by either of the spouses concerned ... may ... make one or more of the following orders:
>
> (a) an order –
>
> (i) providing for the conferral on one spouse either for life or for such other period (whether definite or contingent) as the court may specify the right to occupy the family home to the exclusion of the other spouse[44], or
>
> (ii) directing the sale of the family home subject to such conditions (if any) as the court considers proper and providing for the disposal of the proceeds of the sale between the spouses and any other person having an interest therein,
>
> (b) an order under section 36[45],
>
> (c) an order under section 4, 5, 7 or 9 of the Family Home Protection Act, 1976,
>
> ...
>
> (e) an order for the partition of property or under the Partition Act, 1868, and the Partition Act 1876 ...'

Identical directions are contained in s 15(1) of the 1996 Act in relation to an application by either spouse on or after a decree of divorce[46].

[10.15] Both s 10 of the 1995 Act and s 15 of the 1996 Act contemplate applications for sale of matrimonial property by either spouse on or after judicial separation or divorce. Sections 10(1)(a)(ii) and 15(1)(a)(ii) allow the court to order sale of a family home subject to such conditions as the court considers appropriate[47]. In deciding whether to order sale, the court must have regard to a

---

44 For example, the court may grant one of the spouses a right to occupy the property for his or her lifetime (*JC v CC* (15 November 1991, unreported) High Court (RI)) or for a specified period of time eg until the youngest child of the family reaches the age of 18 or finishes his education (*VS v RS* [1992] 2 Fam LJ 52 and *AK v PK* (13 March 2000, unreported) High Court (RI)). In exercising this jurisdiction, the court must have regard to the matters contained in the Family Law Act 1995, s 10(2) or the Family Law (Divorce) Act 1996, s 15(2) as appropriate: see para **[10.15]** below.

45 See paras **[10.39]-[10.43]** below.

46 The court's jurisdiction under the Family Law Act 1995, s 10(1)(a) and the Family Law (Divorce) Act 1996, s 15(1)(a) is not exercisable in respect of a family home in which, following the grant of a decree of judicial separation or divorce, either of the spouses, having remarried, ordinarily resides with his or her spouse: Family Law Act 1995, s 10(3) (as inserted by the Family Law (Divorce) Act 1996, s 52(c)) and the Family Law (Divorce) Act 1996, s 15(3).

47 For example, the court may postpone sale until a specified date or event, or provide that the house should not be sold until a spouse has acquired alternative accommodation. The court may also prescribe the method of sale and its conduct, and fix a reserve price for the property: see generally Shatter, *Family Law* (4th edn, 1997), pp 903-904. The consent requirements of the Family Home Protection Act 1976 will probably be irrelevant in this context.

number of factors set out in the respective Acts. For example, the court should consider the welfare of the spouses and any dependent member of the family, and in particular the fact that on judicial separation or divorce it is no longer possible for spouses to live together and that, where practicable, proper and secure accommodation should be provided for a spouse who is wholly or mainly dependent on the other spouse and for any dependent member of the family[48]. Upon making an order for sale of the family home, the court may distribute the proceeds between the spouses and any other person having an interest in the property such as a mortgagee. However, distribution of the proceeds of sale does not have to be in accordance with the spouses' respective beneficial interests in the property but can be in any manner that the court considers appropriate[49].

[10.16] Sections 10(1)(e) and 15(1)(e) allow the court to order partition or sale of property under the Partition Acts. Thus, where spouses are co-owners of matrimonial property, either one of them may seek a division or sale of the property on or after judicial separation or divorce. An issue that may arise in this context is whether the court's jurisdiction extends to making an order for sale of a family home under the Partition Acts. While it could be argued that the term 'property' in ss 10(1)(e) and 15(1)(e) incorporates a family home, the court may be reluctant to order sale of such property under the Partition Acts in view of the specific power to order sale of a family home conferred by ss 10(1)(a)(ii) and 15(1)(a)(ii). This power of sale is more flexible than sale under the Partition Acts, and its exercise is subject to a number of specific factors that the court must take into account.

[10.17] Accordingly, the court's jurisdiction under ss 10(1)(e) and 15(1)(e) may be confined to other property which spouses hold as co-owners such as land,

---

47 (contd) Under the Family Law Act 1995, s 10(1)(c) and the Family Law (Divorce) Act 1996, s 15(1)(c), the court may make an order dispensing with the need for consent under the Family Home Protection Act 1976, s 4. Thus, if the court considers it appropriate to make an order for sale of the family home in these circumstances, it must also have regarded the case as an appropriate one in which to dispense with consent. Moreover, if the parties are divorced they cease to be spouses and the Family Home Protection Act 1976 no longer applies.

48 Family Law Act 1995, s 10(2) and the Family Law (Divorce) Act 1996, s 15(2). Family Law Act 1995, s 16 and the Family Law (Divorce) Act 1996, s 20 further provide that the court shall have regard to a number of factors including the income, earning capacity, property and other financial resources which each spouse has or is likely to have in the future, the age of the spouses and length of time during which they lived together, and their accommodation needs.

49 See for example, *JD v PD* (9 August 1974, unreported) High Court (RI) (title to family home in joint names but proceeds of sale divided so as to give 83% to the wife and 17% to the husband) and *AO'L v BO'L* [1996] 2 Fam LJ 63. In these circumstances, the court can divide the proceeds of sale according to the needs of each spouse and, for example, award a larger proportion to a dependent spouse with no income or earning capacity: see Walls and Bergin, *The Law of Divorce in Ireland* (1997), p 77. Contrast this with an order for sale under the Partition Acts 1868 and 1876 where each person's share in the proceeds of sale is commensurate to the extent of his beneficial interest in the property.

business property or any other dwelling not occupied by them as a family home[50]. The principles to be applied in partition actions under ss 10(1)(e) and 15(1)(e) are the same as those which would be applied if proceedings under the Partition Acts had been instituted separately by a spouse[51]. However, the fact that the parties to the partition action are spouses may be relevant in these circumstances[52].

3 Proceedings for partition or sale following judicial separation or divorce

[10.18] Applications for sale of a family home under the Partition Acts following judicial separation or divorce may be rare in practice. Circumstances in which spouses would remain joint owners of the family home are not likely to arise frequently, since co-ownership will often come to an end as part of the relevant financial arrangements between the parties.

[10.19] Even if spouses remain co-owners of the family home following judicial separation or divorce and one of them desires a sale of the property, the court may prefer to order sale under the specific provisions contained in ss 10(1)(a)(ii) and 15(1)(a)(ii) of the respective 1995 and 1996 Acts. Moreover, in the event of an application for sale of the family home under the Partition Acts, the court may be unable to make such an order in certain circumstances. For example, the court's jurisdiction under the Partition Acts may be ousted by a property adjustment order that regulates the use and occupation of the family home or the circumstances in which spouses may dispose of the property[53]. Likewise, where the court has granted one of the spouses a right to occupy the family home under s 10(1)(a)(i) of the 1995 Act or s 15(1)(a)(i) of the 1996 Act, the other spouse could not defeat this by bringing an action for sale of the family home under the Partition Acts while the right of occupation persists[54]. If such considerations do

50 Upon making an order for sale of such property under the Partition Acts 1868 and 1876, the court would not have to consider the provisions of the Family Home Protection Act 1976. If the court were to order sale of a family home in these circumstances, the consent requirements of the Family Home Protection Act 1976 would probably be of little practical consequence. The court would be likely to make an order dispensing with the need for such consent under the Family Home Protection Act 1976, s 4 (and see the Family Law Act 1995, s 10(1)(c) and the Family Law (Divorce) Act 1996, s 15(1)(c)) if it were appropriate to order sale of a family home. Moreover, the Family Home Protection Act 1976 would not apply if the parties were divorced and thus no longer spouses.

51 Shatter, *Family Law* (4th edn, 1997), p 908.

52 See para **[10.37]** below.

53 See the discussion in ch 9 above, para **[9.06]** in relation to the corresponding practice in Northern Ireland.

54 However, if the court granted a contingent right to occupy, the non-occupying spouse might be able to obtain an order for sale of the family home under the Partition Acts 1868 and 1876 once the prescribed period of time had expired or the relevant determining event had occurred: see generally ch 9 above, para **[9.06]**.

not arise however, the court might make an ancillary order for sale of the family home under the Partition Acts following judicial separation or divorce[55].

B Judicial separation or divorce not available

[10.20] If judicial separation or divorce is not available, either spouse could conceivably use the Partition Acts to compel sale of the family home[56]. For example, a husband may wish to end the marital relationship but may not have any grounds upon which to petition for judicial separation or divorce. Should he nevertheless wish to realise his share in the family home, the husband could bring an action for sale of the property under the Partition Acts. As there is no petition for judicial separation or divorce, the jurisdiction under the 1995 and 1996 Acts is not exercisable and the court cannot make an appropriate property adjustment order. The court would probably have no option but to entertain the husband's application under the Partition Acts and to determine the action accordingly. However, if the wife subsequently petitioned for a decree of judicial separation or divorce before the partition action had been determined, the court might adjourn the partition action and deal with the family home when determining financial and property issues between the spouses under the 1995 and 1996 Acts[57].

[10.21] Alternatively, spouses may enter into a separation agreement, the terms of which might regulate occupation of the family home following the breakdown of the marital relationship[58]. In these circumstances, it is likely that a non-occupying co-owner would be prevented from compelling partition or more likely sale of the property under the Partition Acts where such an order would be contrary to the terms of the agreement between the parties. The agreement would oust the court's jurisdiction under the Partition Acts[59]. In addition to this, a separation agreement may effect a severance where spouses are joint tenants of the family home or other relevant property[60].

---

55 However, the decision whether to order sale would be influenced by the factors discussed at paras **[10.22]-[10.38]** below.

56 See the comments of Jacobs J in *Tansell v Tansell* (1977) 35 FLR (Aus) 272 at 301.

57 See the cases cited in ch 9 above, para **[9.07]**.

58 As to separation agreements in general, see Shatter, *Family Law* (4th edn, 1997), ch 8.

59 See ch 9 above, para **[9.08]**. However, there must be some form of express agreement between the parties regulating the occupation of the family home and the relevant wording must be explicit: see *Fergus v Fergus* (12 June 1997, unreported) Manitoba Court of Appeal, discussed in ch 9 above, para **[9.08]**. Moreover, such an agreement would only be relevant between co-owners themselves and would not bind third parties (such as lenders) unless the circumstances of a particular case gave rise to an estoppel: see ch 4 above, paras **[4.57]-[4.60]**.

60 See the cases cited in ch 9 above, para **[9.08]**.

C Related issues

[10.22] Irrespective of whether spouses seek an order for partition or, more likely, sale of a family home following judicial separation or divorce, or in situations where such a decree is not available, two factors may influence the court's jurisdiction under the Partition Acts.

1 Family Home Protection Act 1976

[10.23] The consent requirements of the Family Home Protection Act 1976 may be relevant where a spouse seeks to compel partition or sale of the family home against the wishes of the other spouse[61].

(a) Partition of a family home and the 1976 Act

[10.24] Where spouses are co-owners of a family home, the 1976 Act does not prevent the husband from compelling partition of the property against the wishes of his wife[62]. While the parties will have to execute mutual conveyances to each other in order to complete the division of the property[63], the wife cannot defeat the order for partition by alleging that she did not consent to the conveyance that the husband has made in her favour. The requirement of prior written consent under s 3(1) of the 1976 Act only applies in respect of conveyances 'to any person except the other spouse'[64].

[10.25] However, it has been suggested that s 5 of the 1976 Act may prevent the court from ordering partition of a family home[65]. Section 5(1) applies where a spouse 'is engaging in such conduct as may lead to the loss of any interest in the family home or may render it unsuitable for habitation as a family home'. If the court is satisfied that the intention of that spouse is to deprive the other spouse

61 If spouses are co-owners of matrimonial property other than a family home and one spouse seeks to compel partition or sale of such property under the Partition Acts 1868 and 1876, the Family Home Protection Act 1976 does not apply.

62 The principal function of the Family Home Protection Act 1976 is to protect a spouse without legal title. However, the legislation may also be relevant where spouses are co-owners of the family home at law: see paras **[10.34]-[10.35]** below.

63 The order for partition will instruct the parties to execute mutual conveyances in the appropriate form: see ch 12 below.

64 Mee, 'Partition and Sale of the Family Home' (1993) 15 DULJ 78 at 82. In *O'D v O'D* (18 November 1983, unreported) High Court (RI) at 10-11 Murphy J suggested that the court would not order partition of a family home if consent could not be secured in accordance with the Family Home Protection Act 1976. However, it appears that Murphy J overlooked the fact that spouses must execute conveyances to each other if the court orders partition, and that this avoids the need for consent under the Family Home Protection Act 1976, s 3. Mee has suggested that the legislation should be amended to provide that one spouse cannot obtain partition of a family home without the consent of the other spouse: Mee, 'Partition and Sale of the Family Home' (1993) 15 DULJ 78 at 83.

65 Mee, 'Partition and Sale of the Family Home' (1993) 15 DULJ 78 at 82.

or a dependent child of his or her residence in the family home, the court 'may make such order as it considers proper'[66]. Thus, the court might refuse the husband's request for partition in these circumstances if the wife makes an appropriate application under s 5.

[10.26] In view of the practical difficulties associated with partition of a family home, such orders are unlikely to be sought in practice. Sale will usually be preferable to division of a family home. However, the 1976 Act has also raised substantive issues in relation to the court's jurisdiction to order sale of a family home under the Partition Acts.

(b) Sale of a family home and the 1976 Act

[10.27] Different considerations arise where legal title to a family home is vested in one spouse, and where legal title is vested in both spouses.

(i) Title vested in one spouse

[10.28] Where title to a family home is in the sole name of the husband, he may bring an action for sale of the property under the Partition Acts if he and his wife are co-owners in equity[67]. If the court orders sale, the husband will convey the family home to a purchaser, but must obtain his wife's prior written consent in accordance with s 3(1) of the 1976 Act. If consent has not been sought or the wife refuses to consent, the purchaser may still take good title to the property if consent is not required under s 3 of the 1976 Act or the court dispenses with the wife's consent under s 4[68]. However, if neither exception applies and the wife opposes sale of the family home, this raises the question of whether the husband can still obtain an order for sale of the property under the Partition Acts. In other words, does the 1976 Act qualify or restrict the court's jurisdiction to order sale under the Partition Acts where the subject matter of the action is a family home?

[10.29] This issue was considered in *O'D v O'D*[69] in which the husband sought an order for partition or sale of a family home against the wishes of his wife[70]. After deciding that the court has discretion to refuse partition, Murphy J went on to consider whether the husband was entitled to an order for sale under s 4 of the Partition Act 1868. The learned judge suggested that, in the present case, what constituted 'good reason to the contrary' for the purposes of s 4 should 'properly

66 As to the range of potential orders available to the court under the Family Home Protection Act 1976, s 5 see Shatter, *Family Law* (4th edn, 1997), pp 759-768.

67 For example, if the wife has acquired an interest in the property under a resulting or constructive trust. The wife as an equitable co-owner may also bring an action for sale of the family home under the Partition Acts 1868 and 1876: see para **[10.33]** below.

68 See generally paras **[10.06]-[10.07]** above.

69 (18 November 1983, unreported) High Court (RI).

70 Although title to the family home was in the joint names of the spouses, the relevant principles are applicable in this context.

have regard to the rights of the parties under the Family Home Protection Act 1976'[71]. Counsel for the husband argued that, since the Partition Acts had not been repealed by the 1976 Act, an order for partition or sale of a family home was not dependent on the consent of the other spouse being secured in accordance with the 1976 Act. Rejecting this proposition, Murphy J remarked:

> 'There is no reason to suppose that an order for partition or sale in lieu thereof was intended to overreach the provisions of the Family Home Protection Act. Even if an order were made under the 1868 Act it must be recognised that this would not constitute a parliamentary conveyance and would not of itself correct imperfections in title. It would only be the fact that the spouses themselves joined in the conveyance that would overcome the need to procure their consent and it seems to me unthinkable that the Court would direct a conveyance to be made under the 1868 Act without having regard to the right of a spouse to withhold his or her consent and indeed the express duty imposed on the Court not to dispense with consent without taking into account all the relevant circumstances including in particular those specified in [s 4(2)] of the 1976 Act.'

[10.30] He continued:

> 'Counsel on behalf of the Plaintiff/Appellant recognised that this argument entailed acceptance of the proposition that a spouse who had no beneficial interest in the Family Home enjoyed the statutory veto on the sale thereof where another spouse who had a beneficial interest, however minuscule, could have his or her statutory veto overborne by a sale directed under the Partition Acts. In my view a Court would be justified in concluding in the circumstances of present times, under our Constitution and of the rights conferred by the Family Home Protection Act that the loss of the statutory veto represented good reason within the meaning of s 4 of the Partition Act 1868. This interpretation of the relevant legislation is greatly facilitated by the fact that a contrary conclusion would lead to a result which is unjust to the point of absurdity.'[72]

[10.31] In other words, the statutory right of veto enjoyed by a wife with a beneficial interest in a family home cannot be overridden by an order for sale of the property under the Partition Acts at the request of the husband. Moreover, this statutory right of veto under the 1976 Act amounts to 'good reason to the contrary' under s 4 of the 1868 Act[73]. Since the wife in *O'D v O'D* had refused

---

71 (18 November 1983, unreported) High Court (RI), at 10.

72 (18 November 1983, unreported) High Court (RI), at 10-12.

73 A similar interpretation would presumably follow in relation to the Partition Act 1868, s 3. Under s 3, the court 'may' make an order for sale if this would be more beneficial than partition. The husband may bring an action under s 3 where the wife's interest in the family home exceeds his interest. If the wife exercises her statutory right of veto under the Family Home Protection Act 1976 and the court declines to dispense with her consent, it might refuse to order sale under the Partition Act 1868, s 3 even though such an order would be more beneficial than partition.

to consent to sale of the family home and there were insufficient grounds for dispensing with her consent under s 4 of the 1976 Act, the husband was not entitled to an order for sale of the property under the Partition Acts.

[10.32] A similar approach was adopted by Finlay P in *AL v JL*[74]. Title to the family home was vested in the husband[75]. Following the breakdown of the marriage, the wife sought a declaration of the extent of her beneficial interest in the property and an order for sale under the Partition Acts. The Circuit Court judge directed a sale of the family home and declared that the wife was entitled to 40% of the net proceeds of sale. The wife appealed contending that she was entitled to 50% of any such proceeds[76]. However, Finlay P refused to order sale of the family home on the basis that such an order could not be made under the Partition Acts 'unless the Court [was] ... satisfied that it should dispense with the consent of the non-agreeing spouse under Section 4 of the 1976 Act'[77]. No such grounds existed in this particular case[78].

[10.33] Although he did not specifically refer to *O'D v O'D*[79], it is obvious that Finlay P also regarded the consent requirements of the 1976 Act as paramount in these circumstances. However, the decision in *AL v JL* appears to have wider implications than the former case. The decision in *O'D v O'D* suggests that, where title to a family home is in the husband's name yet both spouses have a beneficial interest in the property, the court may refuse the husband's request for sale under the Partition Acts. In these circumstances, an order for sale cannot be made at the request of the husband as sole legal owner and who 'purports to convey' the family home within s 3(1) of the 1976 Act, without the wife's consent being secured or dispensed with under the 1976 Act. This accords with the ethos of the 1976 Act, namely the protection of the wife as a non-owning spouse. A wife who has an equitable interest in the family home may maintain a partition action as occurred in *AL v JL*[80]. However, if the court orders sale in

---

74 (27 February 1984, unreported) High Court (RI).

75 Although the parties had originally intended to purchase the family home in their joint names, it was placed in the husband's name because the wife was under 21 years of age at the date of purchase.

76 (27 February 1984, unreported) High Court (RI), at 4-6.

77 (27 February 1984, unreported) High Court (RI), at 6.

78 See further *ND v AD* (10 December 1982, unreported) High Court (RI) in which O'Hanlon J ordered sale of property, part of which comprised licensed premises and the other part residential accommodation used as a family home. The property was in the sole name of the husband, and the wife as an equitable co-owner obtained an order for sale under the Partition Acts 1868 and 1876. Although O'Hanlon J did not refer to the Family Home Protection Act 1976, this may have been regarded as an appropriate case in which to dispense with the husband's consent under s 4 – the husband also owned an area of farmland, and the two children of the marriage were no longer residing in the family home.

79 (18 November 1983, unreported) High Court (RI).

80 Since she satisfies the *locus standi* test: see ch 4 above, paras **[4.03]-[4.24]**.

these circumstances the subsequent conveyance to the purchaser will have to be made by the husband as legal title owner[81]. According to Finlay P in *AL v JL*, the wife must procure her husband's consent to the proposed sale in these circumstances. If the spouses cannot agree and the court does not consider it appropriate to dispense with the husband's consent under the 1976 Act, the court may refuse to order sale of the family home under the Partition Acts. The decision in *AL v JL* can only be explained on the basis that the wife in these circumstances is regarded as the spouse who 'purports to convey' under s 3(1) of the 1976 Act – notwithstanding that she is the non-owning spouse, a conveyance of the family home to a purchaser would be made pursuant to the wife's partition action. Thus, while it may be true to say that the primary purpose of the 1976 Act is to protect the non-owning spouse, the Act does accord some protection to the legal title owner by requiring his consent in these circumstances. Although the decision in *AL v JL* may not be strictly in keeping with the spirit and intent of the 1976 Act it nevertheless makes practical sense. To hold otherwise would deny any protection to the husband, as he would be forced to convey the family home pursuant to his wife's partition action.

(ii) Title vested in both spouses

[10.34] The 1976 Act is of limited practical application where title to a family home is vested in both spouses[82]. In these circumstances, the fact that both spouses must usually join in any transaction relating to the family home for it to be valid avoids the need for prior written consent under s 3(1). For example, in *Nestor v Murphy*[83] the defendant spouses were joint tenants of a family home which they agreed to sell to the plaintiff. Both spouses signed a contract of sale, but refused to complete the sale and the plaintiff brought an action for specific performance. The defendants argued that the contract was void because the wife had not given prior written consent in accordance with s 3(1) of the 1976 Act. Rejecting this argument, Henchy J observed that the purpose of s 3(1) was to protect against a unilateral alienation by one spouse; it was not intended to apply where both spouses had joined in the relevant conveyance[84]. In other words, where both spouses have joined in conveying an interest in the family home they cannot subsequently invoke the provisions of the 1976 Act to avoid the conveyance.

[10.35] However, the position is different where title to the family home is in joint names and one spouse attempts to convey his or her interest in the property.

---

81 Although the wife may have to join in the conveyance if the purchaser is aware of her prior equitable interest in the family home.

82 Since the primary purpose of the Family Home Protection Act 1976 is to protect a non-owning spouse against the disposition of any interest in the family home by the spouse with title: see paras **[10.04]-[10.05]** above.

83 [1979] IR 326.

84 [1979] IR 326 at 328.

In these circumstances, he or she must secure the prior written consent of the other spouse in accordance with s 3(1) of the 1976 Act[85]. Accordingly, if a husband seeks an order for sale of the family home under the Partition Acts he must obtain his wife's prior written consent to the proposed sale, or apply under s 4 of the 1976 Act for an order dispensing with this consent[86].

(c) Effect of the 1976 Act on partition actions between spouses

[10.36] The 1976 Act has made substantial inroads into the court's jurisdiction under the Partition Acts. Where spouses are co-owners of a family home at law or in equity, and either spouse seeks an order for sale of the property under the Partition Acts, he or she must obtain the prior written consent of the other spouse[87]. Failing this, the court will only make an order for sale if it is appropriate to dispense with the consent of the opposing spouse in accordance with s 4 of the 1976 Act. In other words, the factors which the court takes into account under s 4 of the 1976 Act may be added to the criteria which the plaintiff must satisfy to obtain an order for sale under s 3 or s 4 of the Partition Act 1868[88]. The court's refusal to order sale in these circumstances may be regarded as analogous to the so-called futility cases[89] in which an order for partition is dependent on the consent of a third party[90]. Yet, in the event of refusing sale, the court is not obliged to order partition in the alternative in view of the practical difficulties associated with such an order and the decision in *O'D v O'D*[91] in which Murphy suggested that such an order was at the discretion of the court[92].

---

85 Coughlan, *Property Law* (2nd edn, 1998), p 446. While the primary purpose of the Family Home Protection Act 1976 may be to protect a non-owning spouse, the statutory right of veto under s 3(1) is not so restricted. In *Bank of Ireland v Purcell* [1989] 2 IR 327 the Supreme Court stated that the Family Home Protection Act 1976 should be construed as widely as possible, although the first consideration in construing s 3 was its purpose, namely protection of the interest of a non-owning spouse in a family home.

86 See *O'D v O'D* (18 November 1983, unreported) High Court (RI) discussed at paras **[10.29]-[10.31]** above.

87 Albeit that such consent is unlikely to be forthcoming in view of the need to commence proceedings for sale of the family home under the Partition Acts 1868 and 1876. If a spouse brings a partition action, this is *prima facie* evidence that the other spouse does not agree to the proposed sale of the family home.

88 See Walls and Bergin, *The Law of Divorce in Ireland* (1997), pp 77-78 and Coughlan, *Property Law* (2nd edn, 1998), pp 143-144.

89 See ch 7 above.

90 Albeit that the court may dispense with the need for such consent under the Family Home Protection Act 1976.

91 (18 November 1983, unreported) High Court (RI).

92 See Mee, 'Partition and Sale of the Family Home' (1993) 15 DULJ 78 at 88-89 and 'Judgment Mortgages, Co-Ownership and Registered Land' (1999) 4 Conveyancing and Property Lawyer 28 at 29 where the author contemplates courts in this jurisdiction refusing both partition and sale of a family home because of the provisions of the Family Home Protection Act 1976, notwithstanding the fact that the usual choice under the Partition Acts 1868 and 1876 is between ordering partition and sale.

2 'Family law proceedings'

[10.37] The 1976 Act aside, it appears that the court may apply different considerations to partition actions between spouses than it might otherwise apply to partition actions where the parties are not married. The Judicial Separation and Family Law Reform Act 1989 applies special rules to the conduct of 'family law proceedings' which are intended to make them as informal as is practicable[93]. These include proceedings under the 1989 Act, the Family Law Act 1995 and the Family Law (Divorce) Act 1996[94]. More importantly however, s 30 of the 1989 Act provides that family law proceedings also include proceedings between spouses under the Partition Acts where 'the fact that they are married to each other is of relevance to the proceedings'. This suggests that, where a spouse brings an action for partition or sale of matrimonial property under the Partition Acts, the court may consider factors which are referable to the marriage of the parties in deciding whether to order partition or sale. Furthermore, this stipulation is not confined to partition actions between spouses which are ancillary to a decree of judicial separation or divorce under the respective 1995 and 1996 Acts[95] – it applies to any proceedings between spouses under the Partition Acts[96].

---

92 (contd) Similar views have been expressed in a number of Canadian cases in relation to 'homestead' property. For example, in *Robertson v Robertson* [1951] 1 WWR 183 a wife sought an order for partition or sale of homestead property which she and her husband owned as joint tenants. Section 3 of the Dower Act 1948 (Alb) provided that '[n]o married person shall make any disposition by act, *inter vivos*, of the homestead of the married persons whereby any interest of the married person shall or may vest in any other person ..., unless the spouse consents thereto in writing or unless a judge has made an order dispensing with the consent of the spouse as hereinafter provided for'. Egbert J observed that the Partition Act 1868 ordinarily granted joint tenants and tenants in common a right to partition or sale. However, he continued at 186-187:

> 'The broad general purpose of [the Dower Act 1948 (Alb)] ... is to preserve to the spouse of the owner of the homestead the right to have and to keep a home, and so they provide that this home cannot be disposed of, nor the right of the spouse to occupy that home taken away, unless the spouse consents in writing to release his or her claim ... [W]hen a husband and wife are owners of a homestead as joint tenants or tenants in common, neither one is entitled as against the other to partition or sale of the homestead, because to permit such partition or sale would defeat the intention and purpose of [the Dower Act 1948 (Alb)]'

See further *Kluss v Kluss* [1947] 1 WWR 734 and *Wimmer v Wimmer* [1947] 2 WWR 249.

93 Judicial Separation and Family Law Reform Act 1989, s 33.

94 Judicial Separation and Family Law Reform Act 1989, s 30; Family Law Act 1995, s 38(6); and Family Law (Divorce) Act 1996, s 38(5).

95 See paras **[10.14]-[10.17]** above.

96 However, the Judicial Separation and Family Law Reform Act 1989, s 30 only applies to proceedings between spouses – it does not apply to partition actions between a spouse and a third party such as a lender or the Official Assignee.

3 Criteria for ordering partition or sale

[10.38] Where the property in question is a family home and either spouse seeks an order for sale of the property in lieu of partition, the consent requirements of the Family Home Protection Act 1976 are relevant factors for the court to take into account in deciding whether to order sale. The definition of 'family law proceedings' and the fact that the parties to the partition action are married to each other are also relevant to proceedings under the Partition Acts. Accordingly, the court may adopt a more flexible approach in deciding whether to order sale of a family home in these circumstances and avoid the otherwise narrow discretion that exists under the Partition Acts. Failing this, the arguments put forward in relation to courts in Northern Ireland adopting a more flexible approach in partition actions between spouses may be relevant in this context[97].

D Proceedings under section 36 of the Family Law Act 1995

[10.39] The court may make an order for partition or sale of matrimonial property as incidental to determining questions between spouses in relation to such property. Section 36 of the Family Law Act 1995 replaces s 12 of the Married Women's Status Act 1957, which in turn was based on s 17 of the Married Women's Property Act 1882[98]. Section 36(1) of the 1995 Act allows spouses to apply to court in a summary manner to determine any question arising between them 'as to the title to or possession of matrimonial property'. Section 36(2) continues:

> 'On an application to it under *subsection (1)*, the court may –
>
> (a) make such order with respect to the property in dispute (including an order that it be sold or partitioned) and as to the costs consequent upon the application), and
>
> (b) direct such inquiries, and give such other directions, in relation to the application,
>
> as the court considers proper.'[99]

---

97 See ch 9 above, paras **[9.25]-[9.37]**.

98 For an overview of the practical application of the Family Law Act 1995, s 36 see Shatter, *Family Law* (4th edn, 1997), pp 772-807 and Walls and Bergin, *The Law of Divorce in Ireland* (1997), pp 67-69. Married Women's Property Act 1882, s 17 remains in force in Northern Ireland. For an overview of this provision see ch 9 above, paras **[9.50]-[9.56]**.

99 Proceedings under the Family Law Act 1995, s 36 are available to spouses on or after a decree of judicial separation or divorce: see s 10 of the 1995 Act and the Family Law (Divorce) Act 1996, s 15 discussed at para **[10.14]** above. Where a marriage has been annulled, either spouse may bring proceedings under s 36 of the 1995 Act within three years of the date of annulment: s 36(7). The court's jurisdiction under s 36 also extends to engaged couples.

[10.40] It appears that s 36 is a procedural provision and merely permits the court to determine property disputes between spouses according to established legal principles[100]. Furthermore, it can only declare the existing legal and equitable property rights of the spouses, and cannot order the transfer of any proprietary rights between them[101]. Thus, the court's discretion under s 36 is more restricted than the wording of the provision might suggest.

[10.41] As with s 12 of the 1957 Act, s 36 may be invoked by a spouse (for convenience, a wife) who is seeking to establish a beneficial interest in a family home[102] through direct or indirect contributions. Under s 36, the court now has a specific power to order partition or sale of matrimonial property[103]. It appears that the inclusion of these powers was aimed at simplifying pleadings[104]. Under s 12 of the 1957 Act, it was common practice for a wife to institute proceedings under the 1957 Act, the Partition Acts and the Family Home Protection Act 1976[105]. The wife would seek a declaration that she was beneficially entitled to a share in the family home, an order for sale of the property under s 3 or s 4 of the Partition Act 1868 (depending on the extent of the beneficial interest which the court declared her to be entitled to)[106], and an order dispensing with her

---

99 (contd) Family Law Act 1981, s 5(2) contemplates such an application by a party 'to an agreement to marry which has been terminated', and provides that the court may determine any dispute between the parties or claim by one of them in relation to property 'in which either or both had a beneficial interest while the agreement was in force'. In determining such disputes, the court must apply the same rules as it would apply in relation to spouses and property in which either or both spouses has or have a beneficial interest: Family Law Act 1981, s 5(1). See further the Family Law (Divorce) Act 1996, s 44 which extends s 36 of the 1995 Act to formerly engaged couples.

100 See Shatter, *Family Law* (4th edn, 1997), p 772 discussing the corresponding practice under the Married Women's Status Act 1957, s 12. See further Walls and Bergin, *The Law of Divorce in Ireland* (1997), p 67. There is little case law on the practical application of the Family Law Act 1995, s 36: see para **[10.43]** below.

101 Shatter, *Family Law* (4th edn, 1997), pp 772-773 referring to the corresponding practice under the Married Women's Status Act 1957, s 12 and citing cases such as *DM'C v MM'C* [1986] 6 ILRM 1 and *EN v RN* [1992] 2 IR 116. See further Walls and Bergin, *The Law of Divorce in Ireland* (1997), p 67.

102 Or any other matrimonial property.

103 No such provision was made in either the Married Women's Property Act 1882, s 17 or the Married Women's Status Act 1957, s 12.

104 Shatter, *Family Law* (4th edn, 1997), p 774.

105 See for example, the draft High Court Summons, Special Endorsement of Claim and draft High Court Summons reproduced in Duncan and Scully, *Marriage Breakdown in Ireland* (1990), pp 326-328. See further *ND v AD* (10 December 1982, unreported) High Court (RI), discussed at para **[10.32]** above.

106 If less than 50%, under the Partition Act 1868, s 3; if 50% or more, under the Partition Act 1868, s 4.

husband's consent to sale under s 4 of the 1976 Act. The court then had to consider whether the relevant criteria for ordering sale under s 3 or s 4 of the 1868 Act were satisfied and whether it was appropriate to dispense with the husband's consent under s 4 of the 1976 Act.

[10.42] Where a wife now wishes to establish a beneficial interest in a family home and desires a sale of the property, she does not have to institute separate proceedings under s 36 of the 1995 Act and the Partition Acts because s 36 expressly confers jurisdiction on the court to order partition or sale[107]. However, s 36 does not refer to the court making such an order under the Partition Acts. Thus when ordering partition or, more likely, sale the court would not have to apply the criteria laid down in s 3 or s 4 of the Partition Act 1868. The rights of both spouses should be given equal weight and there should be no bias in favour of ordering partition or sale[108]. The only restriction on the court's jurisdiction to order sale of a family home under s 36 is whether the court considers it appropriate to dispense with the husband's consent to sale in accordance with s 4 of the 1976 Act[109]. In addition to this, s 36 proceedings are only available in respect of a dispute over title to or possession of matrimonial property[110]. In the absence of any such dispute, the court's jurisdiction is not exercisable[111]. Furthermore, s 36 only provides a summary procedure which may not be appropriate if the proceedings raise complicated issues.

[10.43] To date, there is little authority on the practical application of s 36 of the 1995 Act, so that the extent to which the court will exercise the power to order partition or sale in such cases remains to be seen. Proceedings under s 36 are likely to be rare in practice. Both the Family Law Act 1995 and the Family Law (Divorce) Act 1996 empower the court to make property adjustment orders on judicial separation or divorce. In view of the wider powers available to the court

---

107 Shatter, *Family Law* (4th edn, 1997), p 774.

108 See the comments of Steele J in *Re MacDonald and MacDonald* (1976) 73 DLR (3d) 341 in relation to similar provisions contained in the Married Women's Property Act 1970 (Ont). See further *Silva v Silva* (1990) 75 DLR (4th) 415. In other words, the court's jurisdiction under the Family Law Act 1995, s 36 is more flexible than its corresponding jurisdiction to order partition or sale under the Partition Acts 1868 and 1876. However, the ostensibly wide discretion that the court possesses under s 36 is irrelevant in the context of property disputes between spouses which are determined under the Partition Acts 1868 and 1876: see ch 9 above, paras **[9.52]-[9.56]**. The court's jurisdiction under the s 36 and in partition actions between spouses arises in different contexts.

109 Where the property comprising the subject matter of an application under the Family Law Act 1995, s 36 is not a family home, this consideration does not arise.

110 See Shatter, *Family Law* (4th edn, 1997), p 773 and Walls and Bergin, *The Law of Divorce in Ireland* (1997), p 67.

111 See for example, *Martin v Martin* (1992) 85 DLR (4th) 115 referring to the corresponding practice under the Family Law Act 1986 (Ont), s 10.

when making such orders and the fact that they are not dependent on establishing a beneficial interest in the relevant property, a non-owning spouse would be more likely to apply under these provisions than under s 36 on judicial separation or divorce[112]. However, proceedings under s 36 may be relevant where a spouse without legal title seeks to assert a prior beneficial interest in the family home in the event of a third party such as a lender or the Official Assignee acquiring rights in the property[113].

E Partition actions between cohabitees

[10.44] Persons living together in a cohabiting relationship may purchase a dwelling house as joint owners[114]. Unlike spouses, no legislation exists to regulate the distribution of such property between cohabitees when their relationship breaks down. If the parties cannot reach an agreement on the disposal of the property or its continued use and occupation, either one of them may commence proceedings for sale under the Partition Acts.

[10.45] In these circumstances, the difficulties associated with physical partition of a dwelling house would usually give rise to a strong presumption in favour of sale. The provisions of the Family Home Protection Act 1976 are irrelevant in this context and thus cannot be applied in favour of the court adopting a more flexible approach in deciding whether to order sale of property occupied by cohabitees as their home[115]. Thus, the likelihood of a cohabitee obtaining an order for sale of such property under the Partition Acts may be regarded as considerable[116].

---

[112] It appears that proceedings under the Married Women's Status Act 1957, s 12 were common before the Judicial Separation and Family Law Reform Act 1989 which first introduced a power for courts to resolve financial and property issues between spouses upon granting a decree of judicial separation: Shatter, *Family Law* (4th edn, 1997), p 775. See further Duncan and Scully, *Marriage Breakdown in Ireland* (1990), pp 335-336.

[113] For example, a wife may allege that she has a prior beneficial interest in the family home which prevents the entire property from vesting in the Official Assignee or which prevents the lender's security from extending to the entire property: Shatter, *Family Law* (4th edn, 1997), pp 775-776 and see *CD v WD* (5 February 1997, unreported) High Court (RI).

[114] See generally Mee, *The Property Rights of Cohabitees* (1999).

[115] Since the definition of a 'family home' in the Family Home Protection Act 1976, s 2 refers to a dwelling house in which a 'married couple' ordinarily reside.

[116] An issue that may arise in this context is whether the court should adopt a more flexible approach in partition actions between cohabitees than in partition actions in general. For example, the court might be influenced by the fact that the parties occupied the dwelling as their home, and that sale of the property would prejudice a dependent cohabitee and any children residing in the property.

IV Partition Actions by Lenders

[10.46] In Northern Ireland, a significant number of partition actions involving spouses occur in respect of lenders whose security is restricted to an undivided share of a matrimonial home[117]. However, such actions are less common in the Republic of Ireland. In this context, the consent requirements of the Family Home Protection Act 1976 have significant practical implications for the creation of incumbrances on a family home.

A Mortgages and charges affecting a family home

[10.47] The Family Home Protection Act 1976 affects the creation of mortgages and charges on the family home, so that there is little prospect of the lender's security being restricted to an undivided share of the property. Section 3(1) of the 1976 Act provides that where a spouse without the prior written consent of the other spouse purports to convey any interest in a family home to a third party, the conveyance is void. For the purposes of the 1976 Act, a 'conveyance' includes a mortgage, and the definition of 'mortgage' includes both an equitable mortgage and a charge on registered land[118].

1 Title vested in both spouses

[10.48] Where title to a family home is in joint names, both spouses will usually join in creating a mortgage or charge on the property. If the spouses subsequently default on repayments, the lender can exercise his normal powers of possession and sale[119]. There is nothing in theory to prevent the husband from mortgaging his undivided share of the family home in these circumstances. However, this is unlikely to occur in practice. Any such transaction would require the wife's prior written consent in accordance with s 3(1) of the 1976 Act[120]. That aside, most lenders would be unlikely to agree to a mortgage or charge of an undivided share of a family home where title to the property is held in joint names[121].

---

116 (contd) The absence of a specific legislative framework regulating the property rights of cohabitees on the breakdown of their relationship suggests that they should not be treated in a special manner, and that the traditional practice should apply in partition actions involving such persons. However, in the absence of direct case law on the subject, the extent to which courts in the Republic of Ireland will consider themselves bound by the narrow discretion which exists under the Partition Acts 1868 and 1876 or whether they will adopt a more flexible approach when determining partition actions between cohabitees remains to be seen.

117 See generally ch 9 above, paras **[9.43]**-**[9.71]**.

118 Family Home Protection Act 1976, s 1(1).

119 See ch 8 above, para **[8.06]**.

120 See para **[10.49]** below.

121 If such a transaction were to occur, the mortgage would be restricted to the husband's share of the family home so that the lender would have to apply for sale of the property under the Partition Acts 1868 and 1876 in the event of default.

2 *Title vested in one spouse*

[10.49] More substantive issues arise where title to a family home is vested in the husband, yet he and his wife are co-owners of the property in equity. If the husband wishes to create a mortgage or charge on the family home, he must obtain his wife's prior written consent in accordance with s 3(1) of the 1976 Act[122]. The consent must be a voluntary and fully informed consent, and the onus of proving this rests on the lender[123]. Where the wife agrees to the proposed mortgage or charge, the lender's security will usually extend to the entire beneficial interest in the family home[124]. In these circumstances, the wife is estopped from asserting her beneficial interest in the family home against the lender, and the mortgage or charge will be given priority[125]. The lender can then exercise his normal powers of possession and sale in the event of default. However, if the wife refuses to consent or her consent is held to be invalid[126], the purported mortgage or charge will be void unless the lender can avail of s 3(3)(a) of the 1976 Act.

---

[121] (contd) A mortgage or charge might also be restricted to an undivided share of a family home if, for example, the husband forged his wife's signature on the relevant documents creating the security (although there is some uncertainty as to whether the security only extends to the forger's share of the property in these circumstances or whether the transaction is void: see ch 8 above, para **[8.16]**). Again, the lender would have to bring proceedings for sale of the property under the Partition Acts 1868 and 1876 in the event of default. As to the factors that the court might take into account in deciding whether to order sale of a family home in these circumstances, see paras **[10.54]**-**[10.56]** below.

[122] Unless the court elects to dispense with the need for such consent under the Family Home Protection Act 1976, s 4: see generally para **[10.07]** above. As to the standard form of consent used see Wylie, *Irish Conveyancing Law* (2nd edn, 1996), pp 579-580.

[123] See for example, *Allied Irish Banks plc v O'Neill* [1995] 2 IR 473 and *Allied Irish Banks plc v Finnegan* [1996] 1 ILRM 401. Delivering the judgment of the Supreme Court in *Bank of Ireland v Smyth* [1995] 2 IR 459, Blayney J stated that the consenting spouse must have full knowledge of what he or she is doing, and must be given the opportunity to obtain independent legal advice. In *Bank of Ireland v Purcell* [1989] 2 IR 327 it was suggested that, where a spouse had given prior written consent to a specific loan, this did not authorise the use of a family home as security for subsequent advances. However, the position may now be different in light of the Family Home Protection Act 1976, s 3(9) which provides for a general consent to future conveyances of any interest in the family home: see para **[10.05]** above. In any event, it appears that standard form consents used by banks and other lending institutions contemplate the use of a family home as security for both present and future advances: Coughlan, *Property Law* (2nd edn, 1998), p 443 and Shatter, *Family Law* (4th edn, 1997), p 743.

[124] The wife's consent either expressly or impliedly extends the mortgage or charge to her beneficial interest in the family home (see Shatter, *Family Law* (4th edn, 1997), p 744), and effectively operates to postpone her rights in favour of the lender. See however the decision in *Re White (A Bankrupt)* (4 December 1990, unreported) High Court (RI) discussed at para **[10.53]** below.

[10.50] Section 3(3)(a) of the 1976 Act provides that a conveyance shall not be void by reason of s 3(1) 'if it is made to a purchaser for full value'. The definition of 'purchaser' for the purposes of the 1976 Act includes a 'mortgagee, chargeant or other person who in good faith acquires an interest in the property'[127]. If, for example, the husband conceals the fact that he is married from the lender, the mortgage or charge will be valid if the lender has acted in good faith and given full value. The lender's security will take priority over the wife's beneficial interest and he can exercise his normal powers of possession and sale in the event of default. This requirement of 'good faith' under the 1976 Act implies that the lender must not have notice of the fact that the premises comprise a family home when the mortgage or charge is executed[128]. If the lender is fixed with such notice, the purported mortgage or charge will be void. Furthermore, even if the lender is aware of the wife's existence and has procured her prior written consent to the mortgage or charge in accordance with s 3(1) of the 1976 Act, the purported transaction will be void if the lender has notice of the fact that this was not a voluntary and informed consent[129].

[10.51] There is little prospect of a partition action being brought by a security holder in these circumstances, since a mortgage or charge will rarely be restricted to an undivided share of a family home. If the wife's consent is absent or invalid, the mortgage or charge will be void[130]. If the wife gives a valid

---

[125] In *Doherty v Doherty* [1991] 2 IR 458 the wife was estopped from asserting her beneficial interest against the lender, having given her consent to the loan in accordance with the Family Home Protection Act 1976, s 3(1) and having made a statutory declaration that the family home was in the sole name of the husband. See further *Harrison v Harrison* (20 June 1989, unreported) High Court (RI), and *Hibernian Life Assocation Ltd v Gibbs* (23 July 1993, unreported) High Court (RI). For an analysis of the relevant case law and the application of estoppel in this context see Mee, 'The Family Home Protection Act and Priorities in Land Law' (1992) 12 ILT 213.

[126] For example, if the wife's consent has been procured by duress or undue influence (see *Bank of Nova Scotia v Hogan* [1997] 1 ILRM 407), or if the wife has been misled into believing that the proposed security will not affect the family home (see *Bank of Ireland v Smyth* [1995] 2 IR 459).

[127] Family Home Protection Act 1976, s 3(6).

[128] The reference to 'good faith' incorporates the doctrine of notice under the Conveyancing Act 1882, s 3 (see para **[10.06]** above and see generally ch 8 above, paras **[8.17]**-**[8.18]**). Thus the lender must not have actual notice, constructive notice or imputed notice of the fact that the premises comprise a family home and that the wife's prior written consent is accordingly required before a valid mortgage or charge can take place: see for example *Somers v Weir* [1979] IR 94.

[129] See *Bank of Ireland v Smyth* [1995] 2 IR 459.

[130] However, in these circumstances the mortgagee or chargee may still be able to recover his debt by registering a judgment mortgage against the husband's interest in the family home: see generally paras **[10.58]**-**[10.67]** below.

consent to the creation of a mortgage or charge on the family home or the lender can bring himself within s 3(3)(a) of the 1976 Act, his security will usually extend to the entire beneficial interest in the property and the lender may exercise the normal powers of possession and sale in the event of default. The 1976 Act does not prevent a mortgagee or chargee from realising his security without the consent of the wife – it merely prevents creation of the security without her consent. However, ss 7 and 8 of the 1976 Act apply special rules to proceedings for possession and sale of a family home by a mortgagee or chargee which may prevent the lender from realising his security if the wife is financially capable of and willing to discharge the loan payments herself[131].

[10.52] Section 7 provides that, if the wife is capable of paying off the arrears within a reasonable time and meeting all future periodical payments due under the mortgage or charge, the court may adjourn the proceedings 'for such period and on such terms as appear ... to be just and equitable', taking into account the interests of the lender and the respective spouses[132]. If the wife succeeds in making these payments and the court is satisfied that they will continue to be met, the court may make a declaration to this effect under s 8[133]. Upon making such a declaration, any term in the mortgage or charge whereby the default in payment by the husband that gave rise to the proceedings under s 7 has resulted or would have resulted in the entire capital sum advanced thereunder becoming due, shall be of no effect for the purpose of such proceedings[134].

[10.53] Proceedings under the Partition Acts may, however, be relevant in one particular situation. Where title to the family home is in the husband's name and he attempts to mortgage or charge the property, the wife may be able to assert her prior beneficial interest in the family home against the lender notwithstanding that she has consented to creation of the security. In *Re White (A Bankrupt)*[135] a wife was entitled to a 50% beneficial interest in a family home and land attached to it. The wife had consented to a charge on the property executed by her husband, but subsequently argued that she had done so merely to satisfy the requirements of s 3(1) of the 1976 Act and that this could not be

[131] Moreover, if the wife is aware that her husband has defaulted on the mortgage or charge prior to the lender commencing proceedings for possession and sale, the wife may tender such payments and the lender will be obliged to treat them as if they had been made by the husband: Family Home Protection Act 1976, s 6(1). However, the wife may still rely on these payments when claiming an interest in the family home: Family Home Protection Act 1976, s 6(2).

[132] Family Home Protection Act 1976, s 7(1). The court is also obliged to have particular regard to whether the wife has been informed 'by or on behalf of the [lender] ... or otherwise' of the non-payment of the sums in question: Family Home Protection Act 1976, s 7(2).

[133] Family Home Protection Act 1976, s 8(1).

[134] Family Home Protection Act 1976, s 8(2).

[135] (4 December 1990, unreported) High Court (RI).

interpreted as consent to the charge extending to her beneficial interest in the property. Accepting this argument, Hamilton P held that the wife had not consented to the creation of the charge 'as beneficial owner', but as the 'spouse of the [borrower]'. Accordingly, the charge was restricted to the husband's undivided share of the property[136].

[10.54] Where a mortgage or charge is restricted to an undivided share of a family home, the lender will have to bring proceedings for sale of the entire property under the Partition Acts in order to enforce his security[137]. However, since creation of a charge does not involve a transfer of interest from the borrower to the chargee, the latter would not have *locus standi* to bring an action under the Partition Acts and may be unable to realise his security[138]. In contrast, because creation of a mortgage involves a transfer of interest from borrower to lender, the mortgagee would have the necessary standing to maintain a partition action and may enforce his security by seeking an order for sale of the family home under the Partition Acts[139].

[10.55] At a cursory glance, the likelihood of the court ordering sale of a family home under the Partition Acts upon such a request by a mortgagee might be regarded as considerable. Physical partition of a family home will usually be impossible or impracticable, thus giving rise to a strong presumption in favour of sale. The consent requirements of the 1976 Act are irrelevant in this context: since the mortgagee would convey the husband's interest to a purchaser, the wife could not exercise her statutory right of veto under s 3(1) of the 1976 Act[140]. Furthermore, because the normal methods of enforcement are not available to a mortgagee of an undivided share of land, the court may be aware that an order for sale of the family home under the Partition Acts is the only effective method of allowing the lender to recover the debt owed to him[141].

---

136 Hamilton P stated that if the bank had intended the wife's beneficial interest to be subject to the charge, then it should have made that intention clear and 'used unequivocal language such as persons with ordinary intelligence may without any difficulty understand': (4 December 1990, unreported) High Court (RI), at 9.

137 The lender cannot exercise his usual powers of possession and sale in these circumstances

138 See ch 8 above, paras **[8.60]**-**[8.61]**.

139 See ch 8 above, paras **[8.39]**-**[8.42]** and assuming that an equitable mortgagee satisfies the *locus standi* test.

140 Family Home Protection Act 1976, s 3(1) only applies to a conveyance by 'a spouse'. See further the Family Home Protection Act 1976, s 3(3)(b). In addition to this, the mortgagee's partition action would not come within the definition of 'family law proceedings': see para **[10.37]** above.

141 Although the mortgagee could still sell the husband's interest in the property (see ch 8 above, para **[8.37]**), this would probably not raise as much money as sale of the entire property.

[10.56] However, there are several possible obstacles to an order for sale of a family home being granted under the Partition Acts in these circumstances. For example, the court might adjourn the proceedings if it is satisfied that the wife is capable of discharging the mortgage payments in accordance with s 7 of the 1976 Act[142]. The fact that the subject matter of the partition action comprises a family home might also influence the court's decision on whether to make an order for sale. In *First National Building Society v Ring*[143], the fact that the property comprised a family home and sale would be detrimental to the wife were relevant factors for the court to consider when determining an application for sale under the Partition Acts by a judgment creditor. The court might adopt a similar approach in respect of a partition action by a mortgagee. More importantly however, the husband may be able to veto a sale of the family home in these circumstances[144]. If the court orders sale of the property under the Partition Acts, the mortgagee will convey the husband's interest in the family home to a prospective purchaser. As regards the wife's interest in the family home, the order for sale would instruct her to join in the conveyance to the purchaser[145]. While the wife cannot veto a conveyance of her husband's interest by the mortgagee, the husband could veto a conveyance of his wife's interest. On a strict interpretation of the 1976 Act, any such conveyance requires his prior written consent under s 3(1). The court would then have to consider whether it was appropriate to dispense with the husband's consent under s 4 of the 1976 Act before making an order for sale of the family home under the Partition Acts.

[10.57] Applications by a mortgagee or chargee for sale of a family home under the Partition Acts in the Republic of Ireland are difficult to find. In the majority of cases, a mortgage or charge will either extend to the entire beneficial interest in the property, in which case the lender may exercise his normal powers of possession and sale, or it will be void due to non-compliance with the 1976 Act. Accordingly, the Partition Acts have little practical application here.

---

142 The court might also make an appropriate order under the Family Home Protection Act 1976, s 8 if the wife succeeds in keeping up the mortgage payments: see paras **[10.65]-[10.71]** above.

143 [1992] IR 375 discussed at paras **[10.63]-[10.67]** below.

144 Mee, 'Partition and Sale of the Family Home' (1993) 15 DULJ 78 at 90-93 considered at paras **[10.65]-[10.67]** below and suggested in relation to the decision in *First National Building Society v Ring* [1992] IR 375.

145 See generally ch 12 below. If spouses are co-owners of the family home at law, the wife is a necessary party to a conveyance of the property to a purchaser. However, even if spouses are co-owners in equity only, the wife will have to join in the conveyance to ensure that the purchaser takes the property free from her beneficial interest.

B Judgment mortgages affecting a family home

[10.58] If spouses are co-owners of a family home at law or in equity and the husband incurs a debt, the person to whom it is owed may obtain a judgment for this amount and register a judgment mortgage on the husband's interest in the property pursuant to the Judgment Mortgage (Ir) Act 1850[146]. Likewise, where the husband purports to create a mortgage or charge on the family home which is subsequently held to be void due to non-compliance with the 1976 Act, the lender may sue for the amount borrowed and register a judgment mortgage against the husband's share of the family home[147]. In contrast to the practice in respect of mortgagees and chargees, the 1976 Act has few practical implications for judgment creditors. Registration of a judgment mortgage against the husband's interest in the family home is not dependent on the prior written consent of the wife under s 3(1) of the 1976 Act. Since a judgment mortgage is a conveyance by operation of law as opposed to an action by the debtor spouse, there is no conveyance by 'a spouse' for the purposes of s 3(1)[148].

[10.59] In *Containercare (Ir) Ltd v Wycherley*[149] the plaintiff obtained judgment against the husband for £6,000 and registered a judgment mortgage on the husband's share of the family home, which he and his wife held in joint names. In proceedings by the plaintiff for sale of the property, the wife argued that the judgment mortgage was void since it had been registered without her prior written consent as required by s 3(1) of the 1976 Act. Rejecting this argument, Carroll J stated that:

> 'A judgment mortgage is a process of execution under [the 1850 Act] ... A judgment mortgage, if registered against a family home, is not a disposition by a

---

146 As to the enforcement of judgment mortgages affecting an undivided share of land in general, see ch 8 above, paras **[8.86]-[8.103]**. Where spouses are co-owners in equity, the judgment creditor takes his security subject to the wife's prior equitable interest irrespective of the doctrine of notice, since a judgment creditor is a volunteer: *Tempany v Hynes* (1976) IR 101. However, where legal title to a family home is in the husband's name, his wife may prevent registration of a judgment mortgage on the property if the entire beneficial interest in the family home is vested in her: Shatter, *Family Law* (4th edn, 1997), p 750 citing *Wall v Wall and the Official Assignee* (September 1986, unreported) High Court (RI).

147 See *CP v DP* [1983] ILRM 380 and *Bank of Ireland v Purcell* [1989] 2 IR 327.

148 This has been criticised as a 'significant gap' in the protection conferred by the Family Home Protection Act 1976: Coughlan, *Property Law* (2nd edn, 1998), p 440. See further Shatter, *Family Law* (4th edn, 1997), pp 830-832. However, the wife could apply to court before registration of the judgment mortgage against her husband's interest in the family home, asserting that the husband is engaging in conduct which may deprive the wife of her home and asking the court to transfer the husband's interest in the property to her under the Family Home Protection Act 1976, s 5: Shatter, *Family Law* (4th edn, 1997), p 830.

149 [1982] IR 143.

spouse purporting to convey an interest in the family home. It is a unilateral act by a judgment creditor ...'[150]

[10.60] Furthermore, the wife could not rely on s 7 of the 1976 Act in order to persuade the court to adjourn the proceedings if it was satisfied that she might be able to discharge the amount owed to the judgment creditor. Carroll J held that, because s 7 contemplates periodic repayments of principal and interest, this section would not apply to proceedings for possession and sale brought by a judgment creditor[151]. Accordingly, no relief was available to the wife under the 1976 Act.

[10.61] If spouses are co-owners of a family home at law or in equity and a judgment mortgage is registered against the husband's share of the property, the judgment creditor will have to bring an action for sale of the entire property under the Partition Acts to enforce his security[152]. However, the availability of this remedy depends on whether the judgment mortgage affects an undivided share of registered or unregistered land[153]. Since registration of a judgment mortgage on registered land merely operates to charge the interest of the debtor under the Registration of Title Act 1964, the creditor would not have *locus standi* to bring an action for sale of the family home under the Partition Acts and may be unable to realise his security. In contrast, since registration of a judgment mortgage on unregistered land involves a transfer of estate from the debtor to the creditor under the 1850 Act, the creditor would have the necessary standing to maintain a partition action and may enforce his security by seeking an order for sale of a family home under the Partition Acts[154].

[10.62] The next issue that arises in this context is whether the court should grant an order for sale of a family home under the Partition Acts at the request of a judgment creditor. At a cursory glance, the likelihood of the court making an

---

150 [1982] IR 143 at 149-150. See further *Murray v Diamond* [1982] 2 ILRM 113 at 115 in which Barrington J remarked that a judgment mortgage 'comes into existence by operation of the statute, and not by virtue of any positive act by the judgment debtor'.

151 [1982] IR 143 at 150. Furthermore, the wife could not rely on the Family Home Protection Act 1976, s 8 since s 8 only applies where the court has already made an order under s 7: [1982] IR 143 at 151. Family Home Protection Act 1976, ss 7 and 8 were considered at para **[10.52]** above.

152 A judgment creditor cannot exercise his normal remedies of possession and sale in these circumstances because his security is restricted to an undivided share of land: see ch 8 above, paras **[8.97]-[8.98]**.

153 See ch 8 above, paras **[8.97]-[8.98]**.

154 This 'arbitrary inconsistency' in the law has been criticised: see Mee, 'Judgment Mortgages, Co-Ownership and Registered Land' (1999) 4 Conveyancing and Property Lawyer 28 at 31 where it is suggested that reform of the law is necessary to bring the practice in respect of registered land into line with that relating to unregistered land.

order for sale in these circumstances might be regarded as considerable. Since the creditor would convey the husband's interest to a prospective purchaser, the wife cannot exercise her statutory right of veto under s 3(1) of the 1976 Act[155]. Thus, the consent requirements of the 1976 Act are irrelevant in this context. In addition to this, the court cannot adjourn sale under ss 7 and 8 of the 1976 Act because they do not apply in respect of judgment mortgages. However, the fact that the subject matter of the partition action comprises a family home might influence the court's decision on whether to order sale.

[10.63] In *First National Building Society v Ring*[156] the creditor obtained judgment for £160,000 against the husband and registered this against a family home which the spouses owned as joint tenants[157]. Denham J held that, although the wife did not have a right to veto sale under the 1976 Act, the fact that the property comprised a family home was a relevant factor for the court to take into account when exercising its discretion to refuse sale under s 4 of the 1868 Act[158]. The learned judge referred to *O'D v O'D*[159] in which Murphy J had reviewed a number of cases including *Re Whitwell's Estate*[160] and had interpreted Monroe J in that case as suggesting that the court should not make an order for sale under s 4 of the 1868 Act 'if it were likely to prove abortive or if it would involve the parties in accepting a significant sacrifice'[161]. Denham J observed that, in the present case, no inquiries had been made as to the persons interested in the property, the feasibility of sale, and whether the wife might be able to purchase her husband's share of the family home. Moreover, sale of the property would cause enormous disruption to family life, and the wife would be unable to purchase another home with her share of the proceeds of sale[162]. Denham J concluded:

> 'The second defendant who is a co-owner and who is an innocent party and has no judgment registered against her would undoubtedly suffer a significant

[155] Family Home Protection Act 1976, s 3(1) only applies in respect of conveyances by a spouse. See further the Family Home Protection Act 1976, s 3(3)(b).

[156] [1992] IR 375 discussed in ch 8 above, para **[8.99]**.

[157] It appears that Denham J in this case overlooked the fact that the creditor did not have *locus standi* to bring a partition action in view of the fact that the property in question comprised registered land.

[158] [1992] IR 375 at 379-380.

[159] (18 November 1983, unreported) High Court (RI).

[160] (1887) 19 LR Ir 45.

[161] (18 November 1983, unreported) High Court (RI), at 9-10. However, in *Re Whitwell's Estate* (1887) 19 LR Ir 45 the court dealt only with financial considerations. Monroe J referred to an earlier case in which he had refused to order sale on the basis that the land was suffering from a temporary depreciation in value.

[162] [1992] IR 375 at 379-380.

> sacrifice if her property, part of the family home, were now sold. In these circumstances it does not appear appropriate now to order partition or sale in lieu of partition.'[163]

In other words, Denham J refused to order sale of the family home because of the hardship that the wife as an innocent party would suffer upon making such an order.

[10.64] The decision in *First National Building Society v Ring* suggests that a judgment creditor is not automatically entitled to an order for sale of a family home upon registering his security against the debtor's interest in the property[164]. This has been criticised as contrary to the established practice under the Partition Acts[165]. In these circumstances, there should usually be a strong presumption in favour of ordering sale of the family home. The consent requirements of the 1976 Act do not apply here, and physical partition of the property is likely to be impracticable[166]. Since the normal methods of enforcement are not available to a judgment creditor of an undivided share of land, the court may also be aware that an order for sale of the family home under the Partition Acts is the only effective method of allowing the creditor to recover the debt owed to him[167].

[10.65] However, there may be a more fundamental obstacle to a judgment creditor enforcing his security in this manner. Mee has suggested that the consent requirements of the 1976 Act might enable the husband to veto a sale of the family home under the Partition Acts[168]. While the judgment creditor will convey the husband's share of the family home to a purchaser if the court makes an order for sale of the property under the Partition Acts, the order will instruct

---

163 [1992] IR 375 at 381. The learned judge directed inquiries to be made as to the persons interested in the property, their shares and proportions, the current market value of the property, the feasibility of its sale, and an inquiry as to whether the wife might be able to purchase her husband's share at an agreed price.

164 Contrast this with *Containercare (Ir) Ltd v Wycherley* [1982] IR 143 in which Carroll J appeared to take the view that an order for sale should be made upon registration of a judgment mortgage against the family home, albeit that the application concerned the exercise of the creditor's normal power of sale as opposed to an application under the Partition Acts 1868 and 1876.

165 Mee 'Partition and Sale of Family Home' (1993) 15 DULJ 78 at 88-89 and 'Judgment Mortgages, Co-Ownership and Registered Land' (1999) 4 Conveyancing and Property Lawyer 28 at 31. It will be recalled that, in the absence of special circumstances (such as the consent requirements of the Family Home Protection Act 1976) the court's discretion under the Partition Acts 1968 and 1876 is usually restricted to making an order for either partition or sale.

166 In addition to this, the creditor's partition action would not come within the definition of 'family law proceedings': see para **[10.37]** above.

167 Although the judgment creditor could still sell the debtor's interest in the property (see ch 8 above, para **[8.101]**), this would probably not raise as much money as sale of the entire property.

168 Mee 'Partition and Sale of Family Home' (1993) 15 DULJ 78 at 90-93.

the wife to join in conveying her interest in the family home to the purchaser[169]. This falls within s 3(1) of the 1976 Act, so that the wife's conveyance is subject to the prior written consent of the husband. Since the husband is unlikely to consent to the wife's conveyance in these circumstances, he could veto a sale of the family home and prevent the creditor from enforcing the judgment mortgage unless the court dispensed with the husband's consent under s 4 of the 1976 Act.

[10.66] To date, courts in the Republic of Ireland have not had to deal with this suggestion. On the one hand, it provides some measure of protection for the wife as the non-debtor spouse. On the other hand, it seems wrong in principle that a spouse who has incurred a debt that leads to registration of a judgment mortgage on his interest in the family home should be able to avoid the consequences of his actions by exercising a statutory right of veto which has been largely designed to confer protection on an 'innocent' spouse. However, Mee has observed that:

> '[T]he right of veto is a valuable, independent right. It arises in the husband, not because of his own property rights over the home, but because of his wife's ownership of a share in the home.'[170]

[10.67] Furthermore, the fact that the husband might be able to veto a sale of the family home in these circumstances accords with the ethos of the 1976 Act, namely the protection of the family home[171]. However, the husband's actions may still be relevant in one particular context. Whether or not the judgment creditor succeeds in obtaining an order for sale of the family home under the Partition Acts will depend on whether the court considers it appropriate to dispense with the husband's consent under s 4 of the 1976 Act. Section 4 requires the court to have regard to 'all the circumstances' of the case. The fact that the husband has incurred a debt and is trying to prevent this from being enforced even though the creditor has obtained judgment against him and converted this into a judgment mortgage may persuade the court that this is an appropriate case in which to dispense with the husband's consent to a conveyance of his wife's interest in the family home[172].

---

169 See generally ch 12 below. The wife will have to join in the conveyance irrespective of whether she is a co-owner of the family home at law or in equity: see para **[10.56]** above.

170 Mee 'Partition and Sale of Family Home' (1993) 15 DULJ 78 at 91.

171 Mee 'Partition and Sale of Family Home' (1993) 15 DULJ 78 at 93.

172 Mee has suggested that the law should be reformed to protect the family home from judgment mortgages, either by allowing the non-debtor spouse to veto the imposition of a judgment mortgage or by requiring her prior written consent to its enforcement: Mee, 'Judgment Mortgages, Co-Ownership and Registered Land' (1999) 4 Conveyancing and Property Lawyer 28 at 31-32. See further the various suggestions put forward in Shatter, *Family Law* (4th edn, 1997), pp 830-832.

V The Practice on Bankruptcy

A General principles

[10.68] The Bankruptcy Act 1988 is the principal legislation governing personal insolvency in the Republic of Ireland. Where a person is adjudicated bankrupt all property belonging to him at the date of the adjudication vests in the Official Assignee for the benefit of the bankrupt's creditors[173]. The functions of the Official Assignee are to 'get in and realise the property, to ascertain the debts and liabilities, and to distribute the assets' accordingly[174]. In carrying out these functions the Official Assignee has, *inter alia*, power to sell the property by auction or private contract either in whole or in lots[175], as well as power to institute, continue or defend any proceedings relating to the property[176].

[10.69] If a joint tenant or tenant in common is declared bankrupt, his undivided share of the land vests in the Official Assignee[177]. The Official Assignee may bring an action for sale under the Partition Acts and the 1988 Act[178]. As with the corresponding practice in Northern Ireland[179], there is likely to be a strong presumption in favour of the court making an order for sale in these circumstances notwithstanding the objections of the non-bankrupt co-owner, since the Official Assignee is under a statutory duty to realise the bankrupt's property for the benefit of his creditors[180].

B Bankrupt's property comprising a family home

[10.70] Special rules apply to cases in which the bankrupt's assets include a dwelling house that he and his wife occupy as a family home. Where spouses are co-owners of a family home at law or in equity, the Official Assignee may bring proceedings for sale under the 1988 Act and the Partition Acts if he cannot reach an agreement on sale of the property with the spouses. If the court makes an

---

173 Bankruptcy Act 1988, s 44(1). Bankruptcy Act 1988, s 45 lists a number of excepted articles such as personal items and household furniture.

174 Bankruptcy Act 1988, s 61(2).

175 Bankruptcy Act 1988, s 61(3)(a).

176 Bankruptcy Act 1988, s 61(3)(d).

177 Where co-owners are joint tenants, the vesting of the bankrupt's interest in the Official Assignee causes a severance of the joint tenancy by involuntary alienation: see ch 9 above, para **[9.73]**.

178 See *Rubotham (Official Assignee) v Young* (23 May 1995, unreported) High Court (RI) and *Rubotham (Official Assignee) v Duddy* (1 May 1996, unreported) High Court (RI) both of which are discussed below.

179 See ch 9 above, para **[9.73]**.

180 See the comments of Goff J in *Re Densham (A Bankrupt)* [1975] 1 WLR 1519 and see *Re Solomon* [1967] Ch 573. However, a request for sale may be refused if the circumstances of a particular case have given rise to an estoppel between the original co-owners which subsequently binds the Official Assignee: *Re Yale and MacMaster* (1974) 46 DLR (3d) 167 and see ch 4 above, para **[4.60]**.

order for sale of the family home in these circumstances the Official Assignee will convey the husband's interest in the property to a prospective purchaser[181]. The Official Assignee does not have to secure the wife's prior written consent to the conveyance under the Family Home Protection Act 1976 since s 3(3)(b) of that Act provides that such consent is not required in respect of a conveyance by a third party to a purchaser for value[182]. However, the 1988 Act restricts the Official Assignee's power to dispose of a family home.

[10.71] Section 61(4) of the 1988 Act provides that no disposition of a family home within the meaning of the 1976 Act shall be made by the Official Assignee 'without the prior sanction of the Court, and any disposition made without such sanction shall be void'[183]. This provision does not prevent the Official Assignee from realising the bankrupt's interest in the family home. Rather s 61(4) prevents the Official Assignee from disposing of the bankrupt's interest in the property without the court's permission. In addition to this, s 61(5) of the Act provides that:

> 'On an application by the Official Assignee under this section for an order for sale of a family home, the Court, notwithstanding anything contained in this or any other enactment, shall have power to order postponement of the sale of the family home having regard to the interests of the creditors of the spouse and dependents of the bankrupt as well as to the circumstances of the case.'[184]

[10.72] Thus the court may exercise a power to postpone sale, but only upon having regard to the interests of a number of specified parties and all the circumstances of the particular case.

[10.73] Notwithstanding the ostensibly wide discretion to postpone sale under s 61(5), it appears that the court will order sale of a family home in the absence of 'exceptional circumstances' by analogy to the corresponding practice under English case law[185]. In *Rubotham (Official Assignee) v Young*[186] the plaintiff

[181] The order for sale would also instruct the wife to join in any conveyance in respect of her legal or equitable interest in the property.

[182] See generally para **[10.06]** above.

[183] As to the definition of a 'family home' for the purposes of the Family Home Protection Act 1976, see para **[10.04]** above.

[184] Bankruptcy Act 1988, s 61(7) further provides that the exercise by the Official Assignee of the powers conferred on him by s 61 are subject to the control of the court, 'and any creditor or other person who in the opinion of the Court has an interest may apply to the Court in relation to the exercise or proposed exercise of those powers'.

[185] In England (and in Northern Ireland) there is usually a strong presumption in favour of ordering sale of a matrimonial home upon such an application by the trustee in bankruptcy, with the possibility of a short postponement on the grounds of 'exceptional circumstances' such as serious illness. Any suffering or inconvenience which may be caused to the non-bankrupt spouse and other family members as a result of having to leave their home is irrelevant in this context: see generally ch 9 above, paras **[9.76]-[9.80]**.

[186] (23 May 1995, unreported) High Court (RI).

sought an order for sale of a family home which the bankrupt and his wife owned as joint tenants. The property was valued at between £135,000 and £190,000, and approximately £140,000 was owed to the bankrupt's creditors. The wife argued that sale would be traumatic and that it would be impossible for her and the four children still residing in the family home to manage in a smaller property. Accordingly, the court should either refuse to make an order for sale under the Partition Acts or exercise its right to postpone sale under s 61(5) of the 1988 Act. Referring to English case law considering applications for sale of a matrimonial home by a trustee in bankruptcy, McCracken J stated that, although decided under different legislation, they emphasised that 'if discretion is to be exercised in favour of the family of a Bankrupt, this must only be done under exceptional circumstances'[187]. After considering the specific factors prescribed by s 61(5) of the 1988 Act, the learned judge concluded that this was not an appropriate case in which to postpone sale. The husband had been adjudicated bankrupt almost seven years ago, during which time the creditors had been paid nothing and the bankrupt's wife and children (who were now of full age) had lived in the family home at the creditors' expense[188].

[10.74] However, 'exceptional circumstances' were found to exist in *Rubotham (Official Assignee) v Duddy*[189]. The husband's beneficial interest in the family home became vested in the Official Assignee who subsequently sought an order for sale of the property under the Partition Acts and an order sanctioning sale under s 61 of the 1988 Act[190]. Having determined that it was appropriate to make an order for sale, Shanley J went on to consider the interests of the various parties in accordance with s 61(5) of the 1988 Act. Applying the 'exceptional circumstances' test, the learned judge held that the court would be justified in postponing sale for ten years under the 1988 Act. Both the amount of indebtedness and value of the family home (£20,000 and £65,000 respectively) differed significantly from the relevant amounts in *Rubotham (Official Assignee) v Young*[191]. Other circumstances highlighted by Shanley J were the fact that the wife was in poor health[192] and in dire financial circumstances, and

187 (23 May 1995, unreported) High Court (RI), Lexis transcript at 3.

188 The court postponed sale for four months in order to give the defendant an opportunity to acquire a new house with her share of the proceeds of sale.

189 (1 May 1996, unreported) High Court (RI).

190 There appears to have been some confusion in this case as to the applicable section of the Partition Act 1868. Since the husband was entitled to a 40% beneficial interest in the family home, the Official Assignee's action for sale should have been determined under s 3 of 1868 Act. However, Shanley J initially referred to the provisions of s 4, and later to making an order for sale under ss 3 and 4.

191 (23 May 1995, unreported) High Court (RI).

192 The wife suffered from hypertension, arthritis and agoraphobia, and had been under psychiatric care at various times in the past.

had occupied the property for 38 years[193]. While the bankrupt and his wife had no dependent children, a daughter who was residing in the family home was not able to contribute towards the household finances, and two other adult children who did not reside in the property nevertheless had relatively serious medical conditions. As regards the interests of the creditors, while they would not recover their money in the immediate future, the creditors did have the prospect of the property appreciating in value[194].

VI Human Rights Implications

[10.75] Under the terms of the *Good Friday Agreement*, the Irish Government is committed to consideration of incorporating the provisions of the European Convention on Human Rights into domestic law[195]. If this occurs, the same issues as were identified in relation to partition actions involving the matrimonial home in Northern Ireland may arise in the Republic of Ireland[196]. In addition to this, the commitment by the Irish Government to 'ensure at least an equivalent level of protection of human rights as will pertain in Northern Ireland'[197] may give rise to further litigation in this area.

---

193 The learned judge referred to *Re Mott* [1987] CLY 212 in which the court refused a trustee in bankruptcy's request for sale of a matrimonial home under the Law of Property Act 1925, s 30 on the basis that the property had been occupied by the bankrupt's mother and both her late husbands for over 40 years. See however the comments of Harman J in relation to this case in *Judd v Brown* [1998] 2 FLR 360.

194 With respect, the decision in this case is difficult to justify. The bankrupt's children were no longer dependent, and with the exception of one daughter, no longer resided in the family home nor was there any suggestion that they might return to the property at some stage in the future. Even if the other circumstances in the case could be regarded as exceptional, the length of postponement and its justification are questionable. For example, contrast this case with *Re Ravel* [1998] 2 FLR 718 in which the court postponed sale for a short period because of the wife's health problems but refused to delay sale for five years on the basis that such a lengthy postponement would prejudice the creditors: see ch 9 above, para **[9.80]**.

195 *Belfast Agreement*, 'Rights, Safeguards and Equality of Opportunity', para 9.

196 See generally ch 9 above, paras **[9.81]-9.84]**.

197 *Belfast Agreement*, 'Rights, Safeguards and Equality of Opportunity', para 9.

Chapter 11

Accounting Adjustments Between Co-Owners

I Introduction

[11.01] Unity of possession is fundamental to co-ownership. Each co-owner is entitled to use and occupy the entire property, subject to a similar right on the part of the other co-owners[1]. So long as they all share in the occupation and use of the land, and apportion the associated profits and expenses rateably, few difficulties arise. However, this is not always possible in practice. For example, situations frequently arise in which one co-owner occupies the common property to the exclusion of the other co-owners or the latter simply choose not to occupy the land. The co-owner in occupation may be receiving more than his share of profits from the land, as well as incurring more than his share of expenses. Issues that may arise are whether the non-occupying co-owners are entitled to claim a share of the profits and whether the occupant can recover a share of the expenses.

[11.02] Co-ownership does not give rise to a fiduciary relationship between joint tenants or tenants in common which would render them accountable to each other in respect of such payments[2]. However, joint tenants and tenants in common can achieve this by bringing an action of account. If certain criteria are satisfied[3], the court may order that the parties make appropriate payments to each other whilst remaining co-owners of the land. This, of course, assumes that they can reach some sort of agreement as to the future use and occupation of the land. An action of account may be of limited practical value if the relationship between the parties has deteriorated to the extent that common enjoyment of the property is no longer possible. In these circumstances, the only viable solution may be for one or more co-owners to commence proceedings for partition or sale of the land.

---

1 2 *Bl Comm* 181 and see *Bull v Bull* [1955] 1 QB 234.

2 See *Kennedy v De Trafford* [1896] 1 Ch 762 and *Fleet v Fleet* (1925) 28 OWN 193. See further Mendes Da Costa, 'Co-Ownership Under Victorian Land Law' (1961) 3 Melb Univ L Rev 137 at 141 and the cases cited therein. However, the particular factual circumstances of the case and dealings between co-owners may give rise to a fiduciary relationship: see *Hitchins v Hitchins* (11 December 1998, unreported) Supreme Court of New South Wales.

3 These are discussed below.

[11.03] A partition action may include an application for an accounting adjustment to be made between the parties[4]. In other words, one or more co-owners is seeking partition or sale of the land and the court must decide whether to take account of the fact that the parties have not shared in the occupation of or the profits and expenses associated with the land. Any such adjustment may have significant financial implications. This chapter examines the rights and duties which exist between co-owners in this context, and identifies the principles which courts should apply in deciding whether to make an accounting adjustment as incidental to an order for partition or sale of concurrent interests in land[5].

II Historical Background

[11.04] Before considering the specific rules to be applied in this context, it is appropriate to consider the historical development of actions of account in general and in the context of partition actions. Many of the basic rules expounded by the Courts of Common Law and Courts of Equity are still relevant in such actions today.

A Actions of account

[11.05] One consequence of the unity of possession is that one co-owner cannot usually assert a better right to any part of the property than the other co-owners and, *a fortiori*, to any rents and profits derived from the property. The implications of this precept have been apparent from the earliest stages in the development of actions of account[6].

[11.06] At common law, one co-owner could occupy the property and appropriate any rents and profits without extinguishing the titles of his fellow co-owners through adverse possession[7] unless he had evidenced a clear intention to exclude them[8]. However, the occupying co-owner was not accountable to the

4 If the plaintiff does not wish to terminate co-ownership, he may bring an action of account only. However, the plaintiff must choose one form of action of account or the other – he 'cannot have his remedy twice': *Chatterton v Chatterton* (1989) 52 SASR 337 at 343.

5 This chapter considers accounting adjustments in partition actions in general. It is not for the most part concerned with specific rules that apply when there is a particular relationship between the parties, the most obvious being accounting adjustments between spouses and those between lender and borrower.

6 As to the historical development of actions of account see Story, *Commentaries on Equity Jurisprudence* (10th edn, 1870) Vol II, ch 8; Belsheim, 'The Old Action of Account' (1932) 45 HLR 466; and Stoljar, 'The Transformations of Account' (1964) 80 LQR 203. See further Meagher, Gummow and Lehane, *Equity Doctrines and Remedies* (3rd edn, 1993) ch 25.

7 Since possession by one joint tenant or tenant in common was regarded as possession by them all.

8 See *Fisher v Wigg* (1699) 1 Salk 391 and *Fisher v Prosser* (1774) Cowp 218.

others for his sole occupation or for receiving rents and profits, the rationale for this rule being that:

> '[A] co-owner has a right to possession and enjoyment of the entire common property, and simply by its exercise will not be burdened by a claim for compensation at the suit of a co-owner who has failed to exercise his like right.'[9]

[11.07] However, this rule was subject to several exceptions. In the first place, since the reasoning of the court was predicated on the right of all the co-owners to use and occupy the land, the rule did not apply if the occupying co-owner had ousted the others[10]. The excluded co-owners could sue in ejectment or trespass and for mesne profits[11]. The second exception arose where the occupant undertook to act as bailiff for the other co-owners, and was accountable to them not only for revenue which he received in this capacity but for revenue which might have been generated but for his wilful default[12]. Thirdly, the occupant was liable for payments of outstanding rent where he occupied the entire property as tenant of the other co-owners[13]. Co-owners could also bring an action for waste where the occupant's activities tended towards destruction of the joint property[14].

[11.08] This harsh and inequitable practice was amended by the Administration of Justice Act (Ir) 1707, s 23 of which granted joint tenants and tenants in common an action of account against a co-owner who had received more than his share of rents or other revenues from the property[15]. However, this statutory action did not significantly improve the position of parties seeking an account. The courts interpreted the corresponding provision of the Administration of Justice Act 1705[16] as applying only where one co-owner had actually received in excess of his share of such payments from third parties; it did not extend to profits which he derived from his own use and occupation of the land[17].

---

9 Mendes Da Costa, 'Co-Ownership Under Victorian Land Law' (1961) 3 Melb Univ L Rev 137 at 139.

10 See *Rich v Hall* (1661) 1 Keb 18.

11 See *Goodtitle v Tombs* (1770) 3 Wils 118; *Murray v Hall* (1849) 7 CB 441 and *Jacobs v Seward* (1872) LR 5 HL 464.

12 *Co Litt* 200b. See further *Wheeler v Horne* (1740) Willes 208 and *Pulteney v Warren* (1801) 6 Ves 72.

13 See *Leigh v Dickeson* (1884) 15 QBD 60 and Meitus, 'The Rights, Duties and Liabilities of Tenants in Common Inter Se' (1940) 24 Marq L Rev 148 at 151.

14 See Bewes, *The Law of Waste* (1894), pp 263-267 and Mendes Da Costa, 'Co-Ownership Under Victorian Land Law' (1961) 3 Melb Univ L Rev 137 at 140-141.

15 The relevant terms of the Administration of Justice Act (Ir) 1707, s 23 were noted in ch 6 above, para **[6.24]**.

16 Administration of Justice Act 1705, s 27.

17 See *Henderson v Eason* (1851) 17 QB 701 and *Munsie v Lindsay* (1883) 10 PR (Ont) 173.

[11.09] As regards expenditure, one co-owner could not compel the others to contribute towards voluntary repairs and improvements[18] to the property, even if they benefited all the parties[19]. There appear to have been two reasons for this rule. Firstly, a co-owner carrying out repairs and improvements could not impose liability on the other co-owners for something to which they did not consent, yet could not decline any resulting benefit[20]. Secondly, if the former was in sole occupation of the land and thus enjoyed exclusive benefit of these repairs and improvements, it was only fair that he should bear the costs[21]. As regards necessary expenses that gave rise to a duty to make payments, such as rates or taxes, it appears that liability for these devolved equally on all the co-owners. Where one person paid a debt that was jointly incurred by himself and another person, the former had a right to a contribution against the other in respect of such payments[22].

---

17 (contd) Notwithstanding the reference in the Administration of Justice Act 1705, s 27 and the Administration of Justice Act (Ir) 1707, s 23 to the liability of a co-owner 'as bailiff', a joint tenant or tenant in common was only liable to account for rents and profits which he actually received from third parties and not for all that he might have received but for his wilful neglect or default: see *Osachuk v Osachuk* (1971) 18 DLR (3d) 413 at 425-426 and the cases cited therein. See further Heon, 'The Liability of a Cotenant to Other Cotenants for Rents, Profits and Use and Occupation' (1959) 42 Marq L Rev 363 at 364.

18 The position would have been otherwise where the parties were under a common obligation to carry out such repairs or where the co-owner making the repairs had contracted to do so on behalf of the others.

19 See 21 *Halsbury's Laws of England* (1st edn, 1912), p 851 and Weible, 'Accountability of Cotenants' (1944) 29 Iowa L Rev 558 at 577. It has been suggested that there was one exception to this rule at common law. In *Co Litt* 200b it was said that one co-owner could have a writ *de reparatione facienda*, compelling the others to contribute towards repairs to a mill because, as a matter of public policy, houses and mills should be maintained for the use and benefit of man. This writ has been interpreted as allowing one co-owner to compel the others to contribute towards repairs: see for example, Meitus, 'The Rights, Duties and Liabilities of Tenants in Common Inter Se' (1940) 24 Marq L Rev 148 at 152. However, in *Leigh v Dickeson* (1884) 15 QBD 60 at 66-67 Cotton LJ observed that the passage in *Co Litt* was based on writs in *Fitz Nat Brev* p 127 and p 162 which were examples of co-owners being bound to repair a mill as a result of an obligation towards a third party. Such expenditure gives rise to a right to a contribution in respect of necessary expenses: see below.

20 See *Leigh v Dickeson* (1884) 15 QBD 60 at 64-65 per Brett MR and Meitus, 'The Rights, Duties and Liabilities of Tenants in Common Inter Se' (1940) 24 Marq L Rev 148 at 152. This rule also prevented one co-owner from making improvements to the land solely for his benefit and charging them to the other co-owners: Weible, 'Accountability of Cotenants' (1944) 29 Iowa L Rev 558 at 577.

21 Mendes Da Costa, 'Co-Ownership Under Victorian Land Law' (1961) 3 Melb Univ L Rev 137 at 147.

22 See Cooke, 'Equitable Accounting' [1995] Conv 391 at 396 citing *Edgar v Knapp* (1843) 6 Scott NR 707.

[11.10] The common law action of account was procedurally cumbersome[23]. Accordingly, Courts of Equity also exercised an independent jurisdiction to take accounts, albeit that an account in equity would usually only be granted in situations where a similar action lay at common law[24]. Free from many of the procedural requirements that hindered the common law action, it appears that the equitable jurisdiction had superseded its common law counterpart by the mid-eighteenth century[25]. Thereafter, the taking of accounts was essentially a matter for the Court of Chancery[26]. One significant change to the relevant law was introduced by the Real Property Limitation Act 1833. This Act provided that possession of land or receipt of moneys by one co-owner would not be deemed possession or receipt by them all, thus giving rise to the possibility of adverse possession by an occupying co-owner in the absence of an ouster[27].

B Actions for compulsory partition or sale

[11.11] Prior to 1539 in England and 1542 in Ireland, joint tenants and tenants in common of land could not compel partition and therefore could not enjoy their shares in severalty in the event of disagreement as to the continued use and occupation of the property[28]. This situation was exacerbated where one co-owner excluded the others or appropriated all the rents and profits for himself. Since the other co-owners could not compel partition, their only form of redress was to bring an action of account. However, the particular case had to fall within one of the exceptions to the general rule that a co-owner was not accountable for sole

---

23 See Story, *Commentaries on Equity Jurisprudence* (10th edn, 1870), pp 436-440 and Meagher, Gummow and Lehane, *Equity Doctrines and Remedies* (3rd edn, 1993), p 659.

24 '[W]here an action of account will lie, a bill for an account may be sustained': *Denys v Shuckburgh* (1840) 4 Y & C Ex 42 at 52 per Alderson B. For example, one co-owner could bring an action in equity for a share of rents and profits received by his fellow co-owner: *Leake v Cordeaux* (1856) 4 WR 806. Likewise, a co-owner who incurred more than his share of necessary expenditure had an equitable right to a contribution from the other co-owners: *Rogers v MacKenzie* (1799) 4 Ves 752.

25 Meagher, Gummow and Lehane, *Equity Doctrines and Remedies* (3rd edn, 1993), p 659 citing *AG v Dublin Corpn* (1827) 1 Bli (NS) PC and *Sturton v Richardson* (1844) 13 M & W 17. See further 2 *Bl Comm* 183.

26 Both the Judicature Act 1873, s 34(3) and the Judicature (Ir) Act 1877, s 36(5) subsequently assigned all actions for the taking of partnership or other accounts to the Chancery Division.

27 Real Property Limitation Act 1833, s 12 and see *Glynn v Howell* [1909] 1 Ch 666 and *Foisy v Lord* (1911) 2 OWN 1217. In addition to this, one co-owner could no longer defeat a claim for adverse possession against him by a stranger on the basis that another co-owner was in possession of the property: see *Beaumont v Hochkins* (1889) 15 VLR 442 and Mendes Da Costa, 'Co-Ownership Under Victorian Land Law' (1961) 3 Melb Univ L Rev 137 at 149.

28 *Litt* ss 290 and 318, and see ch 3 above.

occupation of the property or receipt of profits[29]. If it did not fall within one of these exceptions, the other co-owners could not take any action unless the circumstances gave rise to an action for waste as conferred on joint tenants and tenants in common by the Statute of Westminister II 1285[30].

[11.12] Joint tenants and tenants in common were eventually granted a right to compel partition at common law by the sixteenth century Statutes of Partition[31]. Thereafter, co-owners who were excluded from the land or receiving a disproportionate share of the associated income could compel partition of the property. However, a fundamental weakness of the common law remedy was that the court could not direct an account between co-owners as incidental to making an order for partition. A co-owner who sought an accounting adjustment had to bring a separate action to this effect[32].

[11.13] The emergence of an equitable jurisdiction to partition vastly improved this situation. Unlike Courts of Common Law, the Court of Chancery could make appropriate accounting adjustments between co-owners as incidental to making an order for partition[33]. These typically took one of two forms. An accounting adjustment could affect the sum of money which one co-owner had to pay the others for equality of partition[34]. Alternatively, if one co-owner had made improvements to a particular part of the property, the court could order that the relevant parcel of land be allocated to him on partition[35]. Following the enactment of the Partition Acts, the Court of Chancery continued to make accounting adjustments as incidental to an order for sale of concurrent interests

---

29 See paras **[11.06]-[11.07]** above.

30 See *Co Litt* 200a and 200b. No such action was conferred on coparceners, since they could stop another coparcener committing waste by compelling partition: 2 *Bl Comm* 187-188.

31 The preamble to An Act Concerning Joint Tenants and Tenants in Common 1539 and An Act for Jointenants 1542 expressly recognised that joint tenants and tenants in common had been left without any assured remedy where one co-owner occupied the entire property or appropriated all the rents, profits and natural produce: see ch 3 above, para **[3.11]**.

32 See Story, *Commentaries on Equity Jurisprudence* (10th edn, 1870), pp 648-649.

33 See generally ch 3 above, para **[3.27]**. For example, in *Lorimer v Lorimer* (1820) 5 Madd 363 Leach VC stated that, if it appeared that the defendant had received more than his share of rents and profits, the Court of Chancery would direct an account and would not, unlike proceedings at common law, confine its relief to a partition. See further *Hyde v Hindley* (1794) 2 Cox 408; *Hill v Fulbrook* (1822) Jac 574; and *Gage v Mulholland* (1869) 16 Gr 145.

34 See the comments of Alderson B in *Lister v Lister* (1839) 3 Y & C Ex 540 at 545 and see *Watson v Gass* (1881) 30 WR 286.

35 See *Wood v Wood* (1869) 16 Gr 471; *Rice v George* (1873) 20 Gr 221; and *McNeill v McDougall* (1896) 28 NSR 296. See further Story, *Commentaries on Equity Jurisprudence* (10th edn, 1870), p 649.

in land[36], adjusting the parties' respective shares in the proceeds of sale accordingly[37].

III Appropriate Accounting Adjustments in Partition Actions

[11.14] The consequences of an accounting adjustment being made in a partition action today are essentially the same as those outlined immediately above. Thus, an adjustment on partition may affect the amount to be paid for equality of partition or the parcels of land allocated to the parties[38], while an adjustment on sale may affect the share of the proceeds of sale to which each party is entitled[39]. The value of the property will usually be determined at the date of the partition action and not, for example, the date on which one co-owner leaves the property or is excluded from it[40]. Where a period of time has elapsed between these dates, the parties will share any increase in value that was not occasioned by the efforts or expense of the occupant, such as natural appreciation[41] or an increase in value resulting from a change in planning policy for the area[42].

[11.15] The accounting adjustments that may be made as incidental to an order for partition or sale of co-owned land typically fall into the following five categories.

A Occupation rent

[11.16] A co-owner who enjoys exclusive occupation of the common property is usually under no obligation to account to the other co-owners for his use and occupation[43]. Exceptions to this rule arise where the other co-owners have been

---

36 Partition Act 1868, ss 3-5 provide that, when making an order for sale, the court may 'give all necessary or proper consequential directions'.

37 For example, in *Burnell v Burnell* (1879) 11 Ch D 213, Jessel MR directed an account of rents and profits received by the plaintiff as incidental to an order for sale under the Partition Acts 1868 and 1876. See further *Parker v Trigg* [1874] WN 27; *Kenrick v Mountsteven* (1899) 48 WR 141; and *Re Cook's Mortgage* [1896] 1 Ch D 923.

38 See Weible, 'Accountability of Cotenants' (1944) 29 Iowa L Rev 558 at 578 and Meitus, 'The Rights, Duties and Liabilities of Tenants in Common Inter Se' (1940) 24 Marq L Rev 148 at 153.

39 See for example, the comments of Girvan J in *Glass v McManus* [1996] NI 401 at 411 and those of Griffiths LJ in *Bernard v Josephs* [1982] 1 Ch 391 at 405. In *McNabb v Fortin* (14 June 1999, unreported) Saskatchewan Queen's Bench, the respondent's contributions towards capital payments and other outgoings on the property greatly exceeded those made by the applicant. McLellan J held that the respondent was entitled to the entire equity in the property, and made an order vesting title in the sole name of the respondent.

40 See *Cramer v Binder* (1993) 76 BCLR (2d) 354.

41 See *Wells v Wells* (1977) 4 Fam LR 57 cited with approval in *Smith v Smith* (1984) 9 Fam LR 1014, and see *Re Kneebone and Matheson* (1981) 124 DLR (3d) 538.

42 Since this is simply regarded as a 'windfall': *Zappacosta v Zappacosta* (1976) 2 Fam LR 11,214 at 11,217 per McCall J.

43 See para **[11.06]** above. See further *Cattoni v Cattoni* (12 March 1980, unreported) Alberta Queen's Bench.

ousted from the property or where special circumstances exist which render the occupant liable for his occupation, such as some form of agreement between the parties[44] or where the occupant has received more than his share of rents and profits from third parties giving rise to an action under s 23 of the Administration of Justice Act (Ir) 1707. These exceptions are equally relevant where an account is sought as incidental to a partition action, and may result in the occupant being charged with an occupation rent[45].

1 Ouster

(a) Circumstances giving rise to an ouster

[11.17] Exclusive possession by itself does not amount to an ouster. Instead, there must be some element of the occupant excluding the other co-owners or refusing to allow them to exercise their right to possession[46]. For example, if one co-owner locks the means of access to the property with the intention of excluding the others, this will be construed as an ouster[47]. Likewise, a joint tenant or tenant in common who evicts another co-owner from the land commits an ouster[48], while a demand of possession by one co-owner and a refusal by the other stating that he claims the whole is also evidence of ouster[49]. One co-owner may carry out reasonable alterations on the property without being liable for any resulting interference with the shared use of the land[50]. However, a co-owner who uses the land in a manner that results in its destruction may be guilty of an

---

44 For example, where the occupant is acting as the bailiff or agent of the other co-owners, or where he is in possession of the land as tenant of the other co-owners.

45 The term 'occupation rent' is used in a broad sense to denote any payment that may be ordered in respect of one co-owner's exclusive occupation of the common property. Where the occupant has a mortgage affecting his undivided share of the land, the occupation rent will be set off against his distributive share of the proceeds of sale but not to the prejudice of his mortgagee: *Hill v Hickin* [1897] 2 Ch 579.

46 See *Wuychik v Majewski* [1920] OWN 207 and *Cardinaels-Hooper v Tierney* (20 December 1995, unreported) Supreme Court of New South Wales.

47 *Jacobs v Seward* (1872) LR 5 HL 464 at 472 per Lord Hatherley LC and *Glass v McManus* [1996] NI 401 at 413 per Girvan J. A co-owner cannot withhold keys from another co-owner or require him to make an appointment if he wishes to visit the property: *Re Hecker's Estate* (28 April 1994, unreported) High Court (RI).

48 *Bull v Bull* [1955] 1 QB 234 at 237 per Denning LJ.

49 See *Doe v Bird* (1809) 11 East 49 and *Adamson v Adamson* (1889) 17 OR 407.

50 For example, the resurfacing of a shared means of access held by adjoining landowners as tenants in common and which results in a temporary disturbance of access does not amount to an ouster: *Ferguson v Miller* [1978] 1 NZLR 819. Likewise, the demolition and rebuilding of a common wall does not constitute an ouster, even though the wall is rebuilt at a greater height: *Cubitt v Porter* (1828) 8 B & C 257. However, in *Stedman v Smith* (1857) 8 El & Bl 1 where the defendant's roof occupied the top of a wall which he and the plaintiff owned as tenants in common, the court held that this was an ouster so as to sustain an action of trespass by the plaintiff.

ouster[51]. The fact that one co-owner resists or simply ignores a request for sale of the property by another co-owner does not constitute a denial of title which would support an ouster[52]. Yet, if a joint tenant or tenant in common denies another co-owner's interest in the property this amounts to an ouster since it is an express denial of the latter's rights as co-owner[53]. The onus of proof is on the co-owner alleging that an ouster has taken place[54].

[11.18] An ouster may also be implied where the occupant's actions fall short of excluding or removing his fellow co-owners. These so-called cases of 'constructive ouster'[55] typically arise where the other co-owners are unable to occupy the property as a result of the occupant's behaviour towards them. A number of principles have emerged from the relevant case law. For example, the fact that one co-owner leaves because of feelings of animosity between the parties, or as the result of a statement to the effect that she could leave the property if she did not like the behaviour of another co-owner does not give rise to an ouster[56]. Likewise, a co-owner who leaves the property voluntarily but would be welcome back is not excluded[57], while a joint tenant or tenant in common who makes life difficult for another co-owner by, for example, bringing a stranger into the property merely exercises rights of ownership[58]. An ouster may be implied where actual or threatened violence by one co-owner means that shared enjoyment of the land is no longer possible[59]. However, a co-owner who

---

[51] For example, in *Wilkinson v Haygarth* (1847) 12 QB 837 the court held that digging and removal of turf by one co-owner which resulted in the destruction of the common property was an ouster.

[52] See *Jager v Jager* 136 NJ Eq 379 (1945) in which the Court of Chancery in New Jersey held that a mere refusal by one co-owner to join in another's deed to sell the property did not constitute an ouster.

[53] Thus in *Biviano v Natoli* (1998) 43 NSWLR 695 the appellant was charged with an occupation fee in respect of her sole enjoyment of the premises from the date on which she filed this particular defence in response to the respondent's application for sale of the family home.

[54] *Chieco v Evans* (1990) 5 BPR 11,297.

[55] Gray, *Elements of Land Law* (2nd edn, 1993), p 472.

[56] *Marriott v Franklin* (1993) 60 SASR 457 and *Diotallevi v Diotallevi* (1982) 134 DLR (3d) 477.

[57] Thus in *Re Pavlou* [1993] 3 All ER 955 where a husband left the matrimonial home but initially would have been welcomed back by his wife, the court held that she did not have to pay an occupation rent in respect of the period before she petitioned for divorce. See further *Andrews v Andrews* (1969) 7 DLR (3d) 744; *Jansen v Jansen* (1976) 30 RFL 214; and *Sloan v Sloan* (21 March 1985, unreported) British Columbia Supreme Court.

[58] *Thrift v Thrift* (1975) 10 ALR 332 at 338-339 per Hutley JA. In *Re Hecker's Estate* (28 April 1994, unreported) High Court (RI), Lynch J stated that a co-owner not only has a right to occupy the property, but can permit a reasonable number of invitees (such as a spouse and children) to live there with him. However, Lynch J stressed that such persons would not be entitled to overcrowd the property so as to impede or prevent the exercise of a right of residence conferred on another co-owner.

[59] *Dennis v McDonald* [1982] Fam 63 and see the comments of Kerr LJ in *Bernard v Josephs* [1982] 3 All ER 162 at 172.

obtains a court order preventing a violent co-owner from residing in the property is not guilty of an ouster[60]. In these circumstances, the mere fact that a co-owner has secured such an order does not prevent the co-owner affected by it from compelling partition or sale of the property[61]. Where the terms of a separation agreement between spouses allow one of them to remain in occupation of the family home, the non-occupying spouse is not regarded as ousted from the property[62].

(b) Consequences of ouster – payment of an appropriate occupation rent

[11.19] If a co-owner has ousted the others, this gives rise to an action for recovery of land (formerly known as ejectment) or for trespass, with mesne profits to compensate for loss suffered as a result of being out of possession[63]. This may be maintained either as an independent action or as part of the relief claimed in a partition action[64]. When an account of this nature is claimed as part of a partition action, it is not restricted to cases in which the occupant seeks a contribution towards expenses from the other co-owners. An action of ejectment or trespass by the excluded co-owners is not dependent on a reciprocal claim because exclusion is a legal wrong and automatically creates a right of action[65]. However, the excluded co-owners should make a specific claim for mesne profits in the partition action. In *Glass v McManus*[66] Girvan J suggested that, because legal liability for such payments does not arise until the plaintiff obtains

60 Since the co-owner is denied access to the property by the court order itself, and not by the actions of the co-owner who secures the order: *Biviano v Natoli* (1998) 43 NSWLR 695 and see *Tracy v Bifield* (1998) 23 Fam LR 260. Although *Biviano* concerned an order against a violent co-owner, it is suggested that the decision is applicable to any case in which a co-owner is denied access to the common property by a court order obtained by another co-owner: see Conway, 'Co-Owners, Ouster and Occupation Fees' [2000] Conv 49.

61 *Revell v Baker* [1984] 3 NZFLR 20.

62 Since mere want of occupation while another co-owner is in occupation is not sufficient to establish such a claim: *Coburn v Coburn* (25 July 1984, unreported) Saskatchewan Queen's Bench, citing *Wuychik v Majewski* (1920) OWN 207. By entering into the separation agreement, the non-occupying spouse has effectively contracted out of his right to use and occupy the property.

63 See para **[11.07]** above. See further *McCormick v McCormick* [1921] NZLR 384 and *Osachuk v Osachuk* (1971) 18 DLR (3d) 413.

64 See for example, *Pascoe v Swan* (1859) 27 Beav 508 and *Luke v Luke* (1936) 36 SR (NSW) 310. In *Biviano v Natoli* (1998) 43 NSWLR 695 at 704 Beazley JA emphasised that any occupation rent which the court imposes in a partition action to take account of an ouster should be regarded as mesne profits arising from the occupant's wrongful exclusion and determined accordingly.

65 See Heon, 'The Liability of a Cotenant to Other Cotenants for Rents, Profits and Use and Occupation' (1959) 42 Marq L Rev 363 at 375 and Mendes Da Costa, 'Co-Ownership Under Victorian Land Law' (1961) 3 Melb Univ L Rev 137 at 143.

66 [1996] NI 401 at 413.

a judgment for mesne profits, the court may not be able to order an inquiry as to mesne profits or direct their payment from the proceeds of sale in the absence of such a claim. Moreover, since the plaintiff in this particular case did not put forward any such claim in the partition action he could not claim mesne profits in separate proceedings – judgment having been given for sale of the disputed property under the Partition Acts, Girvan J indicated that such a claim might be defeated on the grounds of issue estoppel and res judicata[67].

[11.20] Despite the fact that mesne profits are not rent[68], the amount payable to an ousted co-owner in these circumstances is based on the open market value of the premises[69]. Cases such as *Swordheath Properties v Tabbet*[70] have suggested that mesne profits should be calculated according to the full rental value of the premises[71]. However, in *Biviano v Natoli*[72] Beazley JA asserted that this method of assessment fails to take account of the fact that the ousting co-owner remains in occupation of the premises. The learned judge accordingly suggested that the amount of mesne profits (the occupation rent) payable to an ousted co-owner in these circumstances should be determined by the sum that a prospective tenant would be willing to pay in order to share occupation of the particular premises with the ousting co-owner. Aside from the practical difficulties associated with this method of calculation, a rental value based on shared occupation is likely to be significantly less than a full rental value with a corresponding reduction in the occupation rent payable to the excluded co-owner[73]. The alternative method proposed by Cooke[74] arguably provides a more practicable means of ascertaining the amount of mesne profits payable. She suggests that the court should

---

[67] These comments would appear to be equally relevant to other sums claimed by co-owners: for example, a claim under the Administration of Justice Act (Ir) 1707, s 23, and claims where the occupying party is acting as the agent or bailiff of the other co-owners, or occupies the property as tenant of their shares.

[68] *Progressive Mailing House Pty Ltd v Tabili Pty Ltd* (1985) 157 CLR 17 at 39 per Brennan J.

[69] *Biviano v Natoli* (1998) 43 NSWLR 695 citing *Rock Bottom Fashion Market Pty Ltd (In Liq) v HR & CE Griffiths Pty Ltd* (6 March 1998, unreported) Queensland Court of Appeal, as well as comments of Somervell LJ in *Strand Electric and Engineering Co Ltd v Brisford Entertainments Ltd* [1952] 2 QB 246 at 252.

[70] [1979] 1 WLR 285.

[71] In this particular case the Court of Appeal held that the amount of damages should be calculated by reference to the rental income that the subject property might have produced irrespective of any intention to lease the property. See further *Penarth Dock Engineering Co Ltd v Pounds* [1963] 1 Lloyd's Rep 359 and *Inverugie Investments Ltd v Hackett* [1995] 3 All ER 841.

[72] (1998) 43 NSWLR 695.

[73] For a more detailed appraisal of the decision in *Biviano v Natoli* (1998) 43 NSWLR 695 see Conway, 'Co-Owners, Ouster and Occupation Fees' [2000] Conv 49.

[74] Cooke 'Equitable Accounting' [1995] Conv 391 at 402.

determine the full rental value of the premises, and reduce this to take account of the proportionate share of the co-owner who remains in occupation. For example, if A and B are joint tenants of land and A excludes B from the premises, A would have to pay one-half of the full rental value of the property to B to compensate for this.

2 Other specific situations giving rise to an occupation rent

[11.21] The practice in partition actions where a co-owner who is in exclusive occupation may be accountable as agent or bailiff of the other co-owners or for receiving more than his share of rents and profits under s 23 of the 1707 Act is considered below[75]. As regards those situations in which one co-owner occupies the property as a tenant of the other co-owners, the former is not usually accountable for his use and occupation of the land during the continuance of the tenancy[76]. However, he will be obliged to pay an occupation rent if he fails to pay any rent owing during the tenancy, or if he remains in occupation of the land after the tenancy has ended to the exclusion of the other co-owners[77]. It seems likely that this practice would also apply in partition actions[78].

3 Imposition of a general occupation rent?

[11.22] Opinions have differed over whether there is a general right to charge a co-owner with an occupation rent in a partition action where that person has merely enjoyed sole use and occupation of the property[79]. A number of cases originally suggested that the court could impose such payments in proceedings for compulsory partition or sale[80]. However, the better view appears to be that an occupation rent is payable only in cases of ouster or special circumstances which render the occupant accountable. For example, in *McCormick v McCormick*[81] Salmond J remarked:

---

75 See paras **[11.58]-[11.62]** below.

76 Otherwise than in accordance with the terms of the tenancy agreement itself.

77 See *Leigh v Dickeson* (1884) 15 QBD 60 and Mendes Da Costa, 'Co-Ownership Under Victorian Land Law' (1961) 3 Melb Univ L Rev 137 at 142.

78 See the comments of Deane J in *Squire v Rogers* (1979) 39 FLR (Aus) 106 at 123.

79 For a review of the relevant authorities see *Osachuk v Osachuk* (1971) 18 DLR (3d) 413 at 418-424.

80 See the comments of Lord Eldon LC in *Turner v Morgan* (1803) 8 Ves 143 and those of Romilly MR in *Pascoe v Swan* (1859) 27 Beav 508. In *Hill v Hickin* [1897] 2 Ch 579 at 580-581 where an inquiry had been ordered as to the sum owed by the defendant as occupation rent, Stirling J observed that it had 'long been the practice of the Court of Chancery and the Chancery Division to direct such inquiries'. See further 21 *Halsbury's Laws of England* (1st edn, 1912), p 851 citing *Story v Johnson* (1837) 2 Y & C Ex 586; *Pascoe v Swan* (1859) 27 Beav 508; and *Teasdale v Saunderson* (1864) 33 Beav 534.

81 [1921] NZLR 384 at 385-386.

> 'It was contended ... that in a partition suit there exists a special equitable jurisdiction to require an occupying owner to account in all cases for an occupying [sic] rent to his co-owner who has been out of possession. I am not satisfied that any such rule exists. Considerations of justice and convenience have led to the recognition of the general principle that one co-owner cannot by failing to exercise his right of use and occupation establish a claim for compensation against another co owner for the lawful exercise of his own equal right. These considerations are as cogent in a partition suit as in any other proceeding between co-owners.'[82]

[11.23] Endorsing these comments, Long Innes CJ in the subsequent case of *Luke v Luke*[83] drew attention to the 'considerable body of authority' supporting the view that there is no general right to impose an occupation rent in partition actions[84]. Both Salmond J and Long Innes CJ distinguished earlier decisions to the contrary as being more accurately regarded as cases of exclusion[85] or other circumstances giving rise to an occupation rent[86].

[11.24] From *McCormick v McCormick*[87] and *Luke v Luke*[88], it appears that there is no general right in a partition action to impose an occupation rent where the occupant would otherwise incur no liability for his sole use and occupation of

---

82 The learned judge referred to *Griffies v Griffies* (1863) 11 WR 943 in which Kindersley VC observed that, since each co-owner is entitled 'to enter upon the whole property, there could be no claim by any against the others for an occupation rent'.

83 (1936) 36 SR (NSW) 310 at 316 and see the note on this case at (1936) 10 ALJ 103.

84 In particular, the learned judge referred to *M'Mahon v Burchell* (1846) 2 Ph 127 at 134-135 in which Lord Cottenham LC remarked:

> '[T]he effect ... [of this] would be, that one tenant in common, by keeping out of the actual occupation of the premises, might convert the other into his bailiff; in other words, prevent the other from occupying them, except upon the terms of paying him rent. There is nothing ... to lead to that conclusion, which is contrary to the law as clearly established from the time of Lord Coke downwards.'

85 *Turner v Morgan* (1803) 8 Ves 143 and *Pascoe v Swan* (1859) 27 Beav 508. Salmond J observed that an occupation rent in the latter case had been claimed on the authority of *Goodtitle v Tombs* (1770) 3 Wils 118 which was also a case of ouster. *Turner v Morgan* was also described as an exclusion case by Smith CJM in *Osachuk v Osachuk* (1971) 18 DLR (3d) 413 at 421.

86 For example, where the occupant claimed an allowance for improvements to the property, thereby giving rise to a reciprocal claim for occupation rent in a partition action: *Teasdale v Saunderson* (1864) 3 Beav 534 and *Hill v Hickin* [1897] 2 Ch 579. This is discussed at para **[11.26]** below. The decision in *Story v Johnson* (1837) 2 Y & C Ex 586 was also regarded as irrelevant in this context, since it was not a case of the co-owner in question being in personal occupation of the property.

87 [1921] NZLR 384.

88 (1936) 36 SR (NSW) 310.

the property[89]. This is prudent. It has long been established that a co-owner who occupies property in the absence of an exclusion or other specific circumstances cannot be accountable to the other co-owners[90]. The occupant is merely exercising his right to occupy the land, while the other co-owners are treated as having chosen not to exercise this right. Recent cases such as *Edwards v Edwards*[91] and *Forgeard v Shanahan*[92] have reiterated this basic principle[93]. However, Kirby P who delivered the dissenting judgment in *Forgeard v Shanahan*, argued that this rule:

> 'fail[s] to take into account the multitude of reasons which may explain a withdrawal from land held in co-ownership after the breakdown of the personal relationship which occasioned the creation of the co-ownership in the first place.'[94]

[11.25] He accordingly recommended that an occupation rent should be payable in all cases where one co-owner has been in exclusive occupation of the land[95]. Brereton[96] has observed that Kirby P's suggestion 'offends one of the tenets of co-ownership', namely that co-owners have an equal right to occupy the land. Any deviation from the established practice in respect of occupation rent would undermine this basic precept. Moreover, it is suggested that imposing an occupation rent in all such cases would not automatically produce a more equitable result. For example, if a co-owner simply abandons the land and the

---

[89] These cases were followed in *Re Fettell* (1952) 52 SR (NSW) 221; *Scapinello v Scapinello* [1968] SASR 316; *Chatterton v Chatterton* (1989) 52 SASR 337; *Marriott v Franklin* (1993) 60 SASR 457 and *Forgeard v Shanahan* (1994) 18 Fam LR 281. Similar views were expressed in *Rice v George* (1873) 29 Gr 221 and *Wuychik v Majewski* [1920] OWN 207.

[90] See paras **[11.05]-[11.06]** above.

[91] (12 August 1997, unreported) British Columbia Supreme Court.

[92] (1994) 18 Fam LR 281 per Meagher JA and Mahoney JA.

[93] See further *Cardinaels-Hooper v Tierney* (20 December 1995, unreported) Supreme Court of New South Wales and *Henderson v Henderson* (10 January 2000, unreported) British Columbia Court of Appeal. In *Henderson v Henderson* (2000) 184 DLR (4th) 129 the British Columbia Court of Appeal referred to the established legal principle that mere occupation of the entire property by one co-owner in the absence of exclusion does not render him liable to pay an occupation rent. However, the court suggested that this is subject to principles of equity when it finds that the occupying co-owner has been unjustly enriched at the expense of the other co-owners.

[94] (1994) 18 Fam LR 281 at 286.

[95] This view is also implicit in a number of English cases: see for example *Leake v Bruzzi* [1974] 1 WLR 1528 and *Suttill v Graham* [1977] 1 WLR 819. In *Re Pavlou* [1993] 3 All ER 955 at 959 Millett J remarked:

> '[A] court of equity will order an inquiry and payment of occupation rent, not only in the case where the co-owner in occupation has ousted the other, but in any other case in which it is necessary to do equity between the parties that an occupation rent should be paid.'

[96] Brereton, 'The Rights Between Co-owners of Land' (1995) 69 ALJ 316 at 318.

other co-owner is forced to assume sole responsibility for the property, it seems unfair that he should be charged an occupation rent. One situation in which a general occupation rent might be considered desirable is where a disagreement occurs between the parties and a co-owner feels unable to occupy the land due to hostility towards him by an occupying co-owner. However, Brereton suggests that such problems could be overcome by adopting a more liberal view of circumstances that give rise to an ouster or exclusion, rather than by abandoning one of the fundamental principles of co-ownership[97].

[11.26] The established rule that a co-owner in sole occupation of the land should not be charged with an occupation rent in the absence of an ouster or other specific circumstances that would render him accountable has much to recommend it. The occupant has a right to occupy the land and should not be penalised for doing so[98]. There appears to be no reason why this practice should not also apply in partition actions, since to hold otherwise would render the occupant accountable in a partition action when he could not have been charged with an occupation rent in other proceedings[99]. However, this rule is subject to one important exception. In a partition action, the court may take voluntary repairs and improvements made by one of the co-owners into account when adjusting the parties' interests on partition or sale. If an occupying co-owner seeks to be reimbursed for such expenditure, he may be charged with an occupation rent even though he has not excluded the other co-owners and there are no other circumstances that would render him accountable for his use and occupation[100]. The reason for this practice is discussed below[101].

[11.27] The current practice as regards liability for occupation rent may be summarised as follows: a co-owner in sole occupation of the property cannot be charged with an occupation rent in a partition action unless:

(a) he claims for expenditure on improvements, or

---

97 Brereton, 'The Rights Between Co-owners of Land' (1995) 69 ALJ 316 at 318

98 'At common law the occupant is only exercising his legal right and is getting nothing for which he should be bound to account. This legal right to occupy should not depend on the caprice or indolence of the cotenant': Meitus, 'The Rights, Duties and Liabilities of Tenants in Common Inter Se' (1940) 24 Marq L Rev 148 at 149-150. See further Macy, 'Accountability of a Co-tenant for Use and Occupation' (1958) 12 Wyo LJ 156.

99 Mendes Da Costa, 'Co-Ownership Under Victorian Land Law' (1961) 3 Melb Univ L Rev 137 at 138-139 and see *Scapinello v Scapinello* [1968] SASR 316.

100 See *Teasdale v Saunderson* (1864) 33 Beav 534; *Kenrick v Mountsteven* (1899) 48 WR 141; and *Handley v Archibald* (1899) 30 SCR 130. Similar views have been expressed in *McCormick v McCormick* [1921] NZLR 384; *Scapinello v Scapinello* [1968] SASR 316; *Re Kneebone and Matheson* (1981) 124 DLR (3d) 538; *Chatterton v Chatterton* (1989) 52 SASR 337; and *Forgeard v Shanahan* (1994) 18 Fam LR 281.

101 See para **[11.55]** below.

(b) an occupation rent would have been available in other proceedings, namely those arising from an ouster, or an agreement whereby the occupant was a tenant or bailiff of the other co-owners, or the fact that the occupant received in excess of his share of rents and profits contrary to s 23 of the 1707 Act[102].

B Expenditure

[11.28] It is convenient to consider four different types of expenditure.

1 Repairs and improvements

[11.29] The practice in partition actions as regards expenditure on repairs and improvements differs from that in straightforward actions of account. The majority of repairs and improvements to property represent voluntary expenditure. It will be recalled that, in the absence of an express or implied agreement between the parties, one co-owner cannot compel the others to contribute towards these[103]. However, the Court of Chancery applied a different rule in partition actions, notwithstanding the absence of any such agreement[104]. The reason for this practice was explained by Cotton LJ in *Leigh v Dickeson*[105]:

> '[N]o remedy exists for money expended in repairs by one tenant in common, so long as the property is enjoyed in common; but in a suit for partition it is usual to have an inquiry as to those expenses of which nothing could be recovered so long as the parties enjoyed their property in common ...: the property held in common has been increased in value by the improvements and repairs; and whether the property is divided or sold ..., one party cannot take the increase in value, without making an allowance for what has been expended in order to obtain that increased value; in fact, the execution of the repairs and improvements is adopted and sanctioned by accepting the increased value.'[106]

---

102 See the comments of Deane J in *Squire v Rogers* (1979) 39 FLR (Aus) 106 at 123.

103 See para **[11.09]** above and *Lyons v Lyons* (2 September 1987, unreported) Supreme Court of New South Wales. Thus, if the parties have agreed that a particular co-owner will carry out repairs or improvements to the property, the improving co-owner may have a remedy against the others for their share of such expenditure: Meitus, 'The Rights, Duties and Liabilities of Tenants in Common Inter Se' (1940) 24 Marq L Rev 148 at 152 and Mendes Da Costa, 'Co-Ownership Under Victorian Land Law' (1961) 3 Melb Univ L Rev 137 at 143. In contrast, if one co-owner carries out compulsory repairs and improvements to the property pursuant to an obligation that all the co-owners owe to a third party, it is suggested that the improving co-owner will have a right to a contribution from the others since the work represents necessary expenditure. For example, co-owners of leasehold property might be under an obligation to their landlord to carry out certain repairs and improvements.

104 See for example, *Swan v Swan* (1820) 8 Price 518; *Teasdale v Saunderson* (1864) 33 Beav 534; and *Williams v Williams* (1899) 68 LJ Ch 528. See further *Lasby v Crewson* (1891) 21 OR 255 and see the comments of Strong CJ in *Handley v Archibald* (1899) 30 SCR 130 at 141.

105 (1884) 15 QBD 60 at 67.

106 Similar views were expressed by Brett MR and Lindley LJ. See further the comments of North J in *Re Jones* [1893] 2 Ch 461 at 477-478.

[11.30] In other words, co-owners were liable for such expenditure if the repairs and improvements increased the value of the shares that the parties were allocated on partition or if they enhanced the sale price of the land. As Simpson CJ explained in *Boulter v Boulter*[107]:

> 'This course of action cannot inflict any injustice on the other co-owners, for it takes nothing out of their pockets, it only prevents them putting into their pockets moneys obtained by the expenditure of another person, unless they recoup him such expenditure.'

[11.31] In *Brickwood v Young*[108] Griffith CJ described this equitable right to compensation for repairs and improvements as analogous to an equitable charge on the land, running with the land and enforceable by a successor in title of the co-owner who carried out the repairs and improvements[109]. However, he emphasised that this right to compensation was a defensive equity that could not be enforced arbitrarily but only in proceedings for partition or sale[110].

[11.32] This practice still applies today. A co-owner who carries out voluntary repairs or improvements may recover for these, but only in a partition action[111]. In this context it is irrelevant whether the parties are joint tenants or tenants in common[112] or whether the co-owner making the improvements has some additional interest in the property[113]. However, if the co-owner seeking such

---

[107] (1898) LR (NSW) Eq 135 at 137.

[108] (1905) 2 CLR 387 at 396.

[109] See further *Williams v Williams* (1899) 68 LJ Ch 528. Likewise, an improving co-owner may enforce this equitable right against a successor in title of his fellow co-owner, unless the latter is a *bona fide* purchaser for value without notice: *Squire v Rogers* (1979) 39 FLR (Aus) 106 at 124 per Deane J. See however, *Kay v Johnson* (1856) 21 Beav 536 and *Re Leslie* (1883) 23 Ch D 564 in which the respective courts held that this right to compensation is personal to the co-owner asserting it and does not give rise to a lien over the property. If the parties have specifically agreed that the non-contributing co-owner is to derive no benefit from the improvements, the party who bears the costs may have a lien on the property: *Canada Life Assurance Co v Kennedy* (1978) 21 OR (2d) 83.

[110] (1905) 2 CLR 387 at 396.

[111] See *Squire v Rogers* (1979) 39 FLR (Aus) 106; *Lyons v Lyons* (2 September 1987, unreported) Supreme Court of New South Wales; *Chatterton v Chatterton* (1989) 52 SASR 337; *Martin-Smith v Woodhead* [1990] WAR 62; *Van Dongen v Royal* (1990) 72 OR (2d) 533; *Forgeard v Shanahan* (1994) 18 Fam LR 281; and *Warner v Warner* (30 November 1998, unreported) Ontario Court (General Division).

[112] In *Re Byrne* (1906) 6 SR (NSW) 532 at 533 Walker J rejected suggestions that 'an improvement by a joint tenant is a mere speculation [since] he takes his chance of being the ultimate survivor'. Similar views were expressed by Millet J in *Re Pavlou* [1993] 3 All ER 955 at 958 and see Mendes Da Costa, 'Co-Ownership Under Victorian Land Law' (1961) 3 Melb Univ L Rev 137 at 145-146.

[113] For example, in *Boulter v Boulter* (1898) 19 LR (NSW) Eq 135 the improving co-owner was also a lessee of the property (although a lessee cannot recover for improvements which he covenanted to carry out under the lease: see para **[11.34]** below).

compensation has been in sole occupation of the property[114], he must usually agree to pay a reciprocal occupation rent[115], unless he has been in possession with the consent of the other co-owners[116].

(a) Types of repairs and improvements that the courts may consider

[11.33] Expenditure on trivial or insignificant repairs and improvements will not be taken into account. A co-owner cannot recover for repairs which amount to nothing more than periodic maintenance[117]. Repairs must be necessary and of a substantial nature[118]. As regards improvements, it is well established that these must confer some permanent or lasting benefit on the land[119]. A co-owner cannot recover for improvements that merely benefit him in his personal capacity[120]. The fact that repairs or improvements are carried out during joint occupation does not prevent that particular co-owner recovering them at the end of the relationship[121].

[11.34] However, there are three situations in which such expenditure may not give rise to an accounting adjustment in a partition action. Firstly, if the

---

113 (contd) A joint tenant or tenant in common in reversion or remainder who makes improvements to the land during the occupancy of the tenant for life may recover his expenditure from the other co-owners: see *Re Byrne* (1906) 6 SR (NSW) 532 and *Brickwood v Young* (1905) 2 CLR 387 at 395 per Griffith CJ. See however *Lasby v Crewson* (1891) 21 OR 255.

114 Although the right to recover compensation for repairs and improvements in a partition action is not restricted to these circumstances: *Chatterton v Chatterton* (1989) 52 SASR 337.

115 See para **[11.26]** above.

116 *Parker v Trigg* [1874] WN 27. Alternatively, the court may decline to order payment of an occupation rent on the particular circumstances of the case: see *McMahon v Public Curator of Queensland* [1952] St R Qd 197 in which the improvements took the form of a dwelling house erected at the deceased's expense and occupying a very small area of the land held in co-ownership (one-third acre of a farm comprising over 600 acres).

117 *Cardinaels-Hooper v Tierney* (20 December 1995, unreported) Supreme Court of New South Wales, citing *Re Jones* [1893] 2 Ch 461, and see *Deeks v Deeks* [1988] 1 NZLR 664. In *Forgeard v Shanahan* (1994) 18 Fam LR 281 a majority of the court rejected a claim for expenditure on pest control as amounting to maintenance. A co-owner cannot claim for redecoration work such as wallpapering: *Burns v Burns* [1998] NZFLR 654.

118 For example, the respective courts in *Teasdale v Saunderson* (1864) 33 Beav 534 and *Kenrick v Mountsteven* (1899) 48 WR 141 granted an allowance in respect of 'substantial repairs', while Cotton LJ in *Leigh v Dickeson* (1884) 15 QBD 60 at 66 assumed that the repairs executed were 'necessary'.

119 See *Parker v Trigg* [1874] WN 27 where an allowance was made for 'permanent expenditure', while in *Kenrick v Mountsteven* (1899) 48 WR 141 at 142 Cozens-Hardy J directed an inquiry as to expenditure on 'lasting improvements'. In *Brickwood v Young* (1905) 2 CLR 387 at 396 and 399 both Griffith CJ and O'Connor J referred to 'permanent improvements' to the property.

120 Weible, 'Accountability of Cotenants' (1944) 29 Iowa L Rev 558 at 578.

121 *Malcolm v King* [1992] NZFLR 193.

improving co-owner occupies the property as a tenant of the other co-owners' shares, he cannot recover for repairs or improvements that he covenanted to make under the tenancy agreement[122]. Secondly, if one co-owner leases the property to a third party without involving the other co-owners and subsequently has to carry out repairs which are rendered necessary by letting the property, the other co-owners are not obliged to contribute towards these[123]. Thirdly, a right to compensation does not arise if the co-owner carrying out the alterations intended these to be a gift. Thus in *Noack v Noack*[124] where a husband had made improvements to land which he owned jointly with his wife but failed to rebut the presumption of advancement, the court refused to grant him an allowance for his expenditure[125].

(b) Amount recoverable for repairs and improvements

[11.35] If the court makes an order for partition, the improving co-owner may be allocated the area of land upon which improvements have been made[126]. As regards the amount that the court may allow upon making an order for sale, the rule is well established. The improving co-owner may recover either the amount expended on repairs and improvements or the amount by which these have increased the value of the land, depending on which sum is less. As Simpson CJ explained *Boulter v Boulter*[127]:

> 'In no case can the co-owner who has improved the property obtain more than his outlay, though such outlay may have trebled the value of the property. And, on the other hand, the increase in the price obtained is the limit of what he can receive, though his actual outlay may be far larger.'

[11.36] This rule developed in the nineteenth century. In *Re Jones*[128] a tenant in common spent £900 on improvements to land and her successor in title claimed an accounting adjustment upon its sale. North J held that the maximum amount that could be recovered was £900, even if the value of the property had increased

---

122 *Newall v Johnston* (1903) 23 NZLR 406.

123 *Re the Estates of Dugac and the Official Trustee in Bankruptcy* (6 February 1987, unreported) Federal Court of Australia. A joint tenant or tenant in common may lease his share of the land to a third party without the consent of the other co-owners: *Cowper v Fletcher* (1865) 6 B & S 464 and *Re Marcellos* (1941) 41 SR (NSW) 154. However, if one co-owner purports to lease the entire property without the consent of the others, this will be construed as a lease of his share only: *Bellingham v Aslop* (1604) Cro Jac 652.

124 [1959] VR 137 at 146.

125 Similar views were expressed by Ferguson JA in *Mastron v Cotton* (1925) 58 OLR 251 at 255 and see *Clark v Clark* [1961] VR 181.

126 See the cases noted at para **[11.13]** above and see Meitus, 'The Rights, Duties and Liabilities of Tenants in Common Inter Se' (1940) 24 Marq L Rev 148 at 153.

127 (1898) LR (NSW) Eq 135 at 137.

128 [1893] 2 Ch 461.

by more than this amount[129]. More recently this rule has been applied in *McMahon v Public Curator of Queensland*[130], *Forgeard v Shanahan*[131] and *Cardinaels-Hooper v Tierney*[132]. The reason for the limitation appears to be that, if a co-owner who carried out such work was allowed to recoup more than his expenditure or the corresponding increase in value of the property, he would be deriving an unfair advantage from the other co-owners by profiting from his repairs and improvements at their expense. Moreover, because the nature of co-ownership means that a co-owner can make alterations to the land without the approval of the other co-owners and they cannot usually decline any benefit produced by this work, it seems only fair that there should be a limit on the amount recoverable[133].

[11.37] There are two methods of calculating the amount recoverable for repairs and improvements, both of which yield the same practical result. The first is derived from *Re Cook's Mortgage*[134]. Assuming that two co-owners are entitled to equal shares of land, the proceeds of sale are divided equally between them, before half of the money spent on repairs and improvements (or half of the increase in value to the land) is deducted from the share of the non-improving co-owner and added to the other co-owner's share. The second method is derived from *Re Jones*[135]. By this method, the amount spent on repairs and improvements (or the increase in value to the property) is allocated to the co-owner who made the alterations, before the proceeds of sale are divided between the parties.

[11.38] However, there are a number of disadvantages associated with the practical application of the rule governing recovery for expenditure on repairs and improvements upon sale. In the first place, a co-owner will be unable to recoup his expenditure if the alterations do not increase the value of the property,

---

129 This rule was also applied in *Watson v Gass* (1881) 30 WR 286; *Williams v Williams* (1899) 68 LJ Ch 528; and *Kenrick v Mountsteven* (1899) 48 WR 141. Likewise, in *Brickwood v Young* (1905) 2 CLR 387 Griffith CJ directed an inquiry as to the amount expended by the appellant or his predecessors in title on improvements and the amount by which these had increased the value of the property.

130 [1952] St R Qd 197.

131 (1994) Fam LR 281.

132 (20 December 1995, unreported) Supreme Court of New South Wales. See further *Lyons v Lyons* (2 September 1987, unreported) Supreme Court of New South Wales and *Vasili v Cross* (14 December 1995, unreported) Supreme Court of New South Wales.

133 However, if a co-owner receives in excess of his share of rents and profits from third parties as a result of improvements to the land, the other co-owners must allow for the *entire* cost of the improvements if they seek to recover a proportionate share of such rents and profits: see para **[11.60]** below.

134 [1896] 1 Ch 923.

135 [1893] 2 Ch 461.

even if he has spent a considerable sum of money on them[136]. For example, in *Grant v Grant*[137] a co-owner installed a new oil burner which did not increase the value of the property and the court refused to grant him any allowance for this[138]. Likewise, the improving co-owner is entitled to the lesser of the two amounts where a small expenditure results in a substantial increase in the value of the property or where a large expenditure produces a small increase in value. This situation is exacerbated where the improving co-owner has been in sole occupation of the property – the court will almost certainly charge him with an occupation rent and off-set this against a claim for expenditure. Yet the other co-owners will probably derive a functional benefit from the alterations.

[11.39] The second criticism relates to the manner in which courts calculate the amount spent on repairs and improvements. If these are carried out by a third party such as a building contractor, few problems arise. The court will regard the amount spent on repairs and improvements as the total sum paid to the third party[139], which typically includes both labour and materials. The onus is on the applicant to establish the validity of the amounts claimed[140]. However, difficulties arise where such alterations are carried out by one of the co-owners. While the court may have recourse to receipts and invoices to determine the amount spent (assuming that the co-owner has retained these), time and labour may not be taken into account. As Cohen J explained in *Cardinaels-Hooper v Tierney*[141], the outlaying of time or effort cannot be valued unless the court assesses it against some hourly rate of earnings. Difficulties that arise in this context are identifying an appropriate hourly rate, as well as obtaining an accurate statement of the number of hours that a co-owner has spent carrying out repairs and improvements. Although Cohen J did not explore these difficulties, he concluded that such an assessment of earnings would not amount to expenditure by a co-owner[142]. Accordingly, the amount recoverable in these circumstances is essentially the amount spent on materials; the improving co-

---

[136] However, if 'improvements' actually cause the property to diminish in value, the co-owner responsible may be forced to compensate the other co-owners for the amount by which the value has depreciated: see *Marriott v Franklin* (1993) 60 SASR 457.

[137] [1952] OWN 641.

[138] The only advantage to the improving co-owner in these circumstances is that if he fails to recover for improvements then, assuming he has been in sole occupation of the property, he cannot be charged with an occupation rent in the absence of an exclusion or other circumstances that would render him liable.

[139] See for example, *Squire v Rogers* (1979) 39 FLR (Aus) 106.

[140] *Kalita v Freskiw* (10 December 1998, unreported) Ontario Court (General Division). In this case the amount claimed by the applicant was reduced because it was not fully supported by invoices.

[141] (20 December 1995, unreported) Supreme Court of New South Wales.

[142] (20 December 1995, unreported) Supreme Court of New South Wales, Lexis transcript, at 10.

owner receives no allowance for his time and labour. It follows that the amount spent on alterations will probably be less than the increase in value of the property, and the allowance made restricted accordingly.

[11.40] The third criticism relates to the court's failure to take inflation into account where a period of time has elapsed between expenditure on repairs and improvements and termination of co-ownership[143]. Alterations carried out some years prior to a partition action may have increased the current value of the property considerably. However, since the relevant expenditure is the amount spent at the date upon which the repairs and improvements were made, this will frequently be less than the increase in value to the property and the amount recoverable by the improving co-owner restricted accordingly. Thus in *McMahon v Public Curator of Queensland*[144] where the deceased constructed a house in 1870 at a cost of £900 and sale of the land did not take place until 1950, the deceased's widow could only recover this amount. Macrossan J rejected suggestions that a more appropriate test would be the lesser of the increase in value on sale or the current value of the money spent on improvements by the deceased.

[11.41] One possible argument in favour of retaining the standard rule is that, since the property is likely to fetch a higher price on sale due to the alterations, the improving co-owner receives both an allowance for his expenditure and more money when the proceeds of sale are divided. Assume that X and Y are co-owners in equal shares of a house that is worth £100,000 today and that £20,000 of this is attributable to improvements made by X in 1970. These improvements cost £5,000 but would cost £10,000 today. Applying the standard rule, upon sale of the property X is entitled to £5000, which represents his expenditure in 1970 (this being less than the corresponding increase in value) and £47,500, which represents half of the remaining proceeds of sale. It could be argued that X has benefited quite well in these circumstances – he was not obliged to carry out such work, and if no allowance had been made for improvements he would only have received £50,000 as opposed to £52,500. Moreover, if he had not carried out these improvements, he would only have received £40,000. However, it is submitted that a more equitable result would be produced if the court took inflation into account and assessed the amount that would have been required to make such alterations at the date of the hearing. Applying this to the present example, X would be entitled to £55,000 upon sale of the property – the £10,000 that the improvements would cost today (since this is still less than the increase

143 Cooke has observed that the rule relating to recovery for repairs and improvements evolved in the nineteenth century 'when inflation was not the hazard it is today': Cooke, 'Equitable Accounting' [1995] Conv 391 at 395.

144 [1952] St R Qd 197 and noted at para **[11.32]** above.

in value) and half of the remaining proceeds of sale. While this would prevent Y profiting from X's expenditure, Y's contribution to the improvements would still not exceed the financial benefit he has derived from them – even if the current value of X's expenditure was five times that spent in 1970, X's allowance would still be restricted to the increase in value of the property. In other words, the dual limitation in the standard test ensures that the improving co-owner cannot benefit at the expense of the other co-owners, even if the amount spent on alterations were to be adjusted to take account of inflation.

[11.42] Upon a strict application of the rule that the amount payable for repairs and improvements is limited to their cost or the increase in value they produce, whichever is less, it appears that a co-owner who carries out such work may not receive adequate compensation. Perhaps this is one area of the law relating to accounting adjustments that might be open to review in the future, particularly in the situations identified above.

2 Rates and property taxes

[11.43] If one co-owner has been meeting necessary expenses such as rates and property taxes, he will have a right to a contribution from the other co-owners in respect of such payments towards a joint debt[145]. This may be maintained as an independent action or as incidental to an order for partition or sale[146]. However, it appears that this rule is subject to two exceptions. Firstly, a co-owner may not be able to recover such expenditure if he has been given sole responsibility for meeting necessary expenses on the property[147]. Secondly, a right to a contribution may not arise in respect of payments by a husband towards a joint debt incurred by himself and his wife. In these circumstances, such payments might be regarded as an advancement[148], unless the marriage has broken down or

[145] Since all the co-owners are under an obligation to meet these expenses: see para **[11.09]** above and Meitus, 'The Rights, Duties and Liabilities of Tenants in Common Inter Se' (1940) 24 Marq L Rev 148 at 151-152. In *Forgeard v Shanahan* (1994) 18 Fam LR 281 a majority of the Supreme Court of New South Wales held that, if one co-owner pays a joint debt attributable to the entire property, the other co-owner is liable to contribute a rateable amount under the equitable doctrine of contribution. See further the comments of Gibbs CJ in *Muschinski v Dodds* (1985) 160 CLR 583 at 596-597. However, in *Tracy v Bifield* (1998) 23 Fam LR 260 Templeman J refused to allow the defendant to recover a proportionate share of payments towards rates, alleging that such payments were related to occupation of the property.

[146] See *Osachuk v Osachuk* (1971) 18 DLR (3d) 413; *Shore v Shore* (1975) 63 DLR (3d) 354; and *Re the Estates of Dugac and the Official Trustee in Bankruptcy* (6 February 1987, unreported) Federal Court of Australia.

[147] For example, under the terms of a will granting him sole use of the property provided that he meets all such payments: see *Lyons v Lyons* (2 September 1987, unreported) Supreme Court of New South Wales.

[148] *Shore v Shore* (1975) 63 DLR (3d) 354.

there is an agreement between the parties to the effect that both are responsible for the joint debt[149].

[11.44] It has been suggested that this right to a contribution is now part of the law of restitution, since co-owners who have not made any payment towards necessary expenses are unjustly enriched at the expense of the co-owner meeting such payments[150].

3 Mortgage repayments

[11.45] A divergence in practice has arisen as regards the appropriate form of accounting adjustment to be made where one co-owner meets all the mortgage repayments on the property[151]. A number of cases have regarded such payments as equivalent to that party making improvements to the land[152]. One co-owner may claim an allowance for payments of mortgage capital insofar as these increase the value of the equity of redemption in the property. Thus in *Re Pavlou*[153] where the parties were beneficial joint tenants of a matrimonial home and the wife paid the mortgage instalments following the husband's departure, Millett J held that she was entitled to half the increase in value of the equity of redemption resulting from payments of mortgage capital from the date on which the husband left the property. As regards payments of mortgage interest, the learned judge ordered these to be set off against a payment of occupation rent by the wife[154].

---

149 Since the presumption of advancement does not apply after the breakdown of a marriage (*Shore v Shore* (1975) 63 DLR (3d) 354 at 357-358 and see the cases cited therein) or where an oral or written agreement between the parties indicates that they are to share the debt (*Shore v Shore* (1975) 63 DLR (3d) 354 at 358-359)

150 See Cooke, 'Equitable Accounting' [1995] Conv 391 at 396.

151 This discussion is confined to mortgages that have been created by all of the co-owners. Where a mortgage affects the undivided share of one co-owner, that person must meet all the payments since he alone is responsible for the debt: see the comments of Guy JA in *Re Vermette and Vermette* (1974) 45 DLR (3d) 313 at 316-317.

152 See *Cracknell v Cracknell* [1971] P 356 and *Re Pavlou* [1993] 3 All ER 955. A similar approach was adopted by Bisson J in *Bourke v Bourke* [1983] 2 NZFLR 55.

153 [1993] 3 All ER 955.

154 It appears that an occupation rent was imposed to take account of the wife's sole enjoyment of the property after commencing divorce proceedings, which Millett J construed as an ouster of the husband: see para **[11.18]** above. While not adopting the improvements analogy as regards payments of capital, a number of other English cases have held that mortgage interest payments should be set off against an occupation rent, the latter being imposed simply because it is fair to do so on the circumstances of a particular case: see for example, *Leake v Bruzzi* [1974] 1 WLR 1528 and *Suttill v Graham* [1977] 1 WLR 819. The arguments against imposing a general occupation rent in the absence of an ouster or other circumstances giving rise to such liability were discussed above: see paras **[11.22]-[11.26]** above.

[11.46] However, there are a number of difficulties associated with this approach. In *Re Pavlou*[155], Millett J held that the wife was *prima facie* entitled to recover a proportionate share of mortgage interest payments from her husband. Yet, if mortgage repayments by one co-owner are to be equated with improvements to the land, this does not explain why the other co-owners must contribute towards interest payments when these do not increase the value of the equity of redemption[156]. Cooke[157] has also observed that, if the property was worth less than the mortgage debt, mortgage payments by one co-owner would not increase the value of the (non existent) equity of redemption, but would nevertheless reduce the debt which would remain if the property were sold. The fact that such payments did not increase the value of the equity of redemption would, however, preclude their recovery.

[11.47] It is suggested that it is incorrect to equate mortgage repayments with improvements. While it may be true to say that such payments resemble improvements insofar as the former increase the value of the equity of redemption in a manner similar to that in which improvements increase the value of the land itself, there is one significant difference between the two types of expenditure. The majority of improvements represent voluntary expenditure on the land by one co-owner, whereas a mortgage represents necessary expenditure in the sense that all of the co-owners are jointly and severally liable to repay the mortgage debt. In these circumstances, it is difficult to avoid the conclusion that payment of both mortgage capital and interest by one co-owner represents payment of a joint debt which arises because of the obligation which all the co-owners owe to a third party, the mortgagee.

[11.48] This approach is evident in a number of Australian cases which simply regard mortgage payments by one co-owner as necessary expenditure on the property. A co-owner has a right to a contribution from the others in respect of these payments and may recover both principal and interest in an action of account or in a partition action. For example, in *Scapinello v Scapinello*[158] Bright J remarked:

---

[154] (contd) Mortgage interest payments may also be set off against an occupation rent where an action for sale of a family home is brought by the trustee in bankruptcy, and the wife is claiming a share of mortgage payments from her husband (the bankrupt) - see for example, *Re Pavlou* [1993] 3 All ER 955 and *Official Receiver for Northern Ireland v Kearney* (13 January 1999, unreported) High Court (NI). However, in *Re Gorman* [1990] 1 All ER 717 Vinelott J suggested that this practice was simply a rule of convenience and would not always be appropriate in these circumstances.

[155] [1993] 3 All ER 955.

[156] See Cooke, 'Equitable Accounting' [1995] Conv 391 at 397.

[157] Cooke, 'Equitable Accounting' [1995] Conv 391 at 397.

[158] [1968] SASR 316 at 318.

> 'There is a right to a contribution as between joint mortgagors in favour of the one who has paid the obligation. The right to a contribution is not founded on contract, but is the result of a general equity arising at the inception of the obligation on the ground of equality of burden and benefit.'[159]

[11.49] Accordingly, the wife in this particular case had to account for half the mortgage payments made by the husband between the date on which the wife left the property and the date on which she obtained an order for sale of the premises[160].

[11.50] While recognising that a right to a contribution exists in respect of mortgage repayments, a number of Canadian cases have suggested that payments of capital and interest should be kept separate where the co-owner responsible for meeting such expenditure has merely been in sole occupation of the property[161]. In these cases, the respective courts have imposed an occupation rent as a condition of allowing that particular co-owner to recover mortgage interest payments from the other co-owners[162]. However, it is submitted that payments of mortgage interest should not be set off against an occupation rent in these circumstances. A claim for necessary expenditure does not give rise to a reciprocal claim for an occupation rent by the other co-owners in the absence of any other circumstances that would render the occupant liable in this respect[163]. The latter has a right to a contribution in respect of both mortgage interest and capital payments without having to account to the others as regards his occupation of the property.

---

[159] See further, *Carkeek v Tate-Jones* [1971] VR 691; *Re the Estates of Dugac and the Official Trustee in Bankruptcy* (6 February 1987, unreported) Federal Court of Australia; and *Vasili v Cross* (14 December 1995, unreported) Supreme Court of New South Wales. In *Forgeard v Shanahan* [1991] 5 BPR 11,797 at 11,802 Rolfe J at first instance equated mortgage repayments to improvements. However, this analysis was rejected by Meagher JA on appeal: (1994) 18 Fam LR 281 at 299-300.

[160] However, in *Coburn v Coburn* (25 July 1984, unreported) Saskatchewan Queen's Bench, Geatros J refused to allow a husband to recover a proportionate share of mortgage payments where he had undertaken to make such payments as part of his obligations in the divorce settlement with his wife, and they were made in lieu of maintenance.

[161] See *Osachuk v Osachuk* (1971) 18 DLR (3d) 413 at 433-435 and the cases cited therein. See further *Paterson v Paterson* (1979) 108 DLR (3d) 234. In contrast, cases such as *Ruff v Strobel* (1978) 86 DLR (3d) 284 and *Brewin v Ferguson* (1982) 134 DLR (3d) 538 have adopted the same approach as the Australian cases cited immediately above.

[162] The reason for this being that such payments do not increase the value of the property: see para **[11.56]** below. Contrast this with the English cases of *Leake v Bruzzi* [1974] 1 WLR 1528 and *Suttill v Graham* [1977] 1 WLR 819 noted above: see para **[11.45]** above. Although an occupation rent was set off against mortgage interest payments in these cases, the former was imposed simply because it was considered equitable to do so in the circumstances of the case.

[163] See paras **[11.56]**-**[11.57]** below.

4 Insurance premiums

[11.51] Judicial opinions have differed over whether payments by one co-owner towards an insurance policy affecting the property amount to necessary expenditure and thus give rise to a right to a contribution from the other co-owners[164]. In *Forgeard v Shanahan*[165] Meagher JA (with whom Mahoney JA agreed) held that such payments could not be classified either as improvements to the property or as discharge of a joint debt. In his opinion, they merely maintained the property[166]. However, Kirby P held that a co-owner could recover insurance premiums, these being 'directly relevant to the property jointly owned'[167]. Similar views have been expressed in a number of other cases. For example, in *Osachuk v Osachuk*[168] Smith CJM stated that joint tenants were equally liable for any payments required to be made in respect of the property such as insurance, while in *Re Kneebone and Matheson*[169] the court ordered the respective parties to compensate each other for payments of fire insurance premiums which had not been borne equally[170].

[11.52] As a matter of principle it might seem that where co-owners are joint policyholders and only one of them is meeting the insurance premiums, he should be able to recover a proportionate share of these payments from the other co-owners. However, this may depend on the circumstances surrounding the creation of the insurance policy. An accounting adjustment in respect of insurance payments may be justified where the insurance policy represents necessary expenditure on the common property. For example, co-owners are required to take out an insurance policy where purchase of property is financed either wholly or partly by a lending institution. The mortgagee invariably insists on the land being insured to protect his interests under the mortgage. In these circumstances, the insurance policy is rendered necessary by an obligation that

---

[164] In this context it is assumed that the parties originally acted together in taking out an insurance policy on the land, but that one co-owner has been responsible for meeting payments due under the policy.

[165] (1994) 18 Fam LR 281 at 299.

[166] See further *Bourke v Bourke* [1983] 2 NZFLR 55 in which Bisson J refused to allow a claim for insurance payments (as well as payments of mortgage interest and rates) on the basis that they did not enhance the value of the property.

[167] (1994) 18 Fam LR 281 at 292.

[168] (1971) 18 DLR (3d) 413 at 416.

[169] (1981) 124 DLR (3d) 538.

[170] Similar views were expressed in *Re the Estates of Dugac and the Official Trustee in Bankruptcy* (6 February 1987, unreported) Federal Court of Australia, although the co-owner responsible for meeting the insurance payments could not recover them on the particular facts of the case. In *Kalita v Freskiw* (10 December 1998, unreported) Ontario Court (General Division), Gibson J permitted a co-owner to recover half of all payments made towards capital expenses including insurance payments.

the co-owners owe to a third party[171]. If one co-owner makes all the payments, this represents payment of a joint debt and gives rise to a right to a contribution from the other co-owners. This could be maintained either as an independent action or as part of the relief claimed in a partition action.

[11.53] If an insurance policy represents voluntary expenditure in the sense that the policy is not required by a third party but simply represents a desire to protect the property against accidental damage, it could be argued that a co-owner who meets all of the insurance premiums should still be able to recover a proportionate share of these from the other co-owners. Such an obligation arguably arises because the parties have acted together in entering into the insurance policy, thus giving rise to a joint undertaking to meet all payments that arise in this context. However, this might be regarded as inconsistent with the general practice relating to recovery of expenditure by co-owners. Co-owners can only usually recover for necessary expenditure, and if insurance does not result from liability to a third party then it is difficult to see how it is necessary. As regards the other main type of voluntary expenditure on co-owned property, it will be recalled that a co-owner who carries out repairs and improvements does not have a right to a contribution from the other co-owners, and can only recover for these in a partition action[172]. If the same practice were adopted in respect of voluntary expenditure on insurance premiums, the co-owner responsible for meeting these payments would not be entitled to an accounting adjustment. Insurance merely preserves the value of the property as opposed to enhancing its value, which is the basis on which recovery for repairs and improvements is permitted in a partition action.

[11.54] However, there are fundamental differences between these two types of voluntary expenditure. As regards repairs and improvements, one co-owner usually takes it upon himself to carry out such work; there is no sense in which the co-owners assume joint responsibility for these. In contrast, a joint insurance policy is initially created by all of the co-owners. Therefore it could be argued that an insurance policy effected voluntarily by all the co-owners should give rise to a right to a contribution, since the basis of the policy is a joint undertaking by the parties – one co-owner is paying a debt which he and the others owe jointly. In the absence of further judicial clarification, the law in this area must be regarded as unsettled.

[171] For example, in *Scapinello v Scapinello* [1968] SASR 316 Bright J ordered co-owners to account for fire insurance premiums payable under a joint mortgage, but doubted whether this obligation would have arisen but for the obligation under the mortgage. See further *Tracy v Bifield* (1998) 23 Fam LR 260.

[172] See paras **[11.29]**-**[11.32]** above.

5 *Expenditure and payments of occupation rent*

[11.55] An occupation rent may be imposed as a condition of allowing a co-owner who has been in exclusive occupation of the land to recover for repairs and improvements in a partition action[173]. The practice of imposing reciprocal accounting obligations in this particular situation may be regarded as an example of the court applying the maxim 'he who seeks equity must do equity'. Since partition is an equitable remedy[174], and voluntary expenditure on repairs and improvements can only be recovered in a partition action, the occupant must submit to being charged with an occupation rent[175]. The amount of occupation rent imposed should not exceed the amount of expenditure claimed by the occupant[176].

[11.56] A number of Canadian cases have suggested that an occupying co-owner may also be charged with an occupation rent if he claims for necessary expenses on the property, such as property taxes and mortgage interest payments[177]. The reason for this appears to be that such payments do not increase the value of the property, so that it would be unfair to give the occupant credit for his expenditure without subjecting him to an occupation rent[178]. Otherwise, he would be entitled to a contribution from the other co-owners without having to make any allowance for his sole occupation of the property[179]. However, it is

---

173 See para **[11.26]** above. This rule applies even though the occupying co-owner has not excluded the other co-owners and there are no other circumstances that would render him accountable for his use and occupation, such as liability as an agent or bailiff.

174 See ch 6 above and *Chatterton v Chatterton* (1989) 52 SASR 337 at 340 and 342.

175 See the views expressed by Spragge J in *Rice v George* (1873) Gr 221 at 226. See further *Mastron v Cotton* (1925) OLR 251 and *Luke v Luke* (1936) 36 SR (NSW) 310.

176 See *Brickwood v Young* (1905) 2 CLR 387 at 398 per Griffith CJ and cited with approval by Cohen J in *Cardinaels-Hooper v Tierney* (20 December 1995, unreported) Supreme Court of New South Wales. If the amount of occupation rent exceeded the amount recoverable for expenditure, this would be tantamount to the court imposing liability on the occupant for exercising his right to occupy the property: Berger, 'An Analysis of the Economic Relations Between Co-owners' [1979] Ariz L Rev 1015 at 1020 and see *Forgeard v Shanahan* (1994) 18 Fam LR 281 at 300 per Meagher JA.

177 See *Osachuk v Osachuk* (1971) 18 DLR (3d) 413 and *Szuba v Szuba* [1951] 1 DLR 387. See further *Mastron v Cotton* (1925) 58 OLR 251; *Talbutt v Talbutt* [1953] OWN 63; and *McWilliam v McWilliam and Prudential Insurance Co of America* (1960) 31 WWR 480. Again it is assumed that the other co-owners have not been excluded from the land, and that there are no other circumstances which might render the occupant liable to pay an occupation rent.

178 See *Osachuk v Osachuk* (1971) 18 DLR (3d) 413 at 435.

179 These particular cases make no reference to imposing an occupation rent as a condition of allowing an occupying co-owner to recover mortgage capital payments. The reason for this appears to be that, while the other co-owners must make some allowance for them, payments of mortgage capital increase the value of the property on sale so that recovery is not 'one-sided'. The occupant has a right to a contribution, but the other co-owners will receive a larger sum upon division of the proceeds of sale.

submitted that a co-owner should not be charged with an occupation rent simply because he claims for necessary expenditure. In these circumstances, the occupant's right to recover such payments is independent of proceedings for partition or sale of the land. As Meagher JA explained in *Forgeard v Shanahan*[180]:

> 'In the case where one party is claiming an allowance for improvements and the other is seeking to charge an occupation fee, both claims can arise in partition actions ... and only in such actions. Each claim is a potential incident of a partition action. In this context, "no rent if no improvements" makes good sense. The discharging of joint debts stands in a different position. An adjustment occasioned by such a discharge is not necessarily made in a partition action: it could be made in an action for contribution, which could be brought quite independently of a partition action ... In these circumstances, to equate a claim for contribution with a claim for an allowance for improvements does not seem ... to carry much conviction.'[181]

[11.57] Unlike recovery for expenditure on repairs and improvements, the occupant has a right to a contribution for necessary expenses; he is not claiming equitable relief which is only available in a partition action. Accordingly, the occupant should not be charged with an occupation rent in the absence of any other circumstances giving rise to such liability. The other co-owners are regarded as having chosen not to exercise their right to occupy the property, and the occupant's expenditure represents payment of a joint debt for which all the parties are responsible.

C Rents and profits

[11.58] Notwithstanding the repeal of the procedural methods prescribed by s 23 of the Administration of Justice Act (Ir) 1707[182], a co-owner must still account for rents and profits derived from the property which exceed his share[183]. An account of this nature may also be claimed in a partition action and is not

---

[180] (1994) 18 Fam LR 281 at 299-300.

[181] Similar views were expressed by McInerney J in *Carkeek v Tate-Jones* [1971] VR 691.

[182] See generally para **[11.08]** above.

[183] Since the repealing legislation merely regulated the means of enforcing the right, but left the right itself intact: *Kearney v Kearney* (1861) 13 ICLR 314 (considered in ch 6 above, para **[6.23]**) and Dowling, 'The Baby and the Bathwater: The Administration of Justice Act (Ireland) 1707, s 23' (1996) 47 NILQ 428 at 431-432. Similar problems have arisen in Australia. The Administration of Justice Act 1705 remains in force in the majority of states with the exception of New South Wales, Queensland and Victoria. In Queensland, the 1705 Act, s 27 has been replaced by the Property Law Act 1974 (Qd), s 43. However, problems have arisen as regards the relevant law in New South Wales and Victoria due to the repeal of the 1705 Act without any legislative replacement.

restricted to those situations in which the person receiving more than his share is in exclusive occupation of the property[184]. However, a co-owner who has been ousted from the property and who is thus entitled to an occupation rent cannot also claim a share of rents and profits from the occupying co-owner since this would over-compensate him[185].

[11.59] A co-owner does not receive more than his just share simply because he has sole enjoyment of the property or profits from his own efforts or expenditure on the land[186]. An action of account under s 23 is only available where a co-owner receives in excess of his share of rents and profits from a third party[187]. For example, while a co-owner must account for rents received as a result of leasing the common property[188], he need not account for income arising from using such premises as a boarding house since this is generated by his own labour[189]. Likewise, a co-owner who farms land is entitled to the produce and any income derived from its sale[190]. However, an action of account under s 23

---

183 (contd) Considering the repeal of the 1705 Act by the Imperial Acts Application Act 1969 (NSW), Meagher JA in *Forgeard v Shanahan* (1994) 18 Fam LR 281 at 297 concluded that the right to an account conferred by the 1705 Act, s 27 no longer exists so that co-owners are now in the position they would have been in prior to the enactment of the 1705 Act. This view was endorsed by Cohen J in *Cardinaels-Hooper v Tierney* (20 December 1995, unreported) Supreme Court of New South Wales, and it appears that a similar result would arise in Victoria by virtue of the Imperial Acts Application Act 1980 (Vict). One author has described Meagher JA's ruling on the 1705 Act as 'unpalatable' and difficult to reconcile with *Squire v Rogers* (1979) 39 FLR (Aus) 106 where the court held that a co-owner was liable to account for such rents and profits: Brereton, 'The Rights Between Co-owners of Land' (1995) 69 ALJ 316 at 317. In *Hitchins v Hitchins* (11 December 1998, unreported) Supreme Court of New South Wales, Bryson J asserted that the repeal of the 1705 Act was irrelevant since s 27 was merely a procedural provision and equitable claims to this effect were still possible. That aside, it appears that an account of this nature may be claimed in a partition action under the respective Supreme Court Rules of New South Wales and Victoria: Bradbook, MacCallum and Moore, *Australian Real Property Law* (2nd edn, 1997), p 10-27.

184 See *Lorimer v Lorimer* (1820) 5 Madd 363; *Curtis v Coleman* (1875) 22 Gr 561; and *Burnell v Burnell* (1879) 11 Ch D 213. See further *Blacklaw and Blacklaw v Beveridge and Collier* [1939] 3 WWR 511 and *Marriott v Franklin* (1993) 60 SASR 457.

185 Butt, *Land Law* (3rd edn, 1996), p 237 citing *Re Thurgood* (1987) Qd Conv R 54-239.

186 See *Field v Field* (1910) 8 ELR 374 and *Rees v Rees* [1931] SASR 78.

187 See para **[11.08]** above. However, a co-owner is only liable in respect of rents and profits actually received from a third party, and not for what he might have received with better management of the property: *Thrift v Thrift* (1975) 10 ALR 332.

188 See *Marriott v Franklin* (1993) 60 SASR 457.

189 See for example, *Spelman v Spelman* [1944] 2 DLR 74; *King v King* [1944] 4 DLR 796; and *Reid v Reid* (1978) 87 DLR (3d) 370.

190 See *Rees v Rees* [1931] SASR 78 in which Richards J held that the defendants could not recover income generated by the harvesting and sale of crops. In *Gingles v Magill* [1926] NI 234 Wilson J held that grazing sheep does not give rise to an action under the Administration of Justice Act (Ir) 1707, s 23.

may lie in respect of income generated by the sale of material that forms a natural part of the land[191].

[11.60] While a co-owner must account for rents and profits derived from the property that exceed his share, he may be able to claim against the other co-owners in respect of expenses used to generate that income[192]. This is significant where expenses take the form of improvements that result in the property being leased to a third party. It was established in *Squire v Rogers*[193] that, where co-owners seek a share of rents and profits which were derived from improvements carried out by another co-owner, the latter should be entitled to recover the entire cost of the improvements and should not be limited to the amount by which these have increased the value of property[194]. However, this practice may not be applied where the parties seeking a share of rents and profits were unaware that such improvements were being made[195].

[11.61] Where a co-owner receives in excess of his share of rents and profits from a third party and puts these towards payment of a joint debt affecting the property, the other co-owners may be prevented from recovering their share of this income[196].

D Liability as a bailiff or agent

[11.62] If a co-owner agrees to act as bailiff or agent for the other co-owners, he must account to them for any rents and profits that he receives in this capacity[197], and for all that he might have received but for his wilful neglect or default[198]. For example, if the parties enter into an agreement whereby one of them undertakes to manage the property on behalf of the others, that co-owner may be liable in an action of account or in a partition action for any improper management of the property[199]. However, it is not sufficient that management of the property is simply left in the hands of that particular co-owner[200]. An accounting adjustment

191 See *Curtis v Coleman* (1875) 22 Gr 561 at 562 in which Blake VC held that a co-tenant was liable to account for profits derived from the sale of plaster from plaster beds on the land, and suggested that a similar rule would apply in respect of materials such as brick-clay and turf since 'the amounts received ... are obtained by the eating away of the estate'.

192 *Marriott v Franklin* (1993) 60 SASR 457 at 465.

193 (1979) 39 FLR (Aus) 106.

194 See further *Vasili v Cross* (14 December 1995, unreported) Supreme Court of New South Wales. In other words, this practice will benefit an improving co-owner where the cost of improvements is greater than the resulting increase in value to the property. Recovery for improvements in a partition action is usually restricted to their cost or the increase in value which the improvements produce, whichever is less: see paras **[11.35]**-**[11.42]** above.

195 Bradbook, MacCallum and Moore, *Australian Real Property Law* (2nd edn, 1997), p 10-27.

196 *McNabb v Fortin* (14 June 1999, unreported) Saskatchewan Queen's Bench.

197 See para **[11.07]** above. See further *McCormick v McCormick* [1921] NZLR 384 and *Re Tolman's Estate* (1928) 23 Tas LR 29.

198 See *Nash v McKay* (1868) 15 Gr 247 and *Osachuk v Osachuk* (1971) 18 DLR (3d) 413 at 426.

199 See *Wheeler v Horne* (1740) Willes 208 and *Nash v McKay* (1868) 15 Gr 247.

200 *Re Tolman's Estate* (1928) 23 Tas LR 29 and *Rees v Rees* [1931] SASR 78 both citing *Kennedy v De Trafford* [1897] AC 180.

will not be made unless he specifically assumed responsibility for managing the property. In *Osachuk v Osachuk*[201] the parties were co-owners of a house comprising two flats. The upstairs flat had been rented out on a number of occasions, while the plaintiff and the defendant occupied the downstairs flat. Following the plaintiff's departure, the defendant remained in the downstairs flat and the upstairs flat was unoccupied. Smith CJM held that the defendant was not accountable to the plaintiff for failing to rent out the upstairs flat, since the parties had not specifically agreed that the defendant would manage the property or find a tenant for the unoccupied flat. Such an obligation would not be imposed on the defendant simply because he was in occupation of the property and the upstairs flat had been rented out in the past[202].

E Related proceedings

1 Waste

[11.63] To what extent can one co-owner exploit the land without being accountable to the others for his actions? It is well established that joint tenants or tenants in common may bring an action for waste against another co-owner in certain circumstances[203]. If they wish to remain co-owners, the former might seek an injunction restraining further waste[204]. Failing this, co-owners might seek an injunction, or partition or sale of the property under the Partition Acts in the alternative[205]. An action of account may also be available where the co-owner committing waste is receiving more than his share of income from the property[206].

[11.64] A co-owner will not be liable in an action for waste unless the acts complained of tend towards destruction of the common property[207]. However, an injunction will not be granted in respect of waste occasioned by the defendant's

---

201 (1971) 18 DLR (3d) 413.

202 Since the plaintiff had not been excluded from the property, she could have brought prospective tenants to view the house if she had been keen to rent out the upstairs flat: *Osachuk v Osachuk* (1971) 18 DLR (3d) 413 at 432.

203 Notwithstanding the repeal of the Statute of Westminster II 1285 by the Civil Procedure Acts Repeal Act 1879, it appears that this did not affect the concurrent equitable jurisdiction in actions for waste exercised by the Court of Chancery: see Story, *Commentaries on Equity Jurisprudence* (10th edn, 1870), pp 515-519 and pp 524-528.

204 *Bailey v Hobson* (1869) 18 WR 124.

205 See for example, *Goodwyn v Spray* (1786) Dick 667 and *Gingles v Magill* [1926] NI 234.

206 See Mendes Da Costa, 'Co-Ownership Under Victorian Land Law' (1961) 3 Melb Univ L Rev 137 at 141 and the cases cited therein.

207 *Murray v Hall* (1849) 7 CB 441 and see *Arthur v Lamb* (1865) 2 Dr & S 428 in which it was held that wilful or malicious waste in the nature of destruction would be restrained by the court. See further *Hersey v Murphy* (1920) 48 NBR 65. Where such actions result in complete destruction of the property, this may be regarded as an ouster giving rise to a claim in trespass: see *Wilkinson v Haygarth* (1847) 12 QB 837 and *Jacobs v Seward* (1872) LR 5 HL 464.

normal use of the property[208], even though such actions might have amounted to waste if committed by a limited owner[209]. Thus a co-owner may develop and operate mines on the property since each joint tenant or tenant in common is entitled to exercise acts of ownership in respect of the property[210]. Likewise, cutting down trees does not usually amount to waste[211], and one co-owner may extend a shared means of access to the property without giving rise to such an action[212]. An act that would result in destruction of the common property if imitated by the other co-owners is not in itself an act of destruction and consequently cannot be restrained by an injunction[213].

[11.65] A co-owner may be restrained from committing waste where another joint tenant or tenant in common has commenced proceedings for partition or sale of the property[214]. Likewise, an injunction may be granted where one co-owner commits such acts on the property after an order has been made for partition or sale[215]. In *Bailey v Hobson*[216] Giffard LJ stated that the court may grant an injunction to restrain one of the parties from wasting the property or doing anything amounting to an alteration after a decree has been made in a partition action. An injunction is also available at any stage before partition or sale of the land has been completed[217].

---

208 2 *Bl Comm* 183 and Bewes, *The Law of Waste* (1894), p 263. As a general rule, the right to commit waste is regarded as a normal incident of co-ownership: see *Griffies v Griffies* (1863) 11 WR 943.

209 *Goodwyn v Spray* (1786) Dick 667. The fact that the co-owner in question is occupying the land as tenant of the other co-owners appears to be irrelevant in this context: Mendes Da Costa, 'Co-Ownership Under Victorian Land Law' (1961) 3 Melb Univ L Rev 137 at 141 citing the comments of Lord Kenyon CJ in *Martyn v Knowllys* (1799) 8 TR 145 at 146, but see *Twort v Twort* (1809) 16 Ves 128.

210 *Job v Potton* (1875) LR 20 Eq 84.

211 *Goodwyn v Spray* (1786) 2 Dick 667. However in *Hole v Thomas* (1802) 7 Ves 589 it was held that an injunction would be granted to prevent the cutting of immature timber, and see *Proudfoot v Bush* (1859) 7 Gr 518. In *Smallman v Onions* (1792) 3 Bro CC 621 the court granted an injunction to restrain the defendant from cutting trees on the grounds of his insolvency.

212 *Ferguson v Miller* [1978] 1 NZLR 819.

213 In *Gingles v Magill* [1926] NI 234 the fact that the defendant grazed his sheep on the common land during winter contrary to an agreement between the parties did not amount to destruction of the property, even though this result would have arisen had the other co-owners followed his example.

214 *Lassert v Salyerds* (1870) 17 Gr 109.

215 However, it appears that the court will only restrain destructive waste in these circumstances: Bewes, *The Law of Waste* (1894), p 266 citing *Wright v Atkyns* (1813) 1 V & B 313.

216 (1869) 18 WR 124.

217 *Hughes v D'Arcy* (1873) 8 I R Eq 71.

2 Adverse possession

[11.66] Although not strictly relevant to accounting adjustments between co-owners on partition or sale, the issue of adverse possession may arise in this context. One co-owner cannot usually assert a better claim to any part of the land than another co-owner[218]. However, a co-owner who has enjoyed exclusive possession of the common property or receipt of moneys may rely on the doctrine of adverse possession, even though he has not ousted his fellow co-owners[219]. If the occupant has succeeded in extinguishing the titles of the other co-owners and obtained a judgment to this effect, this precludes the other co-owners from bringing a partition action since the property is now that of the occupying co-owner[220]. However, the occupant must account to the other co-owners if, for example, he received more than his share of rents and profits from the land prior to extinguishing their respective titles[221]. If the occupant has instituted separate proceedings under the relevant Statute of Limitations the court might stay a subsequent partition action by the other co-owners, pending the outcome of the adverse possession issue.

[11.67] Alternatively, if the occupant claims that he has extinguished the titles of his fellow co-owners in the course of a partition action brought by them, the court might determine the adverse possession issue as part of the partition action[222]. However, if the occupant does not raise this issue during the partition

---

218 See *Reeves v Morris* (1840) 2 LR Ir 309.

219 As originally enacted by the Real Property Limitation Act 1833, s 12 (see para **[11.10]** above) and confirmed by the Limitation (NI) Order 1989, art 24 and the Statute of Limitations 1957, s 21. However, such possession must be adverse. An occupying co-owner who requests the others to contribute a proportionate amount towards rates and insurance on the property is not in adverse possession: *Webeck v Foley* (1992) 5 BPR 11,694. In *Gorman v Gorman* (6 April 1998, unreported) Ontario Court of Appeal, a wife opposed her husband's partition action on the basis that she had been residing in the family home since the parties separated in 1971 and had extinguished her husband's title. This was rejected by the court – the parties had tried to sell the property several times and the husband had raised the issue of his interest with the wife on several occasions. Where siblings inherit land as co-owners, the fact that one of them is in receipt of all rents and profits as administratrix of her father's estate and thus in a fiduciary capacity prevents her from relying on the Statute of Limitations as a defence to a partition action brought by the other co-owners: *Brown v Dooley* (1903) 36 NSR 56. Acts of leasing the property and collecting rents in these circumstances are not inconsistent with the rights of the other co-owners. As to the law of adverse possession in general see Jourdan, *Adverse Possession* (2000) and Brady and Kerr, *The Limitation of Actions in the Republic of Ireland* (2nd edn, 1994).

220 See the comments of Britton J in *Stroud v Sun Oil Co* (1904) 7 OLR 704 at 705. See further *Thornton v France* [1897] 2 QB 143; *Power v McBride* (1884) 1 QLJ 192; and *Corea v Appuhamy* [1912] AC 230.

221 *Isaryk v Isaryk* [1955] OWN 487.

222 See *Brown v Dooley* (1903) 36 NSR 56; *Shields v London and Western Trusts Co* [1924] SCR 25; and *Lehman v Hunter* (1939) 13 MPR 553.

action and fails to institute such proceedings until after the court has made an order for partition or sale, he may be prevented from asserting that the titles of the other co-owners have been extinguished even though the limitation period expired before the partition action was commenced. In these circumstances the adverse possession issue may be regarded as *res judicata* and thus should be raised during the partition action[223].

3 Trespass and nuisance

[11.68] One co-owner cannot usually maintain an action of trespass against another co-owner, since the parties are each entitled to possession of the entire property. However, an action of trespass may arise where one co-owner excludes another from the premises[224]. It appears that the mere fact of co-ownership does not prevent one co-owner from maintaining an action of nuisance against another co-owner provided that the relevant criteria are satisfied[225].

IV Overview of the Traditional Accounting Rules

[11.69] A partition action may include an application for an accounting adjustment to be made between the parties. The basic principles to be applied when making such an adjustment appear to be well established. However, these are complicated by numerous exceptions and by conflicting judicial dicta as to the manner in which the various rules should be applied and whether they should be modified to take account of modern exigencies. A number of issues have arisen.

[11.70] Most of the rules that apply in this context are derived from cases decided long ago. It could be argued that these rules are inadequate to deal with the modern realities of co-ownership, and in particular the increase in co-ownership of land (especially home ownership) as well as changing social conditions. For example, a co-owner who has enjoyed exclusive possession of the property cannot be charged with an occupation rent in the absence of an ouster or other circumstances that would render him accountable. This arguably fails to take account of the numerous reasons why one co-owner may leave the common property. Moreover, if the occupant has been meeting necessary expenses on the property, he will have a right to a contribution in respect of such expenditure but cannot be charged with an occupation rent[226]. Another issue that typically arises in relation to accounting adjustments on partition or sale is expenditure on voluntary repairs and improvements. In view of the limitation on

---

223 *Tolosnak v Tolosnak* [1957] OWN 273.

224 See para **[11.07]** above.

225 *Ferguson v Miller* [1978] 1 NZLR 819.

226 This may seem unfair since the occupant is doing all the receiving while the absent co-owners are doing all the paying.

the amount recoverable, such expenditure will not be reimbursed if it does not increase the value of the property. Alternatively, if a relatively small expenditure produces a large increase in value, the allowance made to the improving co-owner will be restricted to the former amount. Other problems that arise in this context are appropriate allowances for time and labour where repairs and improvements were carried out by one of the co-owners, and the issue of inflation where a period of time has elapsed between the expenditure and the partition action.

[11.71] It could be argued that some of the traditional rules are ill-equipped to deal with these issues. However, many of these rules flow from the nature of co-ownership itself. This highlights the danger of judges making general statements without proper consideration of the underlying rules and principles, and makes any reform of the law in this area difficult. Brereton[227] has remarked that:

> 'There is little doubt that the old rules are confusing and, in some respects, appear unjust ... It is questionable, however, whether this means that it is either appropriate or desirable to cast the old rules aside. Some of the rules concerning the rights between co-owners flow directly from the fundamental nature of co-ownership in English and Australian law. The rules cannot be rejected without also calling into question the very nature of co-ownership.'

[11.72] By virtue of the unity of possession, each joint tenant or tenant in common is entitled to use and occupy the entire property. To impose an occupation rent simply because one co-owner enjoys exclusive possession of the common property ignores this fundamental precept. If the other co-owners simply decline to exercise their right to occupy the property, they cannot make the occupant liable in this respect. Even if the occupant claims for necessary expenditure, this claim arises from a right to a contribution that is independent of proceedings for partition or sale. Again, by virtue of the unity of possession, co-owners cannot decline the benefit of voluntary repairs and improvements effected by another co-owner. However, the limitation inherent in the amount recoverable for such expenditure in partition actions usually ensures some compensation for the improving co-owner without forcing the other co-owners to make full compensation for something to which they did not consent.

[11.73] Any accounting adjustment inevitably involves a number of competing interests. For example, a co-owner who has been meeting all the expenses associated with the property will almost certainly want the other co-owners to contribute towards these, but will not usually want the others to share in any income that he may be receiving. Likewise, the non-contributing co-owners will almost certainly want to share in the income from the land, but may be reluctant

[227] Brereton, 'The Rights Between Co-owners of Land' (1995) 69 ALJ 316 at 318.

to contribute towards expenses. The law must strike a balance between these competing interests. It could be argued that the traditional rules achieve this to a large extent, apportioning liability between co-owners in an equitable manner and reconciling the conflicting interests within the confines of the law of co-ownership and the basic consequences that flow from this.

Chapter 12

Practice in Partition Actions in Northern Ireland and the Republic of Ireland

I Introduction

[12.01] This chapter considers a number of issues that are relevant to the practice in partition actions in Northern Ireland and the Republic of Ireland. A brief summary of the general procedures to be adopted in proceedings for compulsory partition or sale may be found in the current practitioners' texts[1]. More detailed accounts are contained in some of the older practitioners' texts dealing with the subject[2].

II Courts Having Jurisdiction

[12.02] Prior to 1868, the majority of partition actions were brought in and determined by the Court of Chancery. Section 2 of the Partition Act 1868 retained this practice[3]. Under the Judicature (Ir) Act 1877 all causes and matters relating to partition and sale of real estates were assigned to the Chancery

---

1 In Northern Ireland, the relevant texts are Valentine, *Civil Proceedings – The Supreme Court* (1997) and Valentine, *Civil Proceedings – The County Court* (1999) both of which provide a brief summary of the practice in partition actions at pp 435-436 and p 37 respectively. In the Republic of Ireland, the relevant texts are Deale, *Circuit Court Practice and Procedure* (2nd edn, 1994) and O'Floinn, *Practice and Procedure in the Superior Courts* (1997) both of which contain brief references to the Partition Acts 1868 and 1876 at pp 8-9, 144 and 301, and at pp 544 and 964 respectively.

2 See Carleton, *The Jurisdiction and Procedure of the County Courts in Ireland* (2nd edn, 1891), ch 37; Seton, *Forms of Judgments and Orders in the High Court of Justice and the Court of Appeal* (6th edn, 1901), ch 46; Osborne, *The Jurisdiction and Practice of the County Courts in Ireland in Equity and Probate Matters* (2nd edn, 1910), ch 9; and *Daniell's Chancery Practice* (8th edn, 1914), pp 1170-1189.

3 Partition Act 1868, s 2 specifically conferred jurisdiction on the Court of Chancery or the Landed Estates Court in Ireland. However, the Landed Estates Court could only order sale in situations where it formerly had jurisdiction to order partition (namely where partition was sought as incidental to sale of an undivided share of land and where co-owners agreed a scheme of partition: see ch 3 above, para **[3.01]**) and so long as the conditions in either of the Partition Act 1868, ss 3-5 were satisfied: see generally Madden, *The Law and Practice of the High Court of Justice in Ireland in Relation to Proceedings Before the Land Judge* (3rd edn, 1889), pp 101 and 301.

Division of the High Court of Justice[4]. In addition to this, County Courts in Ireland exercised a limited jurisdiction in partition actions at this time[5].

A Northern Ireland

[12.03] The Government of Ireland Act 1920 substituted the Chancery Division of the High Court of Justice in Northern Ireland as the court having jurisdiction under s 2 of the Partition Act 1868[6]. Notwithstanding the procedural reforms introduced by the Judicature (NI) Act 1978, all matters relating to the partition or sale of land in Northern Ireland today are still assigned to the Chancery Division and s 2 of the 1868 Act should be construed accordingly[7]. Actions will be determined by either the Chancery Master or the Chancery Judge[8]. This practice is not altered by the fact that a partition action is brought by a mortgagee[9] or by a trustee in bankruptcy[10] of an undivided share of land.

[12.04] County courts also may determine partition actions where the net annual value of the disputed land does not exceed £500[11]. The action may be brought in the county court for the district in which the land or any part thereof is situated[12], and will be determined by the county court judge for that particular area. Although agricultural land has no net annual value, an application may be made to the Valuation Office of the Department of the Environment for Northern Ireland for such a valuation to be made. The result will determine whether proceedings for partition or sale should be brought in the County Court or High Court.

4 Judicature (Ir) Act 1877, s 36(5). Although all matters pending in the Landed Estates Court were assigned to the Chancery Division (Judicature (Ir) Act 1877, s 36(3)), the Land Judges retained jurisdiction to determine partition actions which would previously have been brought in the Landed Estates Court: Judicature (Ir) Act 1877, s 7.

5 Partition Act 1868, s 12 only conferred jurisdiction on county courts in England where the value of the disputed land did not exceed £500. The several Civil Bill Courts in Ireland were granted the same power and authority as the High Court of Chancery (as superseded by the Chancery Division) in partition actions where the net annual value of the land in question did not exceed £30: County Courts and Officers (Ir) Act 1877, s 33(g). As to the practice in partition actions in the County Courts in Ireland during this time see 'Suits for Partition in the County Court' (1878) 12 ILTSJ 211 and 'Suits for Partition in the County Courts – II' (1878) 12 ILTSJ 236. See further Connor, *The Equity Practice: Rules and Forms of the County Courts (Ireland)* (1889), pp 108-110.

6 Government of Ireland Act 1920, s 41.

7 Judicature (NI) Act 1978, ss 16 and 122(1) and Sch 5, Pt I. This practice is confirmed by the Rules of the Supreme Court (NI) 1980, Ord 1, r 10.

8 Rules of the Supreme Court (NI) 1980, Ord 1, rr 14 and 15.

9 Rules of the Supreme Court (NI) 1980, Ord 10, r 1(a)(v) and see further Ord 88.

10 Rules of the Supreme Court (NI) 1980, Ord 10, r 1(b).

11 County Courts (NI) Order 1980, art 14(g).

12 County Court Rules (NI) 1981, Ord 1, r 2.

B Republic of Ireland

[12.05] Under the Government of Ireland Act 1920, the Chancery Division of the High Court of Justice in Southern Ireland was substituted as the court having jurisdiction under s 2 of the 1868 Act[13]. Following fundamental changes to the court system introduced by the Constitution of the Irish Free State (Saorstat Eireann) Act 1922 and the Courts of Justice Act 1924[14], the newly established High Court assumed jurisdiction in partition actions[15]. Since 1924 there have been no formal divisions of the High Court, so that a partition action may be assigned to any judge of the High Court. However, in practice it appears that there is an informal division of business similar to that imposed by the Judicature (Ir) Act 1877[16], so that a partition action is likely to be determined by the judge to whom Chancery matters are regularly assigned.

[12.06] In addition to this, Circuit Courts may determine partition actions where the rateable valuation of the subject-land does not exceed £200[17]. The action may be brought in the court for the Circuit in which the land or any part thereof is situated, and will be determined by the relevant Circuit Court judge[18].

III Necessary Parties

A General Requirements

[12.07] The plaintiff must have a legal or equitable estate or interest in possession in the disputed property[19], while all persons having an interest in the property must usually be parties to the action[20]. The persons in whom the legal estate is vested should be before the court in order for them to be bound by the

13 Government of Ireland Act 1920, s 41.

14 See Byrne and McCutcheon, *The Irish Legal System* (3rd edn, 1996), pp 40-44.

15 The High Court assumed the jurisdiction formerly exercised by the High Court of Justice of Southern Ireland under the Government of Ireland Act 1920: Courts of Justice Act 1924, s 17. Subsequent legislation such as the Constitution of Ireland Act 1937 and the ensuing Courts (Establishment and Constitution) Act 1961 and the Courts (Supplemental Provisions) Act 1961 has retained the principal elements of the 1924 system: see generally Byrne and McCutcheon, *The Irish Legal System* (3rd edn, 1996) ch 4 and Delaney, *The Courts Acts 1924-1991* (1994). The relevant Rules of Court are contained in the Rules of the Superior Courts (RI) 1986.

16 Byrne and McCutcheon, *The Irish Legal System* (3rd edn, 1996), pp 45-46.

17 Courts (Supplemental Provisions) Act 1961, s 22 and Sch 3, Ref No 23 as amended by the Courts Act 1971, ss 2(1)(d) and 25(4) and by the Courts Act 1981, ss 2(1)(d) and 33(3).

18 Courts (Supplemental Provisions) Act 1961, Sch 3, Ref No 23 and the Circuit Court Rules (RI) 1950, Ord 2.

19 See ch 4 above, paras **[4.03]**-**[4.24]**.

20 Osborne, *The Jurisdiction and Practice of the County Courts in Ireland in Equity and Probate Matters* (2nd edn, 1910), p 195 and *Daniell's Chancery Practice* (8th edn, 1914), p 1172. Partition Act 1868, s 9 retained the pre-1868 rules relating to parties to a partition action: see ch 5 above, para **[5.03]**.

judgment[21] and to facilitate the execution of the requisite conveyances on partition or sale[22]. Thus a mortgagee of an undivided share must be joined as a party[23], as must a lessee of an undivided share[24]. Where the subject matter of the partition action is trust property[25], the trustees sufficiently represent the beneficiaries[26]. A third party with rights over the entire property need not be made a party to the action, since he will not be affected by an order for partition or sale[27]. Thus, a mortgagee of the entirety is not a necessary party[28].

B Special provisions

[12.08] The Partition Acts contain special provisions designed to overcome difficulties which may arise if there are a substantial number of persons interested in the property and/or there are difficulties in making any such persons parties to the action[29]. This typically occurs where one of the co-owners is out of the jurisdiction or is not yet in existence (whether because an unborn child or because it is not yet certain who will become entitled to an interest in the property). The latter scenario may arise where co-owners of an estate for life or a term of years desire a permanent partition or sale of the property[30]. In these circumstances, problems arise in respect of persons entitled under a limitation to a class[31] or as being the heirs of a living person[32].

1 Section 9 of the Partition Act 1868

[12.09] All of the persons interested in the property need not be joined as defendants. Section 9 of the 1868 Act provides that a partition action will be properly constituted if one or more such persons is named as defendant[33], so

---

21 *Daniell's Chancery Practice* (8th edn, 1914), pp 151 and 1172.

22 Walker, *The Partition Acts, 1868 and 1876* (1882), p 11 and Osborne, *The Jurisdiction and Practice of the County Courts in Ireland in Equity and Probate Matters* (2nd edn, 1910), p 196.

23 *Gibbs v Haydon* (1882) 30 WR 726.

24 *Cornish v Gest* (1788) 2 Cox 27 and *Mason v Keays* (1898) 78 LT 33. See further *Monro v Toronto Railway* (1903) 5 OLR 483.

25 Assuming it does not come within the jurisdiction exception discussed at ch 4 above, paras **[4.40]-[4.41]**.

26 See *Stace v Gage* (1878) 8 Ch D 451; *Simpson v Denny* (1878) 10 Ch D 28; and *Furner v Furner* (1903) 3 SR (NSW) 576. See further *Daniell's Chancery Practice* (8th edn, 1914), p 1172 and Osborne, *The Jurisdiction and Practice of the County Courts in Ireland in Equity and Probate Matters* (2nd edn, 1910), p 196.

27 See ch 4 above, paras **[4.61]-[4.67]**. See further *Daniell's Chancery Practice* (8th edn, 1914), p 1172.

28 *Sinclair v James* [1894] 3 Ch 554.

29 See generally Walker, *The Partition Acts, 1868 and 1876* (1882), pp 50-65.

30 See ch 4 above, para **[4.29]**.

31 *Lees v Coulton* (1875) LR 20 Eq 20.

32 *Basnett v Moxon* (1875) LR 20 Eq 182.

33 See for example, *Mason v Keays* (1898) 78 LT 33 and *Eagles v Eagles* [1960] VR 400. See further Osborne, *The Jurisdiction and Practice of the County Courts in Ireland in Equity and Probate Matters* (2nd edn, 1910), pp 195-196.

long as he is a necessary party to the action[34]. At the hearing of the action, the court may direct such inquiries as to the nature of the property and the persons interested therein as it thinks fit with a view to an order for partition or sale being made on further consideration[35]. However, s 9 further provides that any person interested in the property who has not been joined as defendant must be served with notice of the decree or order on the hearing and will then be bound as if he had been a party to the action.

2 Section 3 of the Partition 1876

[12.10] Initially, the court could not dispense with service of notice under s 9[36], except where the person in question was presumed dead[37]. This practice was subsequently altered by s 3 of the Partition Act 1876. Section 3 allows the court to dispense with service of notice where service is impossible or involves 'expense disproportionate to the value of the property to which the action relates'. The court can make such an order at the request of any person interested in the property, and notwithstanding the dissent or disability of any of the other co-owners. However, the court must then direct the publication of advertisements calling on those persons who were not served with notice of the order to establish their claims in Chambers within a specified time. The court cannot dispense with both service of notice and publication of advertisements – it must order one or the other[38]. Once the relevant date has passed the court may order sale of the property, and any such persons who have not come forward will be bound by the proceedings in the same manner as if they had been parties to the action.

(a) Order for sale only

[12.11] It appears that an order for sale is the only option available to the court in these circumstances[39]. Section 3 provides that, having dispensed with service and given such persons an opportunity to come forward, the court may 'direct a sale of the property and give all necessary or proper consequential directions'.

---

34 Partition Act 1868, s 9 does not apply where the only other party to the action is an unnecessary party (such as a mortgagee of the entirety) who could be dismissed upon an appropriate application: *Eagles v Eagles* [1960] VR 400.

35 See para **[12.31]** below.

36 Problems typically arose where a co-owner was out of the jurisdiction: see *Hurry v Hurry* (1870) LR 10 Eq 346; *Peters v Bacon* (1869) LR 8 Eq 125; and *Teall v Watts* (1871) LR 11 Eq 213.

37 *Jackson v Lomas* (1875) 23 WR 744 and *Rawlinson v Miller* (1875) 1 Ch D 52. See further *Drew v Drew* (1923) 40 WN (NSW) 128.

38 Seton, *Forms of Judgments and Orders in the High Court of Justice and the Court of Appeal* (6th edn, 1901), p 1878 and see *Hacking v Whalley* [1882] WN 135.

39 The wording of the Partition Act 1876, s 3 (as well as the Partition Act 1876, ss 4 and 5) only seems to contemplate an order for sale; there is no reference to the court making an order for partition: 21 *Halsbury's Laws of England* (1st edn, 1912), p 853.

An absent party might subsequently come forward and claim his share of the proceeds of sale as contemplated by ss 4 and 5 of the 1876 Act[40]. In practical terms, it is easier to redistribute the proceeds of sale between the respective parties here than to alter a scheme of partition and re-allocate the divided parcels of land accordingly.

(b) Vesting orders

[12.12] The court may make a vesting order, vesting the share of the absent party in a court-appointed trustee in order to facilitate sale of the land and execution of the requisite conveyances[41]. As originally enacted, s 3 of the 1876 Act referred to the court exercising such jurisdiction under the Trustee Act 1850[42]. Section 30 of the 1850 Act was replaced by s 31 of the Trustee Act 1893. Thereafter, the provisions of the Trustee Act 1893 were substituted into s 3 of the Partition Act 1876. While the jurisdiction to make vesting orders in the Republic of Ireland is still conferred by the 1893 Act, the relevant provisions in Northern Ireland are now contained in s 48 of the Trustee Act (NI) 1958[43] and s 3 of the 1876 Act should be construed accordingly.

[12.13] Independently of the provisions of the respective Trustee Acts, a decree for sale binds the interests of all persons who are not parties to the action, either because they are out of the jurisdiction or not in existence[44]. The legislation facilitates the transfer of the legal estate in these circumstances.

3 Sections 4 and 5 of the Partition Act 1876

[12.14] These provisions come into effect where the court orders sale having dispensed with service of notice under s 3. Sections 4(1) and (2) provide that the proceeds of sale should be paid into court and a date fixed for their distribution[45]. Section 4(3) continues:

> 'The Court shall direct such notices to be given by advertisements or otherwise as it thinks best adapted for notifying to any persons on whom service is dispensed with, who may not have previously come in and established their claims, the fact of the sale, the time of the intended distribution and the time within which a claim to participate in the proceeds must be made ...'[46]

---

40 See paras **[12.14]**-**[12.17]** below.

41 Thus, vesting orders may be made in respect of the interests of persons who are out of the jurisdiction (see *Beckett v Sutton* (1882) 19 Ch D 646 and *Caswell v Sheen* (1893) 69 LT 854) or who are not yet in existence (see the cases noted at para **[12.08]** above).

42 Trustee Act 1850, s 30 was considered in ch 3 above, para **[3.29]**.

43 See generally Carswell, *Trustee Acts (Northern Ireland)* (1964).

44 *Gaskell v Gaskell* (1836) 6 Sim 643 and *Basnett v Moxon* (1875) LR 20 Eq 182.

45 The court may extend this time by further order: Partition Act 1876, s 4(2).

46 See *In the Matter of Softwood Plantations Pty Ltd* (17 October 1995, unreported) Supreme Court of the Northern Territory of Australia. The use of the word 'shall' means that such advertisements are mandatory and cannot be dispensed with by the court: *Phillips v Andrews* (1887) 56 LT 108.

[12.15] Thus where an absent party fails to establish his claim in accordance with s 3, s 4 gives him a further opportunity to participate in the proceeds of sale. If he comes forward within the prescribed time so that the interests of all persons interested in the property are ascertainable, s 4(4) states that the proceeds of sale should be distributed accordingly.

[12.16] However, if the absent party fails to come forward and the court is of the opinion that the respective interests in the property 'cannot be ascertained, or cannot be ascertained without expense disproportionate to the value of the property or of the unascertained interests', s 4(5) comes into effect. In this event, the court must distribute the proceeds of sale in accordance with the rights of those persons whose claims are established, irrespective of whether they are before the court[47]. Although any person who has failed to establish his interest in the property will not receive a share of the proceeds of sale as distributed by the court, s 4(5) provides that an 'excluded person' may recover his share of the proceeds from any other person who has participated in the proceeds of sale.

[12.17] In addition to this, s 5 of the 1876 Act provides that where two or more sales are made in a partition action[48] and an 'excluded person' establishes a claim to participate in the proceeds of a subsequent sale, then the shares of all the other persons interested shall abate to the extent (if any) to which they were increased by the former's non-participation in the previous sale. These sums represent the share that the excluded person would have been entitled to had his interest in the proceeds of the previous sale been established within the stated time[49].

[12.18] To summarise, all of the persons interested in the property should be joined as parties to a partition action, unless they are served with notice under s 9 of the 1868 Act, or the court dispenses with service under s 3 of the 1876 Act[50], or the person in question is presumed dead. An order for partition or sale will not be made unless the court is satisfied that all persons interested are parties[51] or have been served with notice of the judgment[52], or that service has

---

47 Under the Partition Act 1876, s 4(5), the court also has a discretion to make such reservations as it considers appropriate in favour of other persons (whether ascertained or not) who appear, on the evidence before the court, to have *prima facie* rights in the proceeds which should be provided for.

48 For example, where sale of the property takes place in lots.

49 See Charley, *The Real Property Acts 1874, 1875 and 1876* (3rd edn, 1876), p 368.

50 See further the Rules of the Supreme Court (NI) 1980, Ord 44, r 2 and the County Court Rules (NI) 1981, Ord 34, r 6; the Rules of the Superior Courts (RI) 1986, Ord 10 and the Circuit Court Rules (RI) 1950, Ord 6, rr 13-14 and Ord 10, r 9.

51 See *Dodds v Gronow* (1869) 17 WR 511.

52 See *Peters v Bacon* (1869) LR 8 Eq 125; *Hurry v Hurry* (1870) LR 10 Eq 346; and *Teall v Watts* (1871) LR 11 Eq 213.

been dispensed with[53]. If the court dispenses with service under s 3 and orders sale of the property, ss 4 and 5 of the 1876 Act come into effect.

IV Persons under Disability

[12.19] Special rules apply where one of the parties to a partition action is an infant[54] or a person of unsound mind[55]. Section 6 of the Partition Act 1876 provides that a request for sale or an undertaking to purchase[56] may be made on behalf of an infant, person of unsound mind or person under any other disability by the persons authorised to act on his behalf[57]. Where such a request is made on behalf of an infant, s 6 states that the court is not bound to comply unless it is satisfied that the sale or purchase will be for his benefit[58].

[12.20] In both Northern Ireland and the Republic of Ireland, specific persons are appointed to act on behalf of an infant or person of unsound mind[59]. As regards the former, a next friend may bring a partition action on behalf of an infant, while an infant may defend such proceedings by his guardian *ad litem*[60]. Alternatively, if co-owners wish to partition or sell by agreement and one of

---

53 See *Phillips v Andrews* (1887) 56 LT 108.

54 Namely, a person under 18 years of age: Age of Majority Act (NI) 1968, ss 1(1) and 5(1), and the Age of Majority Act 1985, ss 2(1) and 4(1).

55 Prior to 1882, special rules also applied in respect of married women: see ch 3 above, para **[3.35]**. However, the Married Women's Property Act 1882 provided that a married woman could hold and dispose of her property as if she were unmarried: see Ullrich, 'The Reform of Matrimonial Property Law in England During the Nineteenth Century' (1977) 9 Victoria University of Wellington L Rev 13. This enabled married women to make conveyances of property in their own right: see *Broad v Askam* [1909] WN 236 and *Barrett v Watts* [1909] WN 237. Today there are no restrictions on ownership and disposal of property by married women: Law Reform (Husband and Wife) Act (NI) 1964 and Married Women's Status Act 1957.

56 Under the Partition Act 1868, s 5.

57 Prior to this, a number of cases had doubted whether persons under disability could request sale or give an undertaking to purchase under the Partition Act 1868: see for example, *France v France* (1871) LR 13 Eq 173; *Chubb v Petipher* [1872] WN 110; and *Grove v Comyn* (1874) LR 18 Eq 387. Such doubts were resolved by the Partition Act 1876, s 6: see *Watt v Leach* (1878) 26 WR 475; *Grange v White* (1881) 18 Ch D 612; and *Platt v Platt* (1880) 28 WR 533.

58 See *Rimington v Hartley* (1880) 14 Ch D 630 and *Hopkinson v Richardson* (1913) 1 Ch 284. This restriction does not apply to persons of unsound mind: *Wallace v Greenwood* (1880) 16 Ch D 362.

59 Although a number of cases cited in ch 3 above, para **[3.35]** referred to the court making a vesting order under the Trustee Act 1850, s 30 on behalf of infants and persons of unsound mind, it is suggested that this is unlikely to happen today. The relevant legislation and rules of court in both jurisdictions prescribe specific persons to act on behalf of infants and persons of unsound mind, and to execute any necessary conveyances.

60 County Court Rules (NI) 1981, Ord 3, r 11 and the Rules of the Supreme Court (NI) 1980, Ord 80, r 2; the Circuit Court Rules (RI) 1950, Ord 6, rr 5-6 and the Rules of the Superior Courts (RI) 1986, Ord 15, r 16. See *Rimington v Hartley* (1880) 14 Ch D 630.

them is an infant, he may be represented by trustees of the settlement. Section 59 of the Settled Land Act 1882 provides that, for the purposes of the 1882 Act, land held by a minor is deemed to be settled land and the infant tenant for life thereof. In these circumstances, the powers conferred by the Settled Land Acts may be exercised by the trustees of the settlement[61]. These include powers to partition and to sell land[62].

[12.21] As regards persons of unsound mind, the High Court in Northern Ireland may appoint a 'controller' with powers over the patient's property under the Mental Health (NI) Order 1986[63]. These include making orders for 'the sale ... or other disposition of or dealing with any property of the patient'[64], where this is required for the maintenance and care of the patient, or the maintenance of his family[65]. Accordingly, a controller may enter into an agreement to partition or sell land on behalf of a co-owner who is of unsound mind, or represent that person in proceedings under the Partition Acts. In the Republic of Ireland, the President of the High Court has jurisdiction over the property of persons of unsound mind under the Lunacy Regulation (Ir) Act 1871[66]. A person of unsound mind may be made a ward of court and placed under the care of a 'committee' that has control over his property. Section 74 of the 1871 Act provides that the committee may concur with the other co-owners to make partition or sale of the lands and execute any necessary conveyances, provided that it appears to the High Court that such partition or sale is expedient and for the benefit of the person of unsound mind[67]. A person of unsound mind may also be represented by his committee in proceedings for compulsory partition or sale.

61 Settled Land Act 1882, s 60.

62 Settled Land Act 1882, s 3 and see ch 2 above, paras **[2.23]-[2.25]**. However, in a partition action the Settled Land Acts are not relevant and the infant will act by his next friend or guardian *ad litem* as appropriate.

63 The reference to a 'committee' in the Partition Act 1876, s 6 should accordingly be construed as referring to a 'controller' appointed under the Mental Health (NI) Order 1986, art 101: Mental Health (NI) Order 1986, art 136.

64 Mental Health (NI) Order 1986, art 99(1)(b).

65 Mental Health (NI) Order 1986, art 98(2). However, the primary consideration in these cases is the patient's requirements: Mental Health (NI) Order 1986, art 98(2).

66 Courts of Justice Act 1936 and Courts (Supplemental Provisions) Act 1961, and see Delaney, *The Courts Acts 1924-1991* (1994), pp 147-149. Courts (Supplemental Provisions) Act 1961, s 9(3) substitutes the High Court for all references to the Lord Chancellor in the Lunacy Regulation (Ir) Act 1871.

67 The committee may also give or receive any money necessary for equality of partition: Lunacy Regulation (Ir) Act 1871, s 74.

V Form of Pleadings

[12.22] In Northern Ireland, proceedings for partition or sale of land in the High Court are commenced by originating summons[68], while those in the County Courts are commenced by equity civil bill[69]. In the Republic of Ireland, proceedings in the High Court are commenced by originating summons[70], while those in the Circuit Courts are commenced by equity civil bill[71].

A Title of proceedings

[12.23] The proceedings are usually entitled 'In the Matter of the Partition Acts 1868 and 1876'[72]. Since An Act for Jointenants 1542 has been repealed[73], applications for partition should not be based on this Act[74].

B Matters alleged by the plaintiff

[12.24] A number of matters are typically alleged by the plaintiff in the relevant summons or equity civil bill, or in the supporting affidavits.

1 Net annual value/ rateable value

[12.25] Where proceedings are brought in the county courts the equity civil bill should contain a declaration that the net annual value of the land does not exceed £500[75]. Where proceedings are commenced in the Circuit Courts, the equity civil bill should declare that the rateable valuation of the land does not exceed £200[76].

---

68 Rules of the Supreme Court (NI) 1980, Ord 5, r 3 which states that proceedings which must be begun by originating summons are those in which an application is made under any statutory provision. However the Rules of the Supreme Court (NI) 1980, Ord 5, r 4 lists a number of proceedings which may be begun by writ or by originating summons, including proceedings in which there is a substantial dispute of fact. In the Australian case of *Martin-Smith v Woodhead* [1990] WAR 62 at 65, Kennedy J suggested that the originating summons procedure was inappropriate in partition actions where disputes of fact were likely to arise and that such proceedings should be instituted by writ.

69 County Court Rules (NI) 1981, Ord 5, r 1(4). For the appropriate form of equity civil bill in partition actions, see the County Court Rules (NI) 1981, Form 31.

70 Rules of the Superior Courts (RI) 1986, Ord 1. If a mortgagee seeks sale or delivery of possession of property used as security, the proceedings must be commenced by way of 'special summons': Rules of the Superior Courts (RI) 1986, Ord 3(15).

71 Circuit Court Rules (RI) 1950, Ord 5, rr 1-2.

72 Although a number of cases have erroneously referred to 'the Partition Acts 1868 to 1876': see for example, *Northern Bank Ltd v Bell* (9 May 1988, unreported) High Court (NI) and *Blackhall v Blackhall* (18 February 1994, unreported) Supreme Court (RI).

73 See ch 6 above.

74 *O'D v O'D* (November 1983, unreported) High Court (RI).

75 County Court Rules (NI) 1981, Form 31.

76 Circuit Court Rules (RI) 1950, Ord 5, r 2.

2 *Description of the land and remedy sought*

[12.26] The pleadings should contain a general description of the land comprising the subject-matter of the action, and state whether the plaintiff seeks sale of the land and distribution of the proceeds, or partition. It is not uncommon for the plaintiff to seek an order for sale or partition in the alternative, even if he only wants sale[77]. Likewise, where the plaintiff only wants partition, he may nevertheless seek an order for sale in the alternative[78], unless all the co-owners have agreed that partition of the land is desirable but cannot agree on the manner in which this should be carried out[79].

[12.27] The pleadings should identify the particular section of the 1868 Act under which the plaintiff is proceeding, and contain an averment of the matters specified in that section[80]. Accordingly, where the plaintiff brings an action under s 3, he should allege that sale would be more beneficial for all the persons interested in the property than partition for one or more of the reasons specified therein[81]. Where the action is brought under s 4, the plaintiff should specify that he is interested in a moiety or more of the property and desires sale. There is little authority on the form of pleadings to be adopted under s 5 since it is seldom relied on in practice. By analogy to the practice under ss 3 and 4, it may be assumed that the pleadings should allege some reason why sale should be granted instead of partition (this reason not coming within s 3)[82]. If the plaintiff is entitled to less than half of the property but does not specify that he is proceeding under s 3, the court may treat the action as coming within s 5. It will not simply infer that sale would be more beneficial than partition in accordance with s 3 from the description of the property[83].

---

77 See *Northern Bank Ltd v Moore* (4 June 1991, unreported) High Court (NI); *Northern Bank Ltd v Haggerty* [1995] NI 211; and *Glass v McManus* [1996] NI 401. See further *O'D v O'D* (18 November 1983, unreported) High Court (RI).

78 See *Warwick v Warwick* (21 January 1992, unreported) High Court (NI).

79 See *O'Brien & Cronin Ltd v Dillon* (2 February 1977, unreported) High Court (RI).

80 *Evans v Evans* (1883) 31 WR 495 and *Northern Bank v Adams* (1 February 1996, unreported) High Court (NI).

81 The court may declare that sale is more beneficial than partition for all of the persons interested if it is proved at the hearing that they are all parties to the action or before the court: see *Chubb v Petipher* [1872] WN 110; *Re Hardiman* (1880) 16 Ch D 360; and *Willis v Willis* (1889) 61 LT 610. Failing this, the court may direct an inquiry as to whether it is more beneficial for the persons interested to have sale instead of partition: see *Powell v Powell* (1874) 10 Ch App Cas 131 and *Waite v Bingley* (1882) 21 Ch D 674.

82 Since according to *Richardson v Feary* (1888) 39 Ch D 45 the plaintiff must show some reason why the court should order sale under the Partition Act 1868, s 5: see ch 5 above, para **[5.57]**.

83 *Evans v Evans* (1883) 31 WR 495.

3 Standing and interest; ascertainable shares

[12.28] The plaintiff must specify his standing and the interest in the property that gives him a right to apply under the Partition Acts[84]. He must allege his own title with precision[85], but does not have to show a complete title in the defendants – it is sufficient that they are shown to be persons interested in the property[86]. The plaintiff's title should, if not admitted, be clearly proved[87].

[12.29] The court cannot make an order for partition or sale unless it is satisfied that the shares of all the co-owners are ascertainable[88]. For example, if the number of persons interested in the land is uncertain, the court cannot make an appropriate division of the land or proceeds of sale[89]. However, the fact that unascertained persons may become entitled to a specific share of the land is irrelevant in this context[90]. This might occur where an undivided share of land is held by a tenant for life with remainder to his unborn children, and the former brings a partition action[91]. In these circumstances, the court has jurisdiction to determine the action. It only has to know how many persons are interested in the limited interest in order to make an order for sale[92] and to distribute the proceeds among the ascertained parties. Any persons not yet in existence may be able to claim a share of the proceeds at a later date[93].

---

84 Valentine, *Civil Proceedings – The Supreme Court* (1997), p 435.

85 See Osborne, *The Jurisdiction and Practice of the County Courts in Ireland in Equity and Probate Matters* (2nd edn, 1910), p 203 and *Daniell's Chancery Practice* (8th edn, 1914), p 1172. The title alleged must show that each of the several co-owners is entitled to an undivided interest in the land and that their respective shares are ascertainable: 21 *Halsbury's Laws of England* (1st edn, 1912), pp 846-847 citing *Miller v Warmington* (1830) 1 Jac & W 484 and *Miles v Jarvis (No 2)* (1883) 50 LT 48.

86 See 21 *Halsbury's Laws of England* (1st edn, 1912), pp 846-847 and the cases cited therein, and Osborne, *The Jurisdiction and Practice of the County Courts in Ireland in Equity and Probate Matters* (2nd edn, 1910), p 203.

87 Osborne, *The Jurisdiction and Practice of the County Courts in Ireland in Equity and Probate Matters* (2nd edn, 1910), p 203 and *Daniell's Chancery Practice* (8th edn, 1914), p 1172 both citing *Giffard v Williams* (1869) LR 8 Eq 494. See further *Hawkins v Herbert* (1889) 37 WR 300.

88 Since the court does not have jurisdiction to determine a partition action unless the parties are interested in ascertainable shares: see ch 4 above, paras **[4.68]-[4.69]**.

89 *Miles v Jarvis* [1883] WN 203 noted at ch 4 above, para **[4.68]**.

90 21 *Halsbury's Laws of England* (1st edn, 1912), p 842 citing *Wills v Slade* (1801) 6 Ves 498 and *Gaskell v Gaskell* (1836) 6 Sim 643.

91 *Gaskell v Gaskell* (1836) 6 Sim 643.

92 Since the Partition Act 1876, s 3 only seems to contemplate sale in these circumstances.

93 Partition Act 1876, s 4(5).

VI Hearing of the Action

[12.30] The various issues raised by the parties are determined at the hearing of the action and the court will then decide whether to order partition or sale of the property. If the defendant gives an undertaking to purchase the plaintiff's share under s 5 of the 1868 Act, this must be given at the hearing[94]. In addition to this, if any of the co-owners object to sale, these objections must be raised at the hearing or on further consideration of the action; they cannot be raised after directions for sale have been made[95]. The court may, however, amend the order before sale[96]. Where the consent of a third party is necessary before the court can make an order for partition[97], this consent must be produced at the hearing[98].

[12.31] An order for partition or sale should not be made at the hearing unless all the persons interested in the property are before the court and title is proved[99]. Otherwise, the provisions of s 9 of the 1868 Act and s 3 of the 1876 Act apply[100]. Accordingly, where all of the parties interested are not present at the hearing, the court may direct inquires as to the nature of the property, the persons interested therein and any other matters it thinks necessary or proper 'with a view to an order for partition or sale being made on further consideration'[101]. An order for

94 *Drinkwater v Ratcliffe* (1875) LR 20 Eq 528.

95 *Harper v Bird* (1875) 23 WR 646.

96 *Re Martin's Estate* (1879) 3 LR Ir 255.

97 See ch 7 above.

98 See Osborne, *The Jurisdiction and Practice of the County Courts in Ireland in Equity and Probate Matters* (2nd edn, 1910), pp 655-656 and Carleton, *The Jurisdiction and Procedure of the County Courts in Ireland* (2nd edn, 1891), p 1292.

99 Walker, *The Partition Acts, 1868 and 1876* (1882), pp 51-52 and Seton, *Forms of Judgments and Orders in the High Court of Justice and the Court of Appeal* (6th edn, 1901), p 1878. See further *Mildmay v Quicke* (1875) LR 20 Eq 537; *Burnell v Burnell* (1879) 11 Ch D 213; *Gilbert v Smith* (1879) 11 Ch D 78; *Re Stedman* (1888) 58 LT 709; and *McLean v Hodges* (1885) 6 LR (NSW) Eq 61. However, in *Wood v Gregory* (1890) 43 Ch D 82 North J held that a sale could only be ordered at the hearing where all the persons interested were before the court, title to the property was simple and the property itself was of small value. Similar views were expressed in *Goodacre v Goodacre* [1888] WN 138 and *Hawkins v Herbert* (1889) 37 WR 300.

100 See paras **[12.09]-[12.13]** above.

101 Partition Act 1868, s 9. Initially it was held that, where inquiries had been directed under s 9, the court should not order sale at the same time but should postpone such an order until the result of the inquiries had been certified: *Buckingham v Sellick* (1870) 22 LT 370 and *Harper v Bird* (1875) 23 WR 646. However, the practice subsequently developed whereby the court would direct sale subject to the result of the inquiries: see *Senior v Hereford* (1874) 4 Ch D 494; *Waite v Bingley* (1882) 21 Ch D 674; and *Davis v Ingram* [1897] 1 Ch 477. As to the meaning of 'on further consideration', it was held in *Mildmay v Quicke* (1875) LR 20 Eq 537 and *Powell v Powell* (1874) 10 Ch App Cas 131 that these words should not be construed in a strictly technical sense, but as referring to any consideration which the matter receives after inquires have been made.

partition or sale should not be made at any stage of the proceedings unless every person interested in the land is bound by the order, either by being made a party to the action, or being served with notice of the judgment under s 9 of the 1868 Act or an order is made dispensing with service under s 3 of the 1876 Act[102]. Where an order for sale is made dependent on the result of inquiries and sale takes place before the certificate is made, the purchaser may be discharged from the contract of sale[103]. However, if all the persons interested in the land are before the court at the hearing and a good title can be made independently of the 1868 Act, the purchaser may have to accept this title and may not be able to rely on the technical informality of the decree[104].

[12.32] Where there is a dispute over the title to the lands as alleged by the plaintiff, this may be determined by the court at the hearing of the partition action[105]. Likewise, where a dispute arises as to the ownership of the land, this may also be determined in the partition action, so long as the dispute does not involve a third party[106]. Such disputes may arise where one party claims an interest in the property on the principles of resulting or constructive trusts or claims to be sole owner of the property under the doctrine of adverse possession, and must be determined before the court makes an order for partition or sale[107].

[12.33] In practical terms the court is faced with a difficult task when asked to partition property, and may employ the services of an independent surveyor or valuer to carry out this task[108]. Alternatively, if the parties have carried out their

102 Although under the Partition Act 1876, s 3, the legislation only seems to contemplate an order for sale being made in these circumstances: see para **[12.11]** above.

103 *Powell v Powell* (1874) 10 Ch App Cas 131 and *McLean v Hodges* (1885) 6 LR (NSW) Eq 61.

104 *Rawlinson v Miller* (1875) 1 Ch D 52.

105 The original provision to this effect was contained in the Judicature Act (Ir) 1877, s 27(7). As to the relevant provisions today, see the Judicature (NI) Act 1978, s 86(2) and the Courts (Supplemental Provisions) Act 1961, s 8.

106 Where the issues raised involve a third party, then it is likely that the partition action will be adjourned pending resolution of the dispute as to ownership.

107 See for example, *Northern Bank Ltd v Beattie* [1982] 18 NIJB 1 and *ND v AD* (10 December 1982, unreported) High Court (RI). See further *Kulczycki v Kulczycki* [1949] OWN 177; *Hicks v Kennedy* (1956) 4 DLR (2d) 320; *Tolosnak v Tolosnak* [1957] OWN 273; *Re Garnet and McGoran* (1980) 30 OR (2d) 742; and *Croghan v Grosvenor* (1991) 57 SASR 545. In *Ames v Bond* (1992) 39 RFL (3d) 375 the court refused to order sale where one of the parties made a claim for sole ownership of the property which was sufficient to raise a genuine issue for trial. Likewise, in *Blackhall v Jardine* [1958] OWN 457 it was held that any dispute as to ownership of land should be settled before partition is ordered, and the matter tried by the court and not the Master.

108 See for example, the County Court Rules (NI) 1981, Ord 36, r 4. Alternatively, if the land has been subject to an informal division for some years, the court may order partition on those terms: *Warwick v Warwick* (21 January 1992, unreported) High Court (NI).

own valuations, the court may endorse one of these provided there are no substantial differences in the two valuations. Where such differences do arise, the court may employ the services of an independent valuer and confirm the division proposed by him[109].

VII Form of Order

[12.34] In the majority of partition actions, it is likely that the court will order the property to be sold and the proceeds of sale distributed among the parties in accordance with their respective interests in property[110]. However, the court may order partition if neither party desires sale[111], or if a case for ordering sale has not been made out[112]. In dividing the land, the court may consider the personal circumstances of the parties – for example, the fact that one co-owner owns other land adjacent to one of the divided parcels or occupies a home or business on a particular area of the land[113]. Payment of an appropriate sum of money as equality of partition may be required to address any imbalance in the divided parcels of land[114]. Alternatively, the court may order partition of part of the property and sale of the rest[115], or allot a parcel of land to the co-owner who seeks partition while the others remain as joint tenants or tenants in common[116].

---

[109] See for example, *McLaughlin v McLaughlin* (30 January 1995, unreported) High Court (NI). Alternatively, the court may reach its own conclusion on the most appropriate allocation of land on partition, adopting some of the recommendations in both reports: see for example, *O'Brien & Cronin Ltd v Dillon* (2 February 1977, unreported) High Court (RI).

[110] This of course assumes that the relevant criteria for ordering sale in either of the Partition Act 1868, ss 3-5 are satisfied. Alternatively, if the parties have previously entered into a conditional contract for sale, the court may confirm this: see for example, *Grove v Comyn* (1874) LR 18 Eq 387.

[111] See *O'Brien & Cronin Ltd v Dillon* (2 February 1977, unreported) High Court (RI) and *Warwick v Warwick* (21 January 1992, unreported) High Court (NI). See further *De Campo Holdings Pty Ltd v Cianciullo* [1977] WAR 56.

[112] See generally ch 5 above.

[113] See 21 *Halsbury's Laws of England* (1st edn, 1912), pp 856-857 and the cases cited therein.

[114] See 21 *Halsbury's Laws of England* (1st edn, 1912), p 856. In the event of non-payment, the sum owed as equality of partition may be recovered with interest from the date on which the first payment was due: *Stewart v Ferguson* (1842) 5 Ir Eq R 157. While accepting that the court has a broad discretion to make adjustments on partition for the purpose of achieving balance, Esson J in *Haller v Patrick* (1979) 5 WWR 623 at 629-630 suggested that it could not do so by directing the performance of personal obligations such as payments of money or the carrying out of improvements.

[115] See *Roebuck v Chadebet* (1869) LR 8 Eq 127 and *Pennington v Dalbiac* (1870) 18 WR 684. However, in *Blasdell v Baldwin* (1878) 3 OAR 6 it was suggested that such an order should not be made unless it is clearly beneficial to all the parties.

[116] See *Devereaux v Kearns* (1886) 11 PR (Ont) 45.

[12.35] A number of general points may be made in relation to the typical form of order[117].

A Necessary conveyances or transfers

[12.36] Where the court orders partition, the parties must execute mutual conveyances or transfers to give effect to the division[118]. Where the court orders sale of the property, the order typically directs the parties to join in executing the conveyance or deed of transfer to the purchaser[119]. If one of the parties refuses to execute a conveyance as directed by the order, aside from the fact that he will be in contempt of court, the court may appoint someone to execute the conveyance on his behalf[120].

B Delivery of possession

[12.37] If the court makes an order for sale, the order will usually direct the co-owners to deliver up possession of the property within a specified period of time, to facilitate sale with vacant possession[121].

C Accounting adjustments

[12.38] The court may make an accounting adjustment as incidental to an order for partition or sale and direct inquiries to be carried out accordingly[122]. For

---

117 The term 'judgment' includes an 'order': Partition Act 1876, s 2. An order for partition or sale does not constitute a parliamentary conveyance and therefore would not in itself correct any imperfections in title - *Re Martin's Estate* (1879) 3 LR Ir 255 and *O'D v O'D* (18 November 1983, unreported) High Court (RI).

118 In *Warwick v Warwick* (21 January 1992, unreported) High Court (NI), where the plaintiff and the defendant were tenants in common of registered land, the relevant part of the order stated:

> 'AND IT IS ORDERED that the Plaintiff and the Defendant shall execute mutual transfers to each other of the allotted shares according to their respective interests therein.'

119 See the form of order made in *Bank of Ireland v Young* (13 February 1992, unreported) High Court (NI) and in *Glass v McManus* [1996] NI 401. Where a partition action is brought under the Partition Act 1868, s 5 and the plaintiff accepts the defendant's undertaking to purchase, the order for sale must stipulate this: see *Powell v Powell* (1975) 21 RFL 234, decided under the corresponding provision of the Partition Act 1960 (BC).

120 Judicature (NI) Act 1978, s 33. See further the Rules of the Supreme Court (NI) 1980, Ord 45, r 6 and the County Court Rules (NI) 1981, Ord 33, r 16(3)(b). As regards the Republic of Ireland, it appears that this jurisdiction is exercised under the Chancery (Ir) Acts 1834 and 1835: Deale, *Circuit Court Practice and Procedure* (2nd edn, 1994), p 161.

121 Rules of the Supreme Court (NI) 1980, Ord 31, r 1 and the County Court Rules (NI) 1981, Ord 33, r 16(2); the Rules of the Superior Courts (RI) 1986, Ord 51, r 1 and the Circuit Court Rules (RI) 1950, Ord 33, r 2 and Ord 45, r 1. See for example, the form of order made in *Ulster Bank Ltd v McCullough* (25 September 1989, unreported) High Court (NI) (defendants ordered to deliver up possession within four weeks) and in *William Ewing t/a Ewing Brothers v McCann* (26 January 1993, unreported) High Court (NI) (defendants ordered to deliver up possession within three months).

122 See the Rules of the Supreme Court (NI) 1980, Ord 43 and the County Court Rules (NI) 1981, Ord 17; the Rules of the Superior Courts (RI) 1986, Ord 33 and the Circuit Court Rules (RI) 1950, Ord 50. For accounting adjustments generally see ch 11 above.

example, if a co-owner seeks to be reimbursed for his expenditure on improvements, the court may direct inquiries as to the amount expended on improvements and the amount by which these have increased the value of the property[123].

D Incumbrances

[12.39] Irrespective of whether a partition action is brought by a co-owner or a security holder, the court will usually direct inquiries as to incumbrances on making an order for partition or sale[124]. This direction may take the following form:

> 'The following inquiries and account shall be made and taken that is to say:
>
> 1. an inquiry what incumbrances (if any) affect the premises or any and what parts thereof subsequent as well as prior to or contemporaneous with the Plaintiff's demands;
> 2. an inquiry what are the priorities of such incumbrances;
> 3. an inquiry what is due on the foot of such incumbrances for principle and interest respectively...'[125]

[12.40] Where appropriate, the court may also direct inquires as to whether the lender consents to partition or to sale[126].

E Conditions imposed and/or postponement of order

[12.41] Article 49 of the Property (NI) Order 1997 provides that, where the court makes an order for partition or sale under the Partition Acts, it may also impose such stay or suspension or such conditions on the order as it thinks fit[127]. These may be imposed when the court makes the order or at any time before its

[123] See for example, *Cardinaels-Hooper v Tierney* (20 December 1995, unreported) Supreme Court of New South Wales.

[124] As to the general practice where a partition action is brought by a legal or equitable mortgagee or chargee in Northern Ireland, see the Rules of the Supreme Court (NI) 1980, Ord 88 and see further Hunter, *Notes on Procedure by Originating Summons and in Actions by Mortgagees* (2nd edn, 1985). For the corresponding practice in the Republic of Ireland, see the Rules of the Superior Courts (RI) 1986, Ord 3(15) and Ord 54, and see further Scanlon, *Practice and Procedure in Administration and Mortgage Suits in Ireland* (1963).

[125] *Ulster Bank Ltd v McCullough* (25 September 1989, unreported) High Court (NI). Identical directions were given in *Northern Bank Ltd v Moore* (4 June 1991, unreported) High Court (NI) and in *Bank of Ireland v Young* (13 February 1992, unreported) High Court (NI). Although these cases were dealing with partition actions brought by a security holder, similar inquiries have been directed in partition actions between co-owners *inter se*: see *Waite v Bingley* (1882) 21 Ch D 674 at 683-684.

[126] This typically occurs where a partition action is brought by the co-owner who created the security: see ch 8 above.

[127] See ch 7 above, paras **[7.63]-[7.64]**.

enforcement, and may also be revoked or varied by the court. To date, there is no case law on the practical application of art 49[128]. However, this provision allows the court to postpone an order for partition or sale or to attach such conditions as it thinks appropriate in the particular circumstances of the case. For example, the court might postpone sale of a matrimonial home to facilitate the educational needs of children of the family[129]. Alternatively, an order for sale of co-owned property might be postponed to give an opposing co-owner an opportunity to purchase the plaintiff's share and to arrange the necessary finance[130], or on the basis that an immediate sale would be at a loss[131]. Issues which may arise in relation to contributions towards expenditure on and entitlement to income derived from the property are not sufficient reasons for postponing sale, and can be determined as part of an accounting adjustment[132].

[12.42] Although there is no corresponding legislative provision in the Republic of Ireland, courts in this jurisdiction have not confined themselves to merely making an order for partition or sale. For example, in *First National Building Society v Ring*[133] Denham J postponed making an order for sale pending inquiries about the feasibility of sale. In *ND v AD*[134] O'Hanlon J adjourned an application for sale of premises to give the parties an opportunity to reach agreement as to the manner in which the plaintiff could realise her interest, while

---

128 Save to the extent that it does not allow the court to refuse to make an order: *Ulster Bank Ltd v Carter* [1999] NI 93.

129 In *Northern Bank Ltd v Adams* (1 February 1996, unreported) High Court (NI), at 49-50, Master Ellison postponed sale for 18 months (albeit not under the Property (NI) Order 1997, art 49), by which time the eldest son would have reached the age of 18 and the youngest son would have finished his current course of study. A similar approach has been adopted in a number of Canadian cases: see for example *Bruce v Bruce* (1976) 14 NBR (2d) 422 (sale of family home postponed until minor child had completed his education) and *Woodson v Protheroe* (1995) 17 RFL (4th) 104 (sale of matrimonial home delayed until end of school year to minimise disruption for children of the family). In *Berestin v Berestin* (1994) 96 Man R (2d) 198 the court postponed sale of a family home for one year on the grounds that an immediate sale would be too disruptive for the children who were undergoing counselling and therapy.

130 For example, in *Hoggard v Hoggard* (22 November 1996, unreported) British Columbia Supreme Court, the court made an order for sale of one parcel of land but adjourned sale of another to allow the respondents to negotiate with the petitioner for the purchase of her interest in this parcel (this purchase to be financed by the sale as ordered). See further *Cattoni v Cattoni* (12 March 1980, unreported) Alberta Queen's Bench.

131 *Watts v Watts* [1951] 4 WWR 566 (construction of the property was not yet complete and sale would therefore be at a loss).

132 *Varty v Varty* (22 September 1994, unreported) Ontario Court (General Division).

133 [1992] IR 375.

134 (10 December 1982, unreported) High Court (RI).

in *Blackhall v Blackhall*[135] Lardner J made an order for sale under the Partition Acts, but stayed the execution of the order until a later date.

VIII Special Rules Relating to Partition

[12.43] The mutual conveyances or deeds of transfer must be in the appropriate form[136]. Each joint tenant or tenant in common has an equal right to custody of the title deeds or land certificate while the land is held in co-ownership[137]. Following partition of unregistered land, the title deeds may be retained by the person with the largest interest in the property[138] or by the plaintiff where the various interests are equal[139]. The person holding the deeds may have to covenant to produce them at the request of any of the others[140]. As regards registered land, it is likely that one or more new folios will have to be created after partition since only one portion of the divided land can remain in the existing folio[141].

[12.44] When ordering partition, the court need not divide every part of the co-owned property. For example, if A, B and C are co-owners of three houses the court should allocate one house to each person (with appropriate compensation for equality of partition if required) as opposed to one-third of each house to each co-owner. The important thing is to ensure that each co-owner receives a share of the property that corresponds to his undivided interest[142]. However, if lands are held under different estates or tenures, each much be partitioned separately so as to give a portion to every co-owner. For example, the court should not allocate freeholds to one co-owner and leaseholds to another[143]. The court may order easements to be created over the divided parcels to facilitate their use by the former co-owners following partition[144].

---

135 (30 July 1992, unreported) High Court (RI).

136 Where the parties are joint tenants, the conveyance or transfer should be by way of release, and where the parties are tenants in common by transfer: Wylie, *Irish Land Law* (3rd edn, 1997), pp 445-446 and Challis, *The Modern Law of Real Property* (3rd edn, 1911), pp 368-369.

137 If such documents are retained by one co-owner, the others may request that they be produced for inspection: *Lambert v Rogers* (1817) 2 Mer 489.

138 See *Elton v Elton (No 1)* (1860) 27 Beav 632.

139 See *Daniell's Chancery Practice* (8th edn, 1914), p 1174 and 21 *Halsbury's Laws of England* (1st edn, 1912), p 861. Alternatively, where part of the deeds relates to a specific area of the land, it may be retained by the person to whom that parcel of land has been allotted: see *Lowe v Franks* (1828) 1 Moll 137; *Jones v Robinson* (1853) 3 De G M & G 910; and *Dicks v Batten* [1870] WN 173.

140 See *Jones v Robinson* (1853) 3 De G M & G 910 and *Elton v Elton (No 1)* (1860) 27 Beav 632.

141 Moir, *Land Registration Manual* (1994), pp 70-72. Although the author refers to the practice following voluntary partition, it is likely that the same rule would apply in relation to partition actions.

142 *Earl of Clarendon v Hornby* (1718) P Wms 446 and *Peers v Needham* (1854) 19 Beav 316.

143 *Re Foley's Estate* (1862) 7 Ir Jur (NS) 402.

144 See *Lister v Lister* (1839) 3 Y & Coll Ex 540 and *Warwick v Warwick* (21 January 1992, unreported) High Court (NI).

[12.45] Where the parties to a partition action are numerous and the land is held under complicated titles, the court may declare the parties trustees of their respective shares under the Trustee Act 1893 or the Trustee Act (NI) 1958 as appropriate, and vest these interests in a single new trustee with a direction to convey the divided shares of land to the parties[145].

IX Special Rules Relating to Sale

A Method of sale and conduct

[12.46] Sale of the property may take place in court or out of court[146]. The court may permit the person having conduct of the sale to sell the land in any manner he thinks fit. Alternatively, it might order the land to be sold in a particular manner whether by tender, private treaty[147] or public auction[148]. The court may direct a valuation of the property with a view to fixing a reserve price[149]. Where a third party such as a creditor seeks an order for sale in lieu of partition, sale of the property on the open market may be the only way to ensure that he gets full value for his interest[150].

[12.47] Conduct of the sale is usually given to the plaintiff[151]. Under s 6 of the 1868 Act, the court may allow any of the persons interested in the property to bid at the sale. However, if one of the co-owners is given conduct of the sale, he may be prevented from bidding at the sale presumably to avoid any conflict of interest that might otherwise arise[152]. In these circumstances, conduct of the sale may be given to a third party selected by mutual agreement of the co-owners or,

---

145 See *Shepherd v Churchill* (1857) 25 Beav 21 and *Boyce v Woodroffe* (1859) 5 Ir Jur (ns) 57.

146 As to the practice in Northern Ireland upon an order for sale of land, see the Rules of the Supreme Court (NI) 1980, Ord 31 and the County Court Rules (NI) 1981, Ord 33, r 16 and Ord 34. As regards the Republic of Ireland, see the Rules of the Superior Courts (RI) 1986, Ord 51 and the Circuit Court Rules (RI) 1950, Ord 45.

147 See for example, *Gilbert v Smith* (1879) 11 Ch D 78.

148 In *Pitt v White* (1887) 57 LT 650 Kay J held that, where an order was made for sale out of court by public auction, both the reserved bid and the auctioneer's remuneration had to be fixed in Chambers prior to sale and the purchase money then paid directly into court. Identical directions were made in *Willis v Willis* (1889) 38 WR 7.

149 *Wachsmann v Burrowes* (1912) 31 NZLR 833.

150 *Barnes v Kostiuk* (9 March 1999, unreported) British Columbia Supreme Court.

151 See 21 *Halsbury's Laws of England* (1st edn, 1912), p 864 and Valentine, *Civil Proceedings – The Supreme Court* (1997), p 424. See further *Murray v Geoffroy* (1918) 18 SR (NSW) 259. In *ND v AD* (10 December 1982, unreported) High Court (RI), the parties were given joint carriage of the sale.

152 See for example, *Gilbert v Smith* (1879) 11 Ch D 78; *Domville v Berrington* (1837) 2 Y & C Ex 723; and *Pitt v Jones* (1880) 5 App Cas 651. However, in *Pennington v Dalbiac* (1870) 18 WR 684, Malins VC allowed all the persons interested in the property, including those having conduct of the sale, to bid at the sale.

failing this, appointed by the court[153]. If a third party has conduct of the sale, the court may permit all the persons interested in the property to bid at the sale[154]. However, they cannot interfere with the sale without leave of the court[155].

[12.48] The court's primary goal in crafting a process of sale should be fairness to all persons interested in the property, and the court should ensure that they obtain the maximum mutual benefit[156]. The court cannot grant one co-owner a right of first refusal to the exclusion of the others – if it is appropriate to grant such a right, it should be granted to all of the parties[157]. In addition to this, it appears that the court should not make an order directing that the lands be sold to a particular purchaser if one of the co-owners opposes sale to that person[158].

B Application and distribution of the proceeds of sale

[12.49] Section 8 of the 1868 Act applied ss 23-25 of the Settled Estates Act 1856 to money received from a sale of land under the 1868 Act. These sections contained various rules relating to the application of proceeds of sale of settled land[159].

---

152 (contd) Malins VC stated that in certain circumstances the court would allow persons having carriage of the sale to bid. Here the persons interested were numerous, and none of them objected to proceeding in this manner. Hall VC declined to follow *Pennington v Dalbiac* in *Verrall v Cathcart* (1879) 27 WR 645.

153 See *Roughton v Gibson* (1877) 46 LJ Ch 366 and *Dean v Wilson* (1878) 10 Ch D 136.

154 *Roughton v Gibson* (1877) 46 LJ Ch 366.

155 Conduct of the sale having been given to an independent solicitor in *Dean v Wilson* (1878) 10 Ch D 136, Jessel MR granted an injunction to restrain the plaintiff from issuing and circulating advertisements giving notice of the sale.

156 *Jabs Construction Ltd v Callahan* [1992] 1 WWR 748.

157 *Jabs Construction Ltd v Callahan* [1992] 1 WWR 748. See further *Hersog v Hersog* (1978) 5 BCLR 354 and *Manley v Schiller* (1980) 22 BCLR 61. However, in *Martin v Martin* (1992) 89 DLR (4th) 115 the court asserted that neither party should be given a right of first refusal if the property is ordered to be sold (citing *Dibattista v Memecola* (1990) 74 DLR (4th) 569). The court suggested that a right of first refusal often discourages other interested buyers. Moreover, it distorts the market because it provides a benefit to a co-owner which removes the need for him to compete with any other interested purchaser.

158 See *Ruggieri v Desmeth* (1990) 16 RPR (2d) 196. Although an order to this effect was made contrary to the wishes of the defendant in *Deloisio v Dolejs* (1994) 137 NSR (2d) 368, it appears that this particular decision was prompted by the defendant's continuing attempts to frustrate a sale of the property.

159 These provisions remain incorporated into the Partition Act 1868, s 8 notwithstanding the repeal of the Settled Estates Act 1856 by the Settled Land Act 1877 and the re-enactment (with variations) of the Settled Estates Act 1856, ss 23-25 in the Settled Land Act 1877, ss 34-36. 'We must read the Act of Parliament as if all the 23rd to 25th clauses of the Settled Estates Act [1856] were repeated *totidem verbis* in the Partition Act': *Re Barker* (1881) 17 Ch D 241 at 243 per James LJ. See further *Re Morgan* [1900] 2 Ch 474 and Walker, *The Partition Acts, 1868 and 1876* (1882), p 43.

[12.50] Where all the parties interested in the property were before the court then, by analogy to s 23, the proceeds of sale were either paid to trustees approved by the court[160] or, more usually, paid directly into court[161]. The money then had to be applied to one or more designated purposes[162], such as the discharge of any incumbrances[163] or the purchase of other land to be settled in the same manner as the land sold[164]. More importantly, however, the court could apply the proceeds of sale as 'payment to any persons becoming absolutely entitled'[165]. In other words, money derived from a sale of land under the Partition Acts was paid into court and divided between the former co-owners.

[12.51] Although s 8 of the 1868 Act remains in force, it appears that the various methods of applying the proceeds of sale prescribed in ss 23-25 of the 1856 Act are of little practical relevance. Where the court makes an order for sale today, the proceeds of sale may be paid into court and distributed according to the ascertained beneficial interests of the respective co-owners, but subject to any direction as to costs, payment of incumbrances or accounting adjustments between the parties.

C Conversion

[12.52] Following the enactment of the Partition Acts, where a co-owner was both *sui juris* and absolutely entitled to a share of the land, an order for sale converted his share into personalty from the date on which the order was made[166]. However, where a co-owner was under a disability or not absolutely entitled to his share of the land, an equity for reconversion arose by virtue of ss 23-25 of the Settled Estates Act 1856 as incorporated into s 8 of the Partition Act 1868[167]. These sections expressly provided for reinvestment of the proceeds of sale in land[168].

---

160 See *Hayward v Smith* (1869) 20 LT 70.

161 See *Waite v Bingley* (1882) 21 Ch D 674.

162 Settled Estates Act 1856, s 23. Irrespective of whether the proceeds of sale were paid into court or to trustees, only the court could direct which purposes the money should be applied to – the relevant part of s 23 provided that the money 'shall be applied as the court shall from time to time direct'.

163 Alternatively, the money could be used to discharge any incumbrances affecting other lands subject to the same uses and trusts: Settled Estates Act 1856, s 23.

164 See *Langmead v Cockerton* (1877) 25 WR 315.

165 Settled Estates Act 1856, s 23.

166 See *Arnold v Dixon* (1874) LR 19 Eq 113; *Steed v Preece* (1874) LR 18 Eq 192; *Re Beamish's Estate* (1891) 27 LR Ir 326; and *Re Dodson* [1908] 2 Ch 638.

167 See *Re Morgan* [1900] 2 Ch 474.

168 Accordingly, in *Foster v Foster* (1875) 1 Ch D 588, where persons interested in the land included several infants, Jessel MR held that their shares of the proceeds of sale were to be treated as realty under the Partition Act 1868, s 8.

[12.53] The distinction is of little practical importance today following assimilation of the intestacy succession rules relating to real and personal property in Northern Ireland and the Republic of Ireland by the Administration of Estates Act (NI) 1955 and the Succession Act 1965 respectively. It will only be relevant where, for example, a testator's will distinguishes between the disposal of his real and personal property.

X Costs

[12.54] Prior to 1868 the standard practice was that, partition being for the benefit of all the co-owners, the costs should be borne equally by the parties irrespective of their shares in the property[169]. Although the practice subsequently developed whereby the court ordered that the costs of partition should be borne by co-owners in proportion to their respective interests in the property[170], this did not apply to the entire costs of the action. The standard practice was that no costs were given up to the hearing of the partition suit, but that the subsequent costs of issuing, executing and confirming the partition were borne by the parties according to the value of their interests in the land[171].

[12.55] Section 10 of the Partition Act 1868 provided that the court could make 'such order as it [thought] just respecting costs up to the time of the hearing'[172]. However, the practice developed whereby the court, upon ordering sale, directed that the entire costs of the proceedings were paid out of the proceeds of sale[173]. Although the practical effect was the same, where the court made an order for

---

168 (contd) Similar views were expressed in respect of persons of unsound mind (*Re Pares* (1879) 12 Ch D 333) and in respect of married women who had died without electing to treat their property as converted (*Mordaunt v Benwell* (1881) 19 Ch D 302). It appears that the Partition Act 1876, s 6 did not alter this practice: *Re Norton* [1900] 1 Ch D 101 and *Howard v Jallard* [1891] WN 210.

169 In *Nevis v Levene* (1744) 3 Atk 82, where the defendant owned four acres in a much larger property, and wished to surrender his share rather than face the expense of partition, the court ordered partition and imposed half of the costs on the defendant. See further *Metcalf v Beckwith* (1726) 2 P Wms 376.

170 See *Calmady v Calmady* (1795) 2 Ves 568 and *Monyns v Joad* (1840) 4 Y & C Ex 134.

171 See *Herbert v Hedges* (1844) 10 Ir Eq R 479; *Balfe v Redington* (1850) 2 Ir Ch Rep 324; and *M'Bride v Malcomson* (1840) 2 Dr & Wal 700.

172 See *Daniell's Chancery Practice* (8th edn, 1914), pp 1187-1189 and 21 *Halsbury's Laws of England* (1st edn, 1912), pp 854-856.

173 In *Landell v Baker* (1868) LR 6 Eq 268, Romilly MR asserted that the Partition Act 1868, s 10 did not alter the pre-1868 practice as regards costs and that the parties should bear their own costs up to the hearing, while the subsequent costs of effecting the partition should be borne rateably by the parties. However, subsequent cases declined to adopt this approach, deciding instead that the entire costs of the action should be borne rateably by the parties: see for example, *Miller v Marriott* (1868) LR 7 Eq 1; *Leach v Westall* (1869) 17 WR 313; *Cannon v Johnson* (1870) LR 11 Eq 90; *Ball v Kemp-Welch* (1880) 14 Ch D 512; *Thompson v Richardson* (1872) IR 6 Eq 596; and *Trustees, Executors and Agency Company Ltd v Finn* (1891) 17 VLR 609.

partition, the appropriate direction was for the entire costs to be borne rateably by the parties according to their shares in the land[174]. Following the enactment of the Judicature Act (Ir) 1877, s 53 of which provided that 'the costs of ... every proceeding in the High Court of Justice ... shall be at the discretion of the court', s 10 was effectively rendered obsolete and was accordingly repealed[175]. However, the courts continued to apportion costs in partition actions in the manner discussed above[176].

[12.56] While the allocation of costs in general remains at the discretion of the respective courts in Northern Ireland and the Republic[177], it appears that costs in a partition action are still apportioned in accordance with the nineteenth century rules. Thus, where the court orders partition, the entire costs may be borne rateably by the parties[178], while such costs may be deducted from the purchase money if the court orders sale[179]. However, if additional costs are incurred by one of the co-owners, these are borne by that particular person[180]. This typically occurs in two situations.

[12.57] Firstly, if a co-owner has a mortgage or other form of security on his share of the land, that particular co-owner must bear any costs sustained by his lender[181]. Secondly, it is well established that a party who unreasonably resists

---

[174] See *Bowes v Marquis of Bute* (1879) 27 WR 750.

[175] Statute Law Revision Act 1893.

[176] *Daniell's Chancery Practice* (8th edn, 1914), p 1188.

[177] See the Judicature (NI) Act 1978, s 59; the Rules of the Supreme Court (NI) 1980, Ord 62 and the County Court Rules (NI) 1981, Ord 55. As to the general practice in respect of costs in Northern Ireland, see Valentine, *Civil Proceedings – The County Court* (1999), ch 17 and Valentine, *Civil Proceedings – The Supreme Court* (1997), ch 17. As regards the Republic of Ireland, see the Rules of the Superior Courts (RI) 1986, Ord 99, r 1 and the Circuit Court Rules (RI) 1950, Ord 58, rr 1 and 29. As to the allocation of costs generally in the Republic, see O'Floinn, *Practice and Procedure in the Superior Courts* (1997), pp 887-924 and Deale, *Circuit Court Practice and Procedure* (2nd edn, 1994), ch 15.

[178] See for example, *Blacklaw and Blacklaw v Beveridge and Collier* [1939] 3 WWR 511. Alternatively, the court may order that each party bears his own costs: see for example, *Warwick v Warwick* (21 January 1992, unreported) High Court (NI). Where the court appoints a surveyor to inspect the lands, his costs may be borne by all the parties: *McLaughlin v McLaughlin* (30 January 1995, unreported) High Court (NI). However, where each party employs his own surveyor, it is likely that each party must pay his own costs in this respect according to the practice discussed below.

[179] Valentine, *Civil Proceedings – The Supreme Court* (1997), p 436 and Wylie, *Irish Land Law* (3rd edn, 1997), p 445 both citing *Re Mahoney's Estate* [1909] 1 IR 132. See further *Glass v McManus* [1996] NI 401.

[180] See *Cannon v Johnson* (1870) LR 11 Eq 90.

[181] See *Catton v Banks* [1893] 2 Ch 221. The costs sustained by the incumbrancer take the same priority as the incumbrance: see *Ulster Bank Ltd v McCullough* (25 September 1989, unreported) High Court (NI); *Northern Bank Ltd v Moore* (4 June 1991, unreported) High Court (NI); and *Bank of Ireland v Young* (13 February 1992, unreported) High Court (NI).

the partition action must bear any extra costs thereby incurred[182]. In *Schnytzer v Wielunski*[183] Menhennitt J, having found that the plaintiffs had vexatiously insisted on a sale of the property and that the defendants had established 'good reason to the contrary' under legislation similar to s 4 of the Partition Act 1868, continued:

> 'In my view, the whole of the proceedings were brought about by the plaintiffs' insistence upon a sale and their opposition to the partition which was sought by the defendants and which the defendants have established by good reason should be ordered. In these circumstances, it appears to me that the proper exercise of my discretion ... is to order the plaintiffs to pay the whole of the defendants' costs of the action to this date, including any reserved costs.'

[12.58] More recently, this practice was followed in *Glass v McManus*[184]. However, in the Australian case of *Adler v Ferguson*[185] Lowe J refused to depart from the normal rule as to costs in a partition action where the defendant had pleaded a defence which could not be sustained at law, but the plaintiff had failed to take out a summons to strike out the plea before trial.

---

181 (contd) However, only one set of costs may be allowed in respect of each undivided share and taken by the lender in these circumstances: *Catton v Banks* [1893] 2 Ch 186 (rejecting suggestions to the contrary in *Belcher v Williams* (1890) 45 Ch D 510). See further *Ancell v Rolfe* [1896] WN 9; *Re Vase* (1901) 84 LT 761; and *Carroll v Harrison* [1910] WN 104.

182 In *Hill v Fulbrook* (1822) Jac 574, Plumer VC held that, because additional costs were occasioned by the plaintiffs having to prove their title in consequence of the defendant unreasonably disputing it, the defendant had to pay these costs. See further *Morris v Timmins* (1838) 1 Beav 411; *Wilkinson v Castle* (1868) 37 LJ Ch 467; *Harper v Bird* (1875) 23 WR 646; and *Jennings v Foster* [1884] WN 200.

183 [1978] VR 418 at 430.

184 [1996] NI 401. See further *Re Mahoney's Estate* [1909] IR 132; *Bray v Bray* (1926) 38 CLR 542; and *McMahon v Public Curator of Queensland* [1952] St R Qd 197.

185 [1957] VR 317.

Appendix

Precedent I

Deed of Partition of Freeholds Between Two Tenants In Common

Parties

THIS INDENTURE, made the .... day of ...., 20........., BETWEEN .... [A.B.], ...of .... &c., of the first part; [C.D.], of......... &c., of the second part; and [*grantee to uses*], of .... &c., of the third part:

Recital of title

WHEREAS under or by virtue of the will dated the ....day of ...., ..., of [*testator*], late of ...., deceased, who died on the .... day of ...., ..., the said [A.B.] and [C.D.] are now seised of, or entitled to the several messuages and hereditaments hereinafter described, in equal undivided moieties as tenants in common in fee simple in possession free from incumbrances;

Recital of of agreement for partition

AND WHEREAS the said [A.B.] and [C.D.] have agreed to effect a partition of the said messuages and hereditaments in manner hereinafter appearing;

Recital of of agreement as to custody of title deeds

AND WHEREAS upon the treaty for the said partition, it was agreed that the deeds and documents of title relating to the said premises hereinafter described should be retained by the said [A.B.], who should enter into such acknowledgment and undertaking with respect thereto as are hereinafter contained.

Testatum*:* Conveyance by tenants in common

NOW THIS INDENTURE WITNESSETH that in pursuance of the said agreement, and for the purpose of effecting such partition; they, the said [A.B.] and [C.D.], according to their respective shares and interests respectively, hereby grant, and, as beneficial owners, convey unto the said [*grantee to uses*] and his heirs,

Parcels by reference to schedules

ALL THOSE several messuages, closes of land, and hereditaments situate at ...., in the county of ...., and particularly described in the First and Second Schedules hereunder written; Together with all ways and easements now or at any time heretofore used or enjoyed therewith;

Easements *Habendum*

TO HOLD the premises unto the said [*grantee to uses*] and his heirs, **AS TO** the messuages, lands and hereditaments described in the said First Schedule, **TO THE USE**

of the said [A.B.], his heirs and assigns, to be henceforth held by him and them in severalty; **AND AS TO** the messuages, lands, and hereditaments described in the Second Schedule, **TO THE USE** of the said [C.D.], his heirs and assigns to be henceforth held by him and them in severalty.

Acknowledgment and undertaking as to deeds

AND THIS INDENTURE ALSO WITNESSETH that in pursuance of the said agreement in this behalf, and in consideration of the premises, the said [A.B.] hereby acknowledges the right of the said [C.D.] to the production of the several deeds and documents of title mentioned in the Third Schedule hereunder written, and to delivery of copies thereof, and undertakes for the safe custody thereof.

IN WITNESS, &c.

The **FIRST SCHEDULE** above referred to.

The **SECOND SCHEDULE** above referred to.

The **THIRD SCHEDULE** above referred to.[1]

[1] Adapted from Bythewood and Jarman, *A Selection of Precedents in Conveyancing* (4th edn by LGG Robins, 1887) Vol IV, pp 154-156.

Precedent II

Deed of Partition Between Two Co-Owners of Freeholds and Leaseholds, the latter being held under One Lease

Parties

THIS INDENTURE is made the ....day of ....,

BETWEEN [*first co-owner*] of etc. of the one part and [*second co-owner*] of etc. of the other part.

Recitals of title in joint tenancy or tenancy on common.

WHEREAS the said [*co-owners*] are now seised of the freehold hereditaments more particularly described in the first and second parts of the first schedule to these presents as joint tenants [*or* as tenants in common] in fee simple and are also entitled as joint tenants [*or* as tenants in common] to the leasehold hereditaments comprised in and demised by a certain indenture of lease dated the .... day of .... and made between [*parties*] as the same leasehold hereditaments are more particularly described in the first and second parts of the second schedule hereto for all the residue now unexpired of the term of .... years granted by the said indenture of lease.

Recital of agreement to partition

AND WHEREAS the said [*co-owners*] have agreed to make a partition and division of all the said freehold and leasehold hereditaments described in the first and second schedules hereto in manner hereinafter appearing.

Recital of agreement for payment for equality

AND WHEREAS it has also been agreed between the said [*co-owners*] that the sum of £.... should be paid by the said [*second co-owner*] to the said [*first co-owner*] for equality of partition.

Recital as to title deeds[2]

AND WHEREAS it has been further agreed between the said [*co-owners*] that the several instruments and documents short particulars whereof are specified in the third schedule hereto and which relate as well to the hereditaments hereby appropriated to the said [*first co-owner*] as to the hereditaments hereby appropriated to the said [*second co-owner*] shall be retained by the said [*second co-owner*] and that he shall give to the said [*first co-owner*] such acknowledgment and undertaking with respect thereto as is hereinafter contained.

---

[2] This particular form of recital is appropriate in situations where it is not convenient to state how the co-owners derived their title. Where possible, however, it is always desirable to refer to the relevant will or settlement, etc. as in the former precedet.

NOW THIS INDENTURE WITNESSETH as follows:

Conveyance of freeholds

1 In pursuance of the said recited agreements, and in consideration of the sum of £ .... now paid by the said [*second co-owner*] to the said [*first co-owner*] for equality of partition (the receipt whereof the said [*first co-owner*] hereby acknowledges) and in consideration of the assurance and assignment by the said [*second co-owner*] hereinafter in clauses 2 and 4 hereof contained the said [*first co-owner*] as beneficial owner hereby releases and conveys [*or if the co-owners are not joint tenants* grants and conveys] unto the said [*second co-owner*] **ALL THAT** the undivided share and interest of him the said [*first co-owner*] of and in the freehold hereditaments and premises the particulars whereof are set out in the second part of the first schedule hereto and which are delineated upon the map or plan hereto annexed and therein coloured [blue] **TO HOLD** the same unto and **TO THE USE** of the said [*second co-owner*] in fee simple henceforth in severalty.

Reciprocal conveyances of freeholds

2 In further pursuance of the said recited agreements and in consideration of the assurance and assignment by the said [*first co-owner*] in clauses 1 and 3 hereof contained the said [*second co-owner*] hereby as beneficial owner releases and conveys [*or if the co-owners are not joint tenants* grants and conveys] unto the said [*first co-owner*] **ALL THAT** the undivided share and interest of him the said [*second co-owner*] of and in the freehold hereditaments and premises the particulars whereof are set out in the first part of the first schedule hereto and which are delineated upon the map or plan hereto annexed and therein coloured [red] **TO HOLD** the same unto and **TO THE USE** of the said [*first co-owner*] in fee simple henceforth in severalty.

Assignment of leaseholds

3 In further pursuance of the said recited agreements and for the considerations aforesaid the said [*first co-owner*] as beneficial owner hereby releases and assigns [*or if the co-owners are not joint tenants* grants and assigns] unto the said [*second co-owner*] **ALL THAT** the undivided share and interest of him the said [*first co-owner*] of and in the leasehold hereditaments and premises the particulars whereof are set out in the second part of the second schedule hereto and which are delineated in the map or plan hereto annexed and therein coloured [green] **TO HOLD** the same unto the said [*second co-owner*] his personal representatives and assigns henceforth in severalty for all the residue now unexpired of the said term of .... years granted by the said recited indenture of lease **SUBJECT** nevertheless to the payment of the apportioned yearly rent of £ .... and to the performance and observance of such of the covenants, provisions and conditions in the said indenture of lease contained and by the lessee thereunder to be performed and observed as affect the said leasehold premises in the second part of the said second schedule mentioned.

Reciprocal assignment of leaseholds

4 In further pursuance of the said agreements and for the considerations aforesaid the said [*second co-owner*] as beneficial owner hereby releases and assigns [*or if the co-owners are not joint tenants* grants and assigns] unto the said [*first co-owner*] **ALL THAT** the undivided share and interest of him the said [*second co-owner*] of and in the leasehold hereditaments and premises the particulars whereof are set out in the first part of the said second schedule hereto and which are delineated on the said map or plan and therein coloured [brown] **TO HOLD** the same unto the said [*first co-owner*] his personal representatives and assigns henceforth in severalty for all the residue now unexpired of the said term of ….years granted as aforesaid **SUBJECT** nevertheless to the payment of the apportioned yearly rent of £ …. and to the performance of such of the covenants, provisions and conditions in the said recited indenture of lease contained and by the lessee thereunder to be performed and observed as relate to the said leasehold premises in the first part of the said second schedule mentioned.

Mutual covenants as to leaseholds

5 Each of them the said [*co-owners*] hereby for himself and his assigns covenants with the other of them and his assigns that he or his personal representatives or assigns will henceforth during the continuance of the said term of … years:

To pay rent

(a) Duly pay such part of the said yearly rent of £ …. reserved by the said indenture of lease as is hereby apportioned to and made payable by him at the times and in the manner in the said indenture of lease provided

To perform covenants

(b) Perform and observe the covenants and conditions in the said indenture of lease contained and on the part of the lessee thereunder to be performed and observed so far as such covenants and conditions in any way relate to the leasehold hereditaments hereby assigned to him

To indemnify

(c) Indemnify and at all times keep indemnified the other of them his personal representatives and assigns and the leasehold hereditaments hereby assigned to such other against all actions proceedings costs damages expenses claims and demands whatsoever by reason or on account of the non-payment of the apportioned part hereby made payable by such covenanting party of the said yearly rent of £ …. or the breach non-performance or non-observance in respect of the said leasehold hereditaments hereby assigned to him or any part thereof of the said covenants and conditions or any part of them.

Rights on breach of covenant

PROVIDED ALWAYS that if and whenever on account of any such non-payment breach non-performance or non-observance as aforesaid the other of them the said [*co-owners*] or his personal representatives or assigns shall be called upon to pay and shall pay the said apportioned part hereby made payable by the covenanting party of the said rent or any part thereof or shall incur any costs charges damages or expenses in respect of the covenants and conditions affecting the said leasehold premises hereby assigned to the covenanting party as aforesaid then and in every such case the covenanting party will forthwith repay all such sums of money costs charges damages and expenses so paid or incurred to the party so paying or incurring the same his personal representatives or assigns and in case of non-payment such sums of money costs charges damages and expenses shall be recoverable by the party paying or incurring the sale his personal representatives or assigns by entry and distress as for rent in arrear upon the leasehold premises so assigned to the covenanting party as aforesaid.

Acknowledg-ment as to titles deeds

6 In pursuance of the said recited agreement in that behalf and in consideration of the premises the said [*second co-owner*] hereby acknowledges the right of the said [*first co-owner*] to production of the several instruments and documents short particulars whereof are specified in the third schedule hereto and to delivery of copies thereof and undertakes for the safe custody thereof.

IN WITNESS etc.

The **FIRST SCHEDULE** above referred to.

Part I

[Freeholds appropriated to first co-owner.]

Part II

[Freeholds appropriated to second co-owner.]

The **SECOND SCHEDULE** above referred to.

Part I

[Leaseholds appropriated to first co-owner.]

Part II

[Leaseholds appropriated to second co-owner.]

The **THIRD SCHEDULE** above referred to.

[Muniments of title retained by second co-owner.]

[Signatures and seals of both parties.][3]

---

[3] *Encyclopaedia of Forms and Precedents* (1st edn, 1911) Vol IX, , pp 430-435.

Precedent III

Deed of Partition for Registered Land

Deed of Partition

Land Registry

Folio: County:

Registered Owners: AB & CD

THIS DEED OF PARTITION made on the..........................day of..........................19..........................

BETWEEN AB & CD the above named registered owners (hereinafter called "the Co-Owners") of the first part the said AB of etc. (hereinafter called "Mr B") of the second part and the said CD of etc. (hereinafter called "Mr D") of the third part.

WHEREAS:

The Co-Owners have agreed to effect a partition of the land in the above mentioned folio.

NOW THIS INDENTURE WITNESSETH that in pursuance of the said agreement and in consideration of the premises:-

(1) The Co-Owners as settlors hereby transfer to Mr B **ALL THAT** portion of the land comprised in the above mentioned Folio which is shown surrounded by a red line and hatched green on the map annexed hereto ("the green land").

(2) The Co-Owners as settlors hereby transfer to Mr D **ALL THAT** portion of the land comprised in the above mentioned Folio which is shown surrounded by a red line and hatched blue on the map annexed hereto ('the blue land").

(3) **(Insert any easements for the benefit of the green land)**

(4) **(Insert any easements for the benefit of the blue land)**

(5) **(Insert any appropriate stamp duty certificate)**

IN WITNESS etc[4]

---

[4] Moir, *Land Registration Manual* (1994) pp 70-72 and reproduced with the kind permission of Arthur Moir, Registrar of Titles. The author also draws attention to the fact that a counterpart should be prepared for each party, and a new land certificate applied for since only one portion of the land can remain in the existing folio.

Index